The Origins of Accounting Culture

The Origins of Accounting Culture aims at stu [illegible] origins of the accounting culture in Venice, with a specific focus on accounting education. The period covered by the work ranges from Luca Pacioli to the foundation (in 1868) of the Royal Advanced School of Commerce (*Regia Scuola Superiore di Commercio*), which in 2018 is celebrating its 150th anniversary as Ca' Foscari University of Venice.

Ever since the Middle Ages, Venice has been home to a number of favourable circumstances that have been accumulating over the years. As a trading city par excellence, Venice allowed the spread of bookkeeping at first among firms and then in the public administration, which was much in need of sophisticated accounting principles for the purpose of controlling its activities.

Venice was among the first cities to implement the Gutenberg print method and it quickly became the most important city in the world in the publishing industry, allowing printing and spreading the first handbooks about double-entry bookkeeping and merchant studies.

The Origins of Accounting Culture goes beyond the study of Luca Pacioli and tackles in a more organic and holistic way the social and economic conditions that allowed accounting culture to spread in Venice. This book will be a vital resource to academics and researchers in the fields of accounting, accounting history, economic development and related disciplines.

Massimo Sargiacomo is a full professor of Accounting and Public Management in the Department of Management and Business Administration at G. D'Annunzio University of Chieti-Pescara, Italy.

Stefano Coronella is a full professor of Accounting in the Department of Business and Economics at Parthenope University of Naples, Italy.

Chiara Mio is a full professor of Accounting in the Department of Management at Ca' Foscari University of Venice, Italy.

Ugo Sostero is a full professor of Accounting in the Department of Management at Ca' Foscari University of Venice, Italy.

Roberto Di Pietra is a full professor of Accounting in the Department of Business and Law at the University of Siena, Italy.

Routledge New Works in Accounting History
Series Editor:
John Richard Edwards, Richard Fleischman, Garry Carnegie, Salvador Carmona

This innovative series contains volumes on accounting history, auditing, bibliography, development of accounting principles and standards, education and ethics, financial reporting, law and regulations, management accounting, and the theoretical works of leading scholars. Providing students, teachers and researchers with the opportunity to learn more about the discipline of accountancy and its past, this series is a vital addition to any accounting library.

Local Authority Accounting Methods
Hugh J. Coombs, John Edwards

Curtis Jenkins Cornwell & Company
S. V. Cornwell

Contributions of Limperg & Schmidt to the Replacement Cost Debate in the 1920s
Frank L. Clarke, Graeme Dean

Accounting and Food
Some Italian Experiences
Edited by Massimo Sargiacomo, Luciano D'Amico, & Roberto Di Pietra

Memorial Articles for Twentieth-Century American Accounting Leaders
Edited by Stephen A. Zeff

The Italian and Iberian Influence in Accounting History
The Imperative of Power
Edited by Michele Bigoni and Warwick Funnell

The Origins of Accounting Culture
The Venetian Connection
Edited by Massimo Sargiacomo, Stefano Coronella, Chiara Mio, Ugo Sostero, and Roberto Di Pietra

The Origins of Accounting Culture

The Venetian Connection

Edited by Massimo Sargiacomo, Stefano Coronella, Chiara Mio, Ugo Sostero, and Roberto Di Pietra

Routledge
Taylor & Francis Group
NEW YORK AND LONDON

First published 2018
by Routledge
605 Third Avenue, New York, NY 10017

and by Routledge
2 Park Square, Milton Park, Abingdon, Oxon, OX14 4RN

First issued in paperback 2020

Routledge is an imprint of the Taylor & Francis Group, an informa business

Library of Congress Cataloging-in-Publication Data
A catalog record for this book has been requested

ISBN 13: 978-0-367-73471-8 (pbk)
ISBN 13: 978-1-138-10361-0 (hbk)

Typeset in Sabon
by Apex CoVantage, LLC

Contents

Editors

Massimo Sargiacomo is Full Professor of Accounting in the Department of Management and Business Administration at Gabriele D'Annunzio University of Chieti-Pescara, Italy, where he teaches Management Accounting and Public Sector Management. He has been Vice-Rector and President of the Bachelor Degree Course in Economics and Management at the same university, where now he is PhD Director of the Accounting, Management and Business Economics course. Massimo has been President of the Academy of Accounting Historians, a section of AAA. He is member of the Editorial Boards (EB) or Editorial Advisory Boards (EAB) of several journals, including but not limited to *Accounting, Auditing and Accountability Journal*, *Accounting Historians Journal*, *Accounting History*, *Accounting History Review*, *Critical Perspectives on Accounting*, *De Computis*, and *Research in Accounting History*.

Chiara Mio is Full Professor of Accounting in the Department of Management at Ca' Foscari University of Venice, Italy, where she teaches Strategic Planning and Sustainability Management, Management Control, and Corporate Reporting. She is Scientific Director of the postgraduate course MUMISS in social innovation and sustainability, Chair of ESG (Environmental, Social, and Governance) Reporting Task Force at Accountancy Europe (Brussels) and President of the bank Credit Agricole FriulAdria. Her research interests and publications are related to the following areas: sustainability, integrated reporting, and accounting history.

Stefano Coronella is Full Professor of Accounting in the Department of Business and Economics at Parthenope University of Naples, Italy, where he teaches Accounting and Accounting History. He is Editor of the journal *Rivista Italiana di Ragioneria e di Economia Aziendale* (Italian accounting review) and of the Rirea Historica Study Series. He is Vice-Director of his department, member of the Scientific Committee and of the Editorial Board of several Italian journal and study series. He has published works in the area of accounting, financial statements, TV companies, groups, business combinations, commercial credit, and accounting history.

Ugo Sostero is Full Professor of Accounting in the Department of Management at Ca' Foscari University in Venezia, Italy, where he teaches Business Administration, Financial Accounting, Financial Statement Analysis, and Consolidated Financial Statements and Business Combination. He was Vice-Dean at Ca' Foscari University and then member of the management board in the same university. He is member of the Scientific Committee of the journal *Financial Reporting* and of some other Italian journals and study series. His main research interests are in the fields of financial accounting, international accounting, accounting history, and management accounting.

Roberto Di Pietra is Full Professor of Accounting and Head of the Department of Business and Law of the University of Siena, Italy. He is Past President of the Italian Society of Accounting History and Past and Contributing Editor of the *Journal of Management and Governance* (Editor from 2007 to 2015). He received a PhD in Accounting and Business Administration in 1997 (University of Pisa); he also received a specialization in Banking in 1993 (University of Siena). Di Pietra's main research interests are in international accounting, in auditing and in accounting history. He is also an Editorial Board member of *Accounting in Europe*, *Revista Espanola de Contabilidad y Financiacion de Empresa*, and *Financial Reporting*.

Introduction

Accounting Culture in Venice Through the Lenses of the Centuries: An Introductory View

Massimo Sargiacomo, Stefano Coronella, Chiara Mio, Ugo Sostero and Roberto Di Pietra

Premise

The present book aims at studying the origins and the development of the accounting culture in Venice, with a specific focus on accounting education. The period covered by this work ranges from Luca Pacioli to the foundation (in 1868) of the *Regia Scuola Superiore di Commercio* (Royal High School of Commerce), which in 2018 will celebrate its 150th anniversary as Ca' Foscari University of Venice.

Back in the Middle Ages, Venice was home to a number of favourable circumstances that had accumulated over the years. As a trading city par excellence, Venice allowed the spread of bookkeeping at first among firms and then in public administration, which was much in need of sophisticated accounting tools for the purpose of controlling its activities. As it was a very open city, Venice was among the first to implement the Gutenberg print method in Italy, thus quickly turning into the most important city in the world for the publishing industry. For this reason, Venice was responsible for both the divulgation of knowledge and the spread of volumes on double-entry bookkeeping and merchant business affairs.

The idea of this book arises from the opportunity of highlighting the primary role of Venice as cradle for major accounting scholars, at a time when in other places the subject was not drafted yet. Many works of paramount importance were released in Venice. Accounting education, practitioner activity and managerial culture have long been present in Venice, thus accumulating over the years and finally leading to the foundation of the *Scuola Superiore di Commercio*—High School of Commerce—in 1868.

The Accounting Knowledge in Venice

It is traditionally taught by accounting historians (Melis, 1950, pp. 19–20; Masi, 1975, pp. 288–290) that the rise of modern accounting coincides with the first work we know, which was printed in Venice: the *Summa* by Luca Pacioli (Sangster, 2010).

Yet double entry had already been invented and had been in use for over a century in the small business houses of merchants. Its conception tided up with the trade flourish thanks to the development until the end of the fifteenth century of the independent communes, signorias, princedoms and maritime republics and to the connected need to set forth the outcome of business operations. Indeed, at that time companies had grown both in dimension, thus involving a larger number of employees, and in business scope, since they often established branches in several countries.

In the High Middle Ages, thanks to a revival of trade, the development of companies and their growth in complexity, the double-entry method was invented.

> It is [. . .] to Italy that we must turn if we wish to trace the development of account-keeping. When Europe began to wake from the dark centuries that followed the fall of the Western Empire, Italy took the lead, not only in the renaissance of art and learning, but also in commerce, and the vast trade carried on by Italian merchants with other countries was bound to necessitate the invention of some proper form of keeping accounts.
>
> (Woolf, 1912, p. 104)

Moreover, it is worth noting that

> It is obvious that banks which have to carry on such various and multifarious business are bound to keep many kinds of books and to ensure that they are kept in an absolutely proper manner, and the formation of the first banks in Italy must have given a great impetus to the art of keeping accounts.
>
> (Woolf, 1912, p. 104)

Even if the most famous ones were founded in Florence later, it should be borne in mind that the first example of a bank was "the Bank of Venice, the first to be established, having, it is supposed, been founded in 1157" (Woolf, 1912, p. 104). Only in the fourteenth century was the best-known bank instituted, *Banca dei Medici* in Florence; it is important to emphasize that, very recently, new circumstances surrounding the emergence of double entry in early thirteenth-century Italian banks have been illuminated by Sangster (2016). Nevertheless, accounting historians usually credit the 1494 *Summa* by Fra Luca Pacioli to be the first work having popularized double-entry bookkeeping, as Pacioli has been long lauded as the "father of accounting education" (Sangster and Scataglinibelghitar, 2010).

Indeed, it stands as the outcome, the climax of the medieval accounting which evolved among unknown merchants and bookkeepers, taking the stage in business activities between the fourteenth and fifteenth centuries (Masi, 1975, p. 288).

As is apparent, a unanimous consensus on the invention and origin of double-entry bookkeeping has been achieved. Specifically, as for its "paternity", scholars have expressed contrasting views so far, but they all agree that merchants in the High Middle Ages crafted such a method.

Fabio Besta claims Venice as the leader (Besta, 1916, p. 349), while Federigo Melis refers to Tuscany (Melis, 1950, p. 480), but according to other evidence, the origin of double entry has been retraced in Genoa or Milan (Zerbi, 1952).

However, double entry is universally recognized as Venetian since early references to such a style have been already quoted in more ancient ledgers which had to be kept according to the Venetian approach in other cities.[1]

Furthermore, several hints boost the thesis according to which Venice was the city acknowledged as the cradle of double entry.

Among the four maritime republics (Amalfi, Pisa, Genoa and Venice) which dealt with trades and business, Venice was surely the most important, the most enduring and the most active one in cultural exchanges as well as in trade with foreign countries. Moreover, back to the fifteenth century Venice was known as a "very rich city"—more specifically, the richest one in the entire Italian Peninsula (Luzzatto, 1960, p. 70).

> Venice was truly the foremost commercial city of the Renaissance, her greatness arising from her vast commercial empire in the East and her natural advantages as a port [. . .]. She was the active centre of trade between the East and the West and her profits were enormous.
>
> (Peragallo, 1938, p. 32)

For this reason,

> It was natural that Venice should have developed the famous Venetian method of double entry. Her supremacy in commerce is responsible for the spread of the system to other parts of Italy during the fourteenth and fifteenth centuries, and in the sixteenth century, with the help of Venetian writers, throughout Europe.
>
> (Peragallo, 1938, p. 32)

Venice was "the sovereign as well as the moderator of the world trade and boasted the greatest and most experienced companies" for a very long time, hence giving "to [. . .] theoretical accounting its first followers" (Alfieri, 1891, p. 1).

Since the fourteenth century, abacus schools and master charts of accounts were prolific in the city. In such schools pupils received an education in practical and business arithmetic, commercial technique and bookkeeping (Melis, 1950, p. 609).

Some abacus masters were well known in Venice: Çentil da labacho (as shown in cartularies dated 1304 and 1315), his son Bertucium, who took as surname his father's forename, Magister Balsamus *doctor abachi* (abacus master) (quoted in a 1346 document), Michael abacherio de Bononia (who appears in documents back to 1364), his son Jachobi *de labacho* (as testified in cartularies dated 1381 and 1389), Filippus de Pisis *abaci magistri*, Jeronimus *ab abacho*, Jacobeli *alabacho* (documents dated 1381, 1411, 1418 and 1423 made references to them), Magister Troiolus de Cancellariis *alabacho* or *abachista* (quoted in numerous documents from 1421 to 1454), his son Franciscus (mentioned in charts from 1468 to 1473), who kept his father's forename as a surname, thus abandoning "de Cancellariis" as a last name, Alvise de la Karte abacus master, and Bartholomeus *ab abacho* or *magister abachi* (who appears in cartularies from 1467 to 1468) (Besta, 1916, pp. 345–346).

Those preceptors taught business arithmetic as well as basic knowledge of commercial technique and of keeping the accounts. Moreover, it was not unlikely that they also practiced the accounting profession (Coronella, 2016).

Indeed, in Venice the accounting profession ("*quaderniere*"—the bookkeeper henceforth—because he was entrusted with the task of keeping the book—i.e., the ledger) was already enhanced from the early fifteenth century onwards (Melis, 1950, p. 604). The task of "keeping the books" for companies was becoming more prominent, especially for the largest ones, which held several branches and could broaden their business scope outside their home cities.

Surely, the aforementioned elements are key drivers for the rise of accounting literature.

First, because Venice was the main center of trade and had a high number of large and relevant companies, double entries had been widely used here more than anywhere else. Of course, Venice set the scene for the release of the first printed works on accounting (Bariola, 1897, p. 361).

Moreover, abacus schools were much more in need of books for pupils. In companies, the professional practice of accountants prompted core competences and skills which deserved to be disclosed. In fact,

> In the second half of the 15th century [. . .] the accounting literature is in-progress and the abacus masters, the "accountants" and the "bookkeepers" devote much effort on the subject, especially the Venetian accountants because henceforth Venice has the leadership of the worldwide accounting control. Indeed, on the one hand, the accounting practitioners—who have drawn from the heritage of their forebears whose tireless work has been passed by business to business, thus being disseminated—can funnel their skilful experience in long-awaited volumes.
>
> (Melis, 1950, p. 611)

On the other hand, the accounting art was so much "advanced that it would be easy for someone to set its governing and fundamental rules" (Bariola, 1897, p. 360).

For this reason, it is apparent that all the first and most relevant treatises on double-entry bookkeeping saw the light of day in Venice: from the *Summa* by Luca Pacioli (Pacioli, 1494), moving through works by Giovanni

Antonio Tagliente (1525), Domenico Manzoni (1540), Bartolomeo Fontana (1551), and Alvise Casanova (1558), as well as through two anonymous works (1525 and 1529) and then to the belatedly printed treatise by Benedetto Cotrugli (Cotrugli, 1573). With the exception of the small booklet by the mathematician and physician Girolamo Cardano from Milan—whose work slightly lingers on the keeping of accounts (Cardano, 1539)—the first printed work out of Venice dates from 1586 and was released by Angelo Pietra (Pietra, 1586).

This is an interesting point. Indeed, regardless of the precise *locus* in which double entry was invented, it should be borne in mind that its spread originates in Venice especially thanks to the efforts of Venetian printers, thus being exported throughout the Italian Peninsula and then across Europe. Indeed, the first treatises from beyond the Alps had largely taken inspiration from the Venetian ones and saw the light of day only in the half of the sixteenth century (Ympyn, 1543, relating to The Netherlands; Oldcastle, 1543, for England; Schweicker, 1549, for Germany; De Savonne, 1567, for France; Rocha, 1565, for Spain) (Saporetti, 1898, pp. 113–120; Vlaemminck, 1956, pp. 96–119).

A famous scholar effectively stresses the role played by Venice in the development and spread of double entry:

> Double entry was not conceived as a whole, but came about gradually, imperceptibly—the result of efforts of generations of merchants who unwittingly contributed to its origin and evolution by modifying their crude systems of bookkeeping to meet the exigencies of a fast-growing foreign trade [. . .]. The Venetian records reveal the system in full maturity [. . .]. How much Venice contributed to the origin of this system is not known. But one thing is certain, that whatever the origin of double entry, Venice used and developed it, perfected it, and made it her own, and it was under the name of the Venetian method that it became known the world over.
>
> (Peragallo, 1938, p. 37)

The focus and the prominence of Venice for the rise and development of modern accounting stand out with reference to the ancient companies and "*magistrature contabili*"—that is, public institutions—which were compelled to perform both auditing and accounting functions at that time. It is also worth noting the contribution in knowledge provided by the numerous educational establishments which, following the earlier schools of abacus from the fifteenth century onwards, contributed to entrenching accounting training.

Among the best-known ventures dating back to the fifteenth century and whose registers have been preserved so far, we note the Fraterna dei Soranzo Company (1406), the ones by Andrea Barbarigo (1430) and by Giacomo Badoer (1436), the main firms credited by accounting historians. The most important Italian archival records were—in the main—disseminated to the accounting history community through Book 9 of Volume 3 of Fabio Besta's milestone publication entitled *La Ragioneria* (1916), although the ledgers of Andrea Barbarigo were originally mentioned a few decades earlier, in his prolusion *La Ragioneria* (1880). Notably, Besta's excerpts (1916) were referred to by very influential international commentators, like Littleton (1928, 1933), Katz (1930), Peragallo (1938, 1956) and de Roover (1944, 1954, 1956) (Sargiacomo, Servalli and Andrei, 2012; Andrei, Baker and Sargiacomo, 2017). In a related manner, the Venetian archival records portrayed by Fabio Besta were also exported to neighbouring disciplines, contrary to what is generally occurring in accounting history research (Walker, 2005, 2008). For instance, F. C. Lane's (1944) highly regarded book *Andrea Barbarigo, Merchant of Venice (1418–1499)* contains the admission that the primary data for "Barbarigo's journal are reproduced (from Besta) and translated" (1944, p. 148), thus undoubtedly witnessing the dissemination of old Venetian records, culture and thoughts throughout the globe.

As far as the *magistrature contabili* are concerned, they were active since the twelfth century and from the thirteenth century onwards they have been entrusted with accounting and auditing tasks (Corsi, 2010, p. 52), thus triggering pleas for improvements in business professions. It is no accident that the first "*Collegio dei Ragionati*" (accounting board) was established in Venice in 1581. It was the first to take the lead in regulating the accounting profession and was the precursor to all the further regulatory bodies thereafter. For the first time in the whole world, a new occupational group, the "*Rasonato*" or "*Ragionato*"—namely, the "accountant"—was recognized officially and assigned to hold public office in accounting (Corsi, 2010, p. 8).

Appointment to such a position required a successfully passed practical test which aimed at assessing mastery of account keeping (Alfieri, 1891, p. 107).

This witnesses the imbuing culture of good administration, auditing and compliance with reference to the responsible use of public funds. Indeed, at the end of the eighteenth century, before Venice declined under the domination of the Hapsburgs, the republic could be taken as a virtuous example for administrative and technical structures which dealt with managing public affairs (Bergamin Barbato, 2016, p. 19).

The common thread between the aforementioned circumstances stands out as pivotal in order to portray the role played by Venice for the spread and the path towards the development of double-entry bookkeeping.

The High School of Commerce at Venice

The creation of the High School of Commerce at Venice completes the chain which has inspired the drafting of the present volume.

Indeed, its establishment is deemed to be the obvious outcome of a cultural sedimentation which has lasted from the High Middle Ages and involved the *Serenissima* Republic of Venice.

However, the following Hapsburg domination (1797) prompted an institutional and economic downturn, which led to the adoption of a new public management approach. Such a model was lagging behind the previous full-fledged one and this circumstance caused many management problems. Moreover, the Hapsburg Empire shifted the Atlantic trade routes from Venice to Trieste, thus neglecting the pivotal role the former had played over the centuries in promoting trade and maritime activities (Valussi, 1875–76, pp. 273–274; Bergamin Barbato, 2016, p. 19).

Notwithstanding the decadence occurring from the nineteenth century onwards, the business and accounting culture was still alive in Venice under the surface of the economic crisis. A further proof of this insight is the creation in Venice of the first business school in Italy as well as one of the earlier schools in the world soon after the annexation to the Kingdom of Italy (October 1866).

Already in early 1867, the Venice Provincial Council laid the groundwork. In November, a special committee drew up a report which provided the guidelines for a consortium involving the province, the commune and the Chamber of Trade with the prior consent of government.

In April 1868 a combined committee made up of the representatives of the Provincial Council, the Communal Council and the Chamber of Trade submitted the final draft of the creation of the school (Ministero d'Agricoltura, Industria e Commercio, 1868, pp. 18–33).

Such a draft was based on the Anvers and Mulhouse models, according to which the "*Banco commerciale*" (business practice—that is, a wide subject involving applied arithmetic, commercial technique and accounting) was the principal subject of study. Francesco Ferrara was appointed as director of the Business School (*Notizie e dati*, 1871, 1–4) and was in charge continuously for thirty-two years, from the foundation until he passed away (22 January 1900) at the age of 90 years.

Formally established by the Royal Decree of 6 August 1868, no. 4530, the school comprised three addresses or "sections", which were acknowledged only in 1871 (Royal Decree of 13 April 1871, no. 1807):

- The Commercial Department, three-year degree courses;
- The Consular Department, five-year degree courses;
- The Teacher Training Department, of variable length depending on its further subsections.

On 4 December 1868, Professor Luigi Bodio, who was recently appointed together with other five professors, was assigned to deliver the first and solemn prolusion, a preliminary work to the academic year, entitled "On Statistics for Political Economics Relations", which turned out to be the cultural manifesto of the Business School (Berengo, 1989, p. 20).

In the second and third years of coursework much time was devoted to the "*Pratica commerciale*" (a subject also known as "*Banco*"—i.e., business practice), which required about a third of the hours taught (Favero, 2015, p. 29). It is worth mentioning a particular clue. Students attending this degree course were divided into groups and they simulated specific businesses by deploying typical examples of foreign companies.

Indeed, the coursework was scheduled according to job rotation and included tasks such as report and lists drafting and invoice issuing as well as credit letters and bills of exchange. Moreover, they dealt with mock import transactions and arbitrage in securities with foreign companies, kept the accounting books, drew up the financial statements and so forth (Favero, 2015, p. 31).

It is apparent that the pedagogic approach was practice oriented. For this reason, the Venice High School of Commerce can boast of having invented and employed the "case-based method" for the very first time, which has been credited to Harvard Business School, but it was founded later, only in 1908 (Bergamin, 2016, p. 20).

Together with similar institutions which were established between the nineteenth and the twentieth centuries, the High School of Commerce was the very precursor of the modern business schools which would be formally founded in Italy only in 1935 (Coronella, 2012, pp. 21–26).

Book Structure and Content Within Its Three Sections

This volume pursues the challenging goal of collecting stories related to accounting culture within the Venetian scenario through the centuries. The development of this cultural context led to the establishment of the Ca' Foscari University 150 years ago. The whole research project was conceived as a way to build a clear picture of accounting culture within this context. Due to this we have decided to define the different studies along three perspectives: the accounting treaties, the companies and accounting education. In our view these three angles could create a vivid fresco of the relevant role that the Venetian environment has played in a large and continental area in accounting culture. These three perspectives could be considered as the rich cultural ground from which the Ca' Foscari University emerged 150 years ago. In particular, this is related to involvement on the education side, the "production" and dissemination of accounting concepts and theories through accounting treaties and their consequent adoption in the largest companies and entities of that economic scenario.

The aforementioned three perspectives in this book are clearly represented within the corresponding sections. A large group of authors was invited to contribute to the book in order to develop specific studies on the basis of this research project. The call for contributions was defined eighteen months ago and different Italian and non-Italian scholars proposed their specific contributions. Each research was shared and considered through the lens of the overall project. On the basis of this process we have achieved an almost complete and rich view of accounting culture in the Venetian context and this, in our view, represents a crucial element we would adopt to demonstrate the path followed to establish the Ca' Foscari University 150 years ago. At the end of a long process, the different contributions painting this picture became eighteen chapters, six each for the section on accounting treaties, for the section on companies and for the section on accounting education.

The main focus of the first section is related to the treaties and books published within the Venetian environment, witnessing the strong cultural role played by several scholars in developing accounting concepts and theories. This role has long roots dating back to the fifteenth century, with the seminal and paradigmatic publication of Pacioli's treaty. After this historical cornerstone many other treaties were written and published in one of the most stimulating regions of that age throughout Europe: Venice and the Venetian Republic. In the six chapters composing this section we have followed this development from the age of Pacioli and its fundamental contribution to the nineteenth century.

In Chapter 1, Coronella and Santaniello have centred their study on the pivotal role in the cultural leadership played by Venice and by the Venetian treatises in the development of the Italian accounting. In particular, the authors have surveyed the treaties published in Venice in the years starting from the fifteenth century ("*Trattato di mercatura*", 1458, 1475, 1573 by Benedetto Cotrugli; and the printed *Summa*, 1494, by Luca Pacioli). These authors of these treaties are deemed to be, respectively, the first illustrator of the double-entry method and its first "popularizer", thus closing the period of Middle Ages accounting and opening the rise of Renaissance and modern accounting. Hitherto, the direction imbued to accounting is unchanged for the next three centuries, at least until the eighteenth century, which marks the fall of the *Serenissima* Repubblica of Venice, the further rise of foreign domains and a wide decay involving the accounting discipline too. This chapter purposes to frame the Venetian treatises compared with the double-entry works in the entire Italian Peninsula and to supply both a systematic and concise frame of reference of the contributions provided by several authors (Cotrugli, Pacioli, Gian Francesco "Arithmetico", Tagliente, Anonimous, Manzoni, Fontana, Casanova, Grisogono, Moschetti, Agostinetti, Garatti, Cortonovis and Bassaglia, Farghiscoc, D'Anastasio) for the growth of accounting.

A special focus on Pacioli's treaties is proposed in Chapter 2. Sangster has studied the only known Venetian treatise on double-entry bookkeeping that predates Pacioli's *Particularis de Computis et Scripturis*: de Raphaeli's *La Riegola de Libro*, or *The Rules of Bookkeeping*. Written in 1475, this manuscript remained undetected until the 1990s, escaping the attention of Fabio Besta, Vincenzo Vianello and others in the nineteenth and twentieth centuries who desperately sought to disprove Pacioli's authorship of his treatise. Had they found it, a different history would be told, but would Pacioli's place have been usurped? This chapter considers the purpose behind de Raphaeli's instructional manual; his pedagogy, the content—his syllabus—is presented and discussed, and the manner in which he taught bookkeeping is contrasted to those of Pacioli and his successors.

A treatise to which sufficient attention was devoted is the accounting book written by Dominico Manzoni, published in 1540 and titled *Quaderno doppio col suo giornale novamente composto et dilegentissimamente ordinato secondo il costume di Venetia*. The Manzoni book is relevant to the aim of our volume because it confirms the role played by the Venetian context in disseminating accounting culture throughout the years and throughout Europe. In Chapter 3, Mari and Picciaia constantly refer to the Manzoni accounting book in order to highlight its continuous reference to the Paciolian *Summa* and its contents. Manzoni can be considered one of the first "accountants", providing his services to the famous merchants of his time. In his book, it is worth emphasizing the "educational" intention, based on the experience matured at the company of the merchant Alvise Vallaresso in Venice. From Manzoni's book, Mari and Picciaia have clarified his contribution to the advancement of accounting technique.

Chapter 4 is dedicated to the contribution of the Venetian Giovanni Antonio Moschetti and his accounting treatise titled *Dell'Universal Trattato di Libri Doppii* (published in 1610). The authors of this study (Bigoni, Aloisi, Funnell, Risaliti and Verona) clearly explain how Moschetti was able to provide to the merchants a reliable and homogeneous set of accounting practices, perfectly based on a theoretical foundation. Moschetti provided a detailed range of accounting treatments to use with various types of business and introduced innovations related to classifications among different kinds of transactions.

Another author who enriched the list of bookkeeping treaties published in Venice was Francesco Garatti. As it emerges clearly in Chapter 5, by Antonelli, D'Alessio and Cafaro, the various contributions of Garatti could be interpreted as a way to provide the requested response to the cultural and educational needs of the local economic and social context. In three subsequent years Garatti published three different accounting books and in all of them he was able to deepen a complex list of topics consistent with the social and cultural movement involving Italy during the seventeenth century. The three books published by Garatti are *Il Divertimento Aritmetico* (in 1686), *L'Abachino con diversi contarelli* (The abacus) (in 1687) and *Saggio di scrittura doppia di mercantie e di cambia* (Essay of double-entry bookkeeping of commerce and currency transactions) (in 1688).

Niccolò D'Anastasio published in 1803 the last accounting treatise examined in this section. As the authors (Caputo, Coronella, Leopizzi and Venturelli) clearly emphasize in Chapter 6, *La scrittura doppia ridotta scienza* (Double-entry bookkeeping as a science) could be considered a book in which some concepts were anticipated over half a century ahead of time. In this respect, D'Anastasio could be considered a sort of forerunner of scientific accounting, emerging only at the end of the nineteenth century. D'Anastasio was the first author who broke away from mere accounting technique. He was an innovator since he considered double entry not as a simple accounting tool but as a tool useful to connect and coordinate different accounts. His contribution could be considered the first significant sign of discontinuity with respect to the traditional view of the discipline, a sort of "ridge" between traditional and modern accounting.

In the second section, we have decided to collect six studies devoted to the development of accounting practices and their adoption within the experiences matured in companies and business entities operating within the Venetian socio-economic environment. The stories we have included within this section are referring to private sector firms (the Remondini printing house, Baroviere & Toso, Geminiano Cozzi's porcelain factory, the Giovanni Foscari textile industry), the particular case of a bank in Venice (Carive) and public entities (Venetian hospitals).

In the latter case, Di Pietra and Russo analyze the changes that affected the healthcare system at the end of the Venetian Republic (1777–1797) in Chapter 7. This period determined the reorganization of the Venetian hospital system and the creation of the large hospital of SS. [Saints] Giovanni and Paolo. The establishment of this hospital coincided with a movement towards the explicit declaration of public interest in the healthcare system, and the Venetian Senate used accounting information as a tool to highlight the state of crisis to justify a power change in their administration. In the background of relational dynamics among the various individuals, the *accounting and power* paradigm supports the interpretation of data and documents according to a Foucauldian perspective.

Chapter 8 deals with the accounting and managerial practices adopted in the long history of the Remondini printing house operating in Bassano, a town within the Republic of Venice. The authors of this chapter (Marcon, Favero and Sostero) examine the accounting records of Remondini in order to identify the determinants of the company's life, from its expansion to its subsequent long decline. This chapter aims at assessing the real effectiveness of accounting practices, whether they improved over time and the possible explanations for the change in the Remondini accounting system.

The particular story of a bank is examined in Chapter 9, by Mancin, Marcon, Fasan and D'Alessandro. In this chapter the authors analyze the accounting system of Venice's savings bank (*Cassa di Risparmio di Venezia*, Carive), from the Mount of Piety (1853) to its independence. From the annual reports it is possible to highlight the most relevant changes related to some specific financial years (1853, 1863, 1877 and 1888). In this respect, the authors discuss some possible explanations for the factors driving such changes. One of the factors detected could be the changes in Carive's activities (the greater and different kinds of investments and sources of financing required the bank to evolve its financial statements in order to provide a more complete representation). Another factor was the need of Carive to build trust and stronger accountability towards its stakeholders through financial statements.

Chapter 10 offers the intriguing story of one of the oldest companies in the world: the Barovier & Toso artisan factory. Mio and Fasan provide a clear analysis of a family business still in operation, discussing how this company and its long history (dating back to 1295) are related to the history of innovation (modern endogenous growth theory) and technology (internalist and externalist theories). In particular, the authors review the regulations proposed by the Republic of Venice (particularly from 1500 onwards, during the "strong protectionism" period) and discuss the role of such regulations and of guilds in determining the decline of the industry.

In Chapter 11, Saccon and Alexander address the Venetian textile industry. This industry and the merchants related to this activity have greatly contributed as early and evolved adopters of the double-entry system, emerging in practice in Italy in the thirteenth century. The enacting of accounting procedures served specific purposes and as an integral part of governance and controlling or monitoring processes. The authors of this chapter examine the ledger of Giovanni Foscari. This ledger opens important windows on the Middle Ages business and social environment and its contribution to rebuilding a context could be very valuable.

Geminiano Cozzi's porcelain factory offers the opportunity to follow the story of fraudulent investment in Venice in the second half of eighteenth century. The authors (Agostini, Cella and Favero) of Chapter 12 investigate three years (1781, 1782 and 1783) in the history of this company through the main information emerging from its financial statements. The three financial statements analyzed in the chapter were formally prepared by a government official (the *Inquisitorato alle Arti*), but the accounting information was provided by an accountant who was appointed by the principal investor. The company was facing a lack of liquidity, but it was paying high dividends to the investor. On this basis, it was not possible to detect fraud. This chapter aims to investigate accounting fraud at Geminiano Cozzi's factory through analysis of the *Inquisitorato alle Arti*.

The third perspective adopted in this book is related to accounting education. This perspective is particularly relevant if we consider the Venetian environment, especially in the fifteenth and sixteenth centuries. In that age, in fact, Venice was one of the most active places in Europe for publishing. This is particularly true if we consider the publication of accounting books and treaties. At the same time Venice is one the first places in which the accounting profession started its process of institutionalization.

As to the latter point in Chapter 13, Girella and Cordazzo clearly point out the case of the establishment in Venice of the *Collegio de Rasonati and Scuola di Rialto*. The aim of this study is to start investigating, through interdisciplinary and multi-language lenses, the archaeology of education in bookkeeping in fifteenth-century Venice. The authors show that, since the emergence of its teaching, bookkeeping has been part of a wider and articulated educational understanding and architecture that were included in a vision of the merchant's formation that encompassed both practical training and humanistic knowledge. In their study the authors propose that the works of Pacioli could have been influenced by its attendance to the Rialto School as well as by the Ramist method that was infused into the school.

Chapter 14 concerns the establishment in the sixteenth century of the *Scuola Grande di San Rocco* and the first teaching activities devoted to the diffusion of concepts related to management control practices. Such kinds of schools were a relevant economic and social actor in the Republic of Venice: they were privately managed but publicly regulated charitable organizations, sharing a devotional orientation and performing de facto welfare functions. The authors of this chapter (Lusiani, Vedovato and Pancot) analyze balance sheets and administrative documents to follow the rapid growth of this school and to underline the emergence of a need for control and responsibility over the activity and the resources endowed.

Chapter 15, by Sangster, looks at the Venetian context of the commercial world for which Pacioli wrote *Summa Arithmetica*, his compendium of practical mathematics containing his game-changing treatise on double-entry bookkeeping. In particular, this chapter is about the nature of the education forms adopted in the age of Luca Pacioli. In this respect, the author examines the Venetian accounting books published in that age by Soranso Fraterna (1406–1434), Andrea Barbarigo (1418–1449), Jachomo Badoer (1436–1440) and Marino de Raphaeli (1475). The last one could be considered as an instructional manual from which the idea of the Venetian method has emerged. The meaning of the Venetian method of bookkeeping and what Pacioli intended when he described his method as being in the style of Venice are considered together with Pacioli's purpose in preparing his treatise, his pedagogy, the content.

In Chapter 16, Frandsen and Hoskin consider how far accounting innovations may be understood as outcomes of new ways of thinking and acting, focusing on three different Venetian accounting innovations of the sixteenth century: double-entry bookkeeping (DEB) in the Venetian style, a modern-sounding discourse that proposes accounting and management controls to improve the speed, cost and quality of ship building in the Venice state shipyard, the *Arsenale*, and the use of the Venetian DEB layout in the Jesuit examination of conscience to visually account for one's daily good and bad deeds. We observe how each accounting innovation names its object as a "body" (*corpo*) as opposed to an "organization". We note how *human* performance is evaluated through weighing up merits (good deeds) and faults (sins), rather than measuring with a unilinear value scale (e.g., adding merits and subtracting demerits), although DEB does deploy such a scale as all debit and credit entries are monetized. Finally the co-authors suggest that, just as modern governmental management, in Foucault's analysis, manages populations and individuals via an accounting-based "dispositif of security", there may be a similar but different way of managing via accounting in this earlier era, perhaps as a "dispositif of control".

In Chapter 17 Sargiacomo, Servalli and Andrei center their study on the contribution of Fabio Besta and his long service (forty years) as professor at the Ca' Foscari School. This is perfectly consistent with the biographical research field within the accounting education domain; Besta was an eminent educator during his entire life. The authors have also illustrated the contribution by Besta to the development and spread of accounting education and practice, basing their analysis on his books on accounting theory and public sector accounting, as well as on his painstaking work devoted to enshrining and perpetuating old historical Venetian records. Finally, the authors highlight the contribution of Besta in the educational field related to the origins of double-entry bookkeeping, prior to Pacioli's articulation of the technique and its rules. In particular, a comprehensive analysis is offered of the content and impact of the third volume of Besta's major work entitled *La Ragioneria* (The accounting), by tracking direct references to Besta's work in general accounting journals and specialist accounting history journals and books. His book has been deployed to formulate new interpretations of the history of accounting, and has been disseminated for almost a century throughout the planet.

In the final chapter the authors (Agostini, Cordazzo and Saccon) focus their interest on some historical events in Venice in relation to the origin of the accounting profession, especially the establishment of the *Collegio de' Rasonati* (Decree of the Republic of Venice in 1581) and the formal recognition of "accountant-auditors" (*Ragionieri revisori*) in 1828. In particular, they explore the historical origins of the so-called small and medium practices (SMPs), which represent a widespread organizational form for the provision of accounting support in the northeast of the Italian Peninsula. The term SMP has much less general currency than SME (i.e., small and medium enterprises), but it is useful in order to distinguish SMPs from larger accountancy organizations (including both the Big 4 and the mid-tier firms).

Through the three sections composing this book it is possible to see a vivid representation of the richness of a cultural environment that along the history has greatly contributed to the development of accounting culture not only in Italy but also in a large range of countries in Europe. Venice was in the past a cultural center where generations of merchants, entrepreneurs and companies look to run their own business activities. In the heart of Europe at the crossroads between East and West, Venice was the place to diffuse accounting and business culture through the publication of books and through a rooted accounting education system.

Within the foregoing system the Ca' Foscari School represents one of first examples of business schools in the world, dating back 150 years. Through this volume we have attempted to return such inestimable cultural heritage, and hand it out to the future!

Note

1. For instance, in the Raccolta Strozziana in the Florence State Archive there is a register dated 1382 whose first page includes the following sentence: "Questo

libro fue proprio di Paliano di Folcho da Firenze [. . .] e in esso scriverrò chi dovrà dare a me proprio e così avere [. . .] e scriverollo *alla viniziana*, cioè ne l'una carta dare e di rimpetto l'avere" ["this book was owned by Paliano di Folcho from Florence and I will write in it the accounts who must be credited and hence debited and I will use the *Venetian* manner, that is the debit entries in a page and the credit entries in the opposite page"] (quoted in Besta, 1916, p. 328).

References

Alfieri, V. (1891), *La partita doppia applicata alle scritture delle antiche aziende mercantili veneziane*, Paravia, Torino, Roma, Milano, Firenze, Napoli.

Andrei, P., Baker, R. and Sargiacomo, M. (2017), "Public sector accounting in Italy at the beginning of the 20th century: The contributions of Fabio Besta", *The Accounting Historians*, 44(1): 35–50.

Anonymous (1525), *La tenuta del libro mastro pel negoziante e il possidente*, Venezia.

Anonymous (1529), *Opera che insegna a tener libro doppio, novamente stampata*, Venezia.

Bariola, P. (1897), *Storia della ragioneria italiana premiata al Concorso della Società Storica Lombarda*, Tipografia Ambrosiana di Cavalli Salmini & Co., Milano.

Berengo, M. (1989), *La fondazione della Scuola Superiore di commercio di Venezia*, Università degli Studi di Venezia, Venezia.

Bergamin Barbato, M. (2016), "La fondazione di Ca' Foscari ed il corso di laurea in Economia aziendale: due tappe fondamentali nel percorso della cultura manageriale", *Rivista Italiana di Ragioneria e di Economia Aziendale*, (1–4): 15–22.

Besta, F. (1880), *La ragioneria, prolusione*, Tipografia dell'Istituto Coletti, Venezia.

Besta, F. (1916), *La ragioneria, seconda edizione riveduta ed ampliata col concorso dei professori Vittorio Alfieri, Carlo Ghidiglia, Pietro Rigobon, Parte Prima,Ragioneria generale*, Volume 3, Casa Editrice Dottor Francesco Vallardi, Milano.

Cardano, G. (1539), *Practica arithmetice, & mensurandi singularis. In quaque preter alias continentur, versa pagina demonstrabit*, A. Castellioneus per B. Caluscus, Milano.

Casanova, A. (1558), *Specchio lucidissimo, nel quale si vedeno essere diffinito tutti i modi, & ordini de scrittura, che si deve menare nelli negotiamenti della mercantia, cambii, recambii, con li loro corrispondentie, disgarbugliando, & illuminando l'intelletto a negotianti*, Comin da Trino di Monferrato, Venezia.

Coronella, S. (2012), "Ascesa e declino della ragioneria negli insegnamenti universitari", Rivista *Italiana di Ragioneria e di Economia Aziendale*, (1–2): 18–31.

Coronella, S. (2016), "Tra Leonardo Fibonacci e Luca Pacioli: tre secoli poco conosciuti", *Contabilità e Cultura Aziendale*, 16(2): 88–90.

Corsi, C. (2010), *Le magistrature contabili nella Serenissima e il Collegio dei Ragionati*, Rirea, Roma.

Cotrugli, M.B. (1573), *Della mercatura et del mercante perfetto. Libri quattro. Scritti già più di anni CX & hora dati in luce. Utilissimi ad ogni mercante*, All'Elefanta, Venezia.

de Roover, R. (1944), "The early accounting problems of foreign exchange", *The Accounting Review*, 11(3): 405–420.

de Roover, R. (1954), "New interpretations of the history of banking", *Journal of World History*, 2: 56–57.

de Roover, R. (1956), "The development of accounting prior to Luca Pacioli according to the account-books of medieval merchants", in Littleton, A.C. and Yamey, B. (Eds), *Studies in the history of accounting*, Sweet & Maxwell Limited, London, 114–174.

De Savonne, P. (1567), *Instrucion et manière de tenir les livres de compte par parties doubles, soit en compagnie soit en particulier*, edited by Christophle Plantin, Anvers.

Favero, G. (2015), "L'insegnamento delle discipline aziendali a Venezia dalla Scuola superiore di commercio all'Università Ca' Foscari", in Mantoan, D. and Bianchi, S. (Eds), *30+ anni di aziendalisti in Laguna. Gli studi manageriali a Venezia*, Edizioni Ca' Foscari, Venezia, 21–35.

Fontana, B. (1551), *Ammaestramento novo che insegna a tener libro*, Venezia.

Katz, P. (1930), "A surmise regarding the origin of bookkeeping by double entry", *The Accounting Review*, 5(4): 311–316.

Lane, F.C. (1944), *Andrea Barbarigo, Merchant of Venice (1418–1499)*, The John Hopkins Press, Baltimore.

Littleton, A.C. (1928), "Paciolo and modern accounting", *The Accounting Review*, 3(2): 131–140.

Littleton, A.C. (1933), *Accounting Evolution to 1900*, American Institute Publishing Co. Inc., New York.

Luzzatto, G. (1960), *Storia economica dell'età moderna e contemporanea*, Cedam, Padova.

Manzoni, D. (1540), *Quaderno doppio col suo giornale, novamente composto, e diligentemente ordinato, secondo il costume di Venezia. Opera a ogni persona utilissima, & molto necessaria*, Comin da Trino di Monferrato, Venezia.

Masi, V. (1975), *La ragioneria nell'età medievale*, Tamari, Bologna.

Melis, F. (1950), *Storia della ragioneria. Contributo alla conoscenza e interpretazione delle fonti più significative della storia economica*, Dott. Cesare Zuffi, Bologna.

Ministero d'Agricoltura, Industria e Commercio (1868), *Ordinamento della Regia Scuola Superiore di Commercio in Venezia*, Tipografia di G. Barbéra, Firenze.

Notizie e dati raccolti dalla Commissione organizzatrice per la Esposizione internazionale marittima di Napoli aperta il 17 aprile 1871 (1871), Tipografia del Commercio di Marco Visentini, Venezia.

Oldcastle, H. (1543), *A profitable treatyce called the instrument or boke to learn to know the good order of the kepyng of the famouse reconynge, called in Latin, Dare and Habere, and, in English, debtor and Creditor*, edited by John Gouge, London.

Pacioli, L. (1494), *Summa de Arithmetica, Geometria, Proportioni et Proportionalita*, Paganino de Paganini, Venezia.

Peragallo, E. (1938), *Origin and evolution of double entry bookkeeping: A study of Italian practice from the fourteenth century*, American Institute Publishing Company, New York.

Peragallo, E. (1956), "Origin of the trial balance", *The Accounting Review*, 31(3): 389–394.

Pietra, A. (1586), *Indrizzo degli economi, ossia ordinatissima instruttione da regolatamente formare qualunque scrittura in un libro doppio; aggiuntovi l'essemplare di un libro nobile col suo giornale, ad uso della congregation cassinese, dell'ordine di S. Benedetto. Con due tavole, l'una de' capitoli, et l'altra delle cose piu degne, a pieno intendimento di ciascuno. Opera nuova, non meno utile che necessaria, a Religiosi, che vivono delle proprie Rendite, & ad ogni Padre di Famiglia, che si diletti del Libro Doppio*, Per Francesco Osanna, Mantova.

Rocha, A. (1565), *Compendio y breue instruction por tener Libros de Cuenta y Deudas, y de Mercaduria: muy prouechoso para Mercaderes, y toda gente de negocio, traduzido de Frances en Castellano*, Claudio Bornat, Barcelona.

Sangster, A. (2010), "Using accounting history and Luca Pacioli to put relevance back into the teaching of double entry", *Accounting, Business and Financial History*, 20(1): 23–39.

Sangster, A. (2016), "The genesis of double-entry bookkeeping", *The Accounting Review*, 9(1): 299–315.

Sangster, A. and Scataglinibelghitar, G. (2010), "Luca Pacioli: The father of accounting education", *Accounting Education*, 19(4): 423–438.

Saporetti, F. (1898), *Frà Luca Paciolo. Origine e sviluppo della partita doppia*, Stab. Tipo. S. Belforte & Co., Livorno.

Sargiacomo, M., Servalli, S., and Andrei, P. (2012), "Fabio Besta: Accounting thinker and accounting history pioneer", *Accounting History Review*, 22(3): 249–267.

Schweicker, W. (1549), *Zwifach Buchhalten, sampt seinen Giornal des selben Beschlus auch Rechnung zuthun*, Johann Petreius, Nurnberg.

Tagliente, G.A. (1525), *Considerando io Ioanni Antonio Taiente quanto e necessaria cosa a li nostri magnifici gentilhomeni & adaltri mercatanti el laudabile modo de tenere conto de libro dopio cioe, el zornale, el libro con l'alphabetto secondo el consueto de questa inclita città di Venetia, io qui seguendo con l'agiuto del mio carissimo compagno Aluise da la Fontana, vi daremo lo amaestramento che con facilita lo potrete imparare, laqual opera ancor sarà di molta utilità universalmente ad ogniuno, come ne l'opera vedereti*, Venezia.

Valussi, P. (1875–76), "Venezia e il suo avvenire", in *Atti del Reale Istituto Veneto di Scienze, Lettere ed Arti, dal novembre 1875 all'ottobre 1876*, Tip. Grimaldo e C., Venezia.

Vlaemminck, J.H. (1956), *Histoire et doctrines de la comptabilité*, Éditions du Treurenberg—Dunod, Bruxelles-Paris.

Walker, S.P. (2005), "Accounting in history", *The Accounting Historians Journal*, 33(2): 233–259.

Walker, S.P. (2008), "The search for innovation, convergence and argument without end in accounting history", *Accounting, Auditing & Accountability Journal*, 21(2): 296–322.

Woolf, A.H. (1912), *A short history of accountants and accountancy*, Gee & Co., London.

Ympyn, Christoffels J. (1543), *Nieuwe Instructie Ende Bewys der Looffelycker Consten des Rekenboeckse ende Reckinghete houdene nae die Italiaensche maniere allen Cooplieden Rentmeesteren Tollenaren Assysmeesteren zeer nut ende profytelyk*, & Co., Antwerp.

Zerbi, T. (1952), *Le origini della partita doppia. Gestioni aziendali e situazioni di mercato nei secoli XIV e XV*, Dott. Carlo Marzorati Editore, Milano.

Section 1

Accounting Treatises

1 The Venetian Treatises

A Frame

Stefano Coronella and Lucrezia Santaniello

Introduction

It is traditionally taught by accounting historians (Melis, 1950, 19–20) that the rise of modern accounting history coincides with the first printed work we know—that is, the *Summa* by Luca Pacioli.

Yet double entry had already been invented and had been in use for over a century in the small business houses of Italian merchants. Its conception tided up with the flourishing of trade thanks to the development until the end of the fifteenth century of independent communes, signorias, princedoms and maritime republics and to the connected need to control and report acts of management of companies, which had grown in both dimension and business scope (Peragallo, 1938, 1–37; De Roover, 1955, 405–420).

It's hard to know who the first author to write a work about double-entry bookkeeping was, since until the last decades of the fifteenth century Gutenberg printing didn't exist (invented in 1455 and slightly introduced in Italy starting from 1463).

Consequently whoever wrote about the subject before that time couldn't issue his work, which remained as a manuscript, with the exception of Benedetto Cotrugli's (cf. § 3.1), which was rediscovered and printed 115 years after its writing.

Otherwise, already before the publishing of the *Summa* by Pacioli in several towns of the Italian Peninsula there were master charts of accounts bookkeeping and masters who taught double entry (Bariola, 1897, 59–63; Besta, 1916, 345–346; Melis, 1950, 59).

Thus it is probable that those very preceptors, at least some of them, had arranged somewhat structured notes to carry out their work. A well-known example is Master Troilo, quoted in a 1457 ledger and journal belonging to Nicolò and Alvise Barbarigo's brothers. In them the "*quattro soldi lira di grossi*" (four coins of heavy lira) expense is entered to pay "*maistro*" (master) Troilo as a compensation for teaching bookkeeping in the previous six months (Alfieri, 1891, 108–109; Besta, 1916, 345–346, 376–377).

In that period many others taught the double-entry method to merchants and, generally, they were the same teachers of abacus and calligraphy, which were never carried out separately according to the custom of that time.

Actually, by chance, even some of the first printed books—which were issued in low quantity due to the high cost of printing, above all in the early years—could have been lost. Vittorio Alfieri reminds us (Alfieri, 1891, 109) that in a journal dated 1484 entitled "Zornale R" owned by Francesco Minuzani, a Paduan librarian who worked in Venice, there is a list of books of his small business house where works of bookkeeping and abacus are referenced, some of which have not been catalogued in any library.

It is possible that these works contained references to double entry, due to the strict relation of the aforementioned subjects.

According to the updated knowledge, the first author in the timeline who illustrated the double-entry method was Benedetto Cotrugli in a manuscript dated 1458. There is a wider edition too, which has been found only in the 1990s and is known as "Malta's manuscript" (Sangster, 2014). This is also the only celebrated manuscript enshrining double-entry notions which was arranged before the *Summa* by Luca Pacioli.

It is worth noting that the first Italian double-entry treatises were all issued in Venice—from Pacioli up to the early years of the seventeenth century, and thus for over a century—except for a chapter of the 1539 book by Gerolamo Cardano (Cardano, 1539) and the 1586 edition by Angelo Pietra (Pietra, 1586). This witnesses the pivotal and privileged role in cultural hegemony played by Venice for such a long period of time. Starting from the seventeenth century the publication of accounting works spread all over the territory.

The principal aim of this work is to frame the Venetian treatises compared with double-entry works in the Italian Peninsula. Following, the contents of the most relevant writings will be briefly commented on in order to find a "conceptual frame" of the contributions provided by several authors to the growth of accounting. Some of these books are widely commented on in the deepening of the present volume.

The Leadership of the Venetian Treatises in the Italian Peninsula and All Over the World

In order to gain an overview of the Venetian treatises within double-entry Italian works (in the Italian language) a detailed and complete bibliography has to be available.

To do so, the famous "*Elenco cronologico delle opere di computisteria e ragioneria*" ("Chronological list of commercial arithmetic and bookkeeping works") has been gathered, which was edited by Giuseppe Cerboni and published by the Italian General Accounting Department (Cerboni, 1889). As accounting history scholars know, this volume, especially its fourth and last edition, which is the widest and the most updated, is still the largest and most complete bibliography on the issue (Coronella, 2016).[1]

Specifically, this volume lists all the works, manuscripts included, from *Liber Abaci* by Leonardo Fibonacci (1202) to 1888 (year of the end of the inquiry).

Table 1.1 Number of works on accounting divided into centuries

Century	*Fifteenth*	*Sixteenth*	*Seventeenth*	*Eighteenth*	*Nineteenth (up to 1888)*	
Number of works	1	9	17	23	517 among which	
					106 from 1800 to1860	411 from1861 to 1888

Source: Authors' elaboration from Cerboni (1889), VII–IX

Table 1.2 Average span of time occurring between one publication and the following one

Century	*Fifteenth*	*Sixteenth*	*Seventeenth*	*Eighteenth*	*Nineteenth (up to 1888)*	
Average span of time occurring between one publication and the following one	Only one publication in the whole century	11 years and 1 month	5 years and 10 months	4 years and 4 months	2 months, of which	
					7 months From 1800 to 1860	25 days From 1861 to 1888

Source: Authors

Concerning the works about double entry, the analysis of the volume underlines an exponential growth in time, as illustrated in Table 1.1.

The sense of the exponential growth of the accounting works is conceived through the analysis of the two sub-periods of the nineteenth century as preceding and following the unification of Italy (from 1861 to 1888).

In the first sixty years of the nineteenth century more than a hundred works were published—a huge increase compared to previous centuries—whereas in less than thirty years since the unification of the country more than four hundred works have been catalogued.

The relevance of these data lies in the average span of time occurring between one publication and the following one (see Table 1.2).

In the fifteenth century there is only a single printed work of accounting (the *Summa* by Pacioli), in the sixteenth century an average of one publication each eleven years, in the seventeenth century one nearly each six years, in the eighteenth century one every four years and a bit, in the nineteenth century up to the unification of Italy one printed work each seven months and, after the unification, one every twenty-five days—an amazing growing rate.

Therefore, up to the unification of Italy just in Venice the printed works have been listed in Table 1.3.

Table 1.3 Number of accounting works printed in Venice

Fifteenth century	*Sixteenth century*	*Seventeenth century*	*Total up to seventeenth century*	*Eighteenth century*	*Total up to eighteenth century*	*Nineteenth century (up to 1860)*	*Total overall (1494–1860)*
1 Pacioli (1494)	7 Tagliente (1525) Anonymous (1525) Anonymous (1529) Manzoni (1540)[2] Fontana (1551) Casanova (1558) Cotrugli (1573)	4 Grisogono (1609) Moschetti (1610) Garatti (1688) Agostinetti (1679)	**11**	2 Cortinovis (1782) Farghiscoc (1787)	**13**	7 D'Anastasio (1803a; 1803b) Papaziour (1822) Anonymous (1824) De Peretti (1827) Gabelli (1837) Garello (1857) Tonzig (1857–59)	**20**

Source: Authors

Among the ten printed works in Italy between the fifteenth and sixteenth centuries (see Table 1.1) listed in Cerboni's bibliography, eight of them (80%) are Venetian. The only exceptions are the brief essay by Gerolamo Cardano issued in Milan as a part of a work of arithmetic (Cardano, 1539) and the volume by Angelo Pietra issued in Mantua (Pietra, 1586).

The essay by Cardano consists of a brief chapter (a few pages written in Latin),[3] whereas the work by Pietra is the last one issued in the sixteenth century. This means that for a long time Venice had a total "cultural monopoly" in the double-entry field (Zan, 1994, 263–264).

This perspective being strengthened, it is worth noting that in Cerboni's bibliography a further Venetian manuscript dated 1516 (Gian Francesco, 1516) has not been listed.

In the following centuries, double entry and the related treatises spread all over the Peninsula; thus "Venetian leadership" declined as time passed.

Actually, among the several printed works in the further centuries, some Venetian ones stand out as having excellent remarks compared to the mean.

The Venetian Treatises From the Fifteenth to the Nineteenth Centuries: An Overview

The "Trattato di mercatura" *(Treatise of Merchants) by Benedetto Cotrugli (1458, 1475, 1573)*

As far as we know, Benedetto Cotrugli, merchant and diplomatic agent, was the first to illustrate double entry in a manuscript dated 25 August 1458.

His work, entitled "*L'arte di mercatura*" (The art of merchants), although written before the *Summa* by Pacioli, suffered the misfortune of being printed only in 1573 with the running head "*Della mercatura et del mercante perfetto*" ("About the essence of business practice and the proper conduct of a merchant"), moreover with several interventions compared to the original version which took place 115 years after its writing as well as 80 years after the publication of the *Summa* (Cotrugli, 1573).

Unfortunately, the earlier version of the manuscript has not reached the contemporary age, but information about its date is supplied by the following copies of his work (in those days, the print hadn't been invented yet so books were copied by amanuenses or copyists). Nowadays three different manuscripts exist: the first preserved at La Valletta in the National Library of Malta, whose copy was drawn up in Naples in 1475 by Marino de Raphaeli from Ragusa; the second one preserved in the National Library of Florence and ended on 17 March 1484 by Giovanni de Matteo di Giovanni Strozzi; and a third unfinished copy (it ends at the eighteenth chapter of the third book) without any date (but dating back to the fifteenth century) and preserved in the Marucelliana Library in Florence (Coronella, 2014, 56).

The most interesting is the one from Malta, uncovered only at the end of the 1980s. The first accounting history scholars to have dealt with it are

Dutch: Johanna Postma and Anne J. Van der Helm in 1998 (Postma, Van der Helm, 1998). In recent times, a thoroughly detailed work on this manuscript by Alan Sangster (Sangster, 2014) has been issued.

Before 1998, Cotrugli was referred to in the printed 1573 work (composed of 106 charts),[4] whose references to accounting are quite poor.

Indeed, this volume confines itself to a few pages of exposition on the accounting books for merchants and some specific entries, as well as on the closing of accounts in Chapter 13 (entitled "*Dell'ordine di tenere le scritture mercantilmente*" [About the correct posting of entries]) and in Chapter 19 (running head "*Il saldo si deve fare ogni sette anni*" [The closing ought to be carried out every seven years]) of the first book. Actually, it never delves deeper into the bookkeeping method, as Paciolo does (Peragallo, 1938, 54–55).

For this reason, accounting history scholars have rather neglected Cotrugli compared with the ampler coverage they have devoted to the *Summa* by Pacioli.

Nevertheless, unlike the other two already known books as well as the printed work itself, Malta's manuscript includes a broadened appendix, which contains a patrimonial inventory and 266 ledger entries dated 1475,[5] in Naples. This certainly throws a new light on the extent of Cotrugli's work.

Moreover, it is worth noting that compared to the printed work, the various handwritten versions we know do not coincide in many aspects. The printed version largely differs, thus including deletions, amendments and integrations provided by Francesco Patrizi, who edited the issue of the book. Patrizi's interventions were thoroughly warping and caused many biases. Indeed, the 1573 printed work, biased by many arbitrary revisions, shows significant differences compared to the original version. The most affected section is the one devoted to bookkeeping, which turns out to be devalued with regard to the manuscripts.

The few pages of Chapters 13 and 19 (out of a total of fifty-one chapters)[6] suggest a shallow approach to the subject, whereas the volume itself deals primarily with the merchant and its business matters.

Surely, this is the reason Cotrugli's value and work have never aroused interest in accounting historians, at least up to the last decades, when Malta's manuscript with its broadened appendix of accounting entries was unveiled.

In Cotrugli's manuscript, the references on double entry do not appear scant at all. He illustrates the retain and evidential functions of accounting entries, and he lists the books merchants ought to keep: specifically "*Libriccino delle Ricordanze*" (memorandum book), the "*Libro Giornale*" (journal) and "*Libro Grande*" (ledger), which is also named "*Quaderno*" in the 1573 printed book.

Following, two other accounting books have to be added: "*Copia-conti*" (account copying book) and "*Copia-lettere*" (bills of exchange book).

Cotrugli recommends the Venetian way of bookkeeping, specifically how the items have to be entered in the journal, insofar as the prepositions "*per*" (for) and "*a*" (to) are respectively set before the debit entries (i.e., the one referring to the creditor for liabilities) and the credit entries (referring to the debtor for receivables). Hereafter, Paciolo does the same.

Furthermore, he illustrates the closure of the accounts (without any accrual post), and the extraction of a balance, thus singling out earned profits or incurred losses, which have to be transferred to the capital account. He also recommends the settlement of accounts and the collection of payments every six years, while the seventh year (a sort of sabbatical year) has to be devoted to the rest, to the auditing of accounts and to forward budgeting.

As regards the appendix, the inventory is dated 19 December 1475 and refers to Rafael de Nicolo. It is followed by 266 entries and the most interesting ones are those dealing with the chain of silk business, from the purchase of raw materials to the sale of resulting products, through the manufacturing process as well as the construction of a building.

That said, the question is whether Cotrugli would have ever theorized a proper thought on the double-entry system, thus prevailing over Paciolo. Otherwise, he would have merely illustrated the method in its brief treatment as a practical guide, thus strengthening it through a set of specimen accounts (according to what Malta's manuscript reveals).

On this issue, divergent views have been raised. Yet, some argue that Cotrugli's work would not discard the worth Paciolo ought to deserve. Actually, the former limits the scope of his manuscript to a mere description which neither goes beyond practical concerns nor reveals intellectual effort (Tucci, 1990, 12–13). By contrast, Paciolo deserves credit for the double-entry system being theorized and popularized. According to others, Cotrugli can be considered the first theorist of the double-entry method, because he was its first illustrator, although the double-entry practice had long been in use by Italian merchants at that time (Privitera, 2003, 140).

However, compared to Cotrugli, Paciolo has the merit of having illustrated the double-entry method empirically and more in detail. Furthermore, he was able to have his work printed, thus attaining a wider distribution, whereas Cotrugli's work remained unknown until 1573. Anyway, this latter print version fails to comply with the original one and proves to be incomplete because of the lack of appendix, which is included in "Malta's manuscript".

Moreover, with respect to Paciolo's printed exposition, the one by Cotrugli turns out to be both synthetic and rough. In this respect, the purpose of the author has to be singled out: instead of drafting a treatise on the double-entry method, Cotrugli aimed to stress the importance of keeping books and records within the wider range of proficiencies a merchant had to have (Mari, 1998, 357).

The Summa *by Luca Pacioli (1494)*

According to the current outstanding, Benedetto Cotrugli was the first illustrator of double-entry bookkeeping while the Franciscan friar and teacher Luca Pacioli was the first to have popularized it on a large scale.

Undoubtedly, Pacioli took advantage of both the fact that his treatise had been issued in the form of a "printed" publication in copious amounts and, moreover, the fact that the section devoted to double entry came to be composed in a thoroughly detailed way and through pedagogical devices in order to maximize learning (Sangster, Scataglinibelghitar, 2010).

Also known as "Paciolo", he wrote several works on arithmetic and geometry. Unfortunately some of them have not come down to us. Among them, there are some which mark milestones for mathematical studies, specifically the *Divina proportione* and the *Summa de Arithmetica* (Cavazzoni, 2009, 33–72).

Indeed, the *Summa de Arithmetica, Geometria, Proportioni et Proportionalita* elicits our interest. It was published in Venice in 1494 (Pacioli, 1494) and reprinted in Tuscolano del Garda in 1523 (Pacioli, 1523). It is composed of 308 charts, or 616 pages, and the section entirely devoted to double-entry bookkeeping is the one entitled *Tractatus XI* of *Distinctio IX*, with the running head "*De computis et scripturis*", which includes thirty-six chapters (from the front side of chart 197 to 210), and also contains useful suggestions about good management for merchants (Hernández-Esteve, 1994, 67–82).[7]

In his treatise, Pacioli describes double-entry bookkeeping according to the "*modo de Vinegia*" (Venetian manner), which he thought to be the best among the methods long available in the practice of the diverse territories of Italy.

The *Tractatus* is carved up into two sections. The first one deals with "inventory"—that is to say, the assets and the liabilities of the firm—while the second wider part deals with transactions.

In a thoroughly detailed way, Pacioli illustrates three books a merchant has to keep, referring mainly to family business: the "*Memoriale*" (memorandum book), the "*Giornale*" (journal) and the "*Quaderno*" (ledger) (Peragallo, 1938, 55–60).

The format for the journal entries reproduces the typical Venetian one, which remained in use for a few more centuries: preceding the debit entries by the preposition "*per*" (for) and the credit entries by ": *a*" (: to).

Paciolo points out that all the records entered in the journal ought to be counter-debited and credited simultaneously in the ledger. The ledger accounts are chronologically arranged and, in addition, there is an alphabetical list of the same accounts appended to the ledger in order to better thëir search.

With the aim of facilitating the drafter's task, the page numbers of the ledger are copied within the journal next to the records those entries refer to.

Pacioli focuses on the entries concerning goods purchases, barters, relationships with public companies, and expenses, and he broadly illustrates the "*de botega*" account (warehouse account) and the "*pro et danno*" account (profit and loss account).

Further, he illustrates the way to correct errors and the closure of the accounts he suggests to perform each year avoiding the accrual accounts—that is to say, aiming to verify their balancing through the drafting of a trial balance. Hence, Pacioli applies for the determination of the economic result within the profit and loss account, which includes all the revenues and the expenses as well as the goods accounts devoid of any stock inventory. In this regard, Pacioli's balance can be considered as a middle ground between a trial balance and a modern financial statement (Antinori, 1994, 27).

Pacioli launched the path of the "personalization of the accounts" method, which would be further accomplished in the nineteenth century. Although he illustrated only the underlying logic of the double-entry method, he accidentally dealt with accounts, thus framing an early and embryonic stage "theory" which refers to how main accounts work as well as what they are intended for (Poddighe, 1973, 8–9).

In practice, albeit the purpose was to technically illustrate the debits and credits, Pacioli personalized the accounts entitled to things as a pedagogic device, instead of crafting a theory of accounts. Hence, two kinds of accounts arise from the model by Pacioli according to their nature: "personal" accounts, which are entitled to "persons"—that is, to the proprietor or to third debtors or creditors—and "materialistic accounts", standing for cash, stock inventories ("botega"), furniture and so on. For non-personalistic ones a fiction of identifying accounts entitled to "things" with persons is introduced. Through this tool, they get fictitiously "personalized".

"Arithmetico" *(Arithmetic) (1516), a Manuscript by Gian Francesco*

Following the *Summa* by Pacioli, the first known work concerning double-entry bookkeeping is represented by a manuscript which was authored by a mathematician, simply signing as "Gian Francesco" (Yamey, 1967, 74–76). Actually, it is impossible to find any other information about him because the aforementioned work is a manuscript dating back to the early 1500s. The first page is inscribed "*Ego Joanes Franciscus arithmeticus venetiis feci*" (I, Gian Francesco, Venetian mathematicians, wrote this book).

This manuscript has been included into the 1516 Cartulary Code and is preserved in the Correr Museum in Venice. It has been thoroughly analyzed and discussed first by Vincenzo Vianello (Vianello, 1896, 157–163), who describes it as a seventy-chart handwritten work, including a few initial pages of exposition on double-entry bookkeeping as well as contractions and vagueness. Moreover, at certain points it is nearly illegible.

Gian Francesco illustrates double-entry bookkeeping according to the Venetian manner and he lists some books—namely, the journal, the ledger, and the alphabetical list of accounts but not the memorandum book.

The work does not enshrine any particular innovation with respect to the *Summa* by Pacioli except for an operation the author describes. It concerns the assumption of an obligation through an engagement entry which consists of two memorandum accounts intended as a reminder of a ten-year lease agreement for land.

It deals with the first example of an entry in the memorandum accounts within the bookkeeping treatises, since neither Pacioli nor Cotrugli had alluded to it before (Serra, 1999, 148).

This is the only relevant part of the manuscript which is largely devoted to applied arithmetic. It is worth noting the numerous errors contained therein, which suggest that the author was not competent in the keeping of accounts (Serra, 1999, 148).

The "Luminario di Arithmetica" *(Arithmetic Luminary) by Giovanni Antonio Tagliente (1525)*

The Venetian Giovanni Antonio Tagliente was the first who had print issues after Pacioli. The first author to have dealt with his treatise was Pietro Rigobon (Rigobon, 1894).

He was neither merchant nor mathematician, but a calligraphy teacher. For about thirty years, he taught it to the pupils at the chancellor's office of the Venetian Republic as an "appointee of Serenissima". For this reason, he was among the first to have works printed about calligraphy. Moreover, he published volumes on several subjects—for instance, about models of letters according to requirements, a book aiming to teach reading skills in a short time, a book addressed to women about sewing and drawing and a collection of love letters (Coronella, 2014, 75–76).

It might sound curious that he issued a work on accounting entitled "*Luminario di Aritmetica*" (Arithmetic luminary)—it would be better to define it as a booklet because of its brevity—which is carved up into two sections. Actually, he helped his brother Girolamo write an abacus book (Tagliente, 1515); thus he would have not been unfamiliar with the matter and this ought not to be overlooked.

This extremely rare work was published in 1525 with a very long title, which is usually known as "*Luminario di aritmetica, libro ugnolo*" (Arithmetic luminary, single entry) and "*Luminario di aritmetica, libro doppio*" (Arithmetic luminary, double entry) in the abridged form (Tagliente, 1525). The first volume deals with single entry ("*libro ugnolo*" or "*sempio*"—"single book") and the second one with double entry ("*libro doppio*"—"double book"), authored together with Alvise de la Fontana.

Actually, the twenty-eight-chart volume on double-entry bookkeeping does not elicit much interest: devoid of a theoretical section, it strictly follows the approach by Pacioli but it reveals many gaps, such as the lack of closure of accounts, of assessment of entries and of revisions of errors, as well as the lack of a memorandum book (Melis, 1950, 640).

By contrast, the sixteen-chart volume "*Libro ugnolo*" proves to be very interesting, since it represents the first print work illustrating single entry. Although the single-entry method was more ancient than the double-entry method, it had not been exposed in a volume since then. Neither Pacioli, nor Cotrugli, nor Gian Francesco (the arithmetic) had ever been engaged with it.

As far as Tagliente is concerned, he remains the first known author to have focused on this method, thus applying it to small commercial firms and to artisans—that is to say, wherever double entry was too labored. Therefore, he deals with the single-entry method only in the "*Quaderno*" (ledger), thus laying down some rules—for instance, for the opening and the managing of the ledger accounts to be debited or credited; he also appeals for the household costs to be entered while not referring to any journal, thus implying that small commercial firms did not opt for it at that time.

"La tenuta del libro Mastro" *(The Ledger Keeping) (1525) and the* "Opera che insegna a tener libro doppio" *(Essay on the Teaching of Double Entry) (1529) by Anonymous*

In the same year the "*Luminario di Aritmetica*" was published, the volume entitled "*La tenuta del libro mastro pel negoziante e il possidente*" (The ledger keeping for merchant and principal) was issued too. The author has remained unknown and his work, being mentioned within Cerboni's bibliography references (Cerboni, 1889, 24), is described as a brief as well as sheer format booklet, which is composed of six charts. Fabio Besta dismisses it as a "*libercolo*"—that is to say, a "booklet"—"not worth talking about" (Besta, 1916, 380), since it doesn't include a theoretical section and entirely deals with some specimen entries which refer to 1525. Moreover, Besta notes that the title Cerboni mentions within his bibliography references and the one listed in the catalogue of the Marciana Library are both wrong. The original title he believes is "*Opera che insegna a tener conto de libro secondo lo consueto de tutti li lochi della Italia al modo mercantile*" (Essay on the teaching of ledger keeping with respect to praxis among all Italian places in the mercantile field).

According to Besta, the following unknown 1529 work, which is entitled "*Opera che insegna a tener libro doppio . . . novamente stampata*" (Essay on the teaching of double entry . . . printed again) and consists of eight smaller format charts, would be merely a reprint of the first work (Besta, 1916, 380–381).

Notwithstanding, this essay deserves credit, not so much for its nearly zero-value contribution to the development of the discipline as for the attempt it makes to popularize and spread the double-entry system among merchants.

Indeed, merchants were unable to draw from the awkward as well as intensive *Summa* by Pacioli. Actually, the *Summa* had been reprinted earlier, in 1523 (Serra, 1999, 147–148).

Quaderno doppio *(Double Ledger) by Domenico Manzoni (1540)*

In 1540 the *Quaderno doppio col suo giornale* (Double ledger with its journal) by Domenico Manzoni (Manzoni, 1540) was published. Manzoni was a teacher of calligraphy, abacus and bookkeeping and worked as an accountant too. Among the writers of treatises on double entry, he was thus the first to be involved in accountancy on a practical and professional level. His book, which consists of ninety-one pages and a chart, went through a number of editions (1554, 1564, 1573), some with slight changes to the title although the content remained basically unchanged.

The content is subdivided into a theoretical section and a practical one. The former does not differ substantially from Pacioli's *Summa*, from which it borrows several concepts (Della Penna, 1950, 282).

The innovative aspect of Manzoni's work lies in the type of practical application that he proposes, which was not addressed to seasoned experts—as Paciolo's partially did—but to young and aspiring accountants wishing to learn the double-entry method. Manzoni essentially refitted concepts which had already been developed by Paciolo, thus making them accessible to a much wider public. From this point of view, the volume can be compared to modern accounting textbooks used in high schools of accounting (Serra, 1999, 160).

In the theoretical section, Manzoni lays down some basic rules on the existence of capital, the record and the order of the entries, stressing that the latter should not contain erasures or abrasions. In addition, the authentication of the accounts is more advisable (although this was not the custom at the time in Venice). The author's emphasis on the reliability of the entries also emerges from the fact that in the ledger he still uses Roman numerals instead of Arabic ones because they are harder to falsify and thus the ledgers would have a greater probative value in the event of litigation.

It should be pointed out that Manzoni was the first author to include sequential numbers for double entries. Indeed, he argues that the journal and the ledger must contain six things: outgoing, incoming, quality, quantity, time and order (Manzoni, 1540, chap. 13).

As already mentioned, in the practical section, Manzoni seeks to show the bookkeeping of a single company in a very detailed manner (he includes about three hundred types of double entries). He thus supposes the start-up of a business and its relative operations until the closure of the accounts, describing in the margin—with a clearly pedagogic purpose—what each entry refers to.

It is worth remembering that despite adopting the personalistic theory of accounts, he proposes the distinction between "living things" (persons) and "dead things" (goods) and thus distinguishes between accounts in the name of persons and accounts in the name of things. It is probably for this reason that some authors, including Ceccherelli (1915, 64), have seen in Manzoni's work the first attempt to categorize accounts (for people and things).

The Ammaestramento novo *(New Teaching on Bookkeeping) by Bartolomeo Fontana (1551)*

Cerboni's bibliography (Cerboni, 1889, 24) hints at an essay by Bartolomeo Fontana. He was born around 1520 and was a Venetian merchant as well as an abacus master and a calligraphy teacher. The book was published in 1551 as *Ammaestramento novo che insegna a tener libro* (New teaching on bookkeeping).

In particular, in the aforementioned bibliographic note, the following reference is entered:

1551. Fontana Bartolomeo

Ammaestramento novo che Insegna a Tener Libro

Ordinatamente ad uso di questa inclita città di Venetia come etiam di tutta l'Italia. Da componer e metter le partite in Libro del dare et havere, et render robbe a tempo in vari et diversi modi, et tener conto di Botega: Far accordi, accetar promesse et dinari in Bancho, in imprestito. Affittar case, possessioni, accordar sercio, Tirar dinari a Cambio et tener conto de spese de casa [. . .]. Stampato dell'anno MDLI.

(Bibl. Di Osimo)

New Teaching on Bookkeeping

In this glorious city of Venice as undoubtedly all over Italy [the bookkeeping method] is in use. Be laid down entries and in credit and debit book entered, [as well as] be accounted goods for as requested by various manners and times, and be kept the Inventory account: do business, accept payments of debtor warrants and cash to bank [as well as] be granted loans. Properties and lands be rented, accommodation and exchange gains be drawn and the house expenses be taken into account. Printed in the year MDLI.

(Library in Osimo)

A brief marginal note hints that this volume is not mentioned by the well-known "*Biblioteca Matematica Italiana*" (Italian mathematic bibliography) by Riccardi (Riccardi, 1870) and that the essay briefly deals with the single-entry bookkeeping method.

Cerboni's note reports the availability of the work at Osimo Library but that is not so; probably, if this wasn't an error, the book either got lost or was stolen.[8]

Fortunately, the volume was examined by Pietro Rigobon (Rigobon, 1894), who describes it as an eight-page booklet entirely dealing with single entry, thus consisting of a shallow summary of the first volume by Tagliente. Fabio Besta comments on this work too, defining it as a booklet (Besta, 1916, 394–395, n. 8).

Specchio lucidissimo *(Very Clear Mirror) by Alvise Casanova (1558)*

Alvise Casanova was a fiscal accountant in Venice, where he worked as an auditor and taught double-entry bookkeeping, especially to young people.

His book, entitled *Specchio lucidissimo nel quale si vedeno essere diffinito tutti i modi, & ordini de scrittura* (Very clear mirror, in which any way of keeping the accounts is defined) (Casanova, 1558), was published a few years after it was written, having already circulated among his pupils as a manuscript.

The volume is composed of 138 charts and is divided into theoretical and practical sections. The former is rather short and is structured as a dialogue with an interlocutor and also contains comments on the authors of previous treatises, who cannot boast positive judgements.

It is not characterized by originality and new ideas compared to already known works, in particular those by Pacioli and Manzoni (Bariola, 1897, 380).

The practical section is in contrast highly complex and characterized by a certain degree of originality. The examples on double entry, whose items in the journal are highly detailed, in some cases taking up a full page, refer to an imaginary mercantile company founded by two Flemish brothers, Vielmo and Zuane Zanforth. They travel to Venice with a great amount of funds, rent a house, buy furniture and deal with a shipyard in co-ownership with others, with the aim of importing goods from the Middle East and the goal of reselling them in Germany. Besides this, they gain equity stakes in other companies and work as commission agents, running operations on bills of exchange and currency exchange.

Indeed, Casanova illustrates a broad and variegated set of specimen entries and thus he provides a realistic, complete and significant picture of the management of a trading company.

There is no doubt that, according to some authors, thanks to the numerous detailed examples on the posting of entries, Casanova's work marks a considerable step forward in the practice of double entry compared to previous writers. It is the work on double entry which more broadly dealt with the concrete application of accounting entries at that time (Vianello, 1896, 54).[9]

Moreover, those very items reappear decades later, almost unchanged, in the *Mercante Arricchito* (The enriched merchant) by Simone Grisogono (1609) and both in the content and in the layout of the *Dell'Universal Trattato di Libri Doppii* (The universal treatise about double entry) by Giovanni Antonio Moschetti (1610) (Vianello, 1896, 155).

Another important innovation with respect to previous treatises lies in the fact that for the first time, closing goods are evaluated according to "inventory cost", incorporating the expected markup on the goods rather than the book value alone. Thus a process was initiated first with Angelo Pietra and later with Lodovico Flori that would lead to the affirmation of the matching principle. Although Casanova himself was still a long way from this, by including this type of information he prevented the partial economic result of the goods entries from impacting completely on the financial year in which their sale was finalized. In contrast, previous authors had been in the habit of assessing the inventory by its book value, thereby counting the profit or loss from the sale entirely in the year in which it was made, even when this was many years after the goods were purchased.

Another feature in Casanova's book is that the general journal contains the entries for the general closure of accounts at the end of one financial year and those of their reopening in the next one, with the difference, however, that the profits from the previous financial year are not converted into equity but are left in the accounts even after the reopening.

Another feature of the book lies in the presence, scattered among the accounting entries, of numerous calculations, above all concerning exchange rates between the various currencies.

The Mercante arricchito *(The Enriched Merchant) by Simon Grisogono (1609)*

The first Italian written treatise on double-entry bookkeeping appearing in the seventeenth century is the *Mercante arricchito dal perfetto quaderniere* (The enriched merchant by the perfect accountant) by Simon Grisogono (Grisogono, 1609).[10] He was a nobleman of the city of Zara, in Istria.

It consists of 130 pages and six charts, being divided into two parts: a theoretical section and an application section. The first part illustrates the double-entry bookkeeping method while the second one reports a journal with its ledger and the appended alphabetical list.[11]

The volume does not provide any original features concerning contents. Indeed, the application section is almost entirely borrowed from Casanova with little revision. The theoretical one is wider than the work by Casanova as well as more incisive from a didactic perspective (Melis, 1950, 372) except for the innovativeness of its contents.

This treatise displays originality in the layout of the accounts: Grisogono is the first author using the sole preposition "*a*" to separate the debit entries and the credit entries (ahead of the entry being credited) (Melis, 1950, 372; Privitera, 2003, 199).[12] Previously it was customary to insert the preposition "for" ahead of the entry being debited.

Dell'Universal trattato di libri doppii *(Universal Treatise About Double Entry) by Giovanni Antonio Moschetti (1610)*

Giovanni Antonio Moschetti, a double-entry bookkeeping teacher in Venice, published *Dell'Universal trattato di libri doppii* (Universal treatise about double entry) in 1610 (Moschetti, 1610). It is an extremely interesting volume from various points of view; nevertheless it doesn't have the reputation it deserves (Melis, 1950, 672).

The volume consists of 249 pages and it is written in a pretentious style, using many metaphors and allegories as well as hyperboles (e.g., he compares the journal to a heavenly melody) (Coronella, 2010, 112).

Probably, for this reason, the work by Moschetti has been little appreciated by scholars who have mistaken form for substance (Melis, 1950, 673). According to some authors, if the volume by Moschetti had been written in a different era with less challenging prose, it would have been a theoretical bookkeeping treatise of priceless value (Masi, 1997, 180). On the other hand, an author ought not to be seen as dissociated from the time he lived in. Indeed, at that time, Marinism dominated in literature, thus leading to pompous patterns of prose which refer to the Baroque both in art and in architecture (Coronella, 2014, 99).

The volume is carved up into three parts (books). The first one (consisting of only thirty-six pages) is devoted to accounting theory while the other two mainly focus on double-entry typification.

Specifically, the second book deals with the accounting entries of a merchant firm and the third one with those of a manufacturing venture.

Among the volume's noteworthy points, compared to the investigation of the subject at that time, are accounting entries referring to insurance and shipyard companies, as well as a sugar refinery. It also discloses many trial entries which had never been reported in print (e.g., about gained deposits because of the performance of the contract being turned down, discounts for early payments, stealing with stolen goods retrieval, loan losses).

Moreover, in the third section of the volume, which is devoted to a short-term company that processes wool, "in-process goods" accounts are exposed for the first time. These accounts are stated to run on "revenues and expenses", although the author never delves deeper into the determination of the cost allocation for a single product. The third part ends with the closure accounts as well as the transfer of the firm; hence the three proprietors arrange for to share the net worth (both cash funds and inventories, trade receivables) as well as the net income gained, once the involved bookkeeping costs were deducted.

Moschetti's thought on the operation of capital accounts is deemed to be extremely relevant. Actually, he distinguishes among accounts being raised to *assets and liabilities* and those referring to *net changes in equity components*. He also separates "capital facts" into *permutative* and *modificative*, according to a distinction which will occur only in the second half of the nineteenth century. Moreover, he strictly keeps apart from the account "personalization", assuming that the accounts should have been addressed to values (Della Penna, 1946, 271). Because of this, his work has to be considered a forerunner of the value-based theory by Besta, which will prevail at the end of the nineteenth century.

However, Moschetti's volume enshrines a list of "regressions" compared to the advances in accounting thought (Coronella, 2014, 91). Notwithstanding, he has to be credited with a pivotal role regarding several concerns he hinted at, which would be better developed in future times, even centuries later.

Cento e dieci ricordi *(One Hundred and Ten Memories) by Giacomo Agostinetti (1679)*

Giacomo Agostinetti issued a volume about customs and traditions in agriculture entitled *Cento e dieci ricordi che formano il buon fattor di villa*

(One hundred and ten memories of the good farmer) (Agostinetti, 1679).[13] For forty-five years he worked as a farmer for several Venetian and Friulian noblemen, and then he retired to his birthplace, where he started writing the aforementioned work.

It deals with the practice of agriculture and addresses workers in the sector concerning several subjects: the best way of cultivating plant varieties and producing wine, taking care of livestock, the relationships between peasants and farmers, landowners and subordinates and so on, up to bookkeeping.

Specifically, the last subject has been developed in twelve pages of the volume, from "*Ricordo VI*" (Memory VI) to "*Ricordo X*" (Memory X), which cover the following contents: the "*Memorial*" (memorandum book), also called "*squarzo*", the "*Annal*" (record book of lease payment and land fees owed to the proprietor), the "*Libro Zornal*" (journal) and the "*Libro Maestro*" (ledger).

Actually, the author provides neither details nor practical examples in his short discourse. However, he illustrates the contents as well as the recording principles for each book.

The volume does not contribute any technical innovations to the subject but stands out as an interdisciplinary technical manual which embraces business, a work ethic and accounting books.

The Saggio di scrittura doppia *(Essay on Double Entry) by Francesco Garatti (1688)*

The Venetian Francesco Garatti first published two works on applied arithmetic (Garatti, 1686; Garatti, 1687),[14] and then the volume *Saggio di Scrittura doppia di mercantie e di cambii* (Essay on double entry about goods and currency exchanges) (Garatti, 1688) was released in 1668.

This 124-page treatise is almost unknown to accounting historians; only a minority acknowledges it (Cerboni, 1889, 67; Rigobon, 1912, 658–660; Zappa, 1937, 624, fn. 1; Della Penna, 1946, 400, fn. 1, Serra, 1999, 219). Moreover, up to 2014 no one had investigated his work (Antonelli, 2014).

Garatti illustrates double entry as well as how the journal and ledger (called "*Quaderno*") ought to be kept, claiming that the former is a convenience and the latter is necessary (Garatti, 1688, 1). First he provides a brief theoretical description, and then he enlists a large set of specimen entries drawn from operations in the form of complex questions. For each of them he supplies an explanation and the related accounting entry. As Casanova does, he inserts business arithmetic calculations in the entries, demanded by their operability. Following, he provides several examples missing the solution.

From both a formal and substantial perspective, the volume by Garatti does not contain any original content; on the contrary he somewhat steps backwards compared to previous works. In the ledger, he uses the traditional format which puts the prepositions "*per*" (for) and "*a*" (to) before the debit and credit account. Moreover, he discusses neither accrual entries nor the drafting of the financial statement.

However, having examined the memorandum book (called "*Squarzo*"), he briefly illustrates the contents of numerous auxiliary books: the "*Libro delle comprede e vendite o mercantie in monte*" (buying and selling and wares book altogether), the "*Libro delle tratte e rimesse*" (bill of exchange and remittances book), the "*Quaderno dei cambi*" (exchange book), the "*Salda Conti d'Amici*" (fellow close payments book), the "*Salda Conti proprio o nostro*" (proper closing ledger), the "*Copia conti*" (copy account book), the "*Copia partite*" (copy item book), the "*Libro di Cassa*" (cash book), the "*Libro Scontro de Banco*" (clearing book), the "*Bilancietto di Banco*" (bank balance book), the "*Bilancietto de Cambij*" (exchange balance book), the "*Libro de' commissioni e ordini che vanno e vengono*" (front-and-back fee book), the "*Libro de' Ragguagli delle Piazze*" (stock-market update book), the "*Libretto delle Fiere*" (fair booklet) and, finally, the "*Cartafaccio del Giornale*" (journal scratch book), a sort of more advanced memorandum book.

The **Pratica generale dell'aritmetica** *(The General Practice of Arithmetics) by Girolamo Pietro Cortinovis (Giovan-Domenico Bassaglia) (1782)*

The *Pratica generale dell'aritmetica* (The general practice of arithmetics) by Girolamo Pietro Cortinovis covers eight editions since 1751 (Cortinovis, 1751) and was progressively broadened after the author's death by his nephew, as well as pupil, Giovan-Domenico Bassaglia.

The treatise focuses almost entirely on commercial and applied arithmetic and is written in the form of a dialogue with questions and answers. However, since the 1782 edition (Cortinovis, 1782) some references on double entry added by Giovan-Domenico Bassaglia (Coronella, 2014, 164–165) appear. Consequently, the pages on accounting have to be correctly attributed to him.

Specifically, Giovan-Domenico Bassaglia stresses double entry in Chapter 3 of the thirteenth and last treatise (Cortinovis, 1782, 323–368).

In almost more than forty pages, he briefly illustrates the ledger or "*quaderno*" and the journal, then he enlists a set of questions carrying it out, joining its calculus, and he reports the accounting entries to the journal and ledger.

Actually, Bassaglia's contribution deserves to be mentioned for several reasons, not including the double-entry posting. First of all, he provides full-form exercises to be filled in, where applied and business arithmetic and double entry join. Hence, he steps beyond similar manuals, which dealt with arithmetic and accounting separately.

Furthermore, a point eliciting interest is the goods account personalization, which is fictitiously assigned to the proprietor of the firm instead of the consignee (Serra, 1999, 224).

Through a specific example (Cortinovis, 1782, 323–324), Bassaglia proves that the "goods" account always alludes to the proprietor even if it is not entitled to him.

Therefore, Bassaglia clearly demonstrates the logic according to which the accounts to be credited or debited tally with those of the proprietor, thus forerunning the forte proprietor approach by Dégrange (1795) and his followers.

The Trattato di scrittura mercantile *(The Merchant's Bookkeeping Treatise) by Fererio Antonino Farghiscoc (1787)*

In 1787 Fererio Antonino Farghiscoc published the *Trattato di scrittura mercantile* (The merchant's bookkeeping treatise) (Farghiscoc, 1787).

This 207-page essay is almost unknown to accounting historians and is extremely rare too. In the National Library of Rome only the 1816 edition (consisting of two volumes with the modified title) is listed, while as far as the first edition is concerned, only the first volume is mentioned. Consequently, it is supposed that the second volume has never come to light (Besta, 1916, 414; Serra, 1999, 227). The first volume includes journal and ledger keeping as well as some auxiliary books.

Among the first to have added notes, Ernesto Luchini briefly commented on the treatise by Farghiscoc, whose surname he distorted into *Farghisco*, as a thorough work, and it clearly explains the double-entry system as well as the posting entries to be carried to the accounting books (Luchini, 1898, 80).

Fabio Besta reconsiders this work. Whereas in 1787 in Venice the other Venetian works on double entry were overlooked, the one by Fererio Antonino Farghiscoc illustrated it with a certain robustness (Besta, 1916, 413).

Following, Della Penna points out that Farghiscoc dealt with cost accounting with several bank transfer operations (Della Penna, 1950, 299).

La scrittura doppia ridotta scienza *(Double-Entry Bookkeeping as a Science) by Niccolò D'Anastasio (1803)*

In order to end this review of Venetian authors, it is worth introducing the first nineteenth-century writer: Niccolò D'Anastasio, who published a work in two volumes entitled *La scrittura doppia ridotta scienza* (Double-entry bookkeeping as a science) in 1803 (D'Anastasio, 1803a; D'Anastasio, 1803b).

As specified before, the nineteenth century witnessed a huge increase in the number of accounting works, which reached its climax following the 1861 unification of Italy.

It goes without saying that other authors released their treatises in Venice in that century—for instance, Anonymous (1824), De Peretti (1827), Gabelli (1837), Garello (1857) and Tonzig (1857–59)—before 1861. However, almost until 1861, the only Venetian work worth noting is the one by Niccolò D'Anastasio.

So, whereas the later works, some of them written several decades later, confine themselves to illustrating the technical approach to bookkeeping records, D'Anastasio's essay marks a significant advance compared to eighteenth-century "decadent" works (Serra, 1999, 235).

This treatise is divided into two volumes of 270 and 282 pages. It alternates theoretical and applied sections using a simple and fluid language, thus improving on the volumes of the previous century (Cerboni, 1889, 110). The analysis of transactions is deepened and the examples are several and appropriate. For this reason, the first scholars to have dealt with it stated that D'Anastasio's work marks the transition from the declining old accounting to the new developing one (Brambilla, 1901, 98).

As clearly hinted by the title of his work, D'Anastasio wanted to lay the groundwork of a "scientific accounting", and so he is the first to face this issue, albeit in a completely different way from the turn of events at the end of the century. Indeed, he considers the double-entry posting system not only as a mere accounting tool but also as a useful way to connect and coordinate various account and their contents (Masi, 1997, 281).

The author starts with the study of administrative facts of the enterprise which are intended for "shifts" in "wealth". Each "shift" leads to a double impact—that is to say, two accounts are involved—which is identified as "loci" intended for "warehouse" and referring to both subjects and things.

Indeed, in D'Anastasio's approach, each "shift" withdraws an item to place it into another locus (Bariola, 1897, 461): hitherto double entry uses always a debtor and a creditor. He singles out a sole rule to credit and debit accounts (D'Anastasio, 1803a, 27–31).

Although he was a follower of the Italian tradition rather than the French one, he addresses entries to the proprietor instead of the various nominal accounts, the so-called personalistic fiction, showing that at the beginning of the nineteenth century this approach was acknowledged in Italy too (Mattessich, 2003, 131).

From this perspective, D'Anastasio can be considered a Cerbonian forerunner as he clearly refers to entries which are used to stress consignees' and third parties' rights and obligations towards the proprietor. He also points out that regardless of whether accounts were assigned to goods or persons, they ought to refer to the owner. This condition is *tacit*—that is to say, *implicit*—and if it were explicit, an account would be entered to the proprietor, with the consequence that the quadruple entry would occur (Brambilla, 1901, 98; Ceccherelli, 1915, 94).

This thought also recalls the theory by Marchi, who elicits the account entitled to the factor of the business, thus turning the entry from double into quadruple entry (Coronella, 2007, 76–78).

Finally, with effort (Melis, 1950, 730; Guzzo, 2005, 35–39; Guzzo, 2012, 262), D'Anastasio paves the way to the ennoblement of accounting, which would be fulfilled at the end of the century, thanks to Fabio Besta and the rise of "scientific accounting".

Concluding Remarks

Venetian accounting treatises have played and still play a pivotal role in the development of the subject.

As time passed, the fifteenth century had two main authors who illustrated double entry. The first was Benedetto Cotrugli, whose work should be partially revaluated in light of "Malta's manuscript" recovery, copied by Marino de Raphaeli. The latter was Luca Pacioli, who was the very first "popularizer" of the double-entry method. The subject of accounting was better arranged and spread through print. Actually, Pacioli ended the period of Middle Ages accounting and opened the path of Renaissance and modern accounting. Hitherto, the direction taken by accounting would be unchanged for the next three centuries (Amaduzzi, 1953, 47).

The relevant issue is that the first and sole fifteenth-century treatises about accounting on a global scale are Venetian.

During the sixteenth century, Venetian treatises still predominate in Italy and all over the world.

In Italy, Cerboni's bibliography (Cerboni, 1889) lists ten works. Among these, eight are Venetian and, except for the small chapter by Girolamo Cardano, devoted to accounting (Cardano, 1539), the ninth and non-Venetian (Pietra, 1586) work is also the last of the century, thus demonstrating undoubtedly the absolute cultural leadership of Venice regarding double-entry.

Even if we compare other countries, the same conclusions are drawn. The first treatises on double entry published outside Italy date almost fifty years from the *Summa* by Pacioli and largely retrace the contents both of the last and of the other Venetian treatises prior to their publication (Manzoni, 1540).[15]

The first work on the double-entry system issued outside Italy dates back to 1543 by Jan Ympyn Christofells, a merchant from Anversa who stayed for more than twelve years in Venice, where he learned the method's details. The work, which apparently was begun in 1536, was posthumously published in Flemish, edited by his wife, before being translated in the same year (1547) into French and English. The treatise does not provide original content but it was the first to spread the double-entry system in Holland, as well as in other countries and into other languages (Vlaemminck, 1956, 102–105). Several other Flemish authors active in The Netherlands—Valentin Mennher de Kempten, Claes Pietersz de Deventer, Bartholomeus Cloot, Léon Mellema, Barthélémy de Renterghem (whose work was published in French but printed in Anversa), Zacharie van Hoorebeke—issued volumes in Flemish on accounting during the sixteenth century (Vlaemminck, 1956, 96–105).

The first English treatise dates back to 1543, and it was authored by a London schoolteacher, Hugh Oldcastle. However, according to scholars (Brown, 1905, 127), his work is de facto the English translated version of the *Tractatus de computis et scripturis* by Luca Pacioli. Moreover, the work by Oldcastle was copied in its turn in 1588 by John Mellis. Other English authors who focused on double-entry posts were James Peele and John Weddington.

In Germany, the double-entry system was introduced by Wolffgung Schweicker. He dwelled in Venice to get familiar with the Italian method and, in 1549, he released his accounting treatise, borrowing considerably from the work by Manzoni (Vlaemminck, 1956, 107–111; Chatfield, Vangermeersch, 1996, 520). Other sixteenth-century German authors are Heinrich Schreiber, Johann Gotlieb, Sebastian Gammersfelder and Matthaeus Schwarz (but not all of them focus on the double-entry posting system).

In France, double entry was illustrated in an excellent way first by Pierre de Savonne in his 1567 work. The second sixteenth-century French author is Martin Fustel, whose work is mainly devoted to applied arithmetic (Vlaemminck, 1956, 113–116).

In Spain, the first volume on double entry dates back to 1565; it was authored by Antich Rocha and it uses previous practices (it is a translation of Mennher's book, edited in 1550), so it is scarcely usable (Stevelinck, 1970, 13–14). In 1590, a volume by Bartolome Salvador de Solorzano appeared.

Concerning contributions to the growth of the discipline, with respect to the work by Luca Pacioli worth noting, the sixteenth-century Venetian treatises include numerous incremental innovations in accounting practice.

In 1516 Gian Francesco Aritmetico was the first to employ the alphabetic list of accounts, while Domenico Manzoni in 1540 was the first to try to popularize double entry with laymen through a mere didactic manual.

In 1558 the logic of the matching principle was displayed by Alvise Casanova for the first time (with the valuation of goods at inventory cost including the estimated earning on the sales).

It is worth noting that in 1525 Giovanni Antonio Tagliente was the first to illustrate single entry, which was popularized in printed versions later than the double-entry posting system, although it was even more ancient.

The seventeenth-century Venetian authors were Simon Grisogono (1609), Giovanni Antonio Moschetti (1610), Francesco Garatti (1688) and Giacomo Agostinetti (1679).

Moschetti's work deserves to be mentioned in accounting history because he was the first to have introduced specimen entries fitting many types of firms (insurance, shipyard and so on) that were previously neglected. He also illustrated the "in-progress" accounts of a manufacturing firm, as well as crafting a thought which somewhat foreruns the nineteenth-century proprietorship theory.

However, the seventeenth century witnessed the gradual increase of works on double entry both in Italy and abroad (especially in France).

The eighteenth century for Italy is deemed to be a declining century from many points of view, above all because of foreign invasions and related power struggles. The Italian Peninsula entered a period of decline (including economic), which led to the fall of the *Serenissima* Repubblica of Venice under the hegemony of Austria at the end of the century.

Accounting seems to have been involved in this generalized decline. Most accounting history scholars label the eighteenth century as an Italian period of decline and subjugation to foreign authority (above all the French) and the Italian works boast neither innovation nor originality (Bariola, 1897, 419–422; Brambilla, 1898, 4; Ceccherelli, 1915, 75–76; Melis, 1950, 714–715; Giannessi, 1960, 471; Masi, 1997, 233–234; Serra, 1999, 221–222; Privitera, 2003, 211–213; Zan, 1994, 271–272).

During this century, as far as the growth of the discipline is concerned, the "baton" for the growth of the discipline seems to have passed to others (specifically to the French—for instance, Matthieu de la Porte, Bertrand-François Barrême, Edmond Dégrange), while from Pacioli up to the seventeenth century, Italians held the supremacy.[16]

During this time, the only two eighteenth-century Venetian works are those by Cortonovis and Farghiscoc (Cortinovis, 1782; Farghiscoc, 1787). The former is interesting because it somewhat brings forward the personalization of the accounts, which will be further used by the French.

From the nineteenth century up to the unification of Italy (1861), the Italian Peninsula (including Venice) was still subjugated to the foreign domain, which broadens itself to the culture, as well as being rooted in the political and economic field.

Whereas in the previous century, the small Italian states maintained their culture (the Italian signorias were the beacons of European culture during the sixteenth and partially the seventeenth centuries), regardless of the French political hegemony, in the eighteenth century they were cultural subjugated to foreigners, above all to the French. In this respect, the accounting discipline is no exception.

Italian accounting as well as Italian pride would be recovered and restored at the turn of the century. Indeed, Italian accounting scholars would be able to reclaim their leading role, thus boosting accounting to the status of science

However, already during the first sixty years of the nineteenth century, compared to the previous ones, the number of the accounting essays increased and, among these, several are pioneers of modern accounting, which would be developed only from the end of the century.

Among these, chronologically, the first work was released in Venice (D'Anastasio, 1803a; D'Anastasio, 1803b) and differs from all the previous and coeval ones because it lays down the basis for "scientific accounting", at least from a conceptual perspective. Indeed, the theoretical personalization of the account is brought forward by several decades and will be improved by Francesco Marchi (Marchi, 1867) and then by Giuseppe Cerboni (Cerboni, 1873).

Between the nineteenth and the twentieth centuries Fabio Besta's *opera omnia* (Besta, 1891; Besta, 1909; Besta, 1910; Besta, 1916) was published in

Milan, except for the first edition of the first volume (Besta, 1891), published in Venice. For this reason, it is not considered appropriate to include it as a reference for the "Venetian treatises" we are dealing with. However, for almost fifty years Besta held the chair of accounting at the "Ca' Foscari" Business School (from 1872 to 1920), in Venice, and that needs to be noted, bearing in mind the fundamental role he assumed in the development of the theoretical position on accounting in Italy in the twentieth century (Mattessich, 2008, 85–87).

Above all, Fabio Besta authored the definitive shift from "technical" accounting to the dignity of a science as he defined "the science of economic control", which came to be broadened both in knowledge and in duties. Moreover, among accounting scholars, he was the first to adopt the empirical/inductive method, which he combined with the historical one in his own investigations. He also crafted the "value-based theory" of accounts as well as the equity-centered accounting system to be applied to the double-entry method (Antoni, 1970, 45–138; Giannessi, 1980, 117–148; Coronella, 2014, 236–246; Sargiacomo, Servalli, Andrei, 2012). So, the leading personalistic theory of accounts from the Middle Ages was overwhelmed.

Definitely, Besta was the most important accounting scholar in modern times. It is worth noting that he was appointed to the chair of accounting at the most ancient as well as prestigious Italian business school[17] (founded in 1868) and he held this position continuously for nearly half of a century. This is particularly relevant and demonstrates Venetian leadership on the path to the development of modern accounting.

Notes

1. Among the other foreign bibliographies of the same period, this work stands out for its depth and exhaustiveness, as does a work by Reymondin, a Frenchman (Reymondin, 1909), issued two decades later. Others are either short, like the one by Foster, an Englishman (Foster, 1852), and Hagers, a Dutchman (Hagers, 1903), or concise because they refer only to the most important works, like the one included in Appendix I to the volume by Brown, a Scotsman (Brown, 1905), or broad, gathering mainly works which aren't pertinent to accounting, like the one by Torrents Monner, a Spaniard (Torrents Monner, 1902).
2. The work by Manzoni is wrongly listed in the bibliography by Cerboni dated 1534.
3. The *Pratica arithmetice* (Practice of arithmetic) by Cardano consists of sixty-eight chapters, seven of them (from the fifty-third to the fifty-ninth) devoted to business arithmetic and just one, the seventy-sixth, entitled "*De ratione librorum tractandorum*" (About the treatises of bookkeeping), to bookkeeping.
4. The book was then reprinted in Brescia in 1602, for a total of 213 charts (Cotrugli, 1602). A French translation in book form was brought out by Jean Boyron in 1582.
5. In 1475 Cotrugli had been dead for six years. Hence, these accounting entries might have been included by copyist Marino de Raphaeli or he might have updated them in accordance with the year the manuscript was copied down.
6. Cotrugli's volume is carved up in four sections—that is, in fifty-one chapters of variable length. The first section consists of nineteen chapters and includes the

double-entry references, the second one is composed of nineteen chapters, the third one of eighteen and the fourth one of ten.

7. Furthermore, the *Tractatus XI* falls within a context—the "*Distinctio IX*"—of great relevance for accounting history scholars because the other "treatises" (altogether twelve) are entirely devoted to commercial arithmetic, which strictly relates to bookkeeping. In recent times, the *Tractatus XI* has been reprinted, submitted to critical examination and translated into modern Italian and many other foreign languages.
8. A microfilmed copy has survived, supposedly dating back to 1970 and edited by the Institute of Chartered Accountants in England and Wales. Specifically, it is titled "Italian Language Books in the 15th–19th Centuries"; Institute of Chartered Accountants in England and Wales, microfilmed collection of rare works on accountancy, Group B, Italian language, reel 1.
9. Some scholars do not share a positive opinion of Casanova's book and consider it a work which does not provide any contribution to the development of accounting theory (Melis, 1950, 651).
10. Many years later, the book was reprinted: specifically in 1661 (by an unknown editor) and in 1664 in Venice, edited by Francesco Ginami.
11. Oddly, at the end of the book, there is a trade fair calendar about all the cities, with the related dates and duration.
12. Actually, this conduct has not always been homogeneous in the various typifications.
13. The work was printed in the same year by Publishing House Gio. Giacomo Hertz in Venice. Then, it was reedited, sometimes with a varied title, in Bologna in 1681 and in Venice in 1692, 1703, 1704, 1717 and 1749.
14. In the 1686 work, Garatti promised to write a treatise about the double-entry bookkeeping method.
15. Nevertheless, Yamey illustrates the contents of some non-Italian ancient manuscripts older than the printed books (Yamey, 1967).
16. For a minority of scholars the Italian eighteenth century is acknowledged as "the age of enlightenment"—that is to say, an ideal connection between the flourishing seventeenth and positivist eighteenth centuries, thus abandoning the way to see it in a negative perspective, as for its decline (Ferraris Franceschi, 1996; Antonelli, 1996; Antinori, 2006, 206–207; Antonelli, 2012, 3–24; Coronella, 2014, 134–136).
17. The Venetian Business School was also among the first in the world and second only to those of Antwerp (1852) and Paris (1861).

References

Agostinetti, G. (1679), *Cento, e dieci ricordi, che formano il buon fattor di villa*, Stefano Curti, Venezia.

Alfieri, V. (1891), *La partita doppia applicata alle scritture delle antiche aziende mercantili veneziane*, Paravia, Torino-Roma-Milano-Firenze-Napoli.

Amaduzzi, Al. (1953), *L'azienda nel suo sistema e nell'ordine delle sue rilevazioni*, Utet, Torino.

Anonymous (1525), *La tenuta del libro mastro pel negoziante e il possidente*, Venezia.

Anonymous (1529), *Opera che insegna a tener libro doppio novamente stampata*, Venezia.

Anonymous (1824), *Scrittura doppia dei negozianti*, Venezia.

Antinori, C. (1994), *Luca Pacioli e la Summa de Arithmetica*, Istituto Poligrafico e Zecca dello Stato, Roma.

Antinori, C. (2006), "Il Miscroscopio de' Computisti di Giuseppe Carlo Amato ed Urso", in Lipari, C. (a cura di), *Autori di ragioneria a Palermo. XVII–XVIII secolo*, Numero speciale—Anno 2006, Volume 1, Annali della Facoltà di Economia, Università degli Studi di Palermo, Palermo, 151–208.

Antonelli, V. (1996), "Aspetti evolutivi della ragioneria nel secolo XVIII: Pietro Paolo Scali", in Aa.Vv., *Vita economica e storia della ragioneria in Sardegna dalla seconda metà del settecento*, "Atti del III Convegno Nazionale di Storia della Ragioneria", Alghero, 20 e 21 ottobre 1995, Pacini, Pisa, 245–264.

Antonelli, V. (a cura di) (2012), *Tommaso Domenico Breglia nella storia della ragioneria*, Rirea, Roma.

Antonelli, V. (2014), "Il 'Saggio di scrittura doppia, di mercantie, e di cambii' di Francesco Garatti: considerazioni critiche", *Rivista Italiana di Ragioneria e di Economia Aziendale*, Vol. 114, n. 7–9, 276–294.

Antoni, T. (1970), *Fabio Besta. Contributo alla conoscenza degli studi aziendali*, Colombo Cursi Editore, Pisa.

Bariola, P. (1897), *Storia della ragioneria italiana premiata al Concorso della Società Storica Lombarda*, Tip. Ambrosiana, Milano.

Besta, F. (1891), *Corso di ragioneria professato alla classe di magistero nella R. Scuola Superiore di Commercio in Venezia, Parte prima, Ragioneria Generale*, Volume 1, Coi tipi dei Fratelli Visentini, Venezia.

Besta, F. (1909), *La ragioneria*, seconda edizione, Volume 1, Vallardi, Milano.

Besta, F. (1910), *La ragioneria*, seconda edizione, Volume 1, Vallardi, Milano.

Besta, F. (1916), *La ragioneria*, seconda edizione, Volume 3, Vallardi, Milano.

Brambilla, G. (1898), "Gli scrittori di contabilità mercantile dei secoli XVII e XVIII", *Rivista di Amministrazione e Contabilità*, Vol. 18, 3–7.

Brambilla, G. (1901), *Storia della ragioneria italiana*, Attilio Boriglione, Milano.

Brown, R. (1905), *A history of accounting and accountants*, T.C. & E.C. Jack, Edimburgh.

Cardano, G. (1539), *Practica arithmetice, & mensurandi singularis. In quaque preter alias continentur, versa pagina demonstrabit*, A. Castellioneus per B. Caluscus, Milano.

Casanova, A. (1558), *Specchio lucidissimo, nel quale si vedeno essere diffinito tutti i modi, & ordini de scrittura*, Comin da Trino di Monferrato, Venezia.

Cavazzoni, G. (2009), *L'arte contabile, la ragioneria, l'economia aziendale. Da Luca Pacioli a Gino Zappa*, Volumnia, Perugia.

Ceccherelli, A. (1915), *La logismologia*, Vallardi, Milano.

Cerboni, G. (1873), *Primi saggi di logismografia presentati all'XI Congresso degli scienziati italiani in Roma*, Tipografia Militare La Minerva, Firenze.

Cerboni, G. (1889), *Elenco cronologico delle opere di computisteria e ragioneria venute alla luce in Italia dal 1202 sino al 1888*, quarta edizione, Tipografia Nazionale, Roma.

Chatfield, M., Vangermeersch, R. (1996), *The history of accounting (Routledge library editions: Accounting): An international encyclopedia*, Garland Publishing Inc., New York and London.

Coronella, S. (2007), *La ragioneria in Italia nella seconda metà del XIX secolo. Profili teorici e proposte applicative*, Giuffrè, Milano.

Coronella, S. (2010), "I quattrocento anni 'Dell'Universal trattato di libri doppii' di Giovanni Antonio Moschetti", *Contabilità e Cultura Aziendale*, Vol. 10, n. 1, 111–113.

Coronella, S. (2014), *Storia della ragioneria italiana. Epoche, uomini e idee*, Franco Angeli, Milano.

Coronella, S. (2016), "La bibliografia storica delle opere di Computisteria e Ragioneria di Giuseppe Cerboni: un'analisi spazio-temporale", *Rivista Italiana di Ragioneria e di Economia Aziendale*, Vol. 116, n. 1–4, 143–159.

Cortinovis, G.P. (1751), *La pratica generale dell'aritmetica*, Pietro Bassaglia, Venezia.

Cortinovis, G.P. (1782), *Abbaco ovvero pratica generale dell'aritmetica, Riordinata, ampliata, e divisa in tredici Trattati da Gian-Domenico Bassaglia*, Tomo secondo, Gianmaria Bassaglia, Venezia.

Cotrugli, M.B. (1573), *Della mercatura et del mercante perfetto. Libri quattro. Scritti già più di anni CX & hora dati in luce. Utilissimi ad ogni mercante*, All'Elefanta, Venezia.

Cotrugli, M.B. (1602), *Della mercatura et del mercante perfetto*, Libraria del Bozzola, Brescia.

D'Anastasio, N. (1803a), *La scrittura doppia ridotta scienza. Opera divisa in due volumi*, Tomo I, Niccolò Glichi, Venezia.

D'Anastasio, N. (1803b), *La scrittura doppia ridotta scienza. Opera divisa in due volumi*, Tomo II, Niccolò Glichi, Venezia.

Degrange, E. (1795), *La tenue des livres rendue facile*, Chez Hocquart, Paris.

Della Penna, F. (1946), *Le istituzioni contabili*, parte prima, Castellani, Roma.

Della Penna, F. (1950), *Le istituzioni contabili*, parte seconda, Castellani, Roma.

De Peretti, G. (1827), *Guida teoretico-pratica alla Scienza della Contabilità mercantile*, Tipografia di Francesco Andreola, Venezia.

De Roover, R. (1955), "New perspectives on the history of accounting", *The Accounting Review*, Vol. 30, n. 3, 405–420.

Farghiscoc, F.A. (1787), *Trattato di scrittura doppia mercantile e di scrittura economica diviso in due volumi*, Modesto Fenzo, Venezia.

Ferraris Franceschi, R. (1996), "Illuminismo e razionalismo nella ragioneria del secolo XVIII. L'ambiente e l'opera di P.P. Scali", in Aa.Vv., *Vita economica e storia della ragioneria in Sardegna dalla seconda metà del settecento*, "Atti del III Convegno Nazionale di Storia della Ragioneria", Alghero, 20 e 21 ottobre 1995, Pacini, Pisa, 219–244.

Fontana, B. (1551), *Ammaestramento novo che insegna a tener libro*, Venezia.

Foster, B.F. (1852), *The origin and progress of book-keeping: Comprising an account of all the works on this subject, published in the English language, from 1543 to 1852, with remarks, critical and historical*, John Souter, London.

Gabelli, D.P. (1837), *Insegnamenti intorno alle cambiali ed alla scrittura doppia*, Merlo, Venezia.

Garatti, F. (1686), *Il divertimento aritmetico*, Pietro Orlandi, Venezia.

Garatti, F. (1687), *Abachino con diversi contarelli*, Pietro Orlandi, Venezia.

Garatti, F. (1688), *Saggio di scrittura doppia di mercantie, e di cambii*, Pietro Orlandi, Venezia.

Garello, F. (1857), *Lezioni di contabilità agricola*, Venezia.

Gian Francesco (1516), *Manuscript*, Venezia.

Giannessi, E. (1960), *Le aziende di produzione originaria, Volume primo, Le aziende agricole*, Cursi, Pisa.

Giannessi, E. (1980), *I precursori in economia aziendale*, quarta edizione completamente riveduta e corretta, Giuffrè, Milano.

Grisogono, S. (1609), *Il mercante arricchito. Del perfetto quaderniere*, Alessandro Vecchi, Venezia.

Guzzo, G. (2005), "A due secoli da La scrittura doppia ridotta scienza di N. D'Anastasio: contesti e contenuti di un'opera 'contemporanea'", in Aa.Vv., *Cultura Aziendale e Professionale tra passato e futuro*, "Atti del VII Convegno Nazionale della Società Italiana di Storia della Ragioneria", Bari, 5–6 dicembre 2003, 2° Tomo G-Z, Casa Editrice Rirea, Roma, 9–40.

Guzzo, G. (2012), "The 'Contemporary' thought of Niccolò D'Anastasio through La Scrittura Doppia Ridotta Scienza (1803)", in Lipari, C. (a cura di), *Papers on Accounting and Accounting History*, Rirea, Roma, 247–262.

Hagers, J. (1903), *Bouwstoffen voor de geschiedenis van het bockhouden in de Nederlanden*, Delwel, Rotterdam.

Hernández-Esteve, E. (1994), "Luca Pacioli's treatise *de Computi set Scripturis:* a composite or a unified work?", *Accounting, Business & Financial History*, Vol. 4, n. 1, 67–82.

Luchini, E. (1898), *Storia della ragioneria italiana*, Amministrazione del periodico "Il Ragioniere", Milano.

Manzoni, D. (1540), *Quaderno doppio col suo giornale*, Comin da Trino di Monferrato, Venezia.

Marchi, F. (1867), *I cinquecontisti ovvero la ingannevole teorica che viene insegnata negli istituti tecnici del regno e fuori del regno intorno il sistema di scrittura a partita doppia, e nuovo saggio per la facile intelligenza ed applicazione di quel sistema*, Tipografia Ff. Giachetti, Prato.

Mari, L.M. (1998), "Il libro dell'arte della 'mercatura' e il 'mercante perfetto' di Benedetto Cotrugli da Ragusa", in Aa.Vv., *Storia di imprese tra il XVI ed il XIX secolo*, "Atti del IV Convegno Nazionale di Storia della Ragioneria", Perugia, 2–3 ottobre 1997, Rirea, Roma, 341–358.

Masi, V. (1997), *La ragioneria nell'età moderna e contemporanea*, testo riveduto e completato da Carlo Antinori, Giuffrè, Milano.

Mattessich, R. (2003), "Accounting research and researchers of the nineteenth century and the beginning of the twentieth century: An international survey of authors, ideas and publications", *Accounting, Business & Financial History*, Vol. 13, n. 2, 125–170.

Mattessich, R. (a cura di) (2008), *Two hundred years of accounting research: An international survey of personalities, ideas and publications (from the beginning of the nineteenth century to the beginning of the twenty-first century*, Routledge, London and New York.

Melis, F. (1950), *Storia della ragioneria. Contributo alla conoscenza e interpretazione delle fonti più significative della storia economica*, Cesare Zuffi, Bologna.

Moschetti, G.A. (1610), *Dell'Universal trattato di libri doppii*, Luca Valentini, Venezia.

Pacioli, L. (1494), *Summa de Arithmetica, Geometria, Proportioni et Proportionalita*, Paganino de Paganini, Venezia.

Pacioli, L. (1523), *Summa de Arithmetica, Geometria, Proportioni et Proportionalita. Nuovamente impressa in Toscolano su la riva dil Benacense*, Paganino de Paganini, Toscolano.

Papaziour, I. (1822), *Scrittura doppia di commercio*, Tip. Lazzaro, Venezia.

Peragallo, E. (1938), *Origin and evolution of double entry bookkeeping: A study of Italian practice from the fourteenth century*, American Institute Publishing Company, New York.

Pietra, A. (1586), *Indrizzo degli economi, ossia ordinatissima instruttione da regolatamente formare qualunque scrittura in un libro doppio*, Francesco Osanna, Mantova.

Poddighe, F. (1973), *Dai cinquecontisti a Francesco Marchi. Contributo alla conoscenza del processo formativo della logismologia*, Cursi, Pisa.

Postma, J., Van der Helm, A. (1998), "Rewriting the history of accounting?", *Asia-Pacific Journal of Accounting*, Vol. 5, n. 1, 166–166.

Privitera, C. (2003), *Origine ed evoluzione del pensiero ragionieristico*, Giuffrè, Milano.

Reymondin, G. (1909), *Bibliographie méthodique des Ouvrages en langue française parus de 1543 à 1908 sur la science des comptes.* Volume—Brochures—Articles—Manuscrits, Société Académique de Comptabilité—V, Giard et F. Briere, Paris.

Riccardi, P. (1870), *Biblioteca Matematica Italiana dalla origine della stampa ai primi anni del secolo XIX*, Tipografia dell'Erede Soliani, Modena.

Rigobon, P. (1894), "Di Giovanni Antonio Tagliente veneziano e delle sue opere di ragioneria", *Il Ragioniere*, Serie 2, Vol. 10, n. 1–2, gennaio, 1–12.

Rigobon, P. (1912), "Alcuni appunti storico-bibliografici intorno alla partita doppia sintetica applicata alle aziende mercantili", in Aa.Vv., *Monografie edite in onore di Fabio Besta nel XL anniversario del suo insegnamento*, Puntata seconda, Tipografia nazionale di G. Bertero & C., Roma, 657–682.

Sangster, A. (2014), *Libr. XV: Cotrugli and de Raphaeli on Business and Bookkeeping in the Renaissance*, Lomax Press, Stirling.

Sangster, S., Scataglinibelghitar, G. (2010), "Luca Pacioli: The father of accounting education", *Accounting Education: An International Journal*, Vol. 19, n. 4, 423–438.

Sargiacomo, M., Servalli, S., Andrei, P. (2012), "Fabio Besta: Accounting thinker and accounting history pioneer", *Accounting History Review*, Vol. 22, n. 3, 249–267.

Serra, L. (1999), *Storia della ragioneria italiana*, Giuffrè, Milano.

Stevelinck, E. (1970), *La comptabilité à travers les âges. Introduction par le Prof. Raymond de Roover*, Bibliothèque Royale Albert Ier, Bruxelles.

Tagliente, G.A. (1515), *Libro de abaco*, Venezia.

Tagliente, G.A. (1525), *Luminario di aritmetica*, Venezia.

Tonzig (1857–59), *Trattato della scienza di amministrazione e di contabilità privata e dello Stato*, Vol. 1–3, Pietro Naratovich, Venezia.

Torrents Monner, A. (1902), *Diccionario bibliográfico mercantil, económico y marítimo*, Tipolitografia de José Casamajó, Barcelona.

Tucci, U. (a cura di) (1990), *Benedetto Cotrugli raguseo. Il libro dell'arte della mercatura*, Arsenale, Venezia.

Vianello, V. (1896), *Luca Paciolo nella storia della ragioneria, con documenti inediti*, Libreria Internazionale Ant. Trimarchi, Messina.

Vlaemminck, J.H. (1956), *Histoire et doctrines de la comptabilité*, Éditions du Treurenberg—Dunod, Bruxelles-Paris.

Yamey, B.S. (1967), "Fifteenth and sixteenth century manuscripts on the art of bookkeeping", *Journal of Accounting Research*, Vol. 5, n. 1, 51–76.

Zan, L. (1994), "Toward a history of accounting histories: Perspectives from the Italian tradition", *European Accounting Review*, Vol. 3, n. 2, 255–310.

Zappa, G. (1937), *Il reddito di impresa. Scritture doppie, conti e bilanci di aziende commerciali*, seconda edizione, Giuffrè, Milano.

2 A Venetian Treatise Before Pacioli by Marino De Raphaeli

Alan Sangster

Introduction

This chapter looks at the only known Venetian treatise on double-entry bookkeeping that predates Pacioli's *Particularis de Computis et Scripturis*: de Raphaeli's *La Riegola de Libro*, or *The Rules of Bookkeeping*. Written in 1475, this manuscript remained undetected until the 1990s, escaping the attention of Fabio Besta, Vincenzo Vianello and others in the nineteenth and twentieth centuries who desperately sought to disprove Pacioli's authorship of his treatise. Had they found it, a different history would be told, but would Pacioli's place have been usurped? This chapter considers the purpose behind de Raphaeli's instructional manual; his pedagogy, the content—his syllabus—is presented and discussed; and the manner in which he taught bookkeeping is contrasted to those of Pacioli and his successors.

Background

Until the 1990s, a fifteenth-century 36-page instructional manual on Venetian double-entry bookkeeping lay undisturbed in the National Library of Malta. It had been there for over 140 years and had been on the island since at least 1756, when it was acquired by a local Jesuit priest and bibliophile, Dun Ignazio Saverio Mifsud (1722–c. 1773). One reason why the manual went unnoticed for so long is the fact that it is bound in one volume at the back of a manuscript edition of Benedetto Cotrugli's (1458) *Libro de Larte dela Mercatura* (The book of the art of trade). However, that edition of Cotrugli's book also went unnoticed and was not known to Uggo Tucci when he prepared his translation into modern Italian of Cotrugli's book (1990), which was based on later manuscript editions than the one in Malta. The Maltese edition is considered the closest to the original. Cotrugli's book was recently transcribed using all four surviving editions (Ribaudo, 2016) and translated into English (Carraro & Favero, 2017).

This joint binding of the two manuscripts has always been their format, the binding and numbering of the pages of both books in one volume having taken place soon after they were completed. Dun Ignazio was delighted to have added a copy of Cotrugli's book to his collection, and wrote about its addition in his personal diaries. He treated it as very much his own and inserted the book into a pagination sequence running on from his previous diary, numbering the title page of Cotrugli's book '646'. He also gave the book a name: *Liber IX*. The library received the copy of the book between 1843 and 1856. At some point, it renamed the book *Libr. XV*, and this has remained its title to the present day.[1]

The absence of any awareness of the existence of de Raphaeli's manual has led accounting historians, scholars, and many practising accountants to attribute the development of modern accounting to Luca Pacioli because he published the first printed manual of instruction in double entry in 1494. Pacioli certainly influenced practice and instruction in double entry in a way that has survived for over five hundred years, but the real catalyst for the adoption of the Venetian method as the core of modern accounting is the bookkeeping tutors of the fifteenth century. Of them, we know of only one: Marino de Raphaeli; de Raphaeli appears to have influenced Pacioli, who made use of a similar style of introductory tuition in double entry. In addition, many of his examples resonate with examples of de Raphaeli. Our debt as a discipline therefore arguably lies not so much with Pacioli as with de Raphaeli.

Marino de Raphaeli

Of Marino de Raphaeli, we know very little. Because he signed the manuscript acknowledging himself as the scribe, we know that he made the copy of Cotrugli's manuscript that is bound at the front of the bookkeeping manual. In that signature he identified himself as Ragusan. At that time, Ragusa (Dubrovnik) was part of the Venetian Republic, so it is hardly surprising that he wrote in Venetian dialect and used the Venetian method of double entry. In his manual, he uses many variants on his own name, which may indicate the mind of a teacher trying to compartmentalize instruction for his student, or it may be because these were real people. The first accounting scholars to write about this manual, Anne J. van der Helm and Johanna Postma (2000), speculated that he was from an important Ragusan family and was the fifth son of Rafael de Nicolo (c. 1405/9–c. 1465). If so, de Raphaeli would have been in his early thirties when he wrote the bookkeeping manual in 1475. Regardless of whether that speculation has any foundation, the bookkeeping manual reveals a maturity in the Venetian method of double entry that might surprise anyone who thought it reached maturity only after Pacioli printed his treatise.

The earliest known surviving example of a paired Venetian journal and ledger is those of Andrea Barbarigo (1418–1449). De Raphaeli's manual could have been written using Barbarigo's journal as the source for the entries. Many of the names in de Raphaeli's manual may date from the same period. Many of the names de Raphaeli uses are of real people, real banks, and real businesses. It is a manual written to teach a member of a wealthy family how to do the bookkeeping for the family business—who else could afford the services of a scarce and expensive bookkeeping tutor? If more than a few existed, we would have evidence: they would be mentioned in correspondence, account books, wills, and testaments. We have none. It is as if only one double-entry bookkeeping tutor existed before the sixteenth century.

Where did the Venetian method come from? Who thought of the idea of a journal that summarized every transaction and was then used as the source for each and *every* entry in the ledger? The Tuscans certainly did not. Did the Venetian merchants? None did that we know of, not even Barbarigo, who observed the practice of entering in the journal the location of the two ledger accounts for each entry in the journal, but did not maintain his journal in chronological order, so working back from ledger to journal looking for an entry was such that "*we cannot be sure it is not somewhere out of chronological order*" (Lane, 1944, p. 162). It seems that the Venetian method as presented by de Raphaeli was a normative method, in the sense of desirable—one that should be used—but one that practice struggled to adhere to. It was also the method presented by Pacioli as *el modo de Venegia*, and then by Tagliente (1525) and Manzoni (1540), and all the other tutors who published manuals over the following century. It seems that the Venetian method was an ideal, but flawed in practice in the fifteenth century and, perhaps, only because the tutors taught and wrote about the ideal did it eventually become the norm many years later.

The family to whom de Raphaeli's manual was dictated—it was dictated to the pupil by de Raphaeli (Sangster, 2015)—also paid for a copy to be made of Cotrugli's *Art of Trade*. Together they represented a significant investment in the future of a young man about to enter the family business. His name was Zuan de Domenego. We know nothing about him, other than that he was a member of one of the major families of Venice, well-connected, and with the financial backing to embark on the type of business activities described in de Raphaeli's manual. It is thanks to this commission by the family and the binding together of both these manuscripts in one volume that de Raphaeli's manual has survived. Four pages are missing, most likely having been removed at some point because they were about domestic accounting—household accounting, marriage accounting, and dowry accounting. We shall never know but, compared to the manuals of the sixteenth-century tutors Tagliente and Manzoni, these topics are noticeably absent from de Raphaeli and a good fit for the four missing pages (Sangster, 2015).

The Rules of Bookkeeping

The manual from 1475 by Marino de Raphaeli has no title but begins with the statement *Questa sie la riegola de libro, la qual sie fondamento de ogni quadernier* (These are the rules of bookkeeping that are fundamental to any bookkeeper). It originally comprised 40 pages but, as mentioned earlier, four pages have been lost. What remains presents a rich mixture of business practice of a merchant who is involved in import and export, slavery, silk manufacture, building construction, merchandise accounts, and the necessary financial medium for many businesses of that time, bills of exchange. It is a statement of the variety of business practices, the vagaries of commerce, and the manipulation of bills of exchange to make money. Above all, it is an exemplar of how to keep a double-entry journal in the Venetian style.

In that respect it is unambiguous and constant in the format to adopt, mirroring the journal of Andrea Barbarigo in its presentation, and embracing *el modo de Venegia* that was later captured in print by Luca Pacioli (1494). This was Venetian double entry as it should be practised. There are flaws—the dates become confused where Marino de Raphaeli has failed to update them from an earlier assignment and Zuan de Domenego is particularly weak at arithmetic—but the method of double entry is clearly defined and presented. As a first course in double entry for the journal, it is hard to fault; what it lacks in complexity would soon be encountered in practice and solved by his pupil armed with the basics from de Raphaeli's manual. On the subject of this lack of complexity, it is no less the case in all the manuals printed into the seventeenth century—in fact, arguably more so. They covered the basics but they did not get as close to the complexities of business practice as can be seen in the account books of the fourteenth to the seventeenth centuries. All these manuals contained the maxims (Polanyi, 1958, pp. 51–64, 1966, pp. 4–7) of double entry—what can be taught. Practical knowledge and experience were needed to take the learner to the next level, and he would learn that 'on the job'.

The Content of de Raphaeli's *Rules of Bookkeeping*

Table 2.1 presents the syllabus covered in the manual.

The Basics of Double Entry

The first two chapters deal with generic aspects of double entry. The ways entries are prepared in the journal and in the ledger are briefly described and then the focus is on how to make entries, firstly of what is being introduced into a new business by the owner and then, in Section II, entries for purchases and sales.

Section I is very similar to Tagliente's (1525) introduction. At the foot of the first page is an *aventario* of the merchant's capital (*aventario del mio chavedal*). This is then used to make the first entries in the new journal. While this reveals an awareness that the difference between the debits and the credits represents the merchant's capital, it was not in any way what we would consider a trial balance. No indication is given by de Raphaeli of where the *aventario* was to be written.

No examples of an *aventario* have survived, raising doubts that this was anything more than an artificial device created by a tutor to aid instruction. However, Pacioli, in his treatise (1494) also used an *aventario* (which he called an *inventario*) to introduce the journal entries to make at the beginning of a business. It was prepared on a sheet of paper, or in a separate book. In his description of the same process, Tagliente (1525) states that this is a simplified list compared to one that would be prepared in practice,

Table 2.1 The contents, number of journal entries, and changes of 'owner' in the manuscript

Section[2]	*Cartas*[3]	*Began*	*Merchant*	*Topics*	*J/Es*
I	101v–102r	Dec. 19	Rafael de Nicolò	General instructions, *aventario* and its journal entries	7
II	102v–105v	Mar. 1	Rafael (presumably the same person)	Entries of another *aventario*, purchases, sales	57
III	105v–106v	Apr. 11		Buying/selling for account of another	21
IV	107r	May 4		Voyage to Beirut, commissioned to someone	8
V	107v	16		*Camera d'Imprestedi* (Government Bonds)	8
VI	108r	June 6	Rafael de Marin	Partnership, with voyage *in persona* to the Levant	8
VII	108v–109r	14		Voyage to Alexandria, commissioned to someone: 108v purchases, etc. 6 109r shipping 6	12
VIII	109v–111v	Aug. 1	Marin de Rafael[4]	Partnership, with voyage *in persona*: 109v–110v purchases, etc. 15 110v–111v shipping, conduct business by barter in several seaports 16	31
IX	112r–115r	Sep. 4	Zuan de Domenego	Partnership of a 'silk shop', with complete cycle from formation to selling the finished products	55
X	115v–116r	Oct. 1		Construction of a building	18
XI	116v	14		Let of houses, bad debts, and the *decima*	9
	117 & 118 missing				
XII	119r–120r	29		Bills of exchange (with *protesto*) and some instruction	23
XIII	120v–121r	Nov. 2		Maritime insurance and some additional instructions regarding maritime insurance, voyages and balancing the ledger	10
					267

Source: Van der Helm and Postma (2000, p. 174) and Sangster (2015), amended by the author

that it is presented in this abridged form so that the student can better learn and understand the process, and that it is prepared on a sheet of paper. The *aventario* was not, therefore, an artificial device created by the tutors, but something recommended to be used when merchants opened their journal for the first time after starting a business.

☞ Praise to God 1475, on the 29th day of December in Naples.	
Inventory of my wealth.	
☞ First, I find I have cash in coins	ducats 4,000
In the Gueruzzi bank	ducats 2,500
In the State Loan Office, 8,000 cameral ducats at 25 ducats per 100 cameral ducats, totals	ducats 2,000
Houses for rent, 10 in the San Polo district	ducats 8,000
100 loads of '*cholli*' peppers, which I believe are worth 60 ducats per load, totalling	ducats 6,000
Debtor: Ser Antonio Contarini at par on the exchange	ducats 900
Creditor: Ser Francesco Zane for the rest of the cloth	ducats 100

Figure 2.1 De Raphaeli's *aventario*

Concerning the relationship between an *aventario* and a trial balance, de Raphaeli is silent. He teaches only the journal, not the ledger, which seems to have been the second stage in instruction in double entry. As a result, while he does present the journal entries from another *aventario* at the beginning of Section II, it is again for a new business, not one for an existing business transferring balances to a new ledger. To answer this question of its closeness to a trial balance, we must instead look to what we know of Venetian bookkeeping practice.

A trial balance is struck when a ledger is closed. We know from surviving Venetian account books of the fifteenth century that that process revolved around the ledger without involving the journal. Andrea Barbarigo, a merchant in Venice in the first half of the fifteenth century, prepared an account inside his old ledger containing a list of the old ledger balances—a *conto saldo di debitori e creditori* (balance account of debits and credits).[5] This was done to close his ledger and then open a new one. Barbarigo does not total the two sides of the account so, like an *aventario*, its form does not qualify it as a trial balance. It was used solely to effect the transfer of the balances to the new ledger. The difference between Barbarigo's account and de Raphaeli's *aventario*, and those of these other tutors, is that Barbarigo's was recorded on two sides in an account in both the old and new ledger, not on a sheet of paper, and it was not entered in the journal.

Thus, the *aventario* presented by de Raphaeli was a record used solely for opening the journal of a new business and so was ideally suited to be the first exercise included in a manual of instruction on that book. It was not used for anything else. The money of account used in the manual for the entries in the columns to the right of the journal entries was the gold *lire di grossi*, comprising *lire*, *soldi*, *denari*, and *piccoli* in the ratios 1:20:12:32. The exchange rate used with the principal transaction money, the gold ducat, was ten ducats to one lira.

At this point, it should be noted that there are two *manicule* in Figure 2.1. The pointing finger was a sign dating from the twelfth century that was used in books to indicate something important. In de Raphaeli's manual, it is used primarily to indicate the start of a new subject.

Purchases and Sales

At the beginning of Section II, de Raphaeli repeats the exercise of opening a journal for a new business, but does so without first presenting an *aventario*. It seems most probable he had told the student to whom he was dictating the text that he should follow custom and write down the *aventario* on a separate sheet of paper, rather than in his 'journal', for that is what the manual now becomes. The date is the first day of the Venetian calendar year, 1st March, and all the entries relate to a business—none are about personal property: 2,580 ducats in cash, plus nine different products held for sale—ginger (980 lbs), cinnamon (980 lbs), wax (2,480 lbs), cotton (3,984 lbs), brazilwood (8,930 lbs), nutmeg (843 lbs), quicksilver (1,368 lbs), cloves (740 lbs), and French wool (9,360 lbs). The merchant then begins to purchase more inventory: 80 barrels (9,780 lbs) of honey, 142 pieces of moleskin, 140 metres of silk, 5,000 lbs of soap. Sales then follow: all the 980 lbs of ginger, sold at 16 ducats per 100 lbs compared with its value in the *aventario* of 13; all 980 lbs of cinnamon, at a profit of 4 ducats per 100 lbs; all 2,480 lbs of wax, at less than 2 ducats above its *aventario* value; and all the cotton at only 24 ducats more than its *aventario* value.

This was not an abridged list of inventory, nor a list of purchases of a small-sized business. Gone is the simplicity of calculation of the transaction value and the money of account that was evident in the first *aventario*. The amounts are realistic, not artificially low, and some of the calculations are complex, and trade is not always at a good profit. This is the case through most of the manual, but the volume of transactions is kept low, so maintaining a limit on the number of examples to an appropriate amount for a manual of instruction.

Brokerage fees on sales and transaction tax (the *misataria* fee) on all transactions are also introduced. All brokerage fees and the *misataria* fee on

Dr	Ser Ghabriel d'Alban Cr Ginger, 980 lbs at 16 ducats per 100 lbs equals 156 ducats, 9 grossi, 6 piccoli. Reduced by my part of the *Misataria* at 1 per cent, 1 ducat, 13 grossi, 20 piccoli. Leaving net 175 ducats, 5 (grossi), 18 (piccoli).	£ 15	s 10	d 5	p 18
Dr	Ginger Cr Cash, paid to Ser Domenego Falchon for brokerage, 2 ducats, 16 grossi, 0 piccoli.	£ -	s 5	d 4	p -

Figure 2.2 A journal entry for a sale of ginger net of the *misataria* fee, and a journal entry for the brokerage fee on the sale

D^r	Hairy moleskin C^r Ser Marcho Moresini, for 142 pieces at 4 ducats per piece, total value 568 ducats, 0 grossi, 0 piccoli. Reduced by his part of the *Misataria* at 1½ per cent, 8 ducats, 12 grossi, 15 piccoli, leaving net 559 ducats, 11 (grossi), 12 (piccoli).	£ 55	s 18	d 11	p 12
D^r	Moleskin, as above, C^r *L'Ofizio de la Misataria*, on an overall total of 568 ducats at 1½ per cent equals 17 ducats, (0 grossi), 30 (piccoli).	£ 1	s 14	d -	p 30
D^r	Moleskin, as above, C^r Merchandise expense account for lagoon transport and porters, 1 ducat, 15 grossi, 0 piccoli.	£ -	s 3	d 3	p -

Figure 2.3 A journal entry for a purchase of moleskin net of the *misataria* fee, the payment of the fee for the purchase plus the seller's share of the fee, and the merchandise expense account entry on the purchase

purchases were entered separately from the transaction, but the *misataria* fee was subtracted from the amount recorded for purchases and, having deducted the seller's share from the amount to be paid, the purchaser was responsible for paying his share and the seller's share to the office of the *misataria*. The seller made no entry for the *misataria* fee but deducted it from the value of the sale when recording that transaction. As shown in Figure 2.2, the seller debited the brokerage fee on a sale to the account of the item sold—in this case, ginger.

A merchandise expense account was used to record various expenses relating to purchases. In this series of examples, an entry for one can be seen relating to a purchase of moleskin. Venetian merchandise expense accounts were simply holding accounts that were cleared when payment was made. When a merchandise expense was incurred on a purchase, the merchandise account was debited and the merchandise expense account was credited. This can be seen in Figure 2.3.

Then, when the expense was paid, the debit was to the merchandise expense account and the credit to the account of the form of settlement, cash, bank, and so forth.

Buying and Selling on Someone Else's Behalf

Merchants at that time not only bought and sold for themselves but also acted as agents for other merchants, taking commission, which they charged to the cost of the item sold. The next three figures show how this was recorded. Figure 2.4 shows the merchant Rafael's record of the purchase of some cloth purchased on behalf of his client, Ser Nicolò de Zorzi.

Figure 2.5 shows the sale of some wool for the same client, to Ser Anttonio di Lorenzo.

Dr Vicentine cloth purchased on behalf of Ser Nicolò de Zorzi C^r Ser Zuan de Polo de Vizenza, 40 rolls at 18 ducats per roll equals 720 ducats. Reduced by the *Misataria* fee, 1 per cent, 7 ducats, 4 grossi, 25 piccoli, leaving net to pay 712 ducats, 19 grossi, 7 piccoli.	£ 71	s 5	d 7	p 7

Figure 2.4 The recording of a purchase of cloth belonging to a client

Dr Ser Anttonio di Lorenzo C^r Wool belonging to Ser Nicolò de Zorzi, 12 sacks, weighing 4,980 lbs at 12 ducats per 100, equals 597 ducats, 14 denari, 12 piccoli. Reduced for my part of the *Misataria*, 1 per cent, 5 ducats, 23 denari, 13 piccoli. Leaving net 591 ducats, 14 denari, 31 piccoli.	£ 59	s 3	d 2	p 31

Figure 2.5 The recording of a sale of wool belonging to a client

Dr Wool belonging to Ser Nicolò de Zorzi C^r Commission of mine, Rafael, for sales, 597 ducats, 14 denari, 13 piccoli, at 3 per cent, equals 17 ducats, 22 (grossi), 8 (piccoli).	£ 1	s 15	d 10	p 8

Figure 2.6 The recording of the agent's commission on a sale of wool

A few entries later, the agent's commission on the sale of the wool is charged to the wool account (Figure 2.6).

Voyage Accounting

Voyage accounting features in many entries in the manual and is also prominent in the manuals of Tagliente (1525), Manzoni (1540), and Casanova (1558). Pacioli (1494) mentions it but does not go into any details. De Raphaeli presents entries relating to two forms of activity: voyages conducted by an agent (*recommanda*) on behalf of the merchant and voyages conducted in person (*in persona*) by the merchant. He presents a simple case of each of these followed by a more advanced case, in Sections IV and VII for voyages by agents, and in Sections VI and VIII for voyages *in persona*. The first two entries for the first *recommanda* voyage are shown in Figure 2.7. The abbreviation 'KL' at the top represents *kalende*, indicating that these are the first entries for the month of May.

The investment in the voyage is the total of these entries: 40 lire, 13 soldi, 8 denari, 28 piccoli. The voyage made a profit of 14 lire, 6 soldi.

	KL 1475 On day 4 of May				
☞ D^r	Voyage to Beirut entrusted to Ser Iacomo Ghabriel C^r Silver, 50 *miara*, 7 ounces, 3 quarts aboard the galley of Captain Ser Nichollò Vendramin. Total, with all expenses incurred prior to boarding the galley, 337 ducats, 20 denari, 28 piccoli.	£ 33	s 15	d 8	p 28
D^r	Voyage as above C^r Green and black moleskin 12 pieces, 240 *brazza*, entrusted to the aforesaid Ser Iacomo aboard the galley of Captain ser Antonio Grioni. Total, with all expenses incurred in boarding the galley, 69 ducats.	£ 6	s 18	d -	p -

Figure 2.7 The first entries for the voyage by an agent to Beirut

	KL Here begins the journey On the 1st day of August				
☞ D^r	Cash C^r Company of myself, Marin de Rafael, of master goldsmith Zorzi, and Ser Zuan de Fiorio de Raguxa. I hereby give 500 ducats for my share in the profits and losses, by the conditions set out in the agreement of fellowship agreed between us.	£ 50	s -	d -	p -
D^r	as above C^r as above, 500 ducats contributed by master goldsmith Zorzi for his share in the profits and losses.	£ 50	s -	d -	p -
D^r	as above C^r as above, 500 ducats contributed by Ser Zuan de Fiorio for his share in the profits and losses.	£ 50	s -	d -	p -
	On day 2 of the above.				
D^r	Basic cloth, of various types purchased on behalf of the company, C^r Cash, 300 ducats, as shown below: 2 blue pieces; at 12½ ducats per piece, in total 25 ducats, 0 denari 3 scarlet pieces; at 22 ducats per piece, in total 66 ducats, 0 denari 6 dark coloured pieces; at 10 ducats per piece, in total 60 ducats, 0 denari 10 dry pink pieces; at 14 ducats, 21 denari per piece, 149 ducats, 0 denari In total for the cloth 300 ducats.	£ 30	s -	d -	p -

Figure 2.8 The first entries for the voyage *in persona* to Ponente: company formation and the first purchase of goods to be sold on the voyage

The agent reinvested this profit and brought back ginger, cinnamon, and pepper.

For each of the other voyages, a company was formed and items for sale were purchased. Figure 2.8 shows the opening entries for the company formed for the second of the voyages *in persona*.

The voyage begins a week later. The last entries are recorded on the 31st of the month: two barters of wheat for slaves. The wheat, itself, had been acquired six days earlier in a barter for cloth. As can be seen in Figure 2.9, these final transactions are recorded in two stages. First the sale of wheat is recorded and the buyer is made a debtor. Then, the debt is settled by crediting the buyer and debiting an account for slaves. The slaves are then taken to Zaragoza and bartered for sugar, which is taken back to Venice.

	On day 31 of the above				
Dr	Abram Moro Cr Wheat belonging to the company, for 504 bushels, at 2 ducats to the bushel, makes a total of 1,008 ducats. A barter of dark skinned unbaptised slaves, at 24 ducats to the slave.	£ 100	s 16	d -	p -
Dr	Hodonmur Moro and Company Cr Wheat belonging to the company, 4,380 bushels, at 2 ducats to the bushel, makes a total of 8,760 ducats, in barter for unbaptised slaves, 24 ducats to the slave.	£ 876	s -	d -	p -
Dr	Unbaptised slaves, a variety, belonging to the company, [Cr] Abramo Moro. They number 42, of which 30 male and the rest female. Each one at a flat rate of 24 ducats, making overall 1,008 ducats. It was a barter for wheat.	£ 100	s 16	d -	p -
Dr	Unbaptised slaves, a variety, belonging to the company, Cr Odonmur Moro and Company. They number 365, of which 245 male and the rest female, bought at a flat rate of 24 ducats each. It was a barter for wheat. Making overall 8,760 ducats.	£ 876	s -	d -	p -
	Take note that on arrival in Zaragoza I barterd these slaves for sugar. From here I depart with it and return to Venice. And you will be able to take the sugar on the next voyage to Ponente. For that trip, you should make the voyage the debtor.				

Figure 2.9 The entries for two transactions involving barter of wheat for slaves

Investments in Forced Loans

Section V contains eight entries relating to investments in government credits. Four purchases are made on 16th May. Then, on 21st May, interest is received on two of the holdings. The amounts gained are credited to profits and losses and, in a second stage recorded in separate journal entries, the cash received is debited. The system arose because governments in many of the major cities of Europe did not like using direct taxes. Instead, they placed indirect taxes on various commodities and used a system of forced loans to raise money when the need arose, such as to pay for wars. In Venice, the amount required to be paid was based on the ability to pay—that is, individual wealth. Indirect taxation paid the interest on these 'loans' and provided the funds for their repayment, but repayment was relatively rare in the fifteenth century, and they circulated as the equivalent of government bonds:

> Government credits could be transferred by sale, by testamentary bequest, or by contract of gift or dowry; they could be lent, pledged as surety for nearly any kind of transaction, including bank loans, or used as money in payment of private obligations.
>
> (Mueller, 1997, p. 458)

This form of investment was extremely popular in Venice until the mid-fifteenth century, but by the 1470s, market value had fallen—the four purchases recorded in Section V are at a rate of 20% of par value—and interest payments were 20 years in arrears (ibid., p. 463). In 1454, the system was suspended and replaced with a direct tax, the *decima* (ibid., p. 466).

The *Decima* and Property

The *decima* was introduced in 1463 and was a property tax. The final part of Section XI is missing, but the last entry shown is for a payment due for the *decima* relating to property in San Polo. The merchant had houses in that district which he rented out. The tax was offset against the income from these rentals by being debited to the rent (received) account. The rest of this section concerns the rentals and upkeep of these houses. They show that rent was paid in cash and by a barter for wheat. The penultimate entry is for a bad debt relating to a tenant who fled (Figure 2.10). As with the *decima*, the amount of the bad debt is debited to the rent (received) account as an expense.

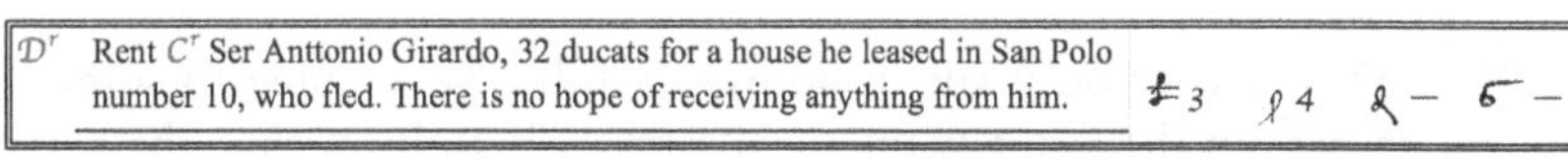

Figure 2.10 The entry for a bad debt

A Silk Shop and Construction of a Building

Sections IX and X contain entries for these two activities. It is here that the focus of the manual switches from what has largely been generic activities of Venetian merchants of that period, such as can been seen in surviving Venetian account books of the fifteenth century. The focus now appears personal to the student, whose name is used as the name for the merchant. Section X has 55 journal entries relating to a silk shop. The silk industry was very active in Venice, which was one of the primary European centres of that industry (Mola, 2000, p. xvi). However, very little is known of the Venetian method of bookkeeping for silk and these examples represent a unique insight into that practice. Section XI contains 18 journal entries relating to construction of a building. It is not a simple dwelling, but one containing sculptured marble balcony, carved columns, two ornate walkways decorated with cherubs and vines, a coat of arms painted on marble, and 20 murals—yet more evidence that this teaching assignment was for a student from a wealthy family.

Bills of Exchange

Section XIII contains 23 journal entries that reveal the mechanism used by merchants to earn profit by issuing bills that were then refused (*protesto*).

	On the 29th day of the above.				
☞ *D^r^*	Ser Zecho de Tomaxo of London *C^r^* Cash, 500 ducats paid in cash to Zuan de Marchanuova for a bill of exchange for London, (at) 56(d) sterling per ducat, according to the custom. Handled by the Cosmo de Medeci (bank).	*£ 50*	*s -*	*d -*	*p -*
…					
*D^r^*	Ser Zuan de Marchanuova *C^r^* Ser Zecho de Tomaxo, 539 ducats, 19 denari, 13 piccoli, for the refusal of a bill (of exchange) of his. It was (issued) at 56½(d) sterling per ducat and returned at 52⅓(d) for its failing to be accepted by the correspondent.	*£ 53*	*s 19*	*d 7*	*p 13*

Figure 2.11 The journal entries to record the issue of a bill of exchange to be drawn in London and to record its refusal

(Note: the second entry contains an error. The bill was issued at 56 sterling, not 56½.)

Bills circulate through the entries, with some advice offered at the end of the section on how to ensure that profits are made:

> Note that when you want to address a bill of exchange to someone, if that person does not want to accept it, it follows that the refusal represents an additional expense. (For this reason) you (should) set the exchange rate to sterling sufficiently high to cover the costs you may incur (if this happens).

This section begins after the missing pages, but the first entry is prefaced with a *manicula*, which, being consistent with the rest of the manual, indicates that this is the beginning of the coverage of this topic.

The bills are issued through the Cosimo de' Medici bank. Two of the first three issued are to be honoured in London, and both are refused, being returned at a poorer exchange rate than the one at which they were issued—this generates a profit for the merchant who issued the bill—and commission is also charged and credited to the agent in London who refused the bill. As a result, after the merchant gave one client 50 lire, when it was refused the client was charged with 53 lire, 19 soldi, 7 denari, 13 piccoli, because the exchange rate to English *sterlini* had fallen, plus a further 4 soldi, 6 denari for commission: a total charge of 54 lire, 4 soldi, 1 denari, 13 piccoli. The profit for the merchant of 3 lire, 19 soldi, 7 denari, 13 piccoli, or 8%, reveals just how profitable giving short-term loans on this basis could be (Figure 2.11).

Maritime Insurance

The final section of the manual includes nine journal entries relating to maritime insurance: premiums paid, recovery of amounts due when pirates steal cargo off two different ships, and recovery of amount due when cargo on a third vessel is lost. This section has far more instruction than the others, including instructions on what to do when you have completed a voyage in person and you have forgotten to enter some expenses against the voyage ("Enter them in the account for profits and losses, so reducing the amount you will earn") and what to do with the account for profits and losses when you close a ledger:

> Record the balance on the account for profits and losses in the capital account. Do not ever think of combining any other profits or losses with that one just mentioned. Pay attention to how much you earn (as shown in that other account) and record it in the capital account.

This appears to be saying that you should keep the profits and losses of each venture separate from any other profits and losses that have been recorded in the account for profits and losses, and post those profits and losses directly to the capital account, not into the account for profits and losses.

Conclusion

In 36 pages, de Raphaeli presents an insight into fifteenth-century Venetian trade and mercantile affairs. He focuses almost exclusively on the journal, with the ledger mentioned in passing on the first and last pages. The sophistication and maturity of the bookkeeping system are far beyond that presented by Pacioli (1494) and Tagliente (1525), and the detail of voyage accounting is far greater than that presented in Manzoni (1540). It is very similar in style to the records on this topic maintained by Andrea Barbarigo. Of the other tutors, only Casanova (1558) offers more on this subject.

The coverage of a silk shop is unique among all the manuals and is the only known example of how the activities of this industry were recorded in Venice. Almost certainly, the detail is due to the personalization of the material for the client, something that could not be replicated in a mass-published book, which is the nature of all the other instructional manuals that have survived.

From records we have of people who lived and worked through this period—bankers, ship captains, merchants, and people of standing—most of those named in the manual are likely to be real individuals, as are many of the transactions, for they are realistic, both in values and in amounts. Obviously, a real merchant would have many more transactions and things would take much longer to unfold, but it is only in the shortening of elapsed time that this manual could be said to lose an air of realism. This attachment to reality makes an even more useful manual for the student who will have heard of many of the people it names.

There are many arithmetical errors in the manual, but perhaps no more than you would expect from a student inexperienced in the calculation of rates of exchange from transaction currencies to moneys of account. On the second page, there is a flawed attempt to perform a multiplication on some blank space and many of the errors in the manual involve weights and measures, suggesting that this student was a novice not just at bookkeeping but also at mercantile arithmetic, and that this manual is the outcome of his simultaneous tuition in both subjects.

Whether that student, Zuan de Domenego, went on to have a successful career in business we are unlikely to ever know, but this manual certainly prepared him in those aspects of Venetian business far beyond the bookkeeping that is the vehicle for their coverage. It is more than a manual on bookkeeping. It is a manual on business and business practice, just as are the manuals of Manzoni and, more so, the manual of Casanova. But de Raphaeli's manual is the only one that gives us insights into a period, the fifteenth century, for which we have very few extant copies of Venetian accounts. Pacioli only scratches the surface, whereas de Raphaeli shows us how it was done.

Finally, de Raphaeli's manual reveals the maturity of the Venetian double-entry system for the journal in the mid-fifteenth century, a maturity that could not have been achieved were the system not relatively widely used. It is different from the Tuscan approach and did not come from there, for the Tuscans had no direct equivalent to the Venetian journal. It is quite likely the manual that gave Pacioli the foundation for his manual—Pacioli is known to have seen Cotrugli's book on the art of trade[6] and the two manuals have been bound together since they were completed in 1475. Regardless of whether it was, it is the only example we have of the approach of fifteenth-century bookkeeping tutors that was embraced by the writers of the printed manuals for at least the following century; and its existence allows us now to finally understand where the approach they adopted originated.

Acknowledgements

The author would like to thank Professor Franco Rossi, former vice-director of the State Archives of Venice and former director of the State Archives of Treviso, for his unselfish and committed efforts to assist in this project, not only for his transcription of the original manuscript and its subsequent translation into Italian but also for all the guidance and assistance he offered throughout.

This research has been supported by a grant from the Chartered Accountants Ireland Educational Trust.

Notes

1. A facsimile edition of *Libr. XV* was published in 2014 (Sangster, 2014).
2. Section numbers have been added. They are not numbered in the manuscript.
3. A carta is a sheet of paper representing two pages, one on the front and the other on the back. Carta 102r is the right-hand page in an open book. 102v is on the back of that page—that is, it is the left-hand page you will see if you turn over page 102r. The pages in the manuscript are numbered in cartas on the right-hand pages.

4. The Italian equivalent of this name, which is in fifteenth-century Venetian dialect, is Marino di Raffaele or, because spelling had not yet become consistent, Marino de Raphaeli.
5. For a fuller description of Barbarigo's bookkeeping, see Lane (1944, pp. 171–183).
6. Van der Helm and Postma (2000) discuss the connection between Pacioli and Cotrugli. Although they express some reservations and suggest that both Pacioli and Cotrugli copied a common source for material, this requires that Cotrugli was a copyist, which seems most unlikely given the nature of his writing of his book in 1458.

References

Carraro, C. and Favero, G. (eds.) (2017). *Benedetto Cotrugli: The Book of the Art of Trade*. Cham, Switzerland: Palgrave Macmillan/Springer.

Casanova, A. (1558). *Specchio lucidissimo nel quale si vedeno essere diffinito tatti i modi . . . che si deve menare nelle negotiamenti della Mercantia*. Venice: Comin da Trino.

Cotrugli, B. (1458). *Libro de Larte dela Mercatura, copy made 1475*. National Library of Malta. Libr. XV: cc. 1r–98v.

de Raphaeli, M. (1475). *La riegola de libro*. National Library of Malta. Libr. XV: cc.101v–121r.

Lane, F.C. (1944). *Andrea Barbarigo: Merchant of Venice, 1418–1449*. Baltimore: Johns Hopkins Press.

Manzoni, D. (1540). *Quaderno doppio col suo giornale, nouamente Composto, & diligentissimamente ordinato, secondo il costume di Venetia . . .* Venetia: Comin de Tridino de Monferrato.

Mola, L. (2000). *The Silk Industry of Renaissance Venice*. Baltimore, MD: Johns Hopkins University Press.

Mueller, R.C. (1997). *The Venetian Money Market: Banks, Panics, and the Public Debt, 1200–1500*. Baltimore, MD: Johns Hopkins University Press.

Pacioli, L. (1494). *Summa de Arithmetica Geometria Proportioni et Proportionalita*. Venice: Paganino de Paganini.

Polanyi, M. (1958). *Personal Knowledge: Towards a Post-Critical Philosophy*. 1998 reprint. London: Routledge.

Polanyi, M. (1966). The Logic of Tacit Inference. *Philosophy*, 41 (155), pp. 1–18.

Ribaudo, V. (2016). *Libro de l'arte de la mercatura*. Venezia: Edizioni Ca' Foscari.

Sangster, A. (2014). *Libr. XV*. Stirling: Lomax Press (www.lomaxpress.co.uk).

Sangster, A. (2015). The Earliest Known Treatise on Double Entry Bookkeeping by Marino de Raphaeli. *Accounting Historians Journal*, 42 (2), pp. 1–34.

Tagliente, A. (1525). *Considerando . . . Diversi Mercanti Et Molti Artesani Li Quali Sanno Le Sue Mercantile Ne Le Loro Botege . . . .* Venetia: Italia.

Tucci, U. (1990). *Benedetto Cotrugli Raguseo: Il libro del l'arte di mercatura*. Venice: Arsenale Editrice.

Van der Helm, A.J. and Postma, J. (2000). La Riegolo de Libro: Bookkeeping instructions from the mid-fifteenth century. In *Accounting and History*, G.J. Previts and E. Hernández-Esteve (eds.). Madrid: Asociación Española de Contabilidad y Administración de Empresas, 147–178.

3 The Spread of the Double-Entry Bookkeeping Method in the Sixteenth Century

The *Quaderno doppio col suo giornale novamente composto et dilegentissimamente ordinato secondo il costume di Venetia* of Dominico Manzoni (Venice, 1540)

Libero Mario Mari and Francesca Picciaia

Introduction

The publication of Luca Pacioli's *Summa* in 1494 marks a fundamental turning point in the history of accounting, as it identified and systematized the rules and relations of the double-entry bookkeeping method. After centuries of merely practical and empirical accounting techniques, for the first time the methodical structure of the Venetian technique was presented. Pacioli's system allowed merchants to identify not only accrued incomes but also lawful and licit ones (Cavazzoni, 2006). Soon after the dissemination of his work, those who kept accounts began to acquire different qualifications, and the art of bookkeeping started to break away from the arithmetic in which it had developed, and professionals began to replace mathematicians as teachers of the art of bookkeeping "in a mercantile way" (Ciambotti, 2016).

Dominico Manzoni, an accountant, played an important role in the development and the spread of double-entry bookkeeping method after Pacioli's *Summa*, with his book *Quaderno doppio col suo giornale novamente composto et dilegentissimamente ordinato secondo il costume di Venetia* (1540). Manzoni, of whose life little is known, was an expert accountant for a well-known Venetian merchant: Alvise Vallaresso. In the first part of his *Quaderno doppio*, he deals with the theoretical part of accounting in a way explicitly inspired by Pacioli's *Tractatus*, and the second part is more practical, full of sample entries (Gordon, 1913; Stoner, 2011). Despite his innovations, however, he has not had the recognition he deserves. The fame of the Paciolian *Summa*, which Manzoni constantly refers to in the theoretical part of his work, has obscured the role and importance of his book. However, there are many interesting perspectives that can be taken from his work. Manzoni was the first accountant, or *quaderniere*, who used the double-entry bookkeeping method to serve the great merchants of the time; then, he described and disseminated accounting techniques according to the Venetian method, for the benefit of all who were interested in them. However, the central contribution of Manzoni's work is doubtless the exemplification of theory, which formed a structural element, with an almost pedagogical intention, taken from his work experience. His aim was not only to empirically apply what is described in the theoretical section of his work but also to make certain technical steps understandable, such as those related to the closing and the reopening of accounts, which were not yet supported by precise theoretical explanations.

Through an analysis of Manzoni's work, this study examines what, and to what extent, Manzoni contributed to the advancement of accounting techniques, considering also the particular widespread reach of the book in the years after its first edition of 1540, as evidenced by the numerous reprints and translations that were made. This chapter is structured as follows. After a brief description of the diffusion of accounting methods before and after the Paciolian *Summa*, the structure of Manzoni's *Quaderno doppio* is presented, in order to highlight commonalities and differences with Pacioli's *Tractatus*. Then, the focus shifts to the sample entries put forward by the author; accounting techniques and the solutions suggested are highlighted, and the contributions of Manzoni to the development and diffusion of double-entry bookkeeping method are isolated.

Pacioli's *Summa* and the Spread of the Venetian Style of the Double-Entry Bookkeeping Method

The first historical evidence of specific environments structured and organized for the tuition of accounting practices is the Italian abacus schools created between the twelfth and thirteenth centuries. These are particular schools (Giusti, 2011; Maraghini, 2011; Sapori, 1997; Sangster, Scataglini-belghitar, 2010; Ulivi, 2002) that were created to transmit knowledge related to so-called practical mathematics, where a teacher (*magister abaci*) prepared pupils to run commercial and artistic activities, through the teaching of mathematics, geometry, and commercial matters. These courses were an alternative to those related to humanistic topics and were

> intended to be addressed to those who were destined to work in trade and trafficking and, therefore, [these schools] elaborated and communicated a different culture, which had to be ready quickly for practical application [. . .] to constitute a dynamic and modern body of accounting techniques.
>
> (Becchi, 2013: 187, our translation)

It is noteworthy that the accounting knowledge of the abacus schools was taught without any theory, but as intuition and necessity dictated (Sosnowski, 2006); in other words, "a theoretical basis was lacking, and this could not be found in mathematical analysis, which examined numbers for their mystical-magical quantity to bring out the factual in a strong and appropriate scientific framework" (Amaduzzi, 2001: 45, our translation). After a few centuries of "practical accountability," the time was ripe for a scholar with deep preparation and eclectic knowledge (Amaduzzi, 2001) who could give the first theorization to the double-entry bookkeeping method (Baskett, 2011; Peragallo, 1938). In this context, Pacioli and his world-famous *Summa Arithmetica, Geometria, Proportioni et Proportionalità* represented a "multidisciplinary upgrade" (Ciambotti, 2011: 295) with regard to the purposes and the functions of accounting in general and the double-entry bookkeeping method in particular. It is probable (Ciambotti, 2011) that he learned the method by reading commercial manuscripts, from some Venetian teacher, or thanks to the patronage of the rich Jewish merchant Antonio Rompiasi; in any case, what is certain is that he immediately understood the importance of the technique and therefore systematized and published the double-entry bookkeeping method through the most important communication channel of the time: the print.

Many studies (i.e., Antinori, Hernàndez-Esteve, 1994; Cavazzoni, 1997, 2003, 2006; Langer, 1958; Sangster, 2007; Turco, 2002) agree in recognizing Pacioli, a Franciscan friar, as the father of accounting. The main aim of his work was to present a guide to all existing mathematical knowledge, of which the double-entry bookkeeping method was an example (Hernàndez-Esteve, 1994). The publication of *Summa* changed how accounting was approached (Fischer, 2000; Peragallo, 1956): the new method, called the Venetian technique, was systematized and thus "the double-entry bookkeeping method, 'produced' at the desks of warehouses, emerges from the closed books of business and becomes available for use by those who, in every environment, run any economic and financial activity" (Catturi, 2009: 6, our translation). In particular, according to Catturi (2009), the role of Pacioli is fundamental and undoubted, because a copy of Paciolian *Tractatus* or the entire *Summa* could be found in most royal or noble libraries, as an essential tool for every merchant (Sangster et al., 2008). This is also true due to the successive reprints of the treatise in the main commercial cities throughout Europe, both as a whole or excerpted as a starting point for the creation of practical handbooks. In fact, and this constitutes a central step in our work, the *Tractatus* became the point of inspiration for the drafting of successive treatises or handbooks on accounting, until the end of the seventeenth century. In other words,

> the spread of Paciolian double-entry bookkeeping technique, from its first publication, was immediate and general, so that the "Venetian," "Italian," or, double-entry, method of accounting was gradually adopted

> and recognized as the most rational and efficient for analyzing and monitoring the activities of warehouses, banks, and public and religious organizations.
>
> (Catturi, 2009: 7, our translation)

However, not all scholars agree on the central role of the *Summa* in the diffusion of accounting technique, precisely because of the characteristics and aims of Pacioli's work. Yamey (2004), for example, suggests that the spread of the double-entry accounting method, especially in the sixteenth century, was independent of Pacioli's work, for several reasons, mostly environmental or intrinsic. He argued that Pacioli was fundamentally a humanistic researcher and the *Summa*, his best-known work, reflected this peculiarity. Further, "few merchants, even Italian merchants, were educated in the humanistic tradition" (p. 144), and this educational distance may have been an obstacle to the adequate diffusion of the book (Yamey, 2010). Yamey also argues that even the physical and intrinsic characteristics of Pacioli's tome slowed the spread of the double-entry method, since the *Summa* is a large book, with more than 600 pages, and the accounting method is described only in one small part. Thus, it was not a handy tool for those who would refer to it for a clarification or explanation of double-entry bookkeeping. Moreover, the *De computis et scripturis* was not a handbook of accounting techniques and does not provide an exhaustive description of all transactions or "an illustrative set of accounting books in which the appropriate entries were entered" (Yamey, 2004: 144).

Of course, as Yamey himself argues, this does not affect the importance of Pacioli's work, since it constitutes the first stone laid down in accounting knowledge. In fact, independently from these considerations, the fundamental role of Pacioli's treatise in the development of the accounting technique is certain, within the broader ways through which the Italian method of double-entry bookkeeping spread all over Europe (Catturi, 2009). Beginning in the sixteenth century, many books about accounting techniques were published, and all were influenced, directly or indirectly, by the *Summa* (Yamey, 2011). Among these works, there is Manzoni's *Quaderno doppio col suo giornale novamente composto et dilegentissimamente ordinato secondo il costume di Venetia*, published in Venice in 1540. It is known that Manzoni was a *computista* (accountant), but little else is known about his life. Thanks to a personal dedication in one of his works, we know that he was born in Oderzo, a town near Treviso and Venice. He lived there, working at the company of Alvise Vallaresso, a well-known merchant (Bariola, 1897; Masi, 1997; Melis, 1950), and teaching as a *magister abaci*, as he himself wrote in the dedication of another work (*La brieve risolutione di aritmetica universale in qual si voglia negotio dove intervenga numero, peso et misura*, Venice, 1553), claiming to have taught double-entry bookkeeping techniques to many people.

The Structure of Manzoni's Book

Several authors (Bariola, 1897; Masi, 1997; Melis, 1950; Saporetti, 1898) consider Manzoni's work to be a mere remake of the *Tractatus*, the best-known work of Luca Pacioli, although it is possible to find interesting and even innovative elements, reflecting the role Manzoni played in the society of the time. Manzoni's professional experience in the mercantile business pervades his entire book, which albeit it in many parts echoes the findings of Pacioli, his most illustrious predecessor, is more essential, freed from many cultural elements that distract from the techniques and rules, and is much better organized and easier to understand (Alfieri, 1891). An example of this ease and linearity can be found in Manzoni's discussion of the logic of double-entry bookkeeping, noting that there will always be "one who gives, the other who receives, and that thing that is given or received, and also the cause or why" (*uno che dà, l'altro che riceve, et quella cosa che vien data o ricevuta, et anche la causa o perché*; Chap. 11, Part 1, our translation). Thus, the presence of examples, appearing for the first time in the history of instructional accounting books, makes Manzoni's work particularly interesting and innovative (Besta, 1922; Lauwers, Willekens, 1994; Masi, 1997; Saporetti, 1898), allowing the reader to follow and understand, with a clear pedagogical approach, all the steps that form the basis of the proper keeping of accounts and registration of entries (Coronella, 2014).

Manzoni's book met with a considerable reception and acquired an enviable reputation, as evidenced by the editions of 1540, 1554, 1564, and 1573 and certain adaptations, such as the book of one Schweicher from Nuremberg, who in 1549 published a work entirely drawn from Manzoni's *Quaderno doppio* (Masi, 1997). In the last two editions of Manzoni's work, the title changed to *Libro mercantile ordinato col suo Giornale e Alfabeto per tenere i conti doppi al modo di Venetia* (Mercantile book ordered according to the ledger and index of account to keep double accounts in the Venetian way; our translation), while the structure remained the same, with a division into two parts. Other changes included the alteration of "*quaderno*" to "*libro grande*" or "*libro mastro*" (ledger) and "*quaderniero*" modified to "*ragionato*" or "*scrivano*" (accountant) (Alfieri, 1891). The structure of the book is very clear and precise. Its two parts show the method of keeping the two main merchant's books: the journal (*giornale*) (Part 1, with 15 chapters and a summary table of 300 accounting entries as examples) and the ledger (*quaderno*) (Part 2, with 12 numbered and 1 unnumbered chapters). The conclusions of the two parts contain examples of the two registers. At the beginning of the book, following Pacioli's example, Manzoni highlights what is absolutely essential to any merchant or to anyone else who wishes to diligently carry on business. He limits himself to indicating only two things: the capital, in the absence of which one is unable to engage in business, and well-ordered accounting, which allows information about what has been done to be obtainable quickly. He does not focus on a third thing, which

Pacioli considered to be equally important: being a good accountant. This omission can be justified by the fact that Manzoni was himself a *computista* (accountant) so he could have considered this to be implicit.

In the introduction to his book, Manzoni notes that he will use examples that, although they cannot cover all the innumerable possibilities that may occur in reality, will allow the reader to acquire the knowledge to resolve any other situation. He also explains that he will follow the Venetian method, which is characterized by the use of two pages for every entry in a *quaderno*: one for the *dare* (give)—that is to say, for debtors—and the other for the *avere* (take)—that is to say, for the creditors. In fact,

> this form of the ledger seems to have been created in Venice and spread from there to Italian cities, replacing other methods, including the Tuscan model, in which the debts were placed over the credits on the same page, and the Genoese model, in which debts and credits were located one next to each other on the same page.
>
> (Yamey, 1994: 115, our translation)

In this first part, Manzoni describes the inventory, the memorial (*Squarza foglio* or *Vachetta*), other smaller books, the journal, the authentication of registers, and the use of currencies. The preparation of the inventory is essential for a merchant, who must know what he owns at the beginning of each year and its subsequent value. This allows the merchant to be aware of the result of the activity, which is always intended to "achieve lawful and competent gain for one's sustenance" (*conseguire licito e competente guadagno per sua sostentazione*; Chap. 2, Part 1, our translation). All goods, starting from the most valuable ones, should be reported on a separate page or in a separate book and transcribed into the journal during a single day. This should be meticulous, careful, and precise work, because from the journal is derived the correct composition of capital, which "is the foundation upon which it is possible to determine and fabricate all operations day by day" (*è fondamento sopra il quale si ha a stabilire e fabbricare tutte le operazioni che di giorno in giorno negotiando accaderanno*; Chap. 4, Part 1, our translation). His brief reference to the inventory is enriched by the details of a concrete case based on his work experience at Alvise Vallaresso's company.

Before transcribing accounting entries into the journal, some merchants would write down the operations that took place into a log, which allowed them to remember what happened during the course of each day: this is the memorial (*memoriale*), a book in which all those who collaborate with the merchant and who carry out work on his behalf can register their activities. The author notes that it is not appropriate to draw up the inventory in the memorial, which often contains information personal to the merchant. This book does not require a particular scriptural technique, and it is permissible to use different currencies. The *quaderniere* must register all operations in the journal, according to an appropriate accounting method and with a single currency. The link between the memorial and the other two main books (the *quaderno* and *giornale*), which must be authenticated, is through the assignment of the same symbol at the beginning of each register: for the first year, a cross (Aho, 2005), and then, in the following years, the letters of the alphabet. Manzoni's invitation of merchants to number the pages to be able to immediately find single transactions and prevent fraudulent behavior must be noted. To facilitate the registration of accounting entries in the journal, and particularly those that regard small, repetitive, and daily expenses, it is possible to use additional books, in the same way as the memorial: at the end of a specific period of time (a week or a month) all these records must be transcribed, in summary fashion, into the journal.

Main Characteristics of Manzoni's Giornale

In the description of the journal, Manzoni focuses both on the formal aspects of the registrations and on the substantial aspects of double-entry methodology. He emphasizes that the *giornale* must have only half of the number of pages of the *quaderno*, precisely because, according to the rules of double entry, for every registration in the first book it is necessary to have two accounting entries in the second, with as many lines drawn in as there are subdivisions of the chosen currency (e.g., *lire*, *soldi*, *grossi*, and *piccoli*).[1] For immediate understanding of the operations, it is very important to use the terms *per* (for) and *a* (to), which always indicate, respectively, debtors and creditors: Manzoni lays great emphasis on this point, believing that one of the main difficulties of the bookkeeping technique consists precisely in making a clear distinction between these two accounts (Amaduzzi, 2001), which, in the journal, are divided by two slanted lines (//), indicating the double registration to be made in the ledger (Geijsbeek, 1914; Yamey, 1994). One innovation Manzoni made is the progressive number assigned to every entry. This is an important feature, although it was not widespread, since it allows the links between the *giornale* and the *quaderno* to be found more easily, helping the merchant "become informed of the number and the amount of operations in the giornale" (*havere notitia del numero overo della quantità de le partite di esso giornale*; Chap. 8, Part 2, our translation) (Alfieri, 1891; Besta, 1922; Coronella, 2014). The accounting entry with which Manzoni begins the examples of the *giornale* is as follows:

Al nome di Dio, 1540 a dì 1° Marzo in Venetia

1 $\frac{1}{2}$ P. *Cassa // A Cavedal de mi Alvise Vallaresso, de mi S. Zacharia, che de contadi me trovo al presente fra oro et moneta, ducati 2.500 g.—val*

1.250 s. - g. - p. -

(Translation: In the name of God, today March, 1st 1540 [. . .] For cash to capital of Alvise Vallaresso [. . .] in gold and money, *ducati*)

In the *giornale*, and consequently in the *quaderno*, there are two very important accounts, which should receive special attention for their representation as accounting entries and for their values on which depends the success of the merchant: the first is the cash account—namely the "bag or any other place where you put and store your money" (*borsa, o altro loco che sia, nel qual intendi riponere e servar li toi denari*; our translation), which can never be a creditor; the second is the capital account—that is to say, "the entire amount of your assets" (*tutto il corpo overo monte del tuo cavedale*; our translation)—which, conversely, cannot be a debtor (Chap. 9, Part 1).

Chapter 13 is dedicated to similarities and differences between the journal and the ledger, as well as the links between these two registers that are put in place to allow any accounting entry to be readily found and to discover errors or possible omissions. The first aspect, common to both registers, is the set of elements that must be considered in each registration:

- *dare* (give), which means "having to give," indicating the debtor;
- *avere* (take), which means "having to take," indicating the creditor;
- *qualità* (quality), which are "the things that you use";
- *quantità* (quantity)—that is, "the number, the weight, or the measure";
- *tempo* (time)—that is to say, "the day, the month, and the year that you are operating in"; and
- *ordine* (order), which "is taught easily in the present book."

One difference between the journal and the ledger is found in the date, which in the journal is placed over the accounting entry, while in the ledger it can be found in the description of the operation. The connection between these two registers is guaranteed, with references to every single operation. The numbers of the pages in the *quaderno* are written one over the other, like a fraction, in the *giornale*, above the accounting entry, while the number of the corresponding page of the *giornale* is listed in the *quaderno* after the transaction. In this part of the book, moreover, the author delves into two more general aspects: the authentication of the registers and the use of the currency. In the first topic, Manzoni does not add anything new to Pacioli, simply underlining the necessity to be explicit about the individuals responsible for the registration and typology of currency used. Everything is certified by an officer, who, affixing his stamp, gives legal value to the registers, which can be used as evidence in court disputes. Manzoni, however, notes that this practice is not widespread in Venice, and many merchants, with fraudulent intent, drew up two sets of registers, with one to show to the buyer and the other to the seller. He also writes that, in his time, many Rialto merchants were discovered and severely condemned for these behaviors.

The section on currency is quite interesting. This is the longest chapter of the entire work. In it, Manzoni explains how, in Venice, two types of systems are usually used. The characteristics of these systems and the passage from

Table 3.1 Conversions among different denominations

First system ("lire de piccoli a moneta comune," *"small lire in common currency"), divided into* lire, soldi, *and* piccolo	*Second system (more common among merchants), divided into* ducati, grossi d'oro, *and* piccoli d'oro	*Third system (used by Manzoni in the book) divided into* lire di grossi, ducati, soldi, grossi d'oro, *and* piccoli d'oro
1 *lira* = 20 *soldi*	1 *ducato* = 24 *grossi d'oro*	1 *lira di grossi* = 10 *ducati* = 20 *soldi*
1 *soldo* = 12 *piccoli*	1 *grosso d'oro* = 32 *piccoli d'oro*	1 *soldo* = 12 *grossi d'oro*
The relationship between these two systems is calculated with *piccoli*: 1 *piccolo d'oro* = 31/16 *piccolo*		1 *grosso d'oro* = 32 *piccoli d'oro*

one currency to another are described in Table 3.1. The monetary system described by Manzoni, with two types of money (gold money and silver money), was maintained for very long time, but with a differentiated use:

> The lira di piccoli was used by the common people, by shopkeepers and small storekeepers, due to the presence of a large amount of transactions of little value, while the state and merchants with larger transactions conducted them in lire di grossi and golden ducati.
>
> (Papadopoli, 1892: 206, our translation)

Moreover, Manzoni explains in this section some practical methods for changing from one system to another, postponing to a future work a complete illustration of the issue.

This first part of the *Quaderno doppio* finishes with a useful summary table of all the operations described in the sections.

Main Characteristics of Manzoni's Quaderno

In the second part of the book the other fundamental register, the *quaderno* (ledger), is described. Manzoni once more discusses the necessity for double registration in the ledger for every single entry in the journal, the importance of the two terms *per* and *a*, and the way to use them correctly. In fact, Manzoni condemns the widespread praxis that reverses this meaning in the ledger, such as Pacioli does, using *a* for the creditor account.[2] Furthermore, the procedural and substantial elements that must be observed to present the accounting records in an orderly fashion are succinctly represented:

- the structure of each accounting entry must be organized in the following way: a descriptive part, a line on the left with the number of the page where the same registration in the journal is collocated, a line on the right indicating the number of the page in the *quaderno* where the other account used in the entry is registered, and as many rows as the subdivisions of the reporting currency (Chap. 1, Part 2);

- at the beginning of each page it is necessary to indicate the year, while the date of the operation should be put in the descriptive part (Chap. 2, Part 2);
- white spaces are not allowed, to avoid possible fraud (Chap. 2, Part 2);
- if there is more than one operation on the same day, the date must be put just in the first registration, while in the following entries must be written "*adi detto*" (Chap. 2, Part 2); and
- when a page is completed, it is necessary to report its result on the first free page available. Only the account balance must be indicated, and the use of the symbol "R" testifies that this is a carryover; in the same place the number of the previous page must be written. This carryover operation does not need to be indicated in the journal (Chap. 2, Part 2).

The passage of an accounting entry from the *giornale* to the *quaderno* is minutely described: the entry in the first one is struck out (a transverse lines on the debtor account, then on the creditor ones) (Chap. 2, Part 2). Near these lines the numbers of the *quaderno*'s pages where the accounts are transcribed must be indicated, as well as the name of the account in a *rubrica* or *alfabeto* (a sort of summary) (Chap. 2, Part 2). This *alfabeto* is very important, and its structure seems to introduce an attempt to reclassify accounts (Alfieri, 1891; Masi, 1997; Melis, 1950; Saporetti, 1898). Manzoni here distinguishes between live things ("here every animated creature is intended"; our translation), on the right side, and dead things ("objects or any other thing are intended"; our translation). This distinction, mostly founded on the

Carta 1 MDXXX—Cassa

			l.	*s.*	*g.*	*p.*			*l.*	*s*	*g.*	*p.*
1	*Cassa di contadi, die dar adì 1° marzo 1540, A Cavedal de mi Alvise Vallaresso de misser Zacharia, che di contadi me trovo al presente fra oro et moneta, in tutto d. 2500*	C.2	250					C.	—	—	—	—

Carta 2 MDXXX—Cavedal

	l.	*s.*	*g.*	*p.*				*l.*	*s*	*g.*	*p.*
C.					1	*Cavedal de mi Alvise Vallaresso de misser Zacharia, die haver, adì 1° Marzo, P. Cassa contadi, mi ritrovo al presente fra oro et moneta in tutto d. 2.500*	C.1	250	—	—	—

form of the accounts, "was used by many people, especially in France and in Germany. Live things are called personal or specific accounts, and dead things impersonal or generic accounts" (Alfieri, 1891: 121, our translation).

Finally, Manzoni illustrates methods for finding possible errors and the techniques that must be used for their correction. Every good merchant must do this systematically, every week, every month, or any other period, must verify the correctness of all the transactions in the journal and in the ledger. For this activity, the help of a second person is necessary, as one checks the journal and the other the ledger, via a cross-checking of the accounts, of the sections of *dare* (give) and *avere* (take) and of the total amounts. The accuracy of the accounting entries is evidenced by a check mark: a line for every account of the ledger and two lines for each entry of the journal. It is a long and demanding process that requires much patience and attention; for this reason, Manzoni proposes ideas that can shorten the time (Chap. 10, Part 2). In the event that an error is encountered, such as an accidental reversal of the sides of the accounts, it is necessary to correct it, and he proposes two different methods:

- make the correct entry and remove, with a cross or any other sign, the wrong one and
- write the correct entry, with a double amount, without canceling the wrong one, although this can not be extended to all errors.

(Yamey, 1994: 170)

However, it is important to not entirely cancel the incorrect operation—that is to say, it is possible to erase it, but the correction should always be legible, otherwise the book could not be presentable in a court case or dispute (Chap. 11, Part 2).

The work ends with a chapter, which is not numbered, dedicated to the way accounting entries and books kept by inexperienced persons or those who are unaware of the complex art of bookkeeping can be sorted and corrected. The starting point is from the signature of the registers with the *alfabeto* (summary) and the numbering of all operations; therefore, it is necessary to do a subdivision into years and, having reached a decade, to archive the registers, creating a "summary of annals" (*sommario di annali*), to proceed to the orderly redefinition of all entries. As in the section related to the *giornale*, this part ends with examples.

The Accounting Technique in the *Quaderno doppio*

As stated in the earlier paragraphs, the most innovative and interesting aspect of Manzoni's work is the presence of a lot of examples, in the form of 300 accounting entries, which enrich what is represented theoretically in the two parts of the book. Manzoni's choice to use Roman numerals ("*figure antique*") instead of Arabic ones is interesting (Brown, 1905). He recommends the use of Roman numerals for the ledger and Arabic numerals in the journal, with the justification that Roman numerals are more difficult to counterfeit, whereas Arabic ones are easy to falsify—for example, by modifying a 6 into a 9, and many others, so that it would be impossible to verify ("*dell'abaco moderno, le qual con facilità, di una se ne potria far un'altra, come è quella del nulla, della quale se ne potria fare un* 6 *o un* 9, *et molte altre se ne potriano mutare che poi con difficoltà se ne accorgerebbe*"; Chap. 2, Part 2). In addition to this practical reason, he also points out that the books with *figure antique* (Roman numbers), if presented in a judgment, will receive greater consideration and are better than others for demonstrating the actual state of affairs ("*quelli come di più autorità sariano creduti, et per ogni somma o gran quantità di denari o robba che fusse, sarian lodati*"). This differentiates the approach of Manzoni from that of Pacioli, who instead used only Arabic numerals, opposing the praxis of the time: the use of Roman numerals in merchants' books is widespread throughout the fifteenth century, although there was already a general acceptation of books with Arabic numerals, which are more generally used beginning with the seventeenth century (Arlinghaus, 2004; Bachi, 1897).

Another peculiarity of the accounting technique proposed by Manzoni regards the typology of registration: all accounting entries are simple—that is, with a single debtor account and a single creditor account.[3] This does not mean that merchants, in Manzoni's time, did not draw up articulated registrations; these, rather, were divided in the *quaderno doppio* into single and simple operations. For example, the operation of purchasing goods, preceded by a down payment and paid for in various forms (cash, barter, and loan disposal), is divided into eight simple entries, also including the payment of the duty. On a more technical level, it should be noted that the reopening of accounts concerns the recognition of all the inventory linked with the *cavedal* (capital) account as the basis of subsequent operations. These are not indications of the theme of the evaluations, instead of Pacioli and his famous assertion "and make it fatter [larger] rather than thin [small]" (*e fallo grasso più presto che magro*; Chap. 12, "De computis et Scripturis," our translation). The accounting entries cover both business and personal affairs of the merchant. In fact it is easy to find in merchants' books, alongside records of transactions of the purchase and sale of goods, special events, such as the wedding of a sister, the dowry received from a wife, the death of the latter and the subsequent funeral expenses, lottery winnings, or a pirate attack on a boat carrying previously purchased goods. The distinction that Manzoni makes between accounts for goods and other things, especially family expenses, must be noted (Masi, 1997). Like the classification in Besta's equity-centered accounting system (Sargiacomo et al., 2012) there is a difference between accounts for products and accounts for periods. The first ones, in fact, with a two-phase functioning, are intended to measure the results achieved with the purchase and sale of every single good, and they converge, over the course of the year, to a synthetic *pro e danno* account (a sort of income statement); the second, instead, with a one-phase functioning, are summarized directly in the *pro and danno* account only at the end of the year.

In the accounts dedicated to goods, the possible inventories at the end of the year are not evaluated and, in the case of total sales of goods, the balance of the account expresses the gain (or loss). The value of the goods includes also the results of purchasing (excluding duties), but only in the year when the goods are completely sold. Regarding the operations at the end of the year, Manzoni does not consider adjustments to entries—that is to say, depreciation, accrual, and prepayment calculations—but just the capitalization of certain expenses. Specifically, he does not evaluate the inventory of goods, because he assumes that everything is sold during the year, making a single exception for *carisee* (light Venetian tissues), which, at the end of the period, are not completely sold, so he calculates the balance of the account

Carta 12 MDXXX—Carisee

		C.	*l.*	*s.*	*g.*	*p.*			C.	*l.*	*s.*	*g.*	*p.*
43	*Carisee de la prima sorte, dieno dar adì 25 Marzo a S. Antonio di Pizoni, per pezze n. 180 a d. 7,5 la pezza, monta d. 1350, battudo per la sua parte della messettaria, a rason di una % d. 13, g. 12 resta netto a pagamento d. 1336, g. 12*	12	133	13			103	*Carisee, a l'incontro, diene haver adì 25 Aprile, P. S. Marcho dal Zio, per l'ammontar di 40 pezze. A d. 9 la pezza, d. 360, et a bon conto di una promessa*	10	36	—	—	—
48	*Ditto, a Officio de la messeteria, per l'ammontare de d. 1350, a 2 %, d. 27*	8	2	14									
49	*Ditto, a Cassa de contadi a S. Augustin Saraco per sua sansaria, d'accordo d. 10*	1	1				R	*Adì 20 Febraro, P. si medesimo porto avanti dover dar, resto per saldo di quelle, pezze n. 140, le qual resta de pezze n. 180, et sta in pretio d. 1013, g. 12*	43	101	7		
	Ducati 1373, g.12							*Ducati 1373, g. 12*					

that must be postponed to a future year, including in this balance any gains and losses related to the sales of this good.

Rental transactions are fully considered on a financial criterion basis, although their accrual basis is in different periods. For this, Manzoni offers the example of the rental operation of a farm for 45 *ducati* per year with a delayed payment. The amount for the first year is entirely destined for the *pro e danno* account.

207	34/34	P.	*S.Jacomo Pavanello mio habitator // A Fitti della possessione de Moian, per fitto di quella, . . ., principiò il suo fitto che fu adì 29 luio, . . . che sono d. 45 all'anno . . .*	l.4	s.10	g.	p.
296	34/44	P.	*Fitti de la possession de Moian // A Pro et danno, per fitto di quella, per l'anno presente, finirà de luio 1541, per saldo di quelli, d.45*	l.4	s.10	g.	p.

There seems to be an exception for the capitalization of the expenses for home and farm furnishings: specifically, three cases are presented, in which the expenses for clothes and the renovation of a villa and a house are postponed to a future year.

284	43/18	P.	*Mobile di casa // A Spese de vestir, per più spese fatte, . . ., le qual porto in quello, resto tratto per saldo de le ditte spese d.12 g.20*	l.1	s.5	g.8	p.

Another difference between Manzoni and Pacioli is the use of the *pro e danno* account in the journal, even during the course of the year. This account is incremented each time goods are entirely sold, and the gain (or loss) is calculated, without the need to wait for the end of the year. Pacioli holds that this synthetic account must not be entered into the journal, but only into the ledger, because it is created and used for the inventory ("*il conto Pro e Danno non bisogna si metta in Giornale, ma basta solo nel Quaderno, perché nasce in quello delle cose avanzate, ovvero mancate in dare e avere*"; Chap. 27, "De Computis et Scripturis"). Manzoni introduces a different approach, since he knows that the *pro e danno* account is used even before the closing of accounts. In the *pro e danno* account are included all proceeds of single goods, as well as all expenses (e.g., household expenses or wage expenses) and revenues (e.g., rental income and interest income) for the period. The balance expresses the final result, which converges on the closing value of the capital.

300	44/33	P.	*Pro et danno // A Cavedal de mi Alvise Vallaresso, per l'utilità seguida de l'anno 1540, tratto in resto, per saldo di quello*	l.136	s.7	g.11	p.15

Finally, Manzoni offers a summary titled "*Summe de tutte le partite poste in Quaderno, sì in dar come ancho in havere*" (Summary of all the entries of the ledger, both in *dare* and in *avere*), a sort of verification statement (not presented in the last two editions of the book; Alfieri, 1891), out of the ledger, with a list "of total debits and credits: each accounting entry of the list is the same in both the debit and in the credit, since this list is drawn up when each account has been balanced and closed" (Yamey, 1994: 178, our translation).

Concluding Remarks: Manzoni's Pedagogical Intent and the Spread of Double-Entry Bookkeeping

It has been determined that the double-entry bookkeeping method is first found in Pacioli's treatise, the milestone of the entire accounting history: as Yamey (2011) wrote, "the publication of Pacioli's *De Scripturis* led the way; others followed" (p. 293). It is important to note, however, the contribution of those others to the dissemination of accounting methods, moreover of those who had educational aims. Manzoni's *Quaderno Doppio* was one of the earliest attempts to formulate general rules for transaction analysis (Chatfield, 2014; Sidebotham, 2014), focusing on its practical and empirical aspects and constituting a sort of accounting handbook. Manzoni's work has a definite educational purpose: his main aim was to teach an accounting method that is difficult but useful (even essential) for achieving lawful and competent gain, for all who, for various reasons, are interested in it. His purpose is evident and pervades all parts of the work, since the author himself declares, many times, that his explanations and structure are easy and simple to understand.

A major element of the *Quaderno doppio* is the long sequence of accounting entries presented as examples. Even though Manzoni asserts that these are taken from the accounts of the merchant Alvise Vallaresso, where Manzoni worked as accountant, the way they are presented implies that this is not quite accurate. Probably these are carefully structured cases, perhaps also inspired by real events (Besta, 1922), as we can observe in subsequent editions, where only the year is changed, while all entries (e.g., also the death of Vallaresso's wife) are presented in the same order, with the same dates and for the same amounts. Manzoni organizes each entry given, for which he presents also a summary table, according to thematic groups, such as purchases, sales, barters, payments, incurring expenses, and so on. For each theme, the transactions are represented in an increasing of difficulty, to guide the reader gradually through each situation. For the same reason, he presents captions indicating the transaction described in each accounting entry (Besta, 1922; Coronella, 2014).

The pedagogical aim is also evidenced by Manzoni's focus on particular topics, such as the way registers can be checked, the use of currencies and changes from one currency to another, corrections of errors and omissions, and whether to use Roman or Arabic numerals. All these elements testify to the great attention paid by Manzoni to empirical matters and the possible solutions inspired by praxis and experience. It must be noted, however, that the accounting technique presented in Manzoni's treatise has not yet been fully perfected. The absence of some elements, such as the evaluation of the accounts at the end of the year or entries for accrual and deferred income, in fact, makes the construction of a final report impossible: these topics will be analyzed by Angelo Pietra and Lodovico Flori some years later, allowing accountants to complete the process of bookkeeping.

Certainly, the representation of the accounting method found within *Quaderno doppio* is significant and, in any case, sufficient to show merchants of the time how to order their accounting and become aware of the trends of their own affairs. Manzoni, with his work, completes what was initially structured by Pacioli in the *Summa*, his most famous treatise, contributing "to disseminate the knowledge and the application of the double-entry bookkeeping method to merchant companies" (Saporetti, 1898: 112, our translation).

Notes

1. These are different Italian currencies of the time.
2. Manzoni, to further emphasize this, presents an example: "*Cassa die dar adì tanti etc A Cavedal et non Per Cavedal, imperoché dicendo Per Cavedal, pareria quasi che 'l Cavedal fusse debitore, essendo però creditore*" (cash *to* capital and not *for* capital, since saying *for* capital it seems that capital account becomes a debtor, but it is a creditor; Chap. 4, Part 2, our translation).
3. For the registration of complex accounting entries it was necessary to wait for the work of Ludovico Flori in 1636 (Mari, 2016).

References

Aho, J. (2005), *Confession and bookkeeping: The religious, moral, and rhetorical roots of modern accounting*, State University of New York Press, New York.

Alfieri, V. (1891), *La partita doppia applicata alle scritture delle antiche aziende mercantili*, Paravia, Torino.

Amaduzzi, A. (2001), *Storia della ragioneria. Uomini, aziende, contabilità*, Collegio dei ragionieri di Bergamo, Erba.

Antinori, C., Hernàndez-Esteve, E. (1994), *500 anni di partita doppia e letteratura contabile 1494–1994*, RIREA, Roma.

Arlinghaus, F.J. (2004), "Bookkeeping, double-entry bookkeeping", in Kleinhenz, C. (ed.), *Medieval Italy: An encyclopedia*, Vol. 1, Routledge, New York.

Bachi, R. (1897), *Alcuni rifacimenti del trattato di Fra Luca Paciolo*, Il Ragioniere. Rivista Scientifica e Professionale, Milano.

Bariola, P. (1897), *Storia della ragioneria italiana*, Tipografia Ambrosiana, Milano.

Baskett, J.H. (2011), "A revisionist history of accounting: From the origins of private property to Venice in the Pacioli era", *International Business & Economic Research Journal*, 1(12), pp. 1–14.

Becchi, E. (2013), "Professionalizzare precocemente: l'acculturazione del mercante in epoca rinascimentale", in Morandi, M. (ed.), *Formare alle professioni*, Franco Angeli, Milano.

Besta, F. (1922), *La Ragioneria*, Vol. 3, Vallardi, Milano.

Brown, R. (1905), *A history of accounting and accountants*, Psychology Press, New York.

Catturi, G. (2009), *Gestazione, 'nascita' e diffusione in Europa del metodo italiano di contabilità. Scuole e libri di abaco dal XIV al XVII secolo*, Asociación Española de Contabilidad y Administración de Empresas, Valladolid.

Cavazzoni, G. (1997), "Luca Pacioli e Lodovico Flori: Due umbri nella storia della ragioneria", *Storia della Ragioneria*, 1, pp. 106–116.

Cavazzoni, G. (2003), "Lettera aperta a Luca Pacioli", in AA.VV., *Contabilità e cultura aziendale*, Istituti editoriali e poligrafici internazionali, Roma.

Cavazzoni, G. (2006), "Alla ricerca dei prodromi del bilancio nell'opera di Luca Pacioli", in AA.VV., *Riferimenti storici e processi evolutivi dell'informativa di bilancio tra teoria e prassi*, RIREA, Roma.

Chatfield, M. (2014), "Manzoni Domenico", in Chatfield, M., Vangermeersch, R. (eds.), *The history of accounting: An international encyclopedia*, Routledge, London.

Ciambotti, M. (2011), "Luca Pacioli, la partita doppia e la storia della contabilità e della società", in Hernàndez-Esteve, E., Martelli, M. (eds.), *Before and after Luca Pacioli*, Centro studi Mario Pancrazi, Perugia.

Ciambotti, M. (2016), "Luca Pacioli e le innovazioni del linguaggio contabile nelle amministrazioni mercantili e nelle signorie del'400", *Cultura Giuridica e Diritto Vivente*, pp. 1–17.

Coronella, S. (2014), *Storia della Ragioneria italiana. Epoche, uomini e idee*, Franco Angeli, Milano.

Fischer, M.J. (2000), "Luca Pacioli on business profits", *Journal of Business Ethics*, 25, pp. 299–312.

Geijsbeek, J. (1914), *Ancient double-entry bookkeeping. Lucas Pacioli's treatise (A.D. 1494—the earliest know writer on bookkeeping)*, J. Geijsbeek, Denver.

Giusti, E. (2011), "Le matematiche dalle scuole d'abaco alle università", in Hernàndez-Esteve, E., Martelli, M. (eds.), *Before and after Luca Pacioli*, Centro studi Mario Pancrazi, Perugia.

Gordon, C. (1913), "Books on Accountancy, 1494–1600", *The Library*, 1(1), pp. 145–170.

Hernàndez-Esteve, E. (1994), "Luca Pacioli's treatise *De Computis et Scripturis*: A composite or a unified work?", *Accounting, Business & Financial History*, 4(1), pp. 67–82.

Langer, C. (1958), "Paciolo-Patriarch of accounting", *The Accounting Review*, 33(3), pp. 482–484.

Lauwers, L., Willekens, M. (1994), "Five hundred years of bookkeeping: A portrait of Luca Pacioli", *Tijdschrift voor Economie en Management*, 39(3), pp. 289–304.

Manzoni, D. (1553), *La brieve risolutione di aritmetica universale in qual si voglia negotio dove intervenga numero, peso et misura*, Al Poggio delle gride in Rialto, Venezia.

Maraghini, M.P. (2011), "Il fenomeno abachistico a supporto dei cambiamenti socio-economici. Arezzo tra il XIII e il XIV secolo", *Pecunia*, 13, pp. 25–58.

Mari, L.M. (2016), *Il bilancio del libro doppio di Lodovico Flori fra tecnica computistica e cultura aziendale*, University Book, Umbertide.

Masi, V. (1997), *La ragioneria nell'età moderna e contemporanea*. Testo riveduto e ampliato da Antinori, C., Giuffrè, Milano.

Melis, F. (1950), *Storia della Ragioneria*, Zuffi, Bologna.

Papadopoli, N. (1892), *Il bimetallismo a Venezia nel Medio Evo*, Rivista Italiana di Numismatica, Milano.

Peragallo, E. (1938), *Origin and evolution of double entry bookkeeping: A study of Italian practice from the fourteenth century*, American Institute Publishing Company, New York.

Peragallo, E. (1956), "Origin of the trial balance", *The Accounting Review*, 31(3), pp. 389–394.

Sangster, A. (2007), "The printing of Luca Pacioli's *Summa Arithmetica* in 1494", *Accounting Historians Journal*, 34(1), pp. 125–146.

Sangster, A., Scataglinibelghitar, G. (2010), "Luca Pacioli: The father of accounting education", *Accounting Education: An International Journal*, 19(4), pp.423–438.

Sangster, A., Stoner, G.N., McCarthy, P. (2008), "The market for Luca Pacioli's *Summa de Arithmetica*", *Accounting Historians Journal*, 35(1), pp. 111–134.

Saporetti, F. (1898), *Frà Luca Paciolo. Origine e sviluppo della partita doppia*, Tip. S. Belforte & Co., Livorno.

Sapori, A. (1997), "La cultura del mercante medievale italiano", in Airaldi, G. (ed.), *Gli orizzonti aperti. Profili del mercante medievale*, Scriptorium, Torino.

Sargiacomo, M., Servalli, S., Andrei, P. (2012), "Fabio Besta: Accounting thinker and accounting history pioneer", *Accounting History Review*, 22(3), pp. 249–267.

Sidebotham, R. (2014), *Introduction to the theory and context of accounting: New dollar edition*, Elsevier, Adelaide.

Sosnowski, R. (2006), *Origini della lingua dell'economia in Italia. Dal XIII al XVI secolo*, Franco Angeli, Milano.

Stoner, G. (2011), "The perseverance of Pacioli's goods inventory accounting system", *Accounting History*, 16(3), pp. 313–329.

Turco, M. (2002), "Finalità e funzioni della contabilità in partita doppia nella prima esposizione teorica di Luca Pacioli", *Contabilità e Cultura Aziendale*, 2, pp. 196–215.

Ulivi, E. (2002), "Scuole e maestri d'abaco in Italia tra Medioevo e Rinascimento", in Giusti, E. (ed.), *Un ponte sul Mediterraneo. Leonardo Pisano, la scienza araba e la rinascita della matematica in Occidente*, Firenze.

Yamey, B. (1994), "Commentario sul De Computis et scripturis di Pacioli", in Pacioli, L. (ed.), *Trattato di partita doppia*, edizione critica, Albrizzi editore, Venezia.

Yamey, B. (2004), "Pacioli's *De Scripturis* in the context of the spread of double entry bookkeeping", *De Computis*, 1, pp. 142–154.

Yamey, B. (2010), "The market for Luca Pacioli's *Summa de Arithmetica*: Some comments", *Accounting Historians Journal*, 37(2), pp. 145–154.

Yamey, B. (2011), "Pacioli, Manzoni, Oldcastle and Ympyn re-visited", in Hernàndez-Esteve, E., Martelli, M. (eds.), *Before and after Luca Pacioli*, Centro studi Mario Pancrazi, Perugia.

4 Giovanni Antonio Moschetti's *Universal Trattato*

An Unexplored Contribution to Accounting Theory and Practice

Michele Bigoni, Tania Aloisi, Warwick Funnell, Gianluca Risaliti and Roberto Verona

Introduction

The analysis of the development of accounting techniques has attracted the attention of numerous international scholars (Jones, 2008; Bryer, 2016). In particular, the development of the double-entry bookkeeping method (Aho, 2005; Lee, 2013) and its diffusion in specific treatises have been, and remain, the topic of lively debate. Numerous studies have sought to elucidate the contribution, to both accounting theory and practice, of such distinguished thinkers as Amaduzzi (Melis, 2007), Besta (Sargiacomo, Servalli and Andrei, 2012), Ceccherelli (Antonelli and Sargiacomo, 2015), De Minico (Fiume, 2007), Littleton (Bedford and Ziegler, 1975), Marchi (Poddighe et al., 2007), Hernàndez Estève (Carmona, 2002) and Kohler (Mautz and Previts, 1977).

The majority of bibliographical works on double-entry bookkeeping have tended to focus on more contemporary authors, while the role of authors from the more distant past has been explored much less, even though their pioneering contributions provided an incomparable impetus to the development of accounting theory and practice. Of particular significance, in terms of the systematization of accounting practice, was undoubtedly the *Dialogus de Scaccarius* by Richard fitz Nigel, published in the twelfth century. This is believed to have been the first example of a comprehensive text on the subject of accounting to appear in the Western world (Jones, 2008), albeit focusing on the charge and discharge system of accounting. In regard to texts relating to the double-entry method, it is not surprising that most of the contributions focus on the work of Pacioli, a Franciscan monk (Coronella, 2010a; Bryer, 2016; Dean, Clarke and Capalbo, 2016; Sangster et al., 2014; Sangster, Stoner and McCarthy, 2008, 2011; Nobes, 1995). He is not considered to be the inventor of the double-entry method, rather the first to have advanced an accounting theory in a treatise dedicated to this topic (Poddighe et al., 2007), thereby facilitating its diffusion. There has been much criticism of the pedagogical effectiveness of this work, as well as of the praxis he set out (Yamey, 2010). Even the originality of Pacioli's work has been questioned, with suggestions he based his work on an already-existing treatise (Sangster,

2015). Among the most prominent non-contemporary authors, other than Pacioli, to have attracted the attention of the scholars of accounting history are the Benedictine monk Pietra and the Jesuit Flori (Quattrone, 2004, 2009; Yamey, 2010). Their works in the sixteenth and seventeenth centuries, though primarily designed for religious institutions, also proved very instructive for merchants and businessmen.

The Venetian Giovanni Antonio Moschetti, who lived in the seventeenth century and, therefore, was almost a contemporary of Pietra and Flori, is much less well known as an important influence in the development and dissemination of accounting practices and theory. His main work, *Dell'Universal Trattato di Libri Doppii* (1610, henceforth *Universal Trattato*), is a pedagogical work that should be of great interest for scholars of accounting history. This chapter will highlight Moschetti's contribution to the development and dissemination of the theory and, more importantly, the practice of accounting, through an analysis of his *Universal Trattato*. This analysis is not merely in terms of the accounting which he advocated but also from a pedagogical perspective. It highlights the features of his very original style, which was very obviously influenced by the era in which he lived. Furthermore, this chapter aims to contribute to the literature on accounting history in response to recent calls urging further in-depth studies on the development of accounting practices (Jeacle, 2011; Walker, 2011), most especially exploring the contribution of authors yet unknown in the international literature. To date, no work of international standing has focused on the work of Moschetti. This, however, does not imply that his work is to be considered in any way of lesser importance. Indeed, the work of Moschetti was widely recognized by the historian Federigo Melis (1950, p. 672), who, in his monumental *Storia della Ragioneria* (History of accounting), noted how Moschetti had been "among the most valuable accounting scholars of the early centuries". He expressed regret that his work had been "neglected by accounting historians, whereas it deserves careful consideration" (p. 673). It is also clear that Moschetti's contribution to accounting studies was well known and appreciated by his contemporaries, at least by accounting scholars. Indeed, the more widely famed Lodovico Flori described him as being among the authors who had contributed most significantly through their treatises to the advancement of accounting practice (Flori, 1677, p. 1).

This work also will contribute to the international debate by focusing on a period of history which still tends to be under-researched. Moreover, it seeks to enrich the international coverage of accounting history by considering the non-Anglo-Saxon context of Italy (Annisette, 2006; Carmona, 2004; Carnegie and Rodrigues, 2007; Williams and Wines, 2006; Jones and Oldroyd, 2015; Fowler and Keeper, 2016). In particular, within the Italian panorama, the case of Venice is of great interest for the purposes of this chapter. The historically renowned commercial vocation of this city, and the consequent flourishing of economic activities that characterized the business world throughout Europe in the seventeenth and eighteenth centuries, facilitated the development of the so-called Venetian method of bookkeeping. This was already used by the Venetian merchants before the publication of Pacioli's *Summa* (Sargiacomo, Servalli and Andrei, 2012), a work which focuses mainly on this method. Not surprisingly, therefore, it was the city of Venice that provided Moschetti with the essential *humus* for the development of his work which had a distinctly operational nature. The desire to contribute to the necessary progress of the city's economy required, according to the author, the development and systematization of accounting practices (Moschetti, 1610, I, chapter 6, p. 5). Hence, there was the need for a new text, the *Universal Trattato*, which could provide existing businesses with effective monitoring tools in such a critical period for the Republic of Venice.

The Seventeenth Century: The Century of Strong Contradictions

Glitzy and ragged, refined and coarse, a backdrop of radical confrontations between despotism and independence, between dogmatism and critical spirit, the seventeenth century was a century of bitter conflict and of great change (Poddighe, 1973, p. 34). This age, characterized by the excessive flaunting of luxury on the part of the aristocracy and a growing poor who crowded the city and the countryside, was devastated by severe agricultural crises and tragic epidemics that resulted in widespread famine. The seventeenth century was one of Catholic, Lutheran and Calvinist intolerance, where even the mere suspicion of atheism or heresy led to the stake; it was the century of the witch hunt. Yet it was also the age that redefined the entire map of the universe. Galileo's discoveries dealt a final blow to the millennial geocentric model of the universe and with the demonstration of the substantial uniformity of the celestial bodies the distinction between Heaven and Earth began to falter. Thus, there was a crisis of all boundaries and all relations of subordination between 'low' and 'high', between 'imperfect' and 'perfect', between 'human' and 'divine'.

In the so-called iron century, the political geography of the world was characterized by a real revolution. Since the last decades of the sixteenth century the stage for decisive action had shifted from the Mediterranean to the Atlantic. This change assured communication links with the colonies of the New World, with Africa and the Orient, via the shipping route of the Cape of Good Hope. Nations which up to then had seemed of secondary importance, such as Holland and England, took on an unimaginable strategic importance, thereby becoming the dominant maritime and colonial powers, at great cost to Venice.

The iron century was, for Italy, an era of severe decline, since the Italian fleets were left operating within a secondary sector of the world stage, the Adriatic and the Mediterranean. The progressive reduction of Italian trading led to an unsustainable increase in the production costs of its wool and silk products for export. Although of higher quality than the Dutch and English fabrics, the Italian production was trapped within a system of ancient guilds, high craftsmanship and professionalism with rigid procedures and little inclination for innovation. This prevented them from reaching wider consumer groups (Lane, 1978). The Counter-Reformation also came down hard on Renaissance culture, conquering and retaining full control of social and intellectual life. It blocked the proposal of any renewal which might challenge the framework of knowledge so jealously defended by the Church.

This state of decline was further aggravated by Spanish misgovernment, beginning in 1559 with the peace treaty of Cateau-Cambrésis between France and Spain. Aside from a punitive taxation system, the domain of the underdeveloped Spanish power had led to *refeudalization*. The middle classes abandoned their entrepreneurial activities for land ownership, becoming patricians living off undeserved parasitic incomes, which were spent on an unquestioning imitation of the squanderous lifestyle of the noble classes. Spain enjoyed direct rule over the Viceroyalties of Sardinia, Sicily and Naples, the Duchy of Milan and the State of the *Presidi* in Tuscany. It also had indirect rule over the State of the Church, which was surrounded by Spanish strongholds, as well as the Republic of Genoa, a long-standing focus of Iberian interests. Furthermore, the Royal House of Savoy in Piedmont, as well as the Medici family in Florence, was indebted to them following the restoration of sovereignty in their respective dukedoms (Diaz, 1976). Amidst this turmoil in Italy, the Republic of Venice was able to maintain its autonomy and independence from the major European powers, managing, moreover, to preserve its own internal order and prevent authoritarian tendencies or dangerous religious radicalism (Von Ranke, 1974). As such, Venice was

> a peaceful place, where everyone, regardless of their nation and religion, could easily ply their trade. The Venetians, in their position between East and West, maintained an independent and proud attitude, just as they did in the conflicts of the great powers.
>
> (Von Ranke, 1974, p. 111)

The Republic of Venice was led by an oligarchy which jealously defended its independence, making the city one of the few oases of ideological tolerance within the Christianity of the Counter-Reformation (Lane, 1978). From a cultural perspective, the University of Padua, under Venetian rule, was one of the centres most open to new developments in secular and religious thought. Together with Bologna, it was also the most renowned institution of higher education in Italy (Grendler, 2002). It is not surprising that such fertile terrain encouraged the development of entrepreneurial activities. Venice, at least until the second half of the sixteenth century, was the most enterprising commercial city in Italy. The manufacture of wool and the production of glass, in particular, both flourished as favoured symbols of power by the rulers of Europe, as did printing activities, away from the ominous influences of the Inquisition. However, this influence was gradually depleted by aggressive competition from the Dutch and the English, by the presence of the Spaniards in Lombardy and by Turkish pressure in the East (Cessi, 1946).

Giovanni Antonio Moschetti, who in 1610 published his *Universal Trattato*, was a prominent figure in these fascinating times. Although no biographical data has survived (Coronella, 2010b; Coronella, 2014), we do know that Moschetti lived in Venice, that he wrote some literary works and that he was the *quaderniere*,[1] or bookkeeper, for several major companies. Hence, he was aware of the commercial dynamics of his city. Moschetti's work is part of the *seventeenth-century style of accountancy* (Melis, 1950).

An Interpretative Analysis of the Style and Purpose of the *Universal Trattato*

Giovanni Antonio Moschetti was a man of the seventeenth century and, as such, an embodiment of the archetypal intellectual of that era.[2] This was the seventeenth-century Baroque era, a period of flair and eccentricity in the arts. In the field of literature this translated into a marked search for the embellishment of expressive forms and the refinement of language. This became a fundamental objective for literary works, often equally as important as the actual content. Clearly then, the sociocultural context of the time (Quattrone, 2009) had a decisive influence on Moschetti's *Universal Trattato*. Although an eminently technical work, it does, however, reflect the seventeenth-century canons of expression without ornament predominating over content.

Analysis of the manuscript style reveals that the metaphor which dominates the pages of the *Universal Trattato* is not a mere rhetorical figure, a sterile embellishment of speech. Rather, it is weighted with greater cognitive value in that, to establish new relationships between words, new links are revealed between certain items. Moschetti's eloquent metaphors, his lively periphrasis, daring hyperboles and surprising allegories enthuse and engage the reader. Accordingly, the *Universal Trattato* could be recognized as being an intellectual pleasure aimed at stimulating the reader's interest or afforded the status of a literary work. For example, in discussing the relationship between arithmetic and the double-entry method Moschetti notes how

> (w)hen comparing those two arts, Double entry bookkeeping and Arithmetics, with these two people, the merchant and the young, or scribe, one could say that Double entry bookkeeping represents the merchant and Arithmetics the scribe. So we sail into the harbour, and having managed to sail across these dangerous Symplegades, like the divine Dove, we enter the safe Maggiore Sea and say that, just as the scribe is without any contradiction at the service of the merchant, so Arithmetics is at the service of Double entry bookkeeping.[3]
>
> (Moschetti, 1610, I, chapter 4, p. 3)

The ultimate goal of seventeenth-century literature was to evoke emotion through the discovery of pleasurable intellectual entertainment. Moschetti was certainly a skilled early advocate of this approach, but it would be too simplistic to relegate his efforts exclusively to a desire to conform to the stylistic tastes of the time. Indeed, the particularly original and complex form of Moschetti's work was probably one of the main causes of the neglect of his work and contributions for such a long period of time. Several accounting historians have emphasized how the continual use of metaphor and linguistic embellishment, more for literary than for research purposes, rendered the work inaccessible (Alfieri, 1918; Masi, 1997). Although relevant, these criticisms do not fully consider the cultural context within which the work was conceived and the related needs of the market for works such Moschetti's at that time. Despite the fact that his treatise was intended for Jesuit establishments, even Flori occasionally resorted to bold metaphors, such as with his affirmation that "the journal is the soul of the ledger, which gives it life and can even resuscitate it after its death, that is, in case the ledger is lost"(Flori, 1677, p. 7; see also Yamey, 2006, p. 449), or when he prayed that the Lord would give us sufficient judgment to avoid "smearing books" with unnecessary detail (Flori, 1677, p. 14).

The seductive literary style of Moschetti's work provides the means to communicate its purpose in an attractive and convincing manner, reducing the gap between theoretical and practical knowledge. Moschetti's starting point was an awareness of the state of neglect that afflicted the science of bookkeeping in his era. In the seventeenth century the arts flourished with the vibrant, generous patronage of the merchant bourgeoisie. They encouraged scientific knowledge to adapt to the needs of a rapidly developing society which was being politically and economically transformed. In this context, bookkeeping was relegated to the rank of a simple *art* (Bariola, 1988), primarily because very few people were committed to articulating and investigating the general principles that could thoroughly explain the causes and roots of accounting practices. Accordingly, Moschetti critically highlights how many qualified contributions can be found in the field of

> Theology, Philosophy, both canon and civil Rhetoric, Music, Arithmetic and the like [. . .] so it is even indecent [. . .] that only a few and with very little detail have written about double-entry bookkeeping (which essentially cannot be compared to the former, even though in many instances is no less important).
>
> (Moschetti, 1610, I, chapter 6, pp. 4–5)

What clearly emerges is Moschetti's need to establish a prominent cultural position for both himself and his 'science'. At the same time he intended to become proactive in the quest to satisfy his society's widespread request for renewal, and go from being a mere repeater of traditional contents to being a witness of the challenges of the new reality.

Moschetti was a keen observer of his surrounding environment. From reading the *Universal Trattato*, what emerges is a great attachment to his *most noble* Venice. This was a city famous not only for the 'Venetian method' of bookkeeping but also for the practice of entering into illegal agreements, minting coins with no intrinsic value and a widespread culture of usury (Moschetti, 1610). In this vibrant economic city, dominated by merchants with their activities and workshops, Moschetti perceived a need on the part of this pulsating sector of society to perfect the tools necessary to study and measure economic affairs, in both their causes and their effects, in order to be able to better manage them (Alfieri, 1994). As a result, particularly pressing for Moschetti was the need to contribute to the progress of accounting practices given their importance for Venetian businesses (Sangster, 2015) to the economic activity of the Republic. He noted with regret that, in his era, the methods of bookkeeping had become too complex, intricate and even subjective. Furthermore, they were often invalidated through errors caused by poor knowledge of the methods. Moschetti even affirmed that "if a young bookkeeper who works for a merchant was to start working for another merchant, he would have to change the way he keeps accounts together with the boss" (Moschetti, 1610, I, chapter 6, p. 5). Thus, Moschetti urged that an accounting treatise to prevent "abuses and confusion" needed to be drafted without delay.

From a methodological perspective, we note once again how Moschetti was truly a Renaissance man. The link between the study of nature and its control for the benefit of mankind (through disciplinary techniques) had been largely fortuitous. The seventeenth-century scientists and intellectuals, however, actively sought to reduce the distance between theoretical knowledge and practical knowledge and, moreover, to come up with findings that could be put to practical use. This can certainly be said of Moschetti. The author devoted 36 pages of his *Universal Trattato* to a theoretical discussion, demonstrating that he had reflected on the logical-technical meaning of accounting and corporate business. To accentuate the practical side of his work he tended to justify himself with his potential interlocutors (henceforth *the Reader*), through his belief that rules are useless if one does not know how to apply them. Moschetti recognized that *the Reader* could accuse him of not providing an explanation in his treatise for every potential doubt or perplexity. He therefore anticipates this by stating that the details are infinite and one cannot provide norms for infinity, other than in very general terms. Moschetti admits that only principles, rules and theoretical knowledge may help in this regard, yet he does not rise to the task of revealing them. He urges *the Reader* to study closely the given examples, in order to deduce a rule and thus overcome any uncertainties. Moschetti warned *the Reader* that

> it is not possible to list in this book all the transactions that a merchant would need to carry out. Suppose that it were; It would be difficult

> and tiring for me, expensive for the printer, and not very useful to you [referring to *the Reader*], because the same knowledge that you would have gained from the longer text you will gain more easily from this one, since it is short, however you will have to use your reasoning skills . . . Finally, study these examples in order to obtain a rule that can be applied to any case which may arise, so if you see the transactions of a Sugar factory, you can then record those of other factories producing Silk, Soap, Weaving fabrics, also the Ternaria [ancient Venetian judiciary responsible for customs duty] Spices, Cured meats and so on. If here you find reference to a shipment of goods sent to Constantinople, you can use the same system to register another for Cloths sent to Alexandria.
>
> (Moschetti, 1610, II, pp. 38–39)

Hence, the expression "reduce the distance between theoretical knowledge and practical knowledge" takes on further interesting and original facets: firstly via the elevation of purely practical and professional subjects to the rank of objects interesting enough for discussion in a monograph, and secondly rendering the very boundary between these two bodies of knowledge less rigid, through a mental process that involves *the Reader* firsthand. The passive *Reader* is urged to take an active, even driving role, in the complex subject matter under discussion.

In the *Universal Trattato*, to reduce the gap between theoretical knowledge and practical knowledge painstaking efforts are put into the teaching of the double-entry method. The methods of keeping the three main accounting books, the *memoir*, the *journal* and the *notebook*, were taught in Venice even before the work of Luca Pacioli (Coronella, 2010a). In a couple of registers dating from 1457 there is an entry relating to the expenditure incurred by the brothers Nicolò and Alvise Barbarigo in favour of Master Troilo for accounting lessons taken over a period of six months (Alfieri, 1994). It should be noted that the bookkeeping masters were also masters of arithmetic and penmanship, disciplines which in practice were closely linked. In seventeenth-century Venice, knowledge of the double-entry method was perceived as essential for those wishing to engage in entrepreneurial activities (Sangster, 2015). Thus, it is fair to say that Moschetti dedicated himself passionately to teaching double-entry bookkeeping. This can be deduced from the strongly didactic tone of the *Universal Trattato*.[4] His treatise is indeed an exemplary work in the teaching of the double-entry method. Moschetti expresses himself clearly and forcefully and appears to be a keen enthusiast of this subject matter. He wanted the approval of the public so as not only to be remembered after his death but also, and above all, to be of use to the merchant class, instructing them in the registration of their financial affairs.

By adopting a writing style in his work methodologically similar to that of the *Dialogus de Scaccarius* (Jones, 2008), consisting of a dialogue between teacher and pupil, Moschetti speaks directly to *the Reader*. However, he uses far more vivid, and sometimes colourful, expressions, such as the use of the word "idiot" to emphasize the severity of the error to be avoided, expressions that capture the attention, persuade and clarify. It is of interest to note how Moschetti often uses strong examples and paradoxes as didactic tools[5] in order to better explain his point, confess it and find shrewd justification.[6] Often his discourse borders on paternalism, but on other occasions he states his point firmly from the typical dominant position of the qualified teacher who would share his knowledge of *come menar le partite in giornale* (how to write entries in a journal). Moschetti's awareness of his own expertise sometimes tends towards self-congratulation, such as when he criticizes the work of other authors in order to highlight the originality and integrity of his own (Moschetti, 1610, chapter 6, p. 6), or when he proffers grave warnings or even makes accusations regarding the accounting practices adopted by certain merchants (Moschetti, 1610, I, chapter 10, p. 10 and II, pp. 38–39).

Moschetti's Contribution to Bookkeeping Techniques

Moschetti's innovative contributions to accounting theory and practice were developed in three books of the *Universal Trattato* (originally four, though the last was not published in line with the author's wishes). The first volume, with its 36 pages, is dedicated to accounting theory. Moschetti supports his approach to the study of bookkeeping and tries to reinvigorate these first steps with a systematic study. The great merit of Moschetti is apparent in the many doctrinal insights that stand out in these first pages. While not expressing his views on the personalistic theory of accounts, Moschetti follows the path marked out by his predecessors, albeit with originality. He introduces personal and inanimate accounts in Chapter 10, which is entitled *Come i debbino portar le partite di Giornal in Libro* (How one should record transactions in a journal), and suggests,

> Let us begin from the alphabet at the letter C, on the left (because cinnamon is neither man nor woman, whose names are placed on the right in this alphabet) you shall write the name of this entry with the number of the page, writing Fine Cinnamon.
>
> (Moschetti, 1610, II, chapter 10, p. 9)

It is interesting to note how Moschetti avoids the artifice of personification for accounts which refer to inanimate objects (Dégrange, 1795) and prefers instead to speak of increase and decrease, hinting for the first time at the *teoria dei conti a valore* (value-based theory of accounts). The continuous use of the terms *accreſciuto*, *accreſca*, *accreſce*, *diminuiſcono*, *accreſcimento*, *diminutione*, *aumenta*, *diminuiſſe* and *riduce* (different expressions to mean "increase" or "decrease") leads us to think of quantities expressible in monetary terms—that is to say, value-based accounts (Besta, 1920). Indeed, Chapter 43 opens as follows:

> A gentleman posed me this query. When I buy a building, a house, a property or whatever else, it is clear that my capital increases. One must write an entry that increases the capital. I replied that it is not true that when buying a house my capital grows because if my home increases, my available funds decrease. The gentleman replied. However, what is important is that this building should be shown in the capital. I rejected this too. Because in the entry 'capital' we should not show the mutation of such things, which were inserted already when the inventory was made. One needs only to make adjustments in terms of an increase or decrease. If not in the specifics, then at least in general. Namely, that we should record in the Capital account that an item therein has increased or decreased; then registering it in the Profit and loss account and finally, at the end of the financial period, reducing the Profit and loss account [overall profit/loss] to Capital.
>
> (Moschetti, 1610, II, chapter 43, p. 30)

There is a clear distinction between 'permutative' and 'modicative' facts.[7] Moschetti was the first to identify such phenomena, but it was Giuseppe Cerboni, more than 200 years later, who introduced them formally with such names. The purchasing of a house increases the asset item 'house' and reduces the amount of cash in hand. This results in two changes in the wealth of the business of the same amount but with reverse effect on the assets concerned, one increasing the account 'house' and one decreasing the account 'cash', which are resolved by the mere substitution of assets. For this reason, Moschetti clarifies that "in the entry 'capital' we should not show the mutation of such things, which were inserted already when the inventory was made". As far as the calculation of the overall profit or loss for the year is concerned, Moschetti expresses himself in the following terms:

> I would appreciate that when the book is finished, or the year, or even both, that the entry Profit and loss [overall profit/loss] be registered in Capital as follows. You shall add up the credits in Profit and Loss because that is the gain (profit), and the debts—that is, the loss—shall be subtracted. For example, if the loss is greater than the gain, you shall write: My Capital = N to Profit and Loss. The capital shall be decreased by that amount. But let us imagine that the earnings are greater than the loss. You will make an entry as follows: For Profit and Loss = My Capital N. The capital shall be increased by that amount.
>
> (Moschetti, 1610, II, chapter 20, p. 17)

The foregoing considerations shed light on another of the author's interesting insights, brought to our attention by Alberto Ceccherelli, whose contribution to accounting history studies has been very significant (Antonelli and Sargiacomo, 2015). Moschetti, without openly discriminating between accounts on the basis of their nature, felt it necessary, nonetheless, to point out the differences between them, hinting at their different functioning and their different purposes (Ceccherelli, 1915, pp. 66–67).

A significant part of Moschetti's first book is dedicated to exemplifying double-entry records of a commercial business, scrupulously reproduced in the second book. It is noteworthy the way the author displays an almost maniacal urge to warn about the huge number of errors that it is possible to make in the practice of double-entry bookkeeping. He is equally thorough in his enumeration of remedies to ascertain, and subsequently correct, those errors. Of undoubted importance is also the multiplicity of questions he covers in depth. The author's attention to detail and his desire to closely guide the bookkeeper are such that he even distinguishes between *Doni*, *Regalie* and *Honoranze* (presents, gratuities and tributes). Furthermore, he provides a meticulous list of "*Fiere principali, che ſi fanno per tutto il mondo, con i loro tempi, quando principiano, & quanto durano*", major trade fairs, which take place all over the world, with their times, start dates and how long they last (Moschetti, 1610, II, pp. 33–36). He also outlines the manner in which charity ought to be dealt with, underlining how accounting can also be a tool for moral improvement (Bigoni and Funnell, 2015).

> I advise you not to record any charity donations you make, as Our Lord says in the Gospel. Do not let your left hand know what the right is doing as regards charity donations. But the entries must be correct, so do as follows. For miscellaneous expenses without specifying the exact reason. So as not to give the impression that you want it to appear that God is indebted to you.
>
> (Moschetti, 1610, II, pp. 30–31)

The second book contains a set of accounts for a sole trader. This exemplifies, with enviable attention to detail, the entries for this type of business. Starting with the definitions and explanations given in the preceding pages, with a clearly didactical objective, Moschetti divides the journal articles into similar classes of corporate situations. Leafing through the pages, we are instructed on the breadth and diversity of possible accounting issues, all anticipated theoretically in the first volume. Examples of these include: "*Caparre guadagnate & perdute*" (down payments made & lost), "*Sconti di tempo*" (time-related discounts), "*Rubbamento & riccuperatione di Mercantia*" (stolen & recuperated goods), or "*Tocchi di sicurtà*" (payments made by insurance companies) (Moschetti, 1610, I, chapter 7, p. 6).

Moschetti also introduces some new features in relation to the accounting practices in force at the time, including the accounts that should be drafted by an insurer. He opens the account *Tocchi di sicurtà* in the Debit column to record insurance costs incurred on the occasion of confirmed incidents. In the Credit column he enters the revenue from collected insurance premiums. The account *Tocchi di sicurtà* is conceived as a two-phase and cumulative account, since it refers to all insured persons, and is duly settled, at the conclusion of the insurance relationship, subsequently flowing into the *Pro e danno* account (profit and loss), either as a Debit or Credit entry depending on whether it has suffered a loss or made a profit (Moschetti, 1610, II, pp. 60–62). For Venetians, a particularly interesting and relevant example of accounts which is provided is commissioning the construction of a ship, equipping it adequately, launching, renting and finally selling it. For didactic purposes only, the author allows an improbable factor: that the entire operation takes place over the span of just two weeks. *Naue vna nomata la Naue dalla Corona di portata di Botte numero 700 di mia ragion* (my ship called the Crowned Ship) and *Sier Andrea Zapparino ſquerarnol* (Mr Andrea Zapparino carpenter) are the two accounts, to be debited and credited respectively, to record the said agreement. It is evident that they serve as memorandum accounts of a commitment system: one party has ordered the construction of a ship and the other has committed to fulfilling the task. The first of the aforementioned accounts is then debited with the construction costs, and later still with maintenance costs. This account is also credited with the balance of the account *Noli della mia naue detta dalla Corona* (revenue from my ship named the Crowned Ship)[8] and at the moment of sale with the price agreed with *Mr Bartolomeo Sora*. The account *Naue vna nomata la Naue dalla Corona di portata di Botte numero 700 di mia ragion* is finally closed and the profit or loss on the transaction calculated through the *Pro e danno* account (Moschetti, 1610, II, pp. 63–66).

Moschetti then moves on to manufacturing and sets out the accounting records of a sugar refinery, making sure to start with those concerned with its set up. The account *Raffinaria di Zuccheri poſta in contrà di Sãta Maria noua* (sugar refinery located in Santa Maria Nova) reports a number of costs on the debit side that, taken as a whole, may be considered as a rough prime cost calculation. A list of the costs of the raw materials, labour and other production-related costs is drawn up. The same account is, however, credited with the revenue from sugar sales. The balance, a sort of primeval gross profit, is summarized in the *Pro e danno* account (Moschetti, 1610, II, pp. 66–70).

In the third book Moschetti moves on to more complex types of businesses. Underlining the advantages of shared ownership in carrying out business activity, he proceeds to set out the accounting records for the entire lifespan of a *Bottega dell'Arte della Lana* (wool workshop), from the drawing up of the Certificate of Incorporation to the preparation of the financial statements. This was undoubtedly one of the most common businesses in Venice, so once again we witness a desire to significantly contribute to the economy of the republic. The account *Bottega di lana di ragion di Compagnia* (wool workshop in the form of a company) presumes the same types of entries as the previously mentioned account *Raffinaria di Zuccheri*.

Unlike the accounting records of his contemporary accountants, who had a strong appreciation of the importance of accounting for costs (Melis, 1950, p. 680), Moschetti's contribution to cost accounting is almost non-existent. There is no theoretical development and no reference to the determination of the cost of the product. Other accounting records at the time reveal that the republic had inaugurated a costing system in its Arsenal, albeit possibly more an accidental by-product of the Senate's attempt to monitor more closely the activities of this strategic site (Zan, 2004; Zambon and Zan, 2007).

Conclusion

This chapter has sought to respond to calls (Jeacle, 2011; Walker, 2011) for a wider study of authors who have contributed to the development of the theory and practice of accountancy. Most of the existing work on the topic has focused on more contemporary authors, with much less written about the contributions of earlier scholars, with the exception of the more renowned Pacioli, Flori and Pietra. Thus, this work has sought to address this by focusing on a period of history still largely unexplored, the seventeenth century. It has considered a non-Anglo-Saxon context to expand the international coverage of accounting history (Annisette, 2006; Carmona, 2004; Carnegie and Rodrigues, 2007; Williams and Wines, 2006; Jones and Oldroyd, 2015; Fowler and Keeper, 2016).

This chapter has examined the figure of Giovanni Antonio Moschetti, still a virtually unknown author in the international accounting literature, despite the wide recognition his contributions received from his contemporaries (Flori, 1677) and by distinguished Italian accounting historians (Melis, 1950). The focus has been on the main volume written by Moschetti, the *Universal Trattato* (1610), and the contribution made by this work to the evolution and diffusion of accounting theory and practice.

The originality of the *Universal Trattato* is immediately apparent in Moschetti's distinctly elegant and refined style of writing, unusual for a work of such technical content, which reflected the influence of the sociocultural context on this work (Quattrone, 2009). This choice of presentation seems to have been dictated not only by the canons of expression of that era and the desire to produce a truly literary work but also by an attempt to surprise and intrigue readers, and thereby to stimulate their interest. The author tries in this way to achieve the goals of his treatise, among which features prominently the need to reduce the gap between theoretical knowledge and practical knowledge. Furthermore, the knowledge promoted by Moschetti was not merely scientific speculation. It represented the dissemination of new techniques which, starting from a solid theoretical foundation, provided a safe point of reference for the economic activities of the republic. This was particularly important in a period in which accounting practice was affected by too many errors and peculiarities, for which the few existing texts of the time provided an inadequate contribution (Moschetti, 1610). This objective was thus pursued through painstaking efforts in teaching the double-entry method, set out in the *Universal Trattato* as a kind of dialogue between teacher and pupil, with *the Reader* actively involved in the learning process.

In Moschetti's work there are clearly discernible some important innovations and ideas that would be implemented only centuries later. In particular, the author avoids the artifice of personification for accounts created for inanimate objects (Dégrange, 1795), focusing on "increases" and "decreases", thereby anticipating by 300 years the theory of value-based accounts developed by Besta (1920). He was also the first to emphasize the distinction between permutative and modicative facts, setting the stage for a full understanding of the different natures of accounts (Ceccherelli, 1915). Moschetti's goal was to contribute to the development of Venetian manufacturing and trade. He did this by starting from the theoretical considerations presented in the first book of his work, developing a very detailed range of possible entries for various types of businesses. These included both sole and collective proprietorships. Moreover, the examples were anchored in the typical activities widespread throughout the republic, such as insurance, sugar processing, wool and navigation.

Although he did not significantly contribute to the development of cost accounting, the work of Moschetti remains of great significance, particularly considering the era in which it was conceived. The author focused more on the discussion of technical issues, rather than the underlying theoretical aspect. He did not, however, ignore the theory and indeed anchored his practical discourse therein. While the many doctrinal insights that transpire from his work are maybe at times vague, nevertheless they have provided excellent stimuli for the writing of subsequent authors.

Notes

1. In the Venetian Republic, a *quaderniere* was the bookkeeper who registered in the *libri maestri* the debits and credits from notebooks or accounting journals of public banks or commercial businesses. See *Encyclopedia Treccani*: www.treccani.it/enciclopedia/ricerca/quaderniere/.
2. Giovanni Antonio Moschetti did not dedicate himself solely to the methodical study of company accounting, to accounting theory and hence the divulgation of double-entry bookkeeping. He was also the author of literary works (*Il pulice* and *La tazza di mercurio, ovvero lettere di vario stile*); he had become involved in the *arte del Quaderno*, or bookkeeping, only as a result of an unexpected opportunity which had arisen. "I was unexpectedly presented with the opportunity to write this book, which, though not entirely appealing to the eye, is rich in content. It is simple, such as my ingenuity was able to offer. I did not want to miss this opportunity, both for the aforementioned reasons, as well as at the insistence of friends and persuasion of the booksellers" (Moschetti, 1610, I, chapter 6, pp. 5–6).

   This quotation from the *Universal Trattato* and all those that follow have been translated from ancient Italian by the authors.
3. Moschetti was a highly cultured man and his writing is full of references to Greek mythology (e.g., the "Divine Dove" and the crossing of the "Symplegades").

4. Despite the lack of bibliographical data, the didactic style of the work and some of the passages would suggest that he probably dedicated himself to teaching. For example, the author explains how he posed a challenging question to a "new student, who had studied with another teacher, to ascertain his level of preparation" (Moschetti, 1610, II, p. 38).
5. The use of simplified examples is an integral part of Moschetti's teaching: "It may happen that in the course of the following books you might find accelerated time references: for example in Travels, exchanges, stores, freight, customs duty, insurance and other actions that it is not humanly possible to carry out in such a short time-span: do not worry, understand that I did this in order to proceed in an orderly fashion and to show them in a simple way, something which otherwise I would not have been able to do. I do not aspire to teaching you the number, the quantity, the time and the names, rather the order, the rule, the method and the course that you must take in order to record these operations"; or "I know that for many people, upon reading this entry, it may seem that I have been imprudent to register such exorbitant profits for a company opened just five months ago. I will merely say that I teach the form rather than the matter and the rule rather than the transaction" (Moschetti, 1610, I, chapter 28, p. 23. See also chapter 40, p. 29).
6. "Pick the rose & leave the thorn. If I jokingly suggested that this might happen to you the reader, you wouldn't be discontent. I would be appealing to your thirst for knowledge, but your sense of reason would not approve" (Moschetti, 1610, I, chapter 40, p, 29).
7. Permutative facts cause a decrease or increase in net equity, while modificative facts have no impact on it.
8. It is a two-phase account which records the rental fees collected in the Credit section, and in the Debit section the portion of the same to be paid to the crew.

References

Aho, J. (2005), *Confession and Bookkeeping: The Religious, Moral, and Rhetorical Roots of Modern Accounting*. Albany: State University of New York.

Alfieri, V. (1918), "Le regole, le classificazioni ed i concetti filosofici nelle opere italiane di ragioneria", *Rivista Italiana di Ragioneria*, 11(3): 59–72.

Alfieri, V. (1994), *La Partita Doppia applicata alle scritture delle antiche aziende mercantili veneziane*. Roma: Edizioni Studium.

Annisette, M. (2006), "People and Periods Untouched by Accounting History: An Ancient Yoruba Practice", *Accounting History*, 11(4): 399–417.

Antonelli, V. and Sargiacomo, M. (2015), "Alberto Ceccherelli (1885–1958): Pioneer in the History of Accounting Practice and Leader in International Dissemination", *Accounting History Review*, 25(2): 121–144.

Bariola, P. (1988), *Storia della Ragioneria Italiana premiata al Concorso della Società Storica Lombarda*. Bari: Cacucci.

Bedford, N. M. and Ziegler, R. E. (1975), "The Contributions of A.C. Littleton to Accounting thought and Practice", *The Accounting Review*, 50(3): 435–444.

Besta, F. (1920), *La Ragioneria, seconda edizione riveduta ed ampliata col concorso dei professori Vittorio Alfieri, Carlo Ghidiglia, Pietro Rigobon*. Milano: Vallardi.

Bigoni, M. and Funnell, W. (2015), "Ancestors of Governmentality: Accounting and Pastoral Power in the 15th Century", *Critical Perspectives on Accounting*, 27: 160–176.

Bryer, R. (2016), "Linking Pacioli's Double-Entry Bookkeeping, Algebra, and Art: Accounting History or Idle Speculation?", *Accounting History Review*, 26(1): 33–40.

Carmona, S. (2002), "Esteban Hernàndez Estève: An appreciation", *Accounting, Business and Financial History*, 12(2): 187–202.

Carmona, S. (2004), "Accounting History Research and its Diffusion in an International Context", *Accounting History*, 9(3): 7–23.

Carnegie, G. D. and Rodrigues, L. L. (2007), "Exploring the Dimensions of the International Accounting History Community", *Accounting History*, 12(4): 441–464.

Ceccherelli, A. (1915), *La Logismologia*. Milano:Vallardi.

Cessi, R. (1946), *Storia della Repubblica di Venezia, Volume secondo*. Milano: Principato.

Coronella, S. (2010a), *Compendio di storia della ragioneria*. Roma: Rirea.

Coronella, S. (2010b), "I quattrocento anni 'Dell'universal trattato di libri doppii' di Giovanni Antonio Moschetti", *Contabilità e Cultura Aziendale*, 10(1).

Coronella, S. (2014), *Storia della ragioneria italiana. Epoche, uomini e idee*. Milano: FrancoAngeli.

Dean, G., Clarke, F., and Capalbo, F. (2016), "Pacioli's Double Entry: Part of an Intellectual and Social Movement", *Accounting History Review*, 26(1): 5–24.

Dégrange, E. (1795), *La tenue des livres rendue facile*. Paris: Hocquart.

Diaz, F. (1976), *Il Granducato di Toscana: i Medici*. Torino: UTET.

Fiume, R. (2007), "Lorenzo De Minico's thought in the Development of Accounting Theory in Italy: An Understated Contribution", *Accounting, Business and Financial History*, 17(1): 33–52.

Flori, L. (1677), *Trattato del modo di tenere il libro doppio domestico col suo esemplare composto dal Padre Lodovico Flori della Compagnia di Gesù per uso delle case, e collegi della medesima Compagnia nel Regno di Sicilia*. 2nd Edition. Roma: Per il Lazzari Varese.

Fowler, C. J. and Keeper, T. (2016), "Twenty Years of Accounting History, 1996–2015: Evidence of the Changing Faces of Accounting History Research", *Accounting History*, 21(4): 389–418.

Grendler, P. (2002), *The Universities of the Italian Renaissance*. Baltimore: Johns Hopkins University Press.

Jeacle, I. (2011), "A Practice of Her Own: Female Career Success Beyond the Accounting Firm", *Critical Perspectives on Accounting*, 22(3): 288–303.

Jones, M. J. (2008), "The Dialogus De Scaccario (c.1179): The First Western Book on Accounting?", *Abacus*, 44(4): 443–474.

Jones, M. J. and Oldroyd, D. (2015), "The 'Internationalisation' of Accounting History Publishing", *British Accounting Review*, 47(2): 117–123.

Lane, F. C. (1978), *Storia di Venezia*. Torino: Einaudi.

Lee, T. A. (2013), "Reflections on the Origins of Modern Accounting", *Accounting History*, 18(2): 141–161.

Masi, V. (1997), *La Ragioneria nell'età moderna e contemporanea. Testo riveduto e completato da Carlo Antinori*. Milano: Giuffrè.

Mautz, R. K. and Previts, G. J. (1977), "Eric Kohler: An Accounting Original", *The Accounting Review*, 52(2): 300–307.

Melis, A. (2007), "Financial Statements and Positive Accounting Theory: The Early Contribution of Aldo Amaduzzi", *Accounting, Business and Financial History*, 17(1): 53–62.

Melis, F. (1950), *Storia della Ragioneria. Contributo alla conoscenza e interpretazione delle fonti più significative della storia economica*. Bologna: Zuffi.

Moschetti, G. A. (1610), *Dell'Universal Trattato di Libri Doppii. Libri tre. Ne' quali con regole universali, & Essempi particolari ampiamente s'insegna il modo di girar in Scrittura Doppia qual si voglia negotio mercantile. Veggonsi distesi con bellissimo, et Semplicissimo ordine varij modi di Comprare, Vendere, & Barattare; di Viaggi fatti in Persona, & raccomandati, di Fattorie, di Fallimenti, d'Alterationi di Prezzo, & lazi nelle monete. Scorgonsi appresso Botteghe di Zuccheri, & Lane, Cambij, Compagnie, Sconti di tempo, Storni di sicurtà, Piezarie, Fabricationi di Naue, & altro. Sono fissi per fine sopra le Partite i titoli, che distinguono una materia dall'altra a maggior intelligenza de' Studiosi.* Venezia: Valentini.

Nobes, C. (1995), "Pacioli's Tractatus: A Note on a Mystery and a Review of Some Commentaries", *Accounting, Business and Financial History*, 5(3): 379–384.

Poddighe, F. (1973), *Dai cinquecontisti a Francesco Marchi. Contributo alla conoscenza del processo formativo della logismologia.* Pisa: Cursi.

Poddighe, F., Coronella, S., Madonna, S., and Deidda Gagliardo, E. (2007), "Francesco Marchi and the Development of Logismology", *Accounting, Business and Financial History*, 17(1): 11–32.

Quattrone, P. (2004), "Accounting for God: Accounting and Accountability Practices in the Society of Jesus (Italy, XVI–XVII Centuries)", *Accounting, Organizations and Society*, 29(7): 647–683.

Quattrone, P. (2009), "Books to be Practiced: Memory, the Power of the Visual, and the Success of Accounting", *Accounting, Organizations and Society*, 34(1): 85–118.

Sangster, A. (2015), "The Earliest Known Treatise on Double Entry Bookkeeping by Marino De Raphaeli", *Accounting Historians Journal*, 42(2): 1–34.

Sangster, A., Stoner, G. N., Scataglini-Belghitar, G., De Lange, P., and O'Connell, B. (2014), "Pacioli's Example Entries-a Conundrum Resolved?", *Abacus*, 50(1): 93–106.

Sangster, A., Stoner, G. N., and McCarthy, P. (2011), "In Defense of Pacioli", *Accounting Historians Journal*, 38(2): 105–124.

Sangster, A., Stoner, G. N., and McCarthy, P. (2008), "The Market for Luca Pacioli's Summa Arithmetica", *Accounting Historians Journal*, 35(1): 111–134.

Sargiacomo, M., Servalli, S., and Andrei, P. (2012), "Fabio Besta: Accounting Thinker and Accounting History Pioneer", *Accounting History Review*, 22(3): 249–267.

Von Ranke, L. (1974), *Venezia nel Cinquecento.* Roma: Istituto della Enciclopedia Italiana.

Walker, S. P. (2011), "Ethel Ayres Purdie: Critical Practitioner and Suffragist", *Critical Perspectives on Accounting*, 22(1): 79–101.

Williams, B. and Wines, G. (2006), "The First 10 Years of Accounting History as an International Refereed Journal: 1996–2005", *Accounting History*, 11(4): 419–445.

Yamey, B. S. (2006), "Duplicate Accounting Records: Historical Notes", *Accounting, Business and Financial History*, 16(3): 447–455.

Yamey, B. S. (2010), "The Market for Luca Pacioli's Summa De Arithmetica: Some Comments", *Accounting Historians Journal*, 37(2): 145–154.

Zambon, S. and Zan, L. (2007), "Controlling Expenditure, or the Slow Emergence of Costing at the Venice Arsenal, 1586–1633", *Accounting, Business and Financial History*, 17(1): 105–128.

Zan, L. (2004), "Accounting and Management Discourse in Proto-Industrial Settings: The Venice Arsenal in the Turn of the 16th Century", *Accounting and Business Research*, 34(2): 145–175.

5 Bookkeeping Treatises in Seventeenth-Century Venice

The Contributions of Francesco Garatti (1686–1688)

Valerio Antonelli, Raffaele D'Alessio and Emanuela Mattia Cafaro

Introduction

Accounting history talks repeatedly of the Italian seventeenth century, a period when the post-Paciolo bookkeeping treatises were consolidated. International historiography focuses on the most prominent authors (Grisogono, Mainardi, Moschetti, Flori, Peri, Pugliesi Sbernia, Venturi, Zambelli), dedicating to them monographic essays or paragraphs in wide universal stories (Brown, 1905; Woolf, 1912; Geijsbeek, 1914; Littleton, 1933; Peragallo, 1938; Chatfield and Vangermeersch, 2014).

There are lesser-known authors deserving recognition. Among these, Francesco Garatti stands out. He is the author of three printed works, all of which were published in Venice between the 1686 and 1688.

There are many interesting aspects to Francesco Garatti's works. Firstly, it is unusual to find in the considered era a practitioner who wrote three volumes of arithmetical and bookkeeping themes. This is mainly due to the lack of bookkeeping schools and academies in the seventeenth century, which is a result of the Venetian merchant's financial struggles. Secondly, Garatti's works have been mentioned in many historical publications but they have never been deeply analysed in international accounting literature. Historiography's focus is mainly concentrated on bookkeeping treatises (Gordon, 1913; Hatfield and Littleton, 1932; Eldridge, 1954; Peragallo, 1956, 1971; Winjum, 1971; Yamey, 1979, 1980, 1981; Chatfield and Vangermeersch, 1996), and on fifteenth- and sixteenth-century bookkeeping practice in Venice (Lane, 1944, 1945, 1977, Peragallo, 1977, 1980; Zan, 2004; Zambon and Zan, 2007; Gleeson-White, 2011; Sargiacomo et al., 2012). Little has been published on the accounting thoughts of the Venetians in the seventeenth century, an era when the republic and its trade went through a difficult phase, 'a real crisis' (Lane, 1973; Pullan, 2013: 59–87).

The objective of this research is twofold. First and foremost, Garatti's works are analysed in depth. Secondly, Garatti's conceptions, drafts and printings are framed in the Venetian context and in the broader overview of accounting literature of previous eras.

There are two sources used to perform the research. The main sources are Garatti's volumes and printing and sources by other Italian authors of previous eras.[1] The secondary sources are Italian accounting history literature and seventeenth-century Venetian history.

To meet our targets, the remaining pages are organized as follows. In the second paragraph, prior literature is presented. The third paragraph shows the political, social and financial contexts that were in place in the latter half of the seventeenth century. The fourth paragraph illustrates Garatti's works by examining the structure, the proposed accountant format, and detected transactions and it gives examples of these. In the fifth, Garatti's volumes are compared with the main treatises published in Italy in the two previous centuries. It continues with the findings, discussion and conclusions about the achieved results, the horizon of possible future research and limitations.

Prior Literature

Bookkeeping treatise history has been widely practised in traditional accounting history, a line of research dominating international literature since the end of the last century (Miller et al., 1991; Miller and Napier, 1993; Carnegie and Napier, 1996; Carmona et al., 2004). Interest in the Italian treatises (mainly Luca Pacioli) has always been very high. Those studies are devoted to analysing accounting practices and theories as answers to business and industrial capitalism (Funnell, 1996; Napier, 2006). Therefore, even accounting change has been explained as an answer to social and financial change, with the focus on evolving nature—basically, a constant and inevitable improvement of the application-related aspects in the transition from one era to the next (Hopwood, 1987; Carnegie and Napier, 1996).

The accounting history literature produced in Italy about the seventeenth century and the bookkeeping treatises published in that period certainly belongs to traditional accounting history (Zan, 1994; Antonelli and D'Alessio, 2014), presenting its typical aspects. In particular, such literature revolves around two interpretative approaches.

The first approach emphasizes the lack of bookkeeping studies in seventeenth-century Italy for the political and financial decadence and for the negative influence of Baroque culture. The interpretation is based on the total lack of new ideas, with the limited exception of Moschetti's and Flori's works. Bookkeeping treatises published in the seventeenth century tend to repeat what was already told by authors from previous eras, mainly Paciolo (Brambilla, 1901: 246; Ceccherelli, 1915: 76; Della Penna, 1946: 273). The Italian political and economic decadence of that time stops the construction of any accurate bookkeeping theory. It keeps the author's attention focused on practical problems that arose from abacus schools, colleges, and monasteries, which were the main users of bookkeeping themes at that time (Catturi, 1989: 116). Sometimes, it is possible to keep up with works published abroad that divulge and refine the Italian accounting method (Masi, 1997:

177). Cartesio's, Galileo's and Newton's ideas do not stimulate in seventeenth-century authors speculative and complex thinking comparable with the thinking in the natural sciences emerging at that time. A bookkeeping science based on the experimental method did not exist (Ceccherelli, 1915: 76). Theoretical accounting problems were not getting the attention they needed due to the negative Baroque culture in search of stylistic refinement and pathological attention to the form. This influence reflects a tendency shared by many seventeenth-century authors to use a refined and pompous language. This language provides little function to the nature of the content so that it is hard to interpret by merchants and scribes, who, often, could barely read and write (Melis, 1950: 672; Antinori, 1991: 360).

The consideration of these three phenomena (political and financial decadence, focus on the practices, Baroque culture) relegates the seventeenth century to "a dark age of Italian accounting", like the following century (Melis, 1950, 561; Coronella, 2011: 29–30).

The Italian academic's negative opinion is shared with non-Italian students who agree on the Italian decadence of studies (Vlaemminck, 1956: 133; Stevenlick, 1970: 94) or, referring to the era between Paciolo's work and the first accounting theories, an "Age of Stagnation" (De Roover, 1955: 409; Littleton and Zimmerman, 1962: 246; Winjum, 1970; Chatfield, 1977: 52–61).

The second approach followed by Italian historiography looks for traces of the gradual evolution of accounting studies towards the current scientific system, according to a trend highlighted recently by various academics (Zan, 1994; Carmona and Zan, 2002; Antonelli and D'Alessio, 2014). Amaduzzi's and Giannessi's periodizations are examples of historical reconstruction. They describe history as a series of long phases where accountancy evolves between a starting point dating back to an ancient era and an end-point (the contemporary scientific ideas). The seventeenth century can be considered an intermediate stage to modern practices (Amaduzzi, 1945: 76: Giannessi, 1960: 461). There are two clear signs of this evolution. Mainly, treatises extend illustrative parts, refine the method and complete the transaction analysis disregarded by Paciolo (Gabrovec Mei, 1999: 84–86; Doni, 2007: 155). Secondly, a slow creation of more ordered and systematic concepts laid the foundations for following studies (Poddighe, 1973: 32; Antinori, 1997: 100; Amaduzzi, 2004: 63).

The differences in these two approaches are the 'profound' forces of the history, which led to the bookkeeping treatise evolution. According to the first approach, this force is the Italian seventeenth century's political and economic decadence. It badly influences the development of accounting literature, reducing its descriptive application ability and minimizing the application volume and its relevance in the evolution (Melis, 1950: 671; Riparbelli, 1952: 27; Poddighe, 1973: 61–64; Masi, 1997: 177–178). In the second approach the elements of bookkeeping treatises published in the seventeenth century (structure, index, contents, style) are part of a long and rough transformation path that goes from the bookkeeping method to the 'theories of accounting systems' (Ferraris Franceschi, 1994: 12–13; Catturi, 1996; Amaduzzi, 2004: 63–64).

Recently, bookkeeping treatises have been studied in the 'new' accounting history perspective by interpreting those volumes as being non-factual and originating from a cultural and social specific context (Quattrone, 2004, 2009). At the same time, interest in double-entry bookkeeping treatises has not decreased, as shown by recent discussions on who created the explanation of the double-entry system, either Cotrugli or Pacioli (Sangster, 2015, 2016; Guidi-Bruscoli, 2016). At the same time, the biographical approach is one of the research areas specifically highlighted in the main taxonomy of accounting history (Previts et al., 1990; Carnegie and Napier, 1996, 2012).

Biographies have to take into consideration the "great men" but also the less famous (Carnegie and Napier, 2012: 339). They have to provide a critical perspective of the subject's life and career in the local, time-specific context, but also to evaluate the contribution to accounting thought and the relapse in the accounting profession and accounting practices (Carnegie and Napier, 1996: 22).

Continuing this historical analysis, as well as the biographical analysis, the contents, the forms, the methodical exposition, the distribution to the public, the anchoring to life and their connections and relapse in the social, financial, and cultural reference environment need to be examined (Flowers, 1974; Yamey, 1967, 1994a; Quattrone, 2004).

Garatti's main book has been studied by Antonelli in a paper published in an Italian refereed journal (Antonelli, 2014). Garatti's works have been mentioned in Italy in the general histories by Luchini (1898: 198), Della Penna (1946: 400), Serra (1999: 219) and Coronella (2014: 121–122). Some of the bookkeeping techniques are highlighted for their similarities to early twentieth-century Italian double-entry theories (Rigobon, 1912: 660; Zappa, 1950: 532). Garatti's works have also been cited in the non-Italian accounting history literature (Brown, 1905: 351; Woolf, 1912: 216; Anonymous, 1927: 21; Hatfield, 1939: 318; Hoock and Jeannin, 1983: 183; Kuter and Gurskaya, 2014: 20). More recently in Bàtiz-Lazo et al.'s (2012: 185) publication, it is argued that Spanish accounting thought between the late seventeenth century and the beginning of the eighteenth century shows several French and Italian influences. They report Peri's, Pugliesi Sbernia's and Garatti's works as influenced by these.

Institutional, Social and Economic Context

The seventeenth century is, in Venetian historiography, considered a politically and socially decadent century (Sestan, 1959: 37). At the beginning of the seventeenth century, Venice faced a period of decline in maritime transport and in the manufacturing industry. These were two driving areas of the seventeenth-century Venetian economy (Benzoni and Cozzi, 1991). Towards the end of the sixteenth century, France and England started to manage

Eastern imports themselves due to the interruption of some of the transport network. In fact, after the Cypriot war, Venetian commercial activities were temporarily frozen (Pullan, 2013: 91). The trade crisis was emphasized, in the first three decades of the 1600s, because of the disappearance of spices on the Eastern markets and the establishment of Nordic seamanship in the Mediterranean Sea (Luzzatto, 1954). Two more events further compromised Venetian trade at that time: the Venetian Plague of 1630 and the war against Turkey for the control of the Island of Candia (Zannini, 1999).

Wool production, being the driving sector of the Venetian economy, was affected by this situation. There were many factors that badly impacted the Venetian wool industry. The first and most influential of these was competition from English and Dutch producers. The English were the first to get into the business of woollen clothing, with lower prices and lower quality (Pullan, 2013: 120). On the other hand, there were some factors making the Venetian wool industry less competitive than the English one. The productive system had strict technical regulations and the labour cost was higher than in other countries. The increase in labour costs was a result of the 1630 plague, which claimed a third of the population, making it difficult to find skilled labour (Pullan, 2013: 139).

Two factors made Venice less competitive—namely, exaggerated export taxes on raw materials and finished products and high custom duties to access Eastern harbours. These started to reduce in Venice at the beginning of the sixteenth century, a long time after that of their English and French competitors (Luzzatto, 1950; Zannini, 1999).

In addition, in 1602 a Navigation Act was issued. It decreed that the Venetian exporter could deal only with national carriers (Pullan, 2013: 120). All these circumstances led during the seventeenth century to an import increase at the expense of the exporter, mainly to Eastern markets (Zannini, 1999). The abolition of the import duties and other trade supporting measures at the end of the seventeenth century had a minimal impact (Costantini, 1993).

The aforementioned financial situation was, to some extent, caused and accentuated by political and institutional contexts of the second half of the seventeenth century. At that time, the Republic of Venice was deployed against the Turkish Empire as it tried to expand in the eastern Mediterranean Sea. The two wars in succession (Siege of Candia from 1645 to 1669 and the Morean War from 1684 to 1699), which lasted until the end of the seventeenth century, put a strain on the Venetian trade and economy. Venice was obliged to enact measures in favour of industry and commerce (Stivieri, 1870: 188).

The Siege of Candia started when the Turkish sultan Ibrahim sent Ottoman troops to besiege the island. The island's control was heavily sought after by Turkey due to its strategic position in the Mediterranean Sea (Mugnai and Secco, 2017: 10). The war ended after twenty-five years of battle with a peace treaty signed on 6th September 1669. Candia was given to Turkey while Venice retained Suda, Clissa and Caradusa and made some territorial gains in Dalmatia (Stivieri, 1870: 184). Hostilities with Turkey started again after a few years with the beginning of the First Morean War, which ended with the siege of Athens in 1688. Due to this siege, Venetians conquered the entire Peloponnese region (Laugier, 1834: 283).

The Venetian conflicts in the second half of the sixteenth century led to an increase in public expenditure, with relevant financial consequences and undermined commercial traffic. The Siege of Candia cost about 125 million ducats (Zannini, 1999).

Despite financial decadence, the publishing industry, after a setback at the beginning of the fifteenth century, had a recovery phase towards the end of the century. The publishing industry and the wool production industry were the driving sectors of the Venetian economy (Benzoni and Cozzi, 1991).

The Books by Francesco Garatti

Francesco Garatti was born in Venice and lived in the second half of the sixteenth century.[2] He declares, "My profession is to educate young pupils who amuse themselves with bookkeeping which is so important for our economy" (Garatti, 1686: 5). He clarifies that the accounting practices he teaches "are commonly used by the merchants who use the new method for its ease and speed" (Garatti, 1688: 5).

His style is intentionally easy because his applications "do not concern the study of the fine arts" (Garatti, 1686: 5). The treatise is not for an advanced-level reader because it is about "basic principles to guide the beginners" (Garatti, 1686: 208).

Garatti is the author of three volumes in the commercial arithmetic and bookkeeping field.

The first text is entitled *Il divertimento aritmetico con diuerse notitie di monete, pesi, misure et curiose pratticbette di conteggiare per aritmetica ordinaria* (Mathematics jokes, with notions about money, measures and practices to count in contemporary arithmetics), published in 1686 in Venice (Figure 5.1).

The dedication of the book is for "the very distinguished Mister Antonio Zinelli" whose identity is unknown.

In the Preface, Garatti specifies that he printed his volume to educate young pupils who study economic subjects. His work is, basically, a mathematic treatise. In the first part, fundamental mathematical operations are explained, while the last part is dedicated to the different sales types of the main merchandise and to the calculation of exchange with the main in-use currency on the major stock exchange.

In this small volume, dedicated to mercantile arithmetic, the index of his next bookkeeping work is announced on pages 124–125. In the volume presentation of 1688, Garatti mentions the promise of this work in *Divertimento aritmetico* (Mathematics jokes) (Garatti, 1688). The volume was published two years later and therefore it is undoubted that Garatti conceived the three works simultaneously.

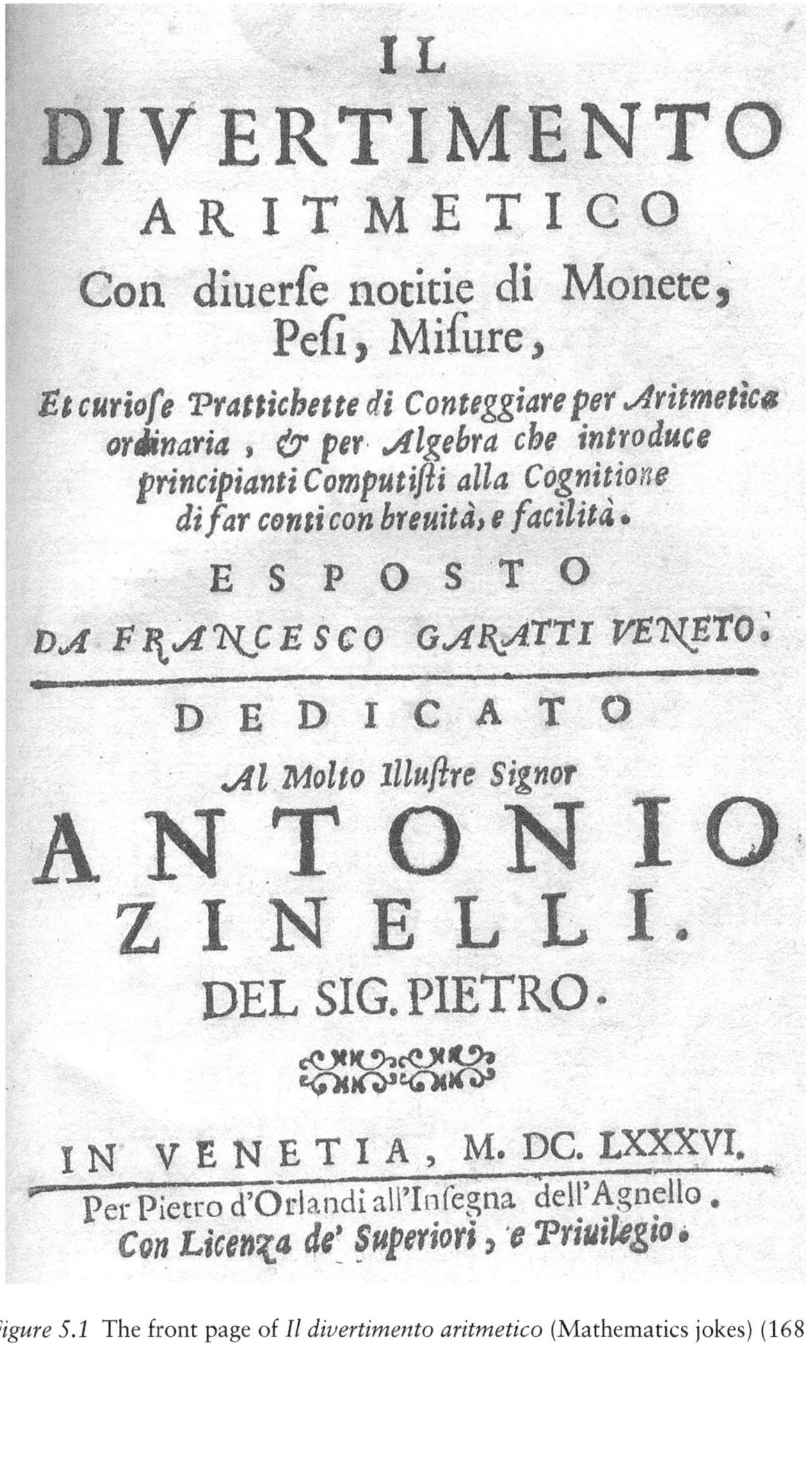

IL
DIVERTIMENTO
ARITMETICO
Con diuerſe notitie di Monete,
Peſi, Miſure,
Et curioſe Prattichette di Conteggiare per Aritmetica ordinaria, & per Algebra che introduce principianti Computiſti alla Cognitione di far conti con breuità, e facilità.
ESPOSTO
DA FRANCESCO GARATTI VENETO.

DEDICATO
Al Molto Illuſtre Signor
ANTONIO
ZINELLI.
DEL SIG. PIETRO.

IN VENETIA, M. DC. LXXXVI.

Per Pietro d'Orlandi all'Inſegna dell'Agnello.
Con Licenza de' Superiori, e Priuilegio.

Figure 5.1 The front page of *Il divertimento aritmetico* (Mathematics jokes) (1686)

ABACHINO
DEL
GARATTI,
Con diverſi contarelli per inſtrutione de principianti, e per ragguaglio del prezzo de Cambij che fanno le Piazze, e Fiere, & altre notitie neceſſarie à qualunque negotiante, nuovamente purgato in queſta quinta impreſſione aggiuntovi le ſerrate & apperte del Banco Giro.
IN VENETIA, M.DCCXI.
Per Pietro d'Orlandi.
Si vende all'Inſegna del Cambio.

Figure 5.2 The front page of *Abachino* (Small abacus) (1687)

Garatti' second work is *Abachino con diversi contarelli* (Small abacus, with various calculations), which was also printed by Orlandi in 1687. The book is a continuation and a summary of the previous one (Figure 5.2).

The book was reprinted after his death with the title *Abachino del gran maestro Garatti, riformato, & accresciuntovi alcuni cambi delle seguenti*

Table 5.1 The index of *Abachino* (Small abacus)

	Page
Account open and closed in the bank of Venice	4
Payment of the exchange letters: When and how to do it	4
Abacus who teaches to multiply	7
Abacus who teaches to divide	16
Way to remove a part from the money	20
Multiplication and division	25
Bank account	32
Discounting	35
Quality of the coins in Venice	41
Method to evaluate the merchandise and make other accounts	42

città, e piazze. Aggiuntovi i tempi delle fiere die alcune citta (Small abacus of the Great Master Garatti, modified and enhanced with money exchange rates of the following cities and markets together with the days when the fairs are hold), in 1713.

Even *Abachino* (Small abacus), as with the previous treatise, is dedicated "*all'istruzione de li principianti*", to the instruction of young pupils interested in the art of bookkeeping and the trade. The index is shown in Table 5.1.

The third work by Garatti is *Saggio di scrittura doppia di mercantie, e di cambi, col quale s'insegna con facilità la vera maniera di scritturare conforme l'uso praticato al presente da Mercanti* (Bookkeeping treatise for merchants, together with money exchange, by which you can easily teach the real way to keep accounts books according to the merchants' use), published by Orlandi in 1688 and reprinted in 1711 after his death (Figure 5.3).

The structure of *Saggio di scrittura doppia*, which consists of 133 pages, is as follows:

- Transcription;
- Presentation;
- Rules of double-entry;
- Recognition of transactions;
- Exercises to do;
- Appendix;
- Ecclesiastical approval.

In the "transcription", dated 12th October 1688, Garatti places himself under the protection of Mr Flospergher (whose identity is unknown). Garatti was friends with Mr Flospergher's children.

In the "presentation" ("To the kind reader"), Garatti addresses young students and explains that accounting practices can be applied to mercantile companies ("Merchants") or farm companies ("Farmers").

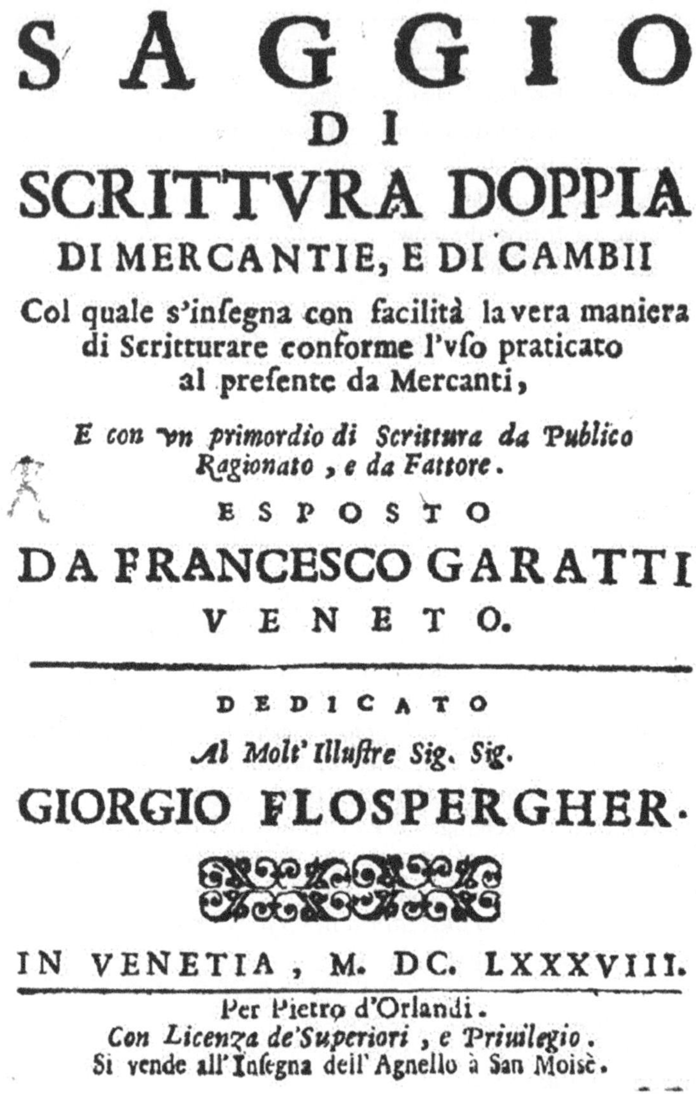

SAGGIO
DI
SCRITTVRA DOPPIA
DI MERCANTIE, E DI CAMBII
Col quale s'infegna con facilità la vera maniera
di Scritturare conforme l'vfo praticato
al prefente da Mercanti,

E con vn primordio di Scrittura da Publico
Ragionato, e da Fattore.

ESPOSTO
DA FRANCESCO GARATTI
VENETO.

DEDICATO
Al Molt' Illuftre Sig. Sig.
GIORGIO FLOSPERGHER.

IN VENETIA, M. DC. LXXXVIII.
Per Pietro d'Orlandi.
Con Licenza de'Superiori, e Priuilegio.
Si vende all'Infegna dell'Agnello à San Moisè.

Figure 5.3 The front page of *Saggio di scrittura doppia* (Bookkeeping treatise) (1688)

On page 92 of the text, Garatti gives more details about his portrayed reader. His work is for accounting students who want to become experts in keeping the journal and the ledger. In the organization of the paperwork in the Venetian companies of his time, the journal keeper is different from the ledger keeper, who records the entries of the first book without having the interpretative skills of the facts of management.

In the introductive theoretical part ("Description of double entry bookkeeping"), included between pages 1 and 14 and in some other parts of the volume, Garatti explains the *rules of double-entry.*

Journal keeping is necessary. There are two main books in the double-entry bookkeeping system. The first is the journal, which could be kept for convenience. The second is the ledger, also called "the book", which is kept for necessity. The journal contains in a single entry what the ledger contains in a double entry. The content of single entries in the journal is of two types: one of them records the transactions in the debit section, and the other one records the transactions in the credit section. The ledger is not sufficient anymore in the mercantile Venetian companies of the fifteenth century; it is necessary to develop chronological entries due to the high number of management operations and the extended number of accounts that need to be opened in order to have efficient control. On one side, the journal logs the transactions; on the other side the many important details of the transactions useful for operational, contractual and financial purpose are elsewhere reported. Garatti, regarding the operation of the account, explains that the entries in the journal and in the ledger are referred to the owner of the goods and not to the goods. The credit or debit refers to the owner too. It is a personification approach, which is typical of literature at that time, even if there is some approximation about how the mercantile accounts work.

The *content of the entries* is illustrated as follows: the two lines in the entry are needed to separate each entry in the journal. The count of journal entries and the dates are missing, while the day, month and year (the facsimiles of documentary evidence) justify the entries in the small volume.

Garatti, like many other previous authors, inserts a fraction on the left margin of each journal entry. This fraction reports the entry recorder in the debit section (because of the serial number of the numerator) and in the credit section (because of the number of the denominator).

When the merchant faces a compound journal entry with a number of accounts movements, he uses a temporary account, known as *Partimenti.* Firstly, a simple entry is detected, which has been used to offset the account *Partimenti*; then with more simple entries (as many entries that are to be recorded in the same section of accounts), each entry is then written off to a permanent account and the temporary one is switched off.

Garatti does not give any details on the way to use the *Partimenti* account. This suggests that the method is well known by those whom it is directed at, and as a result does not need to be explained.

There were many currencies in place in Venice during the period when Marc'Antonio Giustiniani (1684–1688) and Francesco Morosini (1688–1694) were doges, such as the pure gold coin, the silver coin, the ducat and the ecu. Garatti always refers to ecu.

The other "petty cash books" are illustrated on pages 5–12 of the *Saggio* (Table 5.2).

The account codification takes place following the index (*Alfabeto*) (Garatti, 1688: 4). A progressive number corresponds to each of these

Table 5.2 Account books illustrated in the "Double entry bookkeeping treatises"

Book	*Content*
"*Squarzo*"	Prime entry in the strict sense of the term, kept by the "director of the negotiation" and the base for the following entries in the chronological records.
"*Libro delle comprede, e vendite, o Mercantie in monte*"	Records all the purchases and sales of all the goods.
"*Libro delle tratte e rimesse*"	Records the bill of exchange, the receipts, the promissory notes, with all their details.
"*Quaderno dei cambi*"	Reports currency transactions.
"*Salda Conti d'amici*"	A detailed schedule weekly updated with commercial credit/debit and their cash/payment.
"*Salda Conti proprio o nostro*"	A detailed schedule of debit-credit position.
"*Copia conti*"	A stock accounting of where all the loading and unloading of goods are.
"*Copia partite*"	Similar to"*Copia conti*", but refers to"*tutte le partite che si mandano fuori quando sono richieste*".
"*Libro di Cassa*"	Registers cashflow.
"*Libro Scontro de Banco*"	Includes the correspondence to and from the bank.
"*Bilanciетto di Banco*"	Records debit/credit entries into the bank account.
"*Bilancietto de Cambij*"	Comes from "*Salda Conto de' Amici*" and underlines the balance in the foreign market.
"*Libro de' commissioni, ordini che vanno, e vengono*"	Records the commission given to trade intermediaries.
"*Libro de' Ragguagli delle Piazze*"	A handbook of foreigner peso and currency.
"*Libretto delle Fiere*"	A two-phase account where debts and credits towards foreign intermediaries are recorded (intermediaries who negotiate at the main European exhibitions).
"*Cartafaccio del Giornale*"	An advanced prime entry compared to "*Squarzo*"; contains all the auxiliary books and is a draft copy of the journal.

accounts. The pair that refers to the transaction recording each entry is made by "numbers which are on top of each other below the line on the entry margin" (Garatti, 1688: 2). Therefore, Garatti foresees the creation of the chart of accounts prior to double-entry bookkeeping but he does not give any examples, even though he refers to this method often.

The way to record transactions from the journal to the ledger is shown in an example that refers to proposal no. 5, which consists of twelve entries (Garatti, 1688: 93–95).

The ledger has the debit and the credit section placed on opposite pages, according to the typical Venetian form; it has his identification code in correspondence with each transaction record. In fact, the one in the volume seems more a statement of accounts than a ledger because the accounts are not organized on a systematic basis with the sums in debit and credit, of all the variations of the open accounts (Garatti, 1688: 4).

The transaction recording is in the middle of the Garatti's treatise (from page 15 to page 92). It consists of thirty "proposals"—namely, bookkeeping cases (Table 5.3).

Table 5.3 Bookkeeping cases

No.	*Content*
I	Capital in cash
II	Payment of cash in bank
III	Purchase of goods with deferred payment and sale
IV	Advance payment of expenses and commissions of commercial brokerage
V	Purchase and sale of wool, payment through bill
VI	Rice imports from Amsterdam and its export on the London market
VII	Purchase of raw copper, prepayment and cash discount
VIII	Granting a loan
IX	Negotiation of a bill of exchange
X	Trading on the bank of a bill of exchange
XI	Arbitrage in foreign exchange to pay off a debt and related entries
XII	Purchase and sale of foreign currency, with its exchange gains
XIII	Charge of a passive brokerage commission regulated by promissory note
XIV	Acceptance of a bill of exchange
XV	Perception of an active brokerage commission regulated by promissory note
XVI	Purchase of a bill of exchange in foreign currency
XVII	Purchase of a bill of exchange in foreign currency for third parties
XVIII	Issuance of a bill of exchange in foreign currency
XIX	Issuance of a bill of exchange in foreign currency
XX	Discounting of bill in foreign currency
XXI	Arbitrage in foreign exchange to cash a credit and related entries
XXII	Buying and selling currency and creditors
XXIII	Sale with deferred payment with explicit interest
XXIV	Import with deferred payment
XXV	Purchase and sale of wool with commission
XXVI	Purchase and sale of oil with commission
XXVII	Fulfilment of debt by goods
XXVIII	Incense purchase
XXIX	Purchase of a ship, incurring the cost of maintenance
XXX	Shipwreck

From the thirty proposals, the following details emerge.

The account of the owner's assets is *Capital conto di me . . .* (capital account). In the text is the credit section, on the constitution of the company.

The account opens to merchandise (spices, wool, rice, silver, incense, rubber, oil) and the fairs are in the debit and credit section; it holds costs of buying and accessories in the debit section and sales revenue in the credit section, and with the balance they are able to determine the result of each transaction.

The *Cambi in monte* (exchange account) can be recorded in both the debit and credit sections and it reveals credits and debts in the currency. The settlement of the operations with other markets is cash or by bill of exchange.

The accounts of components of income are *Aggi di Banco* (interests and reductions, receivable and payable), *Aggi di valute* (profit and loss on exchange), *Provvigioni, Spese di mercanzia* (additional costs of purchase, transport and commissions) and *Utili e danni* (receivable and payable unexpected occurrence).

The *Nave conto di partecipazione* (ship account) is open to fixed assets in which the capital of the Venetian maritime company can find investment. The purchase cost is mentioned but the other operations are not (maintenance, rights of mooring, enrolment crew), which concerns the cargo, either about the depreciation or about the cost.

The correction of errors, the trial balance and the accounts closing are completely missing.

Regarding the closing journal entries and the trial balance, Garatti is aware of the existence and importance of both of them. Garatti distinguishes the "writing program" (the transaction entries) from the "time of the balance sheet", which he refers to in many parts of the volume and which is always linked to the particular results of the goods (Garatti, 1688: 11). About deferred and prepaid expenses and revenues, Garatti, talking of profit and loss accounts, notes that "if the negotiations have a credit balance then a financial profit will be obtained, if the balance is in the debit section a loss will be achieved (Garatti, 1688: 13). Despite the need of closing journal entries, Garatti does not provide any examples except the indirect reference in the appendix.

The "exercises to do" are helpful to work recipients (Garatti, 1688: 96–114): Garatti observes that the more the reader practises double-entry bookkeeping, the more useful it will be to the resolutions of exercises without a solution (Garatti, 1688: 95).

The appendix is made of two parts: "the opposition against the resolution of Francesco Garatti" (Garatti, 1688: 116–119) and "the answer to the above-mentioned opposition" (Garatti, 1688: 119–124). It is a rhetorical measure where an imaginary speaker contests the biannual compounding of loan interest. Garatti replies by explaining the logic of calculation and presenting the journal entries (the only closing journal entries).

The work ends with the "ecclesiastic approval" released by "The Reformers of Padua" on 28th September 1688, which certifies the lack, in the text, of contents against the Catholic faith or offence towards the institutions and principles (Garatti, 1688: 125).

Comparing Garatti's Works With Main Italian Treatises

The two arithmetical guides and the bookkeeping book by Garatti (1686, 1687) could be listed in a tradition of texts dedicated to mercantile practices and to commercial arithmetic, which has its major successes with Cotrugli's, Peri's and Savary's works (Murray, 1930; Berti, 2009). In the commercial arithmetic works published in Italy and abroad, the contracts, arithmetical calculations, money exchange, units of measurement, the calculations of interest and reduction and many other aspects relevant to the daily activity of the merchants are considered (Geijsbeek, 1914; Swetz and Smith, 1987; Chatfield and Vangermeersch, 1996). Garatti's volumes are not a unique innovation, but what gives them significance is, together with the 1688 bookkeeping work, their origin from the same author, who wrote them with the same publisher within two years. It is an articulated and planned answer to the demand for training and, broadly speaking, for a rational knowledge, typical of trade capitalism, fed by a technical knowledge and by a rhetoric which consolidates the legitimations of merchants (Aho, 1985; Carruthers and Espeland, 1991).

If the two aforementioned works do not present particular innovation for their structure, the bookkeeping work of Garatti (1688) can be compared to more famous previous works. These are defined by Besta (1922: 360) as "Venetian works of double entry bookkeeping" (Pacioli, 1494; Tagliente, 1525; Manzoni, 1540; Casanova, 1558; Grisogono, 1609; Moschetti, 1610), or non-Venetian treatises (Cotrugli, 1573; Pietra, 1586; Flori, 1633; Venturi, 1655; Pugliesi Sbernia, 1671; Zambelli, 1681).

Garatti, like other Venetian writers, refers to the mercantile company as a proprietorship. The only exception is Manzoni (1540), who also deals with the wool mill (the most widespread industrial business at that time) as a partnership. Cotrugli (1573) and Zambelli (1681) do the same.

Venturi (1655) and Pugliesi Sbernia (1671) deal with surveys for the farms while Pietra (1586) and Flori (1633) dedicate their work to the survey of religious organizations, where the Benedictine and the Jesuit respectively belong.

All the volumes have common traits, such as a large illustrative part (except for the *Tractatus* of Pacioli), the limited theoretical part and the lack of a real chart of accounts, and all relate to the social and economic context where their authors are from (e.g., commerce, agriculture, religious life).

In Garatti's works, there is a duality of entries, account sections and books (journal and ledger) (as expressed by Littleton, 1926, 1928). In this regard, except for Tagliente (1525), all writers of previous centuries supported the combined use of the journal and the ledger sometimes associated with the petty cash book (which is called *Memoriale*, *Ricordanze* and so on) (Sangster et al., 2012).

The link between journal and ledger and the indexing accounts are subjects that are outlined by Garatti, but he does not provide an explanation. Such link is largely explained by Manzoni, Moschetti and Flori (Yamey, 1967, 1980).

The journal entries' structure is typical Venetian, as described by Alfieri (1891: 103–147) and by Besta (1922: 380, 395, 400) and then recalled and divulged in the best-known works of traditional accounting history (Littleton, 1933; Peragallo, 1938; Vlaemminck, 1956). Garatti comes back to the original Pacioli accounts form. The journal entries are proposed without date, they have a limited descriptive part and they are not enumerated as it occurs in Paciolo, Casanova, Pietra (while an appropriate cross-reference code lies in Manzoni and Zambelli) (Littleton, 1926; Yamey, 1967).

The accounts are in two sections and allow the calculation of specific results, as related to ship maintenance, to commercial brokering and to commission trade according to accounting forms similar to Paciolo, Manzoni, Casanova, Moschetti, Pietra and Flori (Littleton, 1933; Yamey, 1994b).

In all these considered works, they provide a capital account: *Cavedal* becomes *Capital conto di me* (capital account), or there is the opening of accounts *Monastero nostro* (our monastery) and *Collegio nostro* (our college) in the Benedictine and the Jesuit province of Pietra and Flori (Peragallo, 1938; Nobes, 2015). Moreover, there are one or more accounts open to revenues and expenses (*Pro e danno, Avanzi e disavanzi, Spesa ed Entrata Generale*) (surpluses and deficits, general expenditure and revenue) and a balance summary account of intermediate accounts (Green, 2014; Peragallo, 1956, 1971), called by Garatti "*Negotio in monte*".

Considering the long Venetian tradition in which the *Saggio di scrittura doppia* takes place, the account *Partimenti* by Garatti is a total innovation because all his Venetian predecessors use simple entries. Pietra and Zambelli widely use *Partimenti* accounts, while Flori, Venturi and Pugliesi Sbernia directly use the compound journal entries introduced by expressions like *Lì appresso* e *Infrascritti* (Yamey, 1981). The closing procedures and the balance sheet are totally missing in the *Saggio di scrittura doppia*. The Venetian tradition is, on the contrary, solid: the inventory exists in Paciolo Manzoni, Tagliente and Moschetti, the receivables assessment exists in Paciolo, Moschetti and Casanova, and the trial balance, the closing and opening journal entry exist in Manzoni and Casanova (Peragallo, 1956, 1971; Viganò, 1968; Cavazzoni, 2006).

Even outside Venice, closing entries are not 'invented' by Cotrugli, Venturi and Zambelli. This last one widely develops the correction of errors and the definition of the gross result from the closing procedure related to commercial transactions (Antinori, 1993: 88), while Pietra, Flori and Pugliesi Sbernia write integration entries (especially income and expense accruals on credits for interests and rents) and Pietra and Flori consider the write-off (they record goods receivable). The inventory is partial and it includes fixed property, the warehouse, credits and cash. Inventory use is theorized by Cotrugli, Flori, Pietra and Pugliesi Sbernia. Regarding the balance sheet, Cotrugli, Venturi and Pugliesi Sbernia focus on the drafting of the trial balance, while Flori and Zambelli clearly distinguish this tool from the real balance sheet (Vance, 1943; Peragallo, 1956, 1971).

The *Saggio di scrittura doppia* completely belongs to the Venetian literature tradition, while the volume misses some fundamental expedients of the developmental phase of double-entry bookkeeping, such as the correction of errors, the closing entries and the closing and reopening of accounts.

Discussion and Conclusion

The chapter examines the contribution of one of the 'minor' Venetian writers, who belonged to the long transition existing between the *Tractatus* of Luca Pacioli and nineteenth-century scientific accounting. This is Francesco Garatti, an author nearly unknown to accounting historians, of whom we outlined a biographical profile.

To meet the chapter's objectives we have initially described the state of the historical literature in Italy around the period when Garatti lived, the seventeenth century, and we showed the variety of approaches and the history of each approach.

We have analysed the political, social and economic context in which Garatti worked in Venice at the end of the seventeenth century. Garatti's books have been deeply examined and compared with contemporary and previous works. Considering them in the light of Italian historiography, Garatti's books are not the expression of a decadent period, but, on the contrary, they prove the social and cultural turmoil of the merchant class and of Venetian traders who had a constant need of new manuals.

The character of Garatti clearly emerges, despite the lack of biographical information. Garatti was a merchant but mainly an educator. The *Divertimento aritmetico* was for his students (Garatti, 1686: 5), while the *Saggio di scrittura doppia* was to be used by merchants and it was improved to be easily and quickly used. The writing entries style had already been 'tested' by Venetian merchants (Garatti, 1688: 5) and this is a catchy selling point for the potential customer. The synergies between the practitioner and the educator were, at that time, very important, especially because of operational difficulties due to the manual entries of the accounts. The bookkeeping learning process was organized by privates. It had to be short-term and easy, such as could be found in Pacioli (Sangster and Scataglinibelghitar, 2010). Similarly, commercial arithmetic teaching, intended for merchants who bought and sold goods on their own and to other categories of traders (ship's captain, intermediary, agents, insurance brokers), was structured and followed educational rules designed for easy and quick learning as proved by other experiences—for example, in Florence (Goldthwaite, 1972).

Garatti stands out in all these fields. There are, at least, two demonstrations. The first is that two of the three works were reprinted in 1711 and 1713—namely, twenty-five years after the first edition. These were advertised in other printed volumes (Anonymous, 1711: 180; Pittoni, 1712: 222). The second comes from another seventeenth-century Venetian author who mentions Garatti as an author of that time (seventy years after the publication of his major work) who was still very valued (Cortinovis, 1759: 195).

Publishing represented one of the biggest sectors of the urban Venetian economy during the sixteenth century (Benzoni and Cozzi, 1991). As for other sectors, the book market suffered a crisis towards the end of the sixteenth century and, then, it had a recovery in the last quarter of the century. The printing licenses went from thirty-two titles between 1609 and 1622 to fifty-four between 1686 and 1701 (Benzoni and Cozzi, 1991). Although there was a decrease in the seventeenth century of the high standards of printing and publishing that were achieved in the previous century, it still represented a vital sector as testified by the registration in the art (Zannini, 1999, Ulvioni, 1977, Ciriacono, 1995).

The importance of this sector in Venice is confirmed by Garatti's publisher, Pietro Orlandi, who published between 1684 and 1692 at least seven other treatises concerning the most diverse topics—for example, the use of accents in the Italian language and the pastoral comedies. Despite these considerations, it is unusual for Orlandi to publish three works by the same author within three years, with each work more or less based on accounting themes. This makes us believe there was interest around this topic and that Garatti was well known at that time.

The contribution of this work to accounting history consists, mainly, in enhancing the analysis and evidence about the bookkeeping literature of the seventeenth century, expansion provided with the analysis of the technical accounting aspects presented in the *Saggio di scrittura doppia*. It is a brief text, but very substantial, especially for the wide accounting records shown. It offers an interesting overview of the operations (and how they are represented in the double-entry system) of the main economic Venetian mercantile firms of that time. The other important aspect of this chapter is the role of Garatti in the disclosure of bookkeeping and commercial arithmetic. The skills in this field were taught in private school. Garatti uses his own volumes in the school where he lectured. These works were known and advertised for many years after they were first published (and probably after the author's death).

Our research work is not limitless. The first limit is represented by a significant lack of information about Francesco Garatti's life. The second is the lack of solid facts about the Venetian book market during the time his bestsellers were included.

The chapter opens the way to more research in the same field in at least three possible directions. The first direction is about the knowledge of the Italian seventeenth century and the works published at that time, which is, so far, totally neglected. The second direction is about the historical knowledge, which we touched on in our project, and concerns the relations between mercantile practice and the treatises surrounding accounting surveys. The third, in closing, concerns the chance to compare Garatti's works in the Venetian context of the late 1600s and those published during the same time in other European countries, according to the comparative international accounting history approach (Carnegie and Napier, 2002).

Notes

1. Volumes have been found at the Florence and Rome National Library and at the Venice Historical Library. Research was obtained from a reprint of Luca Pacioli's 1494 works.
2. We do not have biographical notes on Francesco Garatti.

References

Aho, J.A. (1985) Rhetoric and the invention of double entry bookkeeping. *Rhetorica: A Journal of the History of Rhetoric* 3(1): 21–43.

Alfieri, V. (1891) *La partita doppia applicata alle scritture delle antiche aziende mercantili veneziane.* Torino: Paravia & Co.

Amaduzzi, Al. (1945) Sui criteri per la composizione di una storia delle dottrine economico-amministrative. *Rivista Italiana di Ragioneria* 45(7–9): 74–77.

Amaduzzi, An. (2004) *Storia della Ragioneria.* Milano: Giuffrè.

Anonymous (1712) *Istoria dell'Epidemia de' Buoi accaduta l'anno 1711.* Venezia: P. Orlandi.

Anonymous (1927) *A check list of books printed before 1850 in the Montgomery Library of Accountancy.* New York: Columbia University Press.

Antinori, C. (1991) I manuali di computisteria e di ragioneria dal secolo XIII al XVIII. In *L'impresa. Industria Commercio Banca. Secc. XIII–XVIII.* Firenze: Le Monnier, pp. 353–364.

Antinori, C. (1993) *Brescia e la ragioneria.* Brescia: Industrie Grafiche Bresciane.

Antinori, C. (1997) Lettura e interpretazione degli antichi scrittori di ragioneria dal sec. XV al sec. XIX. *Storia della Ragioneria* 1: 90–105.

Antonelli, V. (2014) Il *Saggio di scrittura doppia di mercantie, e di cambii* di Francesco Garatti: considerazioni critiche. *Rivista Italiana di Ragioneria e di Economia Aziendale* 114(7–9): 276–294.

Antonelli, V. and D'Alessio, R. (2014) Accounting history as a local discipline: The case of the Italian-speaking literature (1869–2008). *The Accounting Historians Journal* 41(1): 79–112.

Bátiz-Lazo, B., Borreguero, J.J.H., Maixé-Altés, J.C., and Torrado, M.N. (2012) Adoption, diffusion and appropriation of double entry book-keeping in Mexico and Spain. *América Latina en la Historia Económica*, 19(3): 164–205.

Benzoni, G. and Cozzi, G. (1991) Storia di Venezia. Dalle origini alla caduta della Serenissima. *Istituto della Enciclopedia Italiana* 8.

Berti, M. (2009) Alcune note sulle pratiche di mercatura (secoli XIII–XVIII): dalla Memoria pisana ai manuali del perfetto mercante. In Pierucci, P. (ed) *La contabilità nel bacino del Mediterraneo (secc. XIV–XIX).* Milano: Franco Angeli, pp. 29–83.

Besta, F. (1922) *La ragioneria. Seconda edizione riveduta ed ampliata col concorso dei professori Vittorio Alfieri, Carlo Ghidiglia, Pietro Rigobon, Ragioneria generale*. Volume 3. Milano: Vallardi.

Brambilla, G. (1901) *Storia della Ragioneria italiana*. Milano: Boriglione.

Brown, R. (1905) *A History of Accounting and Accountants*. Edinburgh: TC & EC Jack.

Carmona, S., Ezzamel, M. and Gutiérrez, F. (2004) Accounting history research: Traditional and new accounting history perspectives. *De Computis* 1(1): 24–53.

Carmona, S. and Zan, L. (2002) Special section: Mapping variety in the history of accounting and management practices. *European Accounting Review* 11(2): 291–304.

Carnegie, G.D. and Napier, C.J. (1996) Critical and interpretive histories: Insights into accounting present and future through its past. *Accounting, Auditing and Accountability Journal* 9(3): 739.

Carnegie, G.D. and Napier, C.J. (2002) Exploring comparative international accounting history. *Accounting, Auditing & Accountability Journal* 15(5): 689–718.

Carnegie, G.D. and Napier, C.J. (2012) Accounting's past, present and future: The unifying power of history. *Accounting, Auditing & Accountability Journal* 25(2): 328–369.

Carruthers, B.G. and Espeland, W.N. (1991) Accounting for rationality: Double-entry bookkeeping and the rhetoric of economic rationality. *American Journal of Sociology* 97(1) 31–69.

Casanova, A. (1558) *Specchio lucidissimo, nel qual si vedeno essere diffinito tutti i modi & ordini di scrittura, che si deve menare nelli negotiamenti della mercantia, cambii, recambii, con li loro corrispondenti, disgarbugliando & illuminando l'intelletto a negotianti*. Venezia: Comin da Trino di Monferrato.

Catturi, G. (1989) *Teorie contabili e scenari economico-aziendali*. Padova: Cedam.

Catturi, G. (1996) *Attività ed attori economici nello scenario post-pacioliano*. Padova: Cedam.

Cavazzoni, G. (2006) Alla ricerca dei prodromi del bilancio nell'opera di Luca Pacioli. In *Atti dell'VIII Convegno Nazionale Società Italiana di Storia della Ragioneria, Atri-Silvi 22–23 settembre 2005 Riferimenti storici e processi evolutivi dell'informativa di bilancio tra dottrina e prassi*. Roma, RIREA, pp. 419–438.

Ceccherelli, A. (1915) *La logismologia*. Milano: Vallardi.

Chatfield, M. (1977) *A History of Accounting Thought*. Huntington, NY: Krieger.

Chatfield, M. and Vangermeersch, R. (1996) *The History of Accounting (RLE Accounting): An International Encyclopedia*. London and New York: Routledge.

Chatfield, M. and Vangermeersch, R. (Eds.). (2014) *The history of accounting (RLE accounting): an international encylopedia*. Routledge.

Ciriacono, S. (1995) Manifatture e mestieri in laguna. Equilibri ambientali e sviluppo economico. In Caniato, G. and Turri, E. (eds) *La laguna di Venezia*. Verona: Cierre, pp. 357–383.

Coronella, S. (2011) Il periodo buio della ragioneria italiana. *Contabilità e cultura aziendale* 9(2): 194–196.

Coronella, S. (2014) *Storia della ragioneria. Epoche, uomini, idee*. Milano: Franco Angeli.

Cortinovis, G.P. (1759) *Abbaco ovvero pratica generale dell'aritmetica*. Quarta edizione. Venezia: Bassaglia.

Costantini, M. (1993) La regolazione dei dazi marittimi e l'esperienza del 'porto-franco' a Venezia tra il 1662 e il 1684. In Di Vittorio, A. (ed) *La finanza pubblica in età di crisi*. Bari: Cacucci, pp. 77–88.

Cotrugli, M.B. (1573) *Della mercatura et del mercante perfetto. Libri quattro. Scritti già più di anni CX & hora dati in luce. Utilissimi ad ogni mercante*. Venezia: All'Elefanta.

Della Penna, F. (1946) *Le istituzioni contabili. Parte seconda*. Roma: Castellani.

De Roover, R. (1955) New perspectives on the history of accounting. *The Accounting Review* 30(2): 405–420.

Doni, F. (2007) *La teoria personalistica del conto. Aspetti evolutivi ed approfondimenti critici*. Milano: Giuffrè.

Eldridge, H.J. (1954) *The Evolution of the Science of Bookkeeping*. London: Gee.

Ferraris Franceschi, R. (1994) *Il percorso scientifico dell'economia aziendale*. Torino: Giappichelli.

Flori, L. (1633) *Trattato del modo di tenere il Libro Doppio Domestico con suo essemplare composto dal P. Lodovico Flori della Compagnia di Gesù per uso delle case e dei collegi della medesima Compagnia nel Regno di Sicilia*. Palermo: Decio Cirillo.

Flowers, W.B. (1974) Biography and accounting history. *The Accounting Historians Journal* 1(1–4): 21–22.

Funnell, W.N. (1996) Preserving history in accounting: Seeking common ground between 'new' and 'old' accounting history. *Accounting, Auditing and Accountability Journal* 9(4): 38–64.

Gabrovec Mei, O. (1999) *Il linguaggio contabile. Itinerario storico e metodologico*. Torino: Giappichelli.

Garatti, F. (1686) *Il divertimento aritmetico con diuerse notitie di monete, pesi, misure et curiose prattichette di conteggiare per aritmetica ordinaria*. Venezia: P. Orlandi.

Garatti, F. (1687) *Abachino con diuersi contarelli*. Venezia: P. Orlandi.

Garatti, F. (1688) *Saggio di scrittura doppia di mercantie, e di cambi col quale s'insegna con facilità la vera maniera di scritturare conforme l'uso praticato al presente da Mercanti*. Venezia: P. Orlandi.

Geijsbeek, J.L. (1914) *Ancient Double-Entry Bookkeeping*. Denver: Geijsbeek.

Giannessi, E. (1960) *Le aziende di produzione originaria. Volume I. Le aziende agricole*. Pisa: Cursi.

Gleeson-White, J. (2011) *Double Entry: How the Merchants of Venice Shaped the Modern World and How Their Invention Could Make or Break the Planet*. Sydney: Allen & Unwin.

Goldthwaite, R.A. (1972) Schools and teachers of commercial arithmetic in Renaissance Florence. *Journal of European Economic History* 1(2): 418–435.

Gordon, C. (1913) Books on accountancy, 1494–1600. *The Library* (1): 145–170.

Green, W.L. (2014) *History and Survey of Accountancy (RLE Accounting)*. London and New York: Routledge.

Grisogono, S. (1609) *Il mercante arricchito. Del perfetto quaderniere: ovvero, specchio lucidissimo, nel qual si copre ogni questione, che desiderar si possa per imparare perfettamente a tenere libro doppio*. Venezia: Vecchi.

Guidi-Bruscoli, F. (2016) Libr. XV: Cotrugli and de Raphaeli on business and Bookkeeping in the Renaissance. *Business History* 58(4): 599–600.

Hatfield, H.R. (1939) Origin and evolution of double entry bookkeeping. *Journal of Accountancy* 67(5): 317–320.

Hatfield, H.R. and Littleton, A.C. (1932) A check-list of early bookkeeping texts. *The Accounting Review* 7(3): 194–206.

Hoock, J. and Jeannin, P. (1989) *Ars Mercatoria: Handbücher und Traktate für der Gebrach des Kaufmanns, 1460–1820*. München: Padenborn.

Hopwood, A.G. (1987) The archaeology of accounting systems. *Accounting, Organizations and Society* 12(3): 207–234.

Kuter, M.I. and Gurskaya, M.M. (2014) Main lines of studying genesis and development of accounting. *Independent Auditor/Nezaleznij Auditor* 4(10): 14–29.

Lane, F.C. (1944) *Andrea Barbarigo, Merchant of Venice (1418–1449)*. Baltimore: Johns Hopkins University Press.

Lane, F.C. (1945) Venture accounting in medieval business management. *Bulletin of the Business Historical Society* 19(5): 164–173.

Lane, F.C. (1973) *Venice, a maritime republic*. Baltimore: Johns Hopkins University Press.

Lane, F.C. (1977) Double entry bookkeeping and resident merchants. *The Journal of European Economic History* 6: 177–191.

Laugier, M.A. (1834) *Storia della Repubblica di Venezia dalla sua fondazione sino al presente: Tradotta dal Francese. Tomo V*. Venezia: Palese & Storti.

Littleton, A.C. (1926) Evolution of the ledger account. *The Accounting Review* 1(4): 12–23.

Littleton, A.C. (1928) The evolution of the journal entry. *The Accounting Review* 3(4): 383–396.

Littleton, A.C. (1933) *Accounting Evolution to 1900*. New York: American Institute Publishing Co. Inc.

Littleton, A.C. and Zimmerman, V.K. (1962) *Accounting Theory: Continuity and Change*. New York: Prentice-Hall Inc.

Luchini, E. (1898) *Storia della ragioneria italiana*. Milano: Il ragioniere.

Luzzatto, G. (1950) Le vicende del porto di Venezia dal primo Medio Evo allo scoppio della guerra 1914–1918. In *Il porto di Venezia*. Napoli: S. Candida, pp. 1–35.

Luzzatto, G. (1954) La decadenza di Venezia dopo le scoperte geografiche nella tradizione e nella realtà. *Archivio veneto*: 54–55.

Manzoni, D. (1540) *Quaderno doppio col suo giornale, novamente composto e diligentemente ordinato, secondo il costume di Venezia. Opera a ogni persona utilissima & molto necessaria*. Venezia: Comin da Trino di Monferrato.

Masi, V. (1997) *La ragioneria nell'età moderna e contemporanea*. Milano: Giuffrè.

Melis, F. (1950) *Storia della ragioneria*. Bologna: Zuffi.

Miller, P., Hopper, T. and Laughlin, R.C. (1991) The new accounting history: An introduction. *Accounting, Organizations and Society* 16(3): 395–403.

Miller, P. and Napier, C.J. (1993) Genealogies of calculation. *Accounting, Organizations, and Society* 18(7/8): 631–647.

Moschetti, G.A. (1610) *Dell'Universal trattato di libri doppi, nei quali con regole universali et essempi particolari ampiamente si insegna il modo di girar la scrittura doppia qual si voglia negotio mercantile*. Venezia: Luca Valentini.

Mugnai, B. and Secco, A. (2017) *La guerra di Candia. Vol 1: Assedi e operazioni campali*. Milano: Soldiershop Publishing.

Murray, D. (1930) *Chapters in the History of Bookkeeping, Accountancy & Commercial Arithmetic*. Wylie: Jackson.

Napier, C.J. (2006) Accounts of change: 30 years of historical accounting research. *Accounting, Organizations and Society* 31(4): 445–507.

Nobes, C. (2015) Accounting for capital: The evolution of an idea. *Accounting and Business Research* 45(4): 413–441.

Pacioli, L. (1494) *Tractatus de Computis et Scripturis* (Reprinted Bari: Cacucci, 1987).

Peragallo, E. (1938) Origin and evolution of double entry bookkeeping.

Peragallo, E. (1956) Origin of the trial balance. *The Accounting Review* 31(3): 389–394.

Peragallo, E. (1971) A commentary on Viganò's historical development of ledger balancing procedures, adjustments and financial statements during the Fifteenth, Sixteenth, and Seventeenth centuries. *The Accounting Review* 46(3): 529–534.

Peragallo, E. (1977) The ledger of Jachomo Badoer: Constantinople September 2, 1436 to February 26, 1440. *The Accounting Review* 52(4): 881–892.

Peragallo, E. (1980) Jachomo Badoer, Renaissance man of commerce, and his ledger. *Accounting and Business Research* 10: 93–101.

Pietra, A. (1586) *Indirizzo degli economi, o sia ordinatissima instruttione da regolarmente formare qualunque scrittura in Libro Doppio*. Mantova: Osanna.

Pittoni, G.B. (1712) *Constitutiones pontificiae et Romanarum congregationum decisiones ad episcopos et abbates utriusque cleri spectantes Jo. Baptista Pittono sacerdote Veneto collectore. excudebat Leonardus Pittonus collectoris pater.* Habentur venales sub signo Cambii.

Poddighe, F. (1973) *Dai cinquecontisti a Francesco Marchi*. Pisa: Cursi.

Previts, G.J., Parker, L.D. and Coffman, E.N. (1990) An accounting historiography: Subject matter and methodology. *Abacus* 26(2): 136–158.

Pugliesi Sbernia, O. (1671) *Pratica economica numerale, nella quale si insegna il modo di tenere i Libri de' Conti, con l'essemplare di una Scrittura Signorile, formata al Moderno stile, che per maggiore chiarezza contiene il Giornale col suo Libro Maestro*. Palermo: Bossio.

Pullan, B. (2013) *Crisis and Change in the Venetian Economy in the Sixteenth and Seventeenth Century*. London and New York: Routledge.

Quattrone, P. (2004) Accounting for God: Accounting and accountability practices in the society of Jesus (Italy, 16th–17th centuries). *Accounting, Organizations and Society* 29(7): 647–683.

Quattrone, P. (2009) Books to be practiced: Memory, the power of the visual, and the success of accounting. *Accounting, Organizations and Society* 34(1): 85–118.

Rigobon, P. (1912) Alcuni appunti storico-bibliografici intorno alla partita doppia sintetica applicata alle aziende mercantili. In *Monografie edite in onore di Fabio Besta nel XL anniversario del suo insegnamento*. Roma: Tipografia Bertone, pp. 657–682.

Riparbelli, A. (1952) Il primato italiano nelle applicazioni della ragioneria e negli studi economico aziendali. In *Studi di economia e statistica. Vol. II. Pubblicazioni della Facoltà di economia e commercio*. Catania: Università, pp. 1–35.

Sangster, A. (2015) The earliest known treatise on double entry bookkeeping by Marino de Raphaeli. *The Accounting Historians Journal* 42(2): 1–34.

Sangster, A. (2016) The genesis of double entry bookkeeping. *The Accounting Review* 91(1): 299–315.

Sangster, A. and Scataglinibelghitar, G. (2010) Luca Pacioli: The father of accounting education. *Accounting Education: An International Journal* 19(4): 423–438.

Sangster, A., Stoner, G., De Lange, P., O'Connell, B. and Scataglini-Belghitar, G. (2012) Pacioli's forgotten book: The Merchant's 'Ricordanze'. *The Accounting Historians Journal* 39(2): 27–44.

Sargiacomo, M., Servalli, S. and Carnegie, G.D. (2012) Accounting for killing: Accountability for death. *Accounting History* 17(3–4): 393–413.
Serra, L. (1999) *Storia della ragioneria italiana*. Milano: Giuffrè.
Sestan, E. (1959) La politica veneziana del Seicento. In *La civiltà veneziana nell'età barocca (Florence, 1959)*. Venezia: Sansoni, pp. 35–66.
Stevenlick, E. (1970) *La comptabilité à travers les ages*. Bruxelles: Pragnons.
Stivieri, N. (1870) *Storia di Venezia: dalla sua origine fino ai giorni nostri*. [Stab. di] C. Coen.
Swetz, F. and Smith, D.E. (1987) *Capitalism and Arithmetic: The New Math of the 15th Century, Including the Full Text of the Treviso Arithmetic of 1478, Translated by David Eugene Smith*. La Salle, IL: Open Court Publishing.
Tagliente, G.A. (1525) *Luminario di aritmetica, libro ugnolo e libro doppio*. Venezia.
Ulvioni, P. (1977) Stampatori e librai a Venezia nel Seicento. *Archivio veneto* 109: 93–124.
Vance, L.L. (1943) The authority of history in inventory valuation. *The Accounting Review* 18(3): 219–227.
Venturi, B. (1655) *Della scrittura conteggiante di possessioni*. Firenze: Stamperia Lando Landi.
Viganò, E. (1968) *La tecnica del bilancio di verificazione nell'opera dei primi trattatisti*. Napoli: Giannini.
Vlaemminck, V. (1956) *Histoire et doctrine de la comptabilité*. Bruxelles: Éditions du Treurenberg.
Winjum, J.O. (1970) Accounting in its age of stagnation. *The Accounting Review* 45(4): 743–761.
Winjum, J.O. (1971) Accounting and the rise of capitalism: An accountant's view. *Journal of Accounting Research* 9(2): 333–350.
Woolf, A.H. (1912) *A short history of accountants and accountancy*. London: Gee & Co.
Yamey, B.S. (1967) Fifteenth and Sixteenth century manuscripts on the art of bookkeeping. *Journal of Accounting Research* 5(1): 51–76.
Yamey, B.S. (1979) Compound journal entries in early treatises in bookkeeping. *The Accounting Review* 54(2): 323–330.
Yamey, B.S. (1980) The index to the ledger: Some historical notes. *The Accounting Review* 55(3): 419–425.
Yamey, B.S. (1981) The partiment account: A discarded practice. *Abacus* 17(1): 3–8.
Yamey, B.S. (1994a) Benedetto Cotrugli on bookkeeping (1458). *Accounting, Business & Financial History* 4(1): 43–51.
Yamey, B.S. (1994b) Balancing and closing the ledger: Italian practice, 1300–1600. In Parker, R.H. and Yamey, B.S. (eds) *Accounting History: Some British Contributions*. Oxford: Clarendon Press, pp. 250–268.
Zambelli, A. (1681) *Mercantesche dichiarationi della scrittura doppia, conti de cambii, commissioni, e ragguagli di piazze: Con una tariffa per li pesi, e misure di Brescia con Venetia, & altre città d'Italia*. Brescia: Rizzardi.
Zambon, S. and Zan, L. (2007) Controlling expenditure, or the slow emergence of costing at the Venice arsenal, 1586–1633. *Accounting, Business & Financial History* 17(1): 105–128.
Zan, L. (1994) Toward a history of accounting histories: Perspectives from the Italian tradition. *European Accounting Review* 3(2): 255–307.

Zan, L. (2004) Accounting and management discourse in proto-industrial settings: The Venice arsenal in the turn of the 16th century. *Accounting and Business Research* 32(2): 145–175.

Zannini, A. (1999) L'economia veneta nel Seicento. Oltre il paradigma della 'crisi generale'. In *La popolazione italiana nel Seicento*. Bologna: CLUEB, pp. 473–502.

Zappa, G. (1950) *Il reddito d'impresa*. Milano: Giuffrè.

6 Niccolò D'Anastasio and His *Scrittura Doppia Ridotta Scienza*

Fabio Caputo, Stefano Coronella, Rossella Leopizzi and Andrea Venturelli

Introduction

The aim of this work is to analyze the thought by Niccolò D'Anastasio, through his work entitled *La scrittura doppia ridotta scienza* (Double-entry bookkeeping as a science) (D'Anastasio, 1803a; D'Anastasio, 1803b).

This inquiry has been performed by analyzing the scholar's slants, in relation to the historical time he lived in, and seeking to assess whether and how he contributed to the development of accounting.

Indeed, the work by D'Anastasio displays many insights, which deserve to be highlighted as part of the cultural enrichment path of accounting. This remark is based on the belief that in the evaluation of historical facts, final judgments do not exist and there is always room for further thoughts compared to prior stances (Canfora, 2017).

From a methodological perspective, we have put the author into context in the geographical area and in the historical period in which he lived. So, we have analyzed D'Anastasio's work as a primary source, and the theoretical positions about him over time as a secondary source.

We have followed a horizontal approach, insofar as the analysis of the scholar was carried out with reference both to the hitherto scientific background and to the development of bookkeeping.

Therefore, we have linked the thought by D'Anastasio with the theoretical stances immediately prior and subsequent to him, thus retracing the insights he provided with reference to either social and cultural events or bonds which had marked the development path of accounting practice (Miller, Hopper and Laughlin, 1991; Giannessi, 1992; Keenan, 1998; Amaduzzi, 2004; Carmona, Ezzamel and Gutiérrez, 2004; Antonelli and D'Alessio, 2011).

It is worth noting that our inquiry has not provided any useful information about the life of the scholar. Nothing new has emerged either at the Venice State Archive or at the Historical Library of the University Ca' Foscari of Venice, although extensive investigations have been performed therein, as well as on biographical and bibliographical sources.

That said, from the structure of the work it can be inferred that D'Anastasio might not have been an academic scholar. Such a consideration emerges since he neither mentioned other accounting scholars nor deepened the accounting thought at that time. So, this would be contradictory, insofar as the author dwelled a great deal on the scientific side of his essay as well as on the purpose he envisaged—that is, to set down a theoretic frame for the double-entry method.

Regardless of the rank of science by which D'Anastasio referenced his work, it is acknowledged by accounting scholars that the early nineteenth century marks a fundamental recovery in accounting studies, thus setting the stage for the further upswing in the second half of that century (Coronella, 2007, 119ff.).

In this direction, the switching from stillness to the resumption of scientific outputs is precisely marked by D'Anastasio's work, as is evident from his statement in the preface: "My intention to break the almost universal silence in these theories seemed perhaps too daring" (D'Anastasio, 1803a, 5).

In the period immediately prior to the drafting of the work here discussed, along with economic and social degradation, a significant decline in the quality of the works of Italian accounting scholars occurred (Bariola, 1897, 419–422; Brambilla, 1898, 4; Ceccherelli, 1915, 75–76; Melis, 1950, 714–715; Giannessi, 1979, 232–233; Masi, 1997, 233–234; Serra, 1999, 221–222; Privitera, 2003, 211–213).

The Italian accounting authors of the eighteenth century, although numerous (Giuseppe Vergani, Sanpierdarena Nunzio Giuseppe Carlo Amato ed Urso, Giovanni Cavalà Pasini, Pellegrino Balugani, Vincenzo Maria Arena, Tommaso Domenico Breglia, Pietro Paolo Scali, Giacomo Della Gatta, Giuseppe Enea Marchi, Francescantonio Filonzi, Santi Giusti, Carl'Antonio Monti, Giovan-Domenico Bassaglia, Fererio Farghiscoc Antonino and Giuseppe Forni, as well as several anonymous ones), did not have a great impact (Coronella, 2014, 132–174). On the contrary, from the late eighteenth century and with considerable influence for much of the nineteenth century, scholars from other countries, notably France (in particular Edmond Dégrange) and the UK (Edward Thomas Jones), virtually monopolized European accounting culture, including the Italian one (Brown, 1905, 159–170; Reymondin, 1909, 48–53; Vlaemminck, 1956, 139–149). Their works were translated into numerous languages and, specifically, that by Dégrange was updated and reprinted over a span of more than a century.

In such a fruitless context for Italian accounting, the slants by D'Anastasio emerged. At the beginning of the nineteenth century, compared to the prior Italian "decadent" contribution, he introduced a series of prominent insights, which would have been a forerunner of the further improvements of the discipline.

Literature Review

By the analysis we have performed on both literature and theoretical stances on D'Anastasio, it is acknowledged that several accounting history scholars have dealt with his approach from the late nineteenth century onwards, as witnessed in some works they authored.

Notwithstanding, through an in-depth research on their works (Bonalumi, 1880, 819; Bariola, 1897, 460; Brambilla, 1901, 98; Ceccherelli, 1915, 93ff.; Gomberg, 1912, 48; Besta, 1916, 414; Della Penna, 1946, 280; Melis, 1950, 730; Vlaemminck, 1956, 171; Masi, 1997, 281; Gabrovec Mei, 1999, 104ff.; Serra, 1999, 235–236; Guzzo, 2005; Doni, 2007, 282ff.; Mattessich, 2008, 19ff.; Coronella, 2014, 190ff.) we have found that the references to D'Anastasio are rather few.

So, although some of the greatest accounting history scholars, not just the Italian ones, have turned their attention to this essay, their level of detail is undoubtedly modest, except for a few authors (Coronella, 2014; Guzzo, 2005; Doni, 2007) who have handled the contribution by D'Anastasio. However, except for slight differences among their remarks, their comments on D'Anastasio are rather similar.

As far as his work is concerned, on the one hand, they have noted the lack of scientific robustness, and on the other hand, they have stressed its value, since it is deemed to have marked the qualitative resumption in monographic outputs after a dark period of foreign domination. Moreover, D'Anastasio's thought therein would lay down the basis for the scientific development which a few decades later would characterize the accounting disciplines.

In contrast to the aforesaid reflections, Besta leveled criticism in a brief comment stating that the work by D'Anastasio had added nothing, although it was clear and wide, if compared to the previous Venetian works (Besta, 1916, 414).

Only in recent times D'Anastasio has elicited more attention: first by Guzzo, who reviewed the contents of the essay, putting it into the proper scientific and philosophical perspective (Guzzo, 2005); followed by Doni, who devoted to the hints therein referring to the theory of accounts (Doni, 2007, 283 ff.); finally by Coronella, who provided a summary of the most important elements of the author's contribution to the development of accounting (Coronella, 2014, 190–192).

Background

D'Anastasio's work has to be put into perspective regarding the historical context of his age—that is, the social, cultural, political and economical background of Venice in the eighteenth century. It is deemed to have brought a "scientific break" with respect to the knowledge gained up to that point.

There was no "scientific debate" in accounting, due to weak business trade in the Italian Peninsula (Melis, 1950, 715), which was made up of several independent and different states.

Imperative was the annexation of Venice to the Austrian Empire at the end of the eighteenth century to neglect its pivotal role in the political, economical and cultural fields. Moreover, that was a period of crises both economic (Damerini, 1939; Beltrami, 1954; Berengo, 1956; Cessi, 1968; Lane, 1978;

Panciera, 1998; Venturi, 1980) and in *public administration* (Galasso, 1992) due to the financial deficit as a consequence of the seventeenth-century and early eighteenth-century wars (Errera, 1877).

The budgetary restructuring policies were non-homogeneous and increased the tax burden (Pezzolo, 2006)—the fiscal weight from provisional measures turned into fiscal consolidation—so the social and business weaknesses got worse.

The *maritime traffic* which had played a pivotal role up to then was affected by the development of both the oceanic routes and the shift of trading axis in continental Europe.

Consequently, the other countries had a relevant increase in trades compared to Venice, which had lost its international appeal, turning into a regional harbor for in-going trades to the hinterland (Galasso, 1992, 606).

Although shipbuilding decreased, the dockyard kept its role insofar as the employment rate had remained stable.

Furthermore, *agriculture* was underdeveloped and the peasants' conditions were limited, thus restricting renewal paths of cultivation techniques (Beltrami, 1961) and leading to a growing land abandonment.

As far as *industry* and *manufacturing* (Errera, 1877) are concerned, the textile sector, in particular silk products, had a dominant role, but the lack of equity funding and renewal of productive techniques and growing external competition cannibalized it.

The historical background also provides the rise of *guilds of arts*, which played a central role in the global economic, cultural and social forces at that time (Scarabello, 1981) with reference to the organization of business, mutual protection and employment. They gained such a bargaining power that the central power couldn't regulate the sector.

This remark has to be put into perspective insofar as at that time the welfare state didn't take demands for protection into account.

As for the educational system, it is recognized as a key driver in the spread of knowledge and culture (Gullino, 1973). Nonetheless, it went through a degradation phase because of the lack of funds invested. Only at the end of the eighteenth century, the scholar system underwent a sweeping educational reform aiming at preparing the elites, who could be expected to fill leadership positions (Galasso, 1992, 637ff.)

It goes without saying that the eighteenth century is considered *the dark period of Italy* (Coronella, 2014, 132–136; Melis, 1950, 714–717).

Afterwards, in the nineteenth century, the rebirth of scientific debate paved the way for majestic works in the second part of it.

The most acknowledged schools of that time were the Lombard School with Francesco Villa, the Tuscan School with Giuseppe Cerboni and the Venetian one with Fabio Besta. Their works deserve credit for having privileged the scientific approach of accounting studies, which was bound to the practical approach up to then (Costa, 2001, 24ff.; Melis, 1950, 745ff.; Privitera, 2003, 291ff.).

Indeed, the new investigation of the company phenomenon allows us to stress the economic, patrimonial and financial aspects of the going concern, which are tied up to each other in a systemic way.

Applied accounting comes across as effectively relevant through the widest framework of business administration. This "breakthrough" is the ennoblement of accounting to the rank of a science, thus marking a "scientific break".

As for scientific knowledge laying the basis for such a break, we may quote Niccolò D'Anastasio (D'Anastasio, 1803a; D'Anastasio, 1803b), Giuseppe Bornaccini (Bornaccini, 1818), Lodovico Giuseppe Crippa (Crippa, 1838–39), Antonio Tonzig (Tonzig, 1857–58) and Francesco Villa (Villa, 1840–41; Villa, 1850).

These authors, through their works, actively and concretely started the renewal path of accounting studies, which had completed at the end of the century (Coronella, 2017). This remark stands out as consistent with the accumulation process for scientific knowledge, whereby adding to the fund new challenging advancements, the state of the arts has been developed. Moreover, it goes without saying that accounting studies have to be channeled within the bounds of the economic and management logic they refer to.

With reference to the foregoing, D'Anastasio's work deserves credit as it epitomizes the Italian switch from the stillness of the previous century's accounting community to its further redemption.

In this regard, it is important to point out that he authored his outstanding essay in a historical context—that is, the last years of the eighteenth century, in which deterioration in political matters as well as adverse economic conditions would not have been fertile ground for valuable scientific insights.

This observation takes into account the correlation between the timeline and the evolution of business and accounting practices, insofar as reciprocal influences and mutual spillovers arise between their growth processes and technical accounting improvements (Adamo and Fasiello, 2015).

Prior to the release of *La scrittura doppia ridotta scienza*, the scientific context witnessed a cultural leadership by foreigners rather than Italian scholars, who had a subservient and marginal role (Melis, 1950, 715; Pierucci, 2009).

It was even doubtful whether the cultural root of the double-entry method was firmly Italian (Coronella, 2014, 184).

This was because, as already mentioned, the Italian Peninsula was carved up into a myriad of states, many of which were under a significant foreign influence (Galasso, 1992). Such a scenario fuelled and strengthened cultural leading positions from abroad, which hindered productive and social development in Italy.

This led to a paradox with regard to accounting and trade practices, because Italian traditions were strongly embedded in the process of technical know-how which had been hitherto gathered, but actually they turned out to be degraded.

Significant was the presence of the French at that time and of thought by Edmond Dégrange (Dégrange, 1795). He authored "the theoretic of the five general accounts", whose content certainly provided a useful contribution to the accounting debate at that time. His work followed a series of seminal contributions by other authors (Savary, 1675; Irson, 1678; De La Porte, 1712; Barrême, 1721), who had the merit of formulating the earlier insights which Dégrange subsequently organized, systematized and deepened. Specifically, this approach stressed the proprietor personalistic character of the accounting entries; moreover, the "journal-ledger"—that is, a fusion between ledger and journal—was introduced (Dégrange, 1804), thus providing dynamics and information of the former and the latter jointly in one record only.

It was a useful tool to crowd into a single sheet all the accounting values which pertained to the proprietor for whom the books had to be kept. Notwithstanding, the journal-ledger could not be maintained in practice because of its lack of flexibility in meeting the requirements of the wider business phenomena; otherwise, it would fit only smaller firms.

In the overall theoretical scenario of that time, the Scottish scholar Edward Thomas Jones also played a relevant role since he formulated the method which he renamed with his own (Jones, 1796). Moreover, insights by another Scottish-born author, John Mair, are worth noting, insofar as he sought to clarify some applications of the accounting method with respect to business concerns (Mair, 1736).

The thought by Jones was radically critical of Italian double entry, which he deemed to be complex and not feasible to fit in with practical operations. He maximized his theory by virtue of an alleged broader ease of use, as well as the possibility of having several numerical matches, which would lead to a reliable keeping of the accounts and to the prevention of fraud (Mari, 1996; Coronella, 2007, 192–209).

Within this synthetic overview, it is worth mentioning the Austrian School with reference to the Lombardy-Venetian area. It deserves credit for having set down the cameralistic method, which had to be applied to public administration (Coronella, 2007, 209 ff.). At the core of the cameralistic approach was the cash for collections and payments only. On this subject, particularly insightful is the work by Johann Matthias Puechberg—counsellor to Maria Teresa of Austria and a prominent figure of that time—whose contribution afforded significant progress to the theoretical formulation of this approach and its resulting applications (Puechberg, 1762).

The Work by D'Anastasio: *La Scrittura Doppia Ridotta Scienza* (Double-Entry Bookkeeping as a Science)

Introduction

The essay written by Niccolò D'Anastasio and entitled *La scrittura doppia ridotta scienza* (Double-entry bookkeeping as a science) is divided into two volumes. The first volume alternates theoretical and applied parts, the latter of which, however, is "instrumental" with respect to the theoretical one as he uses examples to illustrate and demonstrate the theoretical topics covered.

Table 6.1 The content of D'Anastasio's work

Volume	*Sections*	*Topics*
Volume 1	First	Portrayal of double-entry bookkeeping, the ledger and the journal
	Second	Double entry for individual firm
	Third	Outflows and inflows
	Fourth	Trial balance for individual firm and companies
	Fifth	Set of example accounting entries for winding-up companies or partner's withdrawal
	Sixth	Auxiliary registers
	Seventh	Errors and their correction
Volume 2	First	Entries for individual firms
	Second	Entries for companies
	Third	Entries for branches and subsidiaries

The second volume is entirely dedicated to practical examples, which are organized in a rigorous manner.

In Table 6.1 we present the synthesis of the contents of the two volumes of the work.

The author aimed to release a work that could provide a "theoretical framework" for "double-entry bookkeeping", thus providing for the lack of similar works up to that moment. Indeed, previous works had investigated accounting topics from a merely operational and practical perspective, and therefore they were totally lacking in a framework that would have illustrated the accounting logic and the dynamics of accounts in a systematic way.

The scholar goes further, thus deeming double-entry bookkeeping a science, but actually he did not delve deeper into this significant consideration.

The work appears to be generally orderly and reasoned. Back to the first volume, the endeavors for such a "systematization" of accounting studies are elicited.

In it, the author identifies a set of principles and axioms that, once understood, allow a bookkeeper to master the theoretical approach for posting entries, as well as the operations of his company (e.g., records of economic transactions being kept), without further studies. This is due to a methodology informed by a specifically pedagogic purpose.

About this point, D'Anastasio states, "The only purpose of my endeavors is to make anyone eligible for handling the Double Entry, without the need for a teacher" (D'Anastasio, 1803a, 7), and again:

> I will prompt the public to thoughts and, whether I would not succeed in making the pupil able to learn the Double Entry by himself and to employ it in any merchant and accounting book, I will boast of deserving

> credits for having laid, at least, the first foundations upon which the most talented to-be would bring forth an entirely perfect work, thus more easily building and broadening the [accounting] pillars further.
> (D'Anastasio, 1803a, 6)

The Method

The author is devoted primarily to the identification of a perimeter of reference in order to set and analyze the conceptual frame of the double-entry working rules.

The methodological rigor the author sets forth in his work is demonstrated by using a method labeled "mathematical". This method is carried out in a series of general principles being applied to any practical case, thus solving any problem of entries, including the most difficult ones.

In essence, D'Anastasio achieves a set of axioms, which he considers the tenets for the running of the aforementioned double-entry frame (D'Anastasio, 1803a, 7).

Insofar as his thought is concerned, the effort to set down an accounting language as a valuable tool for the practitioner emerges. Accordingly, he identifies practitioners as the main beneficiaries of his work, thus having this aim set. Indeed, he maintains that a proper accounting practice lays its basis on the effective theoretical approach, as proved in the premise. The scholar states, "Even though on the scientific part nobody will be found to contradict my statements; I do confess, that in the mechanical [applicative] part, several equivalent methods may exist" (D'Anastasio, 1803a, 7).

It is worth noting the significance of the theoretical frame of the double-entry method, which, starting from the early Middle Ages (Coronella, 2014, 19–26), carries a full-fledge universal language forward (Gabrovec Mei, 1999, 57; Giaccari, 2005).

The double-entry method has found a widespread application to the extent that all the administrative facts—such as purchases, sales, financial, economic (barter) and capital permutations—can be codified into the accounting language (Cassandro, 1985, 502 ff.).

This accounting discourse has conveyed a wider knowledge which gathers a present-day cross-disciplinary track as well as the resource management and stewardship sights of the enterprise. Such a discourse portrays the bounds between accounting practices and socio-economic changes (Salento and Coronella, 2015).

Although Italian scholars deserve credit for the grounding knowledge in the accounting history (Costa, 2001; Coronella, 2014), they are neglected in the international debate.

The Accounting Theory

According to D'Anastasio, the merchant is the reference point of the accounting system, since all the entries related to the events of a merchant's business ought to stress the rights and obligations attributable to him (D'Anastasio, 1803a, 5).

For the first time in a bookkeeping work, the accounts are not directly entered to "persons" and/or "goods" but, regardless of whether they refer to the former or to the latter, the starting point ought to be the "administrative facts"—that is to say, the dynamics of operations.

Delving deeper, we can notice the use of a more definite language for a better interpretation of the aforementioned administrative facts of the enterprise, which are intended for "shifts" (*mosse*) by D'Anastasio.

Such "shifts" trigger a double effect in order to the lead the double-entry record. Indeed, they involve two accounts, which are labeled as two "*loci*" (D'Anastasio, 1803a, 22). The identification of such a "*locus*" gives the idea of "physically" moving the items—referred to either persons or things—which have to be carried to the two accounts.

Moreover, the author also deepens the issue of accounts classification and he deems the double-entry posting system—through the theoretical pattern he has shaped on the operating rules among accounts—a useful way to link and coordinate the relationship between accounts and, therefore, toincrease the quality of disclosure. Consistent with the meaning of the term "shift", the author replaces the preposition "for" with "from", insofar as it can better represent the shift from one place to another, as the result of a given transaction relating to the company.

Although he acknowledged the "personification" of accounts (Guzzo, 2005, 25), the interpretation of operations such as the "shifts" (that involve an item being withdrawn and placed into another locus, intended for the "warehouse") is twofold. First, D'Anastasio introduces an original and innovative approach in accounting thought from a theoretical perspective. Moreover, he simplifies the comprehensibility of the double-entry method, which was not immediately understandable, especially for non-experts.

From this point of view, it is interesting to notice the break with previous authors; furthermore, as far as a conceptual basis can be concerned, his reflection would pave the way for the forthcoming *logismographic* thought (Bariola, 1897, 460), thus witnessing a sort of anticipation of *logismographic* principles.

Indeed, D'Anastasio assesses that even though the accounts were entered to goods or persons, the shifts encompassing them ought to be related to the owner, thus singling out a debtor or a creditor for each shift.

In fact, D'Anastasio's contemporaries—particularly with respect to Dégrange (Dégrange, 1795)—refer the accounts, as appropriate, to third parties towards the firm as well as to the owner, while he stresses that the accounts ought to be referred to the proprietor, although the "warehouses" can be represented either by things or by persons. In so doing, he also underlines that the main purpose of the accounting technique is to better understand the modifying events of wealth components in the company, thus forerunning—albeit in an intuitive and empirical manner—a concept that will be consolidated in Italy only at the end of the nineteenth century (Besta, 1891).

In essence, from the perspective of accounting theory, the approach by D'Anastasio hints at a conceptual effort to overcome the personalistic approach while introducing the concepts of "loci" or the "warehouse". The rule requires that each shift informed by the record of a transaction will prompt the physical or virtual displacement of a given element from one place to another; the word, although not technical, which best represents such a situation is identified by the scholar as the term "warehouse". By this term, the author includes "funds, ware which the merchant might buy or sell, and the persons, with whom the merchant would get into business" (D'Anastasio, 1803a, 5).

It is impossible to determine whether this "vision" was purposeful or the unintended consequence of the illustration of a method which appeals to the "physical" profile (in the sense of "physical shifts") of persons and things from one place (warehouse) to another.

Anyway, consciously or not, it is true that D'Anastasio went beyond the merely personalistic approach typical of the accounting technique of his time and can therefore be interpreted as a "frontier" author.

Moreover, it is worth noting that the array of the various "shifts" of the company appears to be complete, not only as regards the number of events covered and expected but also with respect to the various commercial scenarios.

It is possible to observe a constant reminder of the theoretical axioms that support and explain the practical exemplifications. For instance, in the final part of Chapter 4 of the first volume, the illustrative list of specific principles of operations appears to be effective from a teaching point of view (D'Anastasio, 1803a, 22).

The author pays a great deal of attention to simplifying the logic behind account keeping. Also the breakdown of the "compound shifts" into "simple shifts"—for a better understanding of the dynamics of transactions—is consistent with the need to proceed in an applicative key, thus simplifying the procedural aspects (D'Anastasio, 1803a, 22).

The Accounting Structure and the Financial Statement

The author pays attention to the issue of the technical accounting style—that is to say, the accounting language. Therefore, he considers the trade-off between multiplicity of accounts to be involved and the conciseness of his accounting layout, thus leading to better the quality of the disclosure. To do so, D'Anastasio illustrates many practical applications, insofar as his pragmatic examples can improve understanding as well as facilitate a more consistent application of technical rules for accounting.

It is worth noting the relationship between the double-entry methodological rigor and the administrative facts, which refer to the merchant's business;

furthermore, D'Anastasio's approach has a huge historical significance, as residing in the kind of concern he poses: the need for control, decision making and the consequent activities management, which have involved human beings since ancient times.

For this reason, the author firstly stresses the importance of empirical observation, and following he draws forth the theoretical aspects.

Given the relevance of keeping records of economic transactions, the scholar prioritizes the ledger and the journal, albeit he is aware that larger accounting books can be devoted to the aforementioned purpose (D'Anastasio, 1803a, 3).

By contrast, the authors previous to D'Anastasio did not give such prominence to the ledger and the journal (Coronella, 2014, 136–170). Rather, they considered a huge number of various accounting books and registers, each of which referred to the business one would have dealt with or to its proprietor (mercantile, agricultural, sole proprietorship, baronial). In so doing, "accounting chaos" conditions could have occurred, in spite of the rational and orderly display of the shifts of value by D'Anastasio's approach.

Both ledger and journal are pivotal tools for the double-entry method and, once the pupil achieved a full understanding of the proper way to draft and draw them up, the other auxiliary books would have been an easy thing for him. Indeed, the author states, "a few hints to the reader will be enough to allow him to understand what, if I hadn't, would not be clear, not even with the longest explanation" (D'Anastasio, 1803a, 3).

Therefore, the author says, "Together [the two books] are the substance of Entries; separately examined, they only offer a mere progression of things, passing from the former [the ledger] to the latter [the journal], and the relative need by which they follow" (D'Anastasio, 1803a, 3).

In the drawing up the two accounting books, he suggests a path and a proper format to follow, as well as a matching chart between ledger and journal to be drafted, aiming at keeping records of administrative facts.

The usefulness of this accounting system is apparent, which leads us to understand the going concern of the merchant's firm.

There has always been a *fil rouge* which has linked the evolution of economic events to the development of content of accounting language, referring to both formal and substantial content. This path has been long and complex. It has encompassed simple shapes based on tabular formats of accounts up to complex patterns. This development of accounting issues has been tied up with the qualitative and quantitative growth of enterprise phenomena.

As regards the financial statement, D'Anastasio defines it as "an extract, which is done from the ledger, by which we can thoroughly find out about the state of one's possessions" (D'Anastasio, 1803a, 163).

He handles it with a further deepening on some specific cases—for instance, the individual firms and companies as well as branches and subsidiaries.

According to D'Anastasio, the closing of the ledger has to be done only after having "entered each payment, cash receipts, sale, expense, and any other affair concluded up to that point" (D'Anastasio, 1803a, 198).

He reduces the different conceptual categories of accounts to a single sum, by the means of a sort of settling mechanism, which he defines as "fictitious addition".

Consistently, for each economic track, he makes some adjustments at the end of the year, in order to arrange the worth in line with the shifts which have occurred during the period of reference. Here, the "Statement of Profits and Losses" account is useful and allows us to fully understand the origin of costs and revenues of each transaction.

Moreover, the author makes a distinction between *assets* and *assets of little hope*, which refer to those doubtful and uncollectible accounts receivable—that is to say, "non-performing loans". The latter ought to be entered in balance sheet at the estimated realizable value (D'Anastasio, 1803a, 163ff.).

D'Anastasio focuses on the balance between debit and credit. The eventual lack of this balance would mean making an error, which would need to be corrected following the methods illustrated later in the work.

It is also worth noting the attention the author pays regarding the possibility of keeping other people's things or, on the contrary, having one's own things in the hands of others, providing an rational explanation about such hypothesis.

From the analysis of the work, it is interesting to observe the author's concern about *errors* and the consequent *procedure* to be set out to correct them (D'Anastasio, 1803a, 253ff.). Actually, he devotes a specific section to this issue as a proof of the teaching purpose he envisages. Indeed, D'Anastasio is aware of the difficulties one might fall into which lead one to make errors, and thus he supplies proper tools to rectify them.

The Purpose and the Teaching Approach

The work by D'Anastasio is informed by clear teaching and disclosure purposes, as already said. He sets forth this aim in many points of the first volume. In it, he refers to non-experts and he says that the conciseness of his method would lead them to attain a full understanding and a full mastery of double-entry bookkeeping (D'Anastasio, 1803a, 6–8).

The pedagogical approach emerges firstly on the grounds of the remarks made so far. Actually, such tools as "shifts" and "loci" ("warehouse") that the author uses for the technique of the double-entry method ought to be considered a simplification for educational purposes. In this sense, as already said, at the core of his choice is the desire to find an alternative way to explain the accounting technique so that it could be easily understandable even to those who were completely unaware.

The didactic purpose also emerges from the link between the first and the second volume of the work. In fact, the latter is exclusively dedicated to the illustration of practical examples and, in so doing, D'Anastasio creates a link with the content of the first volume, which includes his theoretical frame and approach.

This requirement is generally taken up and presented in the introductory paragraph of the second volume with the running head "warning":

> To profit from this second volume, we ought to cling to a method: because, unlike almost all other books, in which we progress gradually from the first to the last page, here it is necessary to take a very different path [. . .] and in this way you will come to know where it is possible to find [them] in the first volume, the relative doctrines.
>
> (D'Anastasio, 1803b, 5)

Finally, the teaching purpose arises as well from the careful choice of the succession of the topics, which is set according to a growing level of difficulty, precisely to lead the reader to a progressive learning of the subject. This method demonstrates a modern approach, extremely valuable from a pedagogical point of view.

D'Anastasio, then, is particularly careful about the explanation of the various operations, also in relation to the different phases of life of the company and of the varying complexity that may occur.

In setting practical examples, the author distinguishes the start-up phase of the business, the launch phase and the final winding-up (D'Anastasio, 1803b).

In particular, in the application part devoted to the launch of business, he delves deeper into examples, thus sifting through many events that can normally occur, although in a rough way, this can be linked to the qualitative and quantitative analyses of the variations of the invested assets due to the operations (Cassandro, 1985, 129ff.; Di Cagno, Adamo and Giaccari 2011, 163ff.).

Finally, the author deals with the management of branches and subsidiaries, as well as companies. In the latter case, a partner contributes funds to the capital and the other contributes the labor, as a working partner. On this point, it is interesting to note the lack of a suitable shift for the working partner in the start-up phase. Anyhow, at the close of the accounts, he is mentioned again through his "shift" when checking the profits gained or the losses incurred (D'Anastasio, 1803b, 47).

Conclusions

Through our analysis, we have surmised the attempt by D'Anastasio to provide a theoretical frame, which is settled in the accounting entries, but his thought goes beyond what has been developed by the previous authors.

This feature is especially relevant as far as he belonged to a historical period whereby accounting studies confined themselves to the double-entry method in purely practical terms.

On the contrary, his endeavors intend to grasp the different meanings of shifts which were prompted in the business, as well as the outcome they have for the wealth of the merchant's firm.

D'Anastasio singles out specific axioms behind the functioning of the double-entry method and, moreover, he makes a step forward with respect to previous accounting works, in both the content of the accounts and the boundaries among them. A conceptual stress comes across as transcending double entry as a simple accounting device, launching it towards the noblest paths.

According to D'Anastasio, the tenets and theoretical procedures which underpin the double-entry method are worthy of attention. Indeed, he advocates that only by mastering them can one achieve a full understanding of double entry.

In so doing, although unaware, D'Anastasio is also able to innovate a theoretical approach to the accounts, standing as the forerunner of a materialistic view in which the accounts are all referred to the proprietor, thus laying down basis for an asset-centered accounting theory.

At the core of his slant is the desire for the ennoblement of the method as a science, but actually any particular clue by the author has ever given us the way to appreciate this vision. In this point of view, he attains the climax in a technical-operational topic; actually, his work is a long way off from the very scientific acknowledgment of accounting by Francesco Villa (Villa, 1840–41; Villa, 1850) and subsequently accomplished by Fabio Besta (Besta, 1880; Besta, 1891).

The approach is basically demonstrative and descriptive. However, the analysis is carried out in a detailed and punctual way, with an effective teaching methodology, which stands out as unique compared to the previous scientific works.

In particular, it is useful to emphasize, in that context, the scope of application to which D'Anastasio paid a great deal of attention—that is to say, the winding-up phase and the so-called special cases.

This topic was carried on by taking into account the wider array of cases which could have occurred; for this reason, the work presents insights into companies that are winding down, division of companies into individual firms and the partner's withdrawal.

That being said, the work we have analyzed has played an important role in the development of the discipline. Undoubtedly, it has positively influenced the process of refinement of accounting knowledge for enterprises.

Bearing in mind the period and the context in which the essay matured as well as the fundamental issue that a branch of knowledge advances through further accumulations, even though D'Anastasio's work does not contain any major innovations, his work stands out among those which have to be considered in the development of Italian accounting.

Indeed, his essay is certainly a "frontier" work, which marks a "cutting-edge" switch—that is, it witnesses the transition between the eighteenth

Table 6.2 Elements of originality in D'Anastasio's work

Reference (section)	*Elements of originality in D'Anastasio's work*
Volume 1, Section 1	An attempt to define precise axioms behind the functioning of the double-entry method based on mathematical tenets
Volume 1, Section 2 Volume 2, Section 2	Accounting topics for companies
Volume 1, Section 2 Volume 2, Section 3	Accounting topics for branches and subsidiaries
Volume 1, Section 5	Partner's withdrawal
The whole work	• Hints for further developments of logismologic thought • Innovative interpretation of the logical-technical side of the double-entry method • Partial detachment from the theoretical tenets of the dominant personalistic accounting • High number of exemplifications • Separation between ledger and journal and auxiliary books • Pedagogic approach, methodological rigor and in-depth investigation

century's "decaying" and purely technical accounting and the nineteenth century's strengthened and "scientific" one.

In Table 6.2 we provide an overview of the original features and their related references in D'Anastasio's work, on the basis of the considerations drawn hitherto.

Ultimately, D'Anastasio's use of the term "science" can be more correctly attributed to such aforementioned prominent insights which he laid out with particular care and according to a modern approach. In the following years, they would lay down the basis for a fruitful theoretical debate, which would raise accounting studies to the dignity of a science in the second half of the nineteenth century.

References

Adamo, S., Fasiello, R. (2015), "Attività economica e 'tempo' nei conti dei mercanti medioevali", *Rivista Italiana di Ragioneria ed Economia Aziendale*, n. 10–12, 423–441.

Amaduzzi, A. (2004), *Storia della ragioneria. Percorsi di ricerca tra aziende e contabilità, dottrine e professioni*, Giuffrè, Milano.

Antonelli, V., D'Alessio, R. (2011), *Gli studi di storia della ragioneria dall'unità d'Italia ad oggi. Evidenze, interpretazioni e comparazioni in tema di autori, opere, oggetto e metodo*, Franco Angeli, Milano.

Bariola, P. (1897), *Storia della ragioneria italiana premiata al Concorso della Società Storica Lombarda*, Tip. Ambrosiana, Milano.

Barrême, F.B. (1721), *Traité des parties doubles*, Nyon, Paris.
Beltrami, D. (1954), *Storia della popolazione di Venezia dalla fine del secolo XVI alla caduta della Repubblica*, Cedam, Padova.
Beltrami, D. (1961), *La penetrazione economica dei Veneziani in terraferma. Forza di lavoro e proprietà fondiaria nelle campagne venete dei secoli XVII e XVIII*, Istituto per la collaborazione culturale, Venezia.
Berengo, M. (1956), *La società veneta alla fine del Settecento*, Sansoni, Firenze.
Besta, F. (1880), *La ragioneria. Prolusione letta nella solenne apertura degli studi per l'anno scolastico 1880–81 alla R. Scuola superiore di commercio in Venezia*, Coletti, Venezia.
Besta, F. (1891), *Corso di ragioneria professato alla classe di magistero nella R. Scuola Superiore di Commercio in Venezia, Parte prima, Ragioneria Generale*, Volume 1, Visentini, Venezia.
Besta, F. (1916), *La Ragioneria*, Volume 3, II edizione, Vallardi, Milano.
Bonalumi, F.A. (1880), "Il risveglio degli studi computistici", *Rivista di Contabilità*, Vol. 3, 813–824.
Bornaccini, G. (1818), *Idee pratiche di ragionateria e di doppia registrazione con in fine dei rilievi sul metodo semplice di tenere i registri di commercio di E. T. Jones inglese*, per Marsoner e Grandi, Rimino.
Brambilla, G. (1898), "Gli scrittori di contabilità mercantile dei secoli XVII e XVIII", *Rivista di Amministrazione e Contabilità*, Vol. 18, 3–4.
Brambilla, G. (1901), *Storia della Ragioneria Italiana*, Boriglione, Milano.
Brown, R. (1905), *A History of Accounting and Accountants*, T.C. & E.C. Jack, Edimburg.
Canfora, L. (2017), *La schiavitù del capitale*, Il Mulino, Bologna.
Carmona, S., Ezzamel, M., Gutiérrez, F. (2004), "Accounting history research: Traditional and new accounting history perspectives", *De computis*, Vol. 1, n. 1, 111–120.
Cassandro, E. (1985), *Trattato di Ragioneria. L'economia delle aziende e il suo controllo*, Cacucci, Bari.
Ceccherelli, A. (1915), *La logismologia*, Casa Editrice Dottor Francesco Vallardi, Milano.
Cessi, R. (1968), *Storia della repubblica di Venezia*, Principato, Milano-Messina.
Coronella, S. (2007), *La ragioneria in Italia nella seconda metà del XIX secolo. Profili teorici e proposte applicative*, Giuffrè, Milano.
Coronella, S. (2014), *Storia della Ragioneria Italiana. Epoche, Uomini, Idee*, Franco Angeli, Milano.
Coronella, S. (2017), "I precursori della ragioneria scientifica: gli studiosi italiani del primo Ottocento", *Rivista Italiana di Ragioneria e di Economia Aziendale*, n. 1–4, 117–132.
Costa, M. (2001), *Le concezioni della ragioneria nella dottrina italiana. Profili storici e storiografici nella sistematica delle discipline aziendali*, Giappichelli, Torino.
Crippa, L.G. (1838–39), *La scienza dei conti, ossia l'arte di tenere i registri e compilare i bilanci di ogni azienda*, G.B. Bianchi e Comp., Milano.
Damerini, G. (1939), *Settecento veneziano*, Mondadori, Milano.
D'Anastasio, N., (1803a), *La scrittura doppia ridotta scienza*, Tomo I, Glichi, Venezia.
D'Anastasio, N., (1803b), *La scrittura doppia ridotta scienza*, Tomo II, Glichi, Venezia.

Dégrange, E. (1795), *La tenue des livres rendue facile*, Chez Hocquart, Paris.
Dégrange, E. (1804), *Supplement à la Tenue des Livres rendue facile*, Chez Hocquart, Paris.
De La Porte, M. (1712), *La science des négociants et teneurs de livres*, Charles Osmont, Paris.
Della Penna, F. (1946), *Le istituzioni contabili*, parte prima, Castellani, Roma.
Di Cagno, N., Adamo, S., Giaccari, F. (2011), *Lineamenti di Economia Aziendale. Corso di lezioni*, Cacucci, Bari.
Doni, F. (2007), *La teoria personalistica del conto. Aspetti evolutivi ed approfondimenti critici*, Giuffrè, Milano.
Errera, A. (1877), *Storia dell'economia politica nei secoli XVII e XVIII negli stati della repubblica veneta*, Antonelli, Venezia.
Gabrovec Mei, O. (1999), *Il linguaggio contabile. Itinerario storico e metodologico*, II edizione, Giappichelli, Torino.
Galasso, G. (1992), *Storia d'Italia, volume XII, tomo secondo,La repubblica di Venezia nell'età moderna*, Utet, Torino.
Giaccari, F. (2005), *Lineamenti di ragioneria internazionale*, Cacucci, Bari.
Giannessi, E. (1979), *Appunti di economia aziendale, con particolare riferimento alle aziende agricole*, Pacini, Pisa.
Giannessi, E. (1992), *Considerazioni introduttive sul metodo storico*, Giuffrè, Milano.
Gomberg, L. (1912), *L'économologique (science comptable) et son histoire*, Société Générale d'Imprimerie, Genève.
Gullino, G. (1973), *La politica scolastica veneziana nell'età delle riforme*, Deputazione di storia patria per le Venezie, Venezia.
Guzzo, G. (2005), "A due secoli da la Scrittura doppia ridotta a scienza", *Atti del VII Convegno nazionale della Società Italiana di Storia della Ragioneria*, Bari, 5–6 dicembre 2003, 2° Tomo G-Z, Rirea, Roma, 9–40.
Irson, C. (1678), *Méthode pour bien dresser toutes sortes de comptes à partie double*, Cusson, Paris.
Jones, E.T. (1796), *Jones's English System of Book-Keeping, by Single or Double Eentry*, R. Edwards, Bristol.
Keenan, M.G. (1998), "A defence of traditional acconting history reasearch methodology", *Critical Perspectives on Accounting*, Vol. 9, 641–666.
Lane, F. (1978), *Storia di Venezia*, traduzione italiana, Einaudi, Torino.
Mair, J. (1736), *Book-keeping methodiz'd*, T. and W. Ruddimans, Edinburgh.
Mari, L.M. (1996), "Il nuovo metodo di scrittura mercantile 'ideato' da Edward Thomas Jones—Bristol 1795", *Atti del III Convegno Nazionale di Storia della Ragioneria*, Alghero, 20 e 21 ottobre 1995, Pacini, Pisa, 309–317.
Masi, V. (1997), *La Ragioneria nell'età moderna e contemporanea*, Tamari, Bologna.
Mattessich, R. (ed) (2008), *Two Hundred Years of Accounting Research: An International Survey of Personalities, Ideas and Publications (from the Beginning of the Nineteenth Century to the Beginning of the Twenty-First Century*, Routledge, London and New York.
Melis, F. (1950), *Storia della Ragioneria*, Zuffi, Bologna.
Miller P., Hopper, T., Laughlin, R. (1991), "The new accounting history: An introduction", *Accounting, Organizations and Society*, Vol. 16, n. 5–6, 395–403.

Panciera, W. (1998), *L'economia: imprenditoria, corporazioni, lavoro, in Del Negro—Preto, Storia di Venezia. Dalle origini alla caduta della Serenissima, Vol. VIII. L'ultima fase della Serenissima, Parte II*, Economia e Società, Roma, pp. 479–553.

Pezzolo, L. (2006), *Una finanza d'ancien Regime. La Repubblica Veneta tra XV e XVIII secolo*, ESI, Napoli-Roma.

Pierucci, P. (2009), *La contabilità nel bacino del Mediterraneo (secoli XIV e XIX)*, Franco Angeli, Milano.

Privitera, C. (2003), *Origine ed evoluzione del pensiero ragionieristico*, Giuffrè, Milano.

Puechberg, J.M. (1762), *Einleitung zu einem verbesserten Kameral-Rechnungsfuße, auf die Verwaltung einer Kameral-Herrschaft angewandt*, Johann Thomas Trattner, Wien.

Reymondin, G. (1909), *Bibliographie méthodique des Ouvrages en langue française parus de 1543 à 1908 sur la science des comptes. Volume—Brochures—Articles—Manuscrits*, Société Académique de Comptabilité—V. Giard et F. Briere, Paris.

Salento, A., Coronella, S. (2015), *Trasformazioni dell'accounting e disconnessione dell'impresa. Dal reddito al point-value*, Università del Salento—Coordinamento SIBA, Lecce.

Savary, J. (1675), *Le parfait négociant*, Louis Billaine, Paris.

Scarabello, G. (1981), "Caratteri e funzioni socio-politiche dell'associazionismo a Venezia sotto la Repubblica", in AA.VV., *Scuole di arti mestieri e devozione a Venezia*, Arsenale, Venezia.

Serra, L. (1999), *Storia della Ragioneria Italiana*, Giuffrè, Milano.

Tonzig, A. (1857–58), *Trattato della scienza di amministrazione e di contabilità privata e dello Stato*, Pietro Naratovich, Venezia.

Venturi, F. (1980), *Venezia nel secondo Settecento*, Tirrenia Stampatori, Torino.

Villa, F. (1840–41), *La contabilità applicata alle Amministrazioni private e pubbliche, ossia elementi di scienze economico amministrative applicati alla tenuta dei registri ed alla compilazione e revisione dei rendiconti*, Angelo Monti, Milano.

Villa, F. (1850), *Elementi di amministrazione e contabilità*, Bizzoni, Pavia.

Vlaemminck, J.H. (1956), *Histoire et doctrines de la comptabilité*, Éditions du Treurenberg—Dunod, Bruxelles-Paris.

Section 2

Companies

7 Accounting and Power Relationships at the Origin of the Venetian Hospital of Santi Giovanni e Paolo

Roberto Di Pietra[1] *and Salvatore Russo*[2]

Premise and Historical Background

In the activity of many institutions and/or entities it is common to see some events that are, for sure, exceptional or, better to say, extraordinary. This could be the case of a merger in which different institutions or entities are going to convey their respective activities into a single one. In this process two or more entities have to solve issues related to technical aspects generated by the merging process. At the same time and in a more complex way, the same entities have to start a long process during which they will put together the different managerial cultures characterizing all the entities joining this merger. Each entity is requested to share its own managerial culture with all the others and has to mix the different levels of power in the new entity emerging from the merging process. This process is complex if we consider a shared and mutual consent towards the merger. This process becomes particularly complex if we assume that the merging entities are forced to accept it. In this case we have to consider that some of the entities involved will try to resist the changes. Moreover, all the entities will try to maintain their respective power within the new organization. Some entities use their power to expand it, supporting the merger process and the establishment of the new organization, and others are interested in maintaining their own power, resisting the process. In this contraposition, accounting could be used as a tool with which an entity could support or resist the merging process. Accounting could be settled in a way in which the established power could expand its control of the merged organizations, and/or the pre-existing organizations could use accounting in order to maintain their power, avoiding disclosure and manipulating information. Such issues could be investigated by adopting a historical perspective, as was already done in previous studies (Parker, 1997; Riccaboni *et al.*, 2006; Sargiacomo, 2008; Bracci *et al.*, 2010; Carnegie and Napier, 2012; Leardini *et al.*, 2013). In our study, we have focused our attention on the relevant merger realized during the last years of the Venetian Republic in the healthcare system from which has emerged the Hospital of Santi Giovanni e Paolo. This merger was studied in order to understand which power relations drove this process in order to determine governance and how this has affected the accounting system.

Historically, the establishment of a major hospital in Venice devoted to Santi Giovanni e Paolo is the result of a series of events throughout the centuries, in which retrospectively, three critical components were involved in strict interrelations with each other. Firstly, we have to consider the need of the government of the *Serenissima* Republic to establish an efficient healthcare system for sick and indigent people (*Serenissima* Republic is the historical name for the Republic of Venice). Secondly, we have to look at the events accompanying the end of the *Serenissima* Republic and its transition under the various dominations until the unification of Italy and its effect on the availability of financial resources.

As shown in many studies published on this subject matter, the information received so far mainly comes from the archives of different institutions. According to a historical representation of the facts, our study investigates and interprets by analysing an administrative and accounting data period. In particular, we refer to the last years of the Venetian Republic (1777–1797), when some events profoundly affected the consequential development of the healthcare system in Venice, specifically regarding hospital services, until the unification of Italy.

Combinations of accounting records and archive documents have allowed us to reconstruct some important events preceding the establishment of a unique and large hospital.

In this phase, the hospital underwent the most significant transformations simultaneously during the changes in the governance of the political system that shifted from the Austro-Hungarian Empire to the Kingdom of Italy (Alzetta, 2010).

The decision to focus our attention on the aforementioned period and the choice to study the creation of the Venice hospital were made because this kind of event offers a relevant opportunity to investigate the driving forces and factors that led this momentum forward.

The Venice hospital of Santi Giovanni e Paolo has incorporated different cultural and managerial perspectives from the other various preexisting hospitals. All of these hospitals merged in the Hospital of Santi Giovanni e Paolo and contributed to defining the features and characteristics of the "new entity" and, most importantly, its managerial and governance culture. The establishment of the new hospital requested that the governance structure and its mechanisms were set in a different way in order to manage the new entity and to distribute its organization and a certain level of power to the administration. The main technology in administrators' hands in order to make possible the application of managerial power is based on the accounting system and its characteristics and practices. In the case of the Venice hospital this is particularly relevant because we are referring to a phase in which a relationship was defined between governance and accounting in an entity which emerged from a complex merger.

Adopting the Accounting and Power Framework

In recent years the idea was generally accepted of introducing a critical perspective in designing accounting history studies. Accounting history is both "intellectual" and "utilitarian", and the topic we manage is contemporarily the evidence of this dichotomous relevance. It is "intellectual" from the perspective from which we want to understand the process of the transformation that led to a massive change, with the transition from a system of hospitals essentially based on private contributions to a system based on public financing, even if power remained in the hands of the most representative exponents of higher societal classes. It is "utilitarian" from the perspective that, once both origins and causes of a phenomenon are clarified, it could provide a key to understanding contemporary facts (American Accounting Association, 1970).

The distinction between *old accounting history* and *new accounting history* was finally superseded by a clear adoption of the latter approach. From this perspective scholars "are more likely to see accounting as an instrument of power and domination than as a value-free body of ideas and techniques for putting into effect and monitoring contracts freely entered into between equals" (Carnegie and Napier, 1996: 7–8).

The central claim of this approach from a methodological point of view requires a clear identification of a framework according to which an accounting history research is conceived and conducted. At a social level, accounting is recognized as influential and it functions in a multitude of different and ever changing institutional areas.

This shared thinking makes the idea of accounting as an influencing factor also applicable in past epochs. Even in this space of analysis, accounting seem to plays a decisive role, by offering many uses that are normally linked to its functional attributes, such as providing relevant "information for decision making", fostering the achievement of a "rational allocation of resources", and maintaining and enforcing institutional "accountability" and "stewardship" (Burchell *et al.*, 1980: 5).

Among the many frameworks available to provide a critical narration of the establishment of the Venice hospital (e.g., Foucauldian perspectives, such as governmentality and contingency theory) we believe that the *accounting and power* framework could allow us to enter deeper into this story and to learn how this hospital was created (Gendron and Baker, 2005).

Within the accounting and power framework the observation of the organizational order and its interactions with the social context in which it operates, using a "diachronic" analysis of accounting systems, is already well recognized in other literature contributions. These commonly enhance discussion of the relationship between accounting and power in developing organizations (Hopwood, 1987; Giovannoni and Riccaboni, 2009). The role of accounting as a power tool is unmistakable, and much has been said on "how" accounting can help to strengthen government forms and stimulate an adequate process of accountability. Accounting, however, assumes political and administrative features in the analysis of relationships between power and governance (Mennicken and Miller, 2012).

In its belonging to the "critical accounting" approach, the paradigm is considered to give a biased contribution to the interpretation of the facts, through the combination of the narrative with the interpretation of accounting records. These are mostly found beyond a social practice tool able to influence the decisions in a particular system, as well as in this case by addressing organizational change (Hopwood and Miller, 1994).

"One should power where is exercised over individuals rather than legitimated at centre; explore the actual practices of subjugation rather then the intentions that guide attempts at domination" (Jessop, 2007: 36).

The accounting and power framework concerns "how" accounting is used for governance and, vice versa, "how" accounting can drive governance. This can also be attributed to the observation of "reciprocal relationships between and within two loosely assembled sets of practices", typically in the relationship between public institutions and accounting (Miller, 1990: 316). This theoretical framework highlights "how accounting systems can play an active role in shaping organizational activities and interactions, as well as in the production and maintenance of power" (Riccaboni *et al.*, 2006: 45).

A large body of literature has intervened in this area, proposing a narration of different cases in which it is possible to identify a link between power and accounting, and this could be related to the situation in which power has influenced how the accounting system is defined and operated and, on the contrary, how accounting has found a way to resist this exercise of power. For the reasons outlined, we believe that the episodes that have been discovered in the audit trail, in the manner and for the sequence in which they occurred, can be interpreted as the true key elements of the Venice hospital building.

Methodology

The main question in this research was, "What were the most significant events contributing to the establishment of the Venice hospital Santi Giovanni e Paolo?"

Due to this major question, other subsequent questions have arisen with regard to causes and effects (Boys and Freear,1976). The historical document analysis leads us, in fact, to determine that the prelude of the Venetian hospital Santi Giovanni e Paolo can be found in the succession of episodes that since 1777 have determined the fortunes of the hospital's assistance, across different historical periods until the independence of Italy, within the space of almost one century.

So the main aim of the study is to understand "how", through the historical context and accounting information relating to the crucial steps in change, it is possible to determine the balance generated by the government of public institutions, in healthcare and hospitals. This is intended to investigate both the degree of evolution and refinement of the accounting systems as their ability to provoke organizational tensions (Hopwood, 1987), especially in the course of the consequent changes, which resulted in the fusion of the pre-existing institutions, by highlighting enabling conditions and resistance factors.

More specifically we address our attention to the particular phase in which the Venice hospital Santi Giovanni e Paolo emerged as a result of a complex process of merger and the power at the top and if this hospital defined its governance and consequently defined its accounting system on the ashes of the pre-existing governance structure and accounting systems (Brown, 2014). The analysis of this creative period could shed light on an intriguing situation—that is, the phenomena related to a process of merger. The questions are as follows:

- Who gets the power during a merger process?
- How is the new power in a merger process able to cancel the pre-existing powers and define a new governance structure and its mechanisms?
- What is the interrelationship between the new governance and the characteristics of the newly built accounting system?

The establishment of the Venice hospital and the accounting and power framework could offer an opportunity to address these research questions. The specific focus on the effects of a merger process represents a particular view not fully covered in the existing literature. In order to answer the foregoing research questions, a first screening was based upon the identification of available primary sources.

Over time, these were scattered in different places, but the most significant collections are now at the State Archive of Venice (*Archivio di Stato di Venezia*, AVE) and at the Archive of Hospitalization and Education Institutes (*Archivio degli Istituti di Ricovero ed Educazione*, IRE), a charity whose history is intimately linked to the development of healthcare and charity in Venice (Grandi, 2002).

This study comprises different approaches, by moving along the narrative and interpretational dimensions (Previts *et al.*, 1990a; 1990b). The narrative attitude is used for the illustration of the crucial events that steadily led to the creation of the Venetian hospital, taking into account the role played by the main actors, whereas the interpretive analysis is used to explore both causes and effects of the events by means of the outputs of documents found, such as accounting books, declarations and minutes of meetings (Hopwood, 1983; Roberts and Scapens, 1985). In this chapter the most useful methodology is the examination of actual records and documents, and the analysis of written sources and secondary source material.

The methodology that has enabled us to develop the research was based on the following steps:

- Reconstruction of the historical context in which the events took place, by analysing previous research with a prevailing historiographical approach;
- Access to documents of the superintendents/magistrates on hospitals and holy places of the *Serenissima* Republic (*Provveditori sopra Ospitali e Luoghi Pii*), kept at the AVE and at the IRE archive;
- Analysis of account books of the years from 1776 to 1794, in particular the "common cash" of the four major hospitals (*Cassa Union Quatro Ospitali*", 1776–1794), which can be considered the originating documents of the financial unification of the four hospitals. According to the rules of a normal cash-basis accounting, receipts and expenses are shown for each hospital;
- Consultation of the balance sheets of the four hospitals (*Bilanzi Union 4 Ospitali principali*, 1777–1786); the four hospitals were the Derelicts (*Derelitti*), the Panhandlers (*Mendicanti*), the Incurables (*Incurabili*) and the Mercy (*Pietà*);
- Consultation of the book of charity containing the list of the most important rules and norms of the *Serenissima* Republic from the late eighteenth to the entire nineteenth century;
- Consultation of registers of processes recording cases and debates between administrators and various subjects and organizations;
- Examination of matriculation lists, presenting the updated list of members, the years of membership and the function covered in the confraternity;
- Consultation of books of tenants and freed tenants, identifying each tenant, distinguishing between real estate and land rented out, and periodical payments received;
- Consultation of some historiographical works to better understand the facts and evaluate implications regarding political choices.

The Accounting perspective gave us the opportunity to examine the causes which led to the financial crisis of the four major hospitals and to their progressive union in a single hospital, as an event that drove the transformation of the healthcare system of the *Serenissima* Republic from a private system to a predominantly public one (Colquhoun, and Parker, 2012).

Consisting merely of four different epochs, this construction of events for the establishment of the Venetian hospital is actually the result of a succession of government decisions, for each epoch, which are bound to important economic and financial dynamics, where a key role is assigned to both *accounting records* and the *exercise of power*. Accounting and (the exercise of) power have, therefore, emerged again, demonstrating that, in particular regarding the facts of government dealing with common good and society, accounting information plays a much-needed role in decision making (Coronella et al., 2012).

Venetian Hospitals Across Different Ages

The topic discussed cannot be far away from the idea that the time range being taken under consideration contains several important steps that marked the political, economic and social life of the *Serenissima* Republic. In a certain sense, we can affirm that the end of the *Serenissima* Republic coincided with the end of private healthcare organizations, including great supporters such as senior clergy, dignitaries and prominent citizens over the centuries. Thus they delivered to succeeding generations a system whose principles and values still exist, by empowering government forces, in the belief that the growth of civil society cannot take place without the circumstantial development of forms of protection of both the moral and physical health of individuals. Therefore, in order to build those steps that led to the establishment of the Venice hospital and investigate the main reasons, it's necessary to understand the environment where the initiative developed, and the institutions and individuals who contributed to this development.

An initial consideration is about the way in which healthcare assistance functioned in the *Serenissima* Republic at that time. Since its inception, healthcare assistance in Venice had its own story, because, in the political configuration of the *Serenissima* Republic, the "pious causes" were in a specific position between three main contributing protagonists, the aristocratic power, wealthy Venetian merchants and the Church. As shown by documents and literature, the dispute was deeper between the secular nature of the republic and the Catholic conscience of the same people who founded, managed and maintained, with their legacies and wills, the pious places. For this reason, the charitable institution, created by the Counter-Reformation, is the right compromise and the triumph of the care for the common good (Ellero, 1987).

Thus, in spite of the roots of Venetian philanthropy, which are traced to traditional guidelines by the government, in the late eighteenth century, hospital care was managed mainly by private organizations.

In 1766, Venice had a population of 140,256 inhabitants, with 1,476 under the poverty level, once the distinction between poor, beggars and patients for the hospitals was overcome and all inpatients fell into the latter category (Beloch, 1994: 401). The "structural" poor people in Venice were in their large hospitals and charitable institutes, but the economic decline of the *Serenissima* Republic excluded the "cyclical" poor, the unemployed and those having the habit of almsgiving. These last ones were not only Venetian citizens but also those who came from nearby provinces and other states.

Over time, among the most important organizations, some institutions gained a certain reputation—in particular the four major hospitals:

1. Incurables (*Incurabili*);
2. Derelicts (*Derelitti*);
3. Panhandlers (*Mendicanti*);
4. Mercy (*Pietà*).

Furthermore, other institutions were acting with complementary functions, mainly run by religious orders. The major hospitals were responsible for the hospitalization system, education and general care, being aimed at a large number of people. These were differently treated, depending on age, health conditions and gender. The welfare system, in fact, had grown in the sixteenth century as a part of the new spirit of Catholic reform, through the work of religious people as well as Gerolamo Emiliani, Ignazio Di Loyola, Francesco Saverio and others, by addressing it to those in need and the sick, even creating large hospitals. The numbers fluctuated between 1,500 and 1,600, the *Incurabili*, *Mendicanti* and *Derelitti* hospitals being each able to receive not less than 400 inpatients by counting both patients and orphans.

Thus, different people were cared for in each hospital, including syphilitic patients at the Incurables (*Incurabili*), any kind of feverish people at the Derelicts (*Derelitti*), and beggars at the Panhandlers (*Mendicanti*).

In each hospital orphans were also accepted, under healthy and/or poor conditions, so that they were indoctrinated according to Catholic principles and then were educated in reading, writing and arithmetic. The hospitals were administered by congregations of governors (*Congregazione*), composed of almost forty people, half belonging to the patrician class and the other half to the merchant category. By means of agents or ministers, the governors had to provide for all the needs of patients by means of an efficient management of considerable donations and legacies that the pious places received from different parties and private benefactors (Prieto et.al., 2006; Moggi et al., 2016).

There were numerous legacies and testamentary bequests for the congregations of the religious places in exchange for indulgences. The most common phrase within the testamentary documents is "I leave for my soul an amount of ducats" and the amount given ("*lascio per la mia anima ducati . . . ammontare*"). These are contained in the register called a cadaster (*catastico*), which represents a collection of private documents with the objective of collecting bequests (ASV Ospedali e Luoghi Pii, 890). The bound documents (*filze*) are characterized by the presence in alphabetical order of all parties concerned because of legacies and their amount.

The Four Major Hospitals' Financial Administration

During the middle of the seventeenth century, the governors of the *Serenissima* Republic decided to resort to taking out such loans "*a livello*", so implying that the beneficiary of the loan would be obligated to repay the capital after a fixed period of time.

In this way, hospitals had functions similar to those of a modern savings bank, enticed by the guarantee of substantial deposits by the Republic Mint, which the "holy places" (*luoghi pii*) supported by encouraging Venetian and foreign investors; they were promised a yearly mild interest which was normally considered safer than that offered by traditional banks. The revenues collected were also called—in the Veneto region—*levels*, *census* or *rentals*

(Corazzol, 1979, 1986; Lorenzini, 2009). The term "livello", in particular, could refer to either an agrarian pact or a credit transaction. The *livello affrancabile* was a loan agreement where the borrower, in exchange for the sum of money received, gave the lender his property in the form of guarantees and agreed to pay an annual rent to the lender. By a certain deadline, the borrower could redeem the *livello* by returning the capital received and take ownership of the real estate; otherwise the lender could take possession of the mortgaged property. In the section of revenue of the *Union of Hospitals* we can observe, for instance, the different categories.

The formula adopted was similar to the census annuity (*censo*), with the renunciation by the lender (creditor) to refund the sum granted to the borrower (the congregation), and the provision agreed upon by the borrower of an annual interest. Another feature was about the census (*censo*) distinguished in *censo consegnativo* and *censo riservativo*.

The *censo consegnativo* was similar to the *livello* and was used as a legal credit instrument and also assumed the name of *censo bollare*. According to the criteria imposed by the Church, the interest rate could not exceed 7%, and the goods (land or building) on which the loan was based had to be composed of a property able to generate an income. Finally, the borrower was given the possibility of redeeming the census by returning the capital received. The *censo consegnativo* is a credit instrument widely used in Italy and also in some provinces of the Marciana Republic (Lorenzini, 2009). By the *census riservativo*, a subject gave away real estate, while reserving the right to collect an annual income. This formula did not foresee the return of the capital borrowed (Alonzi, 2005).

More precisely there were two categories of creditors/capitalists. The first category was "capitalists with an annual income", and the second was "capitalists heritor" (*ad heredes*), aiming at handing down the capital to their heirs.

In fact, the hospital institutions were based on a broader system of private care and charity that had initiated within the wealthy classes and had a kind of self-regulation. In this setting, four major hospitals located in different areas of the city were able to distinguish themselves. Ahead is a brief overview of the four major Venetian hospitals, in order to give an understanding of their development, success and status in the final act of the *Serenissima* Republic.

Overview of the Major Hospitals

As mentioned before, the four hospitals operating in the *Serenissima* Republic and involved in the merging process we have examined in this study, highlighting how accounting was used by the Venetian Senate to drive the creation of a unique Hospital entity, were the following: *Pietà* Hospital, *Incurabili* Hospital, *Mendicanti* Hospital and *Derelitti* Hospital. In this section we propose just an overview of their respective establishments, histories and specificities (Chambers, 2001).

Pietà Hospital

It was founded in 1346, through the work of fund raising aiming at saving illegal and abandoned children. The promoter of this initiative was the Franciscan friar *Petruchio* of Assisi and the institution's name derives from the fact that the Franciscan friar collected funds by shouting on the road, "Mercy, mercy!" (*Pietà, pietà!*). The hospital came under the protection of the head of the republic (the doge) from 1353, but at the same time the government of the republic gave out severe penalties for those abandoning their children. The republic contributed by subsidies, consisting of a percentage of the amount of duties and penal fines.

In terms of position, the first location consisted of seventeen houses owned by the noblewoman Lucrezia Dolfin in a different place from what eventually became the permanent seat, during the sixteenth century, when it was considered to be one of the four major hospitals, with the aim of offering admissions to unhappy children, those born from concubinage and/or those rejected by their parents.

Incurabili Hospital

It was founded around 1520 and was originally intended to assist syphilitic patients as well as other similar hospitals in other important cities. The Venetian hospital was supported by Gaetano Thiene and others, before 1522, and quickly won the support of the state (Meijers, 1989: 57). In 1522 the supervisors of health care took care of the syphilis problem by ordering all sick people to leave Venice, or to enter into the *Incurabili* Hospital (ASV, Sanità, reg. 2, c. 31v, 22 February 1522). This hospital expanded its activities, opening the doors to patients affected by other chronic ills which were considered dangerous for the community. Unlike small medieval institutions, this hospital had been founded by a group of benefactors who soon had organized congregations of governors, and had obtained recognition from the republic, as it fulfilled valuable public functions. In 1524 the hospital already had 80 patients, both men and women, who in 1525 increased to 150. The hospital had its own personnel, medical staff and pharmacists. Moreover, also within this hospital an important orphanage was instituted. At the end of the century, a full program of building work led to the construction of wards for both male and female patients, and, in 1601, a hospital pharmacy was built.

Mendicanti Hospital

The origin of this pious institution dates back to the thirteenth century, when the Venetian veterans from Syria returned home, bringing leprosy with them (Bamji et al., 2015).

Nevertheless, the Senate of the republic founded this institution after explicit recommendation of a commission of superintendents/magistrates (*Provveditori sopra ospedali e luoghi pii*). It was, therefore, the result of a striving effort—carried out in the late sixteenth century—in order to completely eradicate all kinds of beggars in the streets of the town and inside the churches. An exception was made only for blind people. Once leprosy was reduced, the Senate ordered, in 1591, that all unnecessary annuities should be used for other pious activities. So the hospital began to place scabby and chronic patients together with old and helpless beggars. Once the needs of the poor lepers and sick people were met, the finances were used for beggars (from which the hospital derives its name).

In 1600 the institute obtained the new larger premises of Santi Giovanni e Paolo, and in the following decades hosted up to 400 patients at once (Pullan, 1971). Among the most generous funders who contributed to the erection of the new hospital were two rich merchants, Bartolomeo Bontempelli and Domenico Biava. The first donated 50,000 ducats, and ordered a *post-mortem* legacy of 100,000 ducats; the second one bestowed 80,000 ducats.

For funding this institution, the revenues of the medieval *San Lazzaro* Hospital were reassigned to the new hospital. As a consequence, the *Mendicanti* Hospital obtained finances for medical purposes, and its directors committed themselves to giving priority to those who were affected by St. Lazarus's disease (this is the name of leprosy); the hospital intended to include patients with not just leprosy but also other skin diseases, especially mange.

Derelitti Hospital (Ospedale Santi Giovanni e Paolo, Hospedaletto)

There are several doubts about the year of its foundation. It is certain that in 1527, for a charity initiative of Bartolomeo Marco, Luigi Marzari and Bartolomeo Boniparte, exactly where today the Venetian hospital complex is located, a hospital was built for poor peasants arriving in Venice because of the famine. The hospice, which was originally called *Spedaletto*, was named *Santa Maria dei Derelitti* in 1527, when Friar Pellegrino Asti from Vicenza and Friar Girolamo Miani added orphans and destitute old people. Since 1542, the hospital took care of the poor sick people of Venice and also from outside; also it offered accommodation and protection to orphans, widows and other poor. In 1569 the registered office was enlarged, so as to expand the scope of its charitable activities. In 1571 a neighbouring property was bought by allowing the opening of a new medical ward, designed to accommodate convalescents, patients with wounds (ASV, Sanità, Reg. 13 cc. 589–91).

From the functioning profile, the numbers are fluctuating, but at the end of the sixteenth century and at the beginning of the next century, the *Incurabili*,

Mendicanti and *Derelitti* hospitals were able to accommodate at least 400 in-patients, by including poor, sick people and orphans. The fundamental reasons for setting up the healthcare and welfare system were actually three. The first reason was the "public order", the second was the "care of the disease" and, finally, the third was the "economy".

Public order would mean stability and it is well known that, in the most important European cities, since 1500, there was a movement for the rationalization of increasing assistance to poor, sick persons and orphans that involved the regulation. Thus, systematic efforts were made for conveying the revenues arising from duties and taxes to those persons most deserving as well as destitute and, above all, resident people.

For achieving this goal, there were often agreements for gathering resources from charity and donations, in order to be entrusted in the distribution of public officials. These initiatives coincided, undoubtedly, with the beginning of reform. The practice of charity was not simply an act of altruism but remained a means by which the soul of the benefactor gained value. One of the main Italian characteristics—more precisely of the individual Italian states, such as the *Serenissima* Republic—was that most cities maintained large hospitals, while in Venice hospitals were much less interesting in terms of dimensions. Despite having different places (hospices, nursing homes, hospitals), such as the *Vecchio Lazaretto* and the *Nuovo Lazaretto*, for the prevention and treatment of plague, and important institutions for the housing of orphans, Venice did not have a large hospital that would serve the general needs of the poor.

So, *Incurabili* Hospital and *Derelitti* Hospital were the result of an initiative driven by religious reasons of members of both the aristocracy and citizen class, supported by representatives of the Catholic reform movement of the sixteenth century (Meijers, 1989: 57).

The private initiative was ratified by the authority in charge of public health (the "magistrate for healthcare") that decreed that all people suffering from syphilis had to be hospitalized in the new hospital. In this way, the decision received public legitimacy and the hospital of *Incurabili* arose as the first general hospital for the whole city. The hospital was built in the south and was especially the living space of the people; it held an important economic role with other institutions, such as the salt warehouses and customs. In 1528, some people offered accommodation to the poor sick who roamed the city, almost on the verge of starvation, because of famine. They were grouped into a laboratory of stonecutters, located behind the choir of the Santi Giovanni e Paolo church, in the northern part of the city. The Venetian government tried to overcome this temporary crisis through the new law, providing a construction of large wooden shelters scattered around the city, just for poor. In such a way the Church of Santi Giovanni e Paolo received the financial resources to build a temporary shed.

Figure 7.1 shows how the four hospitals were operating in different areas and islands of Venice.

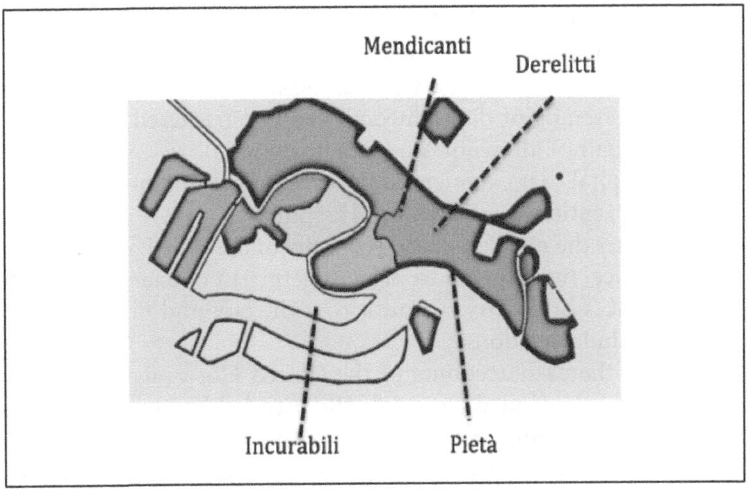

Figure 7.1 Map of the four hospitals

The Financial Crisis of the Four Major Hospitals in the Accounting Books and the Balance of Power

At the end of 1700, because of a series of adverse circumstances in financial administration, three of the four hospitals (*Incurabili*, *Derelitti* and *Mendicanti*) were on the verge of bankruptcy. Since then, the end of an era began and would culminate with the merger of the existing structures and the establishment of the single large hospital, Santi Giovanni e Paolo. For this reason, this study has sought to investigate what occurred during the transition from one government to another, the role of the main actors and the causes of change. Any explanation about these elements is supported by the relevant facts contained in the accounting books and other useful documents.

What happened in the Venetian hospitals was inextricably linked to the governments would succeed and that, in different ways, would strive for reorganization. In particular, it would be the last foreshortening of the *Serenissima* Republic until the Provisional Municipality (1797–1798), the first Austrian government (1798–1805), the annexation of the Napoleonic Kingdom of Italy (1806–1814) and the second Austrian government (1814–1866). Inside the collection of documents and records on assistance and charity of the municipality of Venice, the epochs are distinguished respectively according to the following periodization:

1. Aristocratic epoch;
2. First Austrian epoch;
3. Italian period;
4. Second Austrian period (coinciding with the second Austrian government until the unification of Italy).

The excessive reliance by the hospital's governors on conventional management practice based on testamentary insurance forms, together with the reduction of private donations, was among the principal causes which, in the last foreshortening of the eighteenth century, triggered a financial crisis for more than half of all major Venetian hospitals.

The first hospital that experienced the crisis and, consequently, required a particular intervention was *Incurabili* Hospital.

For some years the most practised economy of the state had tried to reform the public service, by planning to bring together in one large establishment the various places of charity spread across the city and divided into many autonomous administrations.

Throughout the cash accounts of the United Hospitals (*Cassa*) and the balance sheets of the United Hospitals (*Bilanzi dell'Unione degli Ospedali*), we have found emerging criticalities. The *Bilanzi* contain collections and payments, kept on two different pages, made by the United Hospitals, while *Cassa* contains the sheets showing debits and credits of the hospitals in their separate specialties to the same United Hospitals accounts.

As evidenced by the documents, the most financially exposed hospital was, undoubtedly, *Incurabili* Hospital. In practice, the entire income and the full amount of the hospital's capital were under sequestration by depositors, or "capitalists".

According to a review of existing documentation and other previous detailed studies, administrators did not realize the gravity of the situation (Pelizza, 1997: 138). Some fuzzy signals are found among the resolutions of the congregation—for example, in January and February 1775, where the need to make some economies and cost savings is completely unmistakable. Documentary texts highlight the alarm of governors because of the decreased amount of money received as lifetime mortgages in the hospital treasury. However, the sense of an accurate perception of the danger threatening the hospital's survival is not clear.

The repayment of debts had generated additional debt, so the revenues and the total annual revenues were no longer sufficient to pay the interest due to creditors and the payment had been suspended. At this point, any attempt to stop the legal actions of creditors failed.

The balance sheet of the *Hospitals Union* consisted of two prospects: on the left, the total amount of collections, and on the right side the full amount of payments. For each period the accounting records start on 1 March and end on 1 March of the next year. The style of the balance sheet is "narrative-type" and "cash accounting"–based, with the amount of the surplus of the previous year as a first. The incomes are collections made using the cash union where the amounts are derived from legates, pros, rents and deposits out of and in the State Mint. An important detail of the Hospitals Union's balance sheet shows the movements recorded by each hospital towards the Hospitals Union and vice versa. The total amounts are confirmed by the other documents—for instance, in the cash account of the Hospitals Union

(*Cassa Unione degli Ospedali/Scontro*), where each movement is explained with its reason. On the top left, it's possible to read *Cassa retroscritta Deve Dar* and on the top of the right sheet *Cassa controscritta Deve Aver*, according to the rules of a single-entry system. According to the documents that were analysed, there was a perceptible financial crisis in two hospitals, *Incurabili* and *Mendicanti*, given that certain collections were reported to be partly inhibited by creditors. Usually, the sentence adopted was: *in forza degli atti dei creditori del pio luogo*.

There is also a paper attached that shows the debts and credits of the hospitals in their different specializations towards the Hospitals Union (*il debito e il credito degli ospedali nella loro separata spezialità verso l'Unione*).

The first real signs of the financial crisis occurred at *Incurabili* Hospital in 1776, when Marcantonio Priuli, Gerolamo Venier and Giacomo Rizzo were presidents of the "holy place" (*Pio Luogo*) or congregation. At that point, the congregation solicited the work of bookkeeper (*quaderniere*) Pietro Rossi, because he could draw up a balance sheet (Pelizza, 1997). The order was to extend "an exact balance sheet about the revenues and debts" by separating the natural income of the pious place from bequests (*commissarie*), and distinguishing capital *ad he*redes (capital to be assigned to the heirs) from annuities and notes of credits.

On 17 March 1777, the congregation determined to submit to the Senate a petition/request, due to the increase of additional debt, failing to find a solution to meet the pressing demands of creditors. The hospital had entered a vicious circle, since the need to pay an annual interest to those creditors who had deposited their capital (at the same hospital) had forced administrators of *Incurabili* Hospital to increasingly search for new loans. These had been granted, given the confidence of the hospital's solvency, but they had ended up ruining the finances of the pious institution. On 15 April 1777, the congregation of *Incurabili* established that the three inquisitors appointed in the meantime, Nicholas Bon, Zuanne Ruzzini and Marcantonio Priuli, had to hold the legal representation of the congregation and in relations with the *Provveditori sopra ospedali e luoghi pii* (superintendents/magistrates of hospitals and pious institutions), Paolo Girolamo Spinelli, Francesco Angaran and Marin Garzoni, appointed by the Senate of the *Serenissima* Republic, in order to take care of the pious institutions' crisis with creditors *ad haeredes* and annuities.

The first time, the Senate intervened with the Decree of 31 May 1777, which transferred the sum of 3,000 ducats from the charitable fund to that of the superintendents/magistrates of hospitals and pious institutions (*Provveditori sopra ospedali e luoghi pii*), because they were paying, in turn, to the governors of *Incurabili* Hospital. It is remarkable to note the activation of a form of control in such a way that there was a guarantee that the sums were actually paid (ASV, *Provveditori sopra ospedali e luoghi pii, busta* 1, *capitolare* II).

Such an action can historically be considered as the first real intervention by the government of the *Serenissima* Republic in the healthcare financing system. From this initiative, it will gradually become public. The audits by the Senate intensified, by the three superintendents/magistrates, which soon were able to have an effective synopsis of the financial situation.

There was an annual imbalance between expenditure and receipts of 10,083 ducats (*grossi* 6), but apart from the most sensational expenditure item and which was absolutely impossible to meet. It was the yearly burden of 94,004 ducats (*grossi* 16) for the interest to pay to capitalists and annuities to *ad haeredes*. The overall extent of the imbalance was then around 104,000 ducats a year (ASV, *Provveditori sopra ospedali e luoghi pii, busta* 3). In the light of these data the same contribution made by the Senate seemed small compared to the real needs.

So, it was necessary to take new measures to prevent a deteriorated situation. To this end, the Senate strengthened the powers of the three superintendents/magistrates and tried to obtain the release from seizure of the revenues of the hospital that had been frozen by creditors. It also entrusted the superintendents/magistrates themselves with the task of soliciting the congregation to draw up a plan for hospital maintenance.

By a careful reading of the book of *Provveditori sopra ospedali e luoghi pii* (superintendents/magistrates), we can argue that the Venetian Senate encouraged the bailout (financial rescue) and the financial restoration of the hospital, but with a minimum damage for private capitalists and at no cost for the mint.

As often happens in these situations, the voices of a possible hospital failure had an impact on other hospitals, whose financial strength began to waver. The affair of *Incurabili* Hospital, with the suspension of payments of the interests of creditors, and with the subsequent acts by them, also alarmed the creditors of other hospitals. The events triggered a chain reaction, according to which also the creditors of *Mendicanti* Hospital, and consequently the creditors of *Derelitti* Hospital, got alarmed and demanded all together the restitution of their loans. The congregation of *Mendicanti* Hospital therefore decided to submit a request to the Senate, although the situation was less dramatic than that of *Incurabili* Hospital.

It should be noticed that, in some cases, a person could have depositories in more hospitals, so maybe in one this person acted as a capitalist with annuities, and in another as a capitalist *ad haeredes*.

As a result, on 1 September 1777 *Mendicanti* Hospital was subjected to a bankruptcy procedure for a debt of 717,487 ducats, while *Derelitti* Hospital, after taking into consideration different solutions, in 1780 tried to save it by applying a *Tondina* plan with creditors. The fourth largest hospital, *La Pietà*, was in better condition.

In the case of *Mendicanti* Hospital, in March 1777, the imbalance was considerable, and the congregation had tried to prosecute the debtors by trying "to reduce the gap between income and expenses" (Historical Archive of Institutions for Hospitalization and Education, IRE Arch, *busta* MEN G 2).

The propagation of fear about non-repayment had caused a bank run for the reimbursement of funds lent by capitalists, by putting the congregation in a frantic state.

Faced with a complex annual income of about 19,000 ducats—of which 13,000 was conditioned by the will of the testator—*Mendicanti* Hospital had a total amount of expenses for the maintenance of the patients, the levels, perpetual legacies, celebrations of masses (*mansionerie*), taxes and wages for the crew and for the choir of about 18,000 ducats. The actual burden depended on the need to pay creditors annual interest, for a total amount of 36,000 ducats. The hospital's annual imbalance was thus roughly 35,000. At the suggestion of lawyers, hospital administrators decided to pay the instalment of the biannual interest to creditors, amounting to 12,439.90 ducats. However, even this intervention was useless. They had been in office during the mandates of four presidents Gabriel Marcello, Marin Gheltof, Marin Corniani, Maria Biffi.

In the case of *Derelitti* Hospital, superintendents/magistrates had found a financially disastrous situation because the debts amounted to about 260,000 ducats, of which 135,000 was borrowed for capital, compared to total assets of 227,000 ducats. In this case, other than excessive indebtedness, there was also the expenditure for the family—that is, sons and daughters of the institution. The plan called for an immediate freeze of acceptance of new daughters and sons, as well as a somewhat narrow range of savings on food, on clothing and also on *mansionerie*.

During 1779, the situation worsened since in the meantime providers had rejected the hospital governors' request about withdrawing 15,000 ducats from deposits to meet the interest payments on debts.

The refusal was justified by the fact that such a levy would decrease the institution's annuities. The Senate decided to intervene and determined to make another payment of 3,000 ducats, drawing on the "cash charities". It was an emergency solution, which led *Provveditori sopra ospedali e luoghi pii* to develop a comprehensive and decisive plan. This is shown by the correspondence with the Senate containing the overall assessments and advice on particular issues, also from superintendents/magistrates in their personal—and not collegial—capacity (in this period the superintendents/magistrates were: Zuanne Zusto, Marin Garzoni and Giulio Antonio Contarini). The idea of using the revenues from free capital and/or bound by the hospital testers in order to satisfy creditors was not considered sustainable, since the state wanted to guarantee the principle of inalienability for testamentary heritage destinations.

In fact, the state became the guarantor of contracts and legal instruments that had been perfected in accordance with proper means that the law offered throughout the duration of the crisis. The state took on the guise of equidistant supervisor, but also that of a generous benefactor of the four hospitals that were shed by particular funds as well as *Asse gesuitico*, *Cassa opere pie* and *Aggiunto sopra monasteri* and by funds of the superintendents/magistrates with generous amounts until 1797. Therefore, the Senate chose to proceed towards the agreement between hospitals and creditors for a balancing of the respective needs. At the same time, a commission on deputies to charitable causes (*Deputati ad pias causas*), composed of both hospitals' and providers' representatives, was charged with studying subsidy measures and finding new sources of revenue funding for the holy places' citizens (ASV, *Provv sopra osp. e luoghi pii, busta* 1, *Decreto* 21 *Agosto* 1779).

Finally the fourth hospital, *Pietà*, showed the best performance. To cope with the payments, hospital administrators withdrew funds gradually from the mint, thus provoking a decrease in revenues for the maintenance of the patients.

Provveditori sopra ospedali e luoghi pii, in their new guise of supervisors of Venetian hospital affairs, also intervened on the issue by declaring their opinion in the Senate with the letter of 2 October 1777 (ASV, *Provveditori sopra ospedali e luoghi pii, busta* 3).

Specifically, the *Provveditori* signalled that the withdrawal of sums by the agents had become more frequent and therefore demanded an intervention by the government of the *Serenissima* Republic.

Since that event, a dialogue started among supervisors of Venetian hospital affairs and the Senate, albeit with some interruptions. This dialogue lasted until 1797. In fact, the episodes of instability led to exert considerable pressure on the Senate. Senators appointed the superintendents to foster the administrators of *Mendicanti* Hospital in developing programs and measures to cope with the imbalance and the seizures blocking annuities, and also in order to develop a cost-cutting plan.

The Senate declared explicitly that the protection of Venice hospitals was of public interest, but this protection had to be reconciled with the intention to "bring especially the innocent capitalists at the highest possible safe status" (*ricondurre specialmente gli innocenti capitalisti allo stato della maggior possibile sicurezza*).

As a consequence superintendents who were working on the restoration plan for *Incurabili* Hospital were commissioned to develop a similar project for *Mendicanti* Hospital. Both the Senate and superintendents realized that it was necessary in any case to draw up a broader plan, and so the Senate authorized them to request the cooperation of anyone who had ideas on the subject. There were many suggestions made by several citizens (e.g., begging in the state Veneto, use of the overlaps of the Great Schools, establishment of a lottery, additional taxes, a new *Tondina* project, a mixed lottery; *questue nello Stato Veneto, utilizzazione dei sopravanzi delle Scuole Grandi, istituzione di una lotteria, tasse aggiuntive, nuovo progetto di tondina, lotteria mista*).

Among the various emerging proposals, one in particular caught the attention of the supervisors. This was the proposal by Girolamo Gillioli regarding the union of the four major hospitals in one large building and administrative structure, to be placed precisely in the area currently occupied by the civil hospital.

This proposal seemed to be viable, focusing on grouping and a more functional reorganization of the Venetian healthcare system. As shown in the documents, the proposal was inspired by the great metropolises as usual in the main capitals of Europe with a large hospital. In 1780 there were apparently some positive developments since the Senate approved the recovery plan prepared by the administrators of *Mendicanti* Hospital.

In this case, they drew up a maintenance program aiming at a factual return to the origins—that is, to stick to the choices of conduct of the institutions, dating back about 150 years earlier. In the same year the senators approved the most organic plan of agreement, jointly proposed by the governors of *Derelitti* Hospital with the majority of capitalists who had deposited their money there.

The plan was called *Piano di Tondina* and provided that annuities would be reunited into five groups, according to their different ages. From the financial point of view, it provided that the hospital paid each of these categories the interest on the total capital amount that the group members had originally placed in the hospital. This meant that as people belonging to each group died, the perceived interest of the deceased could be divided among the other associates.

Finally, the last survivor of a group would have received the entire amount destined for it. Interest paid would have been different, depending on the age of the participants. For those under the age of 50 years, 3.5%; for those aged between 50 and 60 years, 4%; for those between the ages of 60 and 70 years, 4.5%; from 70 to 75 years, 5%. The interest paid to groups of creditors would be derived from the capital held, in any way, by the hospital in the public mint.

For creditors *ad haeredes* was proposed the payment of interest, drawn from the same source, curtailed from 3% to 2%. The prediction was that the class of younger creditors would be extinguished by 1847, leaving the hospital free from any constraint. The project, despite having weaknesses, allowed the hospital to save itself from the disaster that had involved the other two institutions. The only problem was that many creditors did not want to adhere to this agreement and obtained several judgments in their favour. Therefore, the solution was, in fact, applied until 1806, with very limited effects.

Pietà Hospital deserves separate consideration. In this case the problem persisted and the annual imbalance of 1776 was 32,000 ducats. In 1778, after the first government subsidies, the debt was decreased by 24,000 ducats. The debts to capitalists were smaller than other hospitals, and were secured by the massive amount of stable reserves owned by the hospital. The senators of the republic had allowed the withdrawal of all the sums required by the congregation of governors, so that they could use them for the hospital's temporary sustenance. However, the hospital's situation worsened between 1782 and 1787, when the institution was administered by Father Marchetti. In this case, the Senate established (decree of 30 May 1789) the extraordinary temporary magistrate of the two "deputies" (*deputati alla regolazione dell'ospitale della pietà*), suitably for the regulation of

Pietà Hospital, who were assigned the task of revising accounts, to draw up a precise budget for the annuities, income and expenses, and to elaborate a comprehensive "plan" for general discipline, but also for the individual duties of each administrator operating within the institution.

Different Policies and One Direction in the Hospitals' Reorganization

The crisis of the four major hospitals, as documented, led to the first major proposal aimed at reorganizing hospital care in the republic. This proposal included the aggregation of the four major hospitals, which had already created an institution representing them (the Union), which was approved by the Senate of the republic by a decree of 24 March 1784. Despite its appeal, the proposal was withdrawn in the following month by a decree of the Senate of 23 April 1784.

The congregations of governors of both *Mendicanti* Hospital and *Incurabili* Hospital had dismissed and no longer renewed the new admissions of guests/patients. Subsequently, the survival of the major hospitals, including *Pietà* Hospital, was guaranteed by the government's annual contributions. From that moment on, they actually went about thirteen years. Meanwhile, the republic had fallen, and the Venetian hospital organization, with the strongest of the events reported here, started to take on the present form. At the time of the fall of the republic, *Pietà* Hospital had a deposit of about 430,000 effective ducats, with an annual income of 8,500 ducats; *Incurabili* Hospital was poorer and had a deposit of just over 82,000 ducats, a sum deducted from the seizures practised by creditors in 1777; and *Mendicanti* Hospital had a deposit of 85,000 ducats (*Comune di Venezia, Documenti per la storia della beneficienza in Venezia*).

The real turning point for the four hospitals occurred with the advent of the democratic municipality in 1797. The change is known as the Democratic government stage and dates from 16 May 1797, when French general Baraguay d'Hilliers occupied Venice militarily until 1798 (Ellero, 1987; Pellizza, 2010).

At that time it was to meet a real need of ducats (102,119.14) that corresponded to the maintenance of 3,195 individuals (including 2,627 at *Pietà*, 266 at *Derelitti*, 175 at *Incurabili*, 127 at *Mendicanti*).

On 1 September 1797 a decree established the creation of a single administration for all charities, with a single common fund and managed by a special deputation general administration of pious causes and the institution of the home country. A further decree was promulgated on 7 September 1797, and with this the municipality addressed a matter of extreme importance, the debtor situation of the major hospitals and charities. The establishment of the *Casa Patria* signifies the true unification preamble, before the Austrians conquered Venice. It represented a government's instrument by which the financial resources recovered would flock in various methods. The municipality members had foreseen two main sources of income with the tax breaks and the distribution of the goods confiscated to the traitors to the homeland. To these a legacy was added by one of the sixty municipality members, the patrician Alvise Mocenigo, who had decided to donate to the new welfare institution a property owned by his family (ASV, *Ospedali e luoghi pii*, *Busta* 169, Gatti, 1797, pp. 162–163). The Napoleonic phase was the actual heir of the events here narrated and established the Congregation of Charity (*Congregazione di carità*). This congregation should be considered the most important of the social-political reforms of the French government throughout the Italic kingdom. The strength of this institution together with the prefecture is that, even after its abolition by the Austrian government, it was adopted again in 1861 until 1937. The congregation was established by a special commission for the preparation of the new public charity set up on 10 November 1806, to which Count Daniele Renier was added. The very name "Congregation of Charity" seems to respect the essence of the past tradition. The real news was therefore a direct control of the administration of the state's assistance with an award to the Ministry of the Interior.

Ten other "probe [honest] and zealous citizens" were part of the congregation, or—as in the original decree of 18 June 1806—"Among the most distinguished Tradesmen and Law Officers of the City" and all of them free of charge. There were then three expert committees who twice a week met in the actual management of the three charitable sections in which the congregation was divided:

- Hospitals;
- Hospices and orphanages;
- Charity.

In the congregation, many Venetians who had already been involved in the charitable sector of the former governments were reunited, and on 12 February 1808, all the employees of the old institutes were enrolled in the congregation's Accounting Office (*Archivio Pietà*, *Congregazione di Carità*, *Busta* 4). Every week the congregation was assembled, including the commissioners of the three areas, for ordinary management. "One Cash Only" was to receive all the annuity payments of the various institutes from now on and to execute all individual payments, but the budgets remained separate and distinct for each original body, with the possibility of money transfers among the various institutions. For the first time in the history of Venetian care, the obligation of the budget and the final budget for each institution was laid down not only once a year but also every quarter, to be sent to the ministry responsible for approval in a way that the balance between revenue and expense was always assured.

Up to this point, and for several centuries, the pioneer had set the revenue and outputs in the classic book, the two cashier's editions (daily income and releases) and the master book (by entry or expense chapter), of which the cashier made the closing of the cash at the end of each year in front of the governors' meeting. At times of need, loans secured by hospital properties (levels) or private equity deposits ranged between 3% and 4.5%.

During the Napoleonic period, the functions of the city's health hospital (guaranteed by *Derelitti* Hospital until 1807) were transferred to *Incurabili* Hospital. After the Austrian return, in the same place of *Mendicanti* Hospital, *Derelitti* Hospital (*Hospedaletto*) and the Scuola Grande di San Marco and all around it, all Venetian hospitals (except for *Incurabili* and *Pietà*) gave rise to the current civil hospital, Santi Giovanni e Paolo, close to the homonymous church.

Discussion and Conclusions

What emerged in the research is the demonstration of "how" the episodes between the late seventeenth and early twentieth centuries were decisive in the composition and articulation of the Venice hospital. The accounting and administrative documents of that time (not only today) are the critical factor for understanding how the system affirmed itself in the *Serenissima* Republic and, then, evolved in successive epochs. They are also a testimony to how data, figures, their systematic order and therefore accounting in general play a central role in the policy-making activities and the affirmation of governance models.

The Venetian Senate used accounting information to move the system of hospitals from a private nature (mainly related to the charitable activities of "probe [honest] and zealous citizens") towards a public environment. In order to obtain such a result the accounting system of the Santi Giovanni e Paolo hospital provided data to support this movement, highlighting the losses and situation of difficulties emerging from the merger of the four hospitals operating before.

The era of the crisis of the four major hospitals is certainly the best possible place to read the republic's need to ensure health and hospitalization for the sick and poor, but it is also synonymous with the degree of civilization that an evolved government must provide. The role played by the organs of the republic in rescuing and reorganizing hospitals is an expression of charitable principles, but also a prelude to forms of governance that began to be affirmed, demonstrating the degree of evolution in the order of the *Serenissima* Republic. In this context, the accounting documents, in which relations with third parties are crystallized, define the amount of assets and the entity of the debit/credit positions, which are primarily a precious element in safeguarding the rights of third parties and preserve power in the governance system. All decisions, including subsequent ones, would be made by accounting results and not merely by a political choice.

There are several points that have been made. All decisions regarding the destiny of the four hospitals and their unification process were based on objective findings, real-world comparisons and predictions. Such results gradually determined the congregation petitions, the judgments of the judiciary, the Senate political addresses, and simulations in the proposals. This has meant the strong social and organizational role exercised by accounting. From this, it is possible to affirm the derivation of that kind governmentality, based on investigation and critical reflection.

The successive phases confirm the strong role of accounting because both the Napoleonic phase and the Austrian phase would always be the numbers, or rather, the representation of the numerical quantities by accounting (financial resources, amount of assets, number of employees, number of patients, etc.) to provide the greatest leverage and governance orientation.

Notes

1. Department of Business and Law, University of Siena.
2. Department of Management, University of Venice.

References

Alonzi, L. (2005), *I censi consegnativi nel XVI e XVII secolo tra "finzione" e "realtà"*, in "L'Acropoli", VI, 1.

Alzetta, M. (2010), The St. John and Paul hospital in Venice, in *Journal of Medicine and the Person*, 8(3), 137–139.

American Accounting Association (1970), Committee on accounting history, in *The Accounting Review*, 45, 52–64.

Archivio della Pietà, Congregazione di Carità, busta 4.

Archivio di Stato Venezia, Ospedali e Luoghi Pii, ASV Cassa Union Quatro Ospitali 1776–1794.

Archivio di Stato Venezia, Ospedali e Luoghi Pii, ASV Bilanzi Union Quatro Ospitali 1778–1789.

Archivio Storico delle Istituzioni di Ricovero ed Educazione (Arch IRE), busta MEN G 2.

Bamji, A., Borean, L., and Moretti, L. (2015), *La chiesa e l'ospedale di San Lazzaro dei Mendicanti*, Venezia, Marcianum Press.

Beloch, K. J., Del Panta, L., and Sonnino, E. (1994), *Storia della popolazione d'Italia*, Firenze, Le lettere.

Bembo, P. (1859), D*elle istituzioni di beneficenza nella città e provincia di Venezia, studi storico-economico-statistici*, Venezia, Naratovich.

Boys, P., and Freear, J. (1976), *An Anthology*, Routledge Library Editions: Accounting History 1976–1986, New York.

Bracci, E., Maran, L., and Vagnoni, E. (2010), Saint Anna's hospital in Ferrara, Italy: Accounting and organizational change during the Devolution, in *Accounting History*, 15(4), 463–504.

Brown, R. (2014), *A History of Accounting and Accountants*, Abingdon, UK, Routledge.

Burchell, S., Clubb, C., Hopwood, A., Hughes, J., and Nahapiet, J. (1980), The roles of accounting in organizations and society, in *Accounting, Organizations and Society*, 5(1), 5–27.

Carnegie, G. D., and Napier, C. J. (1996), Critical and interpretive histories: Insights into accounting's present and future through its past, in *Accounting, Auditing & Accountability Journal*, 9(3), 7–39.

Carnegie, G. D., and Napier, C. J. (2012), Accounting's past, present and future: The unifying power of history, in *Accounting, Auditing & Accountability Journal*, 25(2), 328–369.

Chambers, D. S., Fletcher, J., and Pullan, B. S. (2001), *Venice: A Documentary History, 1450–1630* (Vol. 12), University of Toronto Press, Toronto.

Colquhoun, P., and Parker, L. D. (2012), Accounting and the state: An introduction, in *Accounting History*, 17(3–4), 283–286.

Corazzol, G. (1979), *Fitti e livelli a grano. Un aspetto del credito rurale nel Veneto del '500*, Milano, Franco Angeli.

Corazzol, G. (1986), *Livelli stipulati a Venezia nel 1591. Studio storico*, Pisa, Giardini.

Coronella, S., Lombrano, A., and Zanin, L. (2013), State accounting innovations in pre-unification Italy, in *Accounting History Review*, 23(1), 1–21.

Documenti per la Storia della beneficienza in Venezia (1879), Stabilimento Tipografico di Giuseppe Antonelli, Venezia.

Ellero G., (1987), L'archivio IRE. Inventari dei fondi antichi degli ospedali e luoghi pii di Venezia ("Carità e assistenza a Venezia", n. 4). IRE, Venezia.

Gatti, S. (1797), *Raccolta di carte pubbliche, istruzioni, legislazioni, ec.ec.ec. del nuovo veneto governo democratico*, Venezia, I, 46.

Gendron, Y., and Baker, C. R. (2005), On interdisciplinary movements: The development of a network of support around Foucauldian perspectives in accounting research, in *European Accounting Review*, 14(3), 525–569.

Giovannoni, E., and Riccaboni, A. (2009), Editorial: A general overview of perspectives and reflections on accounting's past in Europe, in *Accounting History*, 14(4), 341–355.

Grandi, C. (2002), Assistenza e beneficenza, L'ottocento e il novecento, in *Storia di Venezia*, Treccani, Roma, 865–903.

Hopwood, A. G. (1983), On trying to study accounting in the contexts in which it operates, in *Accounting, Organisations and Society*, 8(2–3), 287–305.

Hopwood, A. G. (1987), The archaeology of accounting systems, in *Accounting, Organizations and Society*, 12(3), 207–234.

Hopwood, A. G., and Miller, P. (1994), *Accounting as Social and Institutional Practice* (Vol. 24), Cambridge, Cambridge University Press.

Jessop, B. (2007), From micro-powers to governmentality: Foucault's work on statehood, state formation, statecraft and state power, in *Political Geography*, 26(1), 34–40.

Leardini, C., and Rossi, G. (2013), Accounting and power in religious institutions: Verona's Santa Maria della Scala monastery in the Middle Ages, in *Accounting History*, 18(3), 415–427.

Lorenzini, M. (2009), "Di solenne e privilegiatissimo credito". Tecniche e strategie di investimento finanziario del convento di Santa Anastasia di Verona (secoli XVII–XVIII), in *Studi storici Luigi Simeoni*, 59, 59–71.

Meijers, D. (1989), L'architettura della nuova filantropia, in Aikema, B., Meijers, D. (eds.), *Nel regno dei poveri*, Arsenale Editrice: Venezia, 43–69.

Mennicken, A., and Miller, P. (2012), Accounting, territorialisation and power, in *Foucault Studies*, (13), 4–24.

Miller, P. (1990), On the interrelations between accounting and the state, in *Accounting, Organizations and Society*, 15(4), 315–338.

Moggi, S., Filippi, V., Leardini, C., and Rossi, G. (2016), Accountability for a place in heaven: A stakeholders' portrait in Verona's confraternities, in *Accounting History*, 21(2–3), 236–262.

Parker, L. D. (1997), Informing historical research in accounting and management: Traditions, philosophies, and opportunities, in *The Accounting Historians Journal*, 24(2), 111–149.

Pelizza, A. (1997), La crisi finanziaria degli ospedali maggiori veneziani fra 1777 e 1797, in *Studi Veneziani*, N. S.(33), 123.

Pelizza, A. (2010), Da "alberghi informi di ammalati" a "fortunati nosocomiali ritiri". Gli ospedali maggiori veneziani tra la fine della Repubblica veneta e le riforme italiche, in *Studi Veneziani*, N. S.(60), 423.

Previts, G. J., Parker, L. D., and Coffman, E. N. (1990a), An accounting historiography: Subject matter and methodology, in *Abacus*, 26(2), 136–158.

Prieto, B., Maté, L., and Tua, J. (2006), The accounting records of the Monastery of Silos throughout the eighteenth century: The accumulation and management of its patrimony in the light of its accounts books, in *Accounting History*, 11(2), 221–256.

Pullan, B. S. (1971), *Rich and Poor in Renaissance Venice: The Social Institutions of a Catholic State, to 1620*, Cambridge, MA, Harvard University Press, 362–371.

Riccaboni, A., Giovannoni, E., Giorgi, A., and Moscadelli, S. (2006), Accounting and power: Evidence from the fourteenth century, in *Accounting History*, 11(1), 41–62.

Roberts, J., and Scapens, R. (1985). Accounting systems and systems of accountability-understanding accounting practices in their organisational contexts, in *Accounting, Organizations and Society*, 10(4), 443–456.

Sargiacomo, M. (2008), Accounting and the "art of government": Margaret of Austria in Abruzzo (1539–86), in *European Accounting Review*, 17(4), 667–695.

Zanaldi, L. (1950), *Notizie preliminari per una storia documentata dell'ospedale civile di Venezia*, Venezia, Carlo Ferrari.

8 Managing the Largest Printing Business in Europe

The Remondini in Bassano (Seventeenth to Nineteenth Century)

Carlo Marcon, Giovanni Favero and Ugo Sostero

Introduction

The Remondini printing house in the Republic of Venice was in the late eighteenth century the largest in continental Europe, with around one thousand employees. Its original specialization in printed objects allowed relevant economies of scale, which were enhanced by vertical integration with the acquisition of a paper mill and a foundry. A later turn to book printing put the company in successful competition with the Venetian guild of book printers. After the fall of the Republic of Venice the obsolescence of a business model fit to the ancient regime went together with the inability to keep pace with technological change.

We find this case interesting to study for three main reasons. First of all, it was a very large and structured organization for that period, with four paper mills, eighteen printing presses, thirty etching presses and a foundry for printed fonts in the late eighteenth century. Not least, the distribution network was composed by some bookshops and stores and some hundreds of street vendors (Tesini) who spread products all over Europe and even in South America. Secondly, this company was not located in Venice but in the hinterland of the *Serenissima* Republic. After a long period of prosperity, the printing and publishing industry in Venice went into crisis in the mid-eighteenth century. To the decline of the Venetian guild of printers corresponded the expansion of the Remondini printing house, which was managed as a modern firm. Therefore, it is interesting to analyse the relationships between Remondini and the government of Republic of Venice on one hand and the competitors belonging to the guild on the other hand. Finally, Remondini implemented a leadership cost strategy, producing printed items at low cost for a wide public, compared to most competitors, which had a completely different business strategy with a more artisanal production for a restricted group of customers.

We deal here with the accounting and managerial practices in use inside of the company, focusing on some surviving accounting records that we consider particularly significant both for their content and for the context in which they were drawn up. We selected these accounting primary sources from a private collection of Remondini family manuscripts covering the years from 1634 to 1827 that are now owned by a family in the surroundings of Bassano (hence BGPC) and the Remondini archive located in the library of the Civic Museum in Bassano (hence BGBM) covering the years from 1634 to 1763.

Despite the previous secondary sources (Infelise, 1980) suggesting that the formal administration of the company was quite undersized with regard to its dimensions, our contribution aims at assessing the real effectiveness of accounting practices, whether they improved over time and the possible explanations of the change in the Remondini accounting system. Using the surviving accounting documents, we will attempt to shed further light also on the determinants of the company's expansion and in particular of its subsequent long decline. We propose then an assessment of the strategic choices the Remondinis made to cope with a context that became extremely turbulent from the 1790s on.

Trying to answer such questions, in the subsequent paragraphs we follow the development of the company all along the two centuries of its life, from its origins in the seventeenth century to its expansion and later decline, up to its closing in 1861.

The Origins of the Remondini Printing Manufactory in Its Context

The Remondini printing house was established in Bassano, a minor city in the Republic of Venice, in 1657, and grew fast in the following decades. If the place was not the classical setting for an activity that usually relied on the vibrant intellectual atmosphere of larger urban centres, also the timing for starting such a business appears surprising to the historian. At the time, book trade in Europe was stagnating, if not declining, after two centuries of continuous expansion and prosperity that followed the introduction in 1454 of Johann Gutenberg's movable-type printing press, which then rapidly spread through Europe and beyond.

During the seventeenth century, the European editorial market experienced in fact a general regression, especially in the Mediterranean regions. The causes of this crisis were manifold. Among the most important it is possible to mention the effects of the Thirty Years' War on continental Europe and the plague outbreaks that concurrently affected in particular the Iberian and Italian peninsulas, together with Counter-Reformation pressures and controls (Infelise, 1989, 11). In this situation, the guilds of printers and booksellers were divided by conflicts between producers and retailers, and suffered the competition of foreign publishers, who enjoyed the advantages of a leaner commercial organization.

However, in the long term the Reformation entailed also a fragmentation of the European book market following the emergence of national languages and the gradual decline of Latin, which remained the language of the Catholic Church. The new pattern of demand in Catholic countries included international ecclesiastical institutions requiring liturgical and scholastic books, local governments and their need to print and circulate official documents, and a literate public which demanded occasional small editions. Such a public was, however, limited to a small elite, given the high levels of illiteracy, which in Southern Europe remained much higher than in France, Britain, The Netherlands and the German area. This situation limited the possibilities for a growth in the scale of production.

In the Italian states, the political division of the peninsula and the lack of a national capital contributed to market fragmentation (Pasta, 2005, 202). Venice was the main Italian printing centre of international relevance since the late fifteenth century, yet its importance declined to a great extent from the early seventeenth century on (Brown, 1891). The emergence of other regional printing centres, such as Padua, with its university, and Bassano, did not compensate for the loss of the strategic cultural function Venice had exerted in the Renaissance. They did, however, entail a recovery of exports. Most of the printers and librarians establishing their activity in the mainland kept their distance from intellectual commitment, focusing on the publishing initiatives that might give a profit.

This was certainly the case of Giovanni Antonio Remondini senior (1634–1711). A Paduan merchant, he moved to Bassano in the 1650s, where he started not only a printing press but also a wool mill, a dyeing plant for wool yarns, a food shop and a paper mill. Still a decade after his death, following the 1725 hereditary division among his sons, printing was not the main activity of the family, being evaluated lower than the value of the wool mill.[1]

Printmaking rather than book printing was the main activity of the Remondini printing house in the beginning and for a long time, as the production of cheap religious or zoomorphic images could find easily a market outlet in the surrounding countryside among a mostly illiterate public. The success of these products pushed Remondini to buy his first specialized printing press for chalcography before 1670. In 1715 a dozen such presses were working in his printing house in Bassano (Infelise, 1990, 109). Itinerant sellers were in charge of the distribution of printing images through the Italian Peninsula and the bordering territories of the Habsburg Empire. Remondini established a special relationship with a small community of flintlock pedlars from Val Tesina, immediately beyond the border. The Tesini took on the risk of sale, buying the images on credit from Remondini and offering their land plots as collateral. This way Remondini became the main landowner in Val Tesina, where a shop was established after 1718[2] to supply the Tesini sellers in their hometown.

Only in 1661 Remondini printed his first known book, authored by Freschi (1661). Two years later he was granted the exclusive privilege of printing and distributing official documents in Bassano under license by G. Pietro Pinelli, the ducal printer (Giachery, 2015, 712). In 1670 Remondini owned four typographic presses. Together with official documents, these printed occasional writings, school textbooks or chivalric tales and above all devotional booklets.

The market success of the printed images and popular booklets convinced Remondini of the necessity of a stable and cheap supply of paper in order to make possible an increase of the scale of production. From 1710 on he probably rented some paper mills, but we do not find clear information on this in the accounting documents.

Notably, there are no accounting records covering the first years of the company's activities. The earliest surviving accounting record is a document dating from 1725 dividing the Remondini house's total wealth into two equal parts. This document was drawn up fourteen years after the death of Giovanni Antonio Remondini, the founder of the Remondini house, since his will had not set out precise provisions regarding the attribution of his legacy. Consequently, his six sons began to quarrel over the breakdown of the inheritance, and the division of the whole business became unavoidable. One half, called *Ramo di Piazza*, was given to his sons Antonio, Giuseppe and Giacomo, while the other, called *Ramo delle Grazie*, was assigned to his other three sons, Francesco, Baldassare and Giambattista. The former was primarily made up of the printing business, and the latter included the woollen mill and silk factory.

This primary source consists of two sheets:[3] the first concerns the business branch *Ramo di Piazza* and the second is dedicated to *Ramo delle Grazie*. Each sheet presents a long and detailed list of properties, business assets and liabilities, which we have summarized in Table 8.1, showing amounts and the composition of the Remondini house's comprehensive wealth in 1725.

As we can see, the total wealth of the Remondini house was enormous for that period. Even more impressive was the rate of accumulation of that amount. Indeed, we do not know the precise financial conditions of Giovanni Antonio Remondini when he moved from Padua to Bassano about seventy years before, but according to the writers of the nineteenth century (Brentari, 1882; Zellini, 1893), he did not have large amounts of money at his disposal. We only know for sure that his wife's dowry in 1655 was 1,923 Venetian lire.

Most of the total wealth (72.9%) was made up of business equity, while only a portion (27.1%) consisted of properties. Moreover, the level of indebtedness was very low, considering that 8.9% of business assets were covered by debt and 91.1% by equity. These numbers show that commercial and manufacturing activities generated satisfactory profits, which were reinvested mainly in the business and partly in investment properties, following wise stewardship. The expansion of the business was supported by retained earnings, without using financial leverage.

While we do not have information on the kind of debt (trade or financial debts) or on the term (short or long), we do have some details about the assets allocated to the main business activities. More than 50% of the assets are credits, which are both trade receivables and loans granted to employees

Table 8.1 Division of the Remondini house in 1725 into two business branches

Ramo di Piazza	*V. lire*[4]	*Ramo delle Grazie*	*V. lire*
Properties	246,469	Properties	246,407
Business assets:		Business assets:	
Inventory of the shop in Piazza	117,094	Inventory of the woollen mill	119,208
Debtors of the shop in Piazza	37,089	Debtors of the woollen mill	186,351
Inventory and debtors of the grocery	26,236	Dry cleaners	5,618
Inventory of the paper mill in Oliero	2,950	Debtors of the shop in Padua	36,348
Inventory of the printing house	125,634	Credits vs employees	23,204
Debtors of the printing house	126,438	Other debtors	150,068
Other debtors	147,260	Silk factory	93,751
Loans granted to Tesini	100,014	Debtors in Trento and Udine	36,284
Cash	19,714	Cash	10,716
Other assets	57,160	Other assets	35,771
Total business assets	759,589	Total business assets	697,319
Liabilities	95,799	Liabilities	33,529
Business equity	663,790	Business equity	663,790
Total (properties + business equity)	910,259	Total (properties + business equity)	910,197

Comprehensive wealth	*V. lire*		
Properties	492,875		27.1%
Business assets	1.456,908	100%	
Liabilities	129,328	8.9%	
Business equity	1,327,580	91.1%	72.9%
Total (properties + business equity)	1,820,455		100.0%

and the Tesini street vendors, who needed money before undertaking their long journeys around Europe. The inventories account for approximately one third of the assets and comprise both stock in trade and fixed assets (working tools), but the distinction between these items is not specified, although it is likely that finished goods and raw materials made up the majority. However, we do not know how the estimates were made: whether the credits were recognized at book value or written off and, in the case, at what rate. Similarly, we do not know whether the stock was valued at cost or market price.

Moreover, it is worth noting that, in the document of division, there are only a few references to some fragmentary personal accounts opened for tracking debtors, but there are no systematic links with the accounting books and ledgers kept for the various business activities. It seems that this document was drawn up *ad hoc* in order to identify and measure the assets and liabilities to be attributed to the two business branches in order to carry out the division. We have not yet found clues that show the existence of a well-organized accounting system meant to support business decisions on resource allocation between different operating segments in the early eighteenth century.

The Largest Printing House in Europe

Following the hereditary division in 1725, the *Ramo di Piazza* of the Remondini family pursued the expansion of the printing activity under the direction of Giuseppe Remondini senior (1672–1742). He reorganized the printing mills, focusing on the vertical integration of paper production and on the definition of a coherent style for the printed images that the Tesini at the time circulated further through the whole Habsburg Empire and beyond, in Central Europe and in the Russian Empire. Since 1730, their travels also penetrated into Spain and Portugal, and from there some of them travelled to the Americas, establishing trading networks that allowed the global diffusion of the "saints" of the Remondinis (Infelise, 1990, 116–117). Such an expansion was in large part the result of the attempts at customizing the production for different markets, collecting feedback from the sellers about local preferences. In 1730, inside the same premises of the printing house in the main square of Bassano, a school of engraving was established: the training of craftsmen was in fact the crucial element in the definition of the product (Infelise, 1990, 109–113).

In order to sustain the growing production, Giuseppe Remondini from 1735 to 1738 rented three different paper mills along the river Brenta upstream of Bassano, in Oliero and Campese, from the noble families that owned the plant and the related water rights (Infelise, 1990, 66–67). Following the large supply of paper available and the possibility of customizing its production, in 1738 also the production of decorated paper was started (Fantinato, 2007, 54).

In this period, the production of books remained a secondary activity, and the number of typographic presses reached the number of six only in 1744. The cause of the stagnation of book production was the obstacles imposed on the Remondini company by the regulations that privileged the members of the Venetian guild of printers and booksellers.

Only a few years after the death of Giuseppe Remondini senior, his sons Giovanni Antonio junior (1700–1769) and Giambattista (1713–1773) presented a plea to the Venetian authorities, asking for admission into the Venetian guild, which was finally forced to admit Giambattista in 1750. Giovanni Antonio junior took on a secondary role in the company since then. Giambattista started also a shop in Venice, which became the official business address for the company. Following the guild's regulations and the 1750 agreement, he should also have transferred its presses to Venice, which he never did, eliciting a reaction from the main Venetian publishers, who were unable to compete with the lower costs of production of the Remondini company (Infelise, 1990, 187–194).

The number of books Remondini printed rapidly multiplied, shifting from an average of four books per year in the first half of the eighteenth century to twenty-four in the second half, following the catalogue of books circulated yearly since 1749, which is the main source on Remondini's book production (Del Sal, 2007). Their editions remained small in size, but multiplied in number, focusing on reprints. The reduction of costs was pursued by reducing the size of fonts and the thickness of paper (Infelise, 1990, 154–155), but also through vertical integration. A foundry for fonts was started before 1767, and in 1766 the largest paper mill in Oliero was finally acquired from the Tiepolo family, in order to introduce new production processes.

In 1764 the typographic presses working in Bassano were eighteen, with hundreds of workers: in the case of printing, the increase of production capacity was attained through additional presses, not by means of a modernization of the process. At the same time, also chalcography and decorated papers increased production (Fantinato, 2007, 54).

In 1764, thirty-two etching presses were working in Bassano, and printed images were sold all over Europe, in particular in Catholic countries. The growing penetration of Remondini's printed images in foreign markets created the occasion for legal and commercial conflicts with other producers and exporters, from the quarrel about plagiarism started by Augsburg printmakers in 1766 (Infelise, 1990, 118–121) to the complaint concerning the circulation of an engraving of the Judgement putting the King of Spain Charles III in the Hell, which forced Giambattista to seek refuge in Castel Tesino, where he died in 1773 (Brentari, 1882).

His son, Giuseppe Remondini junior (1745–1811), was put in charge of coping with the diplomatic consequences of the audacious commercial choices of his father. His education in a Jesuit college and his culture in the humanities have been interpreted as the determinant of a change of attitude in the direction of the family business. Giuseppe also bought a manor with a related noble title in Gorumbergo (Friuli) and joined the Freemasonry. Infelise (1990, 28) suggests that "the Remondini house stopped being the most subversive and disturbing firm of the time" exactly following Giuseppe's adoption of aristocratic behaviour. Such an interpretation may, however, be questioned: some of his choices were made necessary by the new dimensions of the company, and allowed it to become more resilient.

Giuseppe outsourced book printing to Venetian printers, so allowing the Remondini company to become more flexible by decreasing its need for fixed investments, and at the same time acquiring the right to put Venice as the place of publication, as formally required. He also pursued the modernization of the paper mill in Oliero, introducing in 1780 new Dutch machineries that made it the largest and most productive factory in the area. During the 1780s, Giuseppe bought also from their owners the other two paper mills the Remondini company had rented since the 1730s, so increasing the backward vertical integration of the business. Such a strategy, maintaining flexibility downward and consolidating upward the industrial structure, was the main determinant of the business's survival through the difficult decades that followed the fall of the Venetian Republic. Even the 1776 acquisition of the Gorumbergo feudal manor was the occasion to apply to the Slovenian sellers based in San Pietro al Natisone (or *degli Schiavoni*—i.e., of Slovenians) the same logic used with the Tesini.

Figure 8.1 illustrates the organizational complexity and the vertical integration achieved by the Remondini company at the height of its success.

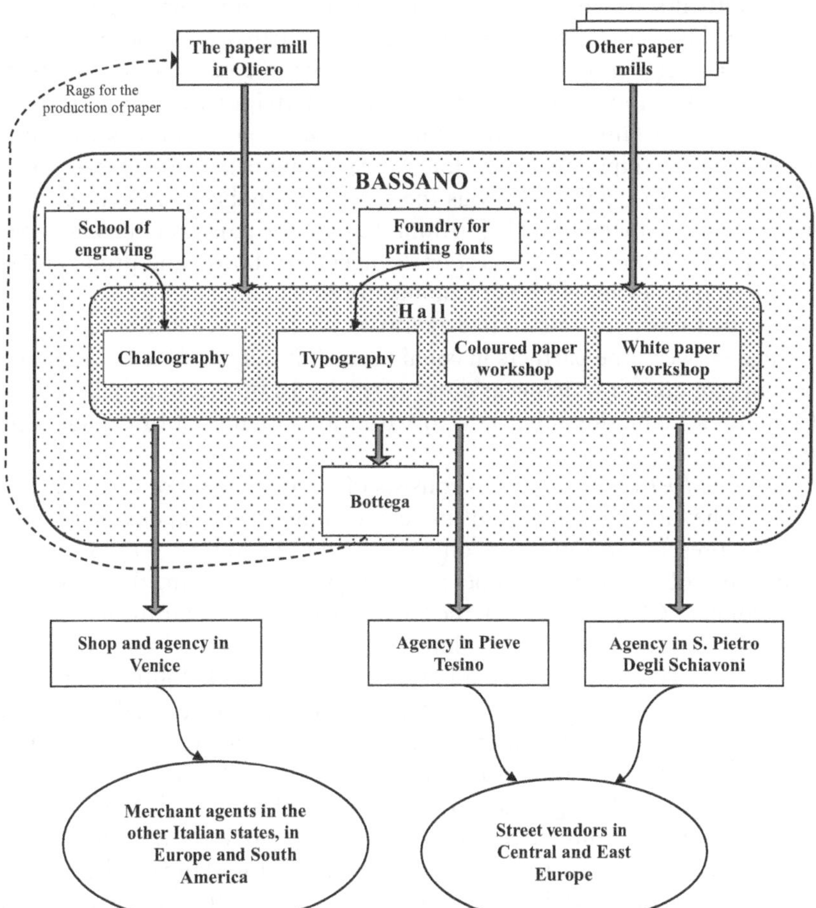

Figure 8.1 The Remondini operations in the second half of the eighteenth century

Changes in the business governance appear even more relevant. Shortly after succeeding his father, Giuseppe put in charge of the business direction Valentino Novelletto, who had represented the Remondini company during the aforementioned trial in Augsburg. Together with him, other specialized collaborators started emerging inside the company in this period. Giuseppe's ability to delegate power inside the company allowed him to cope with the growing complexity of the business, which implied also the necessity to involve experienced merchants in some branches of business, establishing with them *ad hoc* partnerships. Some of the most interesting accounting records surviving from this period are the financial statements (called *Ristretti di Bilanzio*) related precisely to such partnerships between the Remondini company and other merchants.[5]

The *Ristretti di Bilanzio*, now preserved in the private archive of a noble family in the surroundings of Bassano, were presented inside private contracts authenticated by a notary, which founded and regulated partnerships between the Remondini company as capital partner and another partner, usually a merchant or a former employee, who acted as a director of the business. Even though most of the business activities were run directly by the Remondini family, like the printing house, some businesses were managed in partnerships, in order to find the right mix between necessary capital and management skills. This was the case of the haberdashery in Bassano, managed in partnership with Giovanni Fasolo, the paper mill in Vas in partnership with Domenico Gnoato, or the agency of books and prints in Pieve Tesino in partnership with Giovanni Antonio Allieri.

Usually these partnerships had a term of five or ten years. The profits were divided between the partners in equal parts, but only at the end of the partnership, the company acting as director received a further money-benefit and Remondini maintained the right to withdraw an amount of capital before the end.

Not one *Ristretto di Bilanzio* consists of a complete set of financial statements. They are all made up of merely a summarized balance sheet, without the presentation of an income statement. Therefore, we do not have knowledge of the items (revenues and expenses) determining the net income. According to Chatfield (1977), the balance sheet was by far the most important financial statement at that time, and was emphasized by early accounting writers. Users generally paid attention to assets, liabilities and equity, while revenues and expenses were considered merely incidental. Even when a profit and loss account was presented, the main function of this document was to check the accuracy of the profit figure first calculated by comparing the opening and closing balances for net assets (Edwards, 1989).

The main functions of the *Ristretti di Bilanzio* were keeping track of rights and obligations, providing legal evidence for claims to be enforced in court, measuring equity and profit to be divided between partners at the end of a partnership and holding the agent accountable. However, the lack of an income statement did not allow for the use of profit for performance assessment and resource allocation decisions. One could simply know whether he was gaining or losing, and how much. Moreover, the presentation of a profit and loss account would have rendered agents more accountable for their actions.

It is worth noting that assets, liabilities and equity are listed in the balance sheet in reverse order. In other words, in the left-hand section, we find resources received (equity and liabilities) and in the right-hand section we find the resources used (assets such as inventories, trade receivables and cash). In our view, a possible explanation may be connected to the *personalistic* approach, according to which the prefixes *deve dare* (ought to give) and *deve avere* (ought to have) in the balance sheet refer to the director/agent of the business entity. Therefore, the agent ought to give (in the sense of pay back) financial resources and ought to have (in the sense of get) the resources necessary for fulfilling his mandate. However, a number of alternative explanations have been given (see, for the British context, Yamey, 1970).

The *Ristretti di Bilanzio* were not prepared on a regular basis, but only at the end of a partnership's contractual term. Notably, we examined the *Ristretto di Bilanzio* of the haberdashery in Bassano (from 24 January 1776 to 14 March 1778), that of the paper mill in Vas (from 30 October 1767 to 30 October 1778 and from 30 October 1778 to 24 July 1783) and that of the agency of books and prints in Pieve Tesino (from 8 August 1783 to 8 August 1788). However, these documents represented a summarized balance sheet derived from more detailed financial statements, which were prepared annually. Taking into account that profits could not be divided before the end of the partnership, this periodical reporting to owners and managers was a useful mechanism of internal control. This evidence shows how the Remondini company had developed a more organized and systematic accounting system than in the early part of the century, in order to give adequate support to the massive growth of its business.

When we analyse the values found in the *Ristretti di Bilanzio*, some common characteristics can be seen. First of all, the various business initiatives have a low level of debt, as the debts are generally around a third of the sources. The financial liabilities are not always identifiable, but when it is possible to do so, their weight is never excessive. Furthermore, this is not financing from third parties (credit institutions or others) but rather from interest-bearing loans from the Remondinis themselves. The net assets are primarily made up of profits earned during that period and/or by profits maintained within the company. It is therefore self-generated and saved capital rather than capital contributed by partners. In light of these considerations, it seems that the risk of default for these companies was quite limited.

The assets are mainly composed of current assets. The unique fixed assets could be included in the "capital in effect", even though their details are not specified. The most important asset item is the credits, with a weight that is always over 50%. Most of the credits are commercial, but there are also often loans to employees and tenants.

In short, based on the data analysed, the companies, while each operating in different business areas, were solid in their balance sheets and capable of generating good returns, attesting that the Remondini family was adept at administrative management and at choosing valid partners.

Coping With Hard Times

The market for books, and in general the market for printed items, started changing fast during the last quarter of the eighteenth century, when Giuseppe was in charge of the family business. The preference for religious, theological and classical publications declined, in particular following the suppression of the Society of Jesus in many European countries and their colonial empires (Pasta, 1995, 207; Roehner, 1997).

At the same time, the market saw an increasing demand for translations mainly from French, in part related to the circulation of the ideas of the Enlightenment movement, in part related to the interest in a wider literature, including popular fiction and forbidden publications (Darnton, 1996). The latter were, however, not included in the Remondini catalogue, Venetian censorship being quite strict, and Giuseppe Remondini preferring not to start new conflicts with the authorities (Infelise, 1990, 159–161).

After the fall of the republic in 1797, the Remondini company suffered from the increased political turbulence and from the consequences of the Napoleonic military campaigns that passed through Bassano between 1796 and 1797 (Favero, 2013). In these years, only four of the eighteen typographic presses were working, and the production went in large part unsold and remained in stock, waiting for better times (Infelise, 1990, 202).

The end of the ancient regime brought with it also the suppression of the fideicommissum, which entrusted one of the heirs of the full household estate, in order to avoid its fragmentation. As a consequence, Antonio Remondini, a brother of Giuseppe, required in 1798 a division of the family assets, and forced Giuseppe to buy back on credit his part, getting the company heavily in debt with him. Antonio complained about an insufficient attention to costs, the scarce frequency of financial statements and a careless control of the accounts.

The primary source that we consider for this period is the preliminary sales agreement (with attachments) stipulated on 12 March 1798, in which Antonio ceded his half of dues owed from the various activities of the company to his brother, Giuseppe Remondini.[6] According to this agreement, the payment would be split into annual instalments starting from 1803, to be concluded in 1860.

The primary source that we consider for this period is the preliminary sales agreement (with attachments) stipulated on 12 March 1798, in which Antonio ceded his half of dues owed from the various activities of the company to his brother, Giuseppe Remondini.[7] According to this agreement, the payment would be split into annual instalments starting from 1803, to be concluded in 1860.

This primary source interests us for its aspects as follows:

- The insights that can be drawn from the way it is drafted;
- The valuable information it provides about the value of the company's individual businesses;
- The criteria adopted to form these estimates.

There is an eight-page attachment to the preliminary sales agreement labelled "demonstration", which includes a summary of inventory and estimates of the Remondini company's business branches. For each business branch, it shows by whom and when the inventory was made, by whom and when the estimate was carried out and its amount. In some cases, details on the methods of estimation used were also reported. After the "demonstration" paper, there is the detail of all the inventory, estimates and balance sheets mentioned earlier.

Unlike the 1725 document of division, this documentation is much more substantial. The description of assets and the related estimates are more analytical, and explanations are given for the estimation process. There are also many references to accounting records, ledgers and financial statements issued at the individual-business level. From all of this, we can deduce that the Remondini company was equipped with a significant administrative structure which involved many professionals and a well-structured accounting system that evolved over the century in response to the business's increased complexity.

As mentioned, this primary source gives us useful information on the amount and makeup of the company's assets, as seen in Table 8.2. It also allows for a comparison with the situation shown by the 1725 document of division, to understand how the Remondini company evolved over the eighteenth century, although we are aware that the differences may also come from different criteria used in the estimates.

In 1798, net assets were 1,355,830 Venetian lire, or twice what the business branch called 'di Piazza' estimated in 1725, made up of typographic and chalcographic businesses, reflecting the company's strong growth during the century. The financial position at the end of the century still remains solid given that the debts, though higher than those in 1725, account for only 26% of total assets. Looking at the breakdown of businesses, the most important are the following:

- The agencies of Pieve Tesino and San Pietro degli Schiavoni (22.3%). The former was founded between 1718 and 1730, the latter in 1781. Their value, which is mostly made up of loans and trade receivables with street vendors, indicates the enormous importance that this distribution network had for the smooth operation of the company's management;

Table 8.2 Remondini company assets in 1798

1. Paints	15,732	0.9%
2. Paper mill in Oliero	118,865	6.5%
3. Typefaces	33,613	1.8%
4. Tools	21,578	1.2%
5. Copper moulds and wood moulds	182,102	9.9%
6. Prints and decorated paper	64,679	3.5%
7. Bookshop in Piazza	25,895	1.4%
8. Remondini edition books	377,227	20.6%
9. Bookshop in Venice	237,817	13.0%
10. Credits	215,094	11.7%
11. Partnered shop in Tesino	721	0.0%
12. Agencies of Tesino and Schiavonia	407,671	22.3%
13. Grocery in Bassano	19,389	1.1%
14. Cash	43,150	2.4%
15. Other credits	68,265	3.7%
Total assets	1,831,798	100.0%
1. Detraction for the dowry	124,000	
2. Debts of the shop	315,134	
3. Domestic debt of the company	11,876	
4. Expenses for inventory and estimates	12,558	
5. Debts for transport expenses	12,400	
Total liabilities	475,968	26%
Equity	1,355,830	74%

- The books published by Remondini (20.6%), whose share grew notably following Remondini's inclusion in the Venetian printing guild in 1750;
- The bookshop of Venice (13.0%) opened in Merceria San Salvador in the same year, with a wide assortment of books and prints.

Another activity that was improved after 1725 was the paper mill in Oliero, which had previously been rented but was bought in 1766 for 52,700 Venetian lire, whose facilities were renovated starting from 1772, including the purchase of new Dutch machinery in 1780. Similarly, in the 1798 document we see the estimate of the typefaces, as the Remondini company had added an internal foundry. In contrast, by the end of the century, various secondary activities were surrendered or reduced in importance (this is the case for the hardware shop, haberdashery and grocery).

During the eighteenth century, we therefore see a tendency towards the vertical integration of the company, offset by a gradual exit from certain businesses that were no longer considered strategic.

Finally, we found the estimation methods used for the valuation of certain activities in this 1798 document. Specifically, it indicates that the prints were valued at the prices of the last 1797 catalogue, from which an 88% discount was deducted, and Remondini edition books were valued at the prices of the last 1793 catalogue, with an applied discount of 90%. However, surplus was not valued at historical cost but at net realizable value. This criterion and the extent of write-down probably depend on the purpose of the evaluation, but as will be argued, also in the periodic reports drawn up at a later date, we find confirmation of the adoption of net realizable value for the valuation of surplus books and prints. Furthermore, it states that the trade receivables were written off by an average of 50%, while interest-bearing loans granted mainly to street vendors were devalued by 33%. Credits were therefore not recorded at their nominal value, but according to their estimated realizable value, which took into account the quality of the credits, dividing them into good, doubtful and bad.

The 1798 document analysed earlier provides an assessment of the situation of the company on the eve of the deep crisis that hit the whole Venetian area during the following years. Six military campaigns ran over the former territory of the republic from 1796 to 1813. Following the end of the aristocratic republic, Venice passed to the Hapsburgs in 1798.

Under Austrian domination, the company strived to survive under the direction of Bartolomeo Gamba (1776–1841), who was appointed as its director in 1798 (Berti, Ericani and Infelise, 2008). A short-lived recovery allowed ten of the typographic presses to work in 1801 (Infelise, 1990, 205). In 1806 the company still employed three hundred male workers, six women and twenty children (Infelise, 2013, 318). In the same year, however, the Venetian provinces were annexed to the Napoleonic Kingdom of Italy, losing trade access to Central Europe and to the United Kingdom because of the continental blockade. Napoleonic cultural policy favoured the concentration in Milan of publishing activities (Berengo, 1980, 3–32), creating serious difficulties for the Remondini company. As a consequence, in one year the number of employees halved to 150 male workers and fifteen women at the end of 1807.

The most skilled engravers were moving to Milan, and Gamba's efforts to establish relationships with publishers in Milan were not enough: in 1809 only one book was published. Gamba sold the three minor paper mills in the same year, keeping only the Oliero mill, with its modern machines. At the same time, he was involved in family disputes: in 1811, when the younger son Francesco (1777–1820) succeeded Giuseppe, Gamba was forced to resign.

In the difficult years following the 1814 Vienna Congress (Monteleone, 1969), Francesco Remondini focused his attention on chalcography, buying copper plates and six new chalcographic presses in 1816. The next year, he closed down the agency in Pieve Tesino, the distribution hub for the Tesini itinerant sellers. Infelise (1990, 205–206) highlights the absurdity of Francesco's investment in chalcography when lithography was available since

1796 as a cheaper and faster alternative. However, chalcography was still among the most profitable activities of the company during the 1820s, a signal of the backwardness of the local market.

At the same time, Francesco started divesting from manufacturing activity into real estate, a strategy that his widow, Gaetana Baseggio, also pursued after his death despite the obligation to report on her management of family assets in the interest of her minor daughter, Teresa Gioseffa Remondini (1817–1873).

Accounting for the Pupil

For the period from 20 August 1820 to 31 March 1826, there is a quantity of accounting documentation and information on the Remondini company that is not found in any other period of its two centuries of history. This is due to the fact that, at the death of Francesco Remondini in 1820, the business passed to his daughter, Teresa Gioseffa, still a minor. Therefore, her mother Giovanna Gaetana Baseggio, the widow of Francesco Remondini and the daughter of a physician who was also a privileged printer, was named her guardian. For this reason, a judicial inventory was issued of the assets subject to inheritance on 20 August 1820. The guardian was required to present periodic reports on the company and other family assets to the district court of Bassano.

The reports presented totalled five. The first report refers to the period from 20 August 1820 to 31 March 1822 (over nineteen months), while the successive reports all cover a year. The judicial inventory is contained in two substantial volumes (Inventory 1 and Inventory 2) that we found in a collection of Remondini family manuscripts that are now owned by a family in Bassano.[8] Copies of the five reports, however, were not found. It was possible to learn about their contents through the examination of the five respective exculpatory decrees released by the District Court of Bassano. In fact, the transcriptions of these decrees were found in another manuscript volume held in the same private collection.[9] In addition to providing information on the structure and content of the reports examined, the exculpatory decrees also give us other interesting information coming from the judgements expressed regarding the various business branches by the auditors appointed by the District Court of Bassano but also from the advice that the same auditors gave to the guardian in order to preserve and increase the company's profitability.

In more detail, the most interesting insights we can take from these exculpatory decrees concern the following issues:

1. The Company's economic performance and the evolution of its financial position;
2. The methods of bookkeeping and accounting records;
3. The problem of internal transfer prices;

4. The measurement criteria for inventories;
5. The ways of accounting for fixed assets.

The Company's Economic Performance and the Evolution of Its Financial Position

Using the data from the decrees, we reconstructed Table 8.3, which illustrates the economic performance and the evolution of the Remondini company's financial position from 20 August 1820 to 31 March 1826. Evidently, the net assets existing on 20 August 1820, of 494,950 lire, are considerably lower than those of the preliminary sales agreement in 1798 (1,355,830 lire), due mainly to the closure of the historic Pieve Tesino agency in 1817 and of the downsizing of the typographic business and bookshop in Venice.

In economic terms, the company always recorded a profit in the period analysed and the overall profitability is not insignificant, with an ROE that varies from 5.6% to 10.0%. However, less than half of the profit was retained, perhaps demonstrating less interest in the fortunes of the company than in the past.

Compared to the accounting documents analysed in the previous paragraphs, from the exculpatory decrees we can draw valuable information on the profitability of different business sectors and the consequent suggestions from the auditors on pricing policies to adopt, cost containment, the recovery of receivables, the businesses to stop and the activities to invest in.

In the exculpatory decree of the first report,[10] the auditors express very positive final judgments and, in fact, the best economic results out of all five reports presented were obtained here (even recalculating the revenue over twelve months, we get a profit of 80,018.52 lire). However, they report that general expenses seem excessive, urging the guardian to contain them.

In the following years, the main findings of the auditors are concentrated on the typographic business, whose inventory of books seems excessive. Specifically, in the exculpatory decree of the second report[11] they suggest resolving the stock of books by lowering prices compared to competitors and allocating the resources gained to increase the activities of the paper mill, of the coloured papers and of the chalcography, which ensure more reliable and calculable earnings.

However, already in the third report, the auditors' attention turns to chalcography and for the same reason of the typography—namely, a production of prints greater than their sales that generates excessive stock. The advice is the same: to resort to a policy of discounts in order to reduce inventory and increase the turnover of goods.

However, we do not think this management policy turned out to be very effective, given the slow but gradual decrease in profit of typography and chalcography, probably because of the dismantling of the distribution network of street vendors and the decline of Venice in favour of Milan as the capital of Italian publishing.

Table 8.3 The performance and the evolution of the financial position (Lombardo-Venetian lire, also named Austrian lire)

	Judicial inventory	*I Report*	*I Report (with adjusted values)*	*II Report*	*III Report*	*IV Report*	*V Report*
	20/8/1820	*20/8/1820–31/3/1822*	*20/8/1820–31/3/1822*	*1/4/1822–31/3/1823*	*1/4/1823–31/3/1824*	*1/4/1824–31/3/1825*	*1/4/1825–31/3/1826*
Profit for the period		580 days	580 days				
Hall:							
• Chalcography					20,309.10	10,154.55	7,559.37
• Typography				19,659.18	15,106.00	9,686.25	24,417.83
• Coloured paper shop						6,998.77	5,287.14
• White paper						237.62	851.76
Total hall (*)		87,342.00	87,342.00	45,043.37		27,077.19	38,116.10
Bottega				5,224.33		4,760.27	4,282.21
Paper mill				3,556.34	6,430.56	12,421.79	17,851.01
Mezzà (**)				3,618.86		3,946.85	3,357.16
Total profit		128,696.46	128,696.46	57,442.90	56,817.93	48,206.10	63,606.48
Balance sheet							
Typography	323,138.21						
Chalcography	175,782.78						
Tools	10,412.25						
Credits	247,218.35						
Total assets (***)	756,551.59	822,020.65	822,020.65	821,404.21	853,003.01	869,580.74	894,212.34
Liabilities	261,600.65	242,071.88	21,821.58	14,335.10	17,625.90	16,216.60	12,749.79
Equity	494,950.94	579,948.77	800,199.07	807,069.11	835,377.11	853,364.14	881,462.55
Increase in equity		84,997.83		6,870.04	28,308.00	17,987.03	28,098.41
ROE (net income/equity)			10.0%	7.1%	6.8%	5.6%	7.2%

(*) The manufacturing complex in the main square of Bassano.
(**) It dealt with the collection of receivables and the payment of debts.
(***) Does not include cash, which was unique for the entire family's assets.

The agencies of Borgo and Cividale were even at a loss, demonstrating their difficulty in product distribution. The only business with a constantly growing profit was the paper mill in Oliero, whose management was always praised by the auditors.

The auditors, besides paying attention to the high rate of surplus, also indicate that the bulk of receivables located in the accounts of the Mezzà presented some collection difficulties. In the exculpatory decree of the second report,[12] they maintain that the "collection is very low compared to the large sums that remain to be recovered". However, their complaints seem to have produced a positive effect, since in the exculpatory decree of the fifth report[13] they claim that the bulk of receivables had been greatly reduced and propose to recognize "some money-benefits at year's end to the Mezzà agents, based on the sum of old receivables they recovered in three years".

Methods of Bookkeeping and Accounting Records

It is not always easy to understand how the economic performance of each business branch was calculated from the exculpatory decrees, because often it is only the total indicated in the report that is taken.

However, sometimes analytical data is presented, demonstrating the use over time of different techniques.

As an example, the exculpatory decree uses the way of calculating the company's profit, from page E of the first report, in the following way:[14]

Increase of capitals and of credits in		£ 65,162.46
Debts repaid in		£ 33,781.53
Credits towards the family for effective surplus		
Turned	£ 22,445.39	
For giving	£ 336.00	30,025.47
For furniture purchased	£ 7,244.08	
Which gives a total profit of		**£ 128,969.46**

Profit was therefore determined as a change in balance sheet items.

In the later reports, we find examples of profit calculation on the basis of revenues, costs and surplus. For example, in the exculpatory decree of the second report,[15] the annual profit of the paper mill is calculated as the difference between "Ought to give" and "Ought to have" (though not using a table with contrasting sections), where:

- Under the prefix "Ought to give" we find the initial inventories (including tools), the rags supplied by the *bottega* in the square, the checks received from the general fund (we suppose for the payment of the cost of work and all other expenses) and the rental of premises;
- Under the prefix "Ought to have" there are the amounts of paper delivered to the hall and the various final inventories.

The Problem of Internal Transfer Prices

The need to separately monitor the economic performance of various areas of the Remondini company's business made it necessary to develop a system of internal prices in order to measure the transfers of goods and services between the various businesses. This is a typical problem of multi-business companies, which leads to various solutions, ranging from the valuation at cost (full, variable, marginal, etc.) to valuation based on price (market or reconstructed through the application of a margin of sustained costs) (Solomons, 1965; Kaplan and Atkinson, 1989). From the exculpatory decrees,[16] we find the following information on this topic:

- Each activity pays the building administration (which is not part of business but is another activity of the family) a rental for the premises used;
- The *bottega* in Piazza purchases the rags, raw material for the production of paper, and resells it to the Oliero paper mill, making profit on the cost price;
- The paper mill then sells paper to the hall and to the other business activities at a price higher than cost.

The solutions adopted by the company are consistent between one another, following the logic of valuation of transfer on the basis of market prices (or anyway reconstructed with the application of a margin), foreshadowing a trend that, over the next centuries, doctrine will indicate as the most opportune for multi-business companies where a sufficient centralization of decisions remains. Even the auditors agree on the first and last of the solutions indicated (complaining only that there was an effective circle of money, when compensation between internal accounts would be enough), but they emphatically criticize the one for the rags, branding it as an "illusion incompatible with good order, with simplicity and with the proper attribution that must prevail in administration, since all the branches of business equally belong to the girl (Teresa Gioseffa)". According to the auditors, in fact, it was important to identify the most advantageous branches, in order to push the guardian to favour them in future investments, which was not possible with the "confusion in earnings and appropriating a branch of profits from another", observing in fact that if the paper mill did not belong to the same owner it would not buy rags from a third party at a higher price but would open a shop itself to buy them at the best price directly to retail. Forgetting perhaps that the cost of running a shop dedicated to the purchasing of rags could have exceeded the rate applied by the shop in Piazza, they conclude by saying that "it would be fitting therefore if this useless round of apparent profits in favour of the shop were removed".

Valuation Criteria for Surplus Products

Some passages of the exculpatory decrees show us the criteria that were applied for the valuation of stocks, particularly of prints and books. In fact, in the exculpatory decree of the third report[17] the auditors, after claiming that that year, too, more prints had been made than sold, suggest according greater discounts to buyers. To evaluate the sustainability of the discount policy, they present the following information: "prints made that are valued at £ 64,867.08 used to cost only £ 44,696.80 so the profit of over a third that remains can be suitably reduced." It follows that the surplus of products was evaluated at the estimated selling price, and the auditors believed their value should be reduced not to cost but to the selling price that would come from the application of greater discounts suggested by the auditors (Edwards, 1989, 86–87).

The same method of valuation of inventory, based on selling prices net of discounts expected rather than on costs of production, is also applied to the considerable[18] inventory of books. On the same page, it says that typography in the previous year had claimed expenses for the production of books for £83,240.38 and had fabricated books for £194,203.48 gross, which is reduced to £100,985.81 through the established discount of 48%.

Ways of Accounting for Fixed Assets

From the various passages contained in the exculpatory decrees, we can understand that the Remondini company did not use methods of accounting for fixed assets comparable to modern-day ones.

Some goods, which according to current criteria would be classified as fixed assets, are recorded as assets but treated like stocks. For example, the exculpatory decree of the second report[19] determines the total of the inventory belonging to the hall by summing up, in addition to the amounts related to prints, white papers, coloured papers and books, those of the copper moulds, typefaces and tools.

In these inventories of the activities of the various branches, no other fixed assets appear, such as land, buildings, plants and equipment. For example, for typography there is no reference to the printing presses, and for the paper mill no machines for the production of paper.

The absence of land and buildings in these reports is justified by the fact that their management was thought to belong to the building administration and for this reason the productive activities (as mentioned earlier) had to pay rent to that administration. For the other durable goods, we can surmise a different accounting policy. In the exculpatory decree of the second report,[20] in order to justify a decrease in the income of the paper mill compared to the previous year, the auditors comment that "regarding the expenditure of £ 10,285.38 for the renovation of buildings and the cessation of works in the meantime, nothing can plead to the contrary, being certain that it will be compensated in the upcoming years". Thus they were aware of the many-year usefulness of the investments in real estate improvements (leading to larger compensation in the following years), but these were still spent entirely in the year when they were done, depressing the economic result.

A Long Demise in Short

The situation in the 1820s was clearly much different from the late eighteenth century, when the Remondini company reached its largest expansion. However, the company was still one of the most important printing houses in the Venetian mainland, with three hundred merchant agents in the Italian Peninsula and nineteen in Europe in 1820, and a flourishing production of decorated papers (Fantinato, 2007, 56–57).

Not many documents remain on the following years of the company's activity. The absence of sources and information is in itself a signal of its decadence, which lasted for many decades.

During the 1830s Teresa Gioseffa formally took over the inheritance from her mother. Under her direction, the Remondini company gradually reduced its size. During the 1848 revolution only six typographic presses remained. The long siege of Venice convinced her to close down the agency in the city, while starting negotiations to sell the company. Two former workers then took on the production of decorated paper (Fantinato, 2007, 57). But Teresa's efforts to sell the whole company succeeded only in 1859, when she finally married a wealthy landowner and moved with him to Venice. In 1860, when the debt resulting from the 1798 agreement with Antonio's branch of the family was finally extinguished, the company was liquidated, selling all the assets separately.

Conclusion

According to other studies (Infelise, 1980) the administrative structure of the Remondini company was pretty poor and undersized with regard to its dimensions. However, we found several surviving accounting records that provide some valuable information about the amount and composition of the business and some useful insights related to a wide range of accounting issues, including the following: the methods of bookkeeping, the content and structure of financial statements, the periodical reporting, the problems of internal transfer prices, the measurement criteria for inventories and receivables and the accounting treatment of fixed assets.

We consider the accounting primary sources analysed in this chapter significant because they show an evolution of the role played by the Remondini accounting system. Notably, in the early eighteenth century its main functions were keeping track of assets and liabilities and providing legal evidence for claims to be enforced in court; in the second half of the eighteenth century they were measuring profit to be divided between partners and holding the agent accountable (see *Ristretti di Bilanzio*); and finally in the early nineteenth century Remondini developed a well-organized accounting system meant to support business decisions on resource allocation between different operating segments (see the information taken from the exculpatory decrees).

It is likely that the accounting practices used by the Remondini company improved over time in response to: (a) the increased organizational complexity of the business, (b) the growing, even if partial, separation between ownership and management and (c) the reduction of profit margins during the decline period that urged a more sophisticated accounting system.

These findings suggest the opportunity to question in part a reconstruction that identifies in a decline of the entrepreneurial attitude of the family the main cause of the decline of the company's performance since the early 1790s. In particular, the choices Giuseppe Remondini junior made after succeeding his father in 1773 were crucial, if put into perspective, to allow the very long and quite exceptional survival of the company through the wars and revolutions of the early nineteenth century, which not many other firms of the former Venetian Republic did endure. Outsourcing bookprinting to appease guild members, while investing in the modernization of paper production to maintain competitive input costs, made the company much more resilient than it was under Giambattista Remondini's direction.

Appointing a general director to manage the daily operation of the different businesses of the company also allowed it to cope with the growing turbulence that followed the cultural, political and institutional changes of the late eighteenth century. The same is true for the use of partnerships to involve expert merchants with their non-reproducible abilities in specialized businesses.[21]

Family conflicts were then enhanced with the end of the ancient regime in 1797, forcing Giuseppe to get indebted to his brother in order to maintain control of the company. His son Francesco Remondini chose to downsize and retreat to the local market and traditional productions. Despite that, the availability of accounting documents during the tutorship period of Teresa Gioseffa Remondini makes it possible to say that the Remondini company was still in the 1820s making profits and investing in the maintenance and amelioration of plants. A divestment attitude gradually prevailed only following the further difficulties that hit the company in the subsequent decades, and was probably relented by the need to fulfil the repayment of internal family debts on the company budget.

We may then argue that entrepreneurial failure was rather the final consequence of a series of hard crises and difficulties, and not the primary cause of a decline in performance, which was likely to be much more drastic without the innovations introduced on the eve of the age of revolutions.

Notes

1. BGBM, Archivio Remondini, Catastico primo, cc. 232v–233.
2. Infelise (1990, 116) cites different conflicting documents that date the establishment of a local branch of the Remondini company in Pieve Tesino from the end of the seventeenth century to 1730.
3. BGBM, Archivio Remondini, Catastico primo, cc. 232v–233.
4. All the amounts are expressed in Venetian lire. In the original document, the properties are valued in ducats, whereas the assets and liabilities are expressed in Venetian lire. Therefore, in the tables above, we have translated the properties into Venetian lire, at the exchange rate of 1 ducat = 6.2 Venetian lire.

5. BGPC, Catastico 4.
6. BGPC, Catastico A.
7. BGPC, Catastico A.
8. BGPC, *Inventario Remondini*, vol. 1 and vol. 2. Infelise (1990, 207–208) cites the inventory from Zellini (1893, 158).
9. BGPC, *Catastico B*, cc. 34–159.
10. BGPC, *Catastico B*, cc. 54–55.
11. BGPC, *Catastico B*, c. 123.
12. BGPC, *Catastico B*, c. 117.
13. BGPC, *Catastico B*, c. 150.
14. BGPC, *Catastico B*, c. 47.
15. BGPC, *Catastico B*, c. 116.
16. BGPC, *Catastico B*, cc. 40–41, 43.
17. BGPC, *Catastico B*, c. 136.
18. In the exculpatory decree of the second report (BGPC, *Catastico B*, c. 123) the auditors observe that the inventories of books have a value of over four hundred thousand Italian lire and suggest dedicating attention to gaining this inventory capital by applying lower prices. The indicated value, compared with the value of the annual production, lets us understand that book inventories correspond to four times the annual production.
19. BGPC, *Catastico B*, c. 114.
20. BGPC, *Catastico B*, c. 116.
21. For a similar evolution in the ceramic industry, see Favero (2011, 203–207).

References

Berengo, M. (1980). *Intellettuali e librai nella Milano della Restaurazione*. Turin: Einaudi.

Berti, G., Ericani, G., Infelise, M., eds. (2008). *Una vita tra i libri: Bartolomeo Gamba*. Milan: Franco Angeli.

Brentari, O. (1882). *La casa Remondini e la corte di Spagna: aneddoto storico*. Bassano: Pozzato.

Brown, H.F. (1891). *The Venetian Printing Press 1469–1800: An Historical Study Based upon Documents for the Most Part Hitherto Unpublished*. London: Nimmo.

Chatfield, M. (1977). *A History of Accounting Thought*. Malabar, FL: Krieger Publishing Company.

Darnton, R.C. (1996). *The Forbidden Best-Sellers of Prerevolutionary France*. New York: Norton.

Del Sal, R. (2007). I libri. In: *Museo Remodini: guida*. Bassano del Grappa—Cittadella: Comune di Bassano del Grappa—Biblos Edizioni: 59–63.

Edwards, J.R. (1989). *A History of Financial Accounting*. London: Routledge.

Fantinato, M. (2007). Le carte decorate Remondini: tecniche, storia e caratteristiche di produzione. In: *Museo Remodini: guida*. Bassano del Grappa—Cittadella: Comune di Bassano del Grappa—Biblos Edizioni: 49–58.

Favero, G. [Gastone] (2013). Bassano dal 1795 al 1805: le municipalità e la prima dominazione austriaca. In: *di Bassano del Grappa: Vol. 2. L'età moderna*. Bassano del Grappa: Comitato per la storia di Bassano: 343–359.

Favero, G. [Giovanni] (2011). Privilegi d'industria e diritti di proprietà nelle manifatture di ceramica della Repubblica di Venezia (XVII–XVIII secolo). *Quaderni Storici*, 46(136.1): 185–220.

Freschi, G.B. (1661). *L'humiltà sublimata: Pabegrico alle glorie immortali dell'illustriss.mo e reuerendiss.mo sig.re mons. Giuseppe Ciurano*. Bassano: Gio. Antonio Remondin.

Giachery, A. (2015). Pinelli, famiglia. In: *Dizionario biografico degli italiani*. Rome: Istituto dell'Enciclopedia italiana: Vol. 83: 711–717.

Infelise, M. (1980). *I Remondini di Bassano*. Bassano: Tassotti.

Infelise, M. (1989). *L'editoria veneziana nel '700*. Milan: Franco Angeli.

Infelise, M. (1990). *I Remodini di Bassano: stampa e industria nel Veneto del Settecento*. Bassano: Ghedina & Tassotti Editori.

Infelise, M. (2013). La Casa Remondini. In: *Storia di Bassano del Grappa: Vol. 2. L'età moderna*. Bassano del Grappa: Comitato per la storia di Bassano: 305–319.

Kaplan R.S., Atkinson A.A. (1989). *Advanced Management Accounting*. Englewood Cliffs, NJ: Prentice-Hall.

Monteleone, G. (1969). La carestia del 1816–17 nelle provincie venete. *Archivio Veneto*, 5th series, 43(86–87): 23–86.

Pasta, R. (1995). Towards a social history of ideas: The book and the booktrade in eighteen century Italy. In: H.E. Bödeker, ed. *Histoires du livre: nouvelles orientations. Actes du colloque du 6 et 7 septembre 1990, Göttingen*. Paris: IMEC/ Maison des sciences de l'homme: 101–138.

Pasta, R. (2005). The history of the book and publishing in eighteenth-century Italy. *Journal of Modern Italian Studies*, 10(2): 200–217.

Roehner, B.M. (1997). Jesuits and the state: A comparative study of their expulsions (1590–1990). *Religion*, 27(2): 165–182.

Solomons, D. (1965). *Divisional Performance: Measurement and Control*. Homewood, IL: Irwin.

Yamey, B. (1970). Closing the ledger. *Accounting and Business Research*, 1(1): 71–77.

Zellini, L. (1893). *L'arte della stampa a Bassano*. Dissertation. Padua: University of Padua (available at BGBM, mss. 30 B 18–1/2).

9 Carive's Accounting System

An Evolutionary Perspective on Its Early Years

Moreno Mancin, Carlo Marcon, Marco Fasan and Michele D'Alessandro

Introduction

The "Cassa di Risparmio di Venezia" (Carive) was Venice's savings bank and it was the oldest institution of its kind in Italy. Carive was originally created under the initiative of politics, with the aim of keeping the Province of Venice at pace, in terms of the evolution of the financial sector, with other European countries. Ultimately, this institution did lead to significant modernization in the local economic and credit sectors.

This chapter analyses how Carive's accounting system evolved—in terms of presentation rather than measurement—from its independence from the Mount of Piety (1853) until the end of the century. This research question is particularly relevant because we cover a period (1853–1888) that is long enough to capture a number of significant changes in the Carive accounting system. On top of this, Carive used to operate in a substantially deregulated environment, meaning that these changes were caused by Carive itself rather than by external regulation.

We gathered the original Carive annual reports from the bank's historical archives and we analysed them in order to find their most relevant changes, which we found in the financial statements of the following years: 1853, 1863, 1877 and 1888. We found that these changes mainly referred to the structure of the financial statements and the contents of the balance sheet and income statement. Among the main innovations and changes, which are discussed in detail in the third section, there is an increased importance of the income perspective over the patrimonial perspective in the structure of the financial statements. In fact, we found that the earliest Carive financial statements had a mostly patrimonial approach. Together with a more and more detailed representation of costs and revenues, Carive also increased the detail of the representation of equity, which in 1888 was split between different reserves. The bank also introduced, in 1888, a specific figure regarding its charitable activity, in order to increase its accountability towards stakeholders.

We then hypothesize, in the fourth section, some possible explanations for the factors driving such changes. The first one is that the changes were due to changes in Carive's activities. We find that greater (and different) kinds of investments and sources of financing required the bank to evolve its financial statements in order to provide a more complete representation. The second hypothesis, which we also find support for, is that Carive employed financial statements in order to build trust and stronger accountability towards its stakeholders.

The chapter is divided into the following sections: the second section, entitled "The Cassa di Risparmio di Venezia in the Long Nineteenth Century", provides a discussion of the history and evolution of Carive during the nineteenth century. It points out governance, economic and geopolitical events influencing Carive's evolution. The third section analyses the changes in the accounting system. The fourth section relates such changes to the changes in Carive's activities and to its relationships with stakeholders. Finally, the last section provides a conclusion.

The Cassa di Risparmio di Venezia in the Long Nineteenth Century

The Cassa di Risparmio di Venezia (Carive) was one of the first savings banks established in Italy. Its founding in 1822 at the instance of the Habsburgs, then ruling over the Lombardo-Venetian Kingdom, came as part of the wider Western European movement of founding savings banks, which started in the late eighteenth century and gathered steam following the Napoleonic Wars. While unquestionably a sign that the Venetian economy was keeping pace with institutional developments in more advanced areas of Europe, in its early years, Carive had only limited success, mostly because of its close association with the local public pawn-broking institution. Indeed, it was not until it came into its own in the early 1850s that Carive started to establish solid roots in the city's economy and society, by means of (1) an increasingly diversified supply of credit and financial services to both the public and private sectors, and (2) an uninterrupted flow of donations to a host of charitable, educational and health institutions based in Venice and its province. By 1914, while remaining a non-profit organization, subject to government regulation and more risk-averse than commercial and cooperative banks, Carive was by far the largest financial intermediary in Venice in deposits, had started branching out into the province, and held a portfolio largely made up of bills of exchange (23.5%), government bonds (18.7%), mortgage loans (16.9%) and long-term loans to local government bodies (10.1%).

The idea of savings banks as institutions meant to collect deposits from the lower classes and instil the value of thrift is usually traced back to the French Hugues Delestre in 1611 (Bachi 1923: 3; Pohl 1993: 18). It gained traction in Europe in the late eighteenth century when increasing poverty numbers raised concerns about the social order among enlightened social reformers and philanthropists—not to mention political authorities. As noted by Fishlow (1961), in an era of prevailing self-help ideology, savings banks, which promised depositors attractive returns, liquidity and security (Ó Gráda 2009), were regarded by many as an effective way of helping the poor take care of their own needs by setting aside small sums of money for rainy days and old age. Inspired by this concept, savings banks were first established in Hamburg (1778), Oldenburg (1786) and Berne (1787) (Pohl 1993). In Britain, where nearly 500 savings banks were founded between 1810 and 1818, the government had begun regulating them in 1817 (Ó Gráda 2009). By 1820, savings banks had been established in Scandinavia, Paris and Vienna, and were soon to reach Italy, Spain and Portugal. While the principle of the savings bank travelled across borders with little, if any, change, local conditions greatly affected its actual foundation, so we see great variation in the founders, statutes and operations of individual savings banks from country to country and even region to region.

In the Venetian Kingdom, the invitation to set up savings banks came from the imperial government in 1820 and was met by a plan to entrust the local Mount of Piety with the foundation and management of the new institutions (Battistella 1922).[1] Drawn up by an aide of the Venetian governor, the plan envisaged that the sums deposited in the bank would be invested at the pawnshop, with pawned objects serving as a guarantee for depositors. This represented a significant departure from the prevailing British, French and even Austrian models, whereby a group of wealthy bourgeois and noblemen usually acted as promoters, trustees and even managers of the savings banks. More importantly, the two institutions had rather conflicting objectives, as pawnshops catered to current consumption needs, whereas savings banks aimed to spread the habit of saving. Independent of whether the Venetian governor was right in his assessment of local conditions—namely, that Venice lacked philanthropists and wage earners in sufficient numbers and those who earned enough to save were profligate rather than thrifty—it was clear that the integration of the savings bank and the Mount of Piety would better serve the interest of the latter and relegate the former to the role of a captive supplier of funds.[2] To some extent, the situation was further compounded by the fact that—unlike its mainland counterparts—the municipal pawnshop in Venice was a relatively young institution, still seeking a stable institutional arrangement and adequate organization when Carive opened its doors on 12 February 1822.[3]

As a result, the first three decades of Carive proved tortuous, since every step of growth the savings bank made could be easily reversed by the high instability that characterized its "parent" company. Such instability could have a variety of causes: from the ebbs and flows in the demand for credit to fraud committed by the pawnshop's clerks,[4] from changes in supervision[5] to exogenous political shocks.[6] More importantly, the association of Carive with the Mount deprived the savings bank of the trust necessary to elicit deposits from the public, both because of the lack of sound guarantees[7] and because of the dubious reputation associated with the pawnshop. On top of this, as Agostino Sagredo (1848) lamented, a "thick cloud" had always shrouded the administration of the two institutions, preventing the public from acquiring basic information regarding their health status.

The information available—however scant and fragmented—shows that Carive slowly succeeded in attracting a number of depositors. By the end of 1824, they were sixty-nine, with a total of 16,635 Austrian liras—that is, an average of 241 liras per depositor. Twenty years later, in 1845, the figure had risen to 3,429, with an average of 1,033 Austrian liras per depositor, which suggests that Carive's customers were increasingly coming from the middle and wealthy classes, following a pattern common to other Italian and foreign savings banks (Battistella 1922: 228–29; Bembo 1859: 183; De Piante 1929; Fishlow 1961; Monteleone e Stella 1974).[8]

In 1851, a severe crisis hit the Mount, causing a loss in excess of 500,000 Austrian liras, and forced a reluctant Austrian government to effect an additional excise on wine to prevent the pawnshop's bankruptcy. This last straw finally convinced the authorities to sever all administrative and legal ties between the Mount and Carive. On 1 July 1853, the latter moved to a new location, obtained a deposit guarantee from the municipality, and started its new independent life on safer ground (Battistella 1922: 235).

In the second half of the nineteenth century, freer to determine its own path, Carive kept growing, intensifying its interaction with the local economy and managing to carve out a distinct role for itself in the city's credit market. For decades, since the return of the Habsburgs in the mid-1810s, Venice had faced short periods of growth alternating with frequent crises and phases of stagnation. In the new geopolitical setting, besides losing its sovereignty and becoming a province of the Austro-Hungarian Empire, Venice had lost its foreign possessions. Its port, outcompeted by Trieste, had been gradually downgraded to a transit node, serving a greatly reduced hinterland. As Bernardello (2002) puts it, in the years from 1830 to 1866, Venice's economy is best described as a laborious quest for economic modernization conducted by a few amidst a majority of traditional, obsolescent businesses and trades. During this period, old and new members of the city's elite—merchants, private bankers, brokers and noblemen—were ready to invest in modern undertakings as part of a risk diversification strategy—hence the widespread support in the mid-1830s for the railway linking Venice to Milan, seen as a means of besting Trieste; the founding of shipyards and steam shipping companies for inland waterway transport; the establishment of mining companies aimed at reducing dependence on British coal; textile mills, food processing and metallurgical companies that adopted steam power and up-to-date technologies. Nor were services neglected, as attested by the establishment of the Società Veneta Commerciale (1839) and the experiment with joint-stock banking represented by the Stabilimento Mercantile in the 1850s (Bernardello 2002) and, from the 1860s, by the popular banks based on Schulze-Delitzsch's principles.

For some time, Venice's annexation into the Italian Kingdom in 1866 did little to alter this picture of slow change. It was not until the 1880s that the city's economy began to achieve effective integration into the national market.

This development was, to a great extent, the result of (1) Venetian businessmen like Alessandro Rossi and Vincenzo Stefano Breda coming to the fore and getting involved in the major industrial enterprises of the time, and (2) large infrastructure projects aimed at building up capacity and revitalizing port activities (Reberschak 1997; Roverato 1984). In these years, Venice also managed to attract foreign direct investments in a number of sectors, from utilities to manufacturing, insurance and transport services, with French, Swiss and German capital setting up and running city-based companies.

Following the crisis of the late 1880s and early 1890s, economic activity resumed buoyantly, with the city eventually fully embracing modernity at the dawn of the twentieth century. On the one hand, this occurred by putting into effect ambitious plans of business expansion in the Balkans and further east, promoted by Pietro Foscari and Giuseppe Volpi. On the other hand, modernity came with substantial investment in power production and the project of building a vast industrial area in Marghera, south of the lagoon. These plans and projects were backed with strong political support, were funded by national financial institutions, and benefited from ad hoc legislation. Meanwhile, the number of workers in manufacturing increased: from 15,766 in 1885 to 16,629 in 1898 and 22,993 in 1911 (Reberschak 1997).

Against this backdrop of gradually modernizing economic structures, Carive's growth after 1853 proceeded smoothly, keeping with its mission of collecting deposits from the lower classes, which implied cautious investment and credit policies. The savings bank pursued a strategy of portfolio diversification, with private sector customers coming to play a substantial role alongside public sector entities. It started to invest in government securities as a class of highly liquid and relatively safe assets and intensified the accumulation of reserves as a means of strengthening capital and trust. Moreover, true to its philanthropic origin and non-profit nature, from 1874 onwards, Carive kept donating a fraction of its profits to a host of city institutions in the areas of social care, culture and education, which went a long way in earning the bank special consideration from Venice's citizens.

If one excludes the effect of the business cycle on lending policies, major turning points in the bank's evolution in the second half of the nineteenth century seemingly lie in regulation. In this respect, two events stand out. First, the redefinition of its relationship with the Mount of Piety in 1876, whereby all remaining legal ties were definitively cut and the municipality's guarantee on Carive's deposits was withdrawn (Battistella 1922: 235–236). Then, in 1888, the Savings Bank Law, with which the government laid down a comprehensive set of regulations and put a supervisory framework in place that was expressly intended to monitor the behaviour of savings banks.[9] In addition to the many detailed norms regarding savings bank foundation, changes in by-laws, minimum capital, liquidation and so on, the legislation required that savings banks allocate 90% of their annual profit to reserve until the ratio reserves/deposits reached 10%, and that the remaining profit be paid out as charitable donations. It was a set of rules that, after ten years of waiting for the approval of its new by-laws in 1886, Carive was already largely compliant with. Following up on the 1888 law, in 1889 the ministry issued forms (later revised in 1898) for the biannual transmission of financial statements to the government, which set a new accounting standard for savings banks.

The Evolution of Carive's Reporting System: An Accounting Perspective

The aim of this section is to analyse and discuss the evolution of Carive's financial statements, in terms of degree of detail, focus and accountability. We chose to focus on four different reports, published in 1853, 1863, 1877 and 1888. To choose these reports, we first accessed all the reports published by Carive from 1853 on (the year it became an independent institution) and then we selected the reports presenting significant discontinuity from the past in terms of accounting practice.

The first report covers the period from 1 July to 31 December 1853, and it is Carive's first ever financial statement (Figure 9.1). In general, its activity

BILANCIO

della Cassa Risparmio in Venezia da 1.° Luglio a tutto 31 Dicembre 1853

Movimento Capitali ed Interessi a credito degli Azionisti ed a debito della Cassa Risparmio

Numero degli Azionisti	INTROITI	Austriache Lire	C.	Numero degli Azionisti	PAGAMENTI	Austriache Lire	C.
1708	Capitali con interessi consegnati dalla Direzione del Monte a credito degli Azionisti a tutto 30 Giugno 1853	1.907.480	93	464	Capitali ed interessi affrancati da 1. Luglio a tutto 31 Decembre 1853	771,013	94
630	Nuove investite da 1. Luglio a tutto Decembre 1853	702,086	02				
	Competenza interessi da 1. Luglio a tutto Decembre 1853 al 4 per cento	36,627	75				
2338	L.	2,646,194	70		L.	771,013	94
464	Pagate come di contro „	771,013	94				
1874	Residuo Capitale .. L.	1,875,180	76				

Movimento Capitali ed Interessi a credito della Cassa Risparmio ed a debito del Monte di Pietà in Venezia

INVESTITI	Austriache Lire	C.	RITIRATI	Austriache Lire	C.
Capitale rimasto a debito della Direzione del Monte a tutto 30 Giugno 1853 per Capitali ed interessi a credito degli Azionisti, ed assunti dalla nuova Amministrazione.	1,907,480	93	Capitali ritirati dalla Direzione del Monte da 1. Luglio a tutto Decembre 1853	102,609	56
Capitali investiti presso la stessa Direzione del Monte da 1. Luglio a tutto 31 Decembre 1853	28,000	—	Interessi pagati mensilmente dalla suddetta Direzione a tutto Decembre 1853	38,643	16
Interessi scalari del 5 per cento sopra detti Capitali da 1. Luglio a tutto Decembre 1853	46,280	49	L.	141,252	72
L.	1,981,761	05			
Ritirate come di contro .. „	141,252	72			
Residuo Capitale ...... L.	1,840,508	33			

RIEPILOGO

Credito verso la Direzione del Monte	L. 1.840.508.33
Rimanenza di Cassa a tutto 31 Decembre 1853	„ 40.474.83
Credito complessivo	L. 1.880.983.16
Debito per Capitali ed interessi da pagarsi agli Azionisti .	„ 1.875.180.76
Utilità depurata dalle spese d'Amministrazione	L. 5,802.40

Competenza interessi attiva 5 per cento . .		L. 46,280.42
idem passiva 4 per cento	L. 36,627.75	
Onorarj e stampe. . . .	„ 3.849,97	
		„ 40,477.72
Utile come di contro		L. 5,802,40

Venezia li 10 Gennajo 1855.

L'ASSESSORE MUNICIPALE PRESIDENTE
NOB. CAV. PIER GIROLAMO VENIER

Consiglieri
NOB. DOTT. GIO. BATTISTA ANGELI
CONTE CAV. FRANCESCO DONÀ DALLE ROSE
NOB. PIER LUIGI GRIMANI
NOB. CAV. JACOPO TREVES DI BONFILI

GIUSEPPE BAMPO *Ragionato*

Venezia 1855 – G. Longo Tipografo Municipale

Figure 9.1 Carive's report from 1 July 1853 to 31 December 1853

Source: *Archivio storico Carive, "Cassa di Risparmio di Venezia—Bilanci", fascicolo A* (II), 1853–1874

and, consequently, its financial representation were still very much linked to the Mount of Piety. Even though Carive had the power to invest in any activity (being an independent institution since 1 July 1853), most of its investments were still directed towards the Mount of Piety.

The report has two main counterpoised sections: the "Movements of Capital and Interests Credited to the Shareholders and Debited to Carive" and "Movements of Capital and Interests Credited to Carive and Debited to the Mount of Piety", both including stock and flow numbers. The first section (on the left) represents Carive's sources, particularly showing the debts towards shareholders (the exact term "shareholder" is not correctly used, as there was no equity and the creditors were not offering their capital as risk capital) and their changes. Conversely, the second section (on the right) represents the resources of Carive, basically credits towards the Mount of Piety and their changes.

It is interesting to note that, below the main statement, on the left, there is a very brief representation of the net income of the period ("*riepilogo*"). In particular, the net income (5,802 liras) was computed both as the difference between the overall assets (cash and loans) and the overall debts and as the difference between revenues and expenses. Carive did not lend much importance to this elementary income statement, as can be seen by the amount of space devoted to it.

At the end of the first year of reporting, Carive's equity coincides with the generated net income of 5,802 Austrian liras. The bank, in fact, was actually established without any contribution of capital by way of equity. The initial sources of financing, therefore, were made up solely of savings deposits collected from customers. For this reason, the bank had a very low initial leverage ratio of 3.1% (equity/total asset), and for the same reason, savers who had deposits at the bank were identified as shareholders, as they were the only subjects exposed to a risk on capital in the bank (though as liabilities).

The 1863 report introduces an important innovation, as it gives much more importance to the income perspective, compared to previous years (Figure 9.2).

More specifically, next to the balance sheet, there is a statement ("*dettaglio delle rendite e spese dell'amministrazione*") that can be considered a primordial income statement. First, the statement discloses the revenues (e.g., interest revenues on mortgages or on government bonds) and then the costs (i.e., interest expenses to be paid to depositors, salaries or administrative expenses). The difference between revenues and costs ("*totale utilità II semestre* 1863"), amounting to 7,002 Austrian florins, is the net income. The 1863 report uses net income, calculated in such a way to provide a breakdown of the equity. At the bottom of the balance sheet, the report discloses the difference between assets and liabilities (82,411 Austrian florins, "*avanzo di rendita*") and specifies that the equity belonging to previous years was 75,408 Austrian florins and to the current year was 7,002 Austrian florins (i.e., the net income).

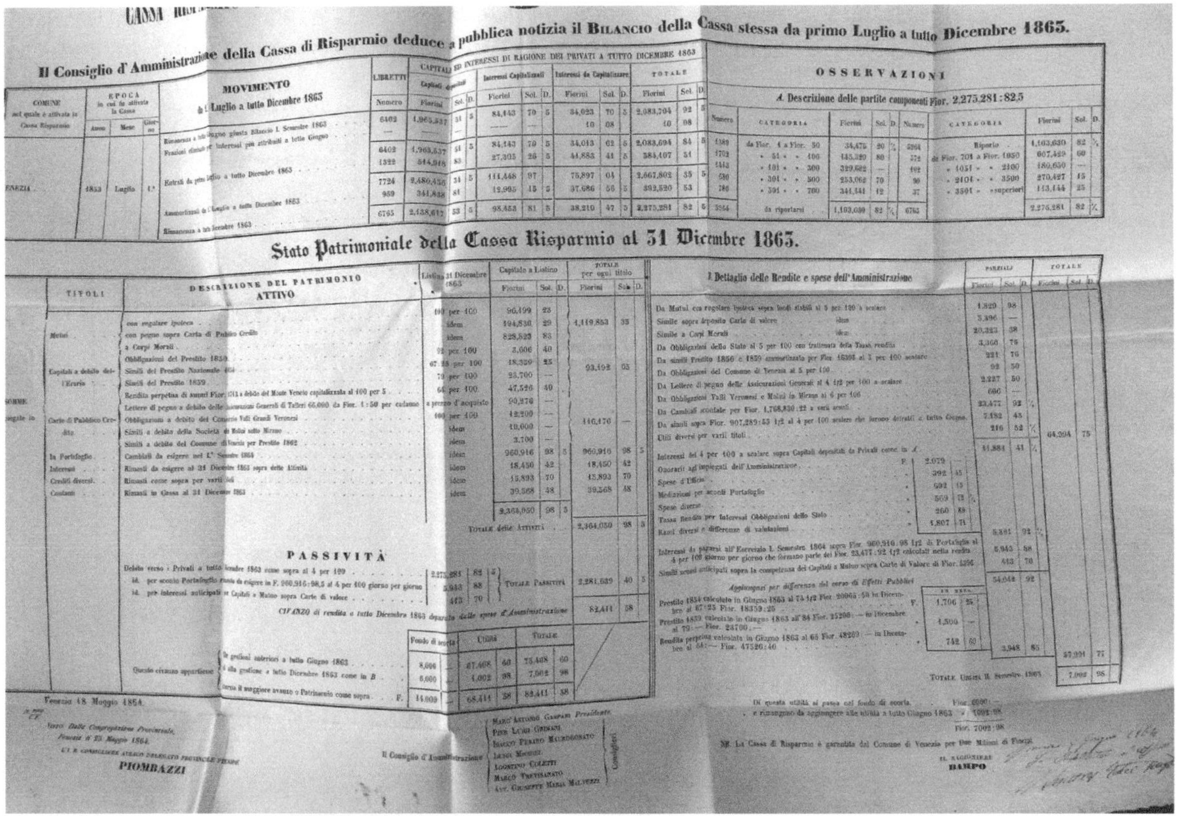

Il Consiglio d'Amministrazione della Cassa di Risparmio deduce a pubblica notizia il Bilancio della Cassa stessa da primo Luglio a tutto Dicembre 1863.

OSSERVAZIONI

Stato Patrimoniale della Cassa Risparmio al 31 Dicembre 1863.

PASSIVITÀ

Figure 9.2 Carive report from 1 July 1863 to 31 December 1863.

Source: Archivio storico Carive, "Cassa di Risparmio di Venezia—Bilanci", fascicolo A (II), 1853–1874).

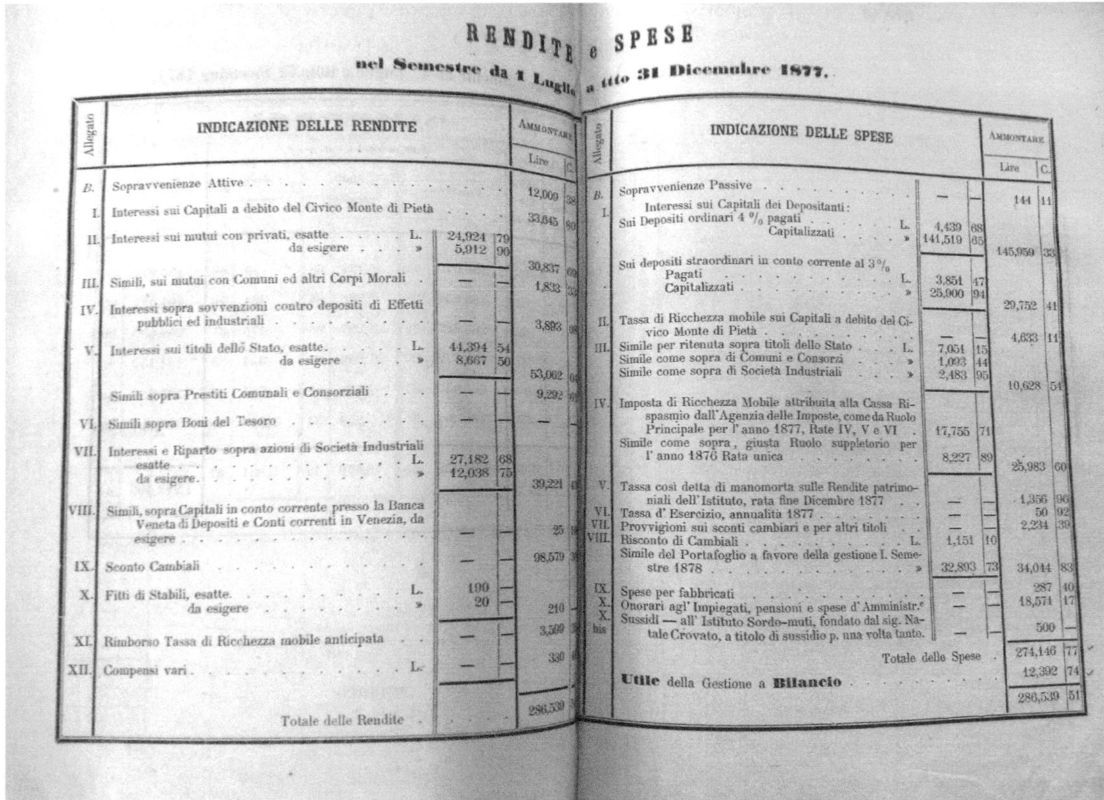

RENDITE e SPESE

nel Semestre da 1 Luglio a tutto 31 Dicembre 1877.

Allegato	INDICAZIONE DELLE RENDITE			Ammontare Lire	C.
B.	Sopravvenienze Attive			12,009	38
I.	Interessi sui Capitali a debito del Civico Monte di Pietà			33,645	80
II.	Interessi sui mutui con privati, esatte . . . L.	24,924	79		
	da esigere . . . »	5,912	90	30,837	69
III.	Simili, sui mutui con Comuni ed altri Corpi Morali	—	—	1,833	33
IV.	Interessi sopra sovvenzioni contro depositi di Effetti pubblici ed industriali	—	—	3,893	[illegible]
V.	Interessi sui titoli dello Stato, esatte . . . L.	44,394	54		
	da esigere . . . »	8,667	50	53,062	04
	Simili sopra Prestiti Comunali e Consorziali	—	—	9,292	[illegible]
VI.	Simili sopra Boni del Tesoro	—	—	—	—
VII.	Interessi e Riparto sopra azioni di Società Industriali esatte . . . L.	27,182	68		
	da esigere . . . »	12,038	75	39,221	[illegible]
VIII.	Simili, sopra Capitali in conto corrente presso la Banca Veneta di Depositi e Conti correnti in Venezia, da esigere	—	—	25	[illegible]
IX.	Sconto Cambiali	—	—	98,579	[illegible]
X.	Fitti di Stabili, esatte . . . L.	190	—		
	da esigere . . . »	20	—	210	—
XI.	Rimborso Tassa di Ricchezza mobile anticipata	—	—	3,509	[illegible]
XII.	Compensi vari . . . L.	—	—	330	[illegible]
	Totale delle Rendite			286,539	[illegible]

Allegato	INDICAZIONE DELLE SPESE			Ammontare Lire	C.
B.	Sopravvenienze Passive	—	—	144	11
I.	Interessi sui Capitali dei Depositanti: Sui Depositi ordinari 4 % pagati . . . L.	4,439	68		
	Capitalizzati . . . »	141,519	65	145,959	33
	Sui depositi straordinari in conto corrente al 3 % Pagati . . . L.	3,851	47		
	Capitalizzati . . . »	25,900	94	29,752	41
II.	Tassa di Ricchezza mobile sui Capitali a debito del Civico Monte di Pietà	—	—	4,633	11
III.	Simile per ritenuta sopra titoli dello Stato . . . L.	7,051	15		
	Simile come sopra di Comuni e Consorzi . . . »	1,093	44		
	Simile come sopra di Società Industriali . . . »	2,483	95	10,628	54
IV.	Imposta di Ricchezza Mobile attribuita alla Cassa Risparmio dall'Agenzia delle Imposte, come da Ruolo Principale per l'anno 1877, Rate IV, V e VI	17,755	71		
	Simile come sopra, giusta Ruolo suppletorio per l'anno 1876 Rata unica	8,227	89	25,983	60
V.	Tassa così detta di manomorta sulle Rendite patrimoniali dell'Istituto, rata fine Dicembre 1877	—	—	1,356	96
VI.	Tassa d'Esercizio, annualità 1877	—	—	50	92
VII.	Provvigioni sui sconti cambiari e per altri titoli	—	—	2,234	39
VIII.	Risconto di Cambiali . . . L.	1,151	10		
	Simile del Portafoglio a favore della gestione I. Semestre 1878 . . . »	32,893	73	34,044	83
IX.	Spese per fabbricati	—	—	287	40
X.	Onorari agl' Impiegati, pensioni e spese d'Amministr.e	—	—	18,571	17
X. bis	Sussidi — all' Istituto Sordo-muti, fondato dal sig. Natale Crovato, a titolo di sussidio p. una volta tanto.	—	—	500	—
	Totale delle Spese			274,146	77
	Utile della Gestione a **Bilancio**			12,392	74
				286,539	51

Figure 9.3 Carive's income statement 1 July 1877 to 31 December 1877

Source: *Archivio storico Carive*, "*Cassa di Risparmio di Venezia—Bilanci*", *fascicolo* A (II), 1853–1874

With the 1877 report, Carive further increases its focus on the income perspective and it presents its first "independent" Income Statement ("rendite e spese"). The document covers a period of 6 months and it is divided into two counterpoised sections. On the left, there are the revenues ("rendite"), which for the most part come from discount of bills and different kinds of interests: (i) for investments in the Mount of Piety ("interessi sui capitali a debito del Civico Monte di Pietà"), (ii) for mortgages ("interessi su mutui con private"); (iii) for investments on government bonds ("Interessi sui titoli dello stato"); (iv) for investments in other firms ("interessi e riparto sopra Azioni di Società Industriali"). Among the costs ("spese"), the most relevant item is interest expenses towards depositors ("interessi sui capitali dei depositanti").

Among the liabilities, for the first time, the report discloses a specific item for equity ("*Fondo di riserva, o Patrimonio proprio della Cassa di Risparmio, per Utili conseguiti da 1 luglio 1853, epoca della nuova sua istituzione, a tutto 31 dicembre 1877*"), including the cumulative income from the foundation of Carive (1 July 1853) to 31 December 1877.

Continuing in our analysis of Carive's reporting methods, 1886 represents an important "breaking point" in the life of the bank: on 22 July, a new statute was approved and legitimized as executive, which called for a series of changes in the governance of the institution and the simultaneous and definitive cessation of any obligation to the Mount of Piety, consequently calling for the repeal of the latter's right to demand subsidies from the savings bank. The same statute establishes (art. 33) that 10% of net profits must be given to works of public utility and charity. Just over a year after the approval of the new statute, the 1888 balance sheet fully implements these innovations, which mark the life and operation of the institution profoundly (Figure 9.4).

One of the main innovations of the 1888 report is the balance sheet structure. While up to this point, Carive was laying out each asset and liability item by item, the 1888 report introduces some more general categories. For instance, instead of listing the credits towards each city (represented by bonds issued by the municipality itself), the report uses the more general category "*Titoli di provincie e comuni*". The aim of this new categorization seems to be that of making the report easier to read for external stakeholders. The representation of the equity ("*patrimonio netto*") was further refined in order to include reserves that were devoted to certain purposes. In particular, Carive created a reserve for covering pension costs for employees or their widows ("*Fondo pensioni vitalizie a favore degli impiegati e loro vedove*") and for changes in the value of bonds included among the assets ("*Fondo di riserva per far fronte alle oscillazioni dei valori pubblici ed industriali*"). Both these reserves make up an allocation in the period of the income statement. Although the original name did not identify them as reserves but as a "provision" ("*Fondi*" in the original Italian), they are a component of equity in all respects (and therefore reserves).

As the income statement increased its degree of detail while maintaining the same structure, Carive introduced another report providing information

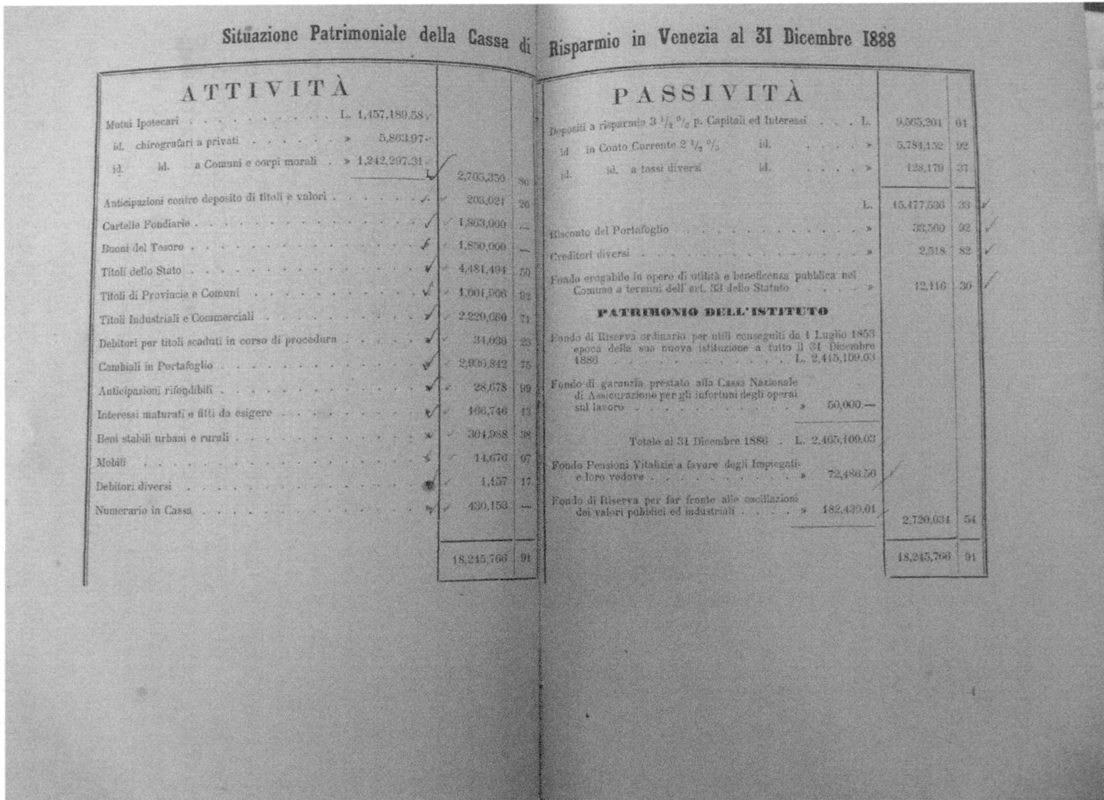

Situazione Patrimoniale della Cassa di Risparmio in Venezia al 31 Dicembre 1888

ATTIVITÀ

Mutui Ipotecari	L. 1,457,189.58		
id. chirografari a privati	» 5,863.97		
id. id. a Comuni e corpi morali	» 1,242,297.31	2,705,350	86
Anticipazioni contro deposito di titoli e valori		203,021	26
Cartelle Fondiarie		1,863,000	—
Buoni del Tesoro		1,850,000	—
Titoli dello Stato		4,481,494	50
Titoli di Provincie e Comuni		1,001,906	92
Titoli Industriali e Commerciali		2,229,080	71
Debitori per titoli scaduti in corso di procedura		34,030	23
Cambiali in Portafoglio		2,930,842	75
Anticipazioni rifondibili		28,678	09
Interessi maturati e fitti da esigere		166,746	13
Beni stabili urbani e rurali		304,988	38
Mobili		14,676	07
Debitori diversi		1,457	17
Numerario in Cassa		430,153	—
		18,245,766	91

PASSIVITÀ

Depositi a risparmio 3 ½ % p. Capitali ed Interessi	L.	9,565,204	04
id. in Conto Corrente 2 ½ % id.	»	5,784,152	92
id. id. a tassi diversi id.	»	128,179	37
	L.	15,477,536	33
Risconto del Portafoglio	»	33,560	92
Creditori diversi	»	2,518	82
Fondo erogabile in opere di utilità e beneficenza pubblica nel Comune a termini dell'art. 33 dello Statuto	»	12,116	30
PATRIMONIO DELL'ISTITUTO			
Fondo di Riserva ordinario per utili conseguiti da 1 Luglio 1853 epoca della sua nuova istituzione a tutto il 31 Dicembre 1886	L. 2,415,109.03		
Fondo di garanzia prestato alla Cassa Nazionale di Assicurazione per gli infortuni degli operai sul lavoro	» 50,000.—		
Totale al 31 Dicembre 1886	L. 2,465,109.03		
Fondo Pensioni Vitalizie a favore degli Impiegati e loro vedove	» 72,486.50		
Fondo di Riserva per far fronte alle oscillazioni dei valori pubblici ed industriali	» 182,439.01	2,720,034	54
		18,245,766	91

Figure 9.4 Carive's balance sheet 1 January 1888 to 31 December 1888

Source: *Archivio storico Carive, "Cassa di Risparmio di Venezia—Bilanci", fascicolo A (II), 1853–1874*

on its charitable activities. This increased the level of disclosure and accountability towards the community, in a period when the Mount of Piety had to deal with some troubles about the way money was given to charity. Some of the resources were given to orphanages ("*alla congregazione di carità per l'orfanotrofio maschile*"), others to institutions taking care of the unemployed ("*al fondo operai disoccupati*") and others to cultural institutions ("*all'Ateneo Veneto pel gabinetto di lettura*"). The report in question provides details of the sums allocated in the corresponding reserve in the balance sheet, equal to 12.116,30 liras, described earlier.

The Evolution of Carive's Reporting System: A Management Perspective

In this section, we will verify if the management trends (interpreted from the information found in the corresponding financial statements) can provide useful information on the reasons that may have led to the changes in Carive's accounting practices.[10]

The 1853–1863 Period

If we look at Carive's balance sheet from 1853 to 1863, a progressive articulation of investments emerges, which increase over the years by type and level of diversification. In 1863 the total assets see an increase of 4,208 thousand liras compared to the corresponding value of investments recorded in 1853, the first year of independent reporting available for Carive. That is an increase in investments of over 258% in just ten years, a fact which testifies to the bank's high dynamism and the strong impact it had in the area (Table 9.1).

The increase in liabilities, and therefore the increased availability of resources, pushes the bank to find new ways of investment, in addition to the traditional mortgages to the Mount of Piety (and to other subjects). In particular, in the period in question we see an explosion of investments in discount of bills: in 1863 they represent the main entry for investments, absorbing 40.6% of the total assets (Table 9.1). Government bonds and other public bonds also increase significantly and, put together, come to a sum that is double the investments made in mortgage loans (8.8% vs 4.1% of total assets).

While the types of investment remain therefore largely unchanged, we see a drastic change in the weight held by each on the total assets in the 1863 balance sheet. The greater fragmentation of investments inevitably led to a greater diversification also in the revenues of Carive, which up to 1859 were almost exclusively concentrated in the interests accumulated by the Mount of Piety.

From the analysis of the annual data from 1863 (Table 9.3), we can see that, in addition to the interests on loans to private and public subjects—equal to

Table 9.1 Composition of Carive's total assets—1853–1888 (in thousands of Italian liras[11]

Year	*Loans to municipalities and consortia*	*Cash*	*Government bonds*	*Discount of bills*	*Subsidies on bonds*	*Mortgages*	*Provincial, municipal and other bonds*	*Various credits*	*Property, plan and equipment*	*Stocks in money issuing institutions*	*Mortgage bonds*	*Unsecured loans to private individuals*	*Total assets*
1853	1,596	35	-	-	-	-	-	-	-	-	-	-	1,631
1856	1,459	49	5	17	88	-	-	-	—	—	—	—	1,619
1859	1,583	29	43	223	187	120	103	27	—	—	—	—	2,315
1863	2,047	98	230	2,373	481	238	287	85	—	—	—	—	5,839
1866	2,247	121	581	62	152	544	415	133	100	—	—	—	4,355
1869	1,842	75	644	539	158	273	470	74	50	-	-	-	4,126
1873	1,737	301	1,367	2,854	115	482	339	35	4	213	—	—	7,509
1876	1,455	109	2,279	4,304	132	1,040	763	57	9	188	-	-	10,336
1877	1,254	157	2,324	4,372	137	1,047	1,039	113	9	190	—	—	10,641
1879	1,082	288	3,505	4,401	87	1,574	1,306	110	14	220	—	-	12,587
1883	1,652	205	5,671	7,164	254	1,313	1,627	104	164	207	805	—	19,179
1886	1,201	148	7,600	3,362	729	1,224	2,336	119	357	217	959	11	18,262
1888	1,242	430	6,331	2,931	203	1,457	3,232	231	320	—	1,863	6	18,246

Source: A. Battistella, *La Cassa di Risparmio di Venezia nel suo primo centenario* (12 febbraio 1922), Venezia, Società Anonima Veneziana Industrie Grafiche, 1922

Table 9.2 Composition of Carive equity and liabilities—1853–1888 (in thousands of Italian liras)

Year	Savings deposits	Deposits in bank accounts	Various creditors	Employee pension fund	Charity fund	Rediscount Portfolio and other activities	Equity		Total liabilities and equity
							Ordinary reserve fund	Investment bond fluctuation	
1853	1,626		—				5		1,631
1856	1,590		—				28		1,619
1859	1,986		254				75		2,315
1863	5,620		16				204		5,839
1866	4,095	—	1			—	259		4,355
1869	3,714	—	1			—	411		4,126
1873	6,647	—	—			22	840		7,509
1876	7,448	1,722	—			37	1,131		10,336
1877	7,495	1,911	—			33	1,202		10,641
1879	7,715	3,165				31	1,676		12,587
1883	10,279	7,128	5	—	—	31	1,736	—	19,179
1886	10,419	5,349	5	—	—	23	2,465	—	18,262
1888	9,565	5,912	3	72	12	34	2,465	182	18,246

Source: A. Battistella, *La Cassa di Risparmio di Venezia nel suo primo centenario* (12 febbraio 1922), Venezia, Società Anonima Veneziana Industrie Grafiche, 1922

Table 9.3 Compositions of Carive Revenues 1853–1888 (in Italian liras)[12]

Year	*Interest on loans to municipalities and consortia (Mount of Piety)*	*Interests and dividends on other bonds*	*Extraordinary income*	*Interests on government bonds*	*Gains on government bonds*	*Interests on mortgages*	*Interests on discount of bills*	*Interests on advances*	*Rent of building*	*Repayment of mobile wealth*	*Interests on property bonds*	*Total profit*
1859	95,688	—	39	8,433	—	-	-	-	-	-		119,370
1863	131,533	7,375	1,162	22,534	6,705	-	-	-	-	-		261,105
1866	112,298	33,270	4,142	46,873	10,337	21,068	19,527	12,031	3,969	—		263,516
1869	94,991	34,339	52,553	50,246	—	16,156	30,121	4,893	3,719	—		287,019
1873	86,514	44,492	29,221	79,500	—	18,759	167,940	3,836	3,930	9,615		443,806
1876	84,627	76,886	22,743	108,330	36,893	50,082	177,964	6,407	456	7,375		571,763
1877	71,902	94,867	25,099	105,059	28,509	88,387	186,610	7,310	522	6,436		614,730
1879	49,585	137,283	51,987	134,943	251,185	82,508	156,155	5,715	534	8,689		878,584
1883	55,260	200,762	4,310	205,841	37,573	87,002	295,979	12,219	4,580	6,035		909,561
1886	53,732	229,971	17,765	293,965	172,522	64,356	145,589	43,804	17,500	5,761		1.044,965
1888	62,197	155,694	5,846	303,844	22,111	56,510	147,122	18,966	11,470	9,720	89,545	883,027

Source: A. Battistella, *La Cassa di Risparmio di Venezia nel suo primo centenario* (12 febbraio 1922), Venezia, Società Anonima Veneziana Industrie Grafiche, 1922

131,533 liras (converted from Austrian florins to Italian liras to make them comparable to the data listed earlier)—revenues from discount of bills (equal to 91,797 liras from a total revenue of 261,105) and interests on government and other public bonds (equal to 29,909 liras) assume significant influence.

As for costs (Table 9.4), while noting the centrality of the cost of passive interests on savings accounts, we see—for the first time in Carive's history—the appearance of costs for taxes on the interests on bonds ("*Imposta da ricchezza mobile su titoli*", equal to 644 liras) and the "*Tassa di Mano Morta e Diverso*" (1,022 liras), which represent the first forms of public taxation the bank is subject to. These two types of costs will assume a significant influence in the Carive accounts due to the increased investments in treasure bonds that will be carried out by the bank in the years to come. In addition to the costs linked to taxes, we also find the costs of personnel (9,325 liras) and administration (22,313 liras) among the expenses in the 1863 income statement, which together account for more than 10% of the interest income generated by the bank.

The 1863–1877 Period

As we discussed in the third section, with the 1877 report, Carive further increases its focus on the income perspective and it presents its first "independent" income statement. The need to provide independent evidence to the income statement compared to the balance sheet—the way of reporting adopted up until the former period—came from the further diversification of the costs and revenues that are found in the 1877 report. While, in the early reporting of Carive, revenues derived almost exclusively from interest on loans to the Mount of Piety, in this report, we can see that the first item of income, based on amount, comes from discount of bills (98,579 liras), followed by interest on government bonds (53,062 liras) and by interests and dividends on bonds issued by industrial corporate entities.

The cost structure of Carive also underwent notable changes, both in the distribution of amounts and in the level of articulation. The main cost entry is obviously still the interest recognized on capitals of depositors (145,939 liras), which goes side-by-side with interests paid on deposits in bank accounts, a new form of collection that Carive used starting in 1875—that is, two years before the adoption of this model of reporting. As we will see, deposits in the form of bank accounts will take on an increasing weight among the sources of financing for the bank in the following years. The 1877 cost structure is also strongly influenced by the configuration of revenues, which is in turn dependent on new forms of investment adopted by the bank. For instance, the cost for the rediscount of bills ("*risconto di cambiali*") is closely linked with the revenues from discount of bills.

Finally, the incidence of taxation costs incurred by the bank increases, amounting to 42,649 liras—thus becoming the second cost item. The high incidence of revenue of interests on bonds (government, issued by private

Table 9.4 Composition of Carive Costs 1858–1888 (in Italian liras)[13]

Year	Interests on savings deposits	Interests on account deposits	Taxes on buildings	Wealth tax on bonds	Institute wealth tax	Tax of mortmain and various	Salaries and compen-sations	Pensions	Adminis-tration costs	Losses on profits and various	Deprecia-tions	Extra-ordinary cost	Total expenses
1858	82,128	-	-	644	-	1,022	10,575	-	-	1,040	-	-	93,743
1859	84,409	-	-	-	-	-	23,862	-	—	—	-	-	108,271
1860	90,251	-	-	-	-	-	12,858	-	—	7,080	-	-	110,190
1861	104,773	-	-	-	-	-	7,506	-	3,912	—	-	-	116,192
1862	141,101	-	-	-	-	-	8,035	-	4,942	—	-	-	154,078
1863	196,195	-	-	-	-	-	9,325	-	22,313	9,754	-	-	229,253
1864	218,140	—	153	1,167	33,437	3,184	10,149	—	9,564	3,668	-	—	279,462
1865	208,635	—	6,542	1,677	7,469	—	10,139	—	9,556	8,217	-	—	252,236
1866	179,977	—	—	1,842	12,359	—	10,331	—	7,319	44,083	-	—	255,911
1867	158,008	—	—	1,921	91,312	—	10,327	—	13,626	—	-	1	275,196
1868	145,352	—	—	2,475	—	—	10,333	—	22,081	—	-	71	180,312
1869	140,027	—	89	4,316	18,621	1,991	10,327	—	7,666	41,155	-	148	224,341
1870	143,153	—	—	2,068	51,746	50	10,579	—	13,608	27,944	-	94	249,244
1871	163,608	—	—	3,228	17,618	50	12,320	346	8,025	—	-	—	205,195
1872	231,274	—	—	13,871	18,731	—	11,350	691	18,839	—	-	107	294,863
1873	251,715	—	—	18,740	35,289	81	19,242	691	13,599	29,790	-	54,257	423,404
1874	275,858	—	—	13,680	65,810	91	16,064	3,528	17,346	—	-	—	392,377
1875	305,059	11,504	—	14,500	35,975	8,925	13,438	3,500	21,439	—	-	—	414,340
1876	296,120	39,158	—	17,362	46,066	2,605	14,111	3,525	64,128	—	-	—	483,103

1877	291,795	57,988	—	20,986	53,163	2,805	17,209	3,525	95,172	—	-	385	543,028
1878	290,837	59,088	—	23,688	48,934	2,967	18,829	3,525	27,370	—	-	—	475,238
1879	292,947	73,944	—	27,845	50,914	3,279	18,997	3,525	59,475	—	-	—	530,927
1880	307,736	88,097	—	35,479	49,187	4,106	19,932	3,525	34,280	117,506	-	—	659,849
1881	328,900	94,226	—	35,694	56,769	4,106	19,022	3,774	37,578	5,010	—		585,078
1882	364,119	105,410	1,191	36,879	57,962	4,398	19,365	3,225	32,056	148,759	126,689	-	900,053
1883	394,669	155,944	1,194	47,087	68,413	3,934	20,199	3,525	49,602	10,752	16,688	-	772,007
1884	406,959	162,718	1,720	60,121	69,505	4,334	22,335	3,525	43,277	—	98,010	-	872,505
1885	399,507	142,171	2,637	63,391	72,804	5,144	22,524	3,525	43,212	41,998	8,276	-	805,188
1886	410,011	123,962	2,385	61,457	61,263	5,370	24,864	2,107	36,939	—	18,712	-	747,070
1887	370,097	133,004	2,598	62,687	62,022	6,224	25,389	8,370	36,388	—	—	-	706,774
1888	337,502	137,632	2,051	61,714	66,555	8,241	34,027	13,566	33,285	—	—	-	694,574

Source: A. Battistella, *La Cassa di Risparmio di Venezia nel suo primo centenario* (12 febbraio 1922), Venezia, Società Anonima Veneziana Industrie Grafiche, 1922

subjects and by municipalities and other public subjects) led to a sharp rise in costs related to the fiscal, compared to previously analysed reports, where this cost component was zero or a negligible amount.

As for the assets, discount billing is the bank's main form of investment, equal to 41.1% of the total assets, followed by investments in government bonds (21.8%) and other public bonds (9,8%). In 1877, therefore, almost a third of Carive's assets are invested in bonds issued by the Italian state or other public entities.

If we analyse the historical data shown in Table 9.1, it is interesting to observe how the investments in discount billing were probably meant to be the bank's "riskiest" investments and the related amounts responded to a clear strategy by the bank's governance. The amount of capital invested in this asset, in fact, increased suddenly when the availability of resources from the bank increased (see the period 1856–1863 in Table 9.1) and decreased just as quickly in the periods of contraction of the collection. From 1863 to 1866, the discount of bills almost completely zeros out their value and, in the same period, the total assets decrease from 5,839 to 4,355 thousands of liras. From 1869 on, we see a progressive increase in the capital collected (from 4,126 to 10,641 thousands of liras in 1877), which is reflected in an equally significant growth in the value of discount of bills (from 539 to 4,372 thousand of liras).

The reading of Carive's balance sheet numbers reflects the administrators' strong sensitivity to implementing strategies of investment aimed at best protecting the capital raised from savers. This was done through prudent policies for investment in low-risk financial instruments, appropriately diversifying the types of investments and favouring investments with high risk levels (and therefore more profitability) only when the bank had growing capital.

As regards liabilities, the 1877 balance sheet is characterized by the presence of amounts collected in the form of bank accounts. Until 1874, in fact, the bank's sources of financing were made up exclusively of equity and savings deposits (Table 9.2). Collections through bank accounts were introduced by Carive in the two years prior to the report year in consideration. From 1876 to 1879 saving deposits are basically the same, while deposits in bank accounts double.

We can, therefore, conclude that the high diversification of investments (Table 9.1)—starting from the second half of the 1860s—led to a consequent and inevitable diversification of the types of revenues (Table 9.3). At the end of the period in question, as concerns revenues, the income statement prevalently features interests drawn from discount of bills operations and interest income on bonds issued by public entities. However, the taxation related to these revenues, during 1870, undergoes a sharp increase and becomes the second cost item, after the passive interests on deposits collected. The balance sheets emphasize how Carive, about twenty-five years after its legal independence from the Mount of Piety (1853), is, in effect, a bank that has reached full managerial autonomy, able to operate freely on the capitals market, on the side both of collection and of investment.

The 1877–1888 Period

One of the main innovations of the 1888 report is the balance sheet structure. The need to make the financial statement more legible comes from the further diversification of investments that the bank enacted from 1877 onwards. The total assets in 1888 are equal to 18,246 thousand liras, compared to 10,641 thousand liras in 1877: over a decade, therefore, the bank's investments basically doubled (Table 9.1). The discount of bills still constitutes an important form of investment, but compared to the 1877 balance sheet (where it accounted for 41.1% of investments), it is down to 16.1%. Bonds issued by the state are the principal form of investment of capitals collected by Carive: 34.7% of the total assets are absorbed by these investments, joined by 1,002 thousand liras more (5.5% of total assets) invested in bonds issued by provinces and municipalities. In 1888, therefore, more than 40% of the bank's assets are invested in bonds issued by public entities.

Another aspect that characterizes the management's evolution in the decade between 1877 in 1888 is the significant growth in deposits into bank accounts (Table 9.2). While in 1877 they made up only 7.9% of sources (compared to 80.9% of savings deposits), in the year in question bank accounts cover 32.4% of the sources, effectively tripling their amount in absolute value over the decade (savings deposits, the first form of collection, represent 52.4% of Carive's sources in 1888).

In addition to savings and bank account deposits, a reserve that identifies the amounts destined for charity appears in the bank's liabilities for the first time in 1877. This reserve, too, has no counterpart in expenses in the income statement, and so must be interpreted as an allocation of the income of the period, however, to the benefit of subjects "outside" the bank. It is interesting, in this regard, to observe how the reserve for covering pension costs for employees was placed within the equity (employees are therefore likened to primary stakeholders of the institution, equivalent to shareholders) unlike the reserve destined for charity works, which is instead qualified as debit and therefore placed among the liabilities (and therefore outside the equity), while finding both the same origin in the allocation and in the net income of the period.

In addition to the two previously mentioned, the 1886 statute introduced important innovations with a significant impact on the representation of net income of the period within the equity, since, ideally, it could be intended for the following:

- Reserves with a specific allocation among the items of equity (reserves for covering pension costs for employees or their widows and reserves for changes in the value of bonds recorded under assets);

- Provisions, placed within liabilities on the balance sheet (provisions for charitable activity);
- A reduction of the value of property, plan and equipment recorded among the assets, by way of amortizations and depreciations, previously booked in the income statement.

However, these elements were not included in the income statement, but rather they represented a part of the allocation of net income.

All of these values, which nowadays are normally included in income statements as reductions of the net income of the period, were treated only patrimonially—probably—because of their "non-monetary" nature. None of these elements, in fact, was associated to a payment or to the emergence of a bond against Carive in a year in which these values were "allocated" in the balance sheet.

Conclusion

We believe that our contribution may be of interest to an accounting historian, because we analyze the evolution of Carive's financial statements in a deregulated environment. In fact, there was no law that regulated the preparation of financial statements of savings banks in Italy during the period from 1853 (the year Carive became an independent institution and presented its first financial statements as separate from the Mount of Piety) to 1888 (when the first savings bank law was issued in Italy, giving the ministry the duty to establish the format of financial statements).

As seen, the focus of our work is on the presentation of financial statements rather than measurement bases or procedures and techniques used in the general accounting system. Even though there were no regulatory constraints, Carive chose to publish its financial reports in order to allow depositors to assess the state of its investments. Moreover, in a context where the accounts of savings banks were free from external regulation, Carive developed a high rate of accounting innovation and several significant changes occurred. The main changes can be summarized in the following aspects:

- Structure of financial statements;
- Content of the balance sheet;
- Content of the income statement.

As for the first point, in 1853, Carive presented a main statement illustrating the changes in deposits (its primary financial source) and in loans to the Mount of Piety (the most important form of capital employed at that time), while below this statement there was a brief balance sheet and a concise income statement, both in scalar format. In 1863, next to the balance sheet was displayed a statement ("*dettaglio delle rendite e spese dell'amministrazione*") that provided greater detail of revenues and expenses compared to previous years. The financial statements in 1877 were made up of two separate and autonomous statements: the balance sheet and the income statement, which analytically disclosed assets and liabilities and revenues and expenses respectively, both in a horizontal format with two counterpoised sections. In 1888, an important innovation was the introduction of another report providing information on its charitable activity. This document increased the level of accountability towards the community. Considering that Carive also began to draw up the notes to financial statements some years later, we can state that, in the late nineteenth century, Carive used to publish a complete set of financial statements.

The degree of informational detail in the items presented on the balance sheets increased gradually over time, passing from a concise balance sheet in 1853 with only two assets (loans to the Mount of Piety and cash) and two kinds of financial sources (deposits and equity made up of the net income for the first period) to a balance sheet with several items, most notably on the asset side. This evolution reflects the greater level of operating autonomy of Carive from the Mount of Piety and allowed external users (particularly depositors) to assess the investment and credit portfolio policies. Only in 1888 did the structure of the balance sheet decrease in degree of detail, presenting some more general categories of assets, instead of displaying each asset item by item. However, this change does not seem to have reduced the level of disclosure but rather to have made the balance sheet easier to read for external users.

In the same year, the balance sheet presented another important innovation; for the first time, the equity was distinguished into many more components than in the past. More specifically, in 1888 the representation of the equity was articulated in ordinary reserves and specific reserves, such as (1) reserves for covering pension costs for employees and their widows and (2) reserves for changes in the value of bonds recognized in the assets. It is worth noting that these two last reserves were created by retained earnings, whereas today the same purposes would be achieved generally by provisions affecting the income statement. Moreover, the 1888 balance sheet presented a new item among the liabilities, which consisted of a provision for charitable activity. Similarly to the specific reserves mentioned earlier, this provision was also created by allocating part of the net income. Still in 1888, the book values of property, plant and equipment began to depreciate, but without determining a depreciation charge, but rather assigning part of the net income. It is therefore interesting to note that all these non-monetary values, which today are generally recognized in the income statement, were treated as allocation of income crediting reserves, provisions and non-current assets respectively.

As for the income statement, its structure and content evolved over time as a consequence both of an increasingly diversified portfolio of assets and of an increasing relevance given to the income approach rather than the asset-liability approach. At the beginning of its activity, the Carive income statement presented only three items (interest income, interest expenses and overall costs) and was set out below the main statement in a residual location, while in 1888, the income statement was a primary statement and comprised several detailed and specific items of revenues and expenses. Nevertheless, the income statement, even in 1888, did not show intermediate margins, and its content was very rich in information that allowed external users to carry out performance assessment.

To sum up, we can say that Carive's financial statements evolved over time towards greater financial transparency. The reasons for this evolutionary path can most likely be found in the changes of the statutes approved in 1853 and 1886. The change in 1853 had an indirect impact on financial statements, because it made Carive more independent from the Mount of Piety. Since that time, Carive began to widen and diversify the forms in which the capital was employed and, accordingly, the kinds of revenues and expenses (notably those related to income tax) increased. In other words, the greater level of detail in the content of financial statements seems to be a consequence of the larger operating and organizational autonomy of Carive. Conversely, the change of the statute approved in 1886 had a direct impact on financial statements, since it required the allocation of part of the net income to the creation of some specific reserves, a provision for charitable activities and to feed the depreciation mechanism.

In light of our analysis, the evolution of Carive's financial reports must have been driven by an attempt to meet the informational needs of external users, and in particular of depositors, in order to capture their trust and increase the collection of savings. According to agency theory, which views financial statements as a commodity supplied to meet a demand of financial information, the gradual trend towards increased disclosure may be attributed to the growing pressure for information exerted by external users, in particular depositors in the case of Carive (Edwards 1989, 141–142). The improvements in reporting practices enabled depositors to be better informed on the investment policies and to make their own assessment of performance. It is likely that the increasing rise of deposits may also be due to these improvements, more than just the economic growth of the territory.

It seems that the lack of external regulation on the preparation of financial statements was exploited by Carive to portray underlying economic facts fairly and increase the decision usefulness of external users rather than to meet particular managerial objectives. However, we are not sure that, in the absence of such a good performance, the level of disclosure and accountability would have been so high.

Notes

1. The *montes pietatis* were public pawnshops, mostly dating back to the fifteenth and sixteenth centuries, which extended credit to the poor at a reasonable, regulated price against the pledge of objects as collateral. They represented a means of fighting usury and were a Christian response to the role of the Jews in

local credit markets. In 1760, sixty-seven *montes pietatis* existed in the Venetian region with 16.7 million Venetian lira in loans. By 1795, the number of *montes* had risen to seventy and outstanding loans had increased by 80% to nearly 30 million Venetian lira (Ferlito 2009: 301ff.).

2. The plan would also apply to other cities in the Venetian Kingdom. Of those that obeyed the imperial order, Udine and Monselice had their savings banks closed down within a few months because of a lack of depositors (Battistella 1922: 15; Udine 1891), whereas the Padua savings bank recorded only limited growth until all legal, organizational and managerial links to the local pawnshop were truncated in 1871 (Padova 1898). Totally different was the scheme for the Cassa di Risparmio delle Provincie Lombarde, Milan, which was promoted by a group of notables and kept independent of the local pawnshop (Bachi 1923).
3. For centuries, the government of the Republic of Venice had benefited from the tightly regulated pawnbroking services supplied by the Jewish community, in return for permission to stay in the city. Given this special relationship, the government had repeatedly rejected proposals to set up a local *mons pietatis*, (Ferlito 2006). After Napoleon made the Jews equal to Christians in 1797, in 1806 a municipal *mons pietatis* was eventually created under the name of Banco Pignoratizio Comunale (Bembo 1859: 135ff.; Zorzi 1957: 16–17).
4. The first major fraud led to reorganizing the bank under the name '*Monte di pietà di Venezia*' in 1834. In the mid-1840s, a second fraud resulted in about 500,000 liras in losses (Battistella 1922: 28).
5. In 1839, the government shifted the supervision of the Monte from the municipal to the provincial government and unified bookkeeping of the Monte and of Carive so that the reserves Carive had thus far accumulated passed to the Monte. The move was partially reversed by a new imperial regulation of 1844 that restored a clear separation in the accounts and administration of mounts of piety and savings banks (Battistella 1922: 27–28; Udine 1891: 13).
6. During the revolutionary years 1848–49, the Monte was on the verge of going bankrupt and was rescued by an emergency loan from the republican government.
7. Carive did not have its own funds apart from those resulting from undistributed profit accumulated over time.
8. According to Bernardello's (2002) estimate, from 1830 to 1866, Venice had on average between 115,000 and 120,000 residents.
9. Until the banking reform of 1926, banks of issue and savings banks were the intermediaries subject to regulation in Italy.
10. Note that in the period under examination, from 1853 to 1888, there were no laws that imposed mandatory financial statements for credit institutions.
11. In order to make the data from the historical analysis of Carive comparable, we converted the amounts reported in the balance sheets from Austrian liras to Italian liras. The exchange rate is Austrian liras/Italian liras = 1,1534 (source: our elaborations from the comparison of balance sheet data and data published by A. *Battistella, La Cassa di Risparmio di Venezia nel suo primo centenario (12 febbraio 1922), Venezia, Società Anonima Veneziana Industrie Grafiche, 1922)*
12. We did not include data from the income statement related to the period 1853–1857 since it is related to semesters and therefore is not comparable with the data from following periods, calculated on an annual basis onad referreing to the entire year. For 1858 and 1860, the balance sheets do not report details on the composition of revenues.
13. We did not include data from the income statement related to the period 1853–1857 since it is related to semesters and therefore is not comparable with the data from following periods, calculated on an annual basis onad referreing to the entire year.

References

Bachi, Riccardo (1923), 'Storia della Cassa di Risparmio delle Provincie Lombarde, 1823–1922', *La Cassa di Risparmio delle Provincie Lombarde nella evoluzione economica della regione, 1823–1923* (Milano: Stab. Arti grafiche Alfieri e Lacroix), 1–321.

Battistella, Antonio (1922), *La Cassa di risparmio di Venezia nel suo primo centenario* (Venezia: Società Anonima Veneziana industrie grafiche).

Bembo, Pier Luigi (1859), *Delle istituzioni di beneficenza nella città e provincia di Venezia* (Venezia: Tipografia P. Naratovich).

Bernardello, Adolfo (2002), 'Venezia 1830–1866. Iniziative economiche, accumulazione e investimenti di capitale', *Il Risorgimento*, (1), 5–66.

Cassa di risparmio di Padova (1898), *Notizie e documenti sulla Cassa di risparmio di Padova dal 1822 al 1897* (Padova: R. Stabilimento P. Prosperini).

Cassa di risparmio di Udine (1891), *La Cassa di risparmio di Udine nel suo primo quindennio, 1876–1890* (Udine: Tipografia G.B. Doretti).

De Piante, Giovanni (1929), 'Depositi e investimenti nel I° secolo delle casse di risparmio italiane', *Giornale degli Economisti e Rivista di Statistica*, 69 (a. 44) (10), 745–765.

Edwards, John Richard (1989), *A History of Financial Accounting* (London: Routledge).

Ferlito, Carmelo (2006), 'Su un progetto di istituzione di un monte di pietà a Venezia (1778–1779)', *Mediterranea Ricerche storiche*, 3, 289–312.

——— (2009), *Il Monte di pietà di Verona e il contesto economico-sociale della città nel secondo settecento* (Venezia: Istituto Veneto di scienze, lettere ed arti).

Fishlow, Albert (1961), 'The trustee savings banks, 1817–1861', *The Journal of Economic History*, 21 (1), 26–40.

Monteleone, Giulio and Stella, Aldo (1974), *Centocinquantanni di vita della Cassa di risparmio di Padova e Rovigo, 1822–1972: lineamenti storici* (Padova: Liviana Editrice).

Ó Gráda, Cormac (2009), 'Savings banks, famine and financial contagion: Ireland in the 1840s and 1850s', *Irish Economic and Social History*, 36 (1), 21–36.

Pohl, Hans (1993), 'Introduction', in Manfred Pix and Hans Pohl (a cura di), *L'histoire des caisses d'épargne européennes, 2, La diffusion de l'idée de caisses d'épargne au XIXe siècle* (Paris: Les Éditions de l'épargne), 17–28.

Reberschak, Maurizio (1997), 'L'industrializzazione di Venezia (1866–1918)', in Stefano Gasparri, Giovanni Levi, and Pierandrea Moro (a cura di), *Venezia: Itinerari per la storia della città* (Bologna: il Mulino), 369–404.

Roverato, Giorgio (1984), 'La terza regione industriale', in Silvio Lanaro (a cura di), *Storia d'Italia, Le regioni dall'unità a oggi, Il Veneto* (Torino: Einaudi), 164–224.

Sagredo, Agostino (1848), 'Stato patrimoniale del Monte di pietà e Cassa di risparmio in Venezia al 3 marzo 1848', *Annali universali di statistica, economia pubblica, geografia, storia, viaggi e commercio*, 15 (45), 302–303.

Zorzi, Elio (1957), 'La Cassa di risparmio di Venezia', *La Cassa di risparmio di Venezia: sintesi storica dopo 135 anni dalla fondazione* (Venezia: Officine grafiche Carlo Ferrari), 13–132.

10 Firm, Industry and Institutional Dimensions of the Glassmaking Industry in Venice

The Case of Barovier & Toso

Chiara Mio and Marco Fasan

Introduction

Glassmaking in Venice (and in particular on the island of Murano) has a long tradition, deriving from the tight relationships that Venice traditionally held (and in some ways, still holds) with the Middle East. The glass industry was one of the most profitable and, at the same time, one of the most strictly regulated by the *Serenissima* Republic. Glassmaking activities were located on Murano not only to avoid the risk of fire from the furnaces to the more heavily populated areas of Rivo Alto (Rialto) and Dorsoduro but also because of the necessity to control them. Know-how had to be protected, so workers in the glass industry were not allowed to leave and were basically kept in a "gilded cage".

The aim of this chapter is to study the case of a company (Barovier & Toso) that was founded and developed in the Venice glassmaking industry. Barovier & Toso was started in 1295 and is the oldest glassmaking company still in operation (and the sixth oldest family business in the world). The chapter provides a comprehensive description of the company and of the institutional landscape of the glassmaking industry. More specifically, our study covers the characteristics of the institutional system of the Republic of Venice, as concerns the regulation of the glassmaking industry. It then focuses on the evolution and development of the glassmaking industry and the specific case of Barovier.

Our analysis allows us to identify some interesting relationships between the institutional and economic landscape and the activities of Barovier & Toso. First, the location of Barovier on the island of Murano derives from economic factors (typical of districts), the way the art was passed from master to labourer and industry regulations. Second, the innovation process that allowed the company to become famous at the time (e.g., Angelo Barovier invented "crystal glass") depended on the availability of raw materials, made available by the close relationships Venice had with the Middle East. It is interesting to note that the Republic of Venice used to protect knowledge and innovations through a patent system, which allowed Barovier alone to produce the crystal glass. Third, Barovier, and in general the whole glassmaking industry, suffered from the increasing protectionism of the Republic of Venice. Particularly, from 1500 onwards ("strong protectionism"), the government and the guild made it increasingly harder for foreign products and workers to enter the republic and Murano respectively. This created a sort of "shield" that seemingly protected Murano glassmaking but actually greatly contributed to its demise. It is interesting to note that pressures towards greater protectionism were coming primarily from the guilds themselves.

The Regulation of the Glassmaking Industry

The history and evolution of the Venetian glassmaking industry are closely related to (and influenced by) the history of the Republic of Venice and its regulations. While it is not within the scope of the present chapter to make a complete review of the republic's institutions, it is important to describe the main characteristics of its institutional system, as concerns glassmaking industry regulation.

Starting in the twelfth century, as Murano glass started to become as refined as Oriental glass (Bruni et al., 2002), the *Serenissima* Republic started to increase controls on the glassmaking industry, in order to protect its activities and know-how. Guilds, which glassmakers had to be part of, were the main entity in charge of this. The fact that Venetian glassmakers started to form organizations is proven by the fact that in 1224 the glassmaking guild fined twenty-nine glassmakers for breaching certain internal regulations (Gaspareto, 1958; Ceruti and Dorigato, 1992). In 1261, the *Maggior Consiglio* (or Major Council, one of the most important political organs of the Republic of Venice) mandated the separation of the "*Provveditori alla Giustizia*" into two parts: the "*Giustizia Nuova*" and the "*Giustizia Vecchia*", which was in charge of auditing the guilds. In the following decade, glassmakers created their first regulations and elected the "*gastaldo*", who was in charge of checking up on the actual implementation of the regulation ("*mariegole*") and who was elected from the glassmakers included in the guild. The internal regulations were changed from time to time and the last one was approved in 1766 (Barovier Mentasti, 1982). The first edition of this regulation had been approved in 1271 and had forty-six articles. Some of the requirements were: furnaces had to use only alder or willow wood; glassmakers could work both during the night and during the day seven months out of the year; if a glassmaker worked outside *Serenissima* territory he had to pay a monetary fine in order to be readmitted into the territory.

Therefore, the ordinary regulations ("*mariegole*" and "*capitolare*") were produced by the glassmaking guild, the association of artisans who controlled the practice of their craft. *Mariegole* and *capitolare* used to include instructions on the production process to be followed, the items to be used and the rights and duties of the associates. The *gastaldo* was the head of the guild, and was nominated from among its members. The system was therefore fully corporative. The extraordinary regulations were approved by the Senate or by the *Maggior Consiglio*. Guilds were kept under control by the *Giustizia Vecchia* and by the *Consiglio dei Dieci* (Zecchin, 1987).

Evolution of the Venetian Glassmaking Industry

The glassmaking industry is one of the oldest and most vibrant in Venice. In fact, it still operates today. Glassmaking already existed during the Roman Empire, but it flourished only around AD 600, when the technique of glassblowing was invented and the products were decorated in an artistic fashion (Barovier Mentasti, 2015). The oldest document showing some form of glassmaking activity dates back to AD 982, and can be found in the "*Archivio Storico*" of Venice. It is a document citing Domenico Fiolaro, who donated hand-blown glass to the church of San Giorgio (Zecchin, 1987).

While the first furnaces were located on the island of Torcello, until 1549 glassmaking manufacturers were located throughout the territory of the *Serenissima*, on the mainland as well as on the island of Venice. But already from 1200 on, most of the furnaces were located on Murano. While the real evolution of the glassmaking industry would happen only in 1400, Venice had a significant competitive advantage from the beginning. In fact, while other firms were using local raw materials, Venetian furnaces could make use of particular raw materials—better suited for glassmaking—coming from the Far East. The availability of raw materials was combined—already in 1200—with institutions devoted to developing glassmaking know-how. Gregorio da Napoli founded a school for glass decoration, which indicates the importance of this fast-growing industry (Zecchin, 1987).

During the thirteenth century, protectionism gradually increased, as the *Serenissima* Republic entered its "aristocratic period" (1236–1797), characterized by strong influence from the aristocracy. The *Giustizia Vecchia* was mostly in charge of this process of protectionism, although at some point the *Maggior Consiglio* withdrew the *Giustizia Vecchia*'s possibility of derogating the regulation. Protectionist regulations were approved in 1295, due to the protests of several glassmakers, who were complaining that some of their colleagues were working abroad during the summer and returning to Venice in the autumn. Therefore, from 1295 on, glassmakers working abroad had to pay a fine in order to come back to Venice. Afterwards, however, they were totally banned from the glassmaking activity (Zecchin, 1987).

Originally, glassmakers were located on the island of Torcello but, when the economic centre of Venice was moved from Torcello to Rivo Alto, they moved to Murano. It may be that this shift was aimed at being as close as possible to the demand. In fact, the transportation of glass had significant costs, such as the transport itself and the risk of damaging the product. Clearly, it would have been even more convenient, from this perspective, for the glassmaker to be located in Venice, where the demand originated.

However, this may have been a problem because of the type of activity (risk of fire) and because most of the buildings in the Rivo Alto and San Marco areas were dedicated to institutional and political functions. Moreover, it is important to take into account the mechanisms underlying the transmission of know-how. Apprentices had to work with the glassmaking artisan for several years in order to learn the secrets of the art. Moreover, apprentices were often the sons of the masters, and therefore the incentives to move from Murano were limited. Even though the heart of glass production was Murano, furnaces could have been built on the mainland or on the island of Venice (but not in the Rivo Alto area) until 1549. In that year, the *Consiglio dei Dieci* decided that all furnaces located on the mainland had to be destroyed. From that year onward, all furnaces had to be built only on the island of Murano (Bruni et al., 2002).

The fourteenth century brought the invention of eyeglasses, and the Murano furnaces started producing for this new market as well, after the *Giustizia Vecchia* gave them permission to do so. During this period, the protectionist approach of the republic went through several phases. On the one hand, in 1315 the *Maggior Consiglio* increased the fine for glassmakers leaving Venice in the summertime in order to work abroad. On the other hand, it allowed some glassmakers to return to Venice without any sanctions, because the industry was in need of a qualified workforce. During the first half of the fourteenth century, the increase in trade and improvements in production techniques and in know-how allowed for a decrease in the production cost of Murano glass (Zecchin, 1987).

During the same period (around the middle of the fourteenth century), Venice had to face the plague, which decreased the population of the island by 70%. Many furnaces were shut down, and the total number of workers in the industry dropped dramatically. It was necessary to wait until the fifteenth century for the situation to get back to fourteenth-century levels. Light and shadow characterized the century. On the one hand, the plague severely damaged the economy of the republic, and many glassmakers chose to expatriate in order to avoid their debts to public administration or other merchants. On the other hand, Murano glass was recognized as the best in the world, and the increasing commercial presence of Venice in the Mediterranean Sea allowed the glassmaking trade to expand significantly (Trivellato, 1999).

The fifteenth century represents the "golden age" of the Murano glassmaking industry. In particular, Angelo Barovier invented "*vetro cristallino*" (crystal glass), a certain kind of glass that was particularly "clean". In 1455, the *Serenissima* Republic granted Angelo Barovier the exclusive rights to produce crystal glass. This innovation was a product innovation rather than a process innovation. Process innovations have been very limited in the history of glassmaking and, in a sense, this is a point of industry strength that allowed it to resist through the centuries and into modern times. At the same time, the tradition of commerce of the *Serenissima* made it easier to get acquainted with new materials to use in the production of glass, thus allowing product innovations. Such materials were not only imported from abroad but also discovered on the mainland surrounding Venice. In the *Archivio Storico* of Venice, some documents show that the Venetian Jacobo Rasmini discovered a specific kind of stone near Vicenza that could be used by Murano glassmakers instead of stone coming from Lombardy. In 1452, another artisan from Vicenza discovered a new vein of manganese. The republic allowed him to extract and sell the manganese. It is not clear whether the new manganese vein and the Angelo Barovier crystal glass are linked in any way (Zecchin, 1966).

Not all the glassmakers were as important and rewarded as Angelo Barovier. According to some documents dating back to 1403, many glassmakers were not able to earn enough to maintain their business and their families. The government then intervened again in order to regulate production, and specifically in order to: extend the production period from December 1 to August 15; increase the fines for the glassmakers working abroad; and decrease the amount of glass the furnaces were allowed to produce, in order to increase production quality. In 1415, each glassmaker had to register his own brand in order to increase the recognizability of his products on the market. In 1420, the guild and the government finally allowed glassmakers to work all year long. Many glassmakers, in fact, were forced to leave Venice and work abroad in order to make a living for themselves and their families. They were artisans and it was quite difficult for them to find other jobs during the summer period (Zecchin, 1987).

The growth of the glassmaking industry was clearly closely connected to that of the *Serenissima* Republic. Starting from the sixteenth century, Venice decreased its commercial relationships with other countries, and this had a negative impact on the performance of companies operating in the sector. Moreover, competition within the industry increased significantly in the same period. As a response to that, the government allowed companies to hire workers from abroad in order to decrease the production cost of the products. Previously, the protection of know-how was considered more important, and therefore glassmakers were allowed to hire only workers included in the guild. On top of this, in 1575 and in 1628 Venice was hit by two plagues, and this again caused the population to drop dramatically. The plague hit not only Venice but all of Europe, and this caused the demand for high-quality glass to drop sharply. The demand for high-quality products decreased more sharply than the demand for low-quality products, and this damaged the Murano glassmaking industry, favouring instead other European industries that were able to produce low-quality products (Trivellato, 2000).

From this perspective, the guild system had become in many ways a burden. First, it decreased the ability of companies to innovate. Second, the fact that companies could not employ glassmaking masters from abroad hindered foreign capital and foreign competence. Third, glassmaking masters could not be employed as workers by other furnaces, thus increasing unemployment among masters. Moreover, the demand for glass increased in the following decades, but favoured low-quality products. Given this change in the economic scenario, glassmakers from Murano reached a quality level that was too high to be lowered to a lower standard. On top of that, the guild system did not allow this. Conversely, other European companies not regulated by guilds were free to innovate products and the production process in order to shape their offer to the requirements of the market. Soon, these companies were able to compete in international markets, meeting the growing demand for low-quality glass. Trivellato (2000) argues that, while guilds did firmly oppose any labour-saving innovation, they had a more open approach to incremental capital-saving innovations.

Table 10.1 reports the production costs of a furnace in Murano. The information comes from a quote that was produced in 1779 in order to consider the foundation of a consortium of glassmakers in Murano (Trivellato, 2000). They are the weekly costs of a production site employing 209 workers and 28 furnaces.

It is interesting to note that raw materials and fuel represent by far the most significant cost. More specifically, fuel was the wood that was used by furnaces. According to Trivellato (2000), during the eighteenth century, it became increasingly expensive. In particular, in 1792–1793 the guild protested because of the increasing prices of wood, which at the time was for the most part coming from Istria and Dalmatia. As a consequence, the *Serenissima* allowed some beech trees to be cut down in the Cansiglio area for the use of the glassmaking industry, but this generated some protests from the Arsenal of Venice.

Usually, the low incidence of fixed assets among the production costs is interpreted as a sign of technological backwardness. According to Trivellato (2000), this is not necessarily the case. The industrial revolution, in fact, shifted the attention to the capital employed in the production, while

Table 10.1 Production costs of a furnace in Murano at the end of the eighteenth century

	Windows		*Big mirrors*		*Small mirrors*		*Blown glasses*		*Crystal glasses*	
	Liras	*%*	*Liras*	*%*	*Liras*	*%*	*Liras*	*%*	*Liras*	*%*
Raw materials	436	43	1227	40	980	50	3240	58	3360	66
Fuel	240	24	920	30	440	22	880	16	560	11
Fixed assets	66	6	196	6	78	4	165	3	84	2
Labour	275	27	687	23	463	24	1348	24	1068	21
Total	1017	100	3030	100	1961	100	5633	100	5072	100

some industries—such as the glassmaking industry—were mostly interested in process innovations. This can be interpreted as one of the factors leading to the decline of Barovier and, more in general, of the whole glassmaking industry. The company focused on process innovations, because of the high incidence of the variable costs. Product innovation instead was neglected, despite being the kind of innovation that may have allowed Barovier—and the Venetian glassmaking industry in general—to innovate and compete in the international market. As a matter of fact, Northern European producers managed to win the market by means of a product innovation.

This lack of attention to product innovation was likely influenced by the guilds, which were more prone to fostering process innovations, as will be further discussed ahead. Even if cost accounting emerged as a discipline several centuries later, it does provide a useful interpretative scheme of strategy evolution.

In the eighteenth century, Venice was in decline and the glassmaking industry could no longer count either on the demand from abroad (because of the higher difficulties in commercial routes around the world) or on internal demand. The government reacted to the crisis in two ways. First, the government increased protectionist measures, so that it was completely forbidden to purchase glass from abroad. Second, glass masters tried to imitate glasses made in Bohemia, France and England, as such products were very successful in those years (Bruni et al., 2002). Giuseppe Briati was a glass master who, in 1737, was awarded the exclusive right to produce the glass "*alla boema*" (Bohemian style) by the *Serenissima* Republic. Besides this, glassmakers from Murano were trying to bring Bohemian masters to Murano in order to learn their secrets (Ciriacono, 1996).

The main cost in glass production at that time was that of the workforce. Glassmaking masters had higher salaries, compared to labourers, because of the protectionist activity of guilds (Trivellato, 2000). A master could earn three times the salary of a labourer. During the eighteenth century, the average compensation for a glassmaking master was decreasing. At that time, the guild regulated salaries of masters and labourers and identified three types of furnaces: Bohemian style, "*comuni*" and "*ordinarie*". After Napoleon took power in 1797, the "*mariegole*" stayed in place for a few more years, but finally in 1808, Napoleon abolished guilds and their regulations (Bruni et al., 2002).

After guilds were abolished, furnaces did not have any burden or duty, but were instead operating on a deregulated market. Furnaces could be run by anyone and operate all year long, glassmaking masters were free to go abroad, and there was no quality control or support for unemployed or disabled masters. In this context, Murano furnaces were competing against Northern European producers, who were able to have much lower sale prices. During the Austrian period, the situation got even worse because imported foreign products were taxed much less than products that were produced internally. After Venice became part of the Italian Kingdom (1866), the situation improved. In 1870, only eleven furnaces were still operating in Murano. In this period, the Veneto region slowly began its economic growth, but the Murano furnaces were loyal to tradition and never evolved in terms of production techniques and size. During that period, the museum of glass and the school for glassmakers were created. Production and exports therefore increased again until the First and Second World Wars. In this period, many workers had to serve in the army, so production stopped again (Bruni et al., 2002).

Barovier & Toso

Barovier & Toso is one of the most famous glassmaking companies within the Murano glass district, and is the sixth oldest family firm in the world. The origins of the company can be traced back to Jacobellus Berovierus, and the first documentation of the Barovier family can be dated back to 1295, the year the furnace was founded or acquired. In the thirteenth century, the documents did not refer to the company or to the furnace, but to the master who owned it. There is not much specific information about the production of Barovier from 1300 to 1400, but it is likely that the production was similar to that of other furnaces operating in the period—that is, mostly devoted to the production of glass-blown products and of small bottles. After the first decades of business, the Barovier masters reached a high degree of specialization in glassblowing techniques (Bruni et al., 2002).

We can identify two different periods in the history of Barovier (Figure 10.1). The first one goes from the establishment of the first furnace to 1810, when Barovier shut down for a few years. This period was mainly characterized by the *Serenissima* Republic. The second period goes from 1810 until today.

There is not much information about the first period of activity of the Barovier company. There are no official documents either in the Venice *Archivio di Stato* or in the sources of the company. The first official mention

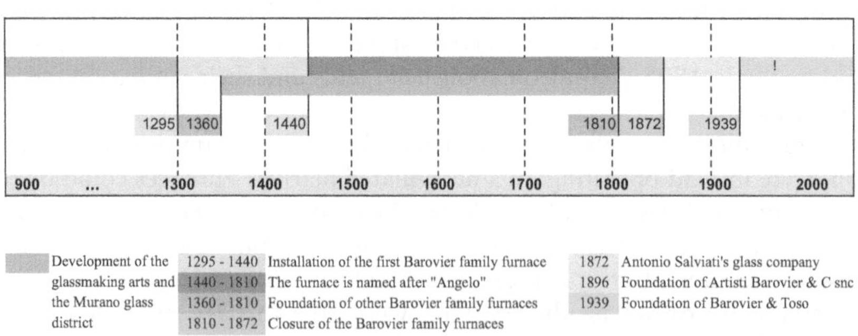

Figure 10.1 Timeline showing the evolution of Barovier & Toso from its foundation to today

of Barovier dates back to February 1324, in a document by the *Podestà* of Murano, where it can be deduced that Jacobellus Berovierius was the owner of a furnace in Murano (Zecchin, 1989). There is no specific information about the production process of Barovier, but we can assume that the company was following the regulations of the guilds. It is important to note that the government decided to move glass production to the island of Murano in 1291, before the establishment of the Barovier company. Some documents, available in the *Archivio Storico*, report some information about the descendants of Jacobellus, Antonio and Bartolomeo. They were defined as glassmakers in documents by the *Podestà* of Murano in 1348. According to Zecchin (1968a), Bartolomeo Barovier had two sons: Jacopo and Antonio. While Jacopo managed a little glass shop in Murano, Antonio worked in the furnace. It is reasonable to think that the two brothers tried to split the business, one focusing on selling, the other on producing.

During the fifteenth century, many of Jacopo's descendants became masters, and some of them were elected as representatives of the guild. In 1440, Angelo Barovier discovered the famous crystal glass, and the furnaces began producing a significant quantity of products with that technique. There are two elements that support this: first, the application to register the production method, which produced particularly pure and transparent glass; second, a document by Antonio Averlino that mentions some very pure glass made by a certain "Mr. Angelo from Murano". During the same period, another production technique was discovered: chalcedony glass. The output of this production was mostly refined objects to be used every day, such as cups that were artistically decorated (Bruni et al., 2002).

During the period of Angelo Barovier, in 1415 the *Serenissima* Republic mandated the use of trademarks in order to make furnaces identifiable. In fact, there are some documents dating to the end of 1400 mentioning the furnace "Angelo". Industrial espionage was used by glassmakers already in this period, in order to get secret production techniques from other masters (Zecchin, 1966). This also had some positive externalities, because it allowed knowledge about production techniques to spread throughout the Murano glass district. After Angelo Barovier died, Giorgio Ballarin, a labourer at the Barovier furnace, managed to steal and make a copy of the recipe book where Angelo had written the famous recipe for crystal glass. Giorgio founded his own furnaces and he had some success, given that he became a glassmaking master and, some years later, was appointed representative of the guild (Bruni et al., 2002). Angelo's two children (Marino and Marietta) kept on producing in the furnace until 1490. Interestingly, it was not common at all for a woman to work in the furnace, and Marietta was in this sense an exception. She became famous because she could create the "rosette millefiori" (Zecchin, 1968b).

Between the fifteenth and sixteenth century, it was common to produce monochromatic cups made of crystal glass, with colourful decorations attached. Such decorations were done mostly in arabesque style, with imaginary animals and mythological representations. Between 1500 and 1600, the Barovier company also started producing mirrors. In 1600, there were some important changes for the Barovier company, mainly due to the fact that the family's proprietary information had spread around Murano and even Europe, despite the *Serenissima* Republic's attempts to protect know-how and keep it on the island of Murano. Despite the new economic scenario (a market increasingly requiring lower-quality products), the company kept on producing high-quality products. At the same time, there were some innovations in production techniques that were then aimed at obtaining a product that was more similar to Bohemian and English glass.

During 1600–1800, the Barovier family kept on producing with Giandomenico, Pietro-Anastasio, Lorenzo, Giuseppe and Giovanni, but there are no records of particular innovations from their side. This lack of new products or production techniques is probably due to the guild system, which hindered innovation, and the demand from the Venetian aristocracy, who kept purchasing the existing kinds of products.

In 1872, Antonio Salviati, owner of the Salviati & Co. Ltd, founded the Venice and Murano Glass and Mosaic Company, in order to boost the industrialization process of the island. Giuseppe Barovier was one of the first to work with Salviati, and together they created a new company, exclusively working with artistic glass, the Salviati dott. Antonio & Co. Other members of the Barovier family followed Giuseppe and joined the company. In 1896 the company "Artisti Barovier & C. snc" was founded. In 1936, the company merged with the *Società Anonima Industrie Artistiche Riunite* (SAIAR), which was managed by the Toso family. In 1939, the company officially became Barovier & Toso. During this period, the company kept on producing—as it still does today—following the traditional methodology, and trying to reach higher sales volumes (Bruni et al., 2002).

The Relationship Between the Institutional and Economic Landscape and the Activity of Barovier & Toso

Location

One of the main features of Barovier & Toso that has been highly influenced by the institutional and economic landscape is its location. In fact, among the regulations promoted by the Republic of Venice and by the guild, some that were particularly relevant were about the location of furnaces. In particular, one of the first regulations about this was issued in 1291, as the guild forbade anyone from building furnaces in the Rivo Alto (Rialto) area in Venice.

It is interesting to note that around the same period, in 1279, most of the furnaces were located on the island of Murano. As a matter of fact, Murano had several advantages: it was located between Venice and Torcello (as pointed out earlier, the first furnaces were located in Torcello), and it was the closest island to Venice having enough space to open production activities, being less heavily populated than Venice. The first furnace by Barovier was founded in 1295, after the 1291 regulation was already in place. There are two possible scenarios. First, it may be that Barovier was the owner of a furnace in the city of Venice. If this were the case, he would have had to move the business to Murano. If, conversely, Barovier already had a furnace in Murano, the legislation did not have any effect on him. Whatever the scenario, when the furnace was founded by Barovier, regulations required the following: furnaces could use only alder wood; they could operate from January to August; if the master was caught practising his art outside Venice, he would be banned from the glassmaking guild or he would pay a fine; it was not allowed to export any scrap material or damaged products. In Altare, a village in the Ligurian hinterland, the statute of the glassmaking guild permitted glassmakers to move elsewhere for work on the condition that they paid a tax to the local administration, did not produce certain types of glass and limited their absence to three months (Belfanti, 2004).

The location of the Barovier furnace is quite important from many perspectives, as it allows us to understand the characteristics of the production process and the relationship between different furnaces. As most furnaces were already located in Murano even before the 1291 regulation, one can deduce that they must have found several advantages on that island. Industrial economics helps to explain this phenomenon, as know-how and competences that are located in a defined area can circulate more easily and effectively (Lucas, 1988). In other words, furnaces located on Murano could have potentially benefited from technology spillovers (Marshall, 1919). Also, Marshall's (1919, p. 86) concept of "industrial atmosphere" may explain why furnaces were concentrated on the island. According to Marshall, when both owners and workers live in the same community, they can benefit because "the secrets of industry are in the air". Moreover, as the case of Giorgio Ballarin shows—Giorgio was the labourer at the Barovier furnace who managed to steal and make a copy of the recipe book by Angelo Barovier—furnaces located in the same area may have benefited by imitating innovations and creations by other furnaces.

Another important factor explaining why most of the furnaces were located on the island of Murano is the way the art was passed from master to labourer. The process was one of "learning by interacting with others" or "learning by doing" (see Arrow, 1962, p. 155), so physical proximity was a necessary condition for such a form of knowledge transmission. We need to keep in mind that labourers had to work with the master for a very long period of time (fifteen years), so it was more difficult to leave the island once the training period was finished. After 1291, the Republic of Venice issued several regulations on the location of the furnaces, so that the fact that furnaces were located on Murano also became a consequence of such regulations.

Innovation

Angelo Barovier invented crystal glass and, in 1455, the *Serenissima* Republic granted him the exclusive rights to produce it. This innovation had a huge impact both on the Barovier company and on the general reputation of Murano glass. It is interesting to note that there was probably a close relationship between this innovation and the context where the company was operating. Angelo Barovier probably did experiments using raw materials coming from abroad. In this sense, the strong relationships existing between the Republic of Venice and the Far East played an important role in the innovation process.

According to Mokyr (2010), modern endogenous growth theory postulated that innovation is produced within the system, and thus it is subject to economic incentives, and should be regarded as an output resulting from inputs (e.g., physical capital, human capital, R&D, economies of scale). In the case of Barovier, it seems that physical and human capital played a major role. More specifically, the progress of technology has been explained by both internalist and externalist theories (Mokyr, 2010). Internalists see an autonomous logic, an evolutionary process where one advance leads to another, in which the past largely determines the future. Externalists, conversely, think of technological change as determined by economic needs, by necessity stimulating invention, by factor prices and by resource endowments. The case of Barovier seems more in line with an externalist approach. In this case, innovation does not come from pressing economic needs, but in the case of Barovier and crystal glass, the availability of this new raw material did play a central role. Several authors, including Mokyr (2010), do not support the idea that economic needs are the main driver of innovation. Modern Western society is by and large wealthy enough not to feel any pressing economic need, yet it is very innovative (Mokyr, 2010, p. 14).

Another important interaction between Barovier and the institutional context happened in 1400. In particular, in 1415, the Republic of Venice required that every furnace and every glass shop had to choose its own brand. This was one of the mechanisms through which the *Serenissima* tried to protect glass production on Murano and to make it more visible. There is no information about the original name or brand of the Barovier furnace. What we do know is that some years later, there was the furnace "all'Angelo" (deriving from the name of Angelo Barovier).

Technology, and knowledge in general, is non-rivalrous, so that the social marginal cost of sharing it is zero. According to Mokyr (2010), since the social marginal product is positive, the optimal static solution is one in which it is made accessible freely to anyone able and willing to use it. Clearly, as pointed out by the same author, under these conditions, there is not much incentive for companies to invest in R&D. The debate on the pros and cons of patents and copyrights has a long history. It is interesting to note that in the case of Barovier, and more generally of the glassmaking industry, the institutions opted for a patent approach.

According to Belfanti (2004), patent laws and craft guilds are two institutions that need to be studied together, as they are apparently dedicated to different objectives but in reality they represent two aspects of the same institutional set-up. On the one hand, patents encourage the spread of technical knowledge by conceding privilege or monopolies to those introducing new products or processes. On the other hand, guilds were traditionally characterized by traditional scholarship as rigidly conservative obstacles to technological progress. According to the authors, patents and guilds were actually parts of an institutional set-up that used to aim to attract craftsmen who knew technical secrets, in an era when the diffusion of technical knowledge depended for the most part on the migration of those in possession of it.

It is interesting to note the case of Marietta Barovier, who became famous because she could create the "rosette millefiori" (Zecchin, 1968b). A woman producing (and innovating) products was not at all common at the time, and it represents in some way an innovation in itself. Innovativeness of the firm and inclusion of a woman seem to be two elements of a virtuous cycle, in which one element reinforces the other. Marietta's activity may have, at the same time, contributed to innovation and may have been allowed by the firm's higher innovative orientation.

Protectionism

An important institutional feature of the Republic of Venice is the degree of protectionism adopted by the government. Broadly speaking, we can see how Venice, in its first period, increased its know-how and prosperity by attracting foreign artists, writers, bankers and so forth. In its second period, the *Serenissima* became more and more closed, increasing protectionism.

With specific reference to the glassmaking industry, the turning points of protectionism by the *Serenissima* can be identified as 1482 and 1489. In these years, regulations allowed only Venetians to open new furnaces and forbade foreigners from owning any furnace.

Before the end of 1400, the approach of the republic can be defined as "weakly protectionist". The regulations from the government and the guild protected the know-how of the master glassmakers, but allowed the inclusion of foreign workers. Consistent with this approach, in 1280 Gregorio da Napoli founded a glassmaking school in Murano. During this phase, guilds were mostly regulating the quality of the products and their certification and trying to avoid the transfer abroad of that know-how developed in Murano.

From 1500 ("strong protectionism"), the government and the guild made it increasingly harder for foreign products and workers to enter the republic and Murano respectively. This created a sort of "shield" that seemingly protected Murano glassmaking, but actually greatly contributed to its demise. As a consequence of strong protectionism, Murano furnaces decreased their possibility of innovating products, as they relied more and more on internal demand and they could not know the characteristics of the foreign production in detail. Clearly there is some literature arguing that guilds were open to innovation. For instance, Trivellato (2000) argues that guilds kept innovation and tradition in tension, allowing one or the other to prevail according to what circumstances required.

The change in the approach of the Republic of Venice towards protectionism can be traced to requests coming from the guilds themselves. Over the years, they had reached high levels of wealth, and by the end of 1400 they were afraid of losing it because of competition coming from abroad. Therefore, glassmakers asked the government and the guild to increase the level of protectionism towards the internal market.

Trivellato (2000) argues that the approach of guilds towards innovation needs to be evaluated by looking at capital-saving innovations and labour-saving innovations separately. According to the author, guilds did not oppose capital-saving innovations, such as those regarding the use of cheaper raw materials. Conversely, guilds did oppose much more firmly labour-saving innovations that would have decreased the need for a qualified workforce. As glassblowing masters forming the guild ultimately made the decisions, any innovation threatening to reduce the qualified workforce was blocked. Only innovations that allowed reducing the non-qualified workforce were accepted, such as those regarding the initial phases of the production process, such as the preparation of the raw materials.

The role of the government and of guilds can be interpreted in the light of the stream of literature on accounting and power (see Hopwood, 1983; Giovannoni and Riccaboni, 2009; Mennicken and Miller, 2012). This framework concerns how accounting is used for governance and "how accounting systems can play an active role in shaping organizational activities and interactions, as well as in the production and maintenance of power" (Riccaboni et al., 2006, p. 45). Guilds likely gathered information (e.g., see Table 10.1 on the production costs of a furnace in Murano) in order to monitor the interests they were most interested in defending. For instance, according to Trivellato (2000), guilds opposed labour-saving innovations, and therefore they were likely to measure the number of workers in a specific field and keep the cost structure of glassmakers under control. This (accounting) information was therefore used in order to shape guild and government policies.

This evolution in protectionism of Venice explains the evolution in the history of Barovier. Between 1600 and 1800, there is no record of any significant innovation, probably due to the fact that the Venetian aristocracy was buying the same products and foreign glass was not pushing Murano furnaces to evolve. The situation collapsed after the end of the republic and the abolition of guilds by Napoleon. At that time, furnaces had to compete on an unregulated market, which Murano glassmakers were not ready for. On top of that, regulations promoted by Napoleon greatly favoured French products, and this hit the Murano glassmaking industry hard. As a matter of fact, Barovier closed in 1800, as a direct effect of such regulations. As the history of Barovier shows, it took several years in order for the company to catch up with the innovations developed by other markets.

Our interpretation of the evolution of Barovier and of the guilds is not consistent with the work by Epstein (1996). The author argues that medieval craft guilds emerged in order to provide transferable skills through apprenticeship and that they sustained interregional specialized labour markets and contributed to technological invention by stimulating technical diffusion through migrant labour. His view about the role of guilds is therefore opposed to the mainstream argument that guilds hindered innovation. With specific reference to the issue of the technological change, Epstein (1996) argues that guilds did not hinder endogenous nor exogenous innovation but rather that craft innovation was the outcome of small-scale and incremental practical experiment and of random variation. Finally, the author recalls the case of Venice, where guilds were not opposed to innovation, but they had to face authorities which often frustrated their activities. Ultimately, according to this argument, Venice's failure to adapt to cheaper foreign competition was due not to the sclerosis of their guilds but to its merchant oligarchy's desire to preserve the quality standards that upheld the city's industrial reputation.

Conclusions

Our analysis allows us to identify some interesting relationships between the institutional and economic landscape and the activities of Barovier & Toso.

First, the location of Barovier on the island of Murano derives from economic factors (typical of districts), from the way the art was passed from master to labourer and from industry regulations.

Second, the innovation process that allowed the company to become famous at the time (Angelo Barovier invented "crystal glass") depended on the availability of raw materials, made available by the close relationships Venice had with the Middle East. It is interesting to note that the Republic of Venice used to protect knowledge and innovations through a patent system, which allowed Barovier alone to produce crystal glass. This finding is consistent with the role patents played in the context of technical change diffusion (Belfanti, 2004) and contributes to previous literature on patents (Calegari, 1969; Berveglieri, 1995; Sabbatini, 1996).

Third, Barovier, and in general the whole glassmaking industry, suffered from the increasing protectionism of the Republic of Venice. Especially from 1500 onwards ("strong protectionism"), the government and the guild made it increasingly harder for foreign products and workers to enter the republic and Murano, respectively. This created a sort of "shield" that seemingly protected Murano glassmaking but actually greatly contributed to its demise. It is interesting to note that pressures towards greater protectionism came, for the most part, from the guilds themselves. This finding is consistent with traditional scholarship (Belfanti, 2004), but at the same time it is opposed to other studies finding that guilds did not oppose innovation (Epstein, 1996).

References

Arrow, K.J. (1962). The economic implication of learning by doing. *Review of Economic Studies*, 29(3), 155–173.

Barovier Mentasti, R. (1982). *Il Vetro Veneziano*. Electa, Milano.
Barovier Mentasti, R. (2015). *Murano una Storia di Vetro*. Gambier Keller Editore, Venezia.
Belfanti, C. (2004). Guilds, patents, and the circulation of technical knowledge: Northern Italy during the early modern age. *Technology and Culture*, 45(3), 569–589.
Berveglieri, R. (1995). *Inventori stranieri a Venezia (1474–1788): Importazione di tecnologia e circolazione di tecnici, artigiani, inventori*. Istituto Veneto di Scienze, Lettere ed Arti, Venezia.
Bruni, G., Campedelli, B., Roffia, P. (2002). *Barovier & Toso vetrerie artistiche reunite: Saggi storici di Ragioneria, Ricerche ed analisi di imprese longeve, vol. 2*. Università degli Studi di Verona.
Calegari, M. (1969). *La Società patria delle arti e manifatture: Iniziativa imprenditoriale rinnovamento tecnologico nel riformismo Genovese del settecento*. Barbera, Siena.
Ceruti, C., Dorigato, A. (1992). *Il Vetro*. De Agostini, Novara.
Ciriacono, S. (1996). *Storia di Venezia: Industria e Artigianato, vol. 3*. Istituto della Enciclopedia Italiana, Roma.
Epstein, S.R. (1996). Craft guilds, apprenticeship and technological change in preindustrial Europe. *The Journal of Economic History*, 58(3), 684–713.
Gaspareto, A. (1958). *Il Vetro di Murano*. Neri Pozza, Venezia.
Giovannoni, E., Riccaboni, A. (2009). Editorial: A general overview of perspectives and reflections on accounting's past in Europe. *Accounting History*, 14(4), 341–355.
Hopwood, A. (1983). On trying to study accounting in the contexts in which it operates. *Accounting, Organisations and Society*, 8(2–3), 287–305.
Lucas, R. (1988). On the mechanics of economic development. *Journal of Monetary Economics*, 22(1), 3–42.
Marshall, A. (1919). *Industry and Trade*. Macmillan, London.
Mennicken, A., Miller, P. (2012). Accounting, territorialisation and power. *Foucault Studies*, (13), 4–24.
Mokyr, J. (2010). The contribution of economic history to the study of innovation and technical change. In: *Handbook of Economics of Innovation by Rosenberg and Hall*, pp. 12–46, Elsevier, Amsterdam.
Riccaboni, A., Giovannoni, E., Giorgi, A., Moscadelli, S. (2006). Accounting and power: Evidence from the fourteenth century. *Accounting History*, 11(1), 41–62.
Sabbatini, R. (1996). *L'innovazione prudente: Spunti per lo studio di un'economia d'ancien régime*. Le lettere, Firenze.
Trivellato, F. (1999). *Arti e mercati: Produzione e commercio del vetro a Venezia nei secoli XVII e XVIII*. Università Bocconi, Milano.
Trivellato, F. (2000). *Fondamenta dei Vetrai, Lavoro, tecnologia e mercato a Venezia tra Sei e Settecento*. Donzelli Editore, Roma.
Zecchin, L. (1966). Angelo Barovier, vetraio del Rinascimento. *Vetro e Silicati*, 11(60), 23–26.
Zecchin, L. (1968a). I Barovier e il vetro cristallino. *Vetro e Silicati*, 13(67), 23–26.
Zecchin, L. (1968b). Maria Barovier e le "Rosette". *Journal of Glass Studies*, 10, 105–109.
Zecchin, L. (1987). *Vetro e vetrai di Murano, vol. I*. Arsenale Editrice, Venezia.
Zecchin, L. (1989). *Vetro e vetrai di Murano, vol. II*. Arsenale Editrice, Venezia.

11 Accounting and the Venetian Merchants

David Alexander and Chiara Saccon

Introduction

This chapter links together several interests of the authors. Two are particularly significant. The first of these, to put it in a fundamental but generalistic way, is that the accounting and reporting function is from every perspective a pragmatic, context-related social construct. At any particular time, and in any particular place, accounting seeks to meet human needs. It seeks to communicate human perceptions which, if understood and accepted within a group of people by "collective intentionality", become "institutional facts" (Alexander and Archer, 2003, p. 5). Since any such agreement is by definition time- and space-specific, and limited in its application and relevance, exploration of, and understanding of, the specific environment is always crucial.

The second interest is in the role of history. Exploration of history constantly reminds us of the practically infinite variations of environment within which the accounting function can operate. It helps us to explore and understand the complex processes through which accounting affects and is affected by the world in which it finds itself. In this context, we are fortunate to have unfettered access to the resources (physical, historical, archival) of Venice. In this chapter, we link these two strands together. In the words of the abstract, the "economic historiography of Venice recognizes merchants as early and creative adopters of the modern accounting tools. The enacting of accounting procedures served specific purposes, as an integral part of governance and controlling or monitoring processes". The chapter therefore uses the Venetian history and scenario as a case study, with reference to a particular surviving set of records relating to Giovanni Foscari, from the middle of the fifteenth century, of our general philosophical standpoint.

Accounting and Its Context

The purpose of this chapter, more precisely, is to study the knowledge of accounting, specifically the origin of the double-entry system, in the context of the late medieval time known as "perhaps the most brilliant and progressive period in the history of accounting" (De Roover, 1956, p. 174). Due to its historical relevance it should be interesting to analyze this process through the theoretical lens of contextual analysis. Accounting is deeply interconnected with the surrounding institutional environment in which it works and which it stems from and, in turn, on which it impacts. Being intended as not merely a technical activity, an "independent art", but instead something that can participate "in constructing the setting in which it forms a part" (Hopwood, 1983), it is considered as being a social practice, having social impact (Carnegie, 2014).

A deep understanding of the nature and dynamics of accounting requires giving prominence not only to its role as a decision-making device but also to the wider institutional and social context in which accounting operates (Hopwood, 1983) in order to examine the diverse arenas in which the calculative practices emerged as significant. This understanding could be positioned in the domain of institutional analysis capable of interrogating the social and cultural underpinning of accounting practices as well as the political and economic forces underlying its development, taking into consideration a three-level analysis: macro-, mezzo- and micro-analysis, mapping the broad domain of institutional research (Arnold, 2009). More precisely, by applying the macro-level institutional analysis attention is paid to examining the ways that accounting practices are embedded in historically determined institutional, societal and cultural contexts (Arnold, 2009, p. 55). An institutional infrastructure comprises public and private rules, conventions and organizations that shape economic behaviour. In contemporary times this includes the economic system, legal system, banking system, taxation system, capital markets, regulatory and enforcement agencies, industry associations and standard-setting bodies (Leuz, 2010), whereas centuries ago a different but corresponding institutional environment existed, even though with obvious characteristics related to the particular time, and was characterized, among other issues, by an economic trade revolution and state intervention in the economy. This context is here briefly outlined.

Accounting contextual linkages are well acknowledged in the literature and they are supposed to cast light in interpreting the ways in which accounting practices have in ancient times followed the path of trade routes, colonial conquests, educational opportunities and state intervention. The aim is to look for insights into the means by which accounting practices responded to contextual change, focusing on its location and mobilization, and on how and why it propagated (Hopwood, 2000).

Legal system, cultural norms and social patterns are intended as exogenous institutions and generally change slowly over time as they are arrangements governing economies as a whole (Wysocki, 2011). More specific and sectorial variables, like the accounting profession, education and mechanisms (e.g., for publications), representing a mezzo-level institutional analysis (Arnold, 2009, p. 53), contribute in deepening knowledge of how (in particular) forms of accounting emerge from, sustain and modify wider institutional and social structures. Mezzo-analysis focuses on the transformations in the institutional arrangements governing the accounting field and profession as a whole. In the Middle Ages, accountants began to be considered professional (Ciambotti, 2007) and so contributed to the development of the double-entry system and its rapid and wide spreading/dissemination. The advance of the accounting profession in the Middle Ages may be interpreted as evidence, at that time, of individual freedom and creativity, projected to understand the world in its many aspects (Sombart, 1922). Values, shared meanings and habits have an influence on decisions and actions, and the so-called institutional thinking (Douglas, 1986), representing the micro-level of analysis, can explain specific accounting decisions or behaviours (Young, 1996). This level of analysis is usually associated with the explanation of continuities between the present and the past in accounting thought and so with a narrow institutional thinking. However, the micro-institutional theory, concentrating on deeply embedded values and social norms, can explain also evolutionary dynamics (Arnold, 2009, p. 53), such as those of the accounting technique in its early times that could be seen as featured by open institutional thinking.

According to business history studies, the Italian Middle Age context is generally characterized by a commercial revolution, a political stability and a cultural renaissance. Nevertheless diverse geographical areas knew specificities/peculiarities, like a predominant maritime commerce, an advanced credit system, a more or less significant intervention of the government in the economic sphere, activities based on partnership and agency, and family ties. In the following section Venetian historical institutions are selected and examined because of their fitting with the general pattern of the three-level institutional analysis, thus representing a reasoned choice of subjects designed to offer an overall view of the institutional context from which accounting practices in the medieval period emerged.

Accounting emanates from the interplay between a series of institutional factors but to understand the social functioning of it a greater contextual analysis is needed in trying to search for accounting as a socially embedded practice and to analyze how it operates in practice. Playing a role in building the setting in which it forms a part, accounting influences organizational and social functioning. So the claim is for conducting "critical and interpretative histories of the nature, role, uses and impacts of accounting within its organizational and social contexts", and investigating the story behind the accounts within the contexts "offers at least potentially more interest and significance under the conception of accounting as a social practice" (Carnegie, 2014, p. 1245). A view of accounting as a socially embedded practice permits, in turn, much profounder and richer understanding not only of accounting but also of the wider social context in which it operates.

Historical Background

According to historians double-entry bookkeeping developed (knowledge of the double-entry system emerged in practice in Italy around 1300; Yamey,

2004, p. 147) in Italy in the thirteenth century mainly due to the development of the regional economy (Mills, 1994). This economic expansion, recognized as a "commercial revolution" (Dyer, 1996, p. 495; Lane, 1977, p. 178), was guided by larger merchants leading trading, commercial and financial firms (Lopez, 1976). Venice belonged to the cities triangle, along with Genoa and Florence, where business activities increased and the accounting technique originated (Mills, 1994). In 1400s, and the subsequent two centuries, the Venetian Republic *Serenissima* experienced a great economic and political power. It represented the commercial crossroads of Mediterranean Europe, a perfect centre of private and public intervention.

During that long and extraordinary period for the Venetian area the need for modern accounting practices arose. Merchants and other economic actors and entities were used to keeping records of activities and transactions. Balancing the books was not the primary objective of medieval accounting. On the contrary, the merchant had begun by 1400 to use accounting as a tool of management or control, developing rudiments of cost accounting, introducing adjustments such as accruals and deferrals and paying attention to the audit of the statements (De Roover, 1956, p. 118), but it took the greater structuring of firms, like the Venetian mercantile companies operating in international trade, and the favouring regulative context, to ask for and need more articulated and organic records (Zerbi, 1952, p. 15). The development, spread and near universal adoption of double-entry accounting helped bridge the late medieval period with that of early modern Europe and formed a base upon which commercial development and modern management were built (Mills, 1994, p. 84).

In the passage from late medieval to early modern Europe, Venice experienced a progressive loss of commercial primacy—in particular the crucial role of brokerage between East and West, with the gradual disappearance of state intervention in the naval system, and the retreat of Venetian shipping in the face of the emergence of more aggressive international competitors, especially North European. Many implications arose: the change of the balance in the Mediterranean in the light of the changes in the political relations between Venice and the Ottoman Empire and the important consequences that this changed landscape involved in the trade between Venice and the East; the various strategies put in place by merchants in order to cope with changed political and economic conditions, with particular attention to the foreign merchant communities active in the lagoon, looking at them as a universe to be understood and to discover, and so generating a flourishing cultural exchange (Dal Grande, 2014); the same vibrant attention towards novelties that gave rise to the profitable maritime commerce and the development of business and accounting practices. Many merchants turned their mercantile capitals towards land and properties investments in the mainland to cope with the riskier activity overseas and reach economic stability.

Double-entry bookkeeping was invented and implemented by large merchants for reasons specific to the economy and culture of northern Italy, probably originating in Genoa (De Roover, 1956, p. 115) or in Florence (Sangster, 2016), but "from there it spread over the trading routes of Europe to become standard business practice" (Mills, 1994, p. 85) and made the fourteenth and fifteenth centuries represent the most brilliant and progressive period in the history of accounting (De Roover, 1956). In this scenario Venice, more than Genoa and Florence, enjoyed the reputation of "maestro" throughout Europe in terms of accounting knowledge and experience (Lane, 1977, p. 152).

Although the double-entry system is not recognized as being invented in Venice, Venice had an undoubted central role in making it a significant business practice, and the context and institutional environment in which this happened deserve our attention and analysis.

Institutional Environment

The origins of the double-entry system are rooted in its relationship to broad economic, technological and intellectual factors (Mills, 1994, p. 84). In medieval times big economic changes came from the transformation of trade. The commercial revolution meant a broad set of activities starting from the extension of a system of international commerce that unified trade routes of Northern and Southern Europe and also those of three continents, then the process of urbanization, the penetration of trade in the most diverse places and in all social classes (Dyer, 1996, p. 495) and associated profound social changes. In the same way, an intensely vibrant economic and social environment characterized the Venetian Middle Ages. But if in the rest of Europe the trade revolution referred to the oceanic expansion of commerce, in Venice it was above all a transformation in business organization and practices (Lane, 1977, p. 177). Certainly an evolving economic environment required more developed accounting techniques able to support the management and control of activities and decision processes, but at the same time improved methods of accounting were deemed one of the causes of new forms of business organization (De Roover, 1956), so giving evidence of the capacity of accounting to both influence and be influenced by context.

The Italian commercial revolution was supported by state institutions that were committed to simplifying and making business more profitable. Because of this orientation, investors

> looked to the State perhaps more in Venice than elsewhere for judicial and regulatory institutions and for a philosophy that would promote a proper balance between regulation and freedom so as to maintain an environment conducive to investment and making profits.
>
> (Mueller, 1997, p. 568)

A prerogative of the Venetian Republic was the control over the commercial sector through rules and protections aimed at protecting sea routes fundamental for the Venice economic domain. From the fourteenth century the Venetian state participated in the management of maritime activity and settled a system of galleys' auction and their organization according to public directives. Great attention was devoted to the management of the main routes of maritime trade towards the East (Romania–Black Sea, Syria-Beirut, Alexandria) and the West (Flanders, Barberia, Aigues-Mortes, Trafego). Thus in order to maintain its predominance as mediator of sea commerce, control over the routes was strategic for Venice. The republic regulated, in timing and organization, long-distance trade. The "*mude*", the naval caravans (perhaps flotillas in modern parlance) composed of groups of galleys, had their precise destination and left Venice according to a strict calendar, taking into consideration seasonal weather conditions and the commercial cycle of the destination. Ensuring regularity in navigation flows favoured the stability of fair-time (large market) events in town, which were linked to the *mude* arrivals and departures, continuous activity in the Arsenal and an increased safety of the convoys (Luzzatto, 1954). The *Serenissima*'s primary objective was to create trade flows covering the entire Mediterranean basin in favour of regular product exchanges and a rapid turnover to allow for rapid reinvestment of capital. The mercantile network that Venice built and the rules it imposed were aimed at consolidating its strategic position, reaffirming its hegemony and ensuring the widest market for its merchandise.

Other institutions were created to make the mercantile activities easier and more profitable. To favour the Venetian commercial interests in important trade cities of the Levant the existence of consulates was fundamental. Consulates were representatives of the *Serenissima*'s government in foreign lands and, at the same time, their activities were greatly influenced by the merchants' interests. The institutional presence of Venice in many Eastern ports represented one of the factors determining the success and the leadership of the Venetian merchants in the Eastern trade, in particular for the recovery of trade with the Levant after the Ottoman embargo (Montemezzo, 2012, p. 8). In supporting their activity merchants counted on the Venetian courts that were aimed at making merchants meet their debts, with bookkeeping acting as a legal record.

The credit system too in Venice contributed to effectively financing and so developing international commerce (Mueller, 1997). Banks were essential for the payment system, and in the fourteenth century the Senate attempted to regulate banking with the aim of increasing the trustworthiness of what was seen as a public service, not only as private enterprises. In medieval and Renaissance Venice the principal structures that sustained the money market were local deposits and transfer banks, international merchant banks, floating debts, public deposit banks and the funded debt; "some of them were relatively unique, others less so, but even those found in other major urban commercial centers attained in Venice a particular renown" (Mueller, 1997, p. 569). The increasing complexity of the business environment, particularly the increase in credit transactions, saw merchants carrying on their trade involving credit, loans, interest negotiable instruments and foreign currencies (Edwards, 1989, p. 50).

The outlined institutional structure, composed of economic, legal and finance factors, manifests the macro environment favouring the conduct of businesses and the need for accounting as a tool of management. The expansion of trade determined the organizational form of enterprises and created the demand for a much improved bookkeeping technique that developed in response to and was dependent upon and adaptable from the nature of the firm (Mills, p. 85).

Towards the end of the thirteenth century in the main Italian cities firms arose based on partnerships between persons, some of whom belonged to the same family (which gave its name to the firm), which conferred capital for the joint venture. Venetian enterprises were constituted as *Fraterne*, partnerships among relatives, taking the family surname (*fraterna* Soranzo, *fraterna* Barbarigo and so on). It was a sort of temporary arrangement established for the duration of a period, from two to twelve years, or a single voyage, especially for Venetian merchants, and closed after its conclusion. At the company's break-up, profits were split and a new partnership was established to advance to the next business phase (Dyer, 1996, p. 498). The accounting representation reflects the fact that the firm is a unit in itself and answers to the need of keeping track of modification of the owners' equity and devising a system producing the measure of profit to be then distributed (De Roover, 1956, p. 116).

Dealing with medieval bookkeeping one must not lose sight of the prevailing way of doing business (De Roover, 1956, p. 117). It bears repetition that the specific activity run by merchants and the way of making it operational impacted on the accounting system, which in turn, using appropriate forms and procedures, favoured the functioning of the economic entity. Venture accounting, coming from the merchants' maritime voyages, characterized Venetians records, keeping note of goods' value and expenses incurred. Many merchants preferred to operate by means of commission agents, sending them wares on consignment to foreign correspondents. Agency impacted the accounting development and explains the use of merchandise accounts in order to keep track of movements between principal and agent; Venetians did not draw up balance sheets at regular intervals but they postponed the closing procedure until after each affair was completely finished. Venetian merchants were often related to agents by kinship, which was considered important in business in the medieval period (De Roover, 1956, p. 117).

The contribution of accounting in holding agents accountable is explored as a reason for the transition from the travelling merchant to the sedentary merchant. According to the literature in favour of this causal relation, accounting played a role in changing the structure of business organizations (Lane, 1977, p. 178), so manifesting an influence in the environment from which it stemmed, and highlighting its effect as an institution. However, even opponents of bookkeeping as a means of affecting business organizations (Yamey, 1975) recognize the merit of accounting in its comprehensiveness and its possibilities for the orderly arrangement of data, and this merit applied in routine administration and the control of assets.

In Venetian medieval times accounting is modelled on the demands of the merchants, the main actors in the economic business scenario, influencing in turn the management of the problems. To the merchants many studies attribute an important role in shaping accounting and contributing to its circulation through mercantile activity. Double entry is referred to mercantile organizations where its proper features matured, and it was considered for a long time a technique proper to the commercial firms, and the Venetian merchants in particular (Tucci, 1996, p. 522). The so-called Venetian method of accounting in the Middle Ages is a testimony of the localization of accounting due to merchants and their involvement in determining its mobilization. It was the Venetian style or version of double-entry bookkeeping that crossed the Alps and disseminated in Flanders, in England and in Germany (Besta, 1929, p. 341).

Accounting comes from practice and its progress comes from there too (Tucci, 1996, p. 517), but other than merchants, educators too are considered an important mechanism for accounting knowledge development and its transmission. Pacioli was a popularizer of the double-entry bookkeeping accounting method through his notable *Summa* (written in Italian, not in Latin) but he was not the inventor; instead he learned about double-entry bookkeeping during his stays in a Venetian family of merchants. Some literature grounds the origin of double-entry bookkeeping in educational advances which occurred in medieval universities from the eleventh century (Hoskin and Macve, 1986). Certainly accounting was taught at universities from the second half of the fourteenth century onwards (Oldroyd and Dobie, 2009, p. 102). On the other hand in medieval times the consideration of accountants as professionals began, responding to the demands from increasing numbers and increasing complexity of commercial transactions. The accounting institutional field, on which the mezzo-level historical analysis focuses, was growing and generating arrangements governing it. The spread of the use of double entry is largely attributed to printed expositions of the system and so to the developed print industry (Besta, 1929; Mills, 1994) but many also argued that the print role is overstated (Yamey, 2004).

From a different approach, doing a micro-level analysis, the double-entry origin and diffusion could be interpreted as an outgrowth of the spirit of Renaissance science. A basic assumption of histories of modern accounting is that double entry arose from a desire on the part of late medieval merchants

> to provide a scientifically precise analysis of the enterprise for use in market forecasting and investment planning. This was presumably inspired by the empirical studies of Copernicus and Galileo, the introduction of Arabic numerology, and the popularization of algebra.
>
> (Aho, 1985, p. 22)

This happened in a period when art, literature, history and philosophy flourished on an unprecedented scale, alongside trade, enterprise, record-keeping and accountability, so determining the "open" institutional thinking of merchants.

Historical Rebuilding Through Original Documents (Ledgers)

The original accounting records presented in the ancient ledgers of Venetian merchants are a great source of information to conduct historical research in accounting. The ledgers of Giacomo Badoer, Andrea Barbarigo and Giovanni Foscari open important windows in the Middle Ages business environment. Those bound volumes tested the passage of time and survived, and their contribution in rebuilding a context could be very valuable. The examination of primary sources of documents in understanding the past, however, must be carefully conducted (Napier, 1989, p. 240) because at the same time they allow descriptions through empirical evidence but they can lead to incorrect generalizations. Any generalization cannot be absolute as the surviving accounts may give a partial picture, many other primary sources being definitely lost. Also interpretations need to offer a degree of coherence in telling the stories behind them.

The books of Venetian merchants Barbarigo and Badoer were analyzed in depth by the historical discipline and the accounting history literature (Lane, 1944; Peragallo, 1977) and they represent valuable open windows in the fifteen-century mercantile environment. In this chapter we look again at that past, trying to see it through the ancient lens of another Venetian merchant, Giovanni Foscari, whose accounting books could be investigated to disclose aspects highlighted through institutional analysis.

Giovanni Foscari

The Foscari family settled in the Venetian lagoon in the eleventh century and soon became a prominent family within the aristocracy. The Foscari members affirmed and distinguished themselves in the economic and political scene, in both commerce and diplomacy activities, through mercantile activities (*mercatura*). The most illustrious and famous member of the Foscari family was Francesco Foscari (1373–1457). He never practised commercial activity through which his father consolidated the family fortune; instead he served the Republic of Venice, taking part in numerous *magistrature*, the main branches of the Venetian state administration, and was distinguished in the military field. In 1423 Francesco became doge of Venice and his was the longest ever *dogado*, lasting thirty-four years. During Foscari's leadership Venice engaged in an expansionist policy for the progressive control of the hinterland regions (Veneto and Friuli) (Lane, 1973, pp. 265–272). Doge Foscari in 1452 built the Ca' Foscari Palace, which is presently (since its foundation in 1868) the headquarters of the University of Venice, which is named after it.

The mercantile tradition of the Foscari family continued with Marco, brother of Francesco, and then Marco's son Giovanni, whose ledgers are here analyzed. Although Marco also embraced a political career, Giovanni concentrated on economic activity based on the sea but also on land businesses. His choice proved to be far-sighted because in a few years the uncertain political situation would not favour trade, while the more localized investments provided the family with greater economic stability.

The merchant Foscari demonstrated a strong involvement in trading with the North European countries. The commercial route towards Flanders allowed the direct importation of tin and wool from England, without intermediation, as well as Flemish wool, linen and hemp. On the other hand those markets absorbed Oriental products, such as alum, silk and spices. But in the last decades of the fifteenth century that route presented many risks generated by the political situation and the Venetian state attempted to promote that route through economic incentives that reduced the costs of running the maritime venture. In his voyages to Flanders in 1463 and 1467 Giovanni Foscari obtained the galleys at a low cost using these incentives.

Giovanni Foscari revealed a deep knowledge of Nordic markets because during his travels he never relied on locals. Instead he himself carried out his business, and also other merchants' businesses for which he was an agent. Furthermore he showed a profound familiarity with the foreign financial system because he made use of local banks despite the strong presence of Italian bankers.

This information stems from the ledgers about the two voyages to Flanders kept by Giovanni Foscari, which are preserved in the State Archives of Venice in the *Fondo Gradenigo* (Montemezzo, 2013).

The accounting information is precious in contributing to recreating the micro and macro environment in which Giovanni Foscari ran his mercantile activity and, at the same time, revealing the institutions affecting and influencing the recording activity, and giving a particular content and form compared to other Italian regions.

First of all the ledger, as a sort of logbook, gave the picture of the geographical and organizational dimension of Venetian state *mude* and the Foscari mercantile itinerary structure and management. Then the trade activity and the merchandise loaded in the *Foscara* (the ship directed by Foscari), exchanged products and commissions received as an agent and a mediator are all revealed. Giovanni Foscari conducted transactions on his own account but also many operations on behalf of other Venetian firms. A ledger was necessary to keep track of all transactions and relationships with other parties. Through accounting entries the personal and commercial linkages of Foscari with foreign merchants or Venetian merchants who resided in foreign countries can be reconstructed in order to understand and evaluate commercial choices (Montemezzo, 2013, p. 68). The partnership underlying the business is the *Fraterna* Foscari, which was run with familiar components and based on trust elements.

The existence of two books referring to the same sort of activity, about two different periods in time, allows a comparative analysis that highlights some aspects that make some economic phenomena emerge, as for example a better situation coming from an increased amount of sales, or some historical facts connected with particular accounting records, like a stable amount of spices against improved revenues due to conflicts with Turkey.

Giovanni Foscari's voyages, venture organization, mercantile customs, improved commercial capacities and financial instruments are all detected from his ledgers.

In 1475 Giovanni Foscari became a resident merchant, having agents and partners working with him who took care of his interests. His attention was on the mainland properties, where he invested money coming from the mercantile activity; in doing this he anticipated a later necessary choice by merchants aimed at diversifying risk as Venice was losing its maritime dominance.

Foscari's bookkeeping throughout his sea and land activity had the functions of tracking rights and obligations, conveying information at a distance, holding agents accountable and, in general, dealing with complexity. It was mainly a venture accounting not closed until the end of the voyage. Double-entry bookkeeping followed the Venetian method, consisting in records using a double entry on adjacent pages of the ledger, providing control of a specific expense, person and so on. Giovanni Foscari represented a man of its time, acting in an institutional context favouring his activities and determining his commercial behaviour. And thanks to his ledgers an economic system and a merchant of a past time can be brought back to life in order to understand them.

Conclusions

In trying to understand the past, consideration of the surrounding context is essential (Miller and Napier, 1993, p. 631). Arguably much more importantly, this statement applies generally to the development of the accounting function in all its aspects, indeed in all times and in all places. We take the proposition that the accounting function is from every perspective a pragmatic context-related social construct, and apply it to the very specific vibrant economic and social environment which characterized the Venetian scenario in the Middle Ages.

Merchants were the main actors in the medieval economic scene and early adopters of accounting tools in Venice and in other Italian important commercial cities—in particular maritime merchants who experienced complicated business operations and foreign business environments, travelling and operating with Northern and Eastern countries. From an institutional perspective macro analysis highlighted a context clearly demanding and favouring an accounting evolution, and the mezzo and micro analysis emphasized a corresponding answer given by professional education and open thinking, leading to the rise of double-entry bookkeeping (DEB). The importance of education based on the professionalization of DEB through manuals has been appreciated over time, considered as the most important source of development in accounting practice for merchants (Sangster et al., 2008), but also criticized because it was evaluated as unhelpful from a practical point of view (Yamey, 2010).

But what could be said that distinctively emerges is the extraction of a unique capacity of the prevailing player in this commercial context, the Venetian merchants, in showing an unexpectedly wide economic culture. Focusing on the inherent nature of accounts, instead of their content, and so on the ability to keep control of activities, presupposes familiarity with a technical practice and this leads to questioning the cultural phenomena producing these dynamics (Goldthwaite, 2015, p. 613).

The micro level of analysis leads us to consider DEB's origin and diffusion as an effect of the Renaissance spirit. The cultural dimension of merchants, stemming from their institutional thinking, derives from a higher "meta-macro" atmosphere, partly independently from the existence of accounting manuals, which are the product of a practice to be tentatively described in written texts trying to systematize and summarize.

The Foscari mercantile life, as an example of merchants of his time, shows, according to a first investigation of his commercial experience, how an economic knowledge and understanding and a correlated accounting attitude was developed. This embraced knowledge of foreign markets in their economic and financial aspects and investment abilities, diversifying risks, anticipating trends and using accounting tools to properly track and manage activities as an agent or as a travelling and resident merchant. In this period merchants were very careful observers (Montemezzo, 2013, p. 23), evidenced by open institutional thinking, including that related to accounting mentality and familiarity.

The Foscari ledgers represent a narrative discourse about the fifteenth-century Venetian context. The ledgers relating to the galley voyages of Giovanni Foscari are very beneficial in giving a "ships log", both in the literal sense and more metaphorically of the time, institutions and cultural phenomena emphasized by Goldthwaite (2015) that impact on the detail of the technical thinking and practices.

References

Aho, A. J., "Rhetoric and the invention of double entry bookkeeping", *Rhetorics: A Journal of the Histories of Rhetoric*, vol. 3, n. 1, Winter 1985, pp. 21–43.

Alexander, D. and Archer, S., "On economic reality, representational faithfulness and the 'true and fair view override'", *Accounting and Business Research*, vol. 33, n. 1, 2003, pp. 3–17.

Arnold, P. J., Institutional perspectives on the internationalization of accounting, in Chapman, C. C., Cooper, D. J. and Miller, P. B. (edited by), *Accounting, Organizations, and Institutions: Essays in Honour of Anthony Hopwood*, Oxford University Press, Oxford, UK, 2009.

Besta, F., *La Ragioneria*, 2nd edition, vol. 3, Vallardi, Milan, 1929.

Carnegie, G. D., "The present and future of accounting history", *Accounting, Auditing & Accountability Journal*, vol. 27, n. 8, 2014, pp. 1241–1249.

Ciambotti, M., Cenni storici della Ragioneria e della professione contabile, con particolare riferimento alla realtà marchigiana,in Iacomucci B. (edited by), I conti tornano. Storia del Collegio dei Ragionieri di Pesaro e Urbino, Tipolitografia Grafica vadese, Pesaro, 2007.

Dal Grande, N., "*Del 'Golfo di Venezia' e della sua storia*" 21.12.2014, www.tuttostoria.net/medio-evo.aspx?code=833

De Roover, R., "The development of accounting prior to Luca Pacioli according to the accounts-books of medieval merchants", in Littleton A. C. and Yamey B. S. (edited by), *Studies in the History of Accounting*, Richard D. Irwin Inc., Homewood, IL, 1956.

Douglas, M., *How Institutions Think*, Syracuse University Press, Syracuse, 1986.

Dyer, C., Il commercio nell'Europa medievale, in Castronovo V. (edited by), *Storia dell'economia mondiale: Permanenze e mutamenti dall'antichità al medioevo*, Laterza, Bari, 1996.

Edwards, J. R., *A History of Financial Accounting*, Routledge, London, 1989.

Goldthwaite, R., "The practice and culture of accounting in Renaissance Florence", Enterprise & Society, vol. 16, n. 3, 2015, pp. 611–647.

Hopwood, A. G., "On trying to study accounting in the context in which it operates", *Accounting, Organizations and Society*, vol. 8, n. 2/3, 1983, pp. 287–305.

Hopwood, A. G., "Understanding financial accounting practice", *Accounting, Organizations and Society*, vol. 25, n. 8, November 2000.

Hoskin, K. W. and Macve, R., "Accounting and the examination: A genealogy of disciplinary power", *Accounting, Organizations and Society*, vol. 1, n. 2, 1986, pp. 105–136.

Lane, F. C., *Andrea Barbarigo, Merchant of Venice: Venice and History*, Johns Hopkins University Press, Baltimore, 1944.

Lane, F. C., "Double entry bookkeping and resident merchants", *Journal of European Economic History*, vol. 6, n. 1, Spring 1977, pp. 177–191.

Lane, F. C., *Venice, a Maritime Republic*, Johns Hopkins University Press, Baltimore, 1973 (tradotto in italiano con il titolo Storia di Venezia, Einaudi, Torino, 1978).

Leuz, C., "Different approaches to corporate reporting regulation: How jurisdictions differ and why", *Accounting and Business Research*, vol. 4, n. 3, 2010.

Lopez, R. S., *The Commercial Revolution in the Middle Ages*, Cambridge University Press, New York, 1976.

Luzzatto, G., "Per la storia delle costruzioni navali a Venezia nei secoli XV e XVI", in *Studi di storia economica veneziana*, Cedam, Padova, 1954, pp. 37–51.

Melis, F., *Storia della Ragioneria*, Zuffi, Bologna, 1950.

Miller, P. and Napier C., "Genealogies of calculation", *Accounting, Organizations and Society*, vol. 18, n. 7/8, 1993, pp. 631–647.

Montemezzo, S., *Giovanni Foscari. Viaggi di Fiandra, 1463–1464 e 1467–1468*, La Malcontenta, Venezia, 2013.

Montemezzo, S., "*Scambi commerciali e reti mercantile fra Asia ed Europa. Le aziende veneziane nella seconda metà del Quattrocento*" Paper, Dottorato di Ricerca in Storia Economica—XXVI ciclo, Università di Verona, 2012.

Mueller, R. C., *The Venetian Money Market: Banks Panic and the Public Debt 1200–1500*, Johns Hopkins University Press, Baltimore, 1997.

Napier, C. J., "Research directions in accounting history", *The British Accounting Review*, vol. 21, n. 3, 1989, pp. 237–254.

Oldroyd, D. and Dobie, A., "*Bookkeeping*", in *Routledge Companion to Accounting History*, Routledge, London, 2009.

Peragallo, E., "The ledger of Jachomo Badoer: Constantinople September 2, 1436 to February 26, 1440", *The Accounting Review*, vol. 52, n. 4, October 1977, pp. 881–892.

Sangster, A., "The genesis of double entry bookkeeping, the accounting review", *American Accounting Association*, vol. 91, n. 1, 2016, pp. 299–315.

Sangster, A., Stoner, G. N. and McCarthy, P., "The market for Luca Pacioli's Summa Arithmetica", *Accounting Historians Journal*, vol. 35, n. 1, June 2008, pp. 111–134.

Sombart, W., Luxus und Kapitalismus, Duncker & Humblot, Munchen, 1922.

Tucci, U., "Le tecniche di contabilità", in Castronovo V. (edited by), *Storia dell'economia mondiale. Dall'antichità al medioevo*, vol. 1, Laterza, Bari, 1996.

Yamey, B. S., "The market for Luca Pacioli's Summa de Arithmetica: Some comments", *Accountinh Historians Journal*, vol. 37, n. 2, 2010, pp. 145–154.

Yamey, B. S., "Notes on double-entry bookkeeping and economic progress", *The Journal of European Economic History*, vol. 4, n. 3, Winter 1975.

Yamey, B. S., "Pacioli's De Scripturis in the context of the spread of double entry bookkeeping", *De Computis*, December 2004.

Young, J. J., "Institutional thinking: Financial instruments", *Accounting, Organizations and Society*, vol. 21, n. 5, 1996, pp. 487–512.

Wysocki, P., "New institutional accounting and IFRS", *Accounting and Business Research*, vol. 41, no. 3, August 2011, pp. 309–328.

Zerbi, T., *Le origini della partita doppia: Gestioni aziendali e situazioni di mercato nei secoli XIV e XV*, Carlo Marzorati, Milano, 1952.

12 The Fraudulent Investor

An Accounting Investigation of a Venetian Manufactory, 1778–1784

Marisa Agostini, Riccardo Cella and Giovanni Favero

Introduction

Studying fraud in pre-codification historical contexts raises some problems of definition, as most definitions of fraud focus on the violation of regulations (Jones, 2011). The case of the Venetian Republic, studied here, is no exception, as there was no explicit regulatory framework in place concerning accounting practices. However, a state authority, the *Inquisitori alle Arti*, was in charge of controlling guilds and manufacturers and of resolving their conflicts. In doing so, it resorted to accounting statements, where necessary requiring them to be produced in order to collect material for its investigations, even if, in some cases, the *Inquisitori* eventually concluded that such statements did not present a fair picture and falsified reality with potentially deleterious consequences.

Given the foregoing, we may apply here Garner's (2009, 731) suggestion to generally identify as fraudulent any "knowing misrepresentation of the truth or concealment of a material fact to induce another to act to his or her detriment". This identifies as crucial the detriment of other parties—ignoring the extreme variation and dis-homogeneity of the accounting criteria in use, in so far as these were "harmless", at least as far as the intentions of those applying them were concerned. Such a working definition of fraud allows a classification of fraudulent behaviour even where and when no apposite regulation existed. However, it does not solve the historical question of discerning how the motivations, the meaning and the mechanisms of such behaviour might change in relationship with the institutional context, and why.

The Context: A Turbulent Industry, an Indebted Business

In order to gain a better understanding of accounting fraud dynamics in the Republic of Venice, we focus on a case which appears odd according to present-day criteria, as the roles of the investor partner, of the managing partner, of the accountant and of the state authority do not fit into the script that we logically expect. The case concerns Geminiano Cozzi's privileged Venetian factory producing porcelain, majolica and earthenware during the late 1770s and the early 1780s. The ceramic industry in Europe underwent many changes during the eighteenth century, and in the Venetian Republic it struggled with repeated changes in fashions and materials in use, which brought in their wake waves of competitive imports. As a consequence, the republic granted privileges and exemptions to manufacturers able to imitate foreign imported novelties (Favero, 2011).

The porcelain industry is particularly interesting for us, as it displays some technical peculiarities creating a need for advanced money and requiring complex financial and accounting solutions. Porcelain was a new industry in Europe in the eighteenth century: the production of "china", as it was named indeed, commenced only in 1708, when a first factory was established in Meissen (Saxony), following the identification of the raw material up to then employed to produce exclusively Chinese porcelain, kaolin. In 1718 another factory was set up in Vienna, and in 1720 in Venice the young nobleman Giovanni Vezzi invested up to 50,000 ducats to start a similar production. The latter was, however, not backed by state protection or subsidies, and in 1727 was forced to give up following a huge indebtment deriving from the low profitability and the high costs of this production, which still had a very high ratio of broken or faulted pieces, despite the recent discovery of a local kaolin quarry at Mount Tretto on the mainland, which made it possible to avoid expensive imports from Saxony (Stazzi, 1967).

China production in the Venetian state started again only with the arrival in 1758 of Saxon artisans fleeing the Seven Years' War. A couple of them, the Hewelcke spouses, established a porcelain factory in Udine, moving it to Venice in 1761, where they found a backer in Geminiano Cozzi. In 1763 they decamped back to Saxony without reimbursing their main creditor, who was left with the equipment and raw materials, and restarted production, obtaining in 1765 tax exemptions and a small subsidy from the republic (Stazzi, 1981, 22–24).

Cozzi remained the sole porcelain producer in the state only until 1768, when Antonibon, the owner of a large majolica factory in Nove, a village on the mainland, was also granted tax and customs exemptions for china manufacture. As competition between the two producers increased, in 1769 Cozzi also started producing majolica, using a single kiln for the lower-temperature decoration of both kinds of wares. Such production economies offset an increase in the cost of local kaolin due to the intensified exploitation of the Tretto quarry (Stazzi, 1981, 53–54). The situation was, however, complicated by the increased competitiveness of imported china. The early 1770s saw a new wave of novel imported majolica wares, and most of all the importation of white earthenware "made in the English way", following Josiah Wedgewood's introduction of the new material to England during the early half of the century (Young, 1995).

During the 1770s, then, the financial situation of Cozzi's factory failed to improve. Difficulties became evident in 1777, as a result of his evident inability to abide by deadlines for payments to his creditors. Over the preceding years,

Cozzi had borrowed 11,000 ducats from Marquis Aleduse Buzzaccarini from Padua, 7,500 from Count Spiridion Peruli and 10,300 from Bonaventura Marinoni (Stazzi, 1981, 63). It was the latter who forced Cozzi to close down the company and establish a new partnership between himself, Cozzi and his brother Vincenzo. Marinoni paid in another 3,700 ducats, and became the owner of 10 of the 24 shares, the Cozzi siblings owning the remaining 14, 2 of which were pledged against Buzzaccarini's loan; Count Peruli provided the company with a further 7,000 ducats as an external backer. Marinoni and the Cozzi brothers were jointly responsible for company agreements (Stazzi, 1981, 64). The Cozzi brothers kept the technical direction of the factory, but forfeited any salary and left to Marinoni the management of any income. Marinoni entrusted an accountant, Giustino Pasquali, to give priority to the yearly liquidation of debts out of cash income. This was the premise to the fraud we are going to study in greater depth.

Although the refinancing of the new company entailed Cozzi losing control over its financial management, it allowed him to invest in the production of English-style earthenware. In 1780 he was able to make a request for the exclusive rights for earthenware, applying at the same time for a public loan, and soliciting the banning of china imports. In 1781 the *Cinque Savi alla Mercanzia*, the Venetian authority overseeing trade, extended his customs exemptions, granted him a monopoly in the production of earthenware in Venice, but denied the requested public loan, assigning instead a four-ducat premium for every 100 *libbre sottili* of exported ceramics. They also banned for a decade the establishment of new china factories in the republic, imposed new duties on European china and barred the importation and sale of Oriental china (Stazzi, 1981, 73–76).

However, new difficulties came from a fall in china sales in the early 1780s, due in part to increased competition from other Venetian manufacturers and in part to the continuing illegal import of porcelain. In 1784 Cozzi's factory had a stockpile of 118,000 unsold pieces of china, most of which were out of fashion. Marinoni feared for his capital and in September 1784, he requested the liquidation of the company, prompting an investigation by the *Inquisitori sopra le Arti*, who checked Pasquali's accounts and, following their examination, discovered the "fraud", finally deciding for liquidation (Stazzi, 1981, 89–90).

As a result, the Cozzi brothers were once again enabled to run the factory on their own, but at the price of having to pay off their huge debts in extended instalments. Even the new company would prove short-lived, however. In June 1791, Geminiano Cozzi gave up his rights over the factory in favour of his brother Vincenzo, and in 1792, Vincenzo was granted the privileges of the previous companies. In 1793 Geminiano asked for the cancellation of the handover, but withdrew this claim in 1794. The military and political events which brought about the fall of the republic hastened its closure, which occurred a decade later, after the death of Vincenzo Cozzi in 1804 (Stazzi, 1981, 121–123).

In the following paragraphs, we focus our attention on the early 1780s, on the accounting budgets produced by Pasquali and on the report prepared by the *Inquisitori alle Arti* following the request for liquidation of the partnership between Marinoni and the Cozzi brothers. The aim is to reconstruct the fraud mechanism and, most of all, its rationale. We will then analyze the accounting documents in detail, and apply a game-theory interpretive framework in order to understand the institutional mechanisms that provide an answer to our questions.

Determinants of the Accounting Fraud

Accounting fraud has been defined by the technical literature as "accounting practices which are outside those permitted by the regulatory framework" (Jones, 2011, 9). As emphasized in the introduction, at the time of Geminiano Cozzi's manufacture (in the second half of the eighteenth century) there was no such regulatory accounting framework.[1] So, fraud in the analysis of the present historical case can be defined, in a more general way, as "a deception or misrepresentation that an individual or entity makes knowing that misrepresentation could result in some unauthorized benefit to the individual or to the entity or some other party" (ACFE, 2010, 10–14). Garner emphasizes that fraud is a "chameleon-hued word" (Garner, 2001, 374) and defines "fraud in fact" as "concealment or false representation by means of a statement or conduct that causes injury to another" (Garner, 2009, 731).

This is exactly the type of fraud that will be examined in the present chapter. It is also comes well within the definition of accounting fraud since in the case of Geminiano Cozzi's factory the misrepresentations have to do with financial statements, prepared for the years 1781, 1782 and 1783. There were, to be sure, specific historical determinants, such as the disappointing economic results and the disagreement between Geminiano Cozzi and Bonaventura Marinoni. The first is strictly related to the economic crisis of the pottery sector at that time, as explained in the introduction. This sector was characterized by a long working capital cycle. The company paid the suppliers of the main raw material (called "white clay") immediately (on delivery) in cash, but it took a long time to collect its receivables (many receivables, as explained ahead, were also irrecoverable). Moreover, the final goods required a long process of ageing: there was no way of rapidly converting inventory into cash and this aggravated a cash dependency on customer payments and loans. The second determinant (i.e., the disagreement between Geminiano Cozzi and Bonaventura Marinoni) concerns the internal governance structure of the company. Geminiano Cozzi desired to be the sole owner of the firm and he resented the presence of Bonaventura Marinoni, who did not fulfil an active role inside the company (Stazzi, 1981, 89). The disagreement between Geminiano Cozzi and Bonaventura Marinoni worsened the economic crisis of the pottery firm and it was noticed by the government official Alvise Zusto, delegated by the *Inquisitorato alle Arti* (Stazzi, 1981, 89).

These historical events are not the only determinants of the case. There were other relevant (but less evident) peculiarities in the internal governance structure of the company. Firstly, Bonaventura Marinoni was both banker to and partner of the company. He (or rather his father) lent Geminiano Cozzi's company the same amount in ducats as Count Spiridion Peruli, but only Bonaventura Marinoni became a business partner: Count Spiridion Peruli continued to be only a lender. Secondly, Giustino Pasquali, who was the bookkeeper of the company, was paid in proportion of the returns due to Bonaventura Marinoni. So, the same person was employed to verify the accounts of the company and acquired the right to receive a portion of the returns recorded in the accounting books of the company (Stazzi, 1981, 64). The last, but most important, peculiarity is related to the aforementioned absence of accounting law in that historical moment: the company started to draw up financial statements only in 1777 in order to monitor the evolution of its economic results in the interest of the lender Bonaventura Marinoni. There was a voluntary commitment to analyze its economic performance. This influenced also the (mild) consequences (described ahead) of the discovery of the accounting fraud by the *Inquisitorato alle Arti*.

Ways of Implementing the Accounting Fraud

The present section analyzes three financial statements of Geminiano Cozzi's company for the years 1781, 1782 and 1783 (Figure 12.1).

These financial statements were formally prepared by the government official (the *Inquisitorato alle Arti*) on the basis of the accounting information provided by Giustino Pasquali, who was the bookkeeper of the company, as emphasized in the previous paragraphs. They reported profits for all the years 1781, 1782 and 1783, although the firm had significant liquidity problems that were exacerbated by the disagreement between Geminiano Cozzi and Bonaventura Marinoni. This second partner (i.e., Bonaventura Marinoni, who was both banker to and partner of the company) asked the government official (called *Inquisitorato alle Arti*) to audit the accounts of the company in order to protect his credit. This inspection entailed the auditing of the financial statements for the three years 1781, 1782 and 1783. The results were a list of doubts (called "*Quesiti*"; Stazzi, 1981) about the accuracy of the accounts and some considerations (called "*Riflessioni*"; Stazzi, 1981) especially about the financial statements of the last year (i.e., 1783). These doubts and considerations are here rehearsed and investigated. In particular, they regard fixed assets, inventory, receivables, debts and revenues.

The fixed assets of the company were recorded at their full cost. Their booked amounts (Table 12.1) did not consider at all their market values and the time period over which the firm expected that such assets would have been useful. This should have been done especially for the buildings of the company given the depreciation of their realizable value. In the financial statement of the year 1783 a write-down should have been recorded in order

Financial statement of Geminiano Cozzi's company for the year 1781				
A Porcellane in esser rissultanti dal Invent.o		L.	60019	7
A Majoliche in esser simili		L.	15376	15
A Terraglie in esser simili		L.	4894	10
A Negozio S. Salvador sim.e		L.	4316	1
A Generi da consumo, rimanenze trovate la sera 31/ Xbre 1781		L.	46646	14
A detti Mineral da Verona ad'uso Terrag.e		L.	1300	
A Crediti da riscuottere, con quelli S. Salvad.r con diffalco Xci per %		L.	43494	12
A Detti per Generi fuori di mano, alcuni col sud.to diff.co		L.	17845	15
A Utensili di Fabrica		L.	9550	17
A Spese Erezion di Fabb.e		L.	26584	
A Burchio e suoi Atrecj		L.	4960	
A Forno per calcinar Piombo		L.	2000	
A Edificcj in Treviso		L.	11000	
A Acquisto Casotto in Brescia		L.	4863	18
A Burchio conto Utili dell'anno 1781		L.	482	12
A Fra.lli Cozzi conto sovenzioni da restituir		L.	13593	5
A Cassa soldo essistente		L.	1901	12
A Merci in Monte		L.	1319	10
		L.	270149	8
HAVER				
Per Co. Spirid.n Perulli Co. Di Cap.l a Depos.o a 4 per %		L.	68200	
Per Franc.o Marinoni qm Bort.o Co. Dett.		L.	86800	
Per Gim.o Cozzi rapp.e li NN. HH. M.si Buzzac.ni Co. Det.		L.	40300	
Per Fra.lli Cozzi per subingresso né Cap.li affranc. Con prò 4 p. %		L.	12400	
Per Co. Spirid.n Perulli Co. Prò		L.	2273	
Per Franc.o Marinoni Co. Det.o		L.	10416	
Per Gim.o Cozzi rapp.e li N.N. H.H. M.si Buzzac.ni Co. Det.		L.	1612	
Per Fra.lli Cozzi Co. Det.o		L.	561	17
Per Bonavven.a Marinoni Co. Utili		L.	4953	10
Per Giusto Pasquali Co. Detto		L.	638	17
Per Fra.lli Cozzi Co. D'Utili		L.	9550	13
Per li seguenti D. 4000 Eff.vi incassati la Dita Gemin.o Cozzi e Compagni dall'off. Del nuovo Stalaggio à tenor del Dec.to 3 Maggio 1781 per restar fondo stabile sino allo scioglim.to della Comp.a 18 Maggio 1778 val	L. 32.000	L.	32000	
Per Gemin.o e Vic.o Fra.lli Cozzi per li Caratti 14 - d'essi rappresentanti	L. 18666.13			
Per Bonav.a Marinoni per Car.ti 18	L. 10666.14			
Per Giusto Pasquali per Car. 2	L. 2666.13			
		L.	269706	3
Utili spetanti a Gem.o e Vic.o Fra.lli Cozzi in ragguag.				
Di Caratti 14	L. 258.10-8			
Sim.e à Bonav. A Marinoni 8	L. 147.14-8			
Sim.e à Giusto Pasquali 2	L. 36.18-8			
		L.	443	4
		L.	270149	7

Figure 12.1 Financial statements (expressed in lira) of Geminiano Cozzi's company for the years 1781, 1782 and 1783 (*Archivio di Stato* in Venice, *Inquisitor alle Arti*, b. 98)

Financial statement of Geminiano Cozzi's company for the year 1782

A Porcellane in esser			L.	65023	17
A Majoliche			L.	28900	9
A Terrag.e			L.	6390	
A Sud.o Mineral di Verona			L.	1300	
A Dep.o S. Salvad.r			L.	4165	16
A Generi da consumo			L.	34765	1
A Crediti da riscuottere con diffalco Xci per %			L.	44495	11
A Detti per Generi fuori di mano, alcuni col sud. to diff.co			L.	14495	11
A Utensili di Fab.a			L.	9550	17
A Spesa Erezion di Fab.a			L.	26584	
A Burchio e suoi Atrecj			L.	4960	
A Forno per calcinar Piombo			L.	2000	
A Edificcj in Treviso			L.	11000	
A Acquisto Casotto in Brescia			L.	4863	18
A Burchio conto Utili			L.	259	
A Fra.lli Cozzi Conto Corr.e			L.	7485	13
A Cassa soldo Nulla			L.		
HAVER					
Per Co. Spirid.n Perulli Co. Di Cap.l a Depos.o a 4 per %			L.	62000	
Per Franc.o Marinoni qm Bort.o Co. Dett.			L.	86800	
Per NN. HH. M.si Buzzac.ni Co. Det.			L.	37200	
Per Fra.lli Cozzi per subingresso né Cap.li affranc. Con prò 4 p. %			L.	12400	
Per Co. Spirid.n Perulli Co. Prò			L.	2066	13
Per Franc.o Marinoni Co. Det.o			L.	13888	
Per N.N. H.H. M.si Buzzac.ni Co. Det.			L.	1488	
Per Bonav.a Marinoni Co. Utili			L.	5101	4
Per Giust. Pasquali Co. Detto			L.	675	15
Per Fra.lli Cozzi Co. D.to			L.	9809	4
Per Detti Co. Prò			L.	1057	17
Per li seguenti D. 4000 Eff.vi incassati la Dita Gemin.o Cozzi e Compagni dall'off. Del nuovo Stalaggio à tenor del Dec.to 3 Maggio 1781 per restar fondo stabile sino allo scioglim.to della Comp.a 18 Maggio 1778 val	L.	32.000			
Per Gemin.o e Vic.o Fra.lli Cozzi per li Caratti 14 - d'essi rappresentanti	L.	18666.13			
Per Bonav.a Marinoni per Car.ti 18	L.	10666.14			
Per Giusto Pasquali per Car. 2	L.	2666.13	L.32000		
			L.	264486	14
Utili spetanti a Gem.o e Vic.o Fra.lli Cozzi in ragguag.					
Di Caratti 14	L.	1022.16.08			
Sim.e à Bonav. A Marinoni 8	L.	584.06.08			
Sim.e à Giusto Pasquali 2	L.	146.01.08			
			L.	1752	19
			L.	266239	13

Figure 12.1 (Continued)

Financial statement of Geminiano Cozzi's company for the year 1783

A Porcellane in esser compreso il Neg.o S. Salvad.o prezzi Costo		L.	86335	9
A Majoliche in esser per Simile		L.	20334	17
A Terraglie per simile		L.	10553	16
A Generi da consumo rillevanti dalla nota a Costo		L.	39077	19
A Crediti rissultanti dal Qud. e Libro debitori minuti raguagliati con il diffalco del 10 per cento		L	49101	3
A Utensili di Fabrica		L.	9550	17
A Spese Erezione di Fabbrica		L.	26584	
A Burchio e suoi Atrezzi valutato in presente		L.	2790	
A Forno per calcinar Piombo		L.	2000	
A Edificcj in Treviso		L.	11000	
Acquisto Casotto in Brescia		L.	4863	18
A Fra.lli Cozzi Conto Corrente per Sovvenzioni		L.	13437	13
A Cassa per rimanenza della sera 31 Dicem.e 1783		L.	425	13
A Fra.lli Cozzi Conto Affrancazione di Capitali a norma del Cap.o della Scr.a di Compagnia 18 Maggio 1778		27900		
		L.	303955	5
HAVER				
Per Co. Spiridion Perulli Conto Di Capital a deposito al quattro p. %		L.	62000	
Per Franc.o Marinoni qm Bortolo conto Sud.o al quattro p. %		L.	86800	
Per Nobb.SS.ri Marchesi Buzzacarini conto Suddetto a 4 p. %		L.	34100	
Per Giminiano e Vincenzo Fra.lli Cozzi per Subingresso né Cap.li affranc. Con il prò 4 p. %		L.	12400	
Per Co. Spiridion Perulli conto Prò		L.	4546	13
Per Francesco Marinoni qm Bortolo conto Prò		L.	17360	
Per Giminiano e Vincenzo Fralli Cozzi conto Prò		L.	1553	17
Per Bonavventura Marinoni conto Utili p. K.ti 8		L.	5685	11
Per Giminiano e Vincenzo fra.lli Cozzi Sim.e per K.ti 14		L.	10831	15
Per Giustino Pasquali Conto simile per K.ti 2		L.	825	17
Per li seguenti D. 4000 Eff.vi incassati dall'off. Del nuovo Stallaggio per esser imputati per conto di Capitale cioè				
Per Geminiano, e Vincenzo Fra.lli Cozzi p. K.ti 14	L. 18666.13			
Per Bonavventura Marinoni per K.ti 8	L. 10666.14			
Per Giustinoo Pasquali p. K.ti 2	L. 2666. 13	L.	32000	
Per li seguenti D. 4500 con.ti Capitali affrancati dalla Cassa della Compagnia		L.	27900	
Per Geminiano, e Vincenzo Fra.lli Cozzi per K.ti 14	L. 16275			
Per Bonavventura Marinoni per K.ti 8	L. 9300			
Per Giustinoo Pasquali per K.ti 2	L. 2325			
Per detti conto Prò sopra li D. 4500 da p.o 1780 a tutto 31 Dicemb.e 1783		L.	295999	13
Con.o D. 450		L.	2790	
		L.	298789	13
Utili spettanti a Fra.lli Cozzi per K.ti 14	L. 3013.05.04			
a Bonav.a Marinoni per K.ti 8	L. 1721.17.04			
a Giustino Pasquali per K.ti 2	L. 430.09.04			
		L.	5165	12
		L.	303955	5

Figure 12.1 (Continued)

Table 12.1 Fixed assets in the financial statements (expressed in lira) of Geminiano Cozzi's company for the years 1781, 1782 and 1783 (*Archivio di Stato* in Venice, *Inquisitor alle Arti*, b. 98)

	1781		*1782*		*1783*	
A Utensili di Fabrica	L.	9550	L.	9550	L.	9550
A Spese Erezion di Fabb.e	L.	26584	L.	26584	L.	26584
A Burchio e suoi Atrecj	L.	4960	L.	4960	L.	2790
A Forno per calcinar Piombo	L.	2000	L.	2000	L.	2000
A Edificcj in Treviso	L.	11000	L.	11000	L.	11000
A Acquisto Casotto in Brescia	L.	4863	L.	4863	L.	4863
Total reported amount	L.	58957	L.	58957	L.	56787

Table 12.2 Inventory in the financial statements (expressed in lira) of Geminiano Cozzi's company for the years 1781, 1782 and 1783 (*Archivio di Stato* in Venice, *Inquisitor alle Arti*, b. 98).

		1781		*1782*		*1783*	
Finished goods	*A Porcellane in esser rissultanti dal Invent.o*	L.	60019	L.	65023	L.	86335
	A Majoliche in esser simili	L.	15376	L.	28900	L.	20334
	A Terraglie in esser simili	L.	4894	L.	6390	L.	10553
	A Negozio S. Salvador sim.e	L.	4316	L.	4165	L.	-
Raw materials	*A Generi da consumo, rimanenze trovate la sera 31/Xbre 1781*	L.	46646	L.	34765	L.	39077
	A detti Mineral da Verona ad'uso Terrag.e	L.	1300	L.	1300	L.	-
Total reported amount		L.	132551	L.	140543	L.	156299

to reduce the book values of such assets that were overvalued compared to their market worth. So, the carried-forward values of the assets could no longer be justified and the likelihood of receiving (in case of sale) the full cost was seriously questionable.

The same considerations apply to inventory (Table 12.2). It was recorded on the debit side of the company's statements. So, the reader of the statements would assume that the inventory was made up of goods that could have been sold to produce revenue, and materials that would be turned into final goods. The items of the analyzed company stocked into inventory were mainly raw materials (e.g., the white clay scheduled to be used in making the final products) and finished goods (ready for sale to customers). Inventory represented in the statements a future economic value and it was reported "at cost". The reader of the statements was induced to think that such reported value would have been lower than the retail price at which the company would ultimately have sold those items. The real situation was different from that described in the accounts prepared by Giustino Pasquali. There were two main problems here: inventory needed to be monitored more closely, and an important part of the inventory purchased for future use became obsolete. Too much stored and unsold inventory resulted in cash flow problems (and probably in unrecorded additional expenses). Thus the company was not able to maintain an optimal inventory level, nor did it pursue the goal of inventory minimization. This meant it was not able to integrate accurate demand forecasting with inventory management: there was perhaps an established procedural way of working based on looking at past averages. This was one of the main causes of the long working capital cycle of the company. The company kept high inventory levels and it suffered from problems such as obsolescence. Perishable raw materials (e.g., clay) had by their nature a short shelf life. This could be further reduced by inadequate storage and handling. Moreover, many finished goods (at the end of their product life cycle) were not sold out for long periods of time. Inventory write-downs ought to have been applied. The company did not recognize in its accounts that the value of inventory had declined: the inventory was not correctly estimated to be worth less than the value shown in the accounting records. The inventory asset was too high, so it was misleading to readers of the company's statements. Large amounts of obsolete inventory to write off would have been a warning sign to the *Inquisitorato alle Arti*: they would have been symptomatic of poor products, poor management forecasts of demand, and poor inventory management. The company was purchasing excessive inventory because it had lost track of certain items or it was using existing inventory inefficiently. The company did not want to admit such problems and did not reduce the huge size of the obsolete or unusable inventory. The company should have written down the value of its inventory to more accurately reflect the value of the company's assets. This constituted, in effect, a sort of inventory fraud.

Moreover, a significant part of the company receivables was recorded on the debit side of the company's statements (Table 12.3), but was not collectable. It should have been written off in pursuit of accounting accuracy

Table 12.3 Receivables in the financial statements (expressed in lira) of Geminiano Cozzi's company for the years 1781, 1782 and 1783 (*Archivio di Stato* in Venice, *Inquisitor alle Arti*, b. 98)

	1781		*1782*		*1783*	
A Crediti da riscuottere, con quelli S. Salvad.r con diffalco Xci per %	L.	43494	L.	44495	L.	49101

objectives. However late in paying were the company's customers, the company continued to carry the obligation as receivables. We do not know if the company used any means of encouraging the customer to pay, nor do we find a specified cut-off period beyond which the firm had to choose to write off the obligation. The company reduced receivables by only 10%, but the government official ("*Riflessioni*"; Stazzi, 1981) stated that the total amount of such receivables should have been equal to one third of the amount recorded in the statement of 1783.

The government official (the *Inquisitorato alle Arti*) did an accurate job and in his final document ("*Riflessioni*"; Stazzi, 1981) emphasized that a large write-off should have been recorded in the statement of the year 1783 in order to reflect the definitive reduced value of the inventory, obsolete fixed assets and uncollectable accounts receivable. Moreover, he highlighted an additional debt amount of 7,030 ducats and some missed revenues, such as those related to the rent of some of the company's buildings.

Consequences of the Accounting Fraud

The previous section regards the specific determinants and the peculiar ways of implementing the examined accounting fraud. The number of incorrect issues is impressive with regard both to the examined financial statements and to the internal governance structure of the company. The consequences of such matters are lessened because of the aforementioned absence of accounting law at that historical moment. The company started to draw up the financial statements in 1777 in order to monitor the evolution of its economic results. There was a voluntary commitment to analyze its economic performance even though this led to the discovery of a sort of accounting fraud by the *Inquisitorato alle Arti*. After these events, Geminiano Cozzi's factory was closed down primarily due to the disagreement between Geminiano Cozzi and Bonaventura Marinoni. The providential moderating work done by the government official and the other stakeholders allowed a final agreement (September 1, 1784) that entailed the business's survival. This agreement sanctioned Marinoni's exit from the company, which became again wholly owned by the Cozzi brothers. This was the most relevant consequence for Bonaventura Marinoni's position. In spite of the responsibility in the discovered fraud, the consequences were in reality minimized for both Bonaventura Marinoni and the bookkeeper Giustino Pasquali. Bonaventura Marinoni was still entitled to obtain his capital, albeit with deferred payments and deadlines longer than those envisaged for the other investors. The bookkeeper Giustino Pasquali remained in his workplace and continued to draw up the financial statements of Geminiano Cozzi's factory. The only relevant difference for him was a change in the way his remuneration was calculated: his wage, after the final agreement in 1784, would be calculated in relation to the sales cash flow.

Discussion

After considering the economic context and the accounting misrepresentations, in this last paragraph we are going to examine in greater depth issues concerning the liquidity and the internal governance structure of the examined company. As a starting point of our discussion we will define two basic terms: "stakeholder" and "property rights". Adopting a broad definition, we can consider stakeholders as persons or institutions exposed to risk from the activity of a firm—for example, shareholders, options and debt holders, employees, local communities, environment, the government, customers and suppliers (Clarkson, 1995). However, for the purposes of this study, given the organizational structure of the Cozzis' firm, we can limit our analysis to three categories: the state, the investor (debt or shareholders) and the entrepreneur.

Property rights can be considered as "sanctioned behavioral relations among decision makers in the use of potentially valuable resources; such sanctioned behaviors allow people the right to use resources within the class of non-prohibited uses" (Asher, Mahoney and Mahoney, 2005, 7). If property rights can be considered as rights to use resources, we have to connect them to the different priorities of the stakeholders. For example, the state is interested in collecting taxes, in maintaining employment levels and (if subsidies or monetary privileges have been conceded) in getting back the money lent; the entrepreneur will generally be concerned for the firm's value maximization in a long perspective; investors are mainly interested in safeguarding their investments.

Stakeholders, therefore, can use their property rights to mitigate the risk involved in their relations with a firm. When a firm faces the risk of default, stakeholders react in different ways according to their interests. On one side the investor's main objective is the immediate bankruptcy declaration in order to save his or her investment; on the other side, the entrepreneur may try to hide the default and continue to manage the firm in order to maximize his gains or divert funds. Between these two extreme points we find the public authority. At a first stage the state can try to save the firm in order to achieve the goals of maintaining the employment rate and collecting taxes, but when the default of the firm is unavoidable the main objective is to save its money.

Even when property rights are not well defined due to the lack of an efficient legal framework, stakeholders can try to negotiate a different distribution of power within a firm. This case study shows that a financial crisis can make room for a shift in the allocation of decision power.

Aghion and Bolton (1992) proposed a pecking-order theory of three possibly efficient governance structures (unilateral control by the entrepreneur, unilateral control by shareholders and contingent control): as long as the shareholder's rights are properly protected the unilateral control of the entrepreneur is preferred; otherwise a contingent control represents a second best;

finally, if the protection granted to the shareholder is not yet adequate, the investor's unilateral control should be chosen.

Utilizing this model, Cella (2012) shows that the governance structure of the Cozzi firm has been characterized by the presence of these three forms:

1. Before 1777: unilateral control by Geminiano Cozzi;
2. 1777–78: contingent control;
3. After 1778: unilateral control by Bonaventura Marinoni.

The passage from stage 1 to stage 2 was caused by a liquidity crisis that moves from a unilateral control to a joint control; however, this situation did not present a symmetric distribution of power and the establishment of a new company sanctioned a passage from stage 2 to stage 3.

In some ways Marinoni faced a paradox: on one side the company was suffering from a lack of liquidity, and on the other he needed to prove the existence of profitable assets in order to obtain his money. As shown previously, in the ceramic industry the productive cycle resulted in a misalignment between positive and negative cash flows; especially when a particular production had just been launched (in this case earthenware in 1780), negative cash flows largely exceed positive ones.

Under the complete control of the investor, the fraud can be interpreted as a means to exercise his decision-making power in order to save his investments. Clearly when liquidity is lacking, a firm cannot pay dividends nor return capital to its investors. Therefore, Marinoni structured his fraud in two stages: firstly, he demonstrated the existence of profits, and then he tried to dissolve the company and force Cozzi to liquidate his investments.

According to the company's statute, the cash was personally managed by Pasquali on behalf of Marinoni (which meant that any expenditure decided by Cozzi had to be approved by Marinoni). The only way to show the existence of profits was the overvaluation of some other assets. Once the financial statement had been accepted by Cozzi, Marinoni could ask for the liquidation of his capital; at this point Cozzi would have to declare bankruptcy, sell the assets and pay back Marinoni even if the company was not in fact producing profits.

As shown by Jones (2011), nowadays it is possible to isolate two typologies of fraud. An excess of power retained by entrepreneurs or managers is usually at the origin of misstatement crimes in continental (European) financial systems, whereas

> In the United States (as in most Anglo-Saxon countries), accounting fraud seems mainly to be the result of pressure to perform that financial investors, market analysts and internal budgeting professionals exert over top and middle managers.
>
> (Agostini and Favero, 2017, 474–475)

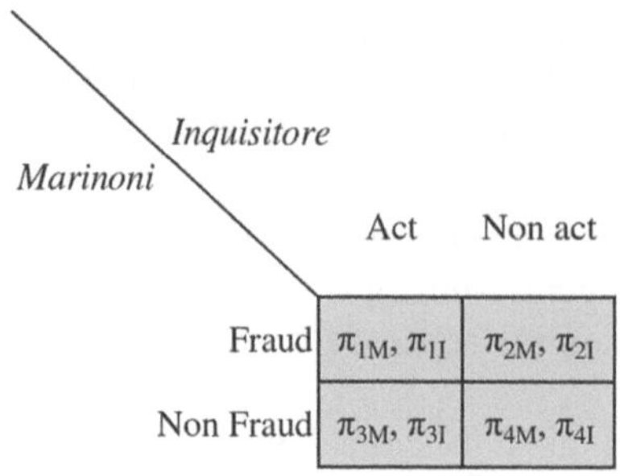

Figure 12.2 Matrix of the game

Managers can be motivated to commit fraud or to indulge in creative accounting by personal incentives or market expectations, and usually increase income and/or assets, decrease expense and/or liabilities, invent sales and/or misappropriate assets.

Comparing the case of Cozzi and Marinoni's company with contemporary cases of fraud, we see some differences and some similarities. The main similarity has to do with the techniques of fraud; we can also observe in this case an overstatement of certain assets. The main difference instead regards the fraudster and his motivations; as shown, the investor perpetrated the fraud and was motivated by the need to protect his investments and get back the money lent.

Why did Marinoni defraud? The situation can be described (Figure 12.2) by a game played by Marinoni and the *Inquisitorato alle Arti*. In the last years, the adoption of game-theoretical approaches in historical studies has shown a great potential. In his survey of the applications of game theory to economic history, Greif (2002, 1991) asserts that "game theory enables the analysis to go further by providing economic history with a theoretical framework suitable for analyzing strategic, economic, social, and political situations". Furthermore, he shows how this theoretical approach can be appropriate to investigate strategic situations perhaps more frequent in premodern economies than in modern ones.

Marinoni has two choices: fraud and non-fraud. The *Inquisitore* can check the correctness of the balance sheet (act) or allow the company to dissolve (non-act). The probability p ($0<p<1$) describes the *Inquisitore*'s belief about the fraudulent behaviour of Marinoni.

The pay-offs are:

- π_{1M} for Marinoni, π_{1I} for the *Inquisitore*: Marinoni defrauds and the *Inquisitore* acts; Marinoni obtains only a part of his money.
- π_{2M} for Marinoni, π_{2I} for the *Inquisitore*: Marinoni defrauds and the *Inquisitore* does not act; Cozzi has to completely repay Marinoni.

- $\pi_{1I} > \pi_{2I}$; $\pi_{2M} > \pi_{1M}$.
- π_{3M} for Marinoni, π_{3I} for the *Inquisitore*: Marinoni does not defraud and the *Inquisitore* acts; Marinoni obtains only part of his money but the *Inquisitore* incurs a cost unnecessarily.
- π_{4M} for Marinoni, π_{4I} for the *Inquisitore*: Marinoni does not defraud and the *Inquisitore* does not act; Marinoni obtains only part of his money.
- $\pi_{4I} > \pi_{3I}$; $\pi_{3M} = \pi_{4M}$.

Moreover, $\pi_{2M} > \pi_{3M} = \pi_{4M}$ (Marinoni prefers to obtain all his money) and $\pi_{4I} > \pi_{1I} > \pi_{2I}$ (the *Inquisitore* prefers "honesty").

The *Inquisitore*'s best response is act if

$$p * \pi_{1I} + (1 - p) * \pi_{3I} > p * \pi_{2I} + (1 - p) * \pi_{4I}$$

that is

$$p > (\pi_{4I} - \pi_{3I})/(\pi_{1I} + \pi_{4I} - \pi_{3I} - \pi_{2I})$$

A crucial point regards the construction of pay-off π_{3I}—that is, the *Inquisitore*'s pay-off when Marinoni does not defraud and the *Inquisitore* acts. In this game pay-off also depends on the difference between the cost of control and the benefits derived. Roughly speaking, when the *Inquisitore* does not act, costs and benefits derived are zero; this situation is described by pay-offs π_{4I} and π_{2I}. When the *Inquisitore* acts, costs rise but not necessarily benefits. In π_{1I} benefits derived cover costs because the fraud is discovered; however, on a first analysis, in π_{3I} benefits derived are zero because there is no fraud to be discovered.

Given that $p > 0$, "high" values (very close to π_{4I}) of π_{3I} make act the *Inquisitore*'s best strategy; π_{3I} arises when control costs decrease—that is, when control is cheap. In general, it is possible to suppose that control costs depend on the establishment of efficient magistracies able to rapidly and economically verify the possibility of fraud. However, the greater part of these costs may be borne by the state in a hypothetical (out-of-the-game) step 0 and the total control cost function can be characterized by decreasing marginal costs. In other words, π_{3I} is "high" when the state bears the greater part of control costs before the game is played. Therefore, these costs can be considered as a deterrent against eventual frauds. For our purpose, the establishment of the magistracy of the *Inquisitorato alle Arti* (in an out-of-the-game step) can provide a qualitative measure of the pay-off and it is possible to suppose a "high" value of π_{3I}.

Another point of interest is the construction of π_{1M}; in particular, we should check whether $\pi_{1M} > \pi_{3M}$ (and π_{4M}) or $\pi_{1M} < \pi_{3M}$ (and π_{4M}).

Nowadays the pay-off of a discovered fraudster (π_{1M} in our game) is the lowest; at least in countries where efficient accounting laws imposing penalties for guilty parties are established, fraudsters are punished. In eighteenth-century Venice, the lack of this kind of normative framework provided room for discretion and arbitrariness on the magistracies' part; therefore, their judgment has to be connected with their priorities among the issues at stake. Generally, as previously said, the state is interested in saving the firm in order to achieve the goals of maintaining employment and collecting taxes; only when the default of the firm is unavoidable does the main objective become to save its money. The questions are the following: was Cozzi's firm close to bankruptcy? Had the company growth prospects?

After 1785 porcelain sales rose (Figure 12.3) and it is possible to say that the company had growth prospects. Therefore, we should suppose that the state was interested in avoiding the company's bankruptcy. However, at the same time Marinoni's will to dissolve the company had to be respected. This situation could potentially make room for a negotiation between Marinoni and Cozzi and, moreover, the involvement of the state would assure Marinoni of the enforcement of its terms. We can capture this situation setting $\pi_{1M} > \pi_{3M} = \pi_{4M}$—that is, for Marinoni "a good negotiation" is better than "honest behaviour".

To sum up, it has been shown that the best strategy of the state is always to act, because an efficient institution had been established in an out-of-the-game stage (the *Inquisitore alle Arti*), and that Marinoni's best strategy is always fraud because at least this action could lead to a "good negotiation". Therefore, the game has a unique equilibrium in which Marinoni defrauds and the state intervenes.

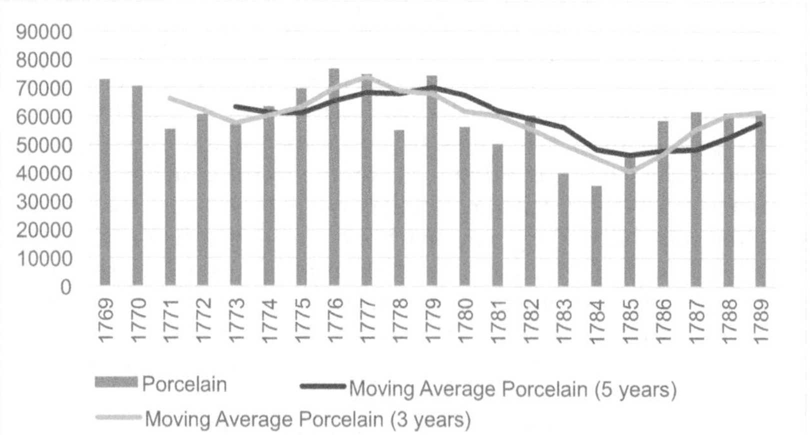

Figure 12.3 Sales of porcelain between 1769 and 1789

Conclusion

The main goal of this essay was to discern in historical perspective how and why the motivations, meanings and mechanisms of fraud change in relationship with the institutional context. We adopted a case study approach in order to answer this research question. The peculiarity of the chosen case lies in the fact that the roles of the investor partner, of the managing partner, of the accountant and of the state authority do not fit into the script that we logically expect. In this perspective, the case is actually questioning our assumptions and playing the role of a paradigmatic example of phenomena that have escaped systematic investigation as far as they were possible only in a different historical context (Ermakoff, 2014, 223–224). After an analysis of the determinants and consequences of the fraud, following authoritative historical economic literature we adopted a game-theoretical approach in order to find an alternative explanation of such opportunistic behaviour in a context characterized by the absence of a well-defined legal framework. We were able to conclude that the accounting fraud can be interpreted in this context not so much as an illegal act but rather as a strategy to negotiate new conditions (in this case between the investor Marinoni and the entrepreneur Cozzi) under the tutelage of the state. Further research on the matter could shed light on the conceptual and theoretical issues such an interpretation raises.

Note

1. Only in 1882 did the Italian Commercial Code include a single article (numbered 176) concerning financial statements: it imposed for the first time rules concerning the functions and the content of the financial statements, it required the profits (or the losses suffered) to be clearly demonstrated and the real social capital and the sum of the payments already made and those in arrears to be clearly stated. It was nothing if not succinct. The Civil Code of 1942 introduced more comprehensive regulations, providing a required minimum content for the balance sheet and establishing a set of rules and evaluation criteria for financial statements.

References

Aghion, Philippe and Patrick Bolton. "An incomplete contracts approach to financial contracting", *Review of Economic Studies* 59 (1992): 473–494.

Agostini, Marisa and Giovanni Favero. "Accounting fraud, business failure and creative auditing: A micro-analysis of the strange case of Sunbeam Corp.", *Accounting History* 22 (2017): 472–487.

Asher, Cheryl Carleton, James M. Mahoney and Joseph T. Mahoney. "Towards a property rights foundation for a stakeholder theory of the firm", *Journal of Management and Governance* 9, no. 1 (2005): 5–32.

Association of Certified Fraud Examiners (ACFE). *Report to the Nation on Occupational Fraud and Abuse.* Austin, TX: Association of Certified Fraud Examiners, 2010. Retrieved from http://butest.acfe.com/rttn/rttn-2010.pdf. May 25, 2013.

Cella, Riccardo. "Finanziamento e governance in un'impresa veneziana del Settecento", *Studi e note di economia* 17, no. 2 (2012): 297–322.

Clarkson, Max B.E. "A stakeholder framework for analyzing and evaluating corporate social performance", *Academy of Management Review* 20, no. 1 (1995): 92–117.

Ermakoff, Ivan. "Exceptional cases: Epistemic contributions and normative expectations", *European Journal of Sociology* 55, no. 2 (2014): 223–243.

Favero, Giovanni. "Old and new ceramics: Manufacturers, products and markets in the Venetian State (17th-18th centuries)", In *At the Center of the Old World: Trade and Manufacturing in Venice and the Venetian Mainland*, 271–315. Edited by Paola Lanaro. Toronto: Centre for Renaissance and Reformation Studies, 2006.

Favero, Giovanni. "Privilegi d'industria e diritti di proprietà nelle manifatture di ceramica della Repubblica di Venezia (XVII–XVIII secolo)", *Quaderni Storici* 46 (2011): 185–220.

Garner, Bryan A. *A Dictionary of Modern Legal Usage*. Oxford: Oxford Universty Press, 2001.

Garner, Bryan A. *Black's Law Dictionary*. 9th edition. Los Angeles, CA: West Group, 2009.

Greif, Avner. "Economic history and game theory: A survey", In *Handbook of Game Theory, Vol. III, 1989–2024*. Edited by Robert J. Aumann and Sergiu Hart. North Holland: Amsterdam, 2001.

Jones, Michael. *Creative Accounting, Fraud and International Accounting Scandals*. Hoboken, NJ: John Wiley & Sons, 2011.

Stazzi, Francesco. *Porcellane della Casa Eccellentissima Vezzi (1720–1727)*. Milan: V. Scheiwiller, 1967.

Stazzi, Francesco. *Le porcellane veneziane di Geminiano e Vincenzo Cozzi*. Venice: Fantoni, 1981.

Young, Hilary. *The Genius of Wedgwood*. London: Victoria and Albert Museum, 1995.

Section 3

Accounting Education

13 Education and Bookkeeping in Fifteenth-Century Venice

A Revisitation and Some Interdisciplinary Insights

Laura Girella and Michela Cordazzo

Introduction

In the last thirty years, the foundation and the developments of professional orders have represented topics that have raised the interest of and that have been explored by scholars at the international level (Abbott, 1988; Macdonald, 1995).

In relation to accounting, works have been advanced from a wide range of countries, especially Anglo-Saxon ones, and perspectives about the rationales that have surrounded the establishment of these associations (Walker, 1991; Willmott, 1986), the selection and examination procedures undertaken, the rules that have disciplined their external and internal activities (Greenwood, 1957), and the logics that have driven their attitude towards other professional terrains (Coronella et al., 2015) have been provided.

However, in taking a broader view, it is worthy of note that in the accounting arena the educational background that can have formed the basis for and "nurtured" the birth of these professional bodies is investigated in isolation, if not under-investigated. Put differently, the ways in which the accounting craft has been moulded within the scholarly system and the extent to which it has contributed to the professionalization process within ad hoc structures are still somehow vague.

As stated by Ross forty years ago (1976),

> What do we know about the education of boys and young men in Venice in this period? Who dispensed instruction, who received it, and who paid for it? What intellectual baggage did the élite of the young Venetian patricians take with them to the Studium of Padua, the sole center of advanced learning sanctioned by the Serenissima?
>
> (p. 521)

Similar questions could be posed also nowadays.

Indeed, although some initial answers have been offered internationally—for example, by McCarthy et al. (2008), Sangster and Scataglinibelghitar (2010) and Thompson (1991)—they have been to some extent myopic.

Firstly, they have mainly focused on the figure of Luca Pacioli, and secondly, they have provided a partial and somehow a "mono-disciplinary" view of the overall scholarly system that could have contributed to education in bookkeeping in that period.

To put it differently, despite several calls for a "new accounting history" (Miller et al., 1991) able to open up and "laterally expand" (ibid., p. 397) the contours of the discipline to other fields of knowledge as well as to non-Anglo-Saxon settings (Parker, 1993) being advanced since the beginning of the 1990s, a peripheral number of works can be said to have offered significant contributions in this respect. A decade ago, accounting history scholars were still witnessing a stagnation of this kind of study vis-à-vis the hegemony of works strictly related to accounting in and by Anglo-Saxon settings and authors (Carmona, 2004; Zan, 2004).

In relation to the specific theme of accounting education in Italy, Walker (2005) contended that, notwithstanding it is a topic that has been subject to investigation from a historical perspective, no specific reference has been made to Venice (at least within the accounting field, until the middle of 2005). To the best of our knowledge, only recently have brief overviews been advanced (Sangster and Scataglinibelghitar, 2010), but they suffer from the shortcomings mentioned earlier.

Following this line of thought, the aim of the chapter is to start investigating the archaeology of education in bookkeeping in fifteenth-century Venice. In particular, by relying on secondary sources, which are mainly documents belonging to other disciplinary fields (especially literature, philosophy and mathematics), insights into the role that the *abbaco* schools as well as the Rialto School played in the emergence of double-entry bookkeeping will be here presented. Indeed, both of them represent the schools that provided lectures on geometry and mathematics—the accounting fundamentals—to which also Fra' Luca Pacioli, the "father" of double-entry bookkeeping, owes his initial learning.

In this way, the work intends to contribute to the current accounting literature and practice by providing a historical and interdisciplinary perspective on the manners in which education in accounting was organized in fifteenth-century Venice. In particular, interdisciplinary here refers to "any form of dialogue or interaction between two or more disciplines" with a view to "producing new forms of knowledge" (Moran, 2002, p. 16). Accordingly, the remainder of the chapter will be structured as follows. Firstly, an overview on the scholarly system in fifteenth-century Venice will be presented, with a particular focus on the *abbaco* schools. Then, the case of the Rialto School will be described with reference to its origins, its most relevant teachers and its most well-known pupil, Luca Pacioli. Through a commentary of the works by Thompson (1991, 1994), observations in relation to the possible influence that the Rialto School could have had on the works of Pacioli will be illustrated. A final section will propose insights and possible learnings that we can derive by investigating accounting (history) at the interface with other disciplines and languages.

Education in Fifteenth-Century Venice: An Overview

The term "school" derives from the Latin word "*schola*", which means "an ancient Roman association of persons (as military men) sharing a common interest or profession" (*Merriam-Webster Dictionary*). It was in this original sense that confraternities started to be established since the thirteenth century in Venice. Of particular interest for the argument here at stake are the *abbaco* schools. However, for the sake of completeness, a brief illustration of the *Scuole Grandi e Scuole Minori*, which constituted a relevant part of educational system in those decades, will be also given.[1]

Scuole Grandi e Scuole Minori

It was in the Middle Ages that confraternities, *corporationes* of arts and professions and associations of cities started to be established in Venice with the aims of protecting their common interests, assisting its members or offering charity services. However, among these, there were two types of schools quite different in nature: the *Scuole Grandi* and the *Scuole Minori*. The former were confraternities or institutions dedicated to charity activities as well as to public redemption, while the latter tended to bring together those who were doing the same work or who were coming from the same city. In addition, their administration differed quite sharply. The *Scuole Minori* were controlled by the so-called *Gastaldi* (functionaries of the doge), while the *Scuole Grandi* were controlled by the Council of Ten. However, it has to be pointed out that the former do not owe this name to their less importance, but to the little locations that used to host them, such as churches, little squares ("*campielli*") or little facilities. The so-called *Scuole Grandi* were conceived as meeting halls, sometimes articulated on floors and adjacent to churches.

Up to 1552 it was possible to count six *Scuole Grandi*, such as the *Scuola Grande di Santa Maria della Carità*, *Scuola Grande di San Marco*, *Scuola Grande di San Giovanni Evangelista*, *Scuola Grande di Santa Maria della Misericordia*, *Scuola Grande di San Rocco* and *Scuola Grande di San Teodoro*, while there were from two hundred to four hundred *Scuole Minori*.

The Abbaco *Schools*

As described by Sangster et al. (2008) and Sangster and Scataglinibelghitar (2010), it was only after the appearance of the *Liber Abaci* by Fibonacci in 1202 that *abbaco* schools started to flourish in northern Italy. Indeed, the first one that was appointed to teach *abbaco* was Fibonacci himself.

As compared to the types of schools briefly outlined earlier, the *abbaco* schools differed in many respects.

Probably the most significant aspect of distinction was related to the scope of the school, which was to prepare the sons of merchants, after they were taught reading and writing in the vernacular primary schools, for their future life and profession (Sangster et al., 2008). In this respect, it had a practical orientation in instruction and teaching material (the *abbaco* books), combined with a conversational and narrative way of confronting problems and solutions. Indeed, there was no generalization effort, but a case-by-case approach was undertaken. As described by Grendler (2002, p. 420) the schools taught

> how to solve business-related problems, such as calculating interest, discounting loans, money exchange, partnership division, measurement and distance problems, and allegation exercises [. . .]. The mathematics employed combined arithmetic, algorism, algebra, geometry, and what might have called ingenious reasoning.

And these cases were collected and memorized for future reference. As effectively summarized by Gamba and Montebelli (1987) the teaching of the *abbaco* schools was prescriptive and not explicative, as it was based on cases and solutions to be remembered. In this respect, a type of mentality that was highly mnemonic-analogic and operative, rather than deductive, was required. It was relevant to recognize, confront, verify and approximate cases with those recorded in the *abbaco* book, and not to deduct general rules or logically connect similar cases and solutions.

As reported also by Grendler (1991, p. 308),

> Abbaco meant solving practical problems on paper. Nor did abbaco refer to a single mathematic operation or technique. Abbaco used arithmetic, algorism (computing with numbers, especially decimals), algebra, and geometry, all based on the Hindu-Arabic numeral system, to solve business-related problems. The nature of the problems, rather than the mathematical operations, unified abbaco.

Another peculiarity that characterized *abbaco* schools vis-à-vis other schools is the language of teaching, which was vernacular. Indeed, after its appearance, *abbaco* was introduced into vernacular schools, while it never entered Latin schools. The reason for this relied on the conventional wisdom that

> it added nothing to the social status and career goals of their students. The Latin schools sought to train society's leaders and the professionals (chiefly secretaries and lawyers) who aided them. Such men had no need to learn commercial mathematics, or so it was thought.
>
> (Grendler, 1991, p. 311)

Accounting Education: The Case of the Rialto School

Despite the ample body of knowledge that the *abbaco* schools offered to the future merchants, in the view of many it was not considered enough. It is possible to better understand this vision by reading the historical reproductions provided by Nardi (1963) first and by Tucci (1990) after.

In a will dictated by Simone Valentini to the Venetian notary Francesco Polo in 1420, he left detailed dispositions in order to protect his three children until their age of majority. In this respect, firstly, they should start to attend those schools where they could learn how to talk and write appropriately and correctly, according to the rules of grammar (i.e., Latin). Then, they should attend a school of *abbaco*—that is, of "practical arithmetic"—where they could learn bookkeeping to become a merchant. Finally, it would have been appreciated by the parent if they could attend a school of philosophy and logic. This was the way, according to Valentini, through which it was possible to become a good merchant, without looking bad vis-à-vis Byzantine and Arabic peers (Nardi, 1963).

In a similar vein, many decades after, Cotrugli (1453) as reported by Tucci (1990), stated that in order to become "*perfecto* and *compiuto*" (Tucci, 1990, p. 104), the young merchant should have acquired a knowledge that would have gone far beyond the pure technical expertise, but that could have allowed him to communicate with men belonging to different social statuses. In particular, at the basis of the merchant's knowledge there were the abilities to be a good writer, to be able to count and to implement double entry. In addition, the knowledge of grammar as well as of logic, rhetoric, philosophy, astrology and cosmology could have permitted the merchant to be able to succeed in a profession that was imbued with social relations (Tucci, 1990, pp. 104–105).

The foregoing examples of wills appear to be consistent with what was advanced later by Ortalli (1996) and Grendler (2002). According to the former, at that time there was no sharp separation between grammar and *abbaco*, but the mercantile mentality and the humanistic sensitivity coexisted, somehow being intertwined (p. 64). Similarly, Grendler (2002) reported that humanists started to be appointed as professors in universities only around 1425. Indeed, it was believed by early humanists that to study humanism allowed one to "inculcate good morals as well as elegant expression and [. . .] to become responsible and upright leaders of society" (Grendler, 2002, p. 209) and this was possible only in elementary and secondary schools.

It is in this context that it is possible to locate the Rialto School.

The case of the Rialto School (also known as the School of Philosophy) is not completely unknown to historians but it may be to many accounting scholars. Indeed, it has been already investigated by Italian intellectuals, philosophers and historians, such as Bruno Nardi and Arnaldo Segarizzi, as well as by international scholars, such as Ross (1976), who have dedicated articles and book chapters to the understanding of the culture, education and philosophical orientation of the Venetian Republic in the Middle Ages. The very few traces that it is possible to find in relation to this school within the accounting realm are mainly linked to one of the pupils who attended lectures between 1465 and 1471—that is, Luca Pacioli, the "father" of double-entry bookkeeping. However, not a lot is known among accounting scholars about the origins of this school, its internal organization and orientation. Accordingly, by relying on secondary sources that are documents belonging to other disciplinary fields (mainly literature, history, philosophy and mathematics) this section will provide initial insights about the history of the Rialto School.

The Origins of the Rialto School

Despite the relevance gained in the Venetian Republic in the fifteenth and sixteenth centuries, the Rialto School owes its origins neither to an institution that was governing the Venice territory nor to the initiative of a private Venetian citizen, but to a Florentine merchant—namely, Tomà Talenti—who used to travel to Venice and became a citizen of the republic only in 1363. Indeed, it was he who in a will dictated to the notary Iacopo Ziera in 1397 established a bequest of fifty annual golden ducats to be paid to a master of arts (*magistro artium*), who should have provided lectures of logics and philosophy in Venice to at least six students who would have attended his lectures regularly and continuously. This master should have been of proven science and fame and should have not required any payment by poor students.

> *Item, dimitto pro uno magistro artium sumendo et salariando Venetiis per dictos commissarios de prode meorum imprestitorum annuatim ducatos quinquaginta auri, pro legendo Artes, scilicet Logicam et phylosophiam, volentibus audire et discere in civitate Venetiarum. Et si auditores et scolares non invenirentur continue, diebus ydoneis, ultra sex numero volentes audire, dictum legatum nullius penitus sit valoris, sed in meum residuum convertatur pro tempore quo non fuerint studentes ydonei ad dictum numerum. Et iste magister sit probate scientie atque fame, et non possit exigere a pauperibus scolaribus de iure quicquam.*
> (Nardi, 1963, p. 10)

Tomà Talenti died in November 1403 but it took five years before the Rialto School was formally established in the Church of San Giovanni Elemosinario in Rialto. However, as previously mentioned, the Venetian Republic was already populated by different schools in those years. Schools of grammar, rhetoric and *abbaco* were established both in *sestieri* (city quarters) and in churches and there were convents where monks were educated in order to obtain academic degrees. In addition, private pedagogues were invited by patrician families with the aim to educate their children (as was the case of Luca Pacioli, who, between 1465 and 1471, was hosted for nearly six years by the rich merchant Sier Antonio de' Rompiasi to educate his three sons). However, none of the foregoing schools were similar to the one imagined by Talenti. Indeed, they were mainly schools devoted to the study of humanities and those hosted by convents were highly influenced by the relative religious orders. The school that Talenti had intended to found was firstly a school of logic and philosophy that could prepare students to achieve an academic degree in medicine, mathematics and astronomy, and secondly, it was a secular school, probably the first one in the republic. Another relevant aspect of distinction relied on the philosophical orientation that the school had, as it was Aristotelian and Averroistic in nature. In this respect, it is worthwhile to mention that, a few years before, Talenti used to have quarrels with the Italian scholar and poet Francesco Petrarca (Petrarch) due to their different philosophical credos. The former was indeed Aristotelian and Averroistic, while the latter was Platonic and used to consider the Aristotelic and Avverroistic philosophers as relying on a knowledge that was not that of Jesus Christ (*De sui ipsius et multorum aliorum ignorantia*, 1368). These quarrels, which were initially personal, culminated then in the opposition between the literary disciplines on the one hand and natural philosophy on the other, which became in turn embodied by the San Marco School and the Rialto School.

Accordingly, it can be stated that since its very first inception this school to some extent represented a turning point in the scholarly system of those centuries, as it embodied a completely new educational system in the republic.

The Development of the Rialto School (1420–1480): The Contribution of Paolo della Pergola and Domenico Bragadin

Despite the voluminous information offered by the books of Nardi (1957, 1963) and Segarizzi (1916), the teachers of the Rialto School, especially those who can be said to have mainly influenced its development during the fifteenth century, can be summarized as having been mainly two, Paolo della Pergola and Domenico Bragadin.

Paolo della Pergola, who taught between 1421 and 1454, is not the first teacher of the school (Camillo da Ferrara, Nicolò da Salerno, "M° Sigismondo" preceded him in this) but he is known, among the others, as having been the teacher who provided the school with an organization similar to the one of a university. He introduced statutes as well as the election of a rector. Furthermore, with respect to teaching, he introduced the study of theology as he was both *artium doctor* and *theologiae professor* (Segarizzi, 1916, pp. 666–667), as well as professor of *calculationes* and mathematics (Lepori, 1980, p. 549). In this way, he allowed the school to become very similar to the Studium of Padua. His intention was indeed to create a university ("*Studio generale*") able to compete with it, which at that time was the only one in the Venetian Republic. However, this intention remained as such as the Council of Ten ("Consiglio di Dieci") opposed it. In their view, the Studium of Padua should remain the only one in the Venetian state ("*Studio Pubblico dello Stato Veneziano*").

Another relevant personality in the history of the Rialto School was Domenico Bragadin, who was a student of Paolo della Pergola, before succeeding him as teacher. Bragadin was probably the only teacher well known also by accounting scholars as he taught Luca Pacioli, who attended the school in the six years during which he was hosted by the Rompiasi family on the island of Giudecca. Bragadin was a Venetian patrician who was selected by the signoria as public lecturer in all the sciences (Taylor, 1956). This intervention by the republic in the activities of the Rialto School could have been due to its change of nature. Indeed, initially the school was "public" in the sense that it was open to the public. However, between 1441 and 1455, it became public in statal terms when its financial maintenance became a task of the Treasury and then in 1455, upon Senate decree, 150 golden annual ducats were added to the 50 left by Talenti by the public administration to pay the salary of Bragadin (Ortalli, 1996). It was then that it may be reasonable to think that, in order to become professor at the school, candidates had to pass a rigid examination, in relation not only to their competences and abilities but also to their morals (Taylor, 1956). Bragadin taught at the school for almost thirty years, firstly from 1454 to 1455 as a substitute for his teacher Paolo della Pergola, and then, once having achieved his doctorate, until 1482 as professor.

One Pupil Among the Others: Luca Pacioli

As mentioned in the foregoing section, probably one of the most well-known pupils of the Rialto School was Luca Pacioli (at that time not yet Fra' as he joined the Franciscan order between 1470 and 1477). Indeed, in the six years during which he was hosted as a pedagogue by the Rompiasi family on the island of Giudecca he attended lectures at the school. However, it is worthy of note that it was not the initial place were Pacioli started to be exposed to mathematics. Indeed, before his stay in Venice, he had already attended lessons at an *abbaco* school. As explicitly mentioned by him in his main work, the mathematical compendium *Summa de arithmetica, geometria, proportioni et proportionalità* (1494), he owed his initiation in geometry and algebra to the Rialto School and especially to Bragadin.

As will be better described in the following section, the influence that the attendance of this school had on Pacioli's education, however, relates not only to its syllabus but also to its underlying philosophical orientation. Indeed, as acknowledged by Sangster and Scataglinibelghitar (2010), in spite of the fact that they were both comprehensive merchant school texts, *Summa*, as compared to his earlier work (*Tractatus Mathematicus*), which was prepared in his youth, could be conceived as a "an integrated text on business and business mathematics" (Sangster and Scataglinibelghitar, 2010, p. 424). In addition, it was written in the vernacular (the spoken language), not in Latin. Accordingly, as stated by Sangster and Scataglinibelghitar (2010, pp. 426–427), "Pacioli's choice of the vernacular in writing *Summa Arithmetica* was wholly in keeping with humanist principles and the humanist desire to extend knowledge to everyone, not just those with the wealth to afford it". In a similar vein, Yamey (2016) advanced the view that in order to comprehend *Summa* a humanistic education was required, which merchants usually did not possess. In addition, Rowland (1995) considered *Summa* "the most elegant and compendious of all vernacular manuals" (p. 701).

It is thus reasonable to think that this shift could have been due not only to his *abbaco* school education, as advanced by Sangster and Scataglinibelghitar (2010), but also to his exposure to the humanistic principles (of the Rialto School) during his Venice years.

Indeed, Pacioli visited Venice on many occasions after 1471. Probably one of the most significant for the argument here at stake was that of 1508 when he was invited by Sebastiano Foscarini, at that time the rector of the school, to hold an inaugural lecture at the Church of San Bartolomeo of Rialto on the fifth book of elements of Euclid, on proportions. This choice of topic was not casual. It was in fact only a few years before that Pacioli published his work *Summa de arithmetica, geometria, proportioni et proportionalità* and one year later he would publish the *De Divina Proportione* (1509), which "applies mathematics to the order underlying the cosmos, with particular emphasis on the Golden Section" (Rowland, 1995, p. 701). As stated by Grendler (2002) Euclid's geometry was also conceived as the link between mathematics and astronomy.

A Reconsideration of Grahame Thompson's View

The view is nowadays widely shared that accounting can be seen as, or is similar to, a rhetorical device (Carruthers and Espeland, 1991; Arrington and Schweiker, 1992; Young, 2003). However, upon closer investigation, this approach can be seen as dating back to the origins of double-entry bookkeeping, especially with reference to the works developed by Thompson (1991, 1994). In her two contributions titled "Is Accounting Rhetorical? Methodology, Luca Pacioli and Printing" (1991) and "Early Double-Entry Bookkeeping and the Rhetoric of Accounting Calculation" (1994) she advances the view that double-entry bookkeeping, as proposed by Luca Pacioli, has been influenced by the institutional background that surrounded the social and technological environment it emerged from. In particular, she refers to the influence that the pedagogical reform advanced by the Protestant priest Peter Ramus could have had on the seminal work of Pacioli, by contending that despite the time difference of about fifty years, it is possible to discern some connections. More specifically, she draws a line of conjunction between Ramus's method on the one hand and the project of Pacioli to "re-emphasise a belief in order sanctified by God" (1991, p. 584) on the other one. The former was based on a demise of rhetoric towards an upsurge of dialectic, in that

> It puts Rhetoric under the shadow of the Dialectic, so that it is subject to the ordered dialectic of invention and judgement. The Ramist drive towards curriculum simplification and orderliness hastened this process of denying the rhetorical moment to classroom practice and exercise. The textbook order, so crucial to the Ramist "method", came to dominate its particular conception of rhetoric.
>
> (1991, p. 586)

In particular, it

> came to denote the orderly arrangement of the *topics within* discourse. A "topical logic" was constructed (a form of class logic in fact) in which it was of central importance where things fell in an ordered and hierarchical series of places.
>
> (1991, p. 586)

To put it differently, also thanks to the development of writing and printing, the method proposed by Ramus allowed one to visualize discourse and, through a series of ordered steps, to produce with certain efficiency a desired effect (1991, p. 586).

Thompson maintains that in the *Summa* it is possible to identify a similar structure. She recognizes that Pacioli "paid particular attention to methodological exactness and the mastery of detail" and that "it imposed organization on a subject by imagining it as made up of parts fixed in space" (1991, p. 592). And the introduction of the printing technology permitted this approach to penetrate and had a significant impact on the diffusion of the Venetian method internationally.

Although we share Thompson's view that accounting should be investigated in the context (or how she puts it, "the institutional matrix") it emerges from, and that printing undoubtedly had a relevant impact on the diffusion of bookkeeping (Eisenstein, 1980), in our view the *Summa* might be further appreciated in the light of the case of the Rialto School. Indeed, as previously described it was an Aristotelian and Averroistic school in nature. One of the main tenets of Averroes (Ibn Rushd), a medieval Andalusian polymath to which we own the Latin translations of Aristotle, was the distinction of three different categories of intellects, which correspond to three different degrees of understanding in order to access the truth. At the top of this hierarchy he located the "demonstration man", whose mind proceeds only by way of rigorous arguments and wants to understand the truth by means of pure scientific methods (as it can be conceived the way the reader of the *Summa* could have done). The second degree was embodied by the "dialectical man", who is content with dialectical arguments of a probable type, and, finally, at the lowest degree, it was possible to find the "man of persuasion", for whom we need a form of rhetorical speech, to turn on or to restrain the feelings and passions, to rule, in short, the desires, needs and instincts. According to this perspective, the three levels and ways of understanding the truth correspond to three levels of a hierarchy among men, but through all the three ways it is possible to understand, although by different routes. Indeed, to each of these broad categories the sacred text (in his case the Quran) must be read and interpreted according to the nature of their genius and different intellectual abilities. To put it differently, he posited that any type of discourse must be appropriate to its own addressees (as can be seen in the choice to write *Summa* in the vernacular). So, for the demonstration men it will be possible to interpret the sacred text with the means of rational and scientific thought, until reaching the rational sense of revelation, and capture its intimate correlation with the reasons of philosophy. Others will be limited to a more direct or immediate understanding of its meaning, or to argue dialectically around the data of revelation. But if there seems to be an open conflict between the literal expression of the sacred text and the demonstrative conclusions of reason, in his view it will be the exact interpretation of philosophers to eliminate apparent contradictions and to demonstrate the profound convergence between the rational truth and that revealed.

Another important aspect of Averroes's thought that could be related to Pacioli's background in composing the *Summa*, and in particular the way the treatise is ordered, can refer to the organization of the world. Indeed, one of the characteristics of the *Summa*, identified also by Thompson, is its ordered structure. Interestingly to note, in Averroes's view, and in one of his main works, "The Incoherence of the Incoherence", in which he defends Aristotelian philosophy against al-Ghazali's claims in "The Incoherence of the Philosophers", he rejects the conception of God, proposed by al-Ghazali, as a Lord with absolute arbitrariness, and of a nature in which the phenomena have no causal relationship. On the contrary, he maintains that of course the nature depends on God, but that means that it is organized by him as a set of phenomena characterized by regular and stable causal relationships, according to a necessary order. For this reason, nature can be an object of knowledge.

To us, for the reasons illustrated earlier, this approach advanced by Averroes might be seen as having impacted the *Summa* of Pacioli in a similar vein as the Ramus method could have done, according to Thompson. Furthermore, if our interpretation is followed, it is not surprising that Pacioli, in his later work *De Divina proportione* (Venice, 1509), explicitly refers to Aristotle and Averroes in order to affirm the supremacy of mathematics.

Indeed: "*Ma de le vere, commo afferma Aristotele e Averrois, le nostre mathematici sono verissime e nel primo grado de la certezza e quelle sequitano ogni altre naturali*".

Education in Accounting in Fifteenth-Century Venice: Reflections and Insights From an Interdisciplinary Approach

The aim of the chapter has been to offer insights into the role that the *abbaco* schools as well as the Rialto School played in the accounting education panorama and the emergence of double-entry bookkeeping in fifteenth-century Venice.

Indeed, as mentioned in the introductory remarks, up to now within the accounting history arena very little has been said on the education in bookkeeping in Venice, especially through interdisciplinary lenses. Despite the efforts more or less recently made by international scholars, such as Thompson and Sangster, to "look beyond our (their) historic comfort zone of the mid-to-late nineteenth century" (Annisette, 2006, p. 400) and to study accounting in "other places and in 'other eras' and by other peoples" (Carnegie and Napier, 1996, pp. 27–28), and we would add in "other languages", in our view they have not been fully able to create a "proper" and "beneficial" interaction between different disciplines. Moving from this standpoint, the present work has sought to start filling this paucity. By relying on books and articles published both in Italian and English and belonging to philosophy, history and mathematics, it has sought to provide insights on two theoretical grounds.

Firstly, it has shown that, since the emergence of its teachings, bookkeeping has been part of a wider and articulated educational understanding and architecture that were included in a vision of the merchant's formation that encompassed both practical training and humanistic knowledge (as clearly pointed out by Nardi, 1963; Tucci, 1990). Secondly, it is possible to reconsider Grahame Thompson's contributions (1991, 1994) on the interpretation of accounting as being rhetorical. In particular, a view according to which the works of Pacioli could have been influenced by his attendance at the Rialto School as well as by the Ramist method has been offered.

In this way, the present work represents a further encouragement towards an investigation of accounting in its past, present and future forms at the interface of other disciplines, as has been the case since its emergence.

As stated by Miller et al. (1991, p. 398),

> The social sciences have been interdisciplinary since their inception. Indeed, the history of the social sciences is a history of differentiation, splitting off and cross-fertilization [. . .] this interchange of concepts and methods from one discipline to another is not to suggest that accounting should genuflect to the authority of this or that discipline. Far from it. Instead, it is increasingly a matter of recognizing that accounting researchers have much to contribute to other related fields of enquiry, including organization theory, sociology, economics, history of science, anthropology and sociology.

Note

1. Although we are aware that also the *sestieri* schools (i.e., the schools of the city quarters) embody a significant part within the educational system in Venice, to the best of our knowledge they started to be established only in the middle of the sixteenth century (Grendler, 1991). Accordingly, they are beyond the scope of the present chapter.

References

Abbott, Andrew. *The system of professions: An essay on the division of labor*. Chicago: The University of Chicago Press, 1988.

Annisette, Marcia. "People and periods untouched by accounting history: An ancient Yoruba practice." *Accounting History* 11, no. 4 (2006): 399–417.

Arrington, C. Edward, and William Schweiker. "The rhetoric and rationality of accounting research." *Accounting, Organizations and Society* 17, no. 6 (1992): 511–533.

Carmona, Salvador. "Accounting history research and its diffusion in an international context." *Accounting History* 9, no. 3 (2004): 7–23.

Carnegie, Garry D., and Christopher J. Napier. "Critical and interpretive histories: Insights into accounting's present and future through its past." *Accounting, Auditing & Accountability Journal* 9, no. 3 (1996): 7–39.

Carruthers, Bruce G., and Wendy Nelson Espeland. "Accounting for rationality: Double-entry bookkeeping and the rhetoric of economic rationality." *American Journal of Sociology* 97, no. 1 (1991): 31–69.

Coronella, Stefano, Massimo Sargiacomo, and Stephen P. Walker. "Unification and Dual Closure in the Italian Accountancy Profession, 1861–1906." *European Accounting Review* 24, no. 1 (2015): 167–197.

Eisenstein, Elizabeth L. *The printing press as an agent of change*. Vol. 1. Cambridge: Cambridge University Press, 1980.

Gamba, Enrico, and Vico Montebelli. "La matematica abachistica tra ricupero della tradizione e rinnovamento scientifico." *Cultura, scienze e tecniche nella Venezia del Cinquecento* (1987): 169–202.

Greenwood, Ernest. "Attributes of a profession." *Social Work* (1957): 45–55.

Grendler, Paul F. *Schooling in Renaissance Italy: Literacy and learning, 1300–1600*. Baltimore: Johns Hopkins University Press (JHU), 1991.

Grendler, Paul F. *The universities of the Italian Renaissance*. Baltimore: Johns Hopkins University Press (JHU), 2002.

Lepori, Fernando. *La scuola di Rialto dalla fondazione alla metà del Cinquecento*. In Girolamo Arnaldi and Manlio Pastore Stocchi (Eds.), *Storia della cultura veneta*, vol. III.2, Girolamo Arnaldi and Manlio Pastore Stocchi, 539–605. Vicenza: Neri Pozza, 1980.

Macdonald, Keith M. *The sociology of the professions: Sage Publications*. London: Sage, 1995.

McCarthy, Patricia, Alan Sangster, and Greg Stoner. "Pacioli and humanism: Pitching the text in Summa Arithmetica." *Accounting History* 13, no. 2 (2008): 183–206.

Miller, Peter, Trevor Hopper, and Richard Laughlin. "The new accounting history: An introduction." *Accounting, Organizations and Society* 16, no. 5–6 (1991): 395–403.

Moran, Joe. *Interdisciplinarity* (The new critical idiom: New critical idiom). Abingdon, UK: Routledge, 2002.
Nardi, Bruno. "La scuola di Rialto e l'umanesimo veneziano." *Umanesimo europeo e umanesimo veneziano* (1963): 93–140.
Nardi, Bruno. *Letteratura e cultura veneziana del Quattrocento*. Firenze: Sansoni Editore, 1957.
Ortalli, Gherardo. *Scuole e maestri tra Medioevo e Rinascimento: il caso veneziano*. Bologna: Il Mulino, 1996.
Parker, Robert H. "The scope of accounting history: A note." *Abacus* 29, no. 1 (1993): 106–110.
Ross, James Bruce. "Venetian Schools and teachers fourteenth to early sixteenth century: A survey and a study of Giovanni Battista Egnazio." *Renaissance Quarterly* 29, no. 4 (1976): 521–566.
Rowland, Ingrid D. "Abacus and humanism." *Renaissance Quarterly* 48, no. 4 (1995): 695–727.
Sangster, Alan, and Giovanna Scataglinibelghitar. "Luca Pacioli: The father of accounting education." *Accounting Education: An International Journal* 19, no. 4 (2010): 423–438.
Sangster, Alan, Gregory N. Stoner, and Patricia McCarthy. "The market for Luca Pacioli's Summa arithmetica." *The Accounting Historians Journal* (2008): 111–134.
Segarizzi, Arnaldo. *Cenni sulle scuole pubbliche a Venezia nel secolo 15 e sul primo maestro d'esse*. Venezia: Premiate Officine Grafiche di Carlo Ferrari, 1916.
Taylor, Robert Emmett. *No royal road: Luca Pacioli and his times*. Salem, New Hampshire, Ayer Publishing, 1956.
Thompson, Grahame. "Is accounting rhetorical? Methodology, Luca Pacioli and printing." *Accounting, Organizations and Society* 16, no. 5–6 (1991): 572–599.
Thompson, Grahame. "Early double-entry bookkeeping and the rhetoric of accounting calculation." *Accounting as Social and Institutional Practice* 24 (1994): 40.
Tucci, Ugo. *Benedetto Cotrugli, Raguseo: Il Libro dell'arte di Mercatura*. Venezia: Arsenale Editrice, 1990.
Venice. *Paganinus de Paganinis*. Urbino: Istituto Statale d'Arte, 1509.
Walker, Stephen P. "Accounting in history." *The Accounting Historians Journal* (2005): 233–259.
Walker, Stephen P. "The defence of professional monopoly: Scottish chartered accountants and 'satellites in the accountancy firmament' 1854–1914." *Accounting, Organizations and Society* 16, no. 3 (1991): 257–283.
Willmott, Hugh. "Organising the profession: A theoretical and historical examination of the development of the major accountancy bodies in the UK." *Accounting, Organizations and Society* 11, no. 6 (1986): 555–580.
Yamey, Basil S. "Pacioli's De Scripturis in the context of the spread of double entry bookkeeping." *De Computis-Revista Española de Historia de la Contabilidad* 1, no. 1 (2016): 142–154.
Young, Joni J. "Constructing, persuading and silencing: The rhetoric of accounting standards." *Accounting, Organizations and Society* 28, no. 6 (2003): 621–638.
Zan, Luca. "Writing accounting and management history: Insights from unorthodox music historiography." *The Accounting Historians Journal* (2004): 171–192.

14 The Rise of a Culture of Management Control

The Case of the *Scuola Grande di San Rocco* in the Sixteenth Century

Maria Lusiani, Marco Vedovato and Chiara Pancot

Introduction

This chapter traces the emergence of management control practices in the *Scuola Grande di San Rocco*, as its activity grew in scope and complexity during the sixteenth century.

The *Scuole Grandi* were the main charitable organizations of the Republic of Venice and relevant economic and social actors in the city, as will be discussed. They were a peculiar organizational reality, differing from public institutions, religious bodies, and commercial or manufacturing firms, yet in relation with each one of these actors: they were privately managed, but publicly regulated; they shared a devotional nature, but they were independent from the ecclesiastical administration; they had a non-commercial orientation, but they relied on the profits generated in the city and bestowed to them.

The sixteenth century marked a crucial transition for the *Scuole Grandi*: it is in this period that they moved from the devotional role they were born with to a more widespread and structured social one (providing housing and social assistance to the needy population), in progressive integration with the state (Pullan, 1982). This period of growth is a suitable one for exploring the emergence and the establishment of managerial practices, like forms of planning and control of an increasingly articulated activity.

We focus on the case of *Scuola Grande di San Rocco* (SGSR). Of the six *Scuole Grandi* in Venice, SGSR was probably the richest and most powerful one in the sixteenth century (Pullan, 1982), and—in the future—the only one that would survive through the decline of the Republic of Venice until nowadays. Indeed, even though it developed almost two centuries later than the four established *Scuole Grandi* (Santa Maria della Carità, San Giovanni Evangelista, San Marco and Santa Maria della Misericordia or di Valverde), it grew quickly and achieved a level equal to the others in a few decades. Assuming that this rapid growth and long-lasting success could be explained, at least in part, by an underlying managerial solidity, it is the managerial dimension of SGSR since its foundation (1478) and throughout its first century of activity that we wish to uncover and reconstruct. *What is the inner logic of how SGSR operated and sustained itself over time?* In other words, *what was its underlying business model?*

Empirically, we accessed an extraordinarily rich archive, articulated in two main bodies of hundreds of pieces each, preserved at SGSR's archives and at the State Archive of Venice (for an overview of the contents and structure of this archive, see Sardi & Zanon, 2007). The richness of this archival material has already widely attracted scholarly attention. To our knowledge, extant research mainly covered the topics of SGSR's welfare policies (Pullan, 1982), its real estate and urban planning ventures (Maschio, 1977; Posocco, 1997; Guidarelli, 2003) and its artistic interventions (Valcanover, 1983), or it more generally and thoroughly illustrated the role of SGSR in the social history of Venice (Fortini Brown, 1996; Tonon, 1998, 1999, 2003; Guidarelli, 2011). A contribution from an accounting scholar's perspective not only was missing, then, but also could complement previous research and findings from other disciplines on SGSR. One of the authors spent several months in the archive, scrutinizing a number of primary sources, such as *Registri delle Parti* (i.e., the minutes of the executive board meetings collected in document b. 581, *seconda consegna*), balance sheets and other accounting and administrative documents available for the period under consideration. Additionally, we analysed secondary sources, such as Tonon's meticulous reconstruction of several administrative facts from the first decades of existence of SGSR (Tonon, 1998, 1999, 2003), Pullan's work on the social policy of the Venetian Republic in the sixteenth century (Pullan, 1982) and Ballarin's work on the different forms of financing of SGSR (Ballarin, 1996/97).

With our broad research question in mind, we transcribed and coded all pieces of evidence related to "what SGSR was doing" (main activities); "through which organizational and regulatory configuration" (governance aspects); "with which resources" (its internal economy—i.e., variety of funding sources, amounts and allocations of resources); and "with which forms of control" (planning and control systems and external accountability systems).

Taken together, this provided us with a picture of how the underlying business model of SGSR took shape and changed in its first century of activity, allowing us to advance conclusions on the main factors that favoured its rapid and solid growth—for example, a general accounting accuracy, cautious financial investments, respect for testators' intentions, and credibility to the external parties.

The chapter is structured as follows. After an overview of the broad context of sixteenth-century Venice and of its system of *Scuole Grandi*, the origins and development of SGSR, our focal case, will be presented. Next, we will report our main findings about each one of the dimensions that altogether contribute to reconstruct its business model and to explain its success: main activities, governance aspects, internal economy, planning, control and accountability systems. Our remarks will be then summarized in the concluding section.

The Broad Context: Venice and the *Scuole Grandi* System

At the end of the fifteenth century, Venice was a powerful and aristocratic city-state, with great wealth coming from both its commercial activity and territorial conquests. Its empire extended from the Adriatic coast to the eastern Mediterranean, and through the Po Valley up to the edge of the Duchy of Milan. The Portuguese discovery of the sea route to India had a great impact on the Venetian economy, as its privileged position in the Mediterranean, together with its intermediary role with the Levant, was ultimately compromised. In addition, the navy industry, which constituted the main industrial activity up to this time, was gradually declining. Thus, the crisis of its traditional businesses led to a period of instability and depression on the labour market, which affected the first thirty years of the sixteenth century. Also, recurring epidemics and famines increased the difficult conditions of the city. The problem of poverty and social assistance was therefore clearly a priority for the republic. Not surprisingly, it is in this period that the Republic of Venice started relying heavily on the charitable activity of its system of *Scuole Grandi.*

The term "*Scuola*" identifies a variety of lay devotional associations, which developed in Venice since the thirteenth century. They were divided between *Scuole Grandi* and *Piccole*, in relation to their weight and role in the Venetian society. The *Scuole Piccole* represented the interests of craft guilds or foreign communities, hence variously supporting mutual assistance, defence of common interests and protection of minorities. The *Scuole Grandi* were larger and more powerful confraternities performing more generic charitable roles, all in all playing an important role in connecting the republic to the Venetian population. Each *Scuola* had its own patron saint and held meetings in a church or other annexed locations; was engaged in religious services and collective prayer; and assisted poor and suffering people. They were independent from the ecclesiastical administration, but used to establish relationships with convents, religious bodies and priors for mutual exchange of favours. In general, the rise of this kind of association was concerned with the reforming process of the Catholic Church. Catholics aspired to reconnect with the laity, granting it an active role and new responsibilities inside the community, thereby preventing the dissemination of heretical doctrines (Pullan, 1982, p. 44).

The *Scuole Grandi* managed considerable amounts of economic resources, thanks to the high number of members (500–600 vs 100–200 of the *Scuole Piccole*) paying an annual fee to the confraternity (the *luminaria*) and, particularly, thanks to the legacies from wealthy Venetian citizens and nobles. Officials of the *Scuole* used to take on the responsibility of administering benefactors' estates—namely, landed properties, houses and financial investments—with the aim of providing social assistance to the needy population, especially to confraternity members. By following the terms of the legacy, officials could sell or rent benefactors' properties, or allocate them to the poor. Large amounts of money were invested in public non-profit pawn banks, in the form of bonds issued by the republic, which guaranteed an interest rate up to 5%. In 1538, the government instituted a new system of voluntary loans consisting in temporary deposits in *Zecca*, the official government mint. However, confraternities were more inclined to invest in real estate, since these investments provided better guarantees compared with industrial or financial speculation (Pullan, 1982, pp. 154–156).

Despite their private status, for the social role they performed the *Scuole Grandi* were subject to the supervision of the Venetian judicial authority and particularly to the Council of Ten, one of the major governing bodies of the republic, responsible for state security. In 1401, the Ten assumed the right to approve any change in the *Mariegola* (the statute). In this way, they legitimated their participation in the *Scuole*'s internal affairs and favoured the process of alignment with the republic's interests (Fortini Brown, 1996, pp. 319–320). Initially, the control was limited to the confraternities' meetings and devotional processions to ensure public order and avoid any potential for subversive action; yet, over time, the system of the *Scuole* became also a useful tool for fiscal purposes. On several occasions, throughout the fifteenth century, the state employed financial resources from the *Scuole* (the so-called *galeotti*) to support its military campaigns. From 1509, this practice became official with the institution of a general tax applied to all confraternities, proportionally to the resources they could supply. The Ottoman-Venetian Wars (1537–40 and 1570–73) exerted intense pressure on the city's finances, which needed to be widely supported. Indeed, the *Scuole*'s minutes of the executive board meetings (*Registri delle Parti*) report various decrees about the matter of providing financial and human resources to the republic.

In this context, SGSR represents a peculiarity. Certainly, it shared a common charitable purpose with the other Venetian confraternities, expressed in their *Mariegole*, but unlike others it turned out to have a substantial managerial solidity. The main factors that favoured its success will be analysed ahead.

The Activities (What It Was Doing)

The earliest documentary evidence of SGSR's foundation dates back to 1478, during one of the recurring pestilences afflicting the city. A decade later, the Council of Ten approved the institution of a new confraternity and officially recognized it as a *Scuola Grande* together with the other four already operating in Venice.

An analysis of the board meeting minutes allows us to reconstruct a picture of the main activities SGSR engaged in (Table 14.1). What emerges is a

Table 14.1 SGSR main activities

Type		*Description*	*Illustrative original excerpt*
Devotional and liturgical activity	Prayer, masses, funerals, processions	Brothers were invited to participate in funerals and daily masses, as moments for sharing prayers, remembering dead brothers and offering thanks to God. Also, periodic processions all over the city were organized to exhibit the relics of the saint.	*Mariegola Maior*, Chapter 25: "*Alle essequie delli Frattelli defonti et alle sepolture debbano venir li frattelli di disciplina, tutti sacerdoti e chierici, [. . .] e tutti essi frattelli debbano dir 5 Pater e 5 Ave Marie, overo far elemosina per l'anima di detti defonti*" [b. 581].
Charity	Generic charity (*elemosine*)	Poor brothers were provided with rations of flour (at Christmas and Easter or during famines), daily bread (only for short periods), or with a fixed monthly amount of money (15/20 *soldi*). All brothers were required to contribute economically to charity by paying an annual fee, called *luminaria*.	*Mariegola Maior*, Chapter 13: "*Luminaria almeno di soldi 20 per cadauno siano obligati pagar tutti li frattelli [. . .] et ciò per sostentamento de poveri. Et quelli non havessero dà pagar li sia dato per Amor di Dio*" [b. 581]. 1512, 21 November, in *Capitolo di Banca*: "*Pan, mesi et altre elemosine non possano haver quelli frattelli che haveranno case amore dei, et ciò perché tutti possano essere partecipi de li beneficij della scola*" [b. 581].
	"*Ad pias causas*" (hospitals and religious institutions)	Transfers of money to hospitals and religious institutions were to a lesser extent but equally important and often incentivized by the republic.	1528, 22 March, in *Banca e Zonta*: "*Dell'entrate e beni della Scola per 10 anni solamente sia dato ducato uno al mese all'Ospedal de poveri de a medesima per loro sostentamento*" [b. 581]
	Donzelle	From 1503, the *Scuola* disposed the allocation of dowries to enable *donzelle* (young daughters of poor brothers) to get married. *Donzelle* had to satisfy certain conditions, properly verified by the *degani* in office.	1503, 27 October, in *Capitolo di Banca*: "*Donzelle n°6 siano in avvenire maritate fie di frattelli, cioè una delli dinnari della scola et cinque delle borse de compagni a ducati 10 per una. Con conditione maritandosi in tempo di un anno doppo ballotate [. . .], ma nessun frattello possa metter sua fia se non sarà di anni 16 e se non saranno fie legitime. Ne possa esser messa alcuna fia se il padre non sarà stato in scola anni 5 et haverà tolte tutte le sue luminarie di anno in anno* [. . .]" [b. 581].
	Prisoners	Charity donations were periodically allocated to assist prisoners, especially brothers who were in jail because of debts.	

(*Continued*)

Table 14.1 (Continued)

Type		*Description*	*Illustrative original excerpt*
Social housing		The *Scuola* was deeply engaged in building houses for the needy population, which were assigned for free (*amore dei*) or at low prices. The main areas selected for construction were Santa Maria Maggiore, Castelforte and Santa Maria Zobenigo.	1507, 4 July, in *Capitolo Generale*: "*Case Amore dei per li poveri frattelli di Scola volendo fabricar, sia data facoltà al Guardian Grande e Compagni di convenir con la Serenissima Signoria, o per via di supplica o in altro modo, di comprar il terren hora atterrato in altro loco o in Castel Forte*" [b. 581].
Investments	Bank investments (since 1498)	The *Scuola*'s investments in Monti (public non-profit pawn banks) were aimed at paying the annual rent to Friars Minor. Other forms of bank investments in *Monti*, *Camera d'Imprestidi* or *Zecca* were essentially related to the dead brothers' intentions, expressed in their testaments.	1525, 26 March, in *Banca e Zonta*: "*Dinnari che si scoderanno del capital di ducati 334.20 investiti di soprabondanti di Messe sin'hora, et li prò che si scoderanno de quali va creditrice la Scola per Capital di Monte Novo, siano tutti sempre obligati al livello de li Padri Minori, com'era obligato il cavedal*" [b. 581].
	Real estate investments (since 1529)	Investments included also the purchase of properties in S. Nicolò, S. Stin and Rialto, to be rented to guarantee a safe return.	1545, 21 July, in *Capitolo Generale*: "*Case e botteghe da affittarsi siano dal Guardian Grande, Vicario, Guardian da Matin, degani di mezz'anno poste all'incanto nella scola, e deliberate a quelli più offriranno. E sia il conduttor o conduttori obligati dar buona et idonea pieggiaria e di pagar li affitti alli tempi debiti secondo l'affittanza* [. . .]" [b. 581].
Enlargement and embellishment of own location		Great effort of all brothers was dedicated to the construction and decoration of the church, the chapel and the main location with offices and meeting rooms for the boards.	1489, 26 September, in *Consiglio di Dieci*: "*Chiesa di San Rocco sia permesso alla Scola poter redificar nel loco dove prima era stata principiata alli Frati Minori*". 1491, 6 August, in *Capitolo Generale*: "*Per finir la Chiesa, tutti li frattelli tanto di disciplina quanto che non sono alla disciplina debbano ad ogni richiesta del Guardian Grande e Compagni presentarsi in albergo e sottoscriver un Rodolo, che li sarà presentato, obligandosi alla quantità del dinnaro che li parerà*" [b. 581].

Source: Authors

picture of an institution born with a devotional orientation and increasingly dedicated to charitable, welfare activities, while also increasingly engaged in financial and real estate investments, as a means to provide for its own growth and the redistribution of wealth.

Devotional and Liturgical Activity

Like all other *Scuole Grandi*, SGSR was founded with a devotional intent, in this case devoted to the cult of Saint Roque. Since its foundation, evidence of considerable expenditures and decisions regarding devotional and liturgical activities is there (see also Table 14.3). SGSR's ordinary activity consisted in the organization of daily masses in the Saint Roque Church and funerals for dead brothers, but also of periodic sumptuous processions to the main shrines of the city, in order to exhibit the relics of the saint.[1] During processions, all vestments, standards and candelabras were paraded as a sign of magnificence and wealth; brothers used to wear the traditional *cappa*, pray, sing religious songs and perform public flagellation as a traditional ritual. Processions were thus a central activity for the confraternity, as shown by the high number of brothers with different tasks involved in the organization[2] and the high number of devotees taking part in them, offering money for receiving protection in return.

Charity

The second fundamental activity of SGSR was charity, in various forms. One form was generic charity, in terms of transfer of riches from the wealthier to the neediest parts of the population. The major problems affecting the poor were hunger, rent for housing and marriage of daughters, who could not get married without bringing a dowry. Initially, the *Scuola* could provide support only to its brothers and had limited resources; yet, over time, its activity expanded in scope and number of recipients. The *Mariegola* dwells a great deal on the importance of charity for the confraternity.[3] Many people living in misery needed support, but in turn, they were asked to serve the *Scuola* and pray for the souls of their benefactors. During Easter and Christmas time, or in periods of famine, SGSR used to provide them with flour; from 1535, it provided also a fixed monthly amount of money. Each brother could benefit from only one type of donation at a time, upon a decision of the SGSR governing board, and had to be registered in a specific book to ensure control over the number of people receiving charity.[4]

A second form of charity reported from the extant sources was the transfer of money "*ad pias causas*"—that is, mainly to hospitals and religious institutions. This type of donation was partly regulated by the republic, which addressed the *Scuola* to specific institutions needing financial help.[5]

Third, SGSR took care of the marriage of young women (*donzelle*) who daughters of poor brothers. From 1503, the *Scuola* allocated dowries to those girls who were judged suitable and worthy of receiving it. They had to be at least sixteen years old (their age guaranteed by the father's oath) and behave honestly; the father had to be a member of the confraternity for at least five years; they had to marry no later than one year after the donation. This form of social assistance aimed at preventing them from going down the wrong road ("*andassero a remengo*") because of being economically unable to get married. The *Degano* was charged with verifying their needy condition and their good behaviour; after that, the more deserving ones were elected by the *Banca* by means of the *ballottazione*. Arguably, money for dowries came mostly from the bequests entrusted to the *Scuola*. Indeed, several decrees established a maximum number of dowries to be annually allocated, since the confraternity itself could satisfy only a limited number of requests.[6]

A fourth form of charity donations dealt with prisoners' assistance, especially those who were in jail because of debts.

Social Housing

From 1507, the *Scuola* was also deeply engaged in constructing housing for the needy population. A first set of buildings was erected in Santa Maria Maggiore and the number of accommodations assigned *amore dei* (i.e., for free) grew over the years. More economic resources favoured more investments in real estate and thus more possibilities of providing the poor with housing: in 1527, the *Scuola* started the construction of new sets of houses in Santa Maria Maggiore; in 1538 thirty-two accommodations were registered; and in 1547 the number of people settled in was likely to be five hundred (as reported in the *Registro delle Parti*). Indeed, the *Guardian Grando* asked for the construction of a new well to satisfy the need for water, as many more people were living there. In the same year, the *Scuola* also invested in Castelforte, a terrain set close to the Church of Saint Roque. We know from the *Registro delle Parti* that for the occasion the government took the decision to mobilize part of the funds that were deposited in *Zecca*. Yet, this was not an isolated case: for example, a decree of 3 January 1534 reports the decision to invest the property of the nobleman Maffio Donà in building new houses in Santa Maria Zobenigo.[7]

Investments

SGSR started investing in Monte Novo (pawn bank) in 1498, in order to be able to pay the annual rent to the friars who were originally hosting SGSR. For this purpose, the executive board decreed that all brothers had to provide the *Scuola* with an economic contribution according to their own possibilities, so that the amount collected could be invested in Monte Novo and devoted to paying only the rent.[8] Later, since the sixteenth century, most investments were related to the bequests entrusted to the *Scuola* after the brothers' death. In several cases, they asked specifically to invest their own assets in *Camera d'Imprestidi* or in *Monti*[9] and to address all income to charitable activities—such as transfers of money to poor brothers or prisoners, dowries to young women and construction of houses.

In 1529, the *Scuola* started investing in real estate. Investments consisted in various properties in San Nicolò, San Stin and Rialto (e.g., houses, workshops, unoccupied terrains close to the *Scuola*) that could guarantee a safe return in terms of rent.

Enlargement and Embellishment of Own Location

Pomp and grandeur were the most tangible symbols of prestige, power and quality of the *Scuole*. Therefore, they all dedicated conspicuous amounts of their resources to the embellishment of their location. We have evidence of this attention since the very foundation of SGSR. In 1490, the confraternity returned permanently to Frari, where the construction of the church devoted to Saint Roque had already begun. The priority was clearly to finish the church and to build a chapel to preserve the saint's relics, but the *Scuola* also needed a proper headquarters, where board members could carry out their daily activities and hold their meetings. The governing body established new professional figures in order to manage the construction work: the so-called *Procuratori soprastanti della Fabricha*, including also the *Guardian Grande* (executive director) and *Vicario* (vice-director), who were firstly responsible for raising capital. Fundraising was the main source to sustain not only the construction but also the major decoration works of the *Scuola*. This is the case, for example, of Tintoretto's paintings placed in the rooms of the main location (he worked from 1564 to 1588), largely funded by brothers.

Growth in number and variety of activities certainly means that SGSR had gained a relevant role in society. Indeed, it is clear that the *Scuola* mobilized many resources and needed to respond to a growing set of diverse interests (interests of devotion and prestige, brothers' charity interests, interests of society at large). Clearly, this needed to be well regulated and coordinated.

Governance (the Organizational and Regulatory Configuration)

We will here review how SGSR organized itself to provide these services.

Governing Board

The *Scuola* was led by a small board of eighteen brothers, called *Banca*. The statute (Chapters 2 and 4 of the *Mariegola*), later integrated by a Council of Ten's decree, set out the composition and rules for the members' election. The *Banca* included the *Guardian Grando* (executive director), *Vicario* (vice director), *Guardiano da Matin* (coordination and control functions), *Scrivano* (secretary and bookkeeping functions), twelve *Degani* (functionaries) and two *Messeri* (type of treasurer), and remained in office for one year. This guaranteed a continuous rotation and avoided any potential for establishing positions of power. The *Banca* was in charge of deliberating about spending decisions and ordinary administration. Many of their decisions, especially those concerning important issues, had to be ratified by the plenary assembly, the *Capitolo Generale*, which used to meet twice a year. All brothers participated in these meetings and were invited to listen to the *Guardian Grando*'s annual report, followed by the priests' sermon and the lecture of the statute. Also, during the assembly, new board members were elected out of a range of brothers nominated by the board members who were leaving the *Banca*'s offices. In 1520, the Council of Ten instituted a new government body, called *Zonta*, with the same functions of the *Banca*, and placed it as a functional counterweight. The *Zonta* was composed of twelve members elected by the *Capitolo Generale*, with no family relationship with those of the *Banca*.

Members

All members of SGSR were divided in two categories: the *disciplinati*—that is, those who used to perform public flagellation—and the *esenti*, those who were exempt from it. The statute provides evidence of this separation and points out how the roles should be assigned inside the confraternity. The former group included all poor members, worthy of receiving charity, who offered in return their service in humble works and during procession, masses and funerals. The "exempts" were the richest and privileged members and included governors, nobles and probably brothers with the requirements to access to high government positions. Nobles could join SGSR, but the administrative offices were reserved for the citizen class, normally excluded from the political power of the city. The clergy had an unspecified position inside the confraternity. Priests were excluded from the governing boards and subordinated to their direction, but they could exercise other functions, such as celebrating mass and funeral services, participating in processions and managing the *Mansonerie* for legatees (intercession mass), in accordance with their requirements. Significantly, a decree of 1536 states that the chaplain had to obey the *Guardian Grando*.[10] Brothers not occupying high government positions could hold several other offices. The growth of the *Scuola* and the gradual increase of responsibility led to the creation of new tasks. In 1490, for instance, the *Banca* established the *Procuratori soprastanti della Fabricha* to manage construction work. Another new important role was related to the legacies entrusted to the *Scuola*, rapidly growing in number and substance. The *Commissari* were responsible for their administration. They took part in the *Capitoli* of *Banca* and *Zonta*, whenever important decisions on the assets had to be taken. Also, in 1533 the *Capitolo* approved the institution of the *Reformatori*, tasked with internal control over the use of financial resources to prevent financial waste. The *Reformatori* had a great responsibility, which is why they were chosen among the previous members of *Banca* and *Zonta*.[11]

Commissarìe

Besides this general governing system, SGSR soon added an organization by *Commissarìe*. *Commissarìe* were internal units endowed with their own accountability and financial and managerial autonomy, and organized around a legacy. In other words, they were a type of foundation established by the *Scuola* in order to more directly manage the most important legacies entrusted to it by a dying brother (benefactor).[12] From an analysis of the benefactors' testaments accompanying each legacy, the following main employments of the fund emerged: funds destined for ceremonies (e.g., a benefactor's own funeral service, or annual commemorative masses), construction works for the enlargement of the *Scuola*'s headquarters or its church, financial investments or real estate (houses or land properties).[13]

Each *Commissaria* was managed by a commissioner. Some of them had separate books; for others, accounting data were reported within the *Scuola*'s own books, sometimes in distinct sections. In any case, they all depended on the central administration of the *Scuola* and were required to report periodically on the state of the accounts.

Every decision concerning the *Commissarìe*'s governance or allocation of resources had to be discussed during executive board meetings, in which the related commissioners were invited to participate and had the right to vote. As reported in several decrees about *Commissarìa Donà*,[14] acceptance of any decisions required a two-thirds majority.

Internal Economy (Amounts, Sources and Destination of Resources)

Regrettably, no detailed accounting records from the first centuries of activity survived. However, we accessed a book compiled at the end of the seventeenth century, summarizing the main items of balance sheets for the period 1551–1685.[15] The book displays cash accounting figures of the central administration of SGSR on a simple entry basis. Each year the difference between total inflows and total outflows was balanced by SGSR's own capital, *Conto cavedal* (or *capital*). Note that these were accounts referring to the central administration of SGSR only: they did not include accounting records related to the administration of the *Commissarìe*, mostly held in separate books.

Tables 14.2 and 14.3 report a sample of the main inflow and outflow figures, respectively, for a set of given years of the sixteenth century (1551, 1561, 1571, 1581 and the final recorded year, 1679). Data are approximated and expressed in ducats, the Venetian currency. Together they provide a picture of the internal economy of SGSR.

Table 14.2 Sample of inflows in the sixteenth century

	1551		*1561*		*1571*		*1581*		*1591*		. . . *1679*	
	Ducati	%	*Ducati*	%	*Ducati*	%	*Ducati*	%	*Ducati*	%	*Ducati*	%
Don delle gravezze	8	1	9	0	41	2	15	1	23	1		0
Benintrade dei fratelli (Registration fees)	118	13	421	22	123	7	238	10	131	3	27	1
Intrade da Chiesa (Charity from Church)	87	10	306	16	235	14	501	20	0	0		0
Carità universal (General charity)	125	14	204	11	293	17	278	11	280	7		0
Elemosine in Monte (Donations to pawn banks)	0	0	0	0	3	0	0	0	211	5		0
Intrade de imprestidi (Rents from loans)	120	13	93	5	91	5	279	11	12	0		0
Affitti e livelli (Rents from rentals)	347	38	842	44	386	23	1093	44	1921	46	2373	59
Livello della casa di S. Nicolò/ErediPapaciza per Livello (S. Nicolò)	2		2		2				4		2	
Affitti in Monte	345		840		290		999		1917		2371	
Livelli in Monte					94		94					
Resto maneggio Guardian da Matin (Surplus from Guardian da Matin administration)	4	0	12	1	0	0	50	2	14	0	0	0
Antonio dalla Zucca Guardian da Matin per resto suo maneggio			12									
Zuane Fasini G. da M. per resto suo maneggio							50					
Bortolo de Tomaso forzer fù degan per avanzo de partidori	4											
Cassa conti dal Guardian da Matin per saldo del suo maneggio dell'anno presente									14			
Prelievi da Commissarie (Transfers from *Commissarie*)	0	0	20	1	0	0	25	1	45	1	309	8

Commissaria Bigarelli per officiatura della sua mansionaria			20									
Commissaria Zucca per sua porzion di spese							25		25			
Commisssaria Saba de Piero per sallariati											5	
Commissaria Vecchia per spese									20			
Commissaria Riosa per sallariati											10	
Commissaria Regazzoni per sallariati											10	
Commissaria Giaccomini per sallariati											20	
Commissaria Mauroceni per sallariati											10	
Commissaria Canal per sallariati											20	
Commissaria Capis per sallariati											10	
Commissaria Maccachiò per sallariati											10	
Commissaria Vendramin per sallarriati											10	
Commissaria Gruato per sallariati											20	
Commissaria Alvise Soranzo 1/5 di sua entrata/rendita											24	
Commissaria Todeschi per legato											25	
Eredità Marina Morosini											135	
Entrate diverse (Miscellaneous)	107	12	2	0	530	31	2	0	1505	36	1286	32
Total inflows	917		1910		1702		2482		4142		3995	
Scola San Rocco conto Cavedal = Capital	627		1115		1231		1010		2300		3	

Source: Authors' elaboration from ASV, Sc. Gr. S. Rocco, *seconda consegna*, b. 387

Looking at Table 14.2, we can distinguish three main sources of money: current inflows (from charity and fees), rents from loans or rentals, and transfers from legacies (*Commissarìe*). Initially, the *Scuola* was supported only by charity during religious services ("Charity from Church", ranging between 10% to 20% of total inflows in the sixteenth century) and by generous donations ("General charity", around 11% of total inflows in the period under consideration); as soon as the number of brothers increased, a major source of income came also from registration and annual fees (*benintrade* and *luminarie*, accounting for between 3% and 22% of total inflows in Table 14.2). These current inflows were mainly allocated as follows: (a) to pay the rent to the friars, owners of the premises; (b) one third of all other resources for deposit for extraordinary expenditures (*Banca* and *Zonta* were in charge of choosing whether to invest or spend these amounts);[16] (c) two thirds for current expenditures (salaries, dowries, charity—see also Table 14.3).

Another important source of financing was rents from investments. As we saw, land and housing investments soon became very common for the *Scuola* and probably preferred over financial ones: rents from rentals were the main source of inflows for SGSR, constituting almost half of total inflows in the sixteenth century (Table 14.2).

On top of this, SGSR could benefit from considerable amounts of money and properties coming from legacies. Throughout the sixteenth century, more than sixty bequests can be counted. Some of them supported the *Scuola* directly—namely, it was allowed by testators to employ the money at its own discretion, to cope with current expenses. As for the others, the *Scuola* was usually tasked with managing testators' goods, respecting their intentions—hence the decision of creating separate funds that were more manageable, entrusted to specific commissioners: the so-called and aforementioned *Commissarìe*. Although, as stated, the accounts of *Commissarìe* were kept in separate books, occasionally, transfers from these funds were accorded in order to pay salaries or other ordinary expenses, and these transactions were recorded in the overall balance sheets—a practice that became even more common in later years (Table 14.2).

These resources were mainly dedicated to financing ceremonies, masses and ornaments for the church (Table 14.3 shows how the most consistent item was the set of devotional expenditures, ranging from 38% to 61% of total annual expenditures) and, secondly, to the consistent charitable activity of the *Scuola* (between 15% and 33% for the period under analysis). As we know, a prominent charitable activity of SGSR was the payment of dowries for young women: this item barely appears in Table 14.3 and tends anyway to disappear over time, due to the fact that dowries were progressively supported by *Commissarìe*'s funds and hence accounted for in separate books. Finally, we see how expenditures for *Commissarìe* increase over time, confirming the fact that an increasing number of legacies were entrusted to the *Scuola*.

Table 14.3 Sample of outflows in the sixteenth century

	1551		*1561*		*1571*		*1581*		*1591*		. . .	*1679*	
	Ducati	%	*Ducati*	%	*Ducati*	%	*Ducati*	%	*Ducati*	%		*Ducati*	%
Officio Governatori delle intrade per gravezze	90	6	97	3	381	13	209	6	231	4		431	11
Donzelle per grazie (Dowries for young women)	80	5	85	3	0	0	0	0	0	0		0	0
Elemosine de poveri fratelli (Charity to poor brothers)	503	33	841	28	618	21	747	21	984	15		1598	40
Spese devozionali (Devotional expenditures)	581	38	1211	40	1083	37	1399	40	3949	61		800	20
Cappe di Rassa	124		135		123		91						
Cere in Monte	434		620		490		707		3465			800	
Mansionarij de Chiesa			63		54								
Spese di palme	23								86				
Spese di processioni(e palme)					55								
Spese de Chiesa			393		361		601		398				
Salari (Salaries)	156	10	221	7	252	9	528	15	189	3		428	11
Spese de concieri			47		70		161		101			278	
Spese de salariadi	156		174		182		367		88			150	
Spese diverse (Miscellaneous)	110	7	166	5	211	7	231	7	216	3		49	1
Commissarie	15	1	130	4	350	12	363	10	707	11		472	12
Commissaria Donà per esequi	15												
Commissaria Donà conto prò									80				
Commissaria (Marco) Bigarelli per sua portion d'affitti/per prò			15		15		16		160			16	
Commissaria Marchiò de Antonio (dalla Seda) per prò			15		15		16		16			16	
Commissaria Marchiò de Zuane (Ganassi) per prò			20		20		20		120			15	
Commissaria Cortona per grazie 4/per prò per donzelle/prò di ducati 2000			80		80		80		80			60	

(Continued)

Table 14.3 (Continued)

	1551		*1561*		*1571*		*1581*		*1591*		. . .	*1679*	
	Ducati	%	*Ducati*	%	*Ducati*	%	*Ducati*	%	*Ducati*	%		*Ducati*	%
Commissaria Grimani per prò					120		120		120			90	
Commissaria Zucca per officiatura di mansionaria													
Commissaria Zucca per elemosina di m . . . ducati 4 all'anno si paga al mansionario													
Commissaria Zucca per porzion spetta alla Scola													
Commissaria Vanecca per prò					100		60		60			60	
Commissaria Burato per prò							51		51				
Commissaria Bembo per prò									20			26	
Commissaria Bembo per prozion di spese													
Commissaria Francesco de Zorzi per prò												9	
Commissaria Prè Paulo de Steffano per prò												18	
Commissaria Querini per prò												30	
Commissaria Giacomo Soranzo per prò												15	
Commissaria Capis per prò												1	
Commissaria Canal per prò												66	
Commissaria Fasiol per prò												10	
Commissaria Zorzi per prò												9	
Commissaria Sol per prò												18	
Commissaria Comin per prò												2	
Commissaria Cecilia Soranzo per prò												11	
Altre spese (Other)	9	1	275	9	38	1	16	0	166	3		221	6
Total outflows	1544		3026		2933		3493		6442			3999	

Source: Authors' elaboration from ASV, Sc. Gr. S. Rocco, *seconda consegna*, b. 387

Planning, Control and Accountability Systems

SGSR managed then conspicuous amounts of financial resources. Despite the lacunae regarding the accounting records, through the analysis of the minutes of the board meetings (*Registri delle Parti*) and other documents, we were able to trace evidence of procedural attention for control and accountability since the foundation of SGSR.

Internal Control

Arguably, considerable attention was given by the administration of the *Scuola* to the care of accounting records and to the development of professional roles in charge of bookkeeping, both for the central administration of the *Scuola* as a whole and for the quasi-autonomous administration of the *Commissarìe*.

Regarding the *Scuola* as a whole, a first evidence of attention for internal control derives from the statute itself (*Mariegola*, dated 1490). The statute established, among other things, the role of a *Scrivano*—that is, a person in charge of collecting fees, registering brothers' participation to the meetings, notifying brothers defaulting on their payments and entering all disbursement data in books.[17] Also, the statute established that every six months an overall review of the administration had to be performed by the *Guardian Grando*, *Guardian da Matin* and the *Scrivano*.[18] If this shows the intended care for the administration of the *Scuola*, probably not differing much from similar dispositions in the statutes of the other *Scuole Grandi*, further evidence suggests that this orientation was taken very seriously at SGSR, especially as the *Scuola* grew in activity and complexity.[19]

For example, in 1514 a problem of control is reported: "Scrivani enter data confusingly in the books".[20] This problem of inaccuracy in the accounting data was followed by the decision to establish a second professional (*Quadernier*, literally: "bookkeeper"), exclusively dedicated to the keeping of accounts. The *Quadernier* would be a salaried employee of the *Scuola*, paid five ducats per year as a fixed component, plus a variable component "depending on his operations and his merits".[21]

Furthermore, in 1525, another decree of the SGSR boards stated that the *Scrivano* might not touch the cash without prior control by the designated professional (arguably, the *Quadernier*).[22] This excerpt provides further evidence of the fact that there was a cash balance kept and controlled by a professional *Quadernier*, and an established practice of internal control on the accounts of SGSR overall. Confusion about the functions that the different accounting professionals had in SGSR was probably an issue and an object of continuous interest of the governing boards. Indeed, in 1532 another board decree (applying a disposition of the Council of Ten; see ahead) attempted to provide some order in the accounting functions, naming another role (*Cogitor*), and establishing that the *Scrivano* was in charge of recording the financial transactions, while the *Cogitor* was in charge of transcribing them in the ledger.[23] Although some ambiguity between the roles of *Quadernier* and *Cogitor* persists (Tomasin, 1982), what is clear is that—differently from the *Scrivano*—the *Quadernier* and *Cogitor* had to be professional accountants (*rasonati*), allowing us to conclude that attention to differentiating and professionalizing accounting roles was there.

Regarding the *Commissarìe*, we already noted that the major *Commissarìe* had a separate, internal accountability (own books, own managers—the commissioners—and own bookkeepers). However, the *Guardian Grando* of SGSR was responsible for verifying the accuracy of the books of all *Commissarìe* and reporting any mistakes. The bookkeeper, for his part, was obligated to consign him the books or he was deprived of his salary.[24] Indeed, statements such as "the book of Commissarìa X is confused" and "it must be adjusted by the Quadernier"[25] are not infrequent among the minutes of the *Scuola*. All in all, it is clear that the *Scuola* exercised an important monitoring activity over the accounts of the *Commissarìe* as well.

Evidence of planning practices is scanter in the period under consideration. Yet, while no real plan or other document testifying to a comprehensive periodical planning system was retrieved, several board decrees deliberating about how to spend or allocate the resources can be put together. In some cases, these regarded general dispositions, such as the 1528 rule establishing the allocation of resources among three destinations: (a) rent; (b) two-thirds for current expenditures; (c) one-third for a deposit.[26] In other cases, SGSR was adopting ad hoc dispositions to plan for some particular expenditures. For instance, in 1528 a board decree established that SGSR would donate one ducat to the hospital on a yearly basis and for a period of ten years.[27] Similarly, a (budget) cap of twenty ducats per year was established for devotional expenditures (ceremonies).[28] Also, a sort of "budget" for *donzelle* was deliberated in 1534: the *Scuola* could support no more than eight *donzelle* per year, with ten ducats per *donzella*.[29] Finally, as already noted, the testaments coming along with the major *Commissarìe* constituted a sort of plan of how to spend that fund over time.

Despite the anecdotal nature of these pieces of evidence, the picture that emerges is one of an institution that is particularly attentive to the management of its resources, and to guaranteeing good procedural and substantive control of their uses and records.

External Accountability

As the *Scuole* acquired increasing relevance over time, in terms of administered resources and role played within the Venetian society, they were, not surprisingly, subject to the attention of public regulation. As mentioned, the Council of Ten had supervisory rights over the *Scuole*'s administration and the right to approve any change to the statute. This is important to our aims as it produced interesting evidence of administrative practices suggested by public authorities and an external evaluation of the management of the *Scuole*.

Overall, the available evidence suggests that the financial stability of the *Scuole* was considered of paramount importance by the *Serenissima*'s government. In order to assure a reliable recording of financial transactions, the Council of Ten imposed specific organizational and procedural arrangements. For example, the aforementioned limitation of access to daybooks to *Scrivani* and the prohibition against *Cogitori* touching them was indeed imposed by the Council of Ten in a 1532 pronouncement.[30] The aim of assuring the reliability of accounting information by means of role differentiation is evident also in a 1559 deliberation that required the *Guardiani Grandi* of the *Scuole* to appoint three different *Scrivani*, who should independently record the day-to-day financial transactions.[31]

Likewise, the Council of Ten was determined to prevent the accumulation of seats. In a 1569 pronunciation, it required that those in charge as commissioners in more than one *Scuola* choose one within eight days, resigning from the other positions.[32]

The public interest in the *Scuole*'s administration led also to the establishment of a body of external *Revisori* (auditors). In the year 1558, three citizens not previously involved in the management of the *Scuole Grandi* were elected as auditors.[33] Their task included the identification of any action performed by the *Scuole* against the law or the will of the donors.[34] The number of *Revisori* was raised to six in 1587 and they were elevated to the status of *Magistrato* in 1622.[35]

The aforementioned organizational and procedural arrangements were not sufficient to prevent errors and inaccuracies. On the contrary, in a note dated 1683, the *Revisori* censured the administration of *Scuole Grandi*, highlighting multiple mistakes and abuses. To address such inaccuracies, the *Revisori* directly took charge of the activities necessary to correct the accounts *ex post*, testifying once again how important the *Scuole*'s financial position was. Finally, they designed a set of rules to follow in order to prevent such abuses from happening again. These included the requirement for *Guardiani Grandi* to personally handwrite the accounts and to keep sufficient evidence of transactions recorded to permit a reconstruction of actual cash movements.[36]

Conclusion

In this chapter, we explored the administrative dimension of the *Scuola Grande di San Rocco* in its first century of life, reconstructing the picture of its activity, governance and internal economy, and tracing the accounting practices in use. An understanding of what an organization does and "how it does what it does" is something that remains rather opaque, and even more obscure when it is about organizations of the past. In this chapter, however, thanks to the extraordinarily rich archive we had access to, we could shed some light on the managerial practices of SGSR, which we argue were at least partially responsible for its quick growth.

First, we reconstructed the underlying architecture of this organization, or its underlying "business model", as we would call it today. We showed how devotional activities combined with charity and welfare services in order to attract donations and legacies from wealthy citizens, and how the resulting resources were profitably invested, growing the importance of SGSR for the Republic of Venice.

Most notably, we showed the importance of accounting information and procedures at SGSR, as a fundamental tool to administer an increasing amount of resources and to make decisions about investments and activities to support. Despite the lacunae in the archive of accounting books that SGSR kept, the particular care for control, planning and accountability is proven by the number of decrees through which the governing bodies of the *Scuola* were giving precise guidelines about which books to keep and how to keep them (how to preserve them and copy them, and who was in charge of each function and the professionalization of these roles).

Overall, the extent of legacies endowed directly to SGSR and through the *Commissarìe* system can be interpreted as a signal of the credibility that it was able to build in just a few decades, also thanks to its administrative care and skills. Does this explain the "success" of this case in the panorama of Venetian *Scuole Grandi*? Possibly. What is certain is that the case of *Scuola Grande di San Rocco* testifies to the existence of a culture of managerial control and sensitivity to accounting care in the sixteenth-century Venetian milieu.

Notes

1. Processions were at least four per year during the sixteenth century. In that period, veneration of saints and their relics was an extremely important form of devotion, capable of attracting a high number of devotees. Particularly appealing was the cult of Saint Roque, since he was considered the protector against plague, which periodically affected the Venetian population.
2. See ASV, Sc. Gr. S. Rocco, *seconda consegna*, b. 581, ff. 806–813.
3. See the introduction of the statute reported in Pullan (1982, p. 48).
4. 1553, 8 February, *Parte delli Reformatori approbata in Banca e Zonta*: "*Carità, elemosine et altri beneficij non si possano in modo alcuno concambiar, e chi cambierà sine approbation perda il beneficio che si troverà di havere*" [b. 581].
5. For instance, a 1534 decree allocated five ducats per year for four years to the friars of San Francesco della Vigna; another one established a donation of twenty ducats to the nuns of San Jeronimo, where the nobleman Ser Maffio Donà and his family were buried (see Tonon, 2003, pp. 66–67).
6. For example, in 1534, the executive board stated that the *Scuola* could provide dowries for only eight *donzelle* per year with ten ducats for each one: "*Dell'entrata e beni della Scola non si possano maritar che donzelle n°8 all'anno con ducati 10 per una e non più a tempo di anni tre e non prima, essendo obbligati sempre li Guardiani Grandi che vorranno maritar donzelle per tal conto, metter la parte del detto numero qual s'intenda conforme a quella dell'Eccellentissimo Consiglio*" [b. 581].

7. Decree approved in *Banca e Zonta* together with commissioners responsible for the bequest: "*Che siano col dinaro che resta da investirsi della comissaria stessa in summa di ducati 1400 fabricate dieci case a S. Maria Zobenico, atterrando le vecchie, giusto al disegno del Proto della Scuola*" [ASV, Sc. Gr. S. Rocco, *prima consegna*, b. 19].
8. 1498, 25 May, in *Capitolo di Banca*: "*Sia fatto un rodolo al quale tutti li fratelli della scola che vorranno, si debbano sottoscriver e prometter secondo le possibilità o se non vorrà sottoscriver, dia in contadi. E tutti li dinnari si troveranno, si debbano investir in tanto cavedal di Monte Novo, qual sia conditionato, che non si possa per alcun modo traslar, né vender, né prò né cavedal sotto la maledittione di Dio e di San Rocco. E tutti quelli prometteranno possano esser astretti realmente e personalmente a pagar quello haveranno promesso e sottoscritto* [. . .]" [b. 581].
9. See paragraph *Commissarie*, p. 297.
10. ASV, Sc. Gr. S. Rocco, *seconda consegna*, b. 46.
11. From *Registro delle Parti*, 1553, 23 April: "*Cinque confratelli con titolo di Reformatori siano elletti dalla Banca, e Zonta quali habbino havuto uno delli primi due gradi, debbano riveder tutte le spese che si fanno si delli dannari della Scola, come della borsa propria, e siano tenuti quelle reformar, regolar, corregger, moderar, e scansar in parte o in tutto come li parerà. Non potendosi intrometter nelle parti dell'Eccellentissimo Consiglio di Dieci, né in quelle che dal medesimo sono state approbate, né contro le leggi dello Serenissimo Dominio, che doveranno esser osservate. Possano poner pena a li trasgressori d'esser privi di Scola et di ducati 50 applicati alli poveri. Né possino esser ritornati se non pagati che haveranno essi ducati 50* [. . .]" [b. 581].
12. *Commissarie Grandi* were only four during the sixteenth century, but they managed large amounts of money and properties, and thus needed separate books. The four *Commissarie Grandi* were responsible for the legacies of the nobleman Maffio Donà (1526), Nicolò Moro (1552), Zuane Marzer alla Zucca (1557) and Pietro Cornovi dalla Vecchia (1585).
13. For more details about testaments, see ASV, Sc. Gr. S. Rocco, *prima consegna*, b. 41.
14. See, for example, a decree of 1528 in *Capitolo Generale*: "*Della comissaria sopradetta [Donà] ogni volta si haverà a far ballotatione alcuna, concernente al governo amministratione e dispense della medesima secondo la forma della terminatione del Petition e del testamento, debba intervenirvi il Guardian Grande con li 5 principali alla Banca e li quattro commissari che al presente sono e saranno, e quattro della Zonta da esser deputati di anno in anno, e li quattro defensori che di tempo in tempo si troveranno, e in tutto sono n° 18. Qualo debbano ridursi ogni volta accaderà per detta commissaria far qualche ballotation, dovendo in Guardian Grande farlo saper a tutti che debbano ridursi in tal giorno la mattina a hora terza, e il doppo pranzo a hora di vespro [. . .]. Né alcuna cosa si intenda presa, che con li due terzi delle balle, e le balle delli comissarij siano di differente color, e tutto ciò sarà così deliberato sia valido et essequito. Non potendo operar cos'alcuna contraria al testamento*" [b.581].
15. ASV, Sc. Gr. S. Rocco, *seconda consegna*, b. 387.
16. See the decree of 1527, 20 May, in *Banca e Zonta* (confirmed by the *Capitolo Generale* in 1528) reported ahead, par. 7.1.
17. *Mariegola Maior*, Chapters 2–4.
18. *Mariegola Maior*, Chapter 7.
19. Note that the 1520s are considered to be the most prestigious ones for SGSR, a period of substantial prosperity in the city, reflected in growth in the inflows coming from benefactors and testators, and paralleled by a proportional increase in the charitable activity of the *Scuola* as well (Pullan, 1982).

20. 1514, 15 May, in *Capitolo di Banca*: "*Scrivani mettendo confusamente la scrittura nelli libri della Scola, onde molte cose sono in essi variate e mal messe così in giornal come in libro, invece di scrivan si debba, a tal fontione di scriver in libro, metter un quadernier come hanno le altre scole, e li sia dato di salario ducati 5 all'anno e nell'avvenir poi secondo le operationi e meriti suoi*" [b. 581].
21. Ibid.
22. 1525, 5 August, in *Banca e Zonta*: "*Scrivan non possa girar partita in cassa di dannari che fossero dati et esborsati di sorta alcuna, non contati e consignati in detta cassa, ma debbano prima dalli deputati esser numerati e poi posti in cassa, e fatte all'hora per el scrivan le partite. In pena contrafacendo di ducati 5 da esser scossi da cadauno sarà stato alla Banca*" [b. 581].
23. 1532, 3 September, in *Banca e Zonta*: "*Cogitor non possa scriver più nelli giornali le casse così della Scola, come delle comissarie, nelle quali solo il Scrivan debba scriver quelle, ma solamente debba esso cogitor metter le partite del Giornal nel Libro*" [b. 581].
24. ASV, Sc. Gr. S. Rocco, *seconda consegna*, b. 581.
25. Ibid.
26. 1528, 22 March, confirmed by the *Capitolo Generale*: "*Per conto di entrate della Scola debba cadaun G. Gr., di tutti li dinnari che scoderanno di elemosine si troveranno in Chiesa, di benintrade e luminarie, dati o lasciati per la fabrica o di qualunque altra sorte eccettuati quelli destinati per il livello dei Frati, [debba] far un deposito del terzo, e si debbano poi quelli spender o investir come parerà di tempo in tempo alla Banca, e Zonta e Capitolo General.*" ASV, Sc. Gr. S. Rocco, *seconda consegna*, b. 581
27. 1528, 22 March, in *Banca e Zonta*: "*Dell'entrate e beni della Scola per 10 anni solamente sia dato ducato uno al mese all'Ospedal de poveri de a medesima per loro sostentamento* [b. 581].
28. 1533, 2 August, in *Banca e Zonta*: "*Delli dinnari della Scola per l'avvenire non si possano spender più in palme di ducati 20 all'anno, non computade quelle del Serenissimo. E se li Guardiani da Matin vorran far pompa a spender di più, debbano spender de suo, non potendo li G. Gr. esborsar più di ducati 20. E se più entreranno, non possano li scrivani farli partita di più di essi ducati 20*" [b. 581].
29. 1534, 3 January, in *Banca e Zonta*: "*Dell'entrata e beni della Scola non si possano de cetero maritar che donzelle n°8 all'anno con ducati 10 per una e non più a tempo di anni tre e non prima, essendo obbligati sempre li Guardiani Grandi che vorranno maritar donzelle per tal conto, metter la parte del detto numero qual s'intenda conforme a quella dell'Eccellentissimo Consiglio*" [b. 581].
30. 1532, 3 September, *Terminazione de Capi del Consiglio de Dieci*: "*Scrivan della Scola e successori siano obbligati tenir e scriver nel giornal le casse della Scola com'anco delle comissarie che sono e pervenissero, et in detto giornal scriver alla Banca tutte le cose per giornata si faranno sì di spender come di scoder. Né il cogitor possi scriver in detto Giornal, ma solo metter le partite del giornal in libro. E perché potrebbe trovarsi il scrivan per qualche impedimento abiente onde non potesse scriver a tempo debito, supplisca in tal caso il Vicario o uno delli Degani di mez'anno chi meglio parerà al Guardian Grande fino che il Scrivan possa scriver lui tenendo una vacchetta com'è il solito. E li libri e giornali così della Scola come delle comissarie star debbano nella Scola, né possano essere portati fuori salvo a qualche offitio o per qualche urgente bisogno sempre con licenza del G. Gr. e non altrimenti. In pena a chi non osserverà la presente terminazione di privation de la Banca, e della Scola*" [b. 581].
31. 1559, 9 September, *Terminazione delli Presidenti Deputati del Collegio delle Scole Grandi de Battudi di Venezia*: "*Che li Guardiani Grandi de le Scole*

debbano deputar tre che scrivano per la sua Scola in tre zornali cadauno separatamente" [ASV, Sc. Gr. S. Rocco, seconda consegna, b. 9].

32. 1569, in *Consiglio di Dieci*: "*Che li comissarij de le Scuole Grandi non possano haver più d'una commissaria e chi ne havesse più d'una termine giorni otto dichiari l'unica che intende esercitare, refutando le altre, saldando le casse sue [. . .]. Non possano tener li soldi delle dette commissarie nelle sue habitazioni, ma in cecca nel deposito de particolari, o nel scrigno particolare da esser tenuto o in cecca ovvero nel Banco publico*" [b. 9].
33. 1558, 15 October, in *Consiglio di Dieci*: "*Ellettione di tre cittadini che non habbino havuto manizo di dennari delle Scole Grandi li quali rivedano le casse delli Guardiani Grandi delle medesime dall'anno 1540 in qua*" [b. 9].
34. 1620, 31 August, in *Consiglio di Dieci*: "*Reellettione de sei Revisori sopra le Scole Grandi per la revisione delli maneggi di Guardiani Grandi et altri carichi di cassa, et di tutto ciò fosse stato operato contro le leggi a dispositione de testatori*" [b. 9].
35. 1622, 31 October, in *Consiglio di Dieci*: "*Istituzione del Magistrato Eccellentissimo degli Inquisitori e Revisori sopra le Scuole Grandi con la stessa autorità del Tribunale del Consiglio dei Dieci*" [b. 9].
36. 1683, 7 February, *Terminazione degli Inquisitori e Revisori sopra le Scole Grandi*: "*Gli Eccellentissimi Inquisitori e Revisori sopra le Scole, intesa la deligente relatione del fedel Alvise Vespesiani Raggionato del Magistratto di S.S.E.E. sopra la revisione commessali dal presente Ecc.mo Magistrato degli ultimi undici guardianati della veneranda Scola di San Rocco, et havuto maturo riflesso alli disordini multipli e considerabili scoperti nell'apontadura delli Giornali e Quaderni di essa Scola e rapresentati nella di luj pontuale e distinta scritura; conoscendo necessario d'ordinare a dar regola per l'agiustamento de li errori raccolti da esso Vespesiani e di preseguire insieme le forme da praticarsi in avenire per togliere gli abusi che sono invalsi e per incaminare la scritura con le cautelle necessarie . . . Decretano doversi da chi s'aspetta praticare e eseguire quanto segue:* [. . .]

    - *che il Guardian Grande presente e li sucesori habbino a scriver di proprio pugno, in conformità con il scontro, tutte le partite tanto del scosso, che del speso, e ogni altra che occorrerà chiamando tutti li fondamenti delle medesime cioè le polizze ricevute, instrumenti, fedi, carte e ogni altro necessario requisito, esprimendo in esse partite di loro numeri e conservando in una filza li mandati o boletini autentici delle grazie delle donzelle, principal fondamento delli pagamenti stessi;*
    - *che nel quaderno e nelle partite del medesimo siano poste le circostanze e particolarità necessarie scrivendo per lettera entro delle partite tutte le summe de denaro. E perché li quaderni si attrovano al fine ordenario S.S.E.E. che ne siano fatti altri, perché habino a scrivere per il Guardian Grande presente, e successori e così anco li giornali, quali libri tutti debino essere numerati e segnati in ogni carta col segno della Scola e delle otto Commissarie rispettivamente*" [ASV, Sc. Gr. S. Rocco, *seconda consegna*, b. 114].

References

Ballarin, S., 1996/97, *Finanziamento delle Scuole di devozione: la Scuola Grande di San Rocco dalla fondazione alla fine del Cinquecento*, Università degli studi di Venezia Ca' Foscari, anno accademico (tesi di laurea).

Fortini Brown, P., 1996, *Le scuole grandi in Storia di Venezia, 5, Il Rinascimento*, Società ed Economia, Roma.

Guidarelli, G., 2003, *Una giogia ligata in piombo: la fabbrica della Scuola Grande di San Rocco in Venezia, 1517–1560*, Quaderni della Scuola Grande Arciconfraternita di san Rocco, n. 8, Ed. Helvetia, Venezia.

Guidarelli, G., 2011, *Le Scuole Grandi e il rinnovamento urbano a Venezia tra XV e XVI secolo: il caso della Scuola Grande di San Rocco (1489–1560)*, in Boucheron, P. & Folin, M. (a cura di), *I grandi cantieri del rinnovamento urbano: esperienze italiane ed europee a confronto (secoli XIV–XVI)* Coll. de École française de Rome, Roma.

Maschio, R., 1977, Investimenti edilizi nelle Scuole Grandi a Venezia, in Guarducci, G. (a cura di), *Investimenti e civiltà urbana. Secoli XIII–XVIII. Nona settimana di studi dell'Istituto internazionale di storia economica "Francesco Datini"* Le Monnier, Firenze.

Posocco, F., 1997, *La Scuola Grande di San Rocco, la vicenda urbanistica e lo spazio scenico*, Ed. Biblos, Cittadella.

Pullan, B., 1982, *La politica sociale della Repubblica di Venezia. 1500 1620, 1, Le Scuole Grandi, l'assistenza e le leggi sui poveri*, Il Veltro, Roma.

Sardi, F. & Zanon, E., 2007, *L'Archivio della Scuola Grande di San Rocco a Venezia, Atlante iconografico*, a cura dell'Archivio di Stato di Venezia e della Scuola Grande di San Rocco, Marsilio Editori, Venezia.

Tomasin, G., 1982, *La nascita della professione contabile nel XVI secolo a Venezia*, Istituto per la Revisione e l'Organizzazione, Venezia.

Tonon, F., 1998, *Scuola del Battuti di San Rocco, Documenti sulle origini e illustrazione dei Capitoli delle Mariegole*, Quaderni della Scuola Grande Arciconfraternita di San Rocco n. 5, Ed. Grafiche Veneziane, Venezia.

Tonon, F., 1999, *La Scuola di San Rocco nel Cinquecento, attraverso i documenti delle sue Mariegole*, Quaderni della Scuola Grande Arciconfraternita di San Rocco n. 6, Ed. Grafiche Veneziane, Venezia.

Tonon, F., 2003, *Devotissima Scuola e Fraternità del Glorioso Messier San Rocco, Registro delle Parti 1488–1549*, Quaderni della Scuola Grande Arciconfraternita di San Rocco n. 9, Ed. Grafica & Stampa, Marghera-Venezia.

Tonon, F., 2013, *Il secondo Registro delle Parti della Scuola Grande di San Rocco, 1542–1577*, Quaderni della Scuola Grande Arciconfraternita di San Rocco n. 11, Ed. RanaRossa, Marghera-Venezia.

Valcanover, F., 1983, *Jacopo Tintoretto e la Scuola Grande di San Rocco*, Ed. Storti, Venezia.

15 *Al Nome De Dio E Bon Guadagno*—[1] Pacioli, Venice, Education, and Bookkeeping

Alan Sangster

Introduction

This chapter looks at the Venetian context of the commercial world for which Pacioli wrote *Summa Arithmetica*, his compendium of practical mathematics containing his game-changing treatise on double-entry bookkeeping. This was a world of powerful families, *colleganze*, *mude*, barter, slaves, multiple currencies, complex mathematics, and much-needed mercantile training and control. A world where business far outstripped the ability of one man, where mercantile education was paramount, and insufficient. The nature of this education is described—what it was, how it was delivered, and by whom; along with what it most notably lacked, instruction in double-entry bookkeeping. Extant examples of fifteenth-century Venetian bookkeeping from the account books of the Soranso *Fraterna* (1406–1434), Andrea Barbarigo (1418–1449), and Jachomo Badoer (1436–1440), along with the instructional manual of Marino de Raphaeli (1475), are used to construct a view of bookkeeping in the style of Venice. The meaning of the 'Venetian method' of bookkeeping and what Pacioli intended when he described his method as being 'in the style of Venice' are also considered. Pacioli's purpose in preparing his treatise, his pedagogy, and the content—his syllabus—is presented and discussed; the manner in which he taught bookkeeping is contrasted to those of his predecessors and his successors; and his impact is analysed, both on future authors of manuals of bookkeeping instruction and on the manner in which accounting was practised.

Pacioli, Venice, and Bookkeeping

Luca Pacioli was born in Borgo San Sepolcro, in eastern Tuscany, between October 23, 1446, and June 19, 1447. Orphaned in 1459, he spent five years under the guardianship of wealthy merchant and local politician Folco di Giovanni di Canti Bofolci (Ulivi, 2009, pp. 29–30). In 1464, experienced in mercantile practice, the gifted student of mathematics, who was schooled in the humanist grammar school tradition and in both practical and theoretical mathematics by the renowned artist Piero della Francesca (c.1430–1492), travelled from his hometown to further his studies in theoretical mathematics at the *Scuola di Rialto* in Venice. He stayed for six years in the *Giuedecca*, working for the merchant Antonio Rompiasi. Pacioli would never again re-enter mercantile life, but what he had learnt, both theoretically and practically about business and business practices, gave him the tools to alter forever both how practical mathematics was taught and how double-entry bookkeeping was taught and used.

Thirty years after first entering the city, Pacioli returned to Venice for the printing of his two-volume compendium of practical mathematics, *Summa de Arithmetica Geometria Proportioni et Proportionalita*. Even at over 600 pages, the book sold well for thirty years, educating hundreds of merchants and teachers of future merchants in the more advanced mathematical tools of their trade. Its teachings were disseminated across Europe as merchants took copies home from their travels to the Italian markets, where work mixed with the pleasure of visits to booksellers to view their latest offerings. Buried towards the back of the first 450-page volume of Pacioli's book was a short, 27-page instructional manual on double-entry bookkeeping. It was the first of its kind—the first ever printed manual on this subject. As there was previously a lack of teachers to instruct students of double entry, it filled a void that made it possible for use of the method to spread (Sangster, 2018). In brief, it was a game changer in the history of commerce, providing all merchants with the knowledge to operate their accounting system using double entry.

At almost the same time that the first printing of Pacioli's *Summa Arithmetica* sold out, printed texts began to appear containing only instructions in bookkeeping. The first, by Giovanni Tagliente, was published in 1525. It owed no debt to Pacioli, instead continuing the instruction tradition of the bookkeeping masters that is exemplified by de Raphaeli's manual of 1475. However, with the next book to be printed, Manzoni's in 1540, the tradition was set aside and Pacioli's syllabus formed the spine of bookkeeping texts, arguably to the present day. His presentation of the method of double-entry bookkeeping was also adopted in these books, so standardizing the approach and establishing the Venetian approach to double entry, with its linked journal and ledger, as the way it was practised from that point forward. But what of the circumstances that gave rise to Pacioli's decision to publish *Summa Arithmetica* and include in it a manual on double-entry bookkeeping?

Merchants, Mercantile Education, and Bookkeeping in the Fifteenth Century

Mercantile education in northern Italy can be traced back to the thirteenth century, when a system of schooling in *abaco* (i.e., mercantile or practical) mathematics emerged. The earliest known teacher of *abaco* was Leonardo Pisano, more commonly known as 'Fibonacci', who is also credited with writing the book that gave rise to this form of instruction, *Liber abaci* (1202). Where previously education in mathematics had been of a theoretical nature in grammar schools and church schools, the *abaco* schools provided future merchants and craftsmen with the maths they needed day-to-day. In Tuscany, this education lasted approximately two years and came after a grammar school education. In much of the rest of northern Italy, including Venice, *abaco* was an alternative to a grammar school education (Grendler, 1989, 2002). By the mid-fifteenth century, it is estimated that as many pupils attended Venetian *abaco* schools as attended grammar schools (Sangster et al., 2008).

Bookkeeping was seldom taught in a classroom setting. Instead, it was learnt in merchant apprenticeships, apprenticeships that often began before or during the period when *abaco* was being learnt. It was assumed in the *abaco* classes that pupils were aware of bookkeeping terminology, and it can be seen in some of the mathematical examples and calculations they had to perform. It should be noted that the same terminology—*de dare* (debit), *de avere* (credit), *saldo* (balance), for example—was also in use in single-entry bookkeeping. Thus, the fact someone was learning bookkeeping was sufficient for them to acquire knowledge of the terminology and should not be taken as evidence that all *abaco* pupils knew how to do *double* entry. In fact, they did not, for reasons that can be deduced from the circumstances surrounding Pacioli's inclusion of a manual on double-entry bookkeeping in *Summa Arithmetica* (Sangster, 2018).

There were thousands of merchants in northern Italy at this time. Most stayed at home, but some travelled to conduct their business, often to the fairs scattered across Europe. What they all had in common was a need to record the transactions into which they entered. Although there were exceptions, as in the case of joint ventures or *colleganze* on the galley fleets (*mude*) of Venice, this recording was not done primarily to identify profit. It was done so as to be able to determine obligations, which is why a single-entry system was, in many cases, more than sufficient to meet mercantile bookkeeping needs, especially when merchants were stay-at-home sole proprietors not engaged in international trade.

However, from the mid-twelfth century, the economy began to expand as international trade brought new products and access to new markets. Banks began to appear, loans became a part of trade, and the difficulties of transporting large amounts of coins and bullion fuelled the expansion of an international system of exchange that began through the Knights Templar (c. 1119–c. 1320) and then in the emerging banking systems of Europe. Specie in this period was variable in quality and inconsistent in value and there was not enough to support the growing Italian economy. Merchants reacted by developing or adopting an economic system based on credit, which is why there was a need to maintain a record of obligations (Sangster, 2016).

Notaries were often involved in validating credit agreements but the system was not universal and, by the late fifteenth century, had become the exception, not the rule. Disputes could come down to the word of individuals, one against the other, but a more efficient means to resolution involved a reversion to the principles of Roman times, when a properly maintained ledger was accepted as proof of the existence of an obligation (Martinelli, 1974, p. 178). In Venice, the courts based their deliberation on the ledgers produced from journals kept in double entry and other source documents. In Florence, double-entry journals of the type attributed to Venice and described by Pacioli were not maintained. A merchant's double-entry ledger was the starting point for the deliberation of the courts.

In both locations, the key was the use of double entry. Single-entry ledgers had no more legal status than notes on scraps of paper because they could not prove anything unless they were used to generate the entries to be recorded for the other side of each entry, so converting single entry into double entry. Double entry had this status that single entry lacked because of the rhetorical power of a double-entry ledger, which was derived from its being a closed axiom-based system (Demski et al., 2006, p. 452)—it is a 'closed' system because the entries within it involve only accounts held within it. That is, no entries are made from an account in the system to something outside the system. With an axiomatic-based system, if you accept the axioms upon which it is built, you must accept the output it produces. As a result, when information is produced from a double entry it is an example of demonstrative logic, the only accepted method for demonstrating scientific proof until the seventeenth century (Klarreich and Moncrief, 2002). This is why the courts accepted a double-entry ledger as evidential of the truth. However, while it was of this nature, the axiomatic foundation of double entry was not articulated and was not formally recognized until much later.

The double-entry ledger therefore holds all the knowledge of the individual account entries and balances that are necessary to prove whatever is required to be proved—"*[double entry] may be made to prove anything*" (Cayley, 1894, p. 19). Thus, if a debtor disputed a balance on his account, the merchant's ledger would be consulted and the balance checked. If a debtor disputed the amount of an entry, the merchant's ledger could, again, be consulted to identify the amount involved and its validity could be confirmed by the contra entry within the ledger, plus any external evidence or documentation. In the absence of anything but the word of the debtor, the merchant's position would be upheld. However, while some merchants used double entry, many did not.

Venetian Merchants and Double-Entry Bookkeeping

The earliest extant ledger of a merchant operating in Venice dates from the 1380s. It reflects very clearly the use at that time of banks and credit in business. The merchant involved, Tomasso Talenti, used the bank of Gabriele Soranzo (Mueller, 1997, pp. 19–20), a name that features in all three of the well-known extant Venetian double-entry account books that have survived from the first half of the fifteenth century. The best known of these books are those of Andrea Barbarigo (1418–1449) and Jachomo Badoer

(1436–1440), but there are also the less frequently mentioned books of the Soranzo *Fraterna* (1406–1434) and the reconstructed ledger of the same company (1410–1417). The Soranzo *Fraterna* is an interesting case, for it represents a partially extant ledger from the company and a reconstructed ledger ordered by the court that demonstrates the incomplete and, at the very least, misleading nature of the ledger provided by the *Fraterna*. This case has long been misunderstood by accounting historians but has recently been analysed and its true nature revealed (Ryabova, 2018).

In a relatively small world, as it was then, it is little surprise that both the other merchants for whom we have extant account books had dealings with the Soranzo *Fraterna*. Andrea Barbarigo employed them as his agents in Syria and also used their bank in Venice for some of his financial affairs (Lane, 1945, 1949). And the first three accounts in Jachomo Badoer's ledger are for Pietro Soranzo.

Badoer travelled to Constantinople in 1436 and his ledger covers the three years he spent in that city, acting as a commission agent for other merchants and as a merchant in his own right. His activities

> centred on cloths, copper, furs, slaves, indigo, pepper, salted fish and pork, lead, silk, soap, scammonee, wax, glass, olive oil, tin, velvet, wine, ginger, sugar, hemp for cordage, linen, alum, wood, cloves, incense, damask, millet, iron, various dyes and other items of less importance.
>
> (Var, 1976, p. 17)

In contrast, Barbarigo was based in Venice. He specialized in cotton import, manufacture, and export. While selling some cloth and other items locally, including tin, he made extensive use of the *mude*, the Venetian galley convoys, to buy and sell his wares. He operated merchandise expense accounts, a practice seen in de Raphaeli's manual of 1475 and, like both Badoer and the merchant portrayed by de Raphaeli, he engaged in barter, such as in May 1492, when he received ginger and cinnamon in exchange for tin he had sent on the *muda* to Alexandria (Lane, 1949). In many ways, Barbarigo is the real-life persona of the merchant in de Raphaelli (1475): staying at home, using *mude* to import and export, with some processing, and selling some wares locally, as well as abroad. His journal, ledger, and the index to his ledger have survived.

The Journal

In his analysis of fifteenth-century account books, Frederick C. Lane (1944, p. 158) expresses the view that there was a range of variation in Venetian practice, some of which did not reflect the Venetian method as presented by Pacioli. One that did was the journal of Andrea Barbarigo that starts in January 1430[2] and is the earliest extant journal for which the ledger has also survived. It opens with an entry to the debit of the cash account for receipt

+ In the Name of Christ, 1430, on the 5th of January, in Venice +		
18 7	*By* cash *To* ser Francesco Balbi and Brothers, counted by ser Nicolo de Bernardo and Brothers and ser Mateo and ser Zuan de Gregorij in the name of ser Armano for the balance due for saffron, 4 ducats, 3 denari, 16 piccoli. Value...	L – s 8 d 3 p 16

Figure 15.1 An example of an entry from Barbarigo's journal
(Translation by Martinelli, 1974, p. 870, amended by the author)

in cash of an amount that had been paid into his bank account. It related to the balance due arising from a sale of saffron that had been paid into his account in the bank of Francesco Balbi and Brothers (Figure 15.1).

This entry follows what is acknowledged to be the Venetian sequence:

1. The account to be debited;
2. The account to be credited;
3. The details;
4. The amount.

The date is outside and above the entry. To the left of the entry are two numbers, one above the other. The upper number is that of the left-side page on which the debit entry can be found in the ledger. The lower one gives the location of the right-side page on which is entered the credit. To the right of the entry is the amount translated from the currency of the transaction to the currency of the account. To confirm that the entry has been posted into two accounts in the ledger, it is scored across diagonally twice from bottom to top with slanting lines (//). The first line starts at the bottom-left of the narrative and ends in the middle-top of the same section. The second starts in the bottom-middle of the section and ends at the top-right. In all respects, this is the style of entry described by Pacioli in 1494, including the invocation, the date, and inclusion of the place where the journal is maintained, all entered at the beginning of the book, and each entry is underlined to signal that it is complete.

Neither Jachomo Badoer nor the Soranzo *Fraterna* appear to have kept a journal in this style. Both refer to a journal in some places in their ledgers but what Badoer described as a journal was a petty cash book, possibly containing chronological details of his personal transactions (Lane, 1944, p. 161). Lane's brief discussion of whether the Soranzo *Fraterna* used a Venetian-style journal as described by Pacioli (ibid., pp. 158–159) focused on the *libro nuovo*, which we now know was a court-generated document, not a working ledger (Ryabova, 2018). However, in a footnote, he noted that a journal was used by the Soranzo *Fraterna*, but not for all entries. Thus, neither the Soranzo *Fraterna* nor Jachomo Badoer maintained and used a journal in the manner described by Pacioli, but they did maintain double-entry ledgers.

The Ledger

The entries in Barbarigo's ledger begin with:

1. The name of the account;
2. The verb (representing debit or credit);
3. The date;
4. The name of the contra account;
5. A description, including the amount in the money of the transaction;
6. The number of the page where the entry in the contra account can be found;
7. The amount in the money of account entered in the monetary column to the right.

Again, this is the style of ledger entry described by Pacioli. There is no difference between Barbarigo and Pacioli in the sequencing within the entry. Even the inclusion of the account name and the verb is consistent: they are included in the first debit entry and the first credit entry in an account, but omitted thereafter. The only difference between them in presentation is that Barbarigo placed the page number of the contra entry in a separate column between the narrative and monetary columns, a sequence and practice also adopted by the Soranzo *Fraterna*. Badoer also followed this sequence, but placed the page number of the contra entry at the end of the narrative rather than in a separate folio column, which is how this is presented in Pacioli's treatise.

With one exception among these books, the debit entries are on the left-facing page of the ledger and the credit entries are on the right. The exception is the original ledger (*libro vecchio*) of the Soranzo *Fraterna*, which records both the debit and credit entries on a single sheet, with the debit entries on the left half of a sheet and the credit entries on the right. Thus, a left-side page contains the debit and credit entries for an account and a right-side page contains the debit and credit entries for a different account.

An important feature of these double-entry account books is the use of a 'money of account'—*lire di grossi* in the case of the Soranzo *Fraterna* and Barbarigo, and the Byzantine *hyperpyron*[3] by Badoer. The use of a money of account is an essential feature of double entry and one that distinguishes it from tabular accounting of Roman times that many see as the precursor to the double-entry system—see, for example, Zerbi (1952) and Martineli (1974). Without a money of account, individual accounts and the entire double-entry ledger can balance only if all transactions are in the same currency.

Moneys of Account

Until much later, moneys of account were almost exclusively 'ghost currencies'—that is, they did not physically exist. In Venice, up to the fifteenth century there were several moneys of account, but this stabilized during that century, leaving two principal moneys of account in use: the silver-based *lire di piccoli*, which had three denominations: *lire*, *soldi*, and *piccoli* in the ratio 1:20:12; and the gold *lire di grossi*, which comprised *lire*, *soldi*, *denari*, and *piccoli* in the ratios 1:20:12:32. The *lire* and *soldi* in these two systems shared the same name but had very different values. However, the *piccolo* in both moneys of account had the same metallic-linked value, facilitating translation from one system into the other, which meant that the *lira di grossi* = 32 *lire di piccoli* (Lane and Mueller, 1985, pp. 290–291).

In order to know how to convert transaction moneys into moneys of account, a link is required to 'real' money. From the late 1320s, moneys of account were linked to the silver *soldino* coin (later called *soldo*) but its value fluctuated, not just because the price of silver fluctuated but also because the Venetian government manipulated the official (minimum) exchange rate to reward officials, reduce expenditure, or impose hidden taxes. In 1456, the situation stabilized at 1 ducat = 124 silver *soldi*, an exchange rate that was maintained into the first quarter of the sixteenth century. This rate made one *lira di grossi* equal to ten gold ducats (Lane and Mueller, 1985, p. 338), which is the rate in use in Figure 15.1.

By converting obligations to and from the money of account, the fluctuating values of real coinage were eliminated from the gains and losses incurred in a transaction. That is, when a sale took place, its sale price, 'x', was converted to 'y' *lire di grossi*. When the debt was paid, the cash received, 'z', was equal to 'y' converted at the current exchange rate for the coinage received. In terms of their underlying value in gold or silver, 'x' = 'z', irrespective of how the value of the original coinage recorded in the sale transaction had changed. As a result, the value of the amount received by the seller was the same in gold or silver as it would have been had payment been received when the original transaction occurred. However, this did not prevent disputes when debtors wanted to make payments in the original transaction amount (Lane and Mueller, 1985, pp. 354–355).

The system varied over time and this situation in the fifteenth century had evolved into existence over the previous two centuries. Wholesale prices of goods and services were quoted in moneys of account but the moneys of account changed over time. For example, at the beginning of the fifteenth century, wholesale prices for wool, cotton, and metals were quoted in *lire di grossi*, whereas *lire di piccoli* were used for wheat, and ducats were used for pepper (Lane and Mueller, 1985, pp. 357–358). But ducats were becoming more commonly used, as is reflected in both de Raphaeli's manual of 1475 and Pacioli's of 1494, and also in the few surviving Venetian account books from the fifteenth century.

El modo de Vinegia

These surviving account books are the evidence we have of *el modo de Vinegia*, the Venetian method. It is a small sample, but there is a consistency within them and with Pacioli and de Raphaelli that suggests we can be confident that Pacioli presented a way of maintaining records of transactions that had matured at least 50 years before he wrote his treatise. It differed from the method elsewhere, particularly in Florence, but no double-entry bookkeeping manuals are known to have been written describing the system used there—none, that is, other than Pacioli's. In his treatise Pacioli presented not only the method of double entry used in Venice but also the method of double entry for the ledger used in Florence.

Luca Pacioli's Presentation of Double Entry

From the surviving fifteenth-century account books, we know that the Venetian system of double entry that Pacioli described in Chapters 1–35 of his treatise was how bookkeeping was done in practice. This is what he meant by '*el modo de Venegia*'. It was a simplified description so, for example, the complexities of some typical transactions, such as bills of exchange, were avoided by not explaining how to record them, but this was a manual of instruction in the basics of the method. It laid the foundation and provided the necessary framework from which merchants and bookkeepers could develop their skill to embrace and include those more complex transactions in their account books. The absence of any adjusting entries is no mystery either. This was a period when issues like depreciation, bad debts, and allowances for doubtful debts were rarely recorded—examination of the many surviving Tuscan account books of this period confirms this, and Venetians did not close their account books very often so they had even less need to consider such adjustments as being of importance.

In the main part of his manual, Pacioli implores merchants to close their ledger annually. As mentioned previously, this was not Venetian practice and it is difficult to believe that there was a well-developed method in use in Venice when closing ledgers was the exception, not the rule. But closing ledgers and reopening them on a relatively regular basis were Tuscan practice. The Tuscan technique Pacioli described in the supplementary part of his treatise was very well developed and detailed, as is evident in extant ledgers from that period in the Florentine State Archive. As such, it was as much state-of-the-art as the Venetian method for making entries Pacioli described in Chapters 1 to 35. But Pacioli's Tuscan method was superior in terms of closing and opening a ledger to the one Pacioli presented as the Venetian approach in Chapter 34. The Tuscan approach involved the use of a trial balance. The Venetian approach did not. Instead, in Venice, a double entry was made for each balance, one into the account in the old ledger and the second into the same account in the new ledger (Pacioli, 1494, c. 208r–v).

Frederick C. Lane (1944) drew attention to how Andrea Barbarigo used a much more sophisticated way to close the ledger than was described by Pacioli, though he did so only in 1431, 1435, and 1440. When he closed his ledger in 1435, possibly because he was about to get married, he did not switch to a new ledger, but reopened the account balances carried forward in the same ledger as before (ibid., pp. 172–174). Pacioli did not explain how to create a trial balance in Chapters 1–35 of his treatise. He only described how to prepare a *Summa Summarum*, a much cruder form of check that simply determined whether all entries had been recorded twice, once in debit and once in credit.

Pacioli's description of the Tuscan method of maintaining, closing, and opening a ledger appears only in the first additional chapter after Chapter 35. In that supplementary chapter, in addition to describing how to prepare a trial balance (*bilancio*) and then transfer the balances into a new ledger, Pacioli included how to check the entries and how to mark up the balances. It was much closer to the sophistication of the method adopted by Andrea Barbarigo than that Pacioli himself presented in Chapter 34. However, Barbarigo's approach involved opening an account for the trial balance, entering all the balances, then copying it to the new ledger with the debits and credits transposed, and then making a second entry for each amount on the opposite side to that in which it is shown in the trial balance copied into the new ledger. That is, if the furniture account has a debit balance of 200 lire, it is recorded in the first trial balance as a debit, in the second as a credit, and then entered as a debit in the furniture account in the new ledger. This differs from Pacioli's trial balance only in that Pacioli's trial balance was written only once and was on a sheet of paper rather than in the ledger. However, it is clear from the surviving fifteenth-century account books that preparing a trial balance and even closing a ledger were very seldom done in Venice, so it is not surprising that Pacioli described a very basic approach in Chapter 34.

The inclusion of the supplementary chapter detailing Florentine practice was a natural extension of his exhortation to close the ledger regularly. He had concluded his description of the Venetian method. Now, he showed a better way to close the ledger. However, it was not explained in the text why it was being presented, and it was presented using the layout for ledger entries as followed in Tuscany, not Venice. The same was the case for the banking ledger entries on the final page, which further compounded the mystery. The most likely explanation for the form in which it was presented is that the printer used an early draft of that material rather than the final version prepared by Pacioli. Given that Pacioli was revising the Venetian material and the banking entries in November 1493 (Sangster, 2012) and that the printer used that revision, it seems that the supplementary Tuscan chapter was in a separate document that, for whatever reason, was not included in its final form. Presumably that unused version explained why it was included and also what the relevance was of the example Tuscan banking ledger entries on the final page to the rest of the treatise.

The Origin of Pacioli's Treatise

The naming of a cluster of towns close to Sansepolcro and other places mentioned in the treatise, plus the manner in which they are referred to, suggests very strongly that the main part of the manual—the Venetian part presented in Chapters 1–35—was originally written to be used to teach merchants and craftsmen, both present and future, in Sansepolcro. It also includes references to business practice in Perugia and Venice that Pacioli would have been aware of from his time in both cities; and, we know from one specific example concerning a bank, that some of the treatise had not been updated since 1482 (Nobes, 1995, p. 383). Furthermore, in 1491, he was commanded by his order to close his school in Sansepolcro. Whatever its source, as previously mentioned, the manual was updated in Padova in November 1493 and then given to the printer in Venice (Sangster, 2012).

The inclusion of Tuscan practice in the supplementary part of the treatise has always been considered surprising and out of place. Yet, if we consider all that we know about Pacioli, it is possible to develop a reasonable hypothesis concerning the origin of this material. Pacioli would have used double entry in Venice in the 1460s. That is, he would have learnt how to use the Venetian method. Before this, Pacioli spent five years in the household of a merchant in Sansepolcro. That is where he would have first learnt about bookkeeping and, being in Tuscany, the form of accounting was most likely Tuscan. Pacioli also spent many years in Florence during his lifetime, including 2–3 years he spent there in the 1480s, gathering material for *Summa Arithmetica*. The *abaco* material he was consulting was mainly held in the collections of merchants, not in libraries (Heeffer, 2017). If there was a place where he may have found a manual on double entry, it was in those personal collections. He was also an avid collector of mercantile-related knowledge and was seeking to find as much as possible that was relevant to mercantile activities (Sangster, 2018). Who else would he have spoken with about Tuscan bookkeeping practice if not the merchants whose manuscript collections he was consulting? It was what he did with artists and other craftsmen (Ciocci, 2009), so why not merchants?

Did he find and use a Tuscan manual in the 1480s or did he have his own from his childhood? It is a question that cannot be answered. But had he acquired knowledge of double entry before he went to Venice, it would have increased his chances of a position with a merchant in Venice, a position that gave him the means to study mathematics at the *Scuola di Rialto*. On the balance of probabilities, that is the most likely scenario for where he first learnt of the Tuscan method of bookkeeping.

It is not just Pacioli's inclusion of Tuscan bookkeeping practice that has been questioned. The main, Venetian, part of Pacioli's treatise—Chapters 1–35—is also considered unusual, not just for its simplicity but also for its use of a completely different pedagogy from that used in the manuals of the bookkeeping tutors.

Pacioli's Pedagogy[4]

As a teacher, Pacioli was first and foremost a teacher of mathematics, not bookkeeping. Initially a teacher of practical mathematics in the *abaco* tradition, between 1480 and 1493 he reinvented himself as a theoretical mathematician. In doing so, he transformed the teaching of algebra from rote-based to founded on principles. Underpinning this transformation were the 15 years he spent studying Euclid's *Elements*. Euclid had transformed the teaching of his predecessors by representing geometry using an axiomatic approach whereby all problems could be solved from first principles, using five axioms and five propositions. Pacioli took his *abaco* manual that he completed in 1480 and those of other *abaco* masters and rewrote the algebra in a similar style, presenting 'keys' to specific problem types that he stated were correct and could be applied to solve any problem of this type. He did not identify these as axioms in the modern sense, but they served the same purpose. Mathematicians in the sixteenth and seventeenth centuries evolved his approach into modern algebra, which, like geometry, can be defined axiomatically.

From a mathematical perspective, double entry is an application of the simplest algebraic equation, 'x = y'. It was natural, therefore, for Pacioli to teach it in a similar way to how he taught algebra. In the course of a few pages of his treatise, he sets down five axioms and two postulates that together define how double entry works. As with his coverage of algebra, he never considers them as a whole and never defines the method by presenting them all in one place—to him they would have been obvious and no more necessary than it had been in his coverage of algebra. But they are what guides anyone who then uses his treatise to learn how to do double-entry bookkeeping for transactions, just as his algebra keys guided the learner of algebra. Pacioli's axiomatic definition of double entry is presented in Figure 15.2.

❒ **All transactions involve two elements: an item exchanged and a form of settlement {Axiom 1}** *(Chapter 9)*
❒ **One element is debit and the other is credit {Axiom 3}** *(Chapter 11)*
❒ **Debit = credit {Axiom 4}** *(Chapter 12)*

⇒ The amount of the form of settlement = the amount of the item exchanged [Theorem 1]

❒ The amount of the form of settlement = the amount of the item exchanged [Theorem 1]
❒ **All forms of settlement can substitute for each other {Axiom 2}** *(Chapter 9)*
❒ Cash received is a debit <Postulate 1> *(Chapter 12)*
❒ Cash is a form of settlement *(Chapter 9)*

⇒ If a form of settlement is received, it is a debit [Theorem 2]

⇒ And the item exchanged is a credit [Theorem 3]

❒ The amount of the form of settlement = the amount of the item exchanged [Theorem 1]
❒ **All forms of settlement can substitute for each other {Axiom 2}** *(Chapter 9)*
❒ Cash given is a credit <Postulate 3> *(Chapter 18)*
❒ Cash is a form of settlement *(Chapter 9)*

⇒ If a form of settlement is given, it is a credit [Theorem 4]

⇒ And the item exchanged is a debit [Theorem 5]

❒ **The entries in the money column are to be in one currency only {Axiom 5}** *(Chapter 12)*

Figure 15.2 Pacioli's axiomatic definition of double entry

Pacioli's Presentation of His Instructions

Pacioli prepared readers of his text by advising them in the introduction to his treatise (1494, f. 198v) that they must study the material that preceded it in *Summa Arithmetica*—that is, arithmetic and algebra: "*e chi di questa parte non fosse bene armato: la sequente in vano li sarebbe*" (and who has not understood this part well will read what follows in vain). This was not an attempt to 'sell' the rest of his book—it was his belief that knowledge of these subjects was essential if you were to become a good bookkeeper. Why he believed that this was the case is not surprising when it is considered that Pacioli perceived double entry as something that can be reduced and described using the simplest form of algebra. That is, he believed that if you know how to manipulate algebraic equations, you should be able to do double entry from first principles. This is how he taught it.

The exemplar-based approach of the bookkeeping tutors has come down to us in de Raphaeli (1475), Tagliente (1525), and Casanova (1558). The approach was largely ignored by Pacioli. He begins his treatise by echoing the sentiments of Cotrugli (1458) about what makes a good accountant and why using double entry is beneficial. He then continues in the same way as de Raphaelli and Tagliente, with an *inventario* being used to open the account books of a new merchant, but even at that point, he adopted a different approach—he did not show how to record creditors, even though the final item in his *inventario* was his creditors. This small omission helped to reinforce the constant 'debit-asset-credit-capital' mantra between assets and capital when the former are introduced to a business. Pedagogically, compared with the tutors, it made things clearer and left less room for confusion.

The rest of Pacioli's manual is completely different from the approach of the tutors. He presents instructions and examples of how to make entries in both the journal and the ledger, often together in the context of one transaction. But his treatise lacks examples, the core of the method of the tutors. It covers only entries for purchases and tells the reader that now that he knows how to record purchases, he can work out the entries for sales himself (Pacioli, 1494, c. 204v). In many places in the treatise, he stops and says that he has said enough. Apart from illustrating how to make the opening entries in the journal from the *inventario*, he does not provide more than one example of how to record anything. It is an extremely minimalist approach. Nevertheless, it is sufficient for anyone to learn how to maintain double-entry account books *nel modo de Vinegia*.

Unlike de Raphaeli and Tagliente, Pacioli focuses mainly upon the principles of double entry, laying down a syllabus and sequence to be followed in covering how to record assets, purchases and expenses, barter, and brokers' fees. He never extends his instruction to the specifics of voyage accounting or marine insurance, nor to specialist topics equivalent to accounting for a silk shop or construction of a building, which are both covered in de Raphaeli, nor to marriage and dowry accounting, as covered in Tagliente, and his coverage of bills of exchange is simply to mention them and move on. However, he does cover what would be useful to any small businessman seeking to keep his account books in double entry. In the rest of his text, Pacioli focuses on the form of settlement used for each purchase transaction and for each expense disbursement. As cash, or whatever other form of settlement used, was an outflow rather than an increase, the form of settlement was consistently credited and the other element, the item exchanged, was debited, so reinforcing the mantra that anything given out as a form of settlement was a credit, which meant that the item received in exchange was a debit.

In terms of examples, Pacioli was parsimonious. He included 25 for the journal—7 from the *inventario* plus 18 others scattered across his treatise. These were generally placed in groups focused upon something specific, such as commission, barter, partnership capital, expenses, branch accounts, and banking; there are 19 example entries for the ledger. Two illustrate how to transfer a balance to a new ledger. All the others are linked to the example journal entries.

In addition, Pacioli presents instructions on how to close the existing books and then open up a new ledger and journal, additional details on which de Raphaeli and Tagliente are silent, though de Raphaeli does make a brief comment about closing the ledger on the final page of his text, and how to make entries in a ledger is mentioned (in an incomplete way) in the introduction by both authors. The reason for those two texts not including more material on the ledger was that both de Raphaeli and Tagliente were teaching only the journal. Pacioli was the first to print a manual on double-entry bookkeeping, and he was also the first we know of to include the ledger in an instructional manual on this topic.

Pacioli's Place in the Stream of Venetian Bookkeeping Manuals

De Raphaeli's manual, or one very like it, was the catalyst for Pacioli's text and all those that followed up until at least the middle of the seventeenth century. This is first revealed by considering how the treatise from 1475 begins its instruction in double entry: it explains what a debit entry is and what a credit entry is and then uses a balance sheet that has no capital account and so does not balance—an *aventario*—as the basis for entries in a new journal. Pacioli adopted the same approach and includes examples at that point, and in the rest of his treatise, that are very similar to some of those to be found in the earlier treatise. In doing so, they were presented by Pacioli to illustrate the techniques of double entry, not in order to reinforce learning. In contrast, the aim of the authors who included exemplar entries after their instructions was to reinforce learning. Pacioli made it very clear in his treatise that doing so was unnecessary (Pacioli, 1494, cc. 200r, 203r, 204r–206r).

Pacioli's approach was one he had established after more than 20 years as a teacher of algebra. In adopting it, he is acknowledged as having revolutionized the teaching of that subject, moving it from rote learning based on innumerable examples to learning from principles (Ciocci, 2011; Heeffer, 2012). This is also what he did with double entry (Sangster, 2011): his approach was based upon establishing principles to guide the learner in the entries to make, not upon rote learning using exemplar entries to reinforce the initial instruction. Pacioli's approach was not copied by any of the authors who published bookkeeping texts after Pacioli. They all preferred to use the exemplar approach as presented in de Raphaeli's treatise from 1475.

Pacioli's contribution to accounting education and the development of accounting practice lies in content and sequence. As illustrated in Geisjbeek's comparison (1914, pp. 29, 31) of the technical topics of bookkeeping and accounting and the sequence in Pacioli's treatise of those topics with those in Manzoni (1540) and Pietra (1586), and also in the Dutch treatise of Ympyn (1543), Pacioli established a syllabus of issues concerning the technique of double-entry bookkeeping to be included in a manual of this type. As commented by Geijsbeek (p. 29), "Carefully note the coincidence that even the order in which the chapter is given [in each of these texts] practically remains unchanged from that of Pacioli."

All the Venetian manuals, including de Raphaeli, Pacioli, and Tagliente, begin their instruction using the technique of a balance sheet missing a capital account (called an *aventario* or *inventario*) as the basis for entries in a new journal. In the first of these texts to be published after Pacioli, Tagliente (1525) virtually copied the first two pages of the manual from 1475 (Rossi, 2013)[5] and then inserted instructions or explanations before each of his exemplar entries, many of which were similar or on similar themes to those in the earlier treatise. Tagliente did not include any part of the syllabus of bookkeeping instruction presented by Pacioli, and there is no indication that any of the rest of Tagliente's manual was based upon Pacioli's. The next instructional text was by Manzoni (1540). Its pedagogy was based on the treatise from 1475, but it also drew from Pacioli by taking his syllabus and sequencing and covering it to an equivalent level of detail in the instructional part of the text. This was the basis for virtually all the bookkeeping manuals published until the mid-seventeenth century: Pacioli's technical syllabus and sequence combined with the bookkeeping method and the approach to teaching from 1475. This is illustrated in Figure 15.3.

Thus, while Pacioli's text was undoubtedly influential in defining the Venetian method taught thereafter—*el modo de Venegia*—it was the method presented by de Raphaeli in 1475. Similarly, the concept of including a great many exemplar entries once instruction had finished, which dominates those texts printed after Pacioli's, was the one presented earlier by de Raphaeli. It is, therefore, to de Raphaeli's treatise from 1475 that we should look primarily for the foundations of modern accounting and instruction in double-entry bookkeeping, not Pacioli. Nevertheless, Pacioli can be credited with extending his treatise beyond the journal to include the ledger *nel modo de*

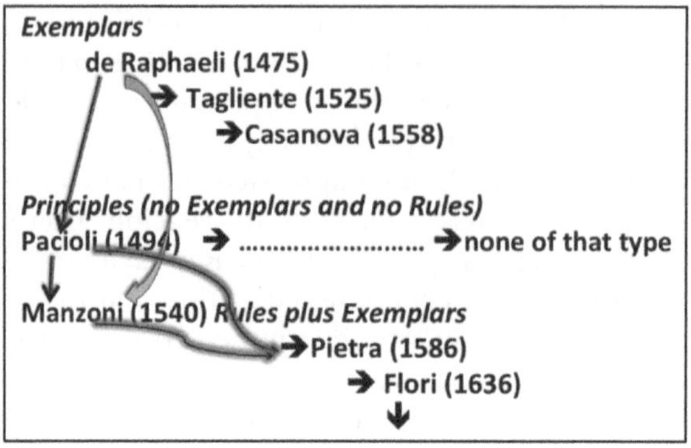

Figure 15.3 The influence of Pacioli and de Raphaeli on the other Venetian printed manuals of double-entry bookkeeping

Venegia, so presenting the foundations upon which later authors presented their coverage of that book, and with establishing the syllabus and sequence of items covered in the instructions of the method.

Notes

1. "In the name of God and good profits"—this is the opening statement in the ledger of Jachomo Badoer (1436–1440), a Venetian merchant based in Constantinople.
2. In the modern calendar, this was 1431. The Venetian year began at the time on 1st March.
3. The *hyperpyron* is most commonly referred to as the *bezant*, *iperpero*, or *perpero*. It was divided into 24 *keratia*, or *carati*. Badoer's transactions involved a range of currencies and the exchange rates used varied. For the gold ducat, it was usually around three *iperperi* six *carati*.
4. For a fuller explanation of this section, see Sangster (2018), upon which this section is based.
5. Dr Franco Rossi is a noted paleographer, former vice-director of the State Archives of Venice, and former director of the State Archives of Treviso.

References

Casanova, A. (1558). *Specchio lucidissimo nel quale si vedeno essere diffinito tatti i modi . . . che si deve menare nelle negotiamenti della Mercantia*. Venice: Comin da Trino.

Cayley, A. (1894). *The Principles of Book-Keeping by Double Entry*. Cambridge: Cambridge University Press.

Ciocci, A. (2009). *Luca Pacioli tra Piero della Francesca e Leonardo*. Sansepolcro, AR: Aboca Museum Edizioni.

Ciocci, A. (2011). "Le matematiche tra Medio Evo e Rinascimento," in Hernández-Esteve, E. and Martelli, M. (eds.), *Before and after Pacioli*. Sansepolcro, Italy: Centro Studi "Mario Pancrazi", 253–285.

Cotrugli, B. (1458). *Libro de Larte dela Mercatura, copy made 1475*. National Library of Malta. Libr. XV: cc. 1r–98v.

Demski, J. S., FitzGerald, S. A., Ijiri, Y., Ijiri, Y., & H. Lin. (2006). "Quantum information and accounting information: Their salient features and conceptual applications." *Journal of Accounting and Public Policy*, Vol. 25(4), pp. 435–464.

de Raphaeli, M. (1475). *La riegola de libro*. National Library of Malta. Libr. XV: cc.101v–121r.

Geijsbeek, J. B. (1914). *Ancient double entry book-keeping*. Denver: Geijsbeek.

Grendler, P. F. (1989). *Schooling in Renaissance Italy: Literacy and Learning, 1300–1600*. Baltimore: The Johns Hopkins University Press.

Grendler, P. F. (2002). *The Universities of the Italian Renaissance*. Baltimore: The Johns Hopkins University Press.

Heeffer, A. 2012. The Genesis of the algebra textbook: From Pacioli to Euler. Almagest Vol. 3(1), pp. 26–61.

Heeffer, A. (2017). Personal communication.

Klarreich, N., & J. W. Moncrief. (2002). Euclid and His Contributions. Mathematics, January (July 2, 2017). Available at www.encyclopedia.com/education/news-wires-white-papers-and-books/euclid-and-his-contributions

Lane, F. C. (1944). *Andrea Barbarigo: Merchant of Venice, 1418–1449*. Baltimore: Johns Hopkins Press.

Lane, F. C. (1945). "Venture accounting in medieval business management." *Bulletin of the Business Historical Society*, Vol. 19, pp. 164–172.

Lane, F. C. (1949). "Ritmo e rapidita di giro d'affari nel commercia veneziano del Quattrocentro," in *Studi in onore di Gino Luzzatto* 4 vols., Vol. 1, Milan: Dott. A. Giuffre, 254–273.

Lane, F. C., & R. C. Mueller. (1985). *Money and Banking in Medieval and Renaissance Venice* (Vol. 1). Baltimore: Johns Hopkins University Press.

Manzoni, D. (1540). *Quaderno doppio col suo giornale, nouamente Composto, & diligentissimamente ordinato, secondo il costume di Venetia* . . . Venetia: Comin de Tridino de Monferrato.

Martinelli, A. (1974). *The Origination and Evolution of Double Entry Bookkeeping to 1440*. Ph.D. Dissertation, North Texas State University.

Mueller, R. C. (1997). *The Venetian Money Market: Banks, Panics, and the Public Debt, 1200–1500*. Baltimore, MD: Johns Hopkins University Press.

Nobes, C. (1995). "Pacioli's Tractatus: A note on a mystery and a review of some commentaries." *Accounting, Business & Financial History*, Vol. 5(3), pp. 379–384.

Pacioli, L. (1494). *Summa de Arithmetica Geometria Proportioni et Proportionalita*. Venice: Paganino de Paganini.

Pietra, A. (1586). *Indrizzo de gli Economi*. Mantova: F. Osanna.

Rossi, F. (2013). Personal correspondence with the author concerning the analysis he had made of these two texts.

Ryabova, M. (2018). "The account books of the Soranzo Fraterna Venice (1406–1434) and their place in the history of bookkeeping." *Accounting Historians Journal*, forthcoming.

Sangster, A. (2011). "Luca Pacioli, school teacher and university professor," in Hernández-Esteve, E. and Martelli, M. (eds.), *Before and after Luca Pacioli*. Sansepolcro: Aboca Edizioni, 457–472.

Sangster, A. (2012). "Locating the source of Pacioli's bookkeeping treatise." *Accounting Historians Journal*, Vol. 39(2), pp. 97–110.

Sangster, A. (2016). "The genesis of double entry bookkeeping." *The Accounting Review*, Vol. 91(1), pp. 299–315.

Sangster, A. (2018). "Pacioli's lens: God, Humanism, Euclid, and the rhetoric of double entry." *The Accounting Review*, Vol. 93(3), pp. 299–314.

Sangster, A., G. N. Stoner, & P. McCarthy. (2008). "The market for Luca Pacioli's Summa Arithmetica." *Accounting Historians Journal*, Vol. 35(1), pp. 111–134.

Tagliente, A. (1525). *Considerando . . . Diversi Mercanti Et Molti Artesani Li Quali Sanno Le Sue Mercantile Ne Le Loro Botege . . . .* Italia: Venetia.

Ulivi, E. (2009). "Documenti inediti su Luca Pacioli, Piero della Francesca e Leonardo da Vinci, con alcuni autografi." *Bollettino di Storia delle Scienze Matematiche*, Vol. 29(1), pp. 9–154.

Var, T. (1976). "The ledger of Giacomo Badoer (1436–39) and the eastern trade." *Accounting History (Journal of the Accounting History Society of the ICAEW)*, Vol. 1(2), pp. 6–22.

Ympyn, J. (1543). *Nieuwe Instructie Ende Bewijs der Looffelijcker Consten des Rekenboeckse ende Reckinghe te houdene nae die Italiaensche maniere*. Antwerp: Jan Ympyn Christoffels.

Zerbi, T. (1952). *Le Origini della partila doppia: Gestioni aziendali e situazioni di mercato nei secoli XIV e XV*. Milan: Marzorati.

16 On the Scope and Significance of the Venetian Accounting Innovations From the Sixteenth Century

Pedagogic Practices, Accounting Statements and Modes of Thinking and Acting

Ann-Christine Frandsen and Keith Hoskin

Introduction: On Studying Accounting Innovations as Ways of Thinking and Acting

The medieval and Renaissance Italian innovations in accounting and management forms are rich and significant, and particularly so, we shall argue here, in their Venetian manifestations. We focus on three particular innovations in this chapter, all with a significant Venetian dimension, and consider in particular their development from the sixteenth century on. In so doing, we seek to identify some key similarities, or even homologies, that run across these innovations, and thereby to pose the question of how these innovations—each of which takes place in a different setting and enacts or makes visible a different aspect or form of accounting—may nevertheless be understood as *three aspects of one more general development*: a development which we shall characterize here at its most general level as being a new 'mode of thinking and acting', which remakes both humans as subjects and the objects which they now come to name as central or regular features of thought, knowledge and so of the world as lived.

We also, having developed that possibility, seek to ask a related or consequent question—namely, how far are these innovations, once thought of as three aspects of one transformation in our human ways of thinking and acting, to be read as anticipations or precursors of modern forms of accounting? Or to put the question at a more general level: do these innovations lead or graft directly onto the modern, or is there a *subsequent* shift in our ways of thinking and acting, of such a transformative kind as to lead to us as human subjects today thinking about both the scope and the specificity of accounting differently than in this Venetian past? Which leads to a more general question still: to what extent are we therefore engaged as subjects in constructing and inhabiting a series of different structures and processes through which accounting is practised and accounting statements articulated in historically differentiable ways, in different eras and places? In other words, how are we to read both the past and the present of accounting?

These are of course big questions which we can only begin to raise here; at the same time, we see the Venetian manifestations of the three innovations we consider here as particularly significant or fertile for engaging in the form of historical and conceptual analysis that we pursue here. As an approach, it draws significantly on the historical-theoretical work of Michel Foucault, and in particular on the growing recognition that in his work he not only engaged extensively in analyses of governmentality or disciplinary power in a general sense, beyond the specific spheres of accounting and management, but also focused specifically and intensively on the specific questions of how accounting and management take differing forms in different times and places, with a particular focus on how management and accounting combine to constitute both a modern form of 'governmental reason' and a new kind of 'economic truth' which places limits on how far the reach of such a reason may extend, but also correlatively on how this modern form emerges out of earlier and systematically different modes of managing and accounting (e.g., Bento da Silva & Quattrone, 2017; Hoskin, 2017; Hoskin & Macve, 2016; Quattrone, 2009). We shall draw on these rereadings of Foucault's forms of analysis in what follows, as one means of contributing to or extending the historical but also conceptual rethinking of accounting and management that may now open up, but of participating in the still unfolding rethinking of our human past, and of its relations to our human present, that has increasingly become a hallmark of historiography in general and accounting historiography in particular.

This, it is increasingly now seen (e.g., Bento da Silva & Quattrone, 2017; Hoskin, 2017), also entails undertaking a form of 'bottom-up' analysis of the kind that Foucault increasingly stressed was necessary if we are to keep a sufficient analytical focus on how different historically constituted modes of governing are constructed. As he put it when he first introduced the term 'governmentality' in the 1978 lecture series, *Security, Territory, Population* (Foucault, 2007), it is necessary that we should avoid the 'overvaluation of the problem of the state' as manifested either in 'the lyricism of the cold monster confronting us' or 'in reducing the state to a number of functions like . . . the development of the productive forces or the reproduction of the relations of production' (2007: 109).

Therefore we seek here to follow the recommendation he makes at the conclusion of the final lecture in the series, to study the state not as 'a transcendent reality' but 'on the basis of men's actual practice, on the basis of what they do and how they think', so that we engage in 'analyzing the state as a way of doing things, [the state as a way of thinking]' (Foucault, 2007: 358, where the phrase in square brackets is restored from the original French text). More particularly we draw upon a recent study (Hoskin & Macve, 2016) which pays close attention to precisely how accounting was used in the governing of the French state, as developed by Colbert in the service of

Louis XIV, in the system widely described as 'governing by inquiry' (e.g., Miller, 1990; Soll, 2009). The analysis traces, for instance, how the use of double-entry bookkeeping (DEB) was restricted to activities such as the forensic audit of the tax payments delivered to the king by tax farmers, as the appointed agents of royal power. But it also traces back this form of governing to the initial emergence of 'inquiry' as a new form of critical reading, in its Latin formulation '*inquisitio*', developed initially in the twelfth century in the cathedral schools in the area around Paris, and first articulated, so far as we know, by Abelard in his *Sic et Non* (c. 1130 CE) as a new form of critical reading of theological commentaries on the Bible, which scholars well knew were riddled with contradictions. Abelard's genius was to propose, in *inquisitio*, a systematic form of reading which, if followed rigorously, would resolve these contradictions and so establish the truth 'beneath the surface', so to speak, of scholarly contradiction.

To approach this form of 'inquiry' as a practice having such transformative effects on our thinking and acting is not something new. Both Erwin Panofsky, in *Gothic Architecture and Scholasticism* (Panofsky, 1957), and Michel Foucault, in his 1973 set of lectures, 'Truth and Juridical Forms'—lectures which precede and foreshadow many of the themes developed in *Discipline and Punish* (1977)—independently make significant claims for inquiry's significance, even if their more detailed analyses differ in some key particulars. So Foucault sees 'inquiry' as first embodying and then disseminating what he calls a new and 'rather characteristic form of truth in our societies' (Foucault, 2001: 4), while Panofsky proposes that with inquiry there emerges a new 'mental habit' (1957: 21), understood in 'its precise Scholastic sense as a "principle that regulates the act", *principem importans ordinem ad actum*'. The Panofsky treatment of inquiry is that its underlying principle is the production from discord of a new and unassailable concord (*concordantia*) since it constitutes a truth that is methodically arrived at through the invariant and methodical system of *inquisitio*. This entails first identifying and enumerating all the relevant passages which contain contradictions for resolving, and then laying them out in a new frame of reference where they can be systematically subjected to a sceptical textual criticism and thus reconstituted and interrelated as a set of consistent and correct observations and arguments. As Abelard himself puts it, 'through doubting (*dubitando*) we come to inquiry (*inquisitio*); through inquiry we perceive the truth (*veritatem*)'.

It is this new approach to establishing the truth that Panofsky then suggests becomes the new 'mental habit' which spreads across not just scholarly settings but also by 1300 out into the fields of architecture, and in particular into the architecture of the Gothic cathedrals. Taking wing initially in a restricted sphere—across 'the period from around 1130–40 to 1270 and within the "100 mile zone around Paris"' (1957: 21)—by the 1300s it becomes embedded in intellectual discourse generally.

Foucault does not see the connection to Abelard; however, he sees the same general progression, whereby inquiry as an old legal or juridical form of truth-seeking is then remade in the same general period, 'the middle of the medieval era' as he puts it (2001: 5), into a new form of truth. As he puts it, 'What is called the inquiry—the inquiry as practiced by philosophers of the fifteenth to eighteenth century, and also by scientists, whether they were geographers, botanists, zoologists or economists—is a rather characteristic form of truth in our societies' (Foucault, 2001: 4). But he also, later in this set of lectures, sees it as having other dimensions that go with the articulation of truth as he contends:

> The inquiry is precisely a political form—a form of management and the exercise of power (the phrase given in French is mistranslated in the English text as 'a form of power, management and exercise') (*une forme de gestion, d'exercice de pouvoir*) that . . . became, in Western culture, a way of authenticating truth, acquiring and transmitting things that would be regarded as true.
>
> (Foucault, 2001: 52)

Furthermore, whereas Panofsky focuses purely on 'inquiry' as practice that constitutes a new (and still potent) way of thinking and acting, Foucault then goes on to suggest that there is a second form of truth which emerges around 1800 to displace or supplement the inquiry: examination. As he goes on to say at that time: "other forms of analysis were invented . . . rather curious and particular forms of analysis that I shall call *examination*' (2001: 5, emphasis in the original).

Hoskin and Macve (2016: 237) suggest that this is a significant form of analysis on the part of both Panofsky and Foucault, whose commonalities outweigh their slightly different emphases. What they take up from Panofsky, and from the form of analysis developed in their initial work together (cf. Hoskin & Macve, 1986), is that the new practice of inquiry does not develop initially as a new *juridical* form of truth, but as a new scholarly practice, whose focus is epistemological and whose purchase on our thinking and acting is *pedagogic*. Young scholars in the generations after Abelard, studying in the institutional settings of twelfth-century cathedral schools and then of the new universities, internalize and then extend the inquisitorial method.

But additionally, their analysis suggests that this new practice of inquiry/*inquisitio* begins to articulate 'two new principles for the production of truth' (Hoskin & Macve, 2016: 237). The first is a new principle of 'graphocentrism', by which they mean that writing definitively displaces speech as the vehicle for truth claims, but also that a certain more methodical and explicit kind of writing is required. Panofsky suggests that alongside *concordantia* as the objective or goal of inquiry, there is a new commitment to a principle of making everything visible or *manifestatio* (1957: 30–31). This *manifestatio* has three requirements: '(1) totality (sufficient enumeration), (2) arrangement according to a system of homologous parts and parts of parts (sufficient articulation), and (3) distinctness and deductive cogency (sufficient interrelation)' (1957: 31). In learning to read and also write in this way, learners internalize the 'mental habit' of seeking to establish truth exclusively through writing, following 'a scheme of division and subdivision, condensable into a table of contents or synopsis, where all parts denoted by numbers or letters of the same class are on the same logical level'. As Panofsky then concludes, this way of thinking and acting now rules knowledge production 'from major works of scholarship' to 'doctoral theses' (1957: 32).

But alongside this graphocentrism, the new mental habit/form of truth entails a new 'synoptic' form of inquiry. All the textual material collected together must be laid out in such a way to enable all relevant material to be both read as a whole and comprehended in all its parts. As Hoskin and Macve put it, this requires the reader/writer first to be on the move around the population of relevant initial texts, assembling the material required and then reassembling it into a readable network of statements. Then comes immobility as the reader/writer must pull together (i.e., comprehend) the initially diverse set of statements and thus come to 'comprehend' them as a set of discordant voices now rendered concordant.

So this new mental habit, this new way of constructing truth as concord out of discord, constitutes a new principle of 'synoptic graphocentrism', and this principle is precisely what is put to use to translate prior forms of accounting into the DEB system, or so Hoskin and Macve then contend (2016: 239–240). First, graphocentrically, there must be, as Panofsky pointed out, a proper *enumeration*, *articulation* and *interrelation* of all entries. So first all relevant transactions, but *only* those, must be entered into the books (sufficient enumeration); second the entries must all be posted twice with cross-referencing, and must also be rewritten and again cross-referenced from journal to ledger (sufficient articulation); and finally the doubled entries must tally with each other, and with the whole population of entries (sufficient interrelation). Only then may the 'balance' be struck, through the synoptic reading of all entries and their interrelations; and only then may conclusions be articulated that will be formally true, so long as all the preceding steps have been properly taken.

So here we propose to consider how far the three accounting innovations that we analyse may be manifestations of a new way of thinking and acting that derives from a new pedagogic practice of inquiry/*inquisitio*. That does not mean that all subjects think and act in the same way, but rather that what we may be observing is a new regularity in ways of thinking and acting, a regularity which is readily adopted by some, and just as readily resisted by others, and not infrequently with success.

Insofar as it is a new regularity, it will, we shall argue, be found simultaneously at the level of the individual subject, at the level of the group or multiplicity, and finally at the level of the large-scale construct, such as the state—and also therefore within the modern era, at the level of that other large-scale construct, the corporate business entity, given how the latter, in its modern multidivisional and transnational forms, can deploy a level of resources and of influence in the world that outstrips the resources and influence of the majority of the world's states.

But equally, insofar as any regularity in ways of thinking and acting establishes itself, it can do so only through constituting for its time and the subjects living in that time a form of speaking truth, or 'veridiction', which is not to say that everything said through such a mode of veridiction will be truth-as-such, as opposed to falsehood or error. Rather what is at stake is what Foucault, writing under the name of Maurice Florence, called a 'critical history of thought' undertaken as a study of 'truth games' and so constituting 'the history of "veridictions", understood as the forms according to which discourses capable of being deemed true or false are articulated upon a domain of things' (Foucault & Florence, 1994: 315).

Taking into account these general methodological guidelines, let us now turn to the particular Venetian innovations that are the object of our interest here.

Three Venetian Accounting Innovations: One Way of Thinking and Acting?

The first innovation we consider is that most famous and intensively studied breakthrough, the Venetian method of double-entry bookkeeping (hereafter DEB). It is now widely understood (see, e.g., de Roover, 1974; Yamey, 1964; Hoskin & Macve, 1986; Sangster, 2016) that the first forms of DEB were established long before 1500; at the same time, DEB gains a level of *conceptual* visibility following the incorporation of a Venetian DEB system into Luca Pacioli's 1494 *Summa de arithmetica, geometria, proportioni et proportionalita*, published of course in Venice, where it is included as Book 9, Tract 11 in the *Summa*, under the title *Particularis de Computis et Scripturis*. We stress here the *conceptual* rather than practical significance of the *de Computis*, accepting here the argument of Yamey (e.g., 2010: 145–148) concerning the implausibility of the notion that Pacioli's text had much practical value to merchants. Yamey notes first the size, cost and unwieldiness of the *Summa* as a text to be used in either learning or entering accounts; but his more important point is that Pacioli provides no clear system which would enable learners to determine the accounts to be debited and credited—a problem that authors of accounting texts as late as 1800 still see as the most difficult and intractable to solve (Yamey, 2010: 146).

Yamey contrasts this deficiency with Manzoni's 1540 text, the *Quaderno Doppio col sui giornale*, also published in Venice, which provides the learner with the basis of a proper understanding through providing, as he puts it, a

> model journal and ledger [which] show the appropriate entries for 300 transactions (including the operations necessary for closing the ledger). The transactions, grouped by type, are listed. The 300 items are numbered and keyed to the numbered entries in the journal. Each item in the list also includes the folio numbers of the two ledgers to be debited and credited respectively (Yamey, 2010: 147).

In contrast, Yamey observes, Pacioli does not offer 'any general rule or rules' to guide the reader, and his examples, though many, 'are limited in range, and they are not shown as entries in a model book of accounts reflecting a series of inter-related transactions. Moreover, there is no illustration of the entries necessary for closing a ledger and opening its successor' (2010: 147).

But if Pacioli's contribution is not of any great practical help, it is nevertheless conceptually significant in a first way given that, by its inclusion in his *Summa*, Pacioli signals that he sees DEB as manifesting the conceptual coherence and rigour found in the other mathematical and philosophical systems he discusses in this Neoplatonic work, where conceptual virtue is manifested through adherence to the principles of 'proportion and proportionality'. But it is also significant in a second way through what is signalled at the surface of this accounting text where the objects of accounting are named in certain regular and specific terms which are not necessarily the terms which we have developed since. So for instance, what we might now call 'capital' is named '*substantia*', the business entity the '*corpo*', and control '*dispone*' (or 'disposition'). The specificity and difference of these terms from those we have developed since are one object of our analysis here.

The second innovation we consider is also long known, but until recently less *well* known, and consists of four texts from the 1580s and 1590s concerning the form and quality of management at the Venetian state's shipbuilding site, the *Arsenale*. These texts, two by Baldissera Drachio and two by Bortolamio Tadini, set out proposed improvements, in Drachio's case, in the provision, storage and use of materials collected in the *Arsenale* for the building of ships for the state (what we would now call 'logistics'); in Tadini's case, the improvements proposed would have enabled the development of a more efficient and effective approach to constructing ships on time and to a consistent quality (e.g., Lane, 1934; Davis, 1991; Rossi, 1996; Zan, 2004; Zan & Deng, 2017).

In the event, neither sets of proposals were adopted and the running of the *Arsenale* continued much as before, in a form of what we might call a 'principal-agent' set-up, but a form where, both at the day-to-day level of activity and in the planning and management of projects, it was not the '*principals*' (i.e., the representatives of the state who controlled what took place) but the agents—that is, the artisan masters who directed the making of the key ship components (e.g., oars, masts, and sails) and in particular the *Marangoni* who directed the construction from these components of a given ship. However, as has been rightly noted, there is articulated here a very modern-sounding form of 'management *discourse*'—named indeed as such in Drachio's first 1586 text as a '*discorso del maneggio*' (Zan, 2004: 153).

Finally and third, the Jesuit Spiritual Exercises have long been an object of study in religious and ecclesiastical history, but only more recently considered as a form of caring for the self via a systematic *accounting for* and so developing one's self in relation to God (Quattrone, 2004, 2015; Bento da Silva & Quattrone, 2017; Bento da Silva, Llewellyn & Gough-Anderson,

2017). The Jesuits have of course various ties and connections to Venice (beginning with the sojourn of Ignatius Loyola in the city before proceeding to Rome to found the Society of Jesus), even though the Society's scope and vision from the outset reached far beyond one city. At the same time, there is one particular Venetian dimension to the form of accounting for one's self undertaken as a means of developing the self within the 'examination of conscience' as analysed in this more recent work (see esp. Quattrone, 2015).

This is a textual borrowing from the Venetian DEB layout, where debits and credits are set out in matching rows on opposing pages so that a 'synoptic' view of each particular pair of debit-credit entries is presented to the viewer/reader, as the entry-point to a more general synoptic viewing of the network of each and every initial debit-credit pair, through the use of text, page and line references, enabling the swift and certain tracking of entry pairs and the entry sets made up of such pairs. As Quattrone (2015: 423–424) explains, 'a specific visual inscription was prescribed for the examination of conscience', which he then displays, taking the image from the 1666 edition of Loyola's *Ezercizi Spirituali* (2015: 424, Figure 3).

The inscription's centrepiece is a book open to a double page, with a series of seven double lines on each page, with each set of double lines preceded by a capital letter. The letters designate the given day of the week (so starting with D for *Domenico*/Sunday, and ending with S for *Sabato*/Saturday). But interestingly the length of the lines on the left-hand page decreases each day, while correlatively that of the lines on the right-hand page increases. Each exercitant must then undertake a twice-daily examination of one's sins (to be entered on the left page) and one's good acts (entered on the right). So as *Quattrone* then says,

> For each sin committed from the moment of rising until the first examination, the exercitant was required to enter a dot (a *punctus*) on the upper line of the first series of lines . . . ; after supper . . . other dots were placed on the lower line of the series for that day.

The visual inspection or reading of one's performance in terms of both bad and good acts was then first the occasion of a 'resolution to do better', and an account of one's level or lack of improvement. And across the week, improvement was both visualized and motivated through the correlative decreasing and increasing of the space available for recording, respectively, sinful and virtuous acts.

Now these three innovations have perhaps up to now been read, perfectly reasonably, as three distinct or discrete innovations. And to read them in this way makes a particular sense, given the way in which accounting has been typically divided up in both professional and academic categorizations of its forms or manifestations over the past century.

So the first innovation, DEB, is legitimately read as located within the general field of financial accounting, where it initiates new forms of undertaking and managing mercantile or merchant-plus-banking activity, or more extensively of managing the activity of the household or estate (e.g., Goldthwaite, 2015). As a financial device it enables a new level of comprehension and valuing of incomings and outgoings, both through the regular and regulated form in which entries are made where the account writer deploys the debit and credit system of entry properly and consistently, and through the second and equally significant aspect of DEB, the monetizing of all entries into a currency of choice (so that even multiple currency transactions are translated into one 'value metric').

Explanations of its genesis at this particular historical juncture (i.e., temporally from around 1300 CE, and geographically in Western or 'Latin' Europe, most specifically in the mercantile world of the Italian city-states) are typically predicated on a focus on the mercantile setting and the intensification and expansion of trade both within Europe (e.g., through the great fairs and the provision of banking facilities by networks of merchant-bankers for the wider and more general networks of merchants) and beyond. In the latter instance, the significance of the Italian port cities, particularly Genoa and Venice, as the European termini of the 'Silk Routes' from the East is regularly noticed.

The second innovation, the development of a management discourse within the context of the *Arsenale*, which as Zan (2004) observes was perhaps the most extensive manufacturing site in Europe of its day, falls more easily within the frame of management and cost accounting, as developed since the nineteenth century, and particularly in the context of developing the large coordinated form of entity described by Chandler (1977) as the 'modern business enterprise', as an entity which combines, in his analysis, a new form of 'organizational' *structure*, the line-and-staff set up where every line unit has a staff office or staff function within it, with a new form of *process*, entailing the constant prescribing, tracking and evaluating of the performance of each and every unit through the continuous gathering within each node of the staff function of accounting and statistical information which comes to cover every aspect of activity within and across each and every line and all its units. In this set-up, every unit 'has its own administrative office (and) own set of books and accounts which can be audited separately' (Chandler, 1977: 1–3), and as the aggregated information is regularly relayed up to the entity's top or 'head office', it can also be translated into new plans, strategies and budgets, derived but not totally determined by the performance of the immediate and more long-term past.

Hence, for Chandler, there emerges the 'modern business enterprise' whose distinctive feature is an 'administrative coordination' which internally 'routinises transactions, reduces information costs, enables effective scheduling of flows (and) generates more certain cash flow and . . . payment for services rendered' (1977: 6), thus across groups of firms adopting the principles and practices of administrative coordination 'permitted greater productivity, lower costs and higher profits than coordination of market mechanisms', and so ultimately (in Chandler's deeply subversive conclusion) rendered redundant at the macro-economic level the possibility of competitive markets with perfect competition, producing instead the historically unprecedented outcome where market sectors would increasingly become dominated by a few large firms constituting an oligopoly (and indeed an oligopsony) dominating each sector, so that the economic world becomes one that manifests 'imperfect competition and misallocation of resources' (1977: 6).

The framing of the management and accounting innovations at the *Arsenale* thus becomes one in which they are read either as some form of precursor or as anticipation of either more contemporary management and accounting practices or of the 'way of seeing' which thinks of management as taking place within modern *organizational* forms or settings where, as Chandler observes (1977: 3–4), the mix of structure and process means that necessarily managers manage other managers in hierarchies, but also that the performance and indeed 'conduct' of each and every manager and employee can be rendered accountable through the setting of targets and measuring actual activities and outcomes against targets. Thus it becomes possible to construct not only financial profit and loss statements and balance sheets but also measures of human performance where actual outcomes are measurable against preset standards, targets or norms, and so to articulate a kind of accounting for human performance and conduct which can construct both individuals and sets of individuals as subject to norms or 'normalized'.

Finally, there is the Jesuit innovation which of course not only articulates a form of accounting for conduct which evokes comparisons to the kinds of accountability systems developed in the managerially run 'modern business enterprises', but also combines this exercise of a 'pastoral power' (Bento da Silva & Quattrone, 2017: 115) with a more general financial managing of the resources of the Society of Jesus through the dissemination of DEB-form accounting across each house within each province of the Society. Thus a form of line-and-staff structure is enacted across the Society, and within each of its provinces and houses: a financial accounting is combined with a form of accounting for the subject that both examines and evaluates each member of the Society and promotes a constant self-examination and self-evaluation as well.

But at this point we may begin to see how the supposed separation of these three innovations is less than complete. The Jesuit system evokes the Chandlerian model in its structure and its insistent processes of generating a range of accounting and statistical information, but insofar as it does so it has affinities in terms of structure and process with the new accounting and management discourse that circulates in the *Arsenale*. But the DEB system also manifests an internal structural coherence which constitutes a form of 'administrative coordination' of the affairs of the merchant, bank or household, albeit at a textual level; and as it tracks incomings and outgoings to the entity through its debit-credit pairs and the set of texts that reframe and rewrite those pairs, it also renders the subjects both within the entity and beyond it subject to forms of valuing: as good or bad members of the entity, and as good or bad debts.

So the first question that then arises is how far initially apparent differences between these accounting innovations may turn out to be versions of the same, which then leads to a second question: how far initially apparent similarities between innovations then and developments traditionally seen as occurring only later may prove to be manifestations of different ways of thinking and acting. It is to an initial investigation of these questions that we now turn. We address first the issue of how far there is a *structural* set-up that is common to all three of our innovations, and how far that structural set-up differs from that articulated in the modern managerial business enterprise. We turn then to the more *processual* issue of how far there is an accounting for, and also valuing of, performance and conduct (financial or human) that is common to all three innovations, and how far that accounting again differs from the accounting forms articulated in modern managerial business and governmental settings. We suggest that there are complex interplays at work; at the same time, there are grounds for making a case that there are two different ways of thinking and acting in play here, each of which produces its own distinctive forms of regularity.

'We Are Not an Organization—We Are a *Corpo*!'

This comment was made to Jose Bento da Silva in the course of undertaking his PhD research into the ways in which the Society of Jesus has been managed across its history. In the course of an interview with a senior member of one of the Society's provinces, he asked the interviewee how he would characterize or describe the Society's organization. The response, made with some passion, forms the heading to this section. One of the current authors, who was supervising the doctoral research, reacted by saying that this was important: the choice of term signalled that, for this senior Jesuit at least, an organizational structure was radically different from that of the Society; in a certain way, the very identity and survival of the Society were tied up in this difference.

One significant difference that then emerged between the Society as a *corpo* or corpus and the modern organization was how little the structure of the corpus has changed across the five and a half ensuing centuries. The specifics of the Society's structure as spelled out in its constitutions have hardly altered over that time; and the robustness of the structure is in a sense borne out by what happened during and after the 'Great Suppression' of the Society, when from the 1750s various states banned or banished the Jesuits, and then in 1773 the then pope, Clement XIV, declared a formal Papal Suppression in which the Church decided to 'suppress and abolish' the Society. But when the ban was reversed in 1814, the Society was able rapidly to re-establish itself wherever it was now welcome. Now of course there were many subplots at work in the Great Suppression, and the speed of re-establishment suggests that the Society continued to function informally. But there was arguably a coherence, unity and consistency to the corpus form which differs from that of the modern organization; in the latter the line-and-staff structure tolerates a huge level of variation in the precise form that the organization can take: the U-form, M-form, matrix form and forms that enable temporary and provisional alliances are all feasible. But in the Jesuit case, there is just the *corpo*: this at least is part of the reason, we suggest, that the very suggestion that the Society might be an 'organization' generated such antipathy.

Nevertheless, was the Jesuit corpus a precursor of the organization form: 'a distinct, if early, version of what later emerged as modern organization', as Bento da Silva and Quattrone put it (2017: 130)? In support of the possibility, there is the fact that the Jesuits clearly did develop a form of line-and-staff structure, supported processually by their range of accounting techniques, serving both financial and pastoral functions. On the other hand, we would draw attention to the insistence and persistence of the '*corpus/corpo*' term, even as 'organization' emerges in the late eighteenth century as a new way of thinking about structure—initially applied to the structure of the biological 'organism', understood as a collection of functions, and then applied also to the characterization of social and economic entities. But perhaps even more intriguing is the way in which the term *corpo* surfaces in the context of both our other Venetian accounting innovations.

First, as we have indicated earlier, the *de Computis* section of Pacioli's *Summa* designates the business entity as a *corpo*. This is at the point (Book 9, Chapter 5) where the text turns to the issue of how a business needs to set up its internal coordination or control of its affairs—its 'disposition' or '*dispone*'. The main focus is on how to account for the '*corpo o vero monte de tutto el trafico*'—that is, 'the body or true amount of all the trafficking' that the general business may undertake; a secondary focus is on the affairs of a more focused business—for example, that of a shop or *botega*, and so on how to account for the '*corpo o vero de botega*'.

But finally, the term recurs in the '*discorso del maneggio*' developed at the *Arsenale*. Specifically Drachio proposes that the remaking of the *Arsenale* as a site of proper management requires that the existing 'principal-agent' approach to designing and building ships—that is, where the agents, the master shipwrights and other artisan masters run their own enterprises to their own rhythm—should be dismantled. There should be 'a new standard ship design, to be . . . issued centrally' (Zan, 2004: 156), and to be established initially by requiring seven senior shipwrights 'to produce their individual ideal *sesto* (design)' and then getting an independent group of 'wise men' to 'choose the best one, judging blind' (ibid.). In this way the state could establish 'the principle that the Arsenal "should function as a body with just one head"' (Zan, 2004: 156). Furthermore, the '*corpo*' principal could be extended down into subunits of the workforce, through 'rationalising the number and composition of shipbuilding gangs with the creation of new functionally differentiated divisions (*corpi*, literally bodies)', Zan (2004: 157), numbering seven in all and each owning the responsibility for separate types of activity, rather than being part of an organic team working on whatever project or activity the master they worked for required.[1]

Thus at a structural level, there is an apparent regularity in the way of thinking of what a coherent entity consists in: it does not take a variable form like that of a modern organization. It is a *corpo*, perhaps with one head, as Drachio suggests, or perhaps with a more elaborate structure to ensure the stability of the uniform set-up. In the Society of Jesus, for instance, the superior general might be the head with executive power, but legislative power lay with the General Congregation, an assembly of elected members from all provinces; furthermore the general did not have unlimited power of executive action, since the constitutions also required that he be attended by '*admonitors*', with those designated as '*admonitores ad providentiam*' (usually 12 in number) being tasked with warning the general concerning things to be foreseen (the literal sense of the Latin *pro-videre*), which in practice entailed ensuring that the general did not act outside what was permitted in the constitutions.

So, at the level of structure we see the possibility that all three accounting innovations manifest a way of thinking which thinks of structure *as* the body, the *corpo*, and which also thinks of the members of that structure as 'bodily members'. Those members may be the debits and credits which constitute the textual body/*corpo* which is the business entity, once translated into the sets of accounting statements arrayed in journals and ledgers; they may equally be those subjects who are to make up the reformed *Arsenale* workforce teams that Drachio dreams of, where they will form bodies within an overall body with one head that the *Arsenale* can now become; or finally they may be those religious subjects who give themselves willingly to becoming the members that make up the *corpo* that is the Society of Jesus, thus guaranteeing its coherence and unity across time and space, even as the multiplicity of subjects making up the Society becomes distributed across almost all the states, languages and cultures of the known world, in ever-extending networks of houses and provinces. It is precisely because every limb and member of the *corpo* know its place and role that the integrity and coherence of the whole can endure. What we therefore raise is the possibility that all these entities are first thought of and then enacted as things that are systematically other than 'organizations'.

'Economies of Value' and the Making of Differently Accountable Subjects

But what of the *processual* issue of how far there is an accounting for, and valuing of, performance and conduct (financial or human) that is common to all three innovations? Here we see things as in certain respects more complex, for there are two different 'economies of value'—that is, two different systems of valuing objects and subjects—operating within the three different forms of body/*corpo* we have discussed earlier. The first is an ancient economy of value which operates with binary values—for instance, when it is conduct that is being accounted for, the economy is one of sticks to punish bad acts and carrots to reward good ones. In a different way, 'financial' accounting before double entry also typically operated with binary values, wherein physical inventory would frequently be recorded in material units (as so many arithmetically regularized measures of corn, beer, oil, etc., or so many heads of livestock), and only cash items entered with monetary values. In relation to conduct, Foucault, when analysing the development of the early Christian pastorate within the monastic space in *Security, Territory, Population*, describes this as 'an economy of merits and faults' (2007: 173). In *Discipline and Punish* he describes it as a 'penal accountancy' (Foucault, 1977: 180), but then recognizes the binary nature of the economy, since 'punishment is only one element of a double system: gratification-punishment' (1977: 180).

This ancestral system of binary values is displaced, so far as we can see, only when accounting, in the DEB format, monetizes all entries and expresses them all in a single currency, thus constructing a single, and indeed unilinear, value metric, and in that process making possible the *discourse* of debits and credits and such consequential possibilities as striking a balance, expressing one's '*substantia*' as a specific monetary value, and indeed, one might say, successfully comparing apples and oranges. But at this historical moment, the binary value system continues to operate in the sphere of valuing human conduct and performance. In this respect the borrowing of the Venetian DEB layout for the entry of good and bad acts by the exercitant undertaking the Jesuit examination of conscience is almost poignant, for what is recorded is not a series of debits and credits expressed in a unilinear value metric, but a binary set of discrete sinful and virtuous acts.

A similar way of thinking obtains in the approach adopted for reforming the management of the *Arsenale* by the second author of texts submitted to the Venetian state, Bartolomeo Tadini. Unlike Drachio, who made his recommendations for improving the logistics of the *Arsenale* as an outsider, Tadini made his proposals as an insider, a trained accountant (*rasonato*) who ended up as the chief accountant for the *Arsenale*. His proposals also seek to erase and replace the 'principal-agent' set-up of work and production, and in particular to use accounting and statistical information to do so. Again there is much that echoes modern management, including the setting of targets for the completion of projects, the control of expenditures, and the quality of the finished product, and then tracking actual performance against these various targets on a regular basis—for example, through 'weekly targets and appraisals' (Zan, 2004: 160) plus a regular evaluation or audit of overall outcomes every six months (or semester). This is, as Zan remarks, a highly detailed and sophisticated plan of action (although again we would note that the state never ventures to implement it). However, when Tadini turns to propose his incentive scheme, the scheme he proposes still conforms to the ancestral 'economy of merits and faults'. As Zan puts it,

> At the end of each semester, the work done by each gang and its boss should be examined, with good performance receiving a monetary bonus to be shared by the team . . ., and poor performance being subject to sanctions and punishment, ranging from public shame up to removal of the gang boss from his position.
>
> (Zan, 2004: 160)

What we therefore do not find, within the world of the *corpo*, is the modern type of 'economy of value' where performance is evaluated through a unitary currency of merits and *demerits*. At this point what had previously obtained only for the valuing of entries into the financial books extended also to human performance. In *Discipline and Punish*, Foucault exemplifies the difference in terms of what begins to take place in the Brothers of the Christian Schools once a system is introduced that operates with a currency of privilege and imposition of 'points' or marks. For example, a pupil can gain exemption from a penance 'by accumulating a certain number of privilege points' (1977: 180). So suddenly a running total of plus and minus points can be kept for each pupil; and equally 'by . . . this circulation of awards and debits, thanks to the continuous calculation of plus and minus points, the disciplinary apparatuses hierarchized the "good" and "bad" subjects in relation to one another' (1977: 181). In this new type of economy of value, there is no longer 'a differentiation . . . of acts, but of individuals themselves, of their nature, their potentialities, their level or their value' (1977: 181). This marks the birth of the constantly accountable subject, and the constantly accountable population, now that 'there is this circulation of awards and debits, thanks to the continuous calculation of plus and minus points' (Foucault, 1977: 181).

This, we suggest, is a consequence of moving beyond a world where the form of truth is inquiry, into a world where the form of truth is examination, and in particular the form of constant examination which translates the actions and performance (and so also the 'potential') of each and all into numerical marks or grades. As Foucault concludes, 'By assessing acts with precision, discipline judges individuals "in truth"' (1977: 181).

Conclusion: Accounting and the Construction of Differing Forms of Space-Time-Value 'Dispositif'

For some years we have been pursuing the idea that accounting operates, in all its forms and manifestations across history, as some specifiable form of 'space-time-value machine' (Frandsen, 2009: 125). But we now consider that rather than accounting constituting a 'machine' it opens up the possibility of thinking about and articulating different forms of Foucauldian 'dispositif'.

We raise this only in a preliminary way here, but we see the question as a potentially fertile one going forward, given the fact that in Foucault's analysis, in *Security, Territory, Population*, of the emergence of modern governmental reason, he sees this form of reason as operating not through discipline but through a new form of management, which he names a 'governmental management', and which he says 'has population as its main target and apparatuses (dispositifs) of security as its essential mechanism' (Foucault, 2007: 107–108). But the most intriguing aspect of this analysis for us is that not only is management, in the sense of management of the population, put centre stage as the means of exercising modern governmental reason but also when he explains the nature of the quintessential modern *dispositif* of security, it turns out to be cost-benefit analysis (see Hoskin, 2017: 42–46).

This is made clear right at the start of the first lecture, where Foucault defines 'security' as a construct which asks new types of questions—for instance, in relation to crime. First, he says, it asks statistical ones, such as 'what is the average rate of criminality?' (2007: 4); but these are only preliminary to the central types of questions, which are all questions concerned with the *relative cost* of acting and of not-acting to reduce crime. So the questions are:

> (H)ow much does this criminality cost society, what damage does it cause . . .? What is the cost of repressing these thefts? . . . What, therefore, is the comparative cost of the theft and of its repression, and what is more worthwhile . . .?
>
> (2007: 5)

In other words,

> the apparatus (*dispositif*) of security inserts the phenomenon in question, namely theft, within a series of events . . . the reactions of power to this phenomenon are inserted in a calculation of cost . . . (and) one establishes an average considered as optimal . . . and . . . a bandwidth of the acceptable.
>
> (2007: 6)

Thus it transpires that that the Foucauldian *dispositif* of security, as that articulated in the modern era, is an enactment of a form of 'managing via accounting', with the modern accounting focus on 'cost' as its key object of analysis. So the question for us then emerges—namely, what form of 'dispositif' might be enacted via accounting in this medieval era of Venetian accounting innovation?

To begin answering that question, we consider the contrast that Foucault draws in these lectures between how discipline and governmental reason 'manage' the subject both as individual and in the mass in space and time, for this is a major concern that he addresses in the lectures following from this initial discussion of the nature of the modern *dispositif* of security. The major distinctions he makes are as follows (cf. Hoskin, 2017). Governmental reason operates on a population made up of desiring subjects and manages them in the space-time complex of 'security', which is a space and time made up of certain artificial arrangements but also containing natural elements. Thus the modern governmental problem is to manage as optimally as possible both individual subjects and sets of subjects, with all their diverse and often conflicting desires. So governing must 'work not only on natural givens but also on quantities that can be relatively but never wholly reduced, and, since they can never be nullified, one works on probabilities' (Foucault, 2007: 19).

The first task of the *dispositif* of security is then to recognize that both individuals and the population constitute subjects, in the latter case a 'collective subject-object', that can develop their own 'naturalness' (Foucault, 2007: 70); the second task is then to recognize the population as much as the individual as 'the subject of needs and aspirations, but also the object of government manipulation' (2007: 105).

But discipline as such does not operate on desiring subjects with needs and aspirations. But then Foucault in these lectures now sees discipline as a manifestation of an earlier way of thinking and acting, which must set up a space that is *wholly artificial* (as is the case in a school, a prison, or indeed a religious order, such as the Jesuits) and where there can be total spatial enclosure and the possibility of total time discipline. Within this artificial space-time zone, the individual he says 'is not the primary datum on which discipline is exercised'. Discipline instead is primarily concerned with the *multiplicities* that are made up of individuals: thus

> school and military discipline, as well as penal discipline, workshop discipline, worker discipline, are all particular ways of managing and organizing *a multiplicity*, of fixing its points of implantation, its lateral or horizontal, vertical and pyramidal trajectories, its hierarchy, and so on.
>
> (2007: 12, emphasis added)

What we wish to end with is a brief reflection on what kind of 'dispositif' may be at work in this earlier world of discipline, which is the kind of world that we see as enacted by the Society of Jesus, and as imagined by the would-be reformers of the *Arsenale*. (We assume here that there will be some form of *dispositif* at work, but simply not one whose guiding principle is the manufacture and internalization of 'security' across the population.)

Perhaps, we suggest, in this earlier world of discipline, what is enacted is a *dispositif* of *control*. Etymologically this is historically appropriate, since 'control' is a term that is first apparently coined in the era of inquiry, with its first recorded usage traced to the English court around AD 1220. Here in a governmental space where financial and legislative records were still kept not in book format but in rolls, the terms *contre-rolle* and *contra-rotulus* first appear, signifying not a second copy of an initial book of entry but a text which summarizes key financial or legislative information excerpted from the original rolls to enable the sovereign to govern in an informed and reasoned manner (cf. Hoskin & Macve, 1986). The term we feel is also conceptually appropriate, since a key aspect of governing by inquiry, as taken to its highest expression by Colbert, is the distillation of truth via an excerptive critical reading that reduces complexity and prolixity to simplicity and brevity. Given that, the management of subjects and multiplicities need have little or no concern for satisfying desires and interests; it operates instead through the prescription of things to be done, and of the times and places of their doing, plus a shaping of conduct through an economy of merits and faults.

That at least is a possibility that we hope to pursue in more detail hereafter.

Note

1. Drachio specifies these seven subordinate *corpi* as follows (Zan, 2004: 147, n. 13): first *corpo*: to comprise five gangs to work on building new light galleys; second *corpo*: a single workforce to build great galleys; third *corpo*: a 'new collective' of 50 older workers to undertake preparatory and supplementary activities; fourth *corpo*: a group to manufacture superstructural components such as masts and spars; fifth *corpo*: five gangs to do refurbishment work on old galleys; sixth *corpo*: a group to work together to deal with 'unexpected emergencies (*accidenti dell' Arsenal*); seventh *corpo*: a group 'not to work with iron' (*non lavora ai ferri*) perhaps because experience showed this led to costly and time-consuming errors.

References

Bento Da Silva, J., Llewellyn, N., and Gough-Anderson, F. (2017), "Oral-Aural Accounting and the Management of the Jesuit Corpus", *Accounting, Organization and Society*, Vol. 59, May, pp. 44–57.

Bento Da Silva, J., and Quattrone, P. (2017), "Government at a Distance: The Spiritual Exercises of Saint Ignatius of Loyola." Pp. 115–158, *in* M. Alan and E. Pezet (eds.) *Foucault and Managerial Governmentality: Rethinking the Management and Populations, Organizations and Individual.* New York: Routledge.

Chandler, A. (1977), *The Visible Hand: The Managerial Revolution in American Business.* Cambridge, MA: Harvard Belknap Press.

Davis, R.C. (1991), *Shipbuilders of the Venetian Arsenal: Workers and Workplace in the Preindustrial City.* Baltimore: The John Hopkins University Press.

de Roover, R. (1974), *Business, banking, and economic thought in the late medieval and early modern Europe: selected studies of Raymond de Roover* (ed. Julius Kirshner). London: University of Chicago Press.

Foucault, M. (1977/1975), *Discipline and Punish.* London: Allen Lane.

Foucault, M. (2001), "Truth and Juridical Forms." Pp. 1–89, *in* J. Faubion (ed.) *Power: Essential Works of Foucault, 1954–1984* (volume three). London: Allen Lane.

Foucault, M. (2007), *Security, Territory, Population: Lectures at the Collège de France, 1977–78.* London: Palgrave Macmillan.

Foucault, M., and Florence, M. (1994), "Michel Foucault, 1926–." Pp. 314–319, *in* G. Gutting (ed.) *The Cambridge Companion to Foucault* (first edition). Cambridge: Cambridge University Press.

Frandsen, A.C. (2009), "From Psoriasis to a Number and Back", *Information and Organization*, Vol. 19, No. 2, pp. 103–128.

Goldthwaite, R. (2015), "The Practice and Culture of Accounting in Renaissance Florence", *Enterprise & Society*, Vol. 16, pp. 611–647.

Hoskin, K. (2017), "Getting to the Surface of Things: Foucault as Theorist and Historian of Management Accounting." Pp. 33–53, *in* M. Alan and E. Pezet (eds.) *Foucault and Managerial Governmentality: Rethinking the Management and Populations, Organizations and Individual.* New York: Routledge.

Hoskin, K., and Macve, R. (1986), "Accounting and the Examination: A Genealogy of Disciplinary Power", *Accounting, Organizations and Society*, Vol. 11, No. 2, pp. 105–136.

Hoskin, K., and Macve, R. (2016), "'L'État c'est moi' . . . ou quoi? On the Interrelations of Accounting, Managing and Governing in the French 'Administrative Monarchy': Revisiting the Colbert (1661–1683) and Paris Brothers (1712–1726) Episodes", *Accounting History Review*, Vol. 26, No. 3, pp. 219–257.

Lane, F. (1934), *Venetian Ships and Shipbuilders of the Renaissance.* Baltimore: The John Hopkins Press.

Miller, P. (1990), "On the Interrelations of Accounting and the State", *Accounting, Organizations and Society*, Vol. 15, No. 4, pp. 315–338.

Pacioli, L. (1994/1494), *Particularis de Computis et Scripturis* (Book 9, Tract 11 from the *Summa*). Translated, Cripps, J. Seattle: Seattle University, Pacioli Society.

Panofsky, E. (1957), *Gothic Architecture and Scholasticism.* New York: Meridian Books.

Quattrone, P. (2004), "Accounting for God: Accounting and Accountability Practices in the Society of Jesus." *Accounting, Organizations and Society*, Vol. 29, No. 7, pp. 647–683.

Quattrone, P. (2009), "Books to be Practiced: Memory, the Power of the Visual, and the Success of Accounting", *Accounting, Organizations and Society*, Vol. 34, No. 1, pp. 85–118.

Quattrone, P. (2015), "Governing Social Orders, Unfolding Rationality, and Jesuit Accounting Practices." *Administrative Science Quarterly*, Vol. 60, No. 3, pp. 411–455.

Rossi, F. (1996), "I quadri Direttivi dell'arsenal", *in* U. Tucci, and A. Tenenti (a cura di) *Storia di Venezia, Vol. VII Rinascimento. Societa ed Economia.* Roma: Istituto della Enciclopedia Treccani.

Sangster, A. (2016), "The Genesis of Double Entry Bookkeeping." *The Accounting Review*, Vol. 91, No. 1, pp. 299–315.

Soll, J. (2009), *The Information Master: Jean-Baptiste Colbert's Secret State Intelligence System.* Ann Arbor: University of Michigan Press.

Yamey, B.S. (1964), "Accounting and the Rise of Capitalism: Further Notes on a Theme by Sombart", *Journal of Accounting Research*, Vol. 2, No. 2, pp. 117–136.

Yamey, B.S. (2010), "The Market for Luca Paciolo's Summa De Arithmetica: Some comments", *The Accounting Historians Journal*, Vol. 37, No. 2, pp. 145–154.

Zan, L. (2004), "Accounting and Management Discourse in Protoindustrial Settings: The Venice Arsenal in the Turn of the 16th Century", *Accounting and Business Research*, Vol. 32, No. 2, pp. 145–175.

Zan, L., and Deng, K. (2017), "Micro Foundations in the Great Divergence Debate: Opening Up the Perspectives", *Accounting History*, Vol. 22, No. 4, pp. 530–553.

17 Fabio Besta

Accounting Education and Accounting History Dissemination

Massimo Sargiacomo, Stefania Servalli and Paolo Andrei

Introduction

This chapter[1] seeks to portray the life, principal writings and contribution to accounting education and accounting history dissemination of Fabio Besta, an eminent scholar of Ca'Foscari, where he worked for more than forty years. This study, which is based on Besta's own works and publications referring to his work, attempts to contribute to the literature in three interconnected ways. Firstly the chapter aims to augment biographical studies in accounting history, given that, admittedly, they have been rather neglected by accounting and accounting history academia (Mautz and Previts 1977; Parker 1980; Previts, Coffman and Parker 1990a1990b). Importantly, the relative paucity of biographical research triggered pleas for its regeneration (Edwards 1994; Carnegie and Napier 1996, 2012), to which there was some response (e.g., Parker 1996; Morecroft, Coffman and Jensen 2000; Walker 2006; Reinstein, Gerald and Vangermeersch 2008; Moussalli, Flesher and Lemarchand 2009; Sargiacomo and Gomes (2011); Sargiacomo, Servalli and Andrei 2012; Flesher and Previts 2013; Antonelli and Sargiacomo 2015).

In relation to biographical studies of prominent Italian figures, there have evidently been a considerable number of studies on Pacioli (e.g., Galassi 1996a, 1996b; Nobes 1995), long lauded as 'the father of modern accounting' (Hatfield 1950, p. 3). Much attention has been also devoted to Gino Zappa and his theories (e.g., Galassi 1984, 1996c; Canziani and Rondo Brovetto 1992; Canziani 1994; Biondi, Canziani and Kirat 2005; Capalbo and Clarke 2006; Dagnino and Quattrone 2006), who advanced *Economia Aziendale* (Zappa 1927) in its economic and social context (e.g., Zan 1994; Viganò 1994, 1998; Zambon and Zan 2000; Cinquini 2007; Alexander and Servalli 2011). There have also been celebrations of the work of Federigo Melis (Padroni 1976a, 1976b; Garner 1976) and various other early authors, such as Fibonacci (Antoni 1985a, 1996) and Ludovico Flori (Quattrone 1994), as well as more recent influential scholars, like Lorenzo De Minico (Cinquini and Marelli 2002; Fiume 2007), Francesco Marchi (Poddighe et al. 2007), Aldo Amaduzzi (Melis 2007) and others. In the context of the aforementioned luminaries Fabio Besta continues to be a rather a neglected figure (Sargiacomo, Servalli and Andrei 2012) despite the fact that he was the mentor of Gino Zappa, who described him as '*Maestro insuperato*'—that is, the unsurpassed master (see De Roover 1955, p. 419). The current investigation seeks to address this omission.

A second, related, contribution of this work is to highlight the contribution by Fabio Besta to the development and spread of accounting education and practice. Following Edwards's (1994) suggestion, a critical analysis of the theoretical contributions of Fabio Besta (Ceriani 2006) will serve to enhance understanding of 'the subject's ideas and theories', and assess their impact on accounting practice (Edwards 1994, xiv). In a related manner, his work was also devoted to enshrine and perpetuate old historical Venetian records, and his books on accounting theory as well as on public sector accounting (Andrei, Baker and Sargiacomo 2017) are clearly witnessing his long-lasting contribution to accounting education. This is particularly relevant if we think that nowadays his works are still quoted not only in the Italian and Anglophone literature but also in Russia (e.g., Sokolov 1996; Gurskaya 2013; Kuter 2000, 2013), Spain (e.g., Hernández Esteve 2013), Brazil (D'Auria 1954, Lopes de Sà 2008) and other countries.

Thirdly, the chapter seeks to highlight the contribution of Fabio Besta in the educational field related to the origins of double-entry bookkeeping, prior to Pacioli's articulation of the technique and its rules. In particular, an analysis is offered of the content and impact of the third volume of Besta's major work entitled *La Ragioneria* (The accounting). We argue that the discussion of early double-entry bookkeeping contained in this volume has influenced the educational process of Ca' Foscari students and significantly impacted on research of international scholars on the subject, thus establishing *La Ragioneria* as a key text in accounting history. Basil Yamey (1967, p. 64) described Fabio Besta as 'a leading Italian accounting theorist and historian', having deployed Besta's arguments in *La Ragioneria* against the case for Pacioli as the founder of double-entry bookkeeping. Relatedly, Raymond de Roover argued that Besta's book 'is still considered by many Italians as the Bible for the history of accounting as well as for contemporary problems of theory and practice', and contended that 'the change in the accepted view with regard to the origin of double entry was due mainly to the labours of a few courageous Italian scholars who had done extensive research on early business records, especially account books' (1955, pp. 405–406). Much time has passed since these statements by leading accounting historians, yet an analysis of the content and international impact of Besta's book and his other writings has yet to be undertaken. Given that *La Ragioneria* was published in the early twentieth century it would not be appropriate to measure impact by performing citation analyses (see Gamble, O'Doherty and Hyman 1987; Bricker 1988; Bisman 2011). Rather, our arguments will be supported by an analysis of direct references to Besta's work in general accounting journals and specialist accounting history journals and books. It will be shown that his book has been deployed to formulate new interpretations of the history of accounting.

The remainder of the chapter is organized as follows. The next section offers a brief overview of the socio-economic scenario at the time Besta was writing. There follows a portrayal of the life of Fabio Besta, covering his family background, education and academic life. The section also contains a discussion of his main writings and influence on accounting education and historical studies. The section thereafter firstly illustrates the equity-based accounting system (*sistema patrimoniale*) proposed by Besta, and then unveils its impact on accounting theory, thereby elucidating his profile as an accounting thinker. The main findings on double-entry bookkeeping enshrined in Chapter 9 of Besta's third book on *La Ragioneria* are then related and a discussion is offered on how its content has helped to support the arguments of prominent scholars in their attempts to rewrite the history of accounting prior to Pacioli's articulation of double-entry bookkeeping. The final section outlines the conclusions of the study.

The Socio-economic Context

In order to better understand Besta's work on accounting and his impact, a brief overview of the Italian scenario up to and during the time of his life and writing is offered.

The eighteenth century is known as a period in which the Italian accounting tradition suffered relative decline (Zan 1994, p. 271). This was a period in which French accounting theory took the lead as represented by the fictitious personification of accounts (De La Porte 1712) and the emergence of the 'five-accounts theory' (Dégranges 1795, 1804). Thereafter, and especially in the second part of the nineteenth century, accounting theory development in Italy revived. This was a period in which the number of works on accounting increased and vibrant debates took place in accounting journals and congresses. According to Cerboni (1889) 106 works on accounting were published in Italy between 1800 and 1860. However, 411 were published between 1860 and 1888.

More broadly the second half of the century was characterized by major political changes, most notably the realization of national unity in 1861. In the economic realm the transformation from an agricultural to an industrial base was underway. If the first two decades after national unification were dominated by political concerns (Amaduzzi 2001), the last part of the century was characterized by 'flourishing industrial production' (Toniolo 1990, p. 73). There was a rapid development in manufacturing, realized by the growth of companies and capital investment, and by the development of the metal, chemical and engineering sectors (Toniolo 1990, pp. 75–76). Technology was increasingly deployed in productive contexts.

The achievement of national unity emphasized the need for a concept of economic administration which reflected the departure from the previous configuration of small states and kingdoms. It was in this context of deep political and economic change that the concept of the '*azienda*' (entity) emerged. This was to be an important foundation to the theoretical development of accounting in Italy. It marked the beginning of the path towards a scientifically based accounting and the twentieth-century notion of *Economia aziendale*—where the economics of the business entity is understood as complex and multifaceted.

In the context of rapid economic change, and industrialization in particular, there were calls for improvements in business education. In the second half of the nineteenth century a series of High Schools of Commerce were created. These were based on the Casati Act of 1859, which reformed the Italian education system (Fauri 1998, p. 38). Ca' Foscari in Venice, founded in 1868, was the first High School of Commerce in Italy. In 1884 and 1886 similar institutions were established in Genoa and Bari. The curricula of these schools recognized accounting as a fundamental discipline, not only because it was a core technique for the practical businessman and imbuing of a business culture but also because the schools were an academic training ground for future instructors in the discipline (Fauri 1998, p. 39). Ca' Foscari, in particular, aimed to prepare young people for careers in business or as secondary school teachers of economics, law or accounting (Longobardi 1927, p. 41).

The last part of the nineteenth century was also characterized by the development of the accounting profession, in terms of both its organization and knowledge advance. This was most tangibly displayed by the establishment of a series of congresses, starting with a national congress in Rome in 1879. Congresses were later convened in Florence (1881), Milan (1885) and Bologna (1888) (Servalli 2004, p. 284). These events were not only the occasion for stimulating the creation of local bodies of accountants around Italy but also the arena in which debates took place about accounting methods, education and schools. Among these debates the differing theoretical positions of leading thinkers such as Cerboni and Besta often featured (Belardinelli 1936).

The Life and Works of Fabio Besta

Fabio Besta was born in Teglio di Valtellina (Sondrio, Italy) on 17 January 1845, one of five sons born to Giacomo Enrico Besta and Teresa Bonadei. He spent his early life in Teglio, Lombardy, until December 1861, when the family moved to Sondrio. Besta attended the Royal School for Bookkeepers and Accountants in Sondrio and then moved to the *Scuola Normale* in Treviglio (Bergamo), where he obtained a diploma in primary school teaching in 1864. He returned to Sondrio to begin his work as a teacher, though in the meantime (in Turin) was the teacher in training of gym in high school; with such qualification he was in charge in the Faculty of the Technical Institute for Accountants in Sondrio.[2]

During the academic year 1868–69 he obtained (as a private student) a diploma in accounting at the same Technical Institute where he was working as a gym teacher and by 1871 was in charge of the teaching of bookkeeping and accounting at the same institute. The following year he published his first scientific work, entitled *Sulla capitalizzazione continua degli interessi* (On the continuous capitalization of interest) (Besta 1872). This work was especially appreciated by Luigi Luzzatti, a jurist, economist, member of the Italian Parliament and a prominent figure in the cultural and political milieu of Venice. Luzzatti had also been a staunch supporter and co-founder of Ca' Foscari. In 1871, a few years after its foundation in 1868, Besta was invited to replace Antonio Biliotti, who had been teaching accounting at Ca' Foscari.

The board of Ca' Foscari appointed Fabio Besta to the chair of accounting on 27 December 1872, a position he held continuously until February 1919 (*Scuola Superiore di Commercio* in Venezia 1873). At the beginning of the academic year 1880–1881 Besta was assigned to deliver a prolusion, or preliminary work, entitled *La Ragioneria* (Besta 1880).

During his long career in Venice, Besta combined excellent teaching with his passion for study. He was appreciated by students and colleagues for his ability to combine academic rigour, insight and wisdom. Such qualities led to his appointment to management positions in Ca' Foscari, first as pro-director from 12 February to 14 March 1914 and then as director from 15 March 1914 to 15 March 1917 (Scuola Superiore di Commercio in Venezia 1919, p. 116). Besta was a major influence in the development of the school (Longobardi 1927, p. 46). In October 1917 Ca' Foscari was transferred to the University of Pisa—a safer location following the defeat of the Italian army by Austro-Hungarian and German forces at the Battle of Caporetto. In February 1919 Besta asked to retire, and did so in June 1920. However, this was not the end of his academic career. On 28 October 1921 Besta was awarded the title of professor emeritus. He died in Tresivio (Sondrio) on 3 October 1922.

The scientific contributions of Fabio Besta are mainly to be found in his work *La Ragioneria* (The accounting), which was published in three volumes in 1891, 1909 and 1916 respectively.[3] It has been stated that these books 'will remain forever the largest and most demanding monument of scientific construction in accounting' (Vianello 1932, p. 316). His original intentions went beyond the subjects of the published volumes. As he stated in 1909 (Besta 1909, preface), a second part of the work ought to be devoted to the *Ragioneria Pubblica* (public accounting—or more specifically the accounts of the state), while a third part might have covered the *Ragioneria applicata al commercio e ai banchi* (accounting applied to trade and to banks). However, these parts were never published. In fact, the intended publishing program of *La Ragioneria* followed the development of Besta's 'Course on Accounting', at Ca' Foscari.

Fabio Besta's principal works are shown in Table 17.1. This confirms that his interests were wide-ranging, embracing accounting by private firms, the state, commercial firms and financial institutions, such as banks.

Table 17.1 The main publications of Fabio Besta

Year	*Title*	*Translation*
1872	*Sulla capitalizzazione continua degli interessi*	On the continuous capitalization of interests
1880	*La Ragioneria—Prolusione*	Accounting—prolusion
1886–7	*Computisteria mercantile*	Business arithmetic
1886–7	*Registri e registrature*	Registers and registrations
1891–1916	*La Ragioneria (volume I-II-III)*	Accounting (Volumes 1–3)
1893	*Diagrammi calcolatori e loro applicazione alla ricerca delle parità nei prezzi e nei cambi in piazze diverse*	Calculating diagrams and their use in conversion of prices and measures in different places
1897	*Lezioni di Contabilità di Stato*	State accounting lectures
1898	*Relazione alla R. Commissione per la pubblicazione dei documenti finanziari della Repubblica di Venezia*	Report to the Royal Committee for the publication of financial documents of the Republic of Venice
1908	*Sulle riforme proposte ai nostri istituti di contabilità di Stato: prolusione letta nella solenne apertura degli studi per l'anno 1908–9 dal Prof. Fabio Besta*	About the proposed reforms by our institutes of state accounting: Prolusion read in the solemn opening of the academic year 1808–9 by Prof. Fabio Besta
1912	*Ragioneria: le società anonime*	Accounting: anonymous companies
1920	*Lezioni di Ragioneria: trattati speciali*	Accounting lessons: special treatises

Besta's Contribution to Accounting Education: Accounting Theory and Accounting History

The great contribution of Besta to accounting education is due to two main spheres: accounting theory and accounting history. Considering the first ambit, which will be developed in this section, Besta's theoretical proposal—after a period of 'scientific fights' with the personalistic approach's supporters—was able to affect the educational system and the accounting programs in schools of commerce, universities and technical schools. In relation to the historical dimension, whose analysis is offered in the next sections, the scientific approach of Besta based on a preliminary historical investigation of phenomena and his devotion to archival research represented an element characterizing his educational discourse and stimulating contemporary and future historical investigations.

In his approach to understanding accounting, in the development of his theoretical position Besta was influenced by dominant philosophical discourse, especially as articulated by Spencer and Comte (Canziani 1987,

p. 203). This encouraged his advocacy of a positivist approach and empirical method in the field of accounting. Theoretical principles would be defined and their operations underpinned and illustrated by practical observations (Besta 1920, p. 394). In his own investigations, Besta adopted a combination of historical and empirical methods and considered that a scientific approach was essential to the development of accounting knowledge:

> In general, in all the branches of human activity, art comes before theory [. . .]. Therefore if the scientist doesn't like to build on the hole, he must refer to the alive source of the art and he must study its natural and effective development. This is the empirical method, the immense and continuous growth of the concrete sciences after Bacon and Galileo is indebted to. And this method must be applied to accounting if you want to give it a vital impetus.
>
> (Besta, 1909, pp. 55–56)

He perceived no incompatibility between science and practice. In order to investigate economic control of every kind of *azienda*, the empirical method would be combined with historical investigation (*historicism*). This was key to the construction of his accounting theory and his critical investigation of accounting practice during the fifteenth and seventeenth centuries (Canziani 1998, p. 50).

As indicated earlier, from the mid-nineteenth century, accounting theorization in Italy was based on the concept of the *azienda*, the entity, which is pivotal in the Italian accounting tradition (Zan 1994; Alexander and Servalli 2011). Besta's thinking on accounting accordingly commences from a notion of the *azienda* as 'the sum of phenomena, businesses and relationships which are administrated referred to an amount of capital' (Besta 1909, p. 3). His focus then shifts from the subject to the object of administration. Besta (1909, p. 5) considers the economic administration of the *azienda* as 'the governance of phenomena, businesses and relationships linked with the evolution of the Azienda's wealth'. He argues that the economic administration comprises three functions: '*gestione*' (operations), '*direzione*' (management) and '*controllo*' (control), pointing out that, while operations and management are different from one kind of '*azienda*' to another, economic control in the form of accounting, being a common feature of all economic units, could be the object of a scientific observation and generalization.

His accounting thought is not based on the subjects of the administration, often fictitiously created, as in French accounting theorization during the eighteenth century (De La Porte 1712; Dégranges 1795, 1804). Indeed, Besta also rejected the leading Italian position of the time, focused on the subjects of administration, expressed by Cerboni in his personalistic approach, named logismography. This method was characterized by the personifications of accounts and by the contraposition of the involved interests, represented on the one hand by the owner and on the other hand by the agency, composed by custodians and the debtors and creditors.

The contraposition between the positions of Besta and Cerboni emerged clearly during the first National Accounting Congress, held in Rome in 1879. In his interventions at the Congress, Besta contended that 'To base a theory on fictions appears to give it no solid foundation' (Atti dei Congressi Nazionali dei Ragionieri Italiani 1911, p. 111). Besta also questioned the legal notion of '*azienda*' which underpinned Cerboni's theory, advocating instead an economic concept, founded on wealth. For Besta accounting was the science of the 'economic control of each kind of azienda' (Besta 1909, p. 31). In particular, he identified wealth as the complex of resources of the '*azienda*' at a given moment. This wealth resourced the assets of the economic unit. He thus elaborated an equity-based accounting system (*sistema patrimoniale*). Asset measurement was based on replacement value. In this, he related accounting theory to economic thought, being particularly influenced by Ricardo's theory of value (Schneider 1987, p. 98).

In his *La Ragioneria*, Besta distinguished notions of the accounting method and accounting system. The accounting method refers to the form, order and the links between the entries, whereas the accounting system concerns the object of observation by accounting. Besta (1920, p. 276) was the first author to separate these two concepts and to clarify the relations between them.

Recalling Spencer's classification of sciences Besta underlined the applied, scientific nature of accounting (Besta 1922, p. 31). Accounting was one of the 'concrete sciences' (Spencer 1871) which concerned the study of the laws of 'economic control' in all kinds of entity, with the aim of identifying the norms to be adopted to achieve effective control. Accounting concerned the ordered application of these norms (Besta 1922, p. 31, vol. 1). Realizing the aims of the entity required that its different operations must be founded on the principles of economic administration. Economic control was not only a way of highlighting the stewardship of management but also an instrument of 'administrative enforcement', embracing all those actions which compelled managers and other employees to fulfil their duties with care (Mattessich 2008, p. 87; Galassi and Mattessich 2004). In this theoretical framework accounting moves away from mere bookkeeping activity to a core technique central to the economic control of the entity's wealth. The measurement of that wealth is a basis for rationally making decisions designed to achieve the economic aims of the entity.

Besta's accounting theory aims to investigate the *azienda*'s wealth (object)—considered as a series of resources, composed of positive elements (assets) and negative elements (liabilities). The application of the double-entry method (form) to the proposed accounting system requires that facts are observed in relation to their 'real' aspect—the increases and decreases of assets or liabilities—and in relation to their 'ideal' aspect—increases and decreases in net wealth (Belardinelli 1936, p. 14). Variations of these two aspects are respectively inserted in two series of accounts: elements accounts and net accounts (Besta 1920, p. 326).

In Besta's accounting system, it is necessary to consider all variations as positive or negative elements of wealth. Such variations in wealth stem from administrative facts. These may derive from external events, such as transactions with third parties, or from internal eventualities, such as the deterioration of goods. Administrative facts may be classified as permutative, modificative or mixed. Permutative facts do not modify the *azienda*'s wealth; modificative facts serve to increase or decrease net wealth, while mixed facts are a combination of permutative and modificative facts, involving not only a permutation of single elements of wealth but also an increasing or decreasing of net wealth. Besta's conception of an accounting system assumes an atomistic approach (Zan 1994, p. 290). The quantification of net wealth emerges from the sum of individual positive and negative values, and the calculation of changes in wealth is the sum of net variations in its elements. From this perspective changes in the *azienda*'s wealth is the principal focus and consequently the balance sheet is the core of the financial statement.

This scientific view of accounting, even before becoming the content of Besta's main publications, was the core of the accounting education he offered with his teaching in Ca'Foscari (Coronella 2007). This aspect is testified by the publications he realized to be exclusively used by his students, such as *Corso di Ragioneria professato alla Classe di magistero nella R. Scuola superiore di commercio in Venezia* (Besta 1891), where we see his theory being disseminated in classes to future generations of academics (e.g., Gino Zappa), accountants and businessmen.

In Ca'Foscari classes first and in his publications (including the books for students) then, the coordination between an accounting method (a set of rules applicable for different aims) and an accounting system articulated around the economics of the *azienda* emerged as Besta's most important contributions to accounting thought. These aspects represented a distinctive contribution from prevailing theorizations in Italy and beyond. Indeed, Besta articulated an adhesion between accounting theory and notions of wealth in the *azienda*. He also recognized the need to consider accounting within the complex of disciplines, asserting that he 'studied how to set the principles' of accounting 'in constant harmony with those of the juridical and social sciences' (Besta 1909, I: V). This connection with other sciences is also affirmed in his drawing on the theory of value. While recognizing that this theory might be considered to be beyond the borders of accounting (Besta 1909, p. 215), he emphasizes that accounting—as a technique whose object is to measure wealth—requires investigation of value.

Concluding this section, and as evidence of a bridge between his contribution in terms of accounting theorization and accounting history within the educational system, it is important to underline the impact of Besta on public accounting with his volume *Lezioni di contabilità di Stato* (1897–8) (Lessons on state accounting). In this book, state accounting issues are dealt with considering all the historical antecedents, as clearly testified by his words:

> I assert that the reason of the present is in the past, also for public accounting, as in all other branch of life, of activities, of human progress and that for the study of this discipline—more than for any other branch of social sciences—it suits to follow the *historical and experimental method*. For this reason, I will deal with the evolution that accounting and financial mechanisms had in the most civilized States, being very sorry not to be able to dwell upon this topic as much as I would and as much as its importance would require.
>
> (1897–8, p. 42)

In this volume on state accounting, after an introduction on the public entities and before an in-depth exploration of state accounting, the author explores state accounting in the past, moving from the most ancient, of Athens and Rome, to his contemporary days. In the next sections, his historical approach and his impact on this kind of study, as well as on the education of his scholars, will be further elucidated.

Influence on Historical Studies

As suggested earlier, Ca' Foscari in Venice was the first school of commerce to establish a chair in accounting (in 1872). Fabio Besta was the first holder of this chair (Fauri 1998, p. 39). His work in Ca' Foscari was characterized by an approach to accounting which emphasized its relationship with other disciplines, empiricism and the intimate connections between principle and practice. His approach to accounting education reflected a similar orientation, and is now characterized as the 'Venetian School' (Longobardi 1927, pp. 77–78). In light of this it is not surprising that Besta should engage with the study of history. His attention to history is also demonstrated by the constant encouragement to his pupils to study paleography and to perform research in the public archives (Longobardi 1927, p. 78). His own historical knowledge derived significantly from a comprehensive exploration of original accounting documents in the archives of Venice and other Italian cities. He discovered that 'Only the source was able to satisfy him' (Arena 1974, p. 131).

It was on the basis of his scrutiny of accounting documents that Besta authored the important historical chapters in Volume 3 of *La Ragioneria* (which are discussed in the next section) and generated another important historical publication titled *Collection of the Financial Documents of the Republic of Venice*. This two-volume work was published in 1903 (*Commissione per la pubblicazione dei documenti finanziari della Repubblica di Venezia*, 1903a and b), revised in 1912 and continually updated after his death. Besta's contribution to *Collection* is evident from the introduction to the work. Here, in the 1903 edition, he describes the contents of the historical documents contained therein, including one that appears under the title 'Notes on Drawing Up of General Financial Statements of Fact' ('*Commissione per la pubblicazione dei documenti finanziari della Repubblica di Venezia*' 1903b, VII–XCV). His extensive introduction also opened the work published in 1912 ('*Commissione per la pubblicazione dei documenti finanziari della Repubblica di Venezia*' 1912, XXXV–CCXXIII).

This work on primary documents in Venice represented an essential source for understanding the finances of the Venetian Republic that had yet to receive the attention of historians (Brown 1904, p. 354). Further in his report for the 'Commission for the publication of the Financial Documents of the Republic of Venice' Besta argued that it was important to proceed towards the publication of early examples of double-entry bookkeeping, as represented by the Badoer ledger and the Barbarigo journal. These books of account he later analysed in *La Ragioneria*.[4]

Consistent with his empirical and positivistic approach is Besta's argument against the originality of *Tractatus XI* in Pacioli's *Summa*. Besta performed biographical study of Pacioli and a content analysis of the *Tractatus XI*. His investigation of the life of Pacioli and his activities indicated an absence of experience as a businessman, assistant to a merchant or teacher of accounting. Besta concluded that Pacioli was unlikely to have attained the knowledge necessary to articulate double-entry bookkeeping as in the *Summa* (Besta 1922, pp. 363–364). His analysis of the *Tractatus* text, both in the language deployed and in its structure, as well as a comparison with similar publications from other countries, such as those authored by Oldcastle and Ympyn (Besta 1922, pp. 369, 381), led Besta to conclude that the *Tractatus* is not the source of these latter works. Rather, all of these publications may have had a common origin in a work that appeared in the first part of the fifteenth century, authored by an abacus master with the requisite knowledge, Troilo de Cancellaris. Testing the validity of Besta's argument against the originality of Pacioli's work is not within the scope of the current study. However, one aspect of his methodological approach should be noted. It could be suggested that by extending his vision beyond the country-specific, Besta anticipated the importance of a comparative international approach to investigating the history of accounting (Carnegie and Napier 1996, 2012).

La Ragioneria: A Milestone in Accounting History

From the early part of his career Besta strongly supported a longitudinal, historical approach to studying accounting (Besta 1880, 1916). He asked his readers to

> consider that the past, as in any other branch of life, activity, human progress, even in public accounting, is the reason for the present, and that in the study of such matters, perhaps more than in any other branch of social sciences, it is good to follow the historical experimental method.
>
> (Besta 1897–98, p. 42)

His seminal work on *La Ragioneria* was informed by this perspective and modus operandi. In his recent work Mattessich (2003) listed Besta among eminent Italian scholars but, surprisingly, did not cite *La Ragioneria* among books having a historical focus, perhaps as a consequence of the absence of 'history' in its title. By contrast de Roover (1956, p. 114) made the valid observation that 'The work of Fabio Besta is still authoritative and contains several historical chapters'. In order to confirm de Roover's point, Table 17.2 details the numerous historical sections in *La Ragioneria* as well as their location in the three volumes published from 1891 to 1916.

The richness of the accounting history content of *La Ragioneria* is even more apparent if we consider the state of accounting history research at the time of its publication. While a series of accounting history publications appeared in the late nineteenth century,[5] Besta uniquely extended beyond a purely descriptive approach. This reflected his view that historical investigation was an indispensable element in the construction of his theories of accounting.

That Fabio Besta's work has been a major contribution to the history of double-entry bookkeeping can be demonstrated in several ways. Here we confine our analysis to Book 9 in Volume 3 of *La Ragioneria*, which focused 'on the probable origins and the development of double-entry bookkeeping

Table 17.2 The historical content of *La Ragioneria*

Volume 1 (1891)	*Volume 2 (1909)*	*Volume 3 (1916)*
Book 1 (3 chapters) Book 2 (8 chapters) Chap. 7 Value	Book 3 (4 chapters) Chap. 4 History of Inventories Book 4 (5 chapters) Chap. 5 Reserve accounts Book 5 (3 chapters) Book 6 (5 chapters) Chap. 2, art. 5 The meaning of *dare ed avere*, debit and credit Chap. 3 The development of the accounting theory Chap. 5, art. 3 The remote origins of bookkeeping Book 7 (4 chapters) Chap. 2, art. 3 The development of single entry Chap. 4 Cameralistic bookkeeping	Book 8 (4 chapters) Book 9 (10 chapters) Chap. 9 The development of double entry Chap. 10 The history of accounting literature Book 10 (2 chapters) Book 11 (6 chapters) Book 12 (6 chapters) Chap. 6 The history of auditing

in practice' (Besta 1922, p. 273). Chapter 9 in Book 9 in particular has been of considerable interest to the accounting community. In this section our aim is reveal the significance of Besta's work on the origins of double-entry bookkeeping, as related in Chapter 9 of Book 9, to the research subsequently performed by prominent international scholars exploring the history of accounting in the period prior to the publication of Pacioli's *Summa*.

In Chapter 9 Besta considers pre-Paciolian double-entry bookkeeping registers from Genoa, Lombardy, Venice and Tuscany. Besta starts Chapter 9 with an analysis of the cartularies of the Commune of Genova, and reveals the content of some of the primary data contained there.[6] It was contended that these were the earliest examples of double-entry bookkeeping. The significance of Besta's findings was alluded to by de Roover (1955, p. 405) as follows:

> On the authority of Besta and his students, it was thought until recently that double-entry bookkeeping originated in Genoa around 1340 [. . .]. The theory that the earliest examples of double-entry bookkeeping were Genoese records of the year 1340 was until now accepted by most authorities, including Fabio Besta, Henry Rand Hatfield, A. C. Littleton, Balduin Penndorf, and others.

He later added,

> In recent years Italian and other scholars have done extensive research on medieval business records with the result that we are now much better informed about book-keeping prior to Pacioli than even a decade ago. Under the influence of Fabio Besta, whose treatise first appeared in 1909, the older writers attached much more importance to the matter of form and procedure.
>
> (1956, p. 114)

A. C. Littleton quoted Besta's work in *The Accounting Review* (henceforth *TAR*) in 1928 as part of his discussion of 'the evolution of the journal entry'. Here Littleton (1928, pp. 384, 389) quoted excerpts concerning early ledgers in Tuscany and Venice. Littleton referred more heavily to Besta in his seminal work, *Accounting Evolution to 1900* (1933). Table 17.3 relates the content of Besta's Chapter 9, Book 9, and identifies points at which it was later deployed by Littleton (1933).

Following the impetus provided by Besta examples of accounting from the Commune of Genova and the Banco di S. Giorgio (Bank of St. George) appeared in many other subsequent international and Italian publications. For example, the 'pepper' account ('*piper*' in Latin) illustrated by Besta (1922, pp. 276–279) was also later reproduced in Edward Peragallo's *Origin of Double Entry Book-Keeping* (1938, pp. 7–9). Excerpts of the cartularies also appear in Melis (1950) and Zerbi (1952). Interestingly, Martinelli, in his 'Notes on the Origin of Double Entry Bookkeeping' published in *Abacus*

Table 17.3 Archival sources analysed in *La Ragioneria* and discussed by Littleton (1933)

Examples of important archives on DEB analysed in Volume 3 (1916)	*Location*	*Reproductions in* **Littleton (1933)**
The Genovese cartularies—e.g., Commune of Genoa 1340 Pepper Account, Bank of St George 1408 (Latin)	pp. 273–287	p. 89 (Commune of Genoa 1340—. . . clerk of the Commune of Genoa owes us (*debet nobis*) that which is p. 102 (Commune of Genova, 1340—*Guillielmo Vacha Notarius debet nobis pro Commune Janue unde nobis in isto* . . .) p. 104 (Banco S. Giorgio, 1409—*Die xxvij marcij Bartholomeus de Mari debet nobis pro Francisco Iustiniano et socio massariis in* . . .)
Lombard-style registers: Archives of the Milan Fabbrica of Duomo Cathedral e.g., Management of the Treasury of the town of Piacenza, 1356–1357, and under the dominion of the Visconti, Lords of Milan,1358–59 e.g., State Archive of Reggio Emilia Tariffs and taxes collections, 1317 Register of the Treasurer of the Camera of Reggio, 1385–87	pp. 287–302	p. 102 (1356, Commune of Piacenza, Treasurer—*Guillelmus Bagarotus debet dare. scriptum in credito Beltramo Leccacorno in isto folio* . . .) p. 103 (1359, *Sozius Picollus debet dare scriptum in credito Communi Placentiae* . . .) p. 103 (1385, *Camera illustris principis et magnifici domini nostri* . . .)
Venetian ledgers and journals—e.g., Soranzo Brothers 1406; journal of the properties of the rebels of Padua, 1406; Barbarigo Family 1431; account of Andrea Barbarigo, January 2nd 1430; account of Jacomo Badoer, September 3rd 1436	pp. 302–317	p. 104 (1406, *Fraterna Soranzo—Debitori e creditori tratti del l'estratto fato per ser Jachomo Boltremo de dar per ser Donaldo Soranzo* . . .) p. 104 (1417, *Quaderno possessioni ribelli di Padova—Ser Marcho da Ponte de Venizia die dar per uno quarto de la gastaldia de* . . .)

(*Continued*)

Table 17.3 (Continued)

Examples of important archives on DEB analysed in Volume 3 (1916)	*Location*	*Reproductions in* Littleton (1933)
Tuscan registers—e.g., Yellow Book B of Francesco Datini, Marco's son, 1383; Averardo dei Medici, Francesco's son, 1395; del Bene Merchants, 1392; Filippo Borromeo and London companions Bank, 1436; ledgers of Giovanni Borromej from San Miniato, 1427; Bruges farm, 1438; Americho Benci, Florentine merchant,1459	pp. 317–333	p. 103 (1383, Yellow Book of Francesco di Marco Datini- *Nicholò di Francesco e fratelli da Firenze der dar . . .*) p. 103 (1392—*La chassa dei contanti de dare . . .*) p. 104 (1436, Filippo Borromei -*Ghaleazo Borromei e Antonio Di Francesco e comp. di Londra den dare a di 8 di marzo . . .*) p. 105 (Americho Benci, 1459—*La cassa de contanti de dare a di XXV di marzo . . .*)

(1977), presented an analysis of the main primary sources on double-entry bookkeeping which described many of the archives already identified by Fabio Besta.[7]

De Roover, who researched in the Italian archives, analysed the material relating to the Bank of St George, in his formulation of 'New Interpretations of the History of Banking' which appeared in the *Journal of World History* in 1954. Subsequently commenting on the accounting content of the ledgers of the Bank of 1408, and referring to Besta, he underlined that 'although the balance is little more than a trial balance, there can be no doubt that the Bank of St. George kept its book in double entry' (1956, pp. 134, 136).

It is not only Besta's work on the Genoa archives that has been widely cited; the Venetian ledgers of the fifteenth century have also been important sources for later scholars. For example, Littleton quoted Besta when providing examples of the Venetian *Fraterna Soranzo*—that is, the books of Donaldo Soranzo and Brothers, merchants, of 1406[8]—as well as the *Quaderno delle possessioni dei ribelli di Padova* (Book of the properties of the Paduan rebels), dated 1417.

The Venetian archives are perhaps best known for the ledger of Andrea Barbarigo. Besta originally referred to this source in his 1880 prolusion *La Ragioneria*. Here he discussed the presence of the Barbarigo archives, and showed two items from the first page of the ledger of Andrea Barbarigo of 1430, as well as other examples drawn from the ledger of Nicolò Barbarigo, dated 1457 (Besta 1880, pp. 44, 76). Later, in Volume 3 of *La Ragioneria*, Besta delved deeper in the Barbarigo archives, and provided a number of significant examples, such as the opening balance of 2 January 1430 (1922, p. 305). Besta (1922, p. 309) concluded that 'The Andrea Barbarico *giornale*, to date the oldest known, as well as his *quaderno* must be considered among the outstanding monuments of double-entry bookkeeping history' (emphasis added). Influential scholars later developed their analysis referring to Besta's previous work on these sources. Ed Peragallo, for example, on discussing the 'Origin of the Trial Balance' in *The Accounting Review* in 1956 quoted Besta when arguing that 'in practice, book-keepers were already using the balance account as an account in the ledger for a good many years before Pacioli. Andrea Barbarigo, a Venetian merchant, used such an account in his records of 1434 [Besta 1929, vol. III, p. 308]'.

The Venetian archives are also famed for the ledger of Jacomo Badoer, a commission agent for merchants in Venice who kept books in double entry with separate accounts for each venture. Besta revealed this source in his 1880 prolusion (44), stating that

> In this State Archive, in the bundle number 958 of de' Cinque Savi alla Mercanzia, there is a ledger perfectly kept following the double-entry bookkeeping, in whose first folio it is possible to read << In the name of God and of the good/fair gain the book belongs to me Jac. badoer of Constantinople, that I reached on the day 2 September 1436 . . .>>.

Vittorio Alfieri (1891), one of Besta's followers, later analysed Badoer's ledger more deeply and in 1897 Besta himself argued that the entire ledger, as a very important source on accounting, commerce, taxation, customs duties and foreign exchange issues with East countries, should be published (1922, p. 312) (see report of the *Commission for the Publication of the Venetian Republic Financial Document*).

In 'A Surmise Regarding the Origin of Bookkeeping by Double Entry' Katz (1930, p. 316) referred to Besta to argue that

> A ledger of the year 1436 that has come down to us and once belonged to the Venetian merchant Jachomo Badoer is an instance of factor's bookkeeping, adapted by the owner of the goods to himself. Badoer [. . .] carried with him a cargo belonging partly to other parties and partly to himself and in both instances the entries were identical [Besta 1922, vol. III, p. 311].

Relatedly, de Roover (1944, p. 405) in 'The Early Accounting Problems of Foreign Exchange' published in *TAR* quoted Besta, and indicated that his work had incited a visit to the archives to study the original source:

> According to entries in the ledger of Jacomo Badoer, a Venetian merchant residing in Constantinople in the second quarter of the fifteenth century, Italian transfer banks were operating in that city. Fabio Besta (*La Ragioneria* [3d ed., Milan, 1922], III, p. 313) cites one entry. I've found numerous others in the original account book in Venice.

Moreover, when illustrating the ledger kept by Jacomo Badoer in Constantinople (1436–1439) de Roover (1956) again referred to Besta.

Ed Peragallo (1977, 1983) also later referred to Besta when discussing the closing procedures revealed by Jacomo Badoer's ledgers, arguing (1981, p. 591),

> He uses a balance account called "Closing of this ledger" (Saldo di questo libro). He is not the first to use it. Extant ledgers of the Soranzo brothers in 1406 and of Andrea Barbarigo in 1434, all Venetian merchants, contained such an account (Besta 1929, pp. 303–306).

A number of scholars who intervened later in the debate about the history of double-entry bookkeeping focused on Tuscan practices during the thirteenth century (Melis 1950, p. 872; Castellani 1952, p. 721; de Roover 1956; Lee 1973a, 1973b, 1977). Though sometimes criticized even here Besta's work was recognized. For example, having performed a comprehensive examination of the 'Florentine Bank Ledger Fragments of 1211' (Santini 1887) Lee (1973a, p. 47) observed that

> Since their transcription in 1887 by Pietro Santini, the ledger accounts of 1211 on the flyleaves of the Codex Aedilis 67 in the Biblioteca Medicea-Laurenziana, Florence, have been recognized as the earliest long fragments of pure Italian, and especially Tuscan, prose . . . Historians of accounting, however, have accorded them only brief and summary treatment—Besta in 1922, Melis more fully in 1950, and Raymond de Roover in 1956.

Conclusions

An attempt has been made in this chapter to portray the life and principal writings of Fabio Besta, elucidating his profile as an accounting thinker, capable by his equity-based accounting system (*sistema patrimoniale*) and his theorization founded on value to influence the accounting education of many accounting generations in Italy and beyond. Further we have discussed the content of a chapter in Volume 3 of Besta's *La Ragioneria*, which represented a milestone in in augmenting accounting history knowledge, and a point of departure for subsequent studies on the history of double-entry bookkeeping (DEB), as well as a fundamental reference for his disciples to be educated through a historical investigation of accounting phenomena.

Besta was an eminent scholar who contributed to the development of accounting education in Italy and its tradition of accounting history scholarship. He crafted an accounting system based on the economic dimension of the *azienda* (i.e., wealth), and thereby advanced beyond some of the prevailing national (e.g., Cerboni) and international (e.g., Dégranges) accounting theories of his time. Of particular importance was his articulation of the adhesion of accounting theory and the theory of the *azienda*'s wealth. In the opinion of the authors Besta's contributions, particularly his shift from a personalistic to a materialistic accounting theory, merit his inclusion in the pantheon of 'accounting thinkers' (Edwards 1994, p. ix).

Besta's contribution to establishing the intrinsic value of historical inquiry, its relation to accounting theory, and the rise of accounting to the dignity of a science (Besta 1880, p. 37) was celebrated thus by Tito Antoni in his 'Report on the Fourth International Congress of the History of Accountancy':[9]

> The return of historians to our discipline is rather a recent development although in fact historical research applied to accountancy dated from the 19th century. A detailed reconstruction of the development of the methods of keeping accounts began when this discipline put aside its modest task of meeting the practical accounting needs of business firms to elevate itself to the dignity of a science. This brought with it the necessity, common to all branches of scientific knowledge, for historical inquiry.
>
> It was Fabio Besta who, a century ago, laid the foundations of this investigation, and it is to him that we owe the acknowledged accession of accountancy to its present autonomous existence. He maintained that no theory could have a solid basis unless it was founded in broad and thorough investigations of what had occurred in the past, and what is happening in the present, in firms of all kinds.
>
> (Antoni 1985b, p. ii)

A number of aspects of Besta's work presaged later developments. A century ago he attempted to craft an accounting theory informed by the Ricardian theory of value. He recognized that this theory existed beyond the borders of accounting (Besta 1909, p. 215), and was anxious to identify accounting principles that were in harmony with those prevailing in the juridical and social sciences (Besta 1909, p. v). Besta thereby demonstrated the importance of interdisciplinarity in accounting, anticipating the 'new accounting history' of the 1990s (Miller, Hopper and Laughlin 1991).

Besta was also acutely aware of the importance of history to an understanding of accounting. His empirical approach to historical research emphasized the importance of the archive and he made a major contribution by alerting other researchers to some of their contents. He also revealed to future generations the utility of historical research that ventured beyond the country-specific to embrace international comparisons. This approach was especially evident in his use of the different sources that sustained his arguments against the originality of Pacioli's *Tractatus*.

It has been shown that Besta's work on that subject has influenced numerous scholars in Italy and beyond. His findings on early double-entry bookkeeping practices were widely disseminated via the publications of eminent accounting historians. Of particular importance to revealing Besta's work to a wider audience was Littleton's 1928 paper on the journal entry and his *Accounting Evolution to 1900*, published in 1933. Subsequently, other influential scholars like de Roover and Peragallo used Besta's work to sustain their arguments in debates played out in foremost journals, such as *The Accounting Review*, *Journal of Accounting Research* and *Abacus*. In more recent times Besta has been quoted in papers appearing in specialist accounting history Anglophone journals, such as *Accounting, Business & Financial History* (e.g., Mattessich 2003). Importantly, Besta's works nowadays are still quoted not only in the Italian and Anglophone literature but also in Russia (e.g., Sokolov 1996; Gurskaya 2013; Kuter 2000, 2013), Spain (e.g., Hernández Esteve 2013), Brazil (D'Auria 1949; Lopes de Sà 2008) and other countries, thus undoubtedly witnessing his worldwide accounting education and accounting history dissemination throughout the globe well beyond his national geographic boundaries.

There have been suggestions that the results of accounting history research are insufficiently exported to neighbouring disciplines (Walker 2005, 2008). The same cannot be said of Besta's work. There exist several examples of scholars in other fields who have drawn on Besta's archival studies. For instance, F. C. Lane's (1944) highly regarded book *Andrea Barbarigo, Merchant of Venice (1418–1499)* contains the admission that the primary data for 'Barbarigo's journal are reproduced (from Besta) and translated' (1944, 148). Besta is also referred to in the context of Lane's assertion that an analysis of the ledgers of the Soranzo *fraterna* (1406–36), Andrea Barbarigo (1430–40) and Badoer indicates that 'double entry was well known and commonly used at Venice at the beginning of the fifteenth century' (1944, pp. 153–158). It is also the case that Besta's efforts to document, publicize and reproduce the primary sources located in Venice have proved invaluable to numerous historians, in accounting and beyond.

Notes

1. This chapter is based on the paper 'Fabio Besta: Accounting Thinker and Accounting History Pioneer', which originally appeared in *Accounting History Review* in 2012, 22 (3): 249–267.The authors would like to thank the publisher, Routledge Taylor & Francis, for permission to use this material.
2. The main sources of information about Besta's life are: Alfieri (1922); Amaduzzi (2001, p. 199); Antoni (1970, p. 3); Ceccherelli (1933); D'Alvise (1923); Perrone (1986, p. 55); Mola (1995); and Zappa (1935).
3. *La Ragioneria* comprises three volumes: Volume 1 (1891) contains an introduction, Book 1 (three chapters), Book 2 (eight chapters); Volume 2 (1909) contains Book 3 (four chapters), Book 4 (five chapters), Book 5 (three chapters), Book 6 (five chapters), Book 7 (four chapters); Volume 3 (1916) contains Book 8 (four chapters), Book 9 (ten chapters), Book 10 (two chapters), Book 11 (six chapters), Book 12 (six chapters). The quotations in this paper are taken from the second edition of *La Ragioneria*: Volume 1 (1909), Volume 2 (1920), Volume 3 (1922).
4. It should be noted that the content of the Venetian Archives extends well beyond these well-known sources for accounting historians. In particular, the archive contains important papers relating to accounting in more recent times (e.g., Sargiacomo, Servalli and Carnegie 2012).

5. In this period a number of works on accounting history were published, often stimulated by competitions arranged by scientific academies. Examples include works by Bariola (1897) and Luchini (1898) that were presented at a competition arranged by the Società Storica Lombarda (Lombard Historical Society) and won by Bariola.
6. The existence of the Commune of Genova cartularies—as well as of the archival material relating to the Banco di S. Giorgio (Bank of St George) and the Casa di S. Giorgio (Office of St George)—had originally been brought to wider attention (as acknowledged by Besta) by Cornelio Desimoni, the director of the Genova Archives, during a regional conference in 1865. Some brief excerpts subsequently appeared in Lanfranchi (1891, who quoted Desimoni), Heinrich Sieveking (1898, who referred to evidence presented by Desimoni in 1865), Brambilla (1901), Row Fogo (in Brown 1905, who also quoted Brambilla 1901) and Bagliano (1911). See also Besta (1922, pp. 273–274, note 1).
7. Importantly, Martinelli (1983) also later analysed 'The Ledger of Cristianus Lomellinus and Dominicus De Garibaldo, Stewards of the city of Genoa (1340–41)'.
8. Row Fogo (in Brown 1905, p. 100 et seq.) had previously published some excerpts of the Soranzo Brothers' book which, according to Besta (1922, p. 304), had been sent to Richard Brown by the director of the Venice Archive.
9. It is also possible to argue that without Besta's former abbrivium, and the later impetus provided by subsequent scholars—before and after Tito Antoni—there would not be an increasing interest of historians until the last World Congress of Accounting Historians (Sargiacomo 2017) and onwards.

References

Alexander, D., and Servalli, S. (2011), "Economia Aziendale and Financial Evaluations in Italy: Some Contradictions and Insights", *Accounting History* 16(3): 291–312.

Alfieri, V. (1891), *La partita doppia applicata alle scritture delle antiche aziende mercantili veneziane*. Torino: Paravia e Comp.

Alfieri, V. (1922), "Commemorazione di Fabio Besta", *La Rassegna delle Scienze Economiche e Commerciali*. Supplement to the pamphlet no. 12.

Amaduzzi, A. (2001), *Storia della Ragioneria. Uomini, aziende, contabilità*. Lomazzo (Como): La Tecnografica.

Andrei, P., Baker, R., and Sargiacomo, M. (2017), "Public Sector Accounting in Italy at the Beginning of the 20th Century: The Contributions of Fabio Besta", *The Accounting Historians* 44(1): 35–50.

Antonelli, V., and Sargiacomo, M. (2015), "Alberto Ceccherelli (1885–1958): Pioneer in the History of Accounting Practice and Leader in International Dissemination", *Accounting History Review* 25(2): 121–144.

Antoni, T. (1970), *Fabio Besta. Contributo alla conoscenza degli studi aziendali*. Pisa: Cursi.

Antoni, T. (1985a), "Leonardo Pisano Called Fibonacci, Mathematician and Accountant", In: *Fourth International Congress of the History of Accountancy. Pisa, 23–27 agosto 1984. Congress Proceedings*, Pisa, ETS: 1–10.

Antoni, T. (1985b), "Report on the 'Fourth International Congress of the History of Accountancy'", In: *Fourth International Congress of the History of Accountancy. Pisa, 23–27 agosto 1984. Congress Proceedings*, Pisa: ETS I–III.

Antoni, T. (1996), "Leonardo de Pisa. (Leonardo Pisano) (Fibonacci 11??–12??)", In: Chatfield, M., and Vangermeersch, R. (Eds.), *The History of Accounting: An International Encyclopedia*. New York: Garland Publishing Inc. 377–379.

Arena, G. (1974), "Bibliografia sui contributi di Fabio Besta alla storia ed all'analisi critica in ragioneria", *Rivista Italiana di Ragioneria e Economia Aziendale* 3: 128–131.

Atti dei Congressi Nazionali dei Ragionieri Italiani. (1911), *Adunanza dell'11 ottobre 1879*. Milano: Amministrazione del 'Monitore dei Ragionieri'.

Bagliano, C. (1911), *Sulla Contabilità di Stato in Genova*. Alessandria: Ricerche Alessandria—Tipografia Cooperativa.

Bariola, P. (1897), *Storia della ragioneria italiana premiata al Concorso della Società Storica Lombarda*. Milano: Tipografia Ambrosiana.

Belardinelli, G. (1936), "I principi logismologici di Cerboni, Besta e Zappa", *Rivista Italiana di Ragioneria* 29(1): 12–20.

Besta, F. (1872), *Sulla capitalizzazione continua degli interessi*. Sondrio: Tip. Brughera ed Ardizzi.

Besta, F. (1880), *La ragioneria, prolusione*. Venezia: Tipografia dell'Istituto Coletti.

Besta, F. (1891), *Corso di ragioneria professato alla classe di magistero nella R. Scuola Superiore di Commercio in Venezia. Parte prima*. Vol. 1. Venezia: Tipografia Frat. Visentini.

Besta, F. (1897–98), *Lezioni di contabilità di Stato*. Venezia: Litografie.

Besta, F. (1909), *La ragioneria, Seconda edizione riveduta ed ampliata col concorso dei professori Vittorio Alfieri, Carlo Ghidiglia, Pietro Rigobon. Parte prima*. Vol. 1. Milano: Vallardi.

Besta, F. (1916), *La ragioneria, seconda edizione riveduta ed ampliata col concorso dei professori Vittorio Alfieri, Carlo Ghidiglia, Pietro Rigobon. Parte prima*. Milano: Vallardi.

Besta, F. (1920), *La ragioneria, seconda edizione riveduta ed ampliata col concorso dei professori Vittorio Alfieri, Carlo Ghidiglia, Pietro Rigobon. Parte prima*. Vol. 2. Milano: Vallardi.

Besta, F. (1922), *La ragioneria, seconda edizione riveduta ed ampliata col concorso dei professori Vittorio Alfieri, Carlo Ghidiglia, Pietro Rigobon. Parte prima*. Vol. 3. Milano: Vallardi.

Besta, F. (1929), *La Ragionaria*. Milano: Vallardi.

Biondi, Y., Canziani, A., and Kirat, T. (2005), *The Firm as an Entity: Implications for Economics, Accounting and the Law*. London and New York: Routledge.

Bisman, J. (2011), "Cite and Seek: Exploring Accounting History through Citation Analysis of the Specialist Accounting History Journals, 1996 to 2008", *Accounting History* 16(2): 161–183.

Brambilla, G. (1901), *Storia della Ragioneria Italiana*. Milano: Boriglione.

Bricker, R.J. (1988), "Knowledge Preservation in Accounting: A Citational Study", *Abacus* 24(2): 120–131.

Brown, H.F. (1904), "Documenti Finanziari della Republica di Venezia", *The English Historical Review* 19(74): 354–356.

Brown, R. (ed.) (1905), *A History of Accounting and Accountants*. Edinburgh: Jack.

Canziani, A. (1987), "Sulle premesse metodologiche della rivoluzione appiana", In: AA.VV. (Eds.), *Scritti in memoria di Lino Azzini*. Milano: Giuffrè. 183–248.

Canziani, A. (1994), "Gino Zappa (1879–1960): Accounting Revolutionary", In: Edwards, J.R. (Ed.), *Twentieth-Century Accounting Thinkers*. London: Routledge. 142–165.

Canziani, A. (1998), "Business History: le tracce epistemologiche nella dottrina italiana", In: Società Italiana di Storia della Ragioneria (Ed.), *Atti del IV Convegno Nazionale di Storia della Ragioneria 'Storia di imprese tra il XVI e il XIX secolo'*. Roma: RIREA.

Canziani, A., and Rondo Brovetto, P. (1992), "The Emerging of the Economics of Firms in Continental Europe during the 20s: Economia Aziendale and Betriebswirtschaftslehre as Methodological Revolutions", In: Todd Lowry, S. (Ed.), *Perspectives in the History of Economic thought*. Vol. 7. London. Elgar for the History of Economics Society. 168–191.

Capalbo, F., and Clarke, F. (2006), "The Italian Economia Aziendale and Chambers' CoCoA", *Abacus* 42(1): 66–86.

Carnegie, G.D., and Napier, C.J. (1996), "Critical and Interpretive Histories: Insights into Accounting's Present and Future through Its Past", *Accounting, Auditing & Accountability Journal* 9(3): 7–39.

Carnegie, G.D., and Napier, C.J. (2012), "Accounting Past, Present and Future: The Unifying Power of History", *Accounting, Auditing & Accountability Journal* 25(2): 328–369.

Castellani, A. (1952), *Nuovi testi fiorentini del Dugento*. Firenze: G. C. Sansoni.

Ceccherelli, A. (1933), "In memoria di Fabio Besta", *Rivista Italiana di Ragioneria* 26(2): 73–75.

Cerboni, G. (1889), *Elenco cronologico delle opere di computisteria e ragioneria venute alla luce in Italia dal 1202 sino al 1888*. Roma, IV edizione 1889. Repr., Biblioteca storica di economia aziendale, Bari: Reprint Cacucci Editore, Bari, 1987.

Ceriani, G. (2006), "Il sistema contabile patrimoniale nell'impostazione di Fabio Besta, nella variante corrente ed in quella anglo-americana", *Contabilità e Cultura Aziendale* 6(2): 33–62.

Cinquini, L. (2007), "Fascist Corporative Economy and Accounting in Italy during the Thirties: Exploring the Relations between a Totalitarian Ideology and Business Studies", *Accounting, Business & Financial History* 17(2): 209–240.

Cinquini, L. and A. Marelli (2002), "An Italian forerunner of cost allocation concepts: Lorenzo de Minico and the logic of the flows of services", *Accounting, Business & Financial History* 12(1): 95–111.

Commissione per la pubblicazione dei documenti finanziari della Repubblica di Venezia. (1903a), *Serie seconda, Bilanci Generali, Vol. II, Bilanci dal 1736 al 1755 [scritture e decreti]*. Venezia: Premiato stabilimento grafico Visentini Cav. Federico.

Commissione per la pubblicazione dei documenti finanziari della Repubblica di Venezia. (1903b), *Serie seconda, Bilanci Generali, Vol. III, Bilanci dal 1736 al 1755*. Venezia: Premiato stabilimento grafico Visentini Cav. Federico.

Commissione per la pubblicazione dei documenti finanziari della Repubblica di Venezia. (1912), *Serie seconda, Bilanci Generali, Vol. I, Tomo I, I. Origini delle gravezze e dei dazii principali (976–1579), II. Regolazioni generali delle pubbliche casse e stati generali delle rendite e spese (1577–1641)*. Venezia: Premiato stabilimento grafico Visentini Cav. Federico.

Coronella, S. (2007), *La ragioneria in Italia nella seconda metà del XIX secolo. Profili teorici e proposte applicative*. Milano: Giuffrè.

Dagnino, G.B., and Quattrone, P. (2006), "Gino Zappa and John R. Commons' Accounts of 'Institution' as a Groundwork for a Constructivist View", *Journal of Management History* 12(1): 36–52.

D'Alvise, P. (1923), *In memoria del grande Maestro Gr. Uff. Rag. N. H. Fabio Besta, Professore emerito nella R. Scuola Superiore di Commercio di Venezia.* Roma: Stabilimento Tipografico del Messaggiero.

D'Auria, F. (1949), *Primeiros Principios de Contabilidade Pura.* Sao Paulo: Universidade de Sao Paulo.

Dégranges, E. (1795), *La tenue des livres rendue facile.* Paris: Hocquart.

Dégranges, E. (1804), *Supplément à la Tenue des livres rendue facile ou nouvelle méthode pour tenir les livres par moyen d'un seul register.* Paris: Hocquart.

De La Porte, M. (1712), *La science des Négocians et teneur de livres.* Paris: G. Cavelier.

De Roover, R. (1944), "The Early Accounting Problems of Foreign Exchange", *The Accounting Review* 11(3): 405–420.

De Roover, R. (1954), "New Interpretations of the History of Banking", *Journal of World History* 2: 56–57.

De Roover, R. (1955), "New Perspectives on the History of Accounting", *The Accounting Review* 30(3): 405–420.

De Roover, R. (1956), "The Development of Accounting Prior to Luca Pacioli According to the Account-Books of Medieval Merchants", In: Littleton, A.C,. and Yamey, B. (eds.), *Studies in the History of Accounting.* London: Sweet & Maxwell Limited. 114–174.

Desimoni, C. (1865), "Cristoforo Colombo e il Banco di S.Giorgio", *Atti della Società Ligure di Storia Patria* 3: 585–623. Genova.

Edwards, J.R. (ed) (1994), *Twentieth-Century Accounting Thinkers.* London: Routledge.

Fauri, F. (1998), "British and Italian Management Education before the Second World War: A Comparative Analysis", In: Engwall, L., and Zamagni, V. (Eds.), *Management Education in Historical Perspective.* Manchester: Manchester University Press. 34–49.

Fiume, R. (2007), "Lorenzo de Minico's thought in the Development of Accounting Theory in Italy: An Understated Contribution", *Accounting, Business & Financial History* 17(1): 33–52.

Flesher, D.L., and Previts, G.J. (2013), "Donaldson Brown (1885–1965): The Power of an Individual and His Ideas over Time", *The Accounting Historians Journal* 40(1): 79–102.

Galassi, G. (1984), "Accounting Research in Italy: Past, Present and Future", In: Hopwood, A.G., and Schreuder, H. (Eds.), *European Contributions to Accounting Research: The Achievements of the Last Decade.* Amsterdam: VU Uitgeverij/Free University Press. 163–187.

Galassi, G. (1996a), "Italy, after Pacioli", In: Chatfield, M., and Vangermeersch, R. (Eds.), *The History of Accounting: An International Encyclopedia.* New York: Garland Publishing Inc. 347–350.

Galassi, G. (1996b), "Paciolo, Luca (c. 1445–c.1517)", In: Chatfield, M., and Vangermeersch, R. (Eds.), *The History of Accounting: An International Encyclopedia.* New York: Garland Publishing Inc. 445–447.

Galassi, G. (1996c), "Zappa Gino (1879–1960)", In: Chatfield, M., and Vangermeersch, R. (Eds.), *The History of Accounting: An International Encyclopedia.* New York: Garland Publishing. 617–618.

Galassi, G., and Mattessich, R. (2004), "Italian Accounting Research in the First Half of the 20th Century", *Review of Accounting and Finance* 3(2): 62–83.

Gamble, G.O., O'Doherty, B., and Hyman, L.M. (1987), "The Development of Agency thought: A Citation Analysis of the Literature", *The Accounting Historians Journal* 14(1): 7–26.

Garner, S.P. (1976), "The Melis Testimonial", *The Accounting Historians Journal* 3(1): 13–15.

Gurskaya, M.M. (2013), *Methodology and Methods of Accounting: Genesis and Conceptual Foundations*. Krasnodar: Education, South.

Hatfield, H.R. (1950), "An Historical Defence of Book-Keeping", In: Baxter, W.T. (Ed.), *Studies in Accounting*. London: Sweet & Maxwell. 1–12. First printed in *The Journal of Accountancy*, April, 1924.

Hernández Esteve, E. (2013), *Aproximación al estudio del pensamento contable espanñol*. Madrid: Aeca.

Katz, P. (1930), "A Surmise Regarding the Origin of Bookkeeping by Double Entry", *The Accounting Review* 5(4): 311–316.

Kuter, M.I. (2000), *Theory of Accounting*. Moscow: Finance and Statistics Publ.

Kuter, M.I. (2013), *Introduction to Accounting: A Textbook*. Krasnodar: Prosveshenie-Ug.

Lane, F.C. (1944), *Andrea Barbarigo, Merchant of Venice (1418–1499)*. Baltimore: The John Hopkins Press.

Lanfranchi, G. (1891), *Le origini della partita doppia*. Ferrara: Tipografia sociale.

Lee, G.A. (1973a), "The Florentine Bank Ledger Fragments of 1211: Some New Insights", *Journal of Accounting Research* 11(1): 47–61.

Lee, G.A. (1973b), "The Development of Italian Bookkeeping 1211–1300", *Abacus* 9(2): 137–155.

Lee, G.A. (1977), "The Coming of Age of Double Entry: The Giovanni Farolfi Ledger of 1299–1300", *The Accounting Historians Journal* 4(2): 79–95.

Littleton, A.C. (1928), "The Evolution of the Journal Entry", *The Accounting Review* 3(4): 383–396.

Littleton, A.C. (1933), *Accounting Evolution to 1900*. New York: American Institute Publishing.

Longobardi, E.C. (1927), "Higher Commercial Education in Italy", *Journal of Political Economy* 35(1): 39–90.

Lopes De Sà, A. (2008), *Moderna Análise de Balanços ao Alcance de Todos*. Curitiba: Juruà Editora.

Luchini, E. (1898), *Storia della ragioneria italiana*. Milano: Amministratore del periodico "Il ragioniere", Tipografia Boriglione.

Martinelli, A. (1977), "Notes on the Origin of Double Entry Bookkeeping", *Abacus* 13(1): 3–27.

Martinelli, A. (1983), "The Ledger of Cristianus Lomellinus and Dominicus De Garibaldo, Stewards of the city of Genoa (1340–41)", *Abacus* 19(2): 83–118.

Mattessich, R. (2003), "Accounting Research and Researchers of the Nineteenth Century and the Beginning of the Twentieth Century: An International Survey of Authors, Ideas and Publications", *Accounting, Business & Financial History* 13(2): 125–170.

Mattessich, R. (2008), *Two Hundred Years of Accounting Research: An International Survey of Personalities, Ideas and Publications*. New York: Routledge.

Mautz, R.K., and Previts, G.J. (1977), "Eric Kohler: An Accounting Original", *The Accounting Review* 52(2): 300–307.

Melis, A. (2007), "Financial Statements and Positive Accounting Theory: The Early Contribution of Aldo Amaduzzi", *Accounting, Business & Financial History* 17(1): 53–62.

Melis, F. (1950), *Storia della ragioneria. Contributo alla conoscenza e interpretazione delle fonti più significative della storia economica*. Bologna: Zuffi.

Miller, P., Hopper, T., and Laughlin, R. (1991), "The New Accounting History: An Introduction", *Accounting, Organizations and Society* 16(5–6): 395–403.

Mola C. (ed.) (1995), *Fabio Besta, il Maestro della Ragioneria, nel 150° dalla nascita*. Sondrio: Banca Popolare di Sondrio.

Morecroft, S.E., Coffman, E.N., and Jensen, D.L. (2000), "Coleman Andrews: Crusader for Accountability in Government", *Accounting, Business & Financial History* 10(2): 245–258.

Moussalli, S.D., Flesher, D.L., and Lemarchand, Y. (2009), "Pierre Boucher and the 1803 Edition of La science des negocians: Accounting in the Republic", *Accounting, Business & Financial History* 19(3): 353–364.

Nobes, C. (1995), "Pacioli's Tractatus: A Note on a Mystery and a Review of Some Commentaries", *Accounting, Business and Financial History* 5(3): 379–384.

Padroni, G. (1976a), "A Profile of Melis", *The Accounting Historians Journal* 3(1): 15–18.

Padroni, G. (1976b), "A Bibliography of Melis' Works. Trans. A. Martinelli", *The Accounting Historians Journal* 13(1): 18–21.

Parker, R.H. (1980), *British Accountants: A Biographical Sourcebook*. New York: Arno Press.

Parker, R.H. (1996), "Basil Yamey, Accounting Historian", *Accounting, Business & Financial History* 6(3): 235–246.

Peragallo, E. (1938), *Origin of Double Entry Book-Keeping*. New York: American Institute Publishing Company.

Peragallo, E. (1956), "Origin of the Trial Balance", *The Accounting Review* 31(3): 389–394.

Peragallo, E. (1977), "The Ledger of Jachomo Badoer: Constantinople September 2, 1436 to February 26, 1440", *The Accounting Review* 52(4): 881–892.

Peragallo, E. (1981), "Closing Procedures in the 15th Century Ledger of Jachomo Badoer, a Venetian Merchant", *The Accounting Review* 56(3): 587–595.

Peragallo, E. (1983), "Development of the Compound Entry in the 15th Century Ledger of Jachomo Badoer, a Venetian merchant", *The Accounting Review* 58(1): 98–104.

Perrone, E. (1986), *La dottrina di Fabio Besta nell'evoluzione della Ragioneria*. Siena: Tipografia Senese.

Poddighe, F., Coronella, S., Deidda Gagliardo, E., and Madonna, S. (2007), "Francesco Marchi and the Development of Logismology", *Accounting, Business & Financial History* 17(1): 11–32.

Previts, G.J., Coffman, E.N., and Parker, L.D. (1990a), "Accounting History: Definition and Relevance", *Abacus* 26(1): 1–16.

Previts, G.J., Coffman, E.N., and Parker, L.D. (1990b), "An Accounting Historiography: Subject Matter and Methodology", *Abacus* 26(2): 136–158.

Quattrone, P. (1994), "Lodovico Flori's Accounting thought: An Epistemological Introduction", *Economia Aziendale Review* 13(2): 199–216.

Reinstein, A., Gerald, A., and Vangermeersch, R.G. (2008), "George R. Husband: Contributions to the Development of Accounting thought", *Abacus* 44(1): 82–108.

Row Fogo, J. (1905), "History of Book-Keeping", In: Brown, R. (Ed.), *A History of Accounting and Accountants*. Edinburgh: Jack. 93–133.

Santini, P. (1887), "Frammenti di un libro di banchieri fiorentini scritti in volgare nel 1211", *Giornale Storico della Letteratura Italiana* 10.

Sargiacomo, M. (2017), "Report of the XIV World Congress of Accounting Historians", *The Accounting Historians Journal* 44(1): 97–101.

Sargiacomo, M., and Gomes, D. (2011), "Accounting and Accountability in Local Government: Contributions from Accounting History Research", *Accounting History* 16(3): 253–290.

Sargiacomo, M., Servalli, S., and Andrei, P. (2012), "Fabio Besta: Accounting Thinker and Accounting History Pioneer", *Accounting History Review* 22(3): 249–267.

Sargiacomo, M., Servalli, S., and Carnegie, G.D. (2012), "Accounting for Killing: Accountability for Death", *Accounting History* 17(3–4): 393–413.

Schneider, D. (1987), *Geschichte betriebswirtschaftlicher Theory* [History of the Theory of Business-Economics]. 3rd. Munich: Oldenbourg Verlag.

Scuola Superiore di Commercio in Venezia. (1919), *Annuario della R. Scuola Superiore di Commercio in Venezia (Istituto Superiore di Studi Commerciali) per l'Anno Accademico 1918–1919*. Venezia: Stabilimento tipo-litografico F. Garzia.

Servalli, S. (2004), "La storia della professione di Ragioniere e di Expert comptable", In: Amaduzzi, A. (Ed.), *Storia della Ragioneria: Percorsi di ricerca tra Aziende, Contabilità, Dottrine e Professioni*. Milano: Giuffrè.

Sieveking, H. (1898), "Genueser Finanzwesen vom 12. bis 14. Jahrundert", *Volkswirtschaftliche Abhandlungen der Badischen Hochshulen* 1: 388–389, 481–488.

Sokolov, I.V. (1996), *Accounting: From the Beginning to the Present days: A Manual for Schools*. Moscow: IuNITI Publ.

Spencer, H. (1871), *Classification of Sciences*. London and Edinburgh: Williams and Norgate.

Toniolo, G. (1990), *An Economic History of Liberal Italy, 1850–1918*. London: Routledge.

Vianello, V. (1932), "Pensiero in memoria di Fabio Besta", *Rivista Italiana di Ragioneria* 25(10–12): 316–317.

Viganò, E. (1994), "A Comparative View of Accounting and 'Economia Aziendale'", *Economia Aziendale Review* 13(1): 1–70.

Viganò, E. (1998), "Accounting and Business Economics Traditions in Italy", *European Accounting Review* 7(3): 381–403.

Walker, S.P. (2005), "Accounting in History", *The Accounting Historians Journal* 33(2): 233–259.

Walker, S.P. (2006), "Philanthropic Women and Accounting: Octavia Hill and the Exercise of Quiet Power and Sympathy", *Accounting, Business & Financial History* 16(4): 163–194.

Walker, S.P. (2008), "The Search for Innovation, Convergence and Argument without End in Accounting History", *Accounting, Auditing & Accountability Journal* 21(2): 296–322.

Yamey, B.S. (1967), "Fifteenth and Sixteenth Century Manuscripts on the Art of Bookkeeping", *Journal of Accounting Research* 5(Spring): 51–76.

Zambon, S., and Zan, L. (2000), "Accounting Relativism: The Unstable Relationship between Income Measurement and Theories of the Firm", *Accounting, Organizations and Society* 25(8): 799–822.
Zan, L. (1994), "Towards a History of Accounting Histories: Perspectives from the Italian Tradition", *European Accounting Review* 3(2): 255–307.
Zappa, G. (1927), "Tendenze nuove negli studi di ragioneria", In: *Discorso inaugurale dell'anno accademico 1926–27 nel Regio Istituto Superiore di Scienze Economiche e Commerciali di Venezia*, Milan, Istituto Editoriale Scientifico.
Zappa, G. (1935), *Fabio Besta, il Maestro. Commemorazione letta a Ca' Foscari il 2 febbraio 1935*. Venezia: Tipografia Emiliana.
Zerbi, T. (1952), *Le origini della partita doppia*. Milan: Marzorati.

18 Historical Origins and Evolution of Small and Medium Practices in the Northeast of the Italian Peninsula

Marisa Agostini, Michela Cordazzo and Chiara Saccon

Introduction: Definition and Features of Small and Medium Practices

The latest report issued by the International Federation of Accountants (2016, p. 10) emphasizes that small and medium practices (SMPs) are themselves small and medium enterprises (SMEs), but they are also the main suppliers of accounting support to SMEs. The studies implemented by the Organization for Economic Cooperation and Development (OECD) underline how widely diffused is the presence of SMEs and highlights the key role of these firms in economic development. This is especially relevant in the Italian context, where SMEs are considered the engine of the country. SMEs represent 99.9% of Italian enterprises and account for 80% of the industrial and service labor force (Eurostat, 2011; OECD, 2016). In the Italian economic system, almost half of SMEs have a unicellular structure, with a small number of employees, sole proprietorship and average turnover comparable to that of micro-firms (Unioncamere-Mediobanca, 2016). The Italian share of micro-enterprises is higher than the EU average across all sectors (OECD, 2016). Thus, the role of SMPs is extremely important in the Italian economic system because, as emphasized earlier, they themselves represent a type of SME and are also the main suppliers of accounting support to SMEs. In spite of this relevance, SMPs have not been much studied. The present chapter focuses on SMPs, particularly on their historical origins in the northeast of the Italian Peninsula, starting from their definition and main features.

The first and most widespread definition of small and medium practices (SMPs) has been provided by the International Federation of Accountants:

> They are practices that exhibit the following characteristics: their clients are mostly Small and Medium Enterprises (SMEs);[1] they use external sources to supplement limited in-house technical resources; they employ a limited number of professional staff.
>
> (IFAC, 2010, p. 10)

Moreover, SMPs "do not ordinarily audit the accounts of listed companies, and most of their work is the provision of non-assurance services (e.g., regulatory compliance, tax, advisory services)" (IFAC, 2016, p. 10). These main features are explored in the following pages.

The first part of the definition of SMPs immediately emphasizes the importance of the supply relationship between small and medium practices (SMPs) and small and medium enterprises (SMEs). This relationship is considered a necessary mutual relation, since each needs the other to survive in their economic environment. Small businesses strongly require SMPs' services, especially for legal and fiscal support, in order to produce and to present appropriate documentation to local government agencies. This external support is also sought when there is a change within the enterprise (growth, acquisition, mergers) or a change in the external environment, and there is a lack of in-house expertise (Jarvis and Thompson, 2014). Indeed, most SMEs need to look to external suppliers for the competencies they require. Moreover, these firms are not searching for especially highly qualified accountants, preferring a demonstration of technical competency and giving priority to personalities and to the promptness of advice and support. Once that competency has been established, the relationship tends to go beyond the statutory service provision. Indeed, SMPs' services are requested not only for mandatory tasks but also for advice related to payroll, context-environment, human resources, health and other financial management services. In this way, the building of trust also promotes the development of accountants' non-conventional services and facilitates the understanding of mutual needs and competencies, reducing uncertainty. Accountants enjoy two different levels of trust: the 'institutional' is related to the regulations and norms of conduct laid down by the government, as chartered accountancy is a government-regulated profession, while the 'relational' dimension of trust derives from their particular relationship with clients, especially with SMEs. Because of their repeated provision of services, accountants tend to establish a relation based on trust with their clients (Gooderham et al., 2004). Small enterprises search for quick responses and prefer to have personal face-to-face meetings with accountants, so proximity and responsiveness represent a strong competitive advantage for SMPs (Jarvis and Thompson, 2014). As a consequence, SMPs often empathize with their client, while bigger accountancy firms tend to pass clients from department to department for specific questions to be addressed (IFAC, 2010). Moreover, to be as effective as possible, SMPs always have to maintain close relations not only with clients but also with trusted experts of different economic sectors, such as bankers, lawyers and IT specialists. SMPs provide not only accountancy-based services, such as audits, accounting and tax, but also other forms of value-adding business advisory services (advice on strategic planning, financing, administration and risk and uncertainty management). The main difference between traditional (accountancy-based) and business advisory services regards stakeholders: the first type of service is primarily rendered to external stakeholders, while the latter answers to internal managerial needs (Carey, 2008).

The heterogeneity of the services provided by SMPs brings in the other two features mentioned in their definition—that is, the use of external sources to supplement limited in-house technical resources and the employment of a limited number of professional staff. It is extremely difficult for SMPs to provide a high level of service without the collaboration of external parties, as these relationships play a key role in the world economy (IFAC, 2011) and allow the provision of a variety of services. Indeed, the chartered accountant is a professional who assists and provides advice to businesses and private individuals on issues related to administrative, fiscal and legal practices. She/he needs to be a highly qualified person, with several competences, able to solve the problems faced by her/his clients in a professional manner (Siriwardane and Durden, 2014). The activities affiliated to this profession are many:[2] SMPs can accomplish different functions on behalf of their clients and, in particular, of SMEs according to their structure, strategy adopted and degree of specialization (Attolini, 2012). The most recent studies about SMPs regard the additional roles required in a global accounting environment (Jarvis and Thompson, 2014): the development of features like competency, tacit knowledge and social relations (Blackburn et al., 2014) in order to meet the expectations and requests of emerging businesses; also the type of assistance useful in directing clients towards a consideration of environmental sustainability problems (Agyemang et al., 2012).

The foregoing issues referring to SMPs and their definition are relatively recent, but their origins go much further back in time. It is interesting to consider the features and the development of SMPs at the beginning of their history, before there was any precise definition or relevant debate about their roles. These issues will be considered in the next section, focusing on the northeast of the Italian Peninsula, where a concern with the origins of the profession of chartered accountant has always been lively (ODCEC, 2015). The third section of the chapter describes the main historical events which led to the official recognition of an autonomous role for accountants in the Venetian history. It also emphasizes those main features of SMPs which appear to have persisted from the historical origins of the profession down to our own day, underlining the long duration of the supply relationship between SMPs and SMEs.

Historical Origins of the Profession of Chartered Accountant

In a number of cultural and academic environments, Italian research work on accounting history is considered of particular importance on account of the significant presence of historical archives and public records concerning the birth of specific practices, such as double-entry bookkeeping and scientific thought in the accounting field (Antonelli and D'Alessio, 2011). Roman civilization brought with it the spread of accounting practices (including in the private sector) and saw the birth of early forms of financial statements (Casalena, 2010). Even if accounting records can be found in ancient times, the accountant starts to be considered as a professional in the medieval age in both the public and the private sectors, answering a demand from increasing mercantile activity (Ciambotti, 2007). This development of the accounting profession in the Middle Ages may be considered one of several demonstrations of the freedom and creativity of individuals, seeking to comprehend the world in all its aspects (Sombart, 1921). Professional experience begins to burgeon in several cities. For instance, in Genoa, around the twelfth century, the development of accounting techniques paves the way to the birth of the first banking activities. Further, the need of the administration of public, private and religious entities (e.g., monasteries and abbeys) to record debts and credits begins to rise considerably. In this historical period, it becomes necessary to be able to demonstrate that the calculations related to transactions are correct and new accounting tools are required. As a consequence, two different accounting books start to be employed (Millis, 1994): a simple cash account is used to record cash inflows and outflows, without taking into consideration the nature of the transaction, while a form of venture accounting is organized in paragraphs with long narratives that describe the transaction. As transactions become larger and more difficult to remember, the need for double entry increases.

The year 1202 is crucial for the evolution of accountancy, in that it sees the publication of the *Liber Abaci* by Leonardo Fibonacci. With its publication, Arabic numerals are introduced into our country, an efficient accountancy system starts to appear ('commercial mathematics') and new technical terms are established (e.g., '*debet dare, debet habere*'). Studies and research on the application of accounting and administrative practices have investigated monasteries, churches and abbeys. Thus it is not surprising that the 'father' of double entry is traditionally considered to be a friar who studied in Venice at the 'Rialto Academy' and taught mathematics in Florence, Naples, Bologna and Pisa. Recent studies have, however, emphasized the existence of a textbook containing some accounting exercises written by Marino de Raphaeli in 1475 prior to the publication of Pacioli's work (Sangster, 2015).

In 1494, Fra Luca Pacioli published his *Summa de Arithmetica, Geometria, Proportioni et Proportionalità*, which explained double-entry bookkeeping. This represented a great step forward in accounting techniques. Fra Pacioli writes,

> All creditors must be written on the right side of the Book and all debtors on the left (. . .) All entries in the Book must be double, that is if you make one creditor, you have to make one debtor (. . .) Both sides must be balanced.
>
> (Pacioli, 1494 as translated into English by Brown and Johnston, 1963, 102–104)

All entries have to contain the date of the operation, the amount and the justification. The date on which the debt is written should be the same as that on which the credit is recorded. The book should be compiled always in the same currency and be maintained from the beginning through to the last page. Money values are still recorded in Roman numerals, while paragraphs are kept either vertically or horizontally. Later, the layout with debit on the left side and credit on the right becomes universal. This accounting method, pioneered in Italy, gradually spreads all over the world and terms like 'balance sheet', 'assets', 'revenue', 'loss' and 'inventory' become more common.

The reasons for the Italian accounting technique's rapid spread throughout Europe are related to three phenomena in particular: the improvement of accounting techniques in order to meet the increasingly sophisticated demands of merchants (Millis, 1994); the invention of the printing press, combined with a favorable economic environment encouraging the enhancement of accounting practices and a wider diffusion of business education; and the great economic development of the three main 'city-states'—that is, Venice, Genoa and Florence ('Italy's Golden Triangle'). These three phenomena will now be described in more detail. Firstly, the flow of trade and commerce in Northern Europe causes an increasing demand for more specialized services, although no systematic body of accounting theory will be developed before the nineteenth century, and accounting is left to practitioners facing practical business problems. Venice is the trading center of Europe and becomes the continent's main propagandist of the double-entry accounting system. It cannot be disputed that "modern accounting is the result of a long and arduous problem solving effort, itself related to the increasing complexities of trade in early modern Italy" (Millis, 1994, 83). The other two phenomena are strictly related to the introduction in Germany of movable-type printing (in 1454), which boosts the diffusion of the double-entry technique and the education of merchants thanks to the introduction of books and manuals on accounting. Given its economic development, Venice soon becomes the printing center of Southern Europe, surpassing Genoa and Florence in terms of modernity. A great number of business and accounting books are published in Venice. Following the spread of double entry and the boom in mercantile activity in almost all countries of the Old World during the seventeenth century, there begins to be a progressive specialization of the accounting profession accompanied by initial attempts to confer an autonomous and formalized shape on it. The art of keeping the accounting books differentiates itself from 'arithmetic': accountants, in place of mathematicians, begin to teach merchants the accounting art. This role is performed by professionals who follow the activities of firms in the administrative sector, and is definitively recognized in Venice in 1581 by the republic's Council of Ten,[3] who promulgate a decree for the establishment of a '*Collegio de' Rasonati*'. The Collegio is composed of "knowledgeable and experienced individuals, with specific technical skills" (Cappellaro, 1997, 149).

The Establishment of the *Collegio de' Rasonati*: The First Venetian Accountants' Association

The reasons for the establishment of the accounting profession in the north-east of the Italian Peninsula may be related to the economic and political situation of the Venetian Republic. At that time, Venice was a flourishing and prosperous city, particularly on account of its trade with the Far East. The Venetian Republic stretched over almost all of the Veneto, and parts of both Lombardy and Friuli Venezia Giulia. The need to control both these territories and economic relationships with the Far East progressively gave rise to a massive delegation of power with a consequent creation of magistracies. The bureaucratic apparatus became so large and complex that the competencies of some magistracies overlapped (Zambon, 2002). There arose, therefore, a need for reliable and professional accountants to ensure that the magistracies were enabled to carry out their jobs efficiently. This requirement, related to the economic and political situation of the Venetian Republic just outlined, led to the establishment of the so-called *Collegio de' Rasonati* when a board of accountants was appointed by the Council of Ten on 2 December 1581 (Figures 18.1–18.4). Henceforth, all accountants aspired to join the *Collegio* in order to be considered experts and reliable members of their profession, but this was possible only if they proved their expertise through a series of tests (Edwards, 1994). In particular, an accountant needed to meet the following requirements: never having performed manual work, never having been imprisoned for a serious crime, and being a Venetian citizen or living in Venice for at least five years. Given these three requirements he then had to pass a test to ensure his accounting capabilities and competence. In order to be accepted into the *Collegio*, the applicants had also to undertake a period

MDLXXXI. a' II. Decembre.

IN CONSEGLIO DI X.

ET ZONTA.

In materia de far vn Collegio de Rasonati.

Andarà parte, che sia fatto vn Collegio di Rasonati in questa Città: nel quale chi vorrà entrare, debba esser diligentemente essaminato dalli Rasonati nostri Ducali alla presenza de i Regolatori nostri alla Scrittura, se ve ne saranno, & delli cinque Savij alla Mercantia, dovendosi da essi Rasonati formar alquanti quesiti necessarij per tal essamina. Et fatta la prova del saper di ciascuno in materia di tener ben scrittura, quei che dalli predetti Magistrati nostri assistenti, & cognitori saranno a bossoli, & ballotte con li tre quarti approbati per buoni, s'intendano del detto Collegio. Nel quale siano accettati principalmente Cittadini nostri, conosciuti (come di sopra) per sufficienti a questo carico, potendo anco esser eletti quelli, che havessero habitato in questa Città almeno per anni cinque continui, pur che non essercitino arte mecanica, ò che siano stati in alcun tempo notati di qualche infamia, i quali siano del tutto esclusi da simil carichi; douen-

Figure 18.1 In *Conseglio di 10. Et Zonta. In materia de far vn Collegio de Rasonati*

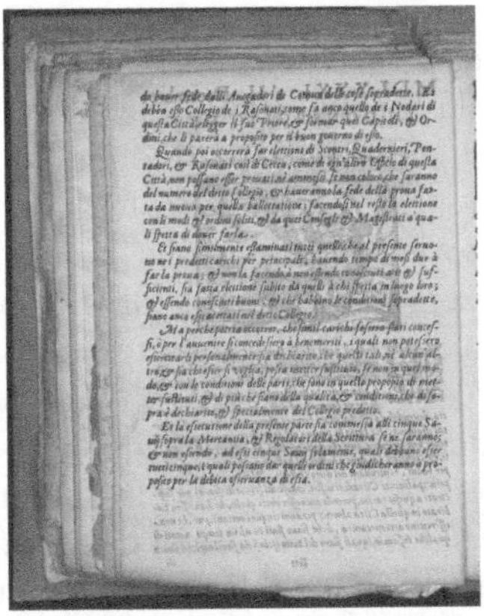

Figure 18.2 In *Conseglio di 10. Et Zonta. In materia de far vn* Collegio de Rasonati

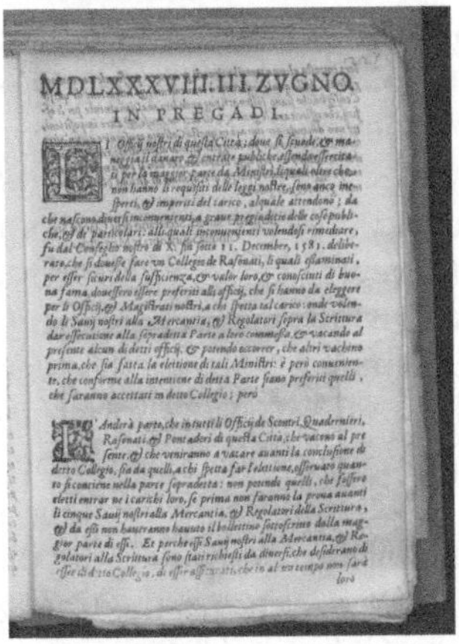

Figure 18.3 In *Conseglio di 10. Et Zonta. In materia de far vn* Collegio de Rasonati

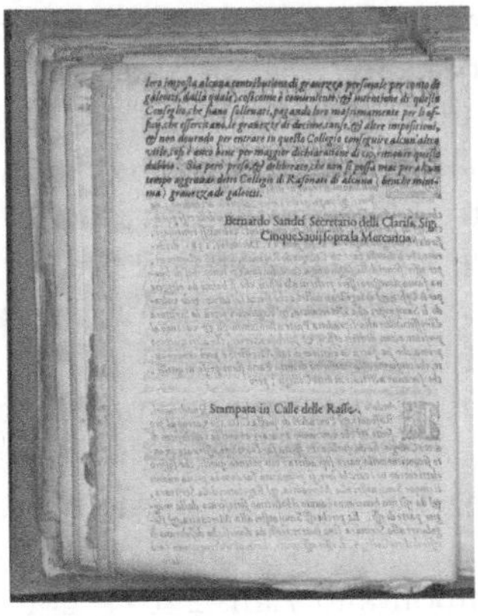

Figure 18.4 In *Conseglio di 10. Et Zonta. In materia de far vn* Collegio de Rasonati

[This document was printed in 1588 and refers to the formal recognition of the *Collegio de' Rasonati* in the Republic of Venice.]

of apprenticeship and pay a fee of fifty ducats. These barriers to entry into the *Collegio* were put in place in order to demonstrate to the outside world the proven professional competence of accountants.

The *Collegio* was created to mold professionals who would perform accounting tasks in a proper and competent way. "All those engaged, either currently or in the future, in bookkeeping, for whatever purposes, had to join the Collegio, as a guarantee of their expertise and competence" (Zambon, 2002, p. 75). The *Collegio* was entrusted by the *Serenissima*[4] with public responsibilities and functions in order to manage accounting issues in the most correct and professional way—that is, under the supervision of the '*Revisori e Regolatori della scrittura*' and of the '*Collegio dei Savi*'. The *Revisori e Regolatori della scrittura*, established on 24 January 1575, revised and fixed the accounting situation after the war in Cyprus,[5] and it had authority over all Venetian offices, including the Council of Ten (and its dependent entities). The *Collegio dei Savi*, founded in 1380 in order to limit the powers of the doge,[6] was one of the older organs of the republic, and was a sort of council of ministers called '*Savi*' (which translates as 'wise men'). There were eleven of these, among whom only five were responsible for the supervision of the *Collegio*. The day-to-day running of the *Collegio* was in the hands of a prior,[7] a deputy prior, two presidents and a chancellor, who were elected by the members of the *Collegio*. These five representatives were part of the '*Colleggetto dei Rasonati*', which expanded from five to fifteen members in 1665. The number of accountants who could be enrolled in the *Collegio* also changed over time: at the outset (in 1589) there was a maximum of twenty accountants, and the upper limit then became twenty-five in 1590, before being raised to fifty in 1592, and finally settling at one hundred in 1633. Notwithstanding the supervision exercised by all the entities mentioned (i.e., the *Revisori e Regolatori della scrittura*, the *Collegio dei Savi* and the *Colleggetto dei Rasonati*), the *Collegio de' Rasonati* remained an independent entity. It established its own 'statutes and orders' and filled the main accounting positions of the time ('*Scontri*', '*Quadernieri*' and '*Pontadori*'). These posts were reserved for members of the *Collegio* only (Figures 18.5–18.8): '*Scontri*' saw that the books were balanced; '*Quadernieri*' were bookkeepers and recorded operations in the historical ledgers; '*Pontadori*' were appointed to supervise the administration of operations carried out by each enterprise. Each role called for a trial two months of practice, after which period the candidate's performance was evaluated and he was accepted or not. Should a candidate fail to come up to scratch, another (meeting the requirements specified earlier) would be chosen. This entrance path emphasizes the key role of the *Collegio* in training accounting professionals.

The *Collegio de' Rasonati* is considered the 'father' of the current professional associations of chartered accountants (Siboni, 2005). It had a positive impact on the implementation of precise accounting procedures, but was not without its critics (Zambon and Zan, 2007). For instance, one drawback was the excessive rigidity imposed by the *Collegio* on accounting procedures.

Figure 18.5 *Parti prese nell'eccellent. Cons. de 10. & Zonta. 1581. Adi 11. Decembre. Et 1588.*

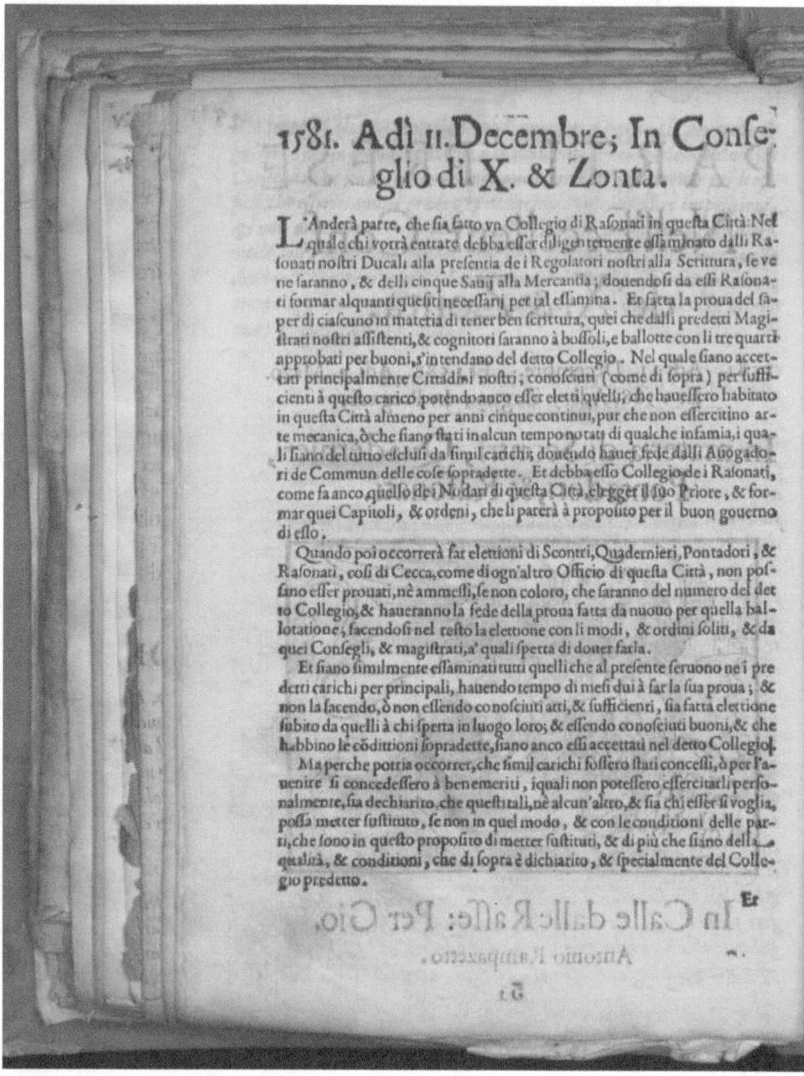

1581. Adì 11. Decembre; In Conseglio di X. & Zonta.

L'Anderà parte, che sia fatto vn Collegio di Rasonati in questa Città: Nel quale chi votrà entrare debba esser diligentemente essaminato dalli Rasonati nostri Ducali alla presentia de i Regolatori nostri alla Scrittura, se ve ne saranno, & delli cinque Sauij alla Mercantia; douendosi da essi Rasonati formar alquanti quesiti necessarij per tal essamina. Et fatta la proua del saper di ciascuno in materia di tener ben scrittura, quei che dalli predetti Magistrati nostri assistenti, & cognitori saranno à bossoli, e ballotte con li tre quarti approbati per buoni, s'intendano del detto Collegio. Nel quale siano accettati principalmente Cittadini nostri, conosciuti (come di sopra) per sufficienti à questo carico potendo anco esser eletti quelli, che hauessero habitato in questa Città almeno per anni cinque continui, pur che non essercitino arte mecanica, ò che siano stati in alcun tempo notati di qualche infamia, i quali siano del tutto esclusi da simil carichi; douendo hauer fede dalli Auogadori de Commun delle cose sopradette. Et debba esso Collegio de i Rasonati, come fa anco quello de i Nodari di questa Città, elegger il suo Priore, & formar quei Capitoli, & ordeni, che li parerà à proposito per il buon gouerno di esso.

Quando poi occorrerà far elettioni di Scontri, Quadernieri, Pontadori, & Rasonati, così di Cecca, come di ogn'altro Officio di questa Città, non possano esser prouati, nè ammessi, se non coloro, che saranno del numero del detto Collegio, & haueranno la fede della proua fatta da nuouo per quella ballotatione; facendosi nel resto la elettione con li modi, & ordini soliti, & da quei Conseglì, & magistrati, a' quali spetta di douer farla.

Et siano similmente essaminati tutti quelli che al presente seruono ne i predetti carichi per principali, hauendo tempo di mesi dui à far la sua proua; & non la facendo, ò non essendo conosciuti atti, & sufficienti, sia fatta elettione subito da quelli à chi spetta in luogo loro; & essendo conosciuti buoni, & che habbino le cõdittioni sopradette, siano anco essi accettati nel detto Collegio.

Ma perche potria occorrer, che simil carichi fossero stati concessi, ò per l'auenire si concedessero à benemeriti, i quali non potessero essercitarli personalmente, sia dechiarito, che questi tali, nè alcun'altro, & sia chi esser si voglia, possa metter sustituto, se non in quel modo, & con le conditioni delle parti, che sono in questo proposito di metter sustituti, & di più che siano della qualità, & conditioni, che di sopra è dichiarito, & specialmente del Collegio predetto.

Et

Figure 18.6 *Parti prese nell'eccellent. Cons. de 10. & Zonta. 1581. Adi 11. Decembre. Et 1588.*

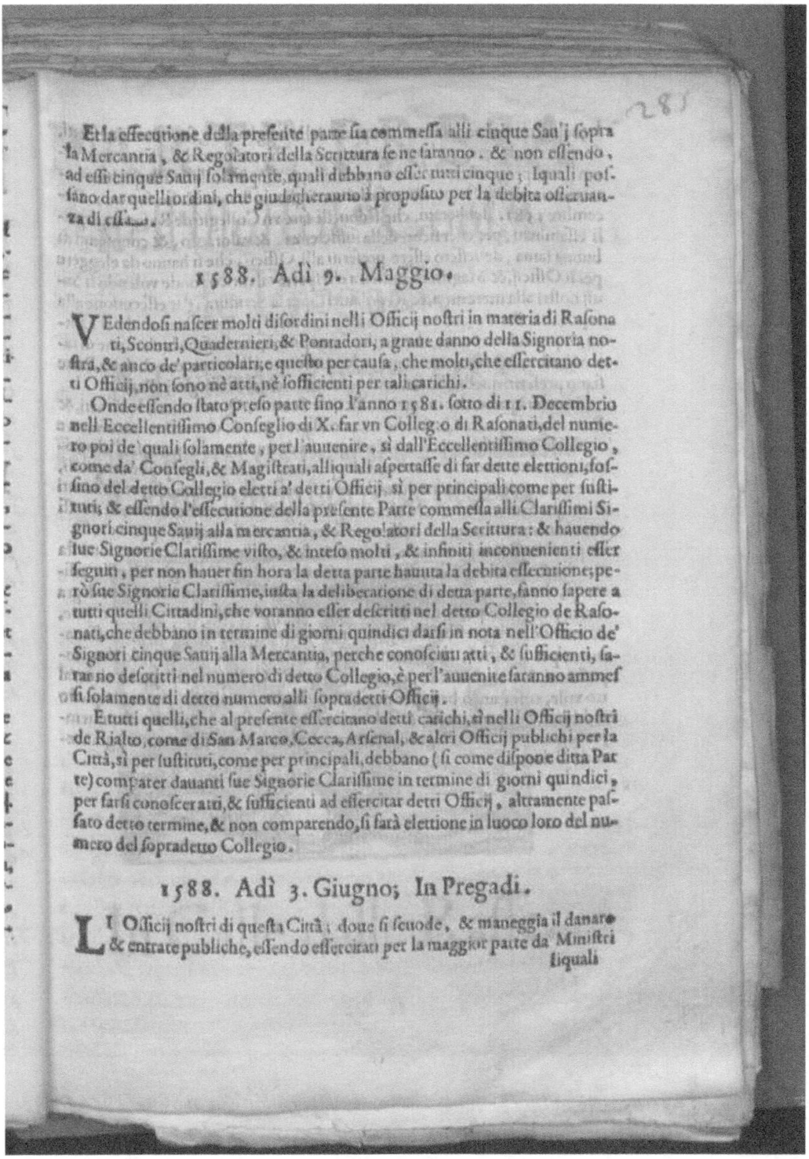

Et la essecutione della presente parte sia commessa alli cinque Savij sopra la Mercantia, & Regolatori della Scrittura se ne saranno. & non essendo, ad essi cinque Savij solamente, quali debbano esser tutti cinque; Iquali possano dar quelli ordini, che giudicheranno à proposito per la debita osservanza di essa.

1588. Adì 9. Maggio.

VEdendosi nascer molti disordini nelli Officij nostri in materia di Rasonati, Scontri, Quadernieri, & Pontadori, a grave danno della Signoria nostra, & anco de' particolari; e questo per causa, che molti, che essercitano detti Officij, non sono nè atti, nè sofficienti per tali carichi.

Onde essendo stato preso parte fino l'anno 1581. sotto di 11. Decembrio nell'Eccellentissimo Conseglio di X. far vn Collegio di Rasonati, del numero poi de' quali solamente, per l'auuenire, sì dall'Eccellentissimo Collegio, come da' Consegli, & Magistrati, alliquali aspettasse di far dette elettioni, fossino del detto Collegio eletti a' detti Officij sì per principali come per sustituti; & essendo l'essecutione della presente Parte commessa alli Clarissimi Signori cinque Savij alla mercantia, & Regolatori della Scrittura: & hauendo sue Signorie Clarissime visto, & inteso molti, & infiniti inconuenienti esser seguiti, per non hauer fin hora la detta parte hauuta la debita essecutione; però sue Signorie Clarissime, iusta la deliberatione di detta parte, fanno sapere a tutti quelli Cittadini, che voranno esser descritti nel detto Collegio de Rasonati, che debbano in termine di giorni quindici darsi in nota nell'Officio de' Signori cinque Savij alla Mercantia, perche conosciuti atti, & sufficienti, saranno descritti nel numero di detto Collegio, è per l'auuenire saranno ammessi solamente di detto numero alli sopradetti Officij.

E tutti quelli, che al presente essercitano detti carichi, sì nelli Officij nostri de Rialto, come di San Marco, Cecca, Arsenal, & altri Officij publichi per la Città, sì per sustituti, come per principali, debbano (si come dispone ditta Parte) comparer dauanti sue Signorie Clarissime in termine di giorni quindici, per farsi conoscer atti, & sufficienti ad essercitar detti Officij, altramente passato detto termine, & non comparendo, si farà elettione in luoco loro del numero del sopradetto Collegio.

1588. Adì 3. Giugno; In Pregadi.

LI Officij nostri di questa Città; doue si scuode, & maneggia il danaro & entrate publiche, essendo essercitati per la maggior parte da Ministri liquali

Figure 18.7 Parti prese nell'eccellent. Cons. de 10. & Zonta. 1581. Adi 11. Decembre. Et 1588.

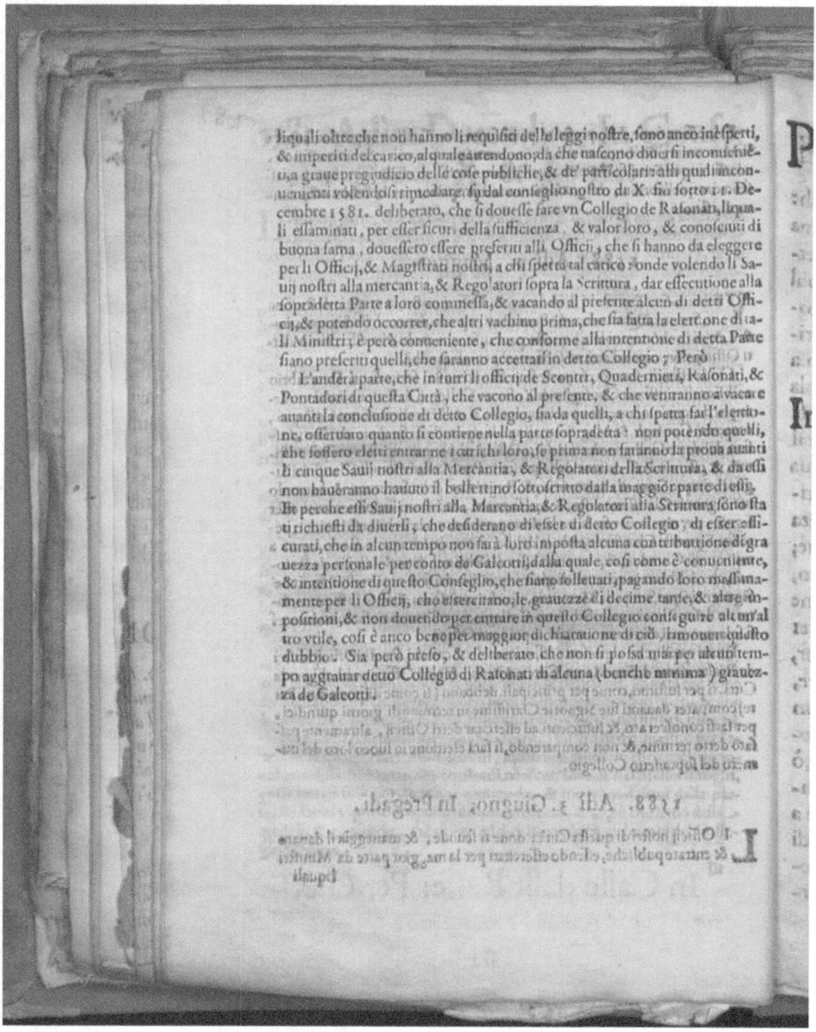

liquali oltre che non hanno li requisiti delle leggi nostre, sono anco inesperti, & imperiti del carico, al quale attendono; da che nascono diversi inconvenienti, a grave pregiudicio delle cose publiche, & de' particolari: alli quali inconvenienti volendosi rimediare, fu dal conseglio nostro di X. fin sotto 11. Decembre 1581. deliberato, che si dovesse fare vn Collegio de Rasonati, liquali essaminati, per esser sicuri della sufficienza, & valor loro, & conosciuti di buona fama, dovessero essere preferiti alli Officij, che si hanno da eleggere per li Officij, & Magistrati nostri, a chi spetta tal carico: onde volendo li Savij nostri alla mercantia, & Regolatori sopra la Scrittura, dar essecutione alla sopradetta Parte a loro commessa, & vacando al presente alcun di detti Officij, & potendo occorrer, che altri vachino prima, che sia fatta la elettione di tali Ministri; è però convenіente, che conforme alla intentione di detta Parte siano preferiti quelli, che saranno accettati in detto Collegio; Però

L'anderà parte, che in tutti li officij de Scontri, Quadernieri, Rasonati, & Pontadori di questa Città, che vacono al presente, & che veniranno a vacare avanti la conclusione di detto Collegio, sia da quelli, a chi spetta far l'elettione, osservato quanto si contiene nella parte sopradetta: non potendo quelli, che fossero eletti entrar ne i carichi loro, se prima non faranno la prova avanti li cinque Savij nostri alla Mercantia, & Regolatori della Scrittura, & da essi non haveranno havuto il bollettino sottoscritto dalla maggior parte di essi.

Et perche essi Savij nostri alla Mercantia, & Regolatori alla Scrittura sono stati richiesti da diversi, che desiderano di esser di detto Collegio, di esser assicurati, che in alcun tempo non sarà loro imposta alcuna contributione di gravezza personale per conto de Galeotti, dalla quale, cosi come è conveniente, & intentione di questo Conseglio, che siano sollevati, pagando loro massimamente per li Officij, che essercitano, le gravezze di decime tanse, & altre impositioni, & non dovendo per entrare in questo Collegio conseguire alcun'altro utile, cosi è anco bene per maggior dichiaratione di ciò, rimovere questo dubbio. Sia però preso, & deliberato, che non si possa mai per alcun tempo aggravar detto Collegio di Rasonati di alcuna (benche minima) gravezza de Galeotti.

Figure 18.8 Parti prese nell'eccellent. Cons. de 10. & Zonta. 1581. Adi 11. Decembre. Et 1588.

[This document was printed in 1588 and refers to the main accounting specializations ('*Scontri*', '*Quadernieri*' and '*Pontadori*') in the *Collegio de' Rasonati* in the Republic of Venice.]

Specific obstacles would slow the takeoff of the *Collegio* from the beginning, as there were no candidates to take the exam before 1588. This may have been related to the reluctance of the candidates to pay the tax called '*gravezza de' galeotti*' from which they were officially exempted by the Senate only in 1588. Moreover, the *Collegio*'s entrance examination was not an easy test and its formulation followed a specific procedure, which consists in the drafting of questions (up to fifteen) by each of the two *Dogal Rasonati*. These questions were put in a locked box and subsequently extracted at random and submitted to each candidate, who was obliged to answer that question. At the end of the examination, the candidates signed their paper, which was then countersigned by the examination supervisors and given to the *Dogal Rasonato* for correction. At the end, the five men of the *Collegetto* would vote on the admission or the rejection of the candidate. Given that the *Collegetto* members and the *Dogal Rasonati* were all of Venetian origins, they tended to favor Venetian citizens against foreign candidates. In the same vein, nepotism was another drawback, facilitating the entrance of members' relatives to the *Collegio*. The main positive point (as far as we are concerned in this chapter) is that the *Collegio* can be considered the first Venetian accountants' association. This official recognition of an autonomous role for accountants with public functions is observable first in Venetian history and only subsequently in a few other cases. In Piedmont and Liguria, a list of '*Liquidatori Giurati*' is established in 1620, following an edict of Carlo Emanuele I of Savoy. In Milan, the '*Collegio dei Ragionati*' is formed (with the same functions of the Venice Collegio) only 161 years after its Venetian counterpart. Finally, in 1828, 'accountant-auditors' are formally and definitively recognized. If the birth of the *Collegio de' Rasonati* is an extraordinary event pioneered by the Republic of Venice, the recognition of 'accountant-auditors' had little to do with Venice. Indeed, after the arrival of Napoleon, who conquered the city in 1797, the Republic of Venice collapses, the *Collegio* ceases to exist and Venice is handed over to the archduchy of Austria, definitively forfeiting its independence. Even when the imperial domination of France falls and the old dominions are reestablished, the city is unable to react, because of the supremacy of Austria, which also obtains in Lombardy and the Veneto. In spite of the absence of geographic independence, all the issues related to economic administration are in fact sensibly faced and improvements in different economic sectors are evident (Cappellaro, 1997). In 1805 a new regulation was introduced covering qualification for the profession of public accountant. It required that future accountants undergo three years of practical training and pass a test in mathematics and bookkeeping. After achieving positive results in the test, candidates were entitled to exercise the profession all over the state (Coronella et al., 2015). This regulation survived the French Empire's fall and was maintained under the Austrian domination practically

Table 18.1 Historical origins of chartered accountants in the northeast of the Italian Peninsula: a chronological table of main events

Year	*Event*
1581	Establishment of the *Collegio de' Rasonati* in the Republic of Venice.
1588	Formal recognition of the *Collegio de' Rasonati* by the Venetian Senate.
1797	Napoleon's invasion and adoption of the Napoleon's Code.
1805	New regulations for qualification to the profession of public accountant.
1807	Creation of '*Corte dei Conti*' (the body in charge of controlling public expenditure).
1828	Formal recognition of the so-called *Ragionieri Revisori* in the Austrian Lombardo-Veneto state.

unchanged (after the final fall of the Napoleonic Empire in 1814 the northeast of the Italian Peninsula remained under Austrian control after the Congress of Vienna on 7 April 1815) (Table 18.1).

Under the Austrian Civil Legislation, the juridical authority decided in 1828 to recognize a limited number (proportional to the importance of each tribunal) of accountants (with at least six years of experience) for the management of sundry accounting tasks. These accountants were called 'accountant-auditors'. Their main function was the auditing of the accounts of government agencies, in particular of the Central Fund. Moreover, they also oversaw the way in which municipalities managed their affairs and audited the accounts of religious foundations. Thanks to these measures, the accounting sector passed through a flourishing period, able to afford substantial help to the administration of that time in exercising efficient and effective supervision (Luchini, 1898).

The formal recognition of these 'accountant-auditors' can be considered a fundamental step that provides a basis for the definitive definition of the figure of the professional accountant. This historical event in 1828 is related to businesses' need for management and auditing of their accounts in a time of industrialization and the creation of small and medium enterprises (especially family-owned ones) in the Lombardo-Veneto state (Becattini and Vaccà, 1994). Given these origins of the profession, the important relation between accounting professionals and SMEs emerges early on and can be identified as a 'persistent' feature in the analyzed geographic territory. Indeed, examining the historical origins of SMPs in the northeast of the Italian Peninsula, we can identify some features as being still characteristic of such practices nowadays. They have been described in the introduction and, in so far as they have persisted (from their outlined historical origins until today), they are briefly recalled here. After the importance of the relationship between accounting professionals and SMEs, another persistent feature regards a desire to differentiate accountants and their work. From their origins, SMPs aimed to distinguish their job, which traditionally consisted in the art of keeping the accounting books, from other disciplines, such as 'arithmetic', in the past. This is related to a desire to be publicly recognized as members of knowledgeable and autonomous institutions (from the *Collegio de' Rasonati* to the more recent accountants' associations). A third persistent feature concerns the formal requirements for entering such institutions and ways of publicly demonstrating the hard-earned professional competence of accountants: a period of apprenticeship and a series of tests have been required since the origins of the profession with a view to building and demonstrating expertise. The acquisition of appropriate and specific competences is another persistent distinguishing feature of these professionals wishing to be regarded as experts and reliable in their work. This is also perhaps related to a persistent fault of over-meticulous precision and excessive rigidity in the procedures and methods traditionally applied by accounting professionals.

Conclusion

This chapter has focused on the profession of chartered accountancy, and especially on Venetian historical events that are at the origin of SMPs (small and medium practices). These represent a specific type of small and medium enterprises (SMEs) and they are also the main suppliers of accounting support to SMEs (IFAC, 2016), which are the most widespread form of economic organization in the Italian context (OECD, 2016). The chapter describes the main features of SMPs and, in particular, 'persistent' features from the historical origins of the profession to our own day. These historical origins are related to the following two main events: first, the establishment of the *Collegio de' Rasonati*, considered the 'father' of the current professional associations of chartered accountants (Siboni, 2005). This official recognition of an autonomous role for accountants who also perform public functions is observable in Venetian history and, later on, in a few other Italian cases. Second, the formal recognition of the so-called accountant-auditors is considered a fundamental step that provides a basis for the definitive definition of the figure of the professional accountant. This historical event in 1828 is related to industrialization and the creation of SMEs in the Austrian Lombardo-Veneto state. From these historical origins onwards, there has been a close relationship between accounting professionals and SMEs that is still especially relevant between SMPs and SMEs in the Italian context. The collection over different years of empirical data about this relationship, which represents one of the persistent features of SMPs emphasized here, may point to a possible future development of the present work. Future research about the topic might focus on the following: the dynamics of the SME-SMP relationship investigated through longitudinal and in-depth case studies; the similarities and differences at regional and international levels analyzed through comparative studies; the concept of trust from the perspective of the relationship between SMPs and SMEs; and the methods and scale of monitoring changes in the accounting profession (IFAC, 2016).

Notes

1. These are not only small organizations but also public sector firms, non-profit organizations and small government agencies.
2. The activities affiliated to this profession are accountancy, tax return preparation, consultancy to companies on fiscal and legal requirements, preparation of financial statements and tax compliance, audit operations and formulation of opinions on the accounts of companies and public or private bodies, operations related to the liquidation/sale of assets, goods or entire businesses, extraordinary operations (e.g., mergers, acquisition, conglomerations), the representation of companies before legal authorities, the evaluation of companies' performance and many other activities relating to the assistance supplied to firms in their day-to-day operations.
3. The Council of Ten, or simply the Ten, was, from 1310 to 1797, one of the major governing bodies of the Republic of Venice. The Council was formally composed of ten members elected for one-year terms and was tasked with maintaining the security of the republic and preserving the government from overthrow or corruption.
4. 'The Most Serene [Republic]' of Venice, sovereign state and maritime republic in the northeast of the Italian Peninsula, which existed for a millennium between the eighth century and the eighteenth century.
5. The Fourth Ottoman-Venetian War, also known as the War of Cyprus, was fought between 1570 and 1573. It was between the Ottoman Empire and the Republic of Venice.
6. The doge was the chief magistrate and titular leader of the Republic of Venice from 697 to 1797.
7. The prior's role lasted one year and could not be re-elected immediately, but had to wait at least another year to reoccupy one of the *Colleggetto* positions.

References

Agyemang G., Rinaldi L., and Spence L.J., "*Environmental Aspects of Sustainability: SMEs and the Role of the Accountant*", ACCA, London, 2012.

Antonelli V., and D'Alessio R., "*Gli studi di storia della ragioneria dall'unità di Italia ad oggi*", Franco Angeli, Milano, 2011.

Attolini G., "*Helping Small and Medium Sized Practices Meet the Challenges and Seize the Opportunities of Tomorrow*", IFAC Small and Medium Practices Committee, March 2012.

Becattini G. and Vaccà S., "*Prospettive degli studi di economia e politica industriale in Italia*", Franco Angeli, Milano, 1994.

Blackburn R., Carey P., and Tanewski G.A., "*Business advice by accountants to SMEs: relationship and trust*". In: 27th Annual Small Enterprise Association of Australia and New Zealand (SEAANZ) Conference 2014: Enhancing SME Success in the Digital Economy; 16–18 Jul 2014, Sydney, Australia. (27th Annual Small Enterprise Association of Australia and New Zealand (SEAANZ) Conference Proceedings), 2014.

Brown, R. Gene, and Kenneth S. Johnston. *Paciolo on accounting*. McGraw-Hill, 1963.

Cappellaro I., "*L'evoluzione storica della professione di Ragioniere*", Storia della Ragioneria, Rirea, Rome, 1997, 144–158.

Carey P.J., "*The Benefits of Services Provided by External Accountants to Small and Medium Sized Enterprises*", PhD thesis, University of New South Wales, 2008.

Casalena A., *"Introduzione alla Storia della Ragioneria"*, Associazione dei Ragionieri d'Abruzzo, 2010.

Ciambotti M., "*Cenni di storia della Ragioneria e della professione contabile*", Tipografia Grafica Valdese, 2007.

Coronella S., Sargiacomo M., and Walker S.P., "Unification and Dual Closure in the Italian Accountancy Profession, 1861–1906", *European Accounting Review* 24 (1), 2015.

Edwards J.D., *Financial Accounting*. New York, NY: McGraw-Hill/Irwin, 1994.

Eurostat, "Key figures on European business – with a special feature on SMEs" Product Code: KS-ET-11-001 ISBN: 978-92-79-20422-7 ISSN: 1830-9720 Digital Object Identifier (DOI): 10.2785/15193 Theme: Industry, trade and services Collection: Pocketbooks Release date: 20/07/2011 http://ec.europa.eu/eurostat/web/products-pocketbooks/-/KS-ET-11-001

Gooderham, P.N., Tobiassen, A., Døving, E., and Nordhaug, O., "Accountants as Sources of Business Advice for Small Firms", *International Small Business Journal*, 22 (1), 2004: 5–22.

IFAC, *"The Role of Small and Medium Practices in Providing Business Support to Small- and Medium-Sized Enterprises"*, March 2010.

IFAC, *"The Role of SMPs in Providing Business Support to SMEs: New Evidence"*, September 2016.

IFAC, *"Small and Medium Practices Committee"*, June 2011.

Jarvis R., and Thompson P., *"The Evolving Advisory Role of SMPs in Supporting the Internationalization of SMEs"*, IFAC, December 2014.

Luchini E., *"Storia della ragioneria italiana"*, Editor: Cacucci, Milano, 1898.

Millis T.G., "Early Accounting in Northern Italy: The Role of Commercial Development and the Printing Press in the Expansion of Double-Entry from Genoa, Florence, and Venice", *Accounting Historians Journal*, June 1994.

ODCEC (Ordine dei Dottori Commercialisti e degli Esperti Contabili) di Padova, *"L'arte del conto a Padova. Dal contador al commercialista in un viaggio attraverso i secoli"*, a cura di Giovanni Borghini, Tipografia Moderna, Montagnana, PD, 2015.

OECD, "Financing SMEs and Entrepreneurs 2016: An OECD Scoreboard", 2016. Available at: www.keepeek.com/Digital-Asset-Management/oecd/industry-and-services/financing-smes-and-entrepreneurs-2016_fin_sme_ent-2016-en#page306.

Pacioli L., *Summa de arithmetica, geometria, proportioni et proportionalita*, Paganino di Paganini, Venice, 1494.

Sangster, A., "The Genesis of Double Entry Bookkeeping", *The Accounting Review* 91 (1), 2015: 299–315.

Siboni B., *"Introduzione allo studio di storia della ragioneria attraverso lo studio e le opere dei suoi maestri"*, Editor: Franco Angeli, Milano 2005.

Siriwardane H.P., and Durden C.H., "The Communication Skills of Accountants: What We Know and the Gaps in Our Knowledge", *Accounting Education* 23 (2), 2014.

Sombart W., *"Luxus und Kapitalismus"*, München: Duncker & Humblot, 1921.

Unioncamere e Ufficio Studi di Mediobanca, *"Le medie imprese industriali italiane"*, May 2016.

Zambon S., *"Locating Accounting in Its National Contest: The Case of Italy"*, Editor: Franco Angeli, Milano 2002.

Zambon S., and Zan L., "Controlling Expenditure, or the Slow Emergence of Costing at the Venice Arsenal, 1586–1633", *Accounting, Business & Financial History* 17 (1), 2007: 105–128.

Index

Page numbers in italic indicate a figure and page numbers in bold indicate a table.

For Product Safety Concerns and Information please contact our EU representative GPSR@taylorandfrancis.com Taylor & Francis Verlag GmbH, Kaufingerstraße 24, 80331 München, Germany